THE NATIONAL MUSEUM & ARCHIVE OF LESBIAN AND GAY HISTORY

The National Museum & Archive of Lesbian and Gay History catalogues the daily lives and political struggles of lesbians and gay men. One of the largest collections of its kind in the country, the Archive is a repository for the personal papers, correspondence, artifacts, and publications of both individuals and organizations. Taken as a whole, it offers a unique view of the many communities that make up the complex tapestry we recognize as the gay and lesbian community.

THE LESBIAN AND GAY COMMUNITY SERVICES CENTER

Founded in 1983, the Lesbian and Gay Community Services Center has grown to become New York City's largest gay-identified community organization. The Center provides twenty-six services and programs specifically designed for the needs and interests of the gay community, including HIV prevention education; AIDS bereavement services; youth support services; Center Kids, a gay and lesbian family program; and numerous recreational, cultural, and public policy programs. Other Center programs include the Pat Parker/Vito Russo Center Library and the National Museum & Archive of Lesbian and Gay History. In its mission to build community, the Center provides a home for more than 300 lesbian and gay organizations representing every facet of the diverse New York metropolitan community. Each week, 5,000 people come to the Center, which exists through the financial support of members of the lesbian and gay community.

The NYC Lesbian and Gay Community Services Center, founded in 1983, is housed in the former Food and Maritime Trade High School on West 13th Street in Greenwich Village. The building is shown here circa 1927, when it was still a school.

THE LESBIAN
ALMANAC

COMPILED BY THE NATIONAL MUSEUM
& ARCHIVE
OF LESBIAN AND GAY HISTORY

*A Program of
the Lesbian and Gay Community Services Center—
New York*

Produced by The Philip Lief Group, Inc.

BERKLEY BOOKS, NEW YORK

THE LESBIAN ALMANAC

A Berkley Book / published by arrangement with
The Philip Lief Group, Inc.

PRINTING HISTORY
Berkley trade paperback edition / June 1996

All rights reserved.
Copyright © 1996 by The Philip Lief Group, Inc.
Produced by The Philip Lief Group, Inc.
Book design by Irving Perkins Associates.
This book may not be reproduced in whole or in part,
by mimeograph or any other means, without permission.
For information address: The Philip Lief Group, Inc.,
130 Wall Street, Princeton, New Jersey 08540.

The Putnam Berkley World Wide Web site address is http://www.berkley.com

ISBN: 0-425-15301-0

BERKLEY®
Berkley Books are published by The Berkley Publishing Group, a member of
Penguin Putnam Inc.,
200 Madison Avenue, New York, New York 10016.
BERKLEY and the "B" design
are trademarks belonging to Berkley Publishing Corporation.

PRINTED IN THE UNITED STATES OF AMERICA

15 14 13 12 11 10 9 8 7 6 5 4

ACKNOWLEDGMENTS

Project manager: Paula Martinac

Research/writing team: Terry Boggis, Richard D. Burns, Jennifer L. Costley, Thom Furr, Stephanie Grant, Katie Hogan, Winnie Hough, Paula Martinac, Gerry Gomez Pearlberg, Penny Perkins, and Judith E. Turkel

Thanks to: Firebrand Books; Frameline; the Gay and Lesbian Alliance Against Defamation; Morgan Gwenwald; Donald Huppert; Lambda Legal Defense and Education Fund; the Lesbian Herstory Archives (especially Polly Thistlethwaite); Naiad Press; The NAMES Project; the NYC Gay and Lesbian Anti-Violence Project; Overlooked Opinions, Inc.; the Pat Parker/Vito Russo Center Library; Seal Press; Rich Wandel; Dr. Barbara Warren; Rhett Wickham; Women Make Movies; and the entire staff of the NYC Lesbian and Gay Community Services Center.

Thanks also to the many lesbian and gay news and culture magazines and newspapers that we used in our research, especially *The Advocate, Deneuve, Out, POZ,* and *The Washington Blade.*

In this almanac, we have attempted to be as up to date as possible, but the lesbian and gay community is constantly changing and growing. If you have information that would help us in updating this book, please write to: *The Lesbian Almanac,* Lesbian and Gay Community Services Center, 208 West 13th Street, New York, NY 10011.

THE LESBIAN ALMANAC

CONTENTS

INTRODUCTION

During Lesbian and Gay Pride Month in June 1994, I spent an afternoon at the "Becoming Visible" exhibit at the New York Public Library, traveling through the history of lesbian and gay culture in New York City before and since the Stonewall riots of 1969. The exhibit brought back many memories, some happy, some bittersweet, but all of them reminding me that as different as we are from one another, we share a common history and are part of a lesbian community.

I came out as a lesbian in New York City in the mid-1970s, a time when many lesbians seemed to look and dress alike, when the only places I knew to go to meet other women were bars, when the word "women" was spelled in more ways than I could keep track of (womyn and wimmin, for example). Nearly fifteen years ago, I met my life partner at the Duchess, a now-defunct Greenwich Village bar that was a landmark for many, many years.

Although my own experiences reflect just a small part of our lesbian community, out of our "well of loneliness" we have created a wonderful, vibrant community and culture. As lesbians, we can be proud to celebrate our diversity as well as our connections, our distinct culture, and a very long and proud history.

This book is both a reflection and a celebration of our accomplishments. In the early 1600s, lesbian sexual behavior could result in a whipping or other public censure. In the late 1900s, we have a lesbian-feminist community with its own newspapers, publishing houses, bookstores, women's centers, music festivals, and coffeehouses. We have elected openly lesbian political representatives across the country. We have witnessed a "lesbian baby boom." We have achieved domestic partnership benefits in our towns, cities, and workplaces. We have watched our lives sensitively depicted on national network television. And, in every field from literature to law to entertainment to sports, we have achieved prominence and recognition. Our triumphs and also our tragedies over the last four hundred years of North American history are the heart of this almanac.

I am thrilled to be part of one of the numerous lesbian and gay community centers that have been founded in the last few decades. Our lesbian and gay community centers have made it possible for our organizations to grow and prosper and for all of us to have places to call home.

This almanac was prepared to enrich your understanding of lesbian history, culture, and life and to be a frequently used reference guide. Here you can find lesbian health tips, information on lesbian legal issues, news from lesbians in cyber-space, resources for lesbian mothers, and the most up-to-date directory available of lesbian and gay community centers across the United States. Lesbian trivia and tidbits are here, too: famous lesbians and their accomplishments, a glossary of lesbian slang, the most popular lesbian vacation spots, spotlights on lesbian sporting events, and lesbian-themed movies by category.

As you wander through the almanac, I hope you will feel proud of all that lesbians have accomplished. I know I do.

—Judith E. Turkel,
President, Lesbian and Gay Community
Services Center–New York
July 1995

PART I

HIGHLIGHTS AND "LOWLIGHTS" OF NORTH AMERICAN LESBIAN AND GAY HISTORY FROM THE SIXTEENTH CENTURY TO THE PRESENT

Butch-femme couples, ca. 1920s *(Collection of the National Museum & Archive of Lesbian and Gay History)*

Do YOU REMEMBER when studying history in school meant reading about wealthy, white, heterosexual men making war with each other? References to the history and lives of women and people of color—when they appeared at all—were relegated to sidebars in our textbooks. Homosexuality was virtually invisible, except as it related to "scandals."

A lot has changed in the last two decades. Social historians influenced by the civil rights and women's movements of the 1960s and the 1970s have been digging into tax records, census reports, court proceedings and criminal records, newspapers, diaries, and church rosters to unearth the history of people who had never been considered important enough to have a history: poor people, women, people of color.

In the aftermath of the Stonewall riots, fueled by the exciting momentum of their own liberation movement, lesbians and gay men started looking for their history, too. Important grassroots projects like the Lesbian Herstory Archives (founded in 1973; see box on page 33) and the San Francisco Lesbian and Gay History Project (1977) used the techniques of the new social history to uncover the pasts of lesbians and gay men, who had been hidden from history just like so many other marginalized people. As lesbian and gay activists create a public presence through organizations, marches, and rallies, lesbian and gay historians, many of whom were self-taught in the techniques of history, began to reclaim our historical presence as well.

Now, lesbian and gay archives have sprouted up across the continent, preserving the documents that will make our history more accessible to the next generations. The field of lesbian and gay studies has burgeoned in the last decade, and there are presently lesbian and gay studies courses and openly lesbian and gay professors in major universities across the United States and Canada. The Center for Lesbian and Gay Studies (CLAGS) at the City University of New York has been a pioneer in advocating the acceptance of lesbian and gay studies as a recognized academic discipline. We used many published histories of lesbians and gay men in compiling this time line, and they are listed on pages 6 to 30.

Lesbian and gay history has never been easy to research, and some of the pitfalls are obvious ones. To this day, homosexuality is viewed by many as a taboo subject, and in some places, it is still a criminal activity. In early American history, sodomy was a capital offense. A lot of what we have learned about lesbians and gay men has come from criminal records. While people certainly engaged in homosexual relations, their "deviant" sexual behavior was not something they very often divulged. It was not a source of pride. Those who did write letters to lovers may have burned them or written in code. Also, though we may now label a man or woman as gay or lesbian by their sexual activities, he or she may not have done so.

Women and people of color have always been more invisible in the annals of history, so the history of lesbians and of lesbians and gay men of color is even more difficult to uncover than that of gay white men. Throughout much of American history, women were the property of men and until very recently were discouraged from exploring their sexuality. Most of the early sodomy laws in the American colonies did not even mention the possibility of sex between women. African-

Americans and Native Americans challenged invisibility and genocide by preserving their histories orally. Sometimes, the whites recorded biased glimpses of their lives. The journals of a number of European explorers, for example, discuss the berdaches among Native Americans. (See the entry for **1804-1810** on page 8.)

Our time line scratches the surface of North American lesbian and gay history. The following list of books used to compile our highlights and "lowlights" is suggested for further reading.

UNITED STATES

Berube, Allan. *Coming Out Under Fire: The History of Gay Men and Women in World War II.* Plume, 1991.

Chauncey, George. *Gay New York: Gender, Urban Culture, and the Making of the Gay Male World, 1890–1940.* Basic Books, 1994.

D'Emilio, John. *Sexual Politics, Sexual Communities: The Making of a Homosexual Minority in the United States, 1940–1970.* University of Chicago Press, 1983.

Duberman, Martin B., Martha Vicinus, and George Chauncey, Jr., eds. *Hidden from History: Reclaiming the Lesbian and Gay Past.* New American Library, 1989.

Faderman, Lillian. *Odd Girls and Twilight Lovers: A History of Lesbian Life in Twentieth-Century America.* Columbia University Press, 1991.

_____. *Gay American History: Lesbians and Gay Men in the U.S.A.* Meridien, 1992.

Katz, Jonathan Ned. *Gay/Lesbian Almanac.* Carroll & Graf, 1994.

Kennedy, Elizabeth Lapovsky, and Madeline D. Davis. *Boots of Leather, Slippers of Gold: The History of a Lesbian Community.* Routledge, 1993.

Marcus, Eric. *Making History: The Struggle for Gay and Lesbian Equal Rights, 1945–1990: An Oral History.* HarperCollins, 1992.

Miller, Neil. *Out of the Past.* Vintage, 1995.

Rutledge, Leigh. *The Gay Decades.* Plume, 1991.

Schwartz, Judith. *Radical Feminist of Heterodoxy: Greenwich Village, 1912–1940.* New Victoria Publishers, 1986.

Thompson, Mark, ed. *Long Road to Freedom:* The Advocate *History of the Gay and Lesbian Movement.* St. Martin's Press, 1994.

CANADA

Adam, Barry. *The Rise of the Gay and Lesbian Movement.* Twain Publishers, 1987.

Body Politic, The. *Flaunting It: A Decade of Gay Journalism from* The Body Politic. Pink Triangle Books and New Star Books, 1982.

Herman, Didi. *Rights of Passage: The Struggle for Lesbian and Gay Legal Equality.* University of Toronto Press, 1994.

Kinsman, Gary. *The Regulation of Desire.* Black Rose Books, 1987.
Stone, Sharon. *Lesbians in Canada.* Between the Lines, 1990.

For a separate time line on the AIDS epidemic, see pages 426–432.

1528–1536: Spanish explorer Alvar Nunez Cabeza de Vaca made the earliest written account of "effeminate" Indians in Florida, who "go about dressed as women, and do women's tasks."

1566: In Florida, Guillermo, a French interpreter accused of being a traitor and "a great Sodomite," was murdered by the Spaniards. Guillermo lived with a local Indian, who was the son of the cacique (chief) of the Guale area and reportedly "loved that interpreter very much."

1610: The Virginia Colony passed the earliest American sodomy law, dictating the death penalty for offenders. It did not include women as potential sodomites.

1613: Francisco de Pareja, a Spanish missionary with the Florida Indians, recorded in his work *Confessionario (Confessional)* the likelihood of sodomy between native men and of sexual acts between native women.

1624: Though the evidence was slim, Richard Cornish, master of the ship *The Ambrose*, was executed by hanging in the Virginia Colony for alleged "buggery" of one of his indentured servants, the ship's steward, William Cowse.

1629: The Virginia Court recorded the first incidence of gender ambiguity among the American colonists. A servant, Thomas/Thomasine Hall, was officially proclaimed by the governor to be both "a man and a woman" and ordered to wear articles of each sex's clothing. (It is unclear if Hall was a hermaphrodite or a biological male who dressed in women's clothes.)

• On board the ship *Talbot,* bound for New England, Rev. Francis Higginson recorded the discovery of "5 beastly Sodomiticall boyes, which confessed their wickedness not to be named." When the ship landed, Higginson reported the incident to the governor of the Massachusetts Bay Colony, who sent the boys "to be punished in old England as the crime deserved." At that time, English law authorized that males over fourteen could be hanged for sodomy. The fate of the boys is unknown.

1636: In the Massachusetts Bay Colony, Rev. John Cotton proposed the death penalty for sixteen crimes, including sodomy, which he called "unnatural filthiness" and defined as "carnal fellowship of man with man, or woman with woman." Though Cotton's code was not accepted, Massachusetts adopted a sodomy law five years later (see **1641**).

• The codification of the laws of Plymouth Colony included eight offenses punishable by death. Included with treason, murder, and witchcraft were "Sodomy, rapes, buggery." The law did not specify if sodomy pertained only to men, or to men and women equally.

1641: The Massachusetts Bay Colony adopted a body of laws (which remained unprinted until 1648), including sodomy as a capital crime. In this code—unlike John Mather's earlier proposal, which included women as potential offenders—

sodomy was defined as a "man lying with mankind as he lies with a woman." The wording is taken straight from Leviticus 20:13.

1642: Connecticut adopted twelve capital crimes, among which was sodomy, defined as "a man lying with a man."

• In Salem, Massachusetts, a servant, Elizabeth Johnson, received a whipping for "unseemly practices betwixt her and another maid."

1646: "Jan Creoli, a negro," was executed by choking in New Netherland for sodomy. Manuel Congo, the ten-year-old whom Creoli allegedly sodomized, received a public flogging.

• In Connecticut, William Plaine, one of the original settlers of the town of Guilford, was accused of committing sodomy twice in England and of corrupting "a great part of the youth of Guilford by masturbations." Plaine was executed at New Haven.

1647: Rhode Island passed a law making sodomy between men a capital offense.

1648: A young soldier in Montreal was charged with "the worst of crimes," interpreted to be sodomy. The Jesuits intervened on the youth's behalf, and his sentence to hard labor was commuted on condition that he become New France's first executioner.

1649: In Plymouth, two married women, Sara Norman and Mary Hammon, were charged with "lewd behavior . . . upon a bed." Hammon, who was fifteen, was cleared of the charges; Norman, apparently older (and referred to throughout the record as "the wife of Hugh Norman"), was required to acknowledge publicly her "unchaste behavior" and received a warning that, if there were any subsequent "carriages," her punishment would be "greater."

1656: New Haven passed a law that punished by death "men lying with men as with women" and women changing "the natural use, into that which is against nature." This law was rare among colonial legislation for its inclusion of women's "unnatural acts."

1660: In New Netherland, Jan Quisthout van der Linde was executed by drowning for sodomy. Hendrick Harmensen, "the boy on whom Quisthout committed by force the above crime," was sentenced to a private whipping.

1665: Conquered by the English in 1664, New Netherland became a proprietary colony of the Duke of York. The following year, representatives from several towns enacted laws that included the death penalty for sodomy between men over the age of fourteen. The law specified that if "one party were Forced," he was exempt from capital punishment.

1668: New Jersey made sodomy between men a capital crime, exempting children under fourteen and victims of force. Plymouth and Connecticut subsequently amended their sodomy laws (in 1671 and 1672, respectively) to include the same exemptions.

1673–1677: Father Jacques Marquette made his first voyage down the Mississippi River and recounted that "some Illinois [Indians], as well as some Nadouessi, while still young, assume the garb of women, and retain it throughout their lives."

1680: New Hampshire passed its first capital laws, including sodomy between men, "unless one party were forced, or were under fourteen years of age."

1682: The Province of Pennsylvania, a Quaker colony, enacted legislation that made sodomy by "any person" a non–capital offense—the first American colony to show such leniency. The punishment was limited to whipping, forfeiting one-third of one's estate, and six months at hard labor. This law was amended in 1700 to require life imprisonment and, for married men, castration for the offense.

1712: Mingo, a slave of Wait Winthrop, chief justice of Massachusetts, was executed in Charlestown for "forcible Buggery."

• South Carolina legislators included the text of the English "buggery law" of 1533, including its death penalty, in their colonial statutes.

1718: Pennsylvania revised its sodomy law, making it a capital offense.

1719: The Delaware Assembly adopted a sodomy law, reproduced from the 1718 Pennsylvania law.

1721: Jesuit explorer Pierre François Xavier de Charlevoix noted in his journal that "effeminacy and lewdness were carried to the greatest excess" by the Iroquois, the Illinois, and other Indian nations of the area that would become Louisiana.

1776: Fleury Mesplet, a friend of Benjamin Franklin and a fellow printer, published the play *Jonathas et David, or Le Triomphe de l'amitie*, which became the first book ever printed in Montreal. The play was a tragedy in three acts, describing the thinly veiled homoerotic relationship between Jonathan and David in the Old Testament.

1778: In the newly formed Continental Army, Lieutenant Frederick Gotthold Enslin was court-martialed for "attempting to commit sodomy."

1782: Deborah Sampson, a descendent of Governor William Bradford, was excommunicated from the First Baptist Church of Middleborough, Massachusetts, for "dressing in men's clothes" and for behaving "very loose and unchristian like."

1798: Moreau de St. Mery, a French lawyer and politician, wrote that women in Philadelphia, where he lived for several years, "are not at all strangers to being willing to seek unnatural pleasures with persons of their own sex."

1804–1810: Nicholas Biddle, a member of the Lewis and Clark expeditions, recorded that "among Minitarees [Indians] if a boy shows any symptoms of effeminacy or girlish inclinations he is put among the girls, dressed in their way, brought up with them, & sometimes married to men. . . . the French called them Birdashes."

1811: In an account of events at Fort Astoria in the Oregon Territory, Gabriel Franchere made the first written reference to a female berdache from the Kutenai Indian nation, who dressed as a man and was accompanied by a "wife."

1824–1826: A printed broadside by Louis Dwight was the first known document in the United States to discuss homosexuality in the country's prisons.

1839: In Montreal, two boys—Thomas Clotworthy, seventeen, and Henry Cole, eleven—both apprenticed to a local gilder, were discovered in bed together, committing sodomy. They were prosecuted, but nothing is known of their fate. This is the only documented North American civilian case of sodomy prosecution resulting from bed-sharing.

1846: Edward McCosker was dismissed from the New York City Police Department for making "indecent" advances to other men while on duty.

1848: The first Women's Rights Convention in Seneca Falls, New York, passed a "Declaration of Sentiments and Resolutions." The forerunner of the modern feminist movement, this convention jettisoned several probable lesbian and bisexual women into the national limelight, most notably Susan B. Anthony.

1860: Walt Whitman published the homoerotic *Leaves of Grass*, which later inspired numerous gay poets.

1866: Horatio Alger, the author of numerous popular books for boys, was accused by the Unitarian Church of Brewster, Massachusetts, of "practicing" on boys "deeds . . . too revolting to relate." Alger neither denied nor confirmed the charges and left town immediately after "for parts unknown."

1870: Bayard Taylor's *Joseph and His Friend,* the first U.S. novel to touch on the subject of homosexuality, was published.

1886: A news story in Montreal's *La Presse* featured the earliest available documentation of gay night life in the city, when it described the activity in a nocturnal cruising spot, the Champs-de-Mars, and the arrest of a gay man, Clovis Villeneuve, through police entrapment.

1892: In Tennessee, Alice Mitchell was tried for the murder of her lover, Freda Ward, and judged to be insane. The teenage girls were "engaged" and planned to marry, with Alice intending to pass as a man. When the affair was discovered and broken up by Freda's older sister, Alice "could not bear the thought of losing her" and slit Freda's throat in a mad fit of passion.

1896: For the first time on the American stage, two women hugged and kissed in a scene of the play, *A Florida Enchantment.* Though the play was not lesbian in content, the scene was so controversial that, at intermission, ushers offered ice water to any audience member who felt faint.

1897: Havelock Ellis wrote in his famous *Sexual Inversion* of "the great prevalence of sexual inversion in American cities." His book was the first to treat homosexuality impartially, but his observations were limited to men.

1901: Influential New York politician Murray Hall died and was revealed to have been a passing woman.

1912: At Polly Halliday's restaurant in New York City, Heterodoxy, a feminist luncheon club for "unorthodox women," began meeting bimonthly. Among its members were many prominent lesbians, including Helen Hull, Katharine Anthony, Dr. Sara Josephine Baker, and Elisabeth Irwin, and bisexual women such as Mabel Dodge Luhan. Heterodoxy met on a regular basis to discuss politics and social issues until the early 1940s.

1914: In Portland, Oregon, a dictionary of criminal slang was published, in which the first printed use of the word "faggot" to refer to male homosexuals appeared.

1916: The Provincetown Playhouse, the first major off-Broadway theater, was founded in New York's Greenwich Village. In its early days, Edna St. Vincent Millay and Djuna Barnes were associated with the theater. In a later incarnation, the theater presented Edward Albee's first play *The Zoo Story* and Charles Busch's *Vampire Lesbians of Sodom.*

1917: In Montreal, nineteen-year-old Elsa Gidlow, a budding writer and a lesbian, started an artists' salon in her parents' home, which welcomed several women writers, a painter, and a gay man named Roswell George Mills, who became her mentor. Subsequently, the salon members published a literary magazine called *Les mouches fantastique,* the informal name of the group. Gidlow later moved to the United States, wrote fifteen books, and became a mentor to a younger generation of lesbian writers.

1919: Dispatching a squad of young enlisted men to act as decoys, the U.S. Navy, by order of under secretary Franklin D. Roosevelt, initiated a search for "sexual perverts" at the Newport (Rhode Island) Naval Training Station. Based on information the plants gathered, twenty sailors and sixteen civilians were arrested on morals charges by naval and municipal authorities.

1920–1935: Referred to as the Harlem Renaissance, this period witnessed an unprecedented flourishing of African-American culture in the United States. Central to this significant time in African-American history were many gay, lesbian, and bisexual writers, artists, and musicians, including Countee Cullen, Claude McKay, Langston Hughes, Bessie Smith, Ma Rainey, Alain Locke, Bruce Nugent, and Ethel Waters.

1923: Sholom Asch's *God of Vengeance,* one of the earliest plays with lesbian content, opened on Broadway. The play was originally written in Yiddish in 1907 and was first produced in Berlin.

1924: Henry Gerber and others founded the Society for Human Rights in Illinois, believed to be the first homosexual organization in the United States. Though it lasted only a few months, the society published two issues of *Friendship and Freedom,* the first homosexual liberation magazine in the country.

1926: *The Captive,* another early play with lesbian content, opened on Broadway, starring Helen Menken, then the wife of Humphrey Bogart. As one newspaper critic put it, "Lesbian love walked out onto a New York stage. . . ." The play raised a flurry of public controversy, and William Randolph Hearst, the newspaper magnate, made it a campaign to "wipe out those evil plays now menacing the future of the theater." *The Captive* was raided and shut down, and the following year the Wade "Padlock" Law was enacted, prohibiting Broadway plays from depicting "sex perversion." Though only occasionally enforced, the law remained on the books until 1967.

  • The journal *Fire!,* a periodical showcasing the work of Harlem Renaissance writers, published its first and only issue. Included was the erotic narrative poem, "Smoke, Lilies and Jade," by Bruce Nugent, which was the first published piece about homosexuality by an African-American writer.

1927: Written and produced by Mae West, *The Drag*, the first play with gay male content to be produced in the United States, debuted in Connecticut on its way to Broadway. It further fueled the controversy started by the Broadway run of *The Captive* and was closed before it reached New York.

1929: New York publisher Covici-Friede was convicted of obscenity for publishing Radclyffe Hall's lesbian novel, *The Well of Loneliness*. The conviction was later appealed and overturned.

1930: Hollywood studios enacted the Motion Picture Production Code, prohibiting all references to homosexuality or "sexual perversion" in the movies. Though initially not enforced, the code was strengthened in 1934 under pressure from the Catholic-led Legion for Decency and remained in effect until the 1960s.

1934: Despite the Padlock Bill, Lillian Hellman's play *The Children's Hour*— about two teachers accused by a student of being lesbians—opened on Broadway. It may have escaped closing because of its moralistic ending: the one character who is indeed a lesbian killed herself.

1942: The U.S. military issued its first official prohibition against homosexuals in the armed forces. Because the country was in the middle of World War II, the policy was not stringently enforced until after the war.

• The book, *A Generation of Vipers*, by Philip Wylie, was published, coining the word "Momism" to blame American mothers for overprotecting their sons and raising unmasculine boys unfit for military service.

• In Los Angeles, Jim Kepner began his private collection of gay-related books, clippings, photographs, and artifacts, which later became the International Gay and Lesbian Archive, the oldest and largest in North America. The archive opened to the public in 1979.

1947: The pseudonymous Lisa Ben (an anagram for "lesbian") began publishing *Vice Versa*, the first U.S. lesbian magazine, in Los Angeles. From her desk as a secretary at RKO Studios, Ben typed each issue twice using four carbons, then circulated the ten copies of the publication to lesbian friends, who in turn passed it on to others.

1948: The Kinsey Institute published its ground-breaking study of sexual behavior in American men. Among its findings were: 50 percent of those surveyed admitted erotic responses to other men; 37 percent had had at least one adult homosexual experience; and 10 percent were exclusively homosexual for at least

A San Francisco lesbian bar scene of the 1940s, from the documentary *Last Call at Maud's*.

three years of their adulthood. The celebrated "Kinsey scale" displayed a significant amount of fluctuation in sexual activity, from 1 (exclusively heterosexual) to 6 (exclusively homosexual). Kinsey's findings shook the heterosexual
world and helped foster a sense of community and self-acceptance among homosexuals. (See **1953**.)

1951: Harry Hay, Chuck Rowland, and others formed the Mattachine Society in
Los Angeles, one of the first gay organizations in the United States and forerunner of the current gay liberation movement.

1952: The United States Congress enacted a law banning lesbian and gay for-
eigners from entering the country. The legislation was on the books until its repeal in 1990.

  • George Jorgensen, a former sergeant in the U.S. Army, underwent his
famous sex-change operation in Denmark, becoming Christine Jorgensen.

1953: President Eisenhower signed Executive Order 10450, making "sexual perversion" grounds for exclusion from federal employment.

  • The magazine *ONE*, designed to air gay and lesbian opinions and concerns to the public, began publication in Los Angeles.

  • The Kinsey Institute published its second historic study on human sexuality, *Sexual Behavior in the Human Female*. Its findings include: 28 percent of
women surveyed responded erotically to other women; 13 percent had had at
least one adult lesbian sexual experience; and between 2 and 6 percent identified their sexual orientation as exclusively lesbian between the ages of twenty
and thirty-five.

  • Dr. Evelyn Hooker began her historic study of male homosexual personality. In the late 1950s, she published the findings of her research in a series
of monographs, reporting that she could find no signs of maladjustment in homosexual men's personalities. Her study thus disputed the prevailing medical
theory that homosexuality was a "sickness."

1954: The Los Angeles postmaster seized copies of *ONE* magazine and refused
to mail them, on the grounds that they were "obscene, lewd, lascivious and
filthy." The incident was sparked by an article about J. Edgar Hoover and his
lover. *ONE* editors challenged the postmaster, but two courts upheld the postal
service's action in 1956 and 1957. Finally, in 1958, the U.S. Supreme Court, in
a "legal and publishing landmark," reversed the rulings of the two lower courts,
ensuring the distribution of lesbian and gay materials through the mail service.

1955: The Daughters of Bilitis, the first lesbian organization in the United States,
was founded in San Francisco by Del Martin and Phyllis Lyon.

1956: *The Ladder*, the official magazine of the Daughters of Bilitis, began publication.

1957: The American Civil Liberties Union (ACLU) adopted a national policy
statement that sustained the constitutionality of state sodomy laws and federal
security regulations denying employment to gay men and lesbians. The ACLU
finally reversed this policy in 1964.

1960: The first national lesbian conference, a convention of the Daughters of
Bilitis, was held in San Francisco.

1961: Illinois became the first state to abolish its laws against consensual homosexual sex.

1964: The first homosexual rights demonstration in New York City took place. Ten participants from the Homosexual League of New York and the League for Sexual Freedom picketed the Army Induction Center on Whitehall Street, protesting the army's dishonorable discharges of gay soldiers.

   • Jane Rule published her first lesbian novel, *Desert of the Heart,* which became an instant classic and was made into the popular movie, *Desert Hearts,* in 1985.

   • The earliest known homosexual rights button was produced for the Washington, D.C., conference of East Coast Homophile Organizations (ECHO).

   • *Two* magazine, whose name was inspired by the U.S. magazine, *ONE,* began publication and continued publishing until 1966. It was the first gay magazine in Canada.

   • The Association for Social Knowledge (ASK), the oldest known homophile organization in Canada, was formed in Vancouver.

1965: The Mattachine Society led a picket in front of the White House, protesting the government's discriminatory employment practices. Seven men and three women participated in the action. The first of its kind ever, the picket received national TV coverage.

1966: The National Organization for Women (NOW) was founded in New York.

   • The SIR Center (Society for Individual Rights) opened in San Francisco, the first gay community center in North America.

   • ASK Community Center opened in Vancouver, Canada, to "serve the homosexual community." It was the first gay community center in Canada.

1967: *The Advocate*, the oldest continuing gay publication in the United States, began publishing in Los Angeles.

   • The Oscar Wilde Memorial Bookshop, the oldest gay bookstore in the United States, opened in New York City on Mercer Street. In 1973, the store relocated to its current site at the junction of Christopher and Gay streets.

   • John Herbert's play about homosexuality in the Canadian prison system, *Fortune and Men's Eyes*, was published in Toronto.

   • In San Francisco, a group of radical gays formed the Circle of Loving Companions and began publishing a monthly called *Vanguard.*

1968: The Metropolitan Community Church was founded in Los Angeles by Rev. Troy Perry for gay people who wanted to worship together.

   • At Johns Hopkins University, Dr. John Money performed the first complete male-to-female sex-change operation in the United States.

1969: In late June, when plainclothes police raided the Stonewall Inn in New York's Greenwich Village, they met violent resistance from gay patrons of the bar and people on the street, including transvestites, butch lesbians, and gay teenagers. The weekend of riots is now viewed as the start of the modern gay liberation movement.

   • Taking its name from the National Liberation Front in Vietnam, the Gay Liberation Front (GLF) was founded in New York by participants in the

Stonewall riots and others in the gay community as an ongoing militant political action group.

• *Time* magazine's "The Homosexual in America" became the first cover story on gay rights in a national magazine.

• *Gay Power* became the first gay newspaper to appear after the Stonewall Riots.

• Amendments to the Canadian criminal code took effect, legalizing private sexual acts between consenting adults over the age of twenty-one.

• The University of Toronto Homophile Association (UTHA), the first gay liberation organization in Canada, began meeting.

1970: The first legislative hearings on gay rights in the United States were convened in New York City by three New York State Assembly members.

• The first march to commemorate the Stonewall Riots was held in New York. Several thousand participants marched up Sixth Avenue to Sheep Meadow in Central Park, where the march was followed by a Be-In.

• Catalyst Press, the first gay press in Canada, was launched in Toronto by Ian Young and published its first book, *Cool Fire*, by Young and Richard Phelan.

• Radicalesbians, a New York–based group of lesbian-feminists who split from the Gay Liberation Front, published the manifesto "The Woman-Identified Woman," which defined a lesbian as "the rage of all women condensed to the point of explosion."

• The first lesbian/feminist bookstore in the United States, Amazon Bookstore in Minneapolis, opened for business. Also that year, A Woman's Place bookstore was started in Oakland, California.

• Robin Morgan published her compilation, *Sisterhood Is Powerful: An Anthology of Writings from the Women's Liberation Movement*.

1971: The Los Angeles Gay and Lesbian Community Services Center was founded, the oldest gay community center still in existence in North America.

• The Furies, a lesbian-feminist separatist collective, was founded by lesbian activists fed up with mainstream women's organizations like the National Organization for Women (NOW). Original members included Joan E. Biren, Rita Mae Brown, Charlotte Bunch, and Helaine Harris.

• NOW approved its first resolution supporting lesbian rights. A similar resolution in the previous year had been attacked and defeated by NOW founder Betty Friedan, who labeled lesbians "the Lavender Menace."

• The American Library Association began awarding an annual Gay Book Award. The first went to Isabel Miller for her novel *Patience and Sarah*.

• A full ten years after Illinois, Connecticut became the second state to repeal its sodomy laws.

• The first francophone gay organization in Canada, Front de liberation homosexuel, was formed in Montreal, and sponsored rap groups and organized the first gay dances in the city.

• The "We Demand" brief—sponsored by Canadian gay groups and calling for legal reform and changes in public policy relating to homosexuals—was presented to the federal government. The first public gay demonstration in Canada took place a week later on Parliament Hill in support of the brief.

Lesbian/gay candlelight march on New York's City Hall, June 1971 *(Photo by Richard C. Wandel)*

The second annual Christopher Street Liberation Day Parade, June 1971 *(Photo by Richard C. Wandel)*

1972: The United States Senate approved the Equal Rights Amendment (ERA), which prohibited discrimination on the basis of gender, and sent the bill to the state assemblies for ratification. Phyllis Schlafly and the Eagle Forum led the fight to block ratification, and after a bitter ten-year fight, the ERA was defeated in 1982.

• A U.S. district judge ruled that the Civil Service Commission could not discriminate against gay employees unless it could prove that being gay would interfere with their jobs.

• The first gay synagogue in the United States, Beth Chayim Chadashim in Los Angeles, was founded. The following year, the second and now the largest gay synagogue in the world, Congregation Beth Simchat Torah in New York, was formed.

• The first Canadian nonfiction book on homosexuality, *A Not So Gay World: Homosexuality in Canada*, was published.

• East Lansing, Michigan, became the first city in the United States to ban antigay bias in city hiring.

• William Johnson became the first openly gay man to be ordained as a minister by a major religious denomination, the United Church of Christ, in California.

• The first issue of *The Other Woman*, a predominantly lesbian feminist publication, was produced in Toronto.

• Toronto Gay Action organized its first Gay Pride Week, August 19–27.

1973: The Supreme Court of the United States ruled in *Roe v. Wade* that constitutional privacy rights included a woman's right to a first-trimester abortion. Twenty years later, Norma McCorvey, a lesbian, revealed herself as "Jane Roe."

• Under the auspices of the YWCA, the first national lesbian conference in Canada was held in Toronto, and Montreal Gay Women was founded as a separatist group the same year. Shortly after, the first lesbian journal in Canada, *Long Time Coming*, began publication in Montreal.

• The Toronto City Council passed a resolution banning discrimination in municipal hiring on the basis of sexual orientation, the first such legislation in North America.

• The National Gay Task Force (later the National Gay and Lesbian Task Force), a civil rights group, was founded in New York. The Task Force opened an office in Washington in 1986.

• The Canadian Gay Archives was founded by *The Body Politic*, with the newspaper's back files as a foundation.

• *Gay Community News* was founded in Boston and was the only lesbian and gay newsweekly in the United States at the time.

• The first pan-Canadian conference of gay organizations, hosted by Centre humanitaire d'aide et de liberation (CHAL) was held in Quebec City.

• Daughters, Inc., a lesbian-feminist publishing house founded by June Arnold and Parke Bowman, published the first edition of Rita Mae Brown's *Rubyfruit Jungle,* which later was sold to Bantam Books as a mass-market paperback.

• Naiad Press was started in Florida by Barbara Grier and Donna McBride. Naiad is now the oldest surviving lesbian book publisher in North America.

• Olivia Records, the leader in women's music, was founded by a lesbian-feminist collective. The company cut its first single the following year, with Meg Christian on one side and Cris Williamson on the other.

• The American Psychiatric Association decided that homosexuality should no longer be classified as a mental disorder.

• The Lesbian Herstory Archives was started in New York City, housed in the apartment of founders Joan Nestle and Deborah Edel, taking as its mission the preservation of the lives and works of all lesbians.

• The American Bar Association passed a resolution recommending the repeal of all state sodomy laws.

• The Supreme Court of the United States restricted the availability of sexually explicit material in two rulings, *Miller v. California* and *Paris Adult Theater I v. Slaton.* The rulings allowed local communities to define obscenity and eliminated a national standard.

• Lambda Legal Defense and Education Fund was founded as a nonprofit gay law firm dedicated to obtaining gay civil rights through the courts.

1974: HR-14752, a bill to prohibit antigay discrimination across the United States—the first of its kind in U.S. history—was introduced into the House of

Joan Nestle (l.), one of the cofounders of the Lesbian Herstory Archives, and Mabel Hampton (1902–1989), lesbian entertainer, domestic worker, and activist (*Copyright © 1984 by Morgan Gwenwald*)

Official opening of the Gay Activists Alliance Firehouse on Wooster Street in New York City, 1971 *(Photo by Richard C. Wandel)*

Representatives by Bella Abzug and Edward Koch. The bill sought to add protections for gays to the 1964 Civil Rights Act.

• Comunidad Orgullo Gay (COG), the first gay and lesbian organization on the island of Puerto Rico, was founded to work for the repeal of the sodomy laws included in the New Penal Code under consideration by the legislature.

• In Milton, Ontario, fundamentalist minister Ken Campbell, outraged by members of a local gay group addressing his daughter's high school class, formed the Halton Renaissance Committee, the forerunner of Renaissance Canada, which became one of the strongest organizations opposing gay rights in Canada.

• *Lesbian Connection*—now the largest-circulation lesbian periodical in the United States—began publication in East Lansing, Michigan, by the Ambitions Amazons collective.

• Elaine Noble, elected to the Massachusetts state legislature, became the first openly gay elected official in the United States.

1975: Santa Cruz County, California, became the first U.S. county to ban antigay discrimination.

• *Consenting Adult*, Laura Z. Hobson's groundbreaking novel about a gay teenage boy, was published.

• In Canada, a joint parliamentary committee on immigration policy recommended that homosexuals no longer be prohibited from entering Canada under the revised Immigration Act.

1976: The lesbian feminist journal, *Conditions*, was founded in New York by Elly

Bulkin, Jan Clausen, Irena Klepfisz, and Rima Shore. The journal was dedicated to publishing the work of lesbians, particularly working-class lesbians and lesbians of color.

• Montreal police launched a series of raids on gay bars designed to clean up the city before the opening of the summer Olympics. The largest gay demonstration at that time, organized by Comite homosexuel anti-repression/Gay Coalition against Repression, was held to protest the raids. The group later evolved into the Association pour les droits des gai(e)s du Quebec (ADGQ).

• In *Rose v. Locke*, the U.S. Supreme Court ruled that cunnilingus was covered by Tennessee's "crimes against nature" statute, even though it was not expressly mentioned there.

• The first Michigan Womyn's Music Festival, a celebration of lesbian culture, included musical performances by Holly Near, Linda Tillery, and Maxine Feldman.

• Armistead Maupin began serializing his famous "Tales of the City" in the *San Francisco Chronicle*.

• The Lesbian Organization of Toronto (LOOT) was founded, with its first priority the establishment of a lesbian center.

1977: Voters in Dade County, Florida, repealed a gay rights law by a two to one margin. The fight to repeal was led by fundamentalist singer, orange juice–industry spokesperson, and former Miss America contestant, Anita Bryant.

• Toronto police raided the offices of *The Body Politic*, Canada's leading gay newspaper, seizing records, manuscripts, and subscription lists. The newspaper was charged with using the mail service to distribute "indecent" material. After a long and costly legal battle (and another police raid in 1982), the paper was acquitted, but its financial problems forced it to cease publication in 1987.

• The Women's Archives was formed in Toronto to preserve and record Canadian women's history.

• The Combahee River Collective, an African-American lesbian feminist group, published "A Black Feminist Statement," a historic manifesto that put forth a political analysis recognizing the interconnectedness of oppressions based on identity.

• Coop-femmes, the first francophone lesbian group in Canada, was founded in Montreal.

• Senior Action in a Gay Environment (SAGE) was founded in New York to serve the social and political needs of older lesbians and gay men.

• The province of Quebec amended its provincial Charter of Human Rights, adding lesbians and gay men to the list of those protected, thus banning antigay discrimination in employment, housing, and public accommodations. It was the first jurisdiction in North America to protect its citizens against discrimination on the basis of sexual orientation.

1978: The U.S. Supreme Court, in *Federal Communications Commission v. Pacifica Foundation*, approved restrictions on broadcast material that was "indecent," but not "obscene." The case was used to block the broadcast of gay-themed programs.

- San Francisco Supervisor Harvey Milk, an out gay man, and Mayor George Moscone were murdered by Dan White.
- The rainbow flag, which is one of the most prominent symbols of lesbian and gay pride, was designed by Gilbert Baker in San Francisco and flew in the Gay Freedom Day Parade there.
- An hour-long radio program, "Gay News and Views," began airing on an Ontario station, the first regularly scheduled gay radio program in Canada.
- *Dancer from the Dance*, by Andrew Holleran, was published and is now considered a classic novel about white gay male life and culture before AIDS.
- Gay and Lesbian Advocates and Defenders (GLAD), New England's nonprofit, public-interest gay and lesbian law foundation, was founded in Boston by John Ward, Richard Burns, Cindy Rizzo, and others.
- California voters defeated the Briggs Initiative, which would have barred lesbians and gay men from teaching in the state's public schools.

1979: The first national March on Washington for Gay and Lesbian Civil Rights drew over one hundred thousand marchers.

- Dan White was acquitted of first-degree murder in the deaths of Harvey Milk and George Moscone and was convicted of the lesser charge of manslaughter. His lawyer successfully argued that White's mental capacity was diminished by his excessive consumption of Twinkies and other junk food. In 1985, White was released from prison and then killed himself.
- *Conditions* magazine published the groundbreaking "Black Women's Issue," later the basis for the anthology *Home Girls,* one of the first titles from Kitchen Table: Women of Color Press (see **1981**).
- The first issue of the francophone journal *Le Berdache* was published in Montreal.
- The U.S. Mint issued the Susan B. Anthony dollar, named for the noted feminist and probable lesbian.
- Fundamentalist minister Jerry Falwell founded the Moral Majority in Lynchburg, Virginia. The organization listed as its goals opposition to abortion, feminism, pornography, communism, and gay rights.
- Stephen Lachs became the first openly gay judge in the United States, appointed to the Superior Court of Los Angeles.

1980: The Gay Community Appeal of Toronto was incorporated and began plans to launch the first United Way–type fund-raising drive in North America.

- Alyson Publications, presently the largest gay press in the United States, was founded in Boston by gay activist Sasha Alyson.
- Mel Boozer, an African-American gay man, became the first openly gay person to have his name placed in nomination as a candidate at the Democratic National Convention. As a vice presidential nominee, he addressed the convention.
- The Canadian Union of Postal Workers ratified a contract that included a nondiscrimination clause protecting gay people. This was the first time gay employees of a federal government anywhere in the world were awarded such protection.
- The Toronto Board of Education amended its policy to ban discrimina-

tion on the basis of sexual orientation, but added a clause forbidding "prosely-tizing of homosexuality in the schools."

• The Fifth Canadian Binational Lesbian Conference drew women from across Canada and resulted in the organization of Canada's first lesbian pride march.

1981: The U.S. Department of Defense revised its policy on lesbians and gays in the military. The new policy barred gay people from serving in the military and required that questions about sexual orientation be asked of all recruits.

• Toronto police undertook a massive raid on gay bathhouses and arrested over three hundred men. It was the largest mass arrest in Canadian history and the largest mass arrest of gay men in North America. The arrests generated a riot that has been called the Canadian Stonewall.

• The *New York Times* reported the first cases of Kaposi's sarcoma, a rare form of cancer, in forty-one gay men. In addition, the Centers for Disease Control (CDC) made known the growing number of cases of Pneumocystis carinii pneumonia (PCP) among gay men.

• A new Kinsey Institute study reported that neither parental nor societal influences have much effect on a person's sexual orientation.

• Governor Jerry Brown of California appointed Mary Morgan to the state supreme court, making her the first openly lesbian judge.

• Kitchen Table: Women of Color Press, the first publishing house in North America devoted to producing works by women of color, was founded in New York by Barbara Smith, Audre Lorde, Cherie Moraga, and a group of other writers and activists.

Barbara Smith (l.), cofounder of Kitchen Table: Women of Color Press, and writer Dorothy Allison *(Copyright © Morgan Gwenwald)*

- The first lesbian pride march in Toronto, "Dykes in the Streets," was sponsored by Lesbians against the Right.
- A group of Los Angeles parents formed the support group Parents and Friends of Lesbians and Gay Men (P-FLAG) to help each other and to help combat society's homophobia against gay people.
- Marilyn Barnett filed a "galimony" suit against her former employer and lover, tennis champion Billie Jean King. King said she was straight, but didn't deny the affair.
- The New York City Gay Men's Chorus became the first gay musical group to perform at Carnegie Hall. A year later, Meg Christian and Cris Williamson became the first out lesbians to play there.

1982: Wisconsin became the first state to enact statewide gay rights legislation.

- A Los Angeles man filed a palimony suit against entertainer Liberace, who denied that he was gay.
- The first Gay Games were held in San Francisco, with 1,300 participants from twelve countries. They were forbidden to use the word "Olympics" by the U.S. Olympic Commission.
- Gay related immune disorder (GRID) acquired the new name of Acquired Immunodeficiency Syndrome (AIDS).
- Gay men in New York founded Gay Men's Health Crisis (GMHC), a social service and education agency, to deal with growing concern over the spread of AIDS among gay men.
- The first Montreal lesbian publications in French, *Amazones d'hier, Lesbiennes d'aujourd'hui* and *Ca s'attrape*, were circulated.
- Byton High in Philadelphia, the first gay high school in the United States, was started as an alternative to the public school system.

1983: Representative Gerry Studds (D-Mass.) declared on the floor of the U.S. House of Representatives that he was gay.

- Howard Cruse's gay comic strip "Wendel" first appeared in *The Advocate*. Alison Bechdel's comic strip "Dykes to Watch Out For" was first published in New York's *Womanews*.
- Les Archives gaies du Quebec opened in Montreal with the mission of collecting books, manuscripts, magazines, newspapers, photographs, films, and objects related to gay life in the province.
- A group of lesbian and gay activists acquired a former public high school building from the city of New York, and the Lesbian and Gay Community Services Center was born. The following year, the building was purchased for $1.5 million.

1984: San Francisco Health Department head Mervyn Silverman closed fourteen gay bathhouses after investigators uncovered high-risk sexual behavior in them.

- Government officials announced the discovery of the "probable cause" of AIDS, then known as HTLV-III, but eventually renamed HIV (human immunodeficiency virus).
- Berkeley, California, became the first city in the United States to extend domestic partnership benefits to lesbian and gay city employees.

• West Hollywood incorporated as a municipality and elected a largely gay city council and a lesbian mayor.

1985: After repeated denials, movie and television actor Rock Hudson finally issued a public statement that he had AIDS and died three months later.

• A test for HIV antibodies was licensed by the U.S. Food and Drug Administration (FDA), allowing for the testing of both individuals and the existing blood supplies.

• The Democratic Party voted to drop official recognition of some caucuses, including the Gay and Lesbian Caucus.

• Canadian customs banned *The Joy of Gay Sex*, one of many such instances of censorship by the Canadian government.

• More than a hundred well-known women—including Lily Tomlin, Yoko Ono, Joanne Woodward, and Joyce Carol Oates—signed a *Ms.* magazine Petition for Freedom of Sexual Choice, condemning all government attempts to interfere in "the sexual lives of consenting adults."

• Angered by the media's poor coverage of the AIDS epidemic, a group of New York activists founded the Gay and Lesbian Alliance against Defamation (GLAAD) during a meeting at the Lesbian and Gay Community Services Center. GLAAD served as a watchdog on the presentation of lesbians and gay men in Hollywood and the media.

• The Harvey Milk School, a public high school for lesbian and gay youth, was started in New York City as a collaborative project of the Hetrick-Martin Institute, a social service agency for gay youth, and the city's public school system.

1986: The province of Ontario, Canada, passed a gay rights ordinance.

• In *Bowers v. Hardwick*, the U.S. Supreme Court upheld the constitutionality of Georgia's sodomy law. In Atlanta in 1982, police tried to serve Michael Hardwick at home with a warrant for a traffic violation and found him having sex with another man. Hardwick was arrested for sodomy, and his appeal went all the way to the Supreme Court.

• The U.S. Public Health Service released the experimental drug AZT to people with Pneumocystis carinii pneumonia (PCP).

• The U.S. Justice Department ended its policy of asking prospective federal prosecutors if they were gay.

• Californians rejected an initiative that called for the quarantine of people with AIDS.

1987: Delta Airlines apologized for arguing in plane crash litigation that it should pay less in compensation for the life of a gay passenger than for a heterosexual one because he might have had AIDS.

• The second national March on Washington for Lesbian and Gay Rights drew approximately a half million participants. During a weekend of events, two thousand lesbian and gay couples participated in a mass wedding in front of the Internal Revenue Service building. Also, the NAMES Project quilt, which was the size of two football fields, was displayed on the mall in front of the U.S. Capitol.

• President Reagan underwent testing for HIV when he became concerned about the blood transfusions he received when he was shot in 1981. According to a White House spokesperson, he tested negative.

• Massachusetts Representative Barney Frank told an interviewer in the *Boston Globe* that he was gay.

• Robert Bork, who openly opposed gay rights, was rejected as a candidate for the U.S. Supreme Court.

• Vermont became the first state to distribute condoms to prison inmates.

• At a meeting at the New York Lesbian and Gay Community Services Center, activist Larry Kramer and others started the AIDS Coalition to Unleash Power (ACT UP), a direct action group whose purpose was to draw public and government attention to the need for AIDS funding and research.

• The *Lambda Book Report* began publication, the first journal devoted to reviews of works by lesbian and gay writers.

1988: The first World AIDS Day, organized by the World Health Organization, was held.

• On October 11, the first anniversary of the historic 1987 lesbian and gay march on Washington, National Coming Out Day was first celebrated, set aside as a day when gay people could each make a step toward coming completely out of the closet.

• Citizens of Oregon repealed a ban on antigay job discrimination, paving the way for the antigay initiatives in Oregon in the early 1990s.

• In Canada, sodomy and anal intercourse between consenting adults over eighteen were eliminated as criminal offenses.

• President Reagan's newly founded National AIDS Commission released a report, with over five hundred recommendations for addressing the epidemic. A presidential adviser reduced the list to ten items.

• *OUT/LOOK*, a national lesbian and gay magazine of politics and culture, began quarterly publication.

• Democrat Svend Robinson became the first member of the Canadian Parliament to come out as gay.

1989: In *Watkins v. United States Army,* a federal court ordered the reinstatement of Perry Watkins, who had been dismissed from the service because he was gay.

• The U.S. Supreme Court, in *Price Waterhouse v. Hopkins,* ruled that the accounting firm violated sex discrimination laws by dismissing a woman for "masculine behavior."

• The Corcoran Art Gallery in Washington, D.C., canceled a retrospective of Robert Mapplethorpe's photographs after the exhibit was attacked by Senator Jesse Helms and others for its homoerotic content. The director of the gallery resigned, and in the ensuing brouhaha, Mapplethorpe's name became a household word, synonymous with artistic censorship.

• The first annual Lambda Literary Awards for excellence in lesbian and gay writing were held at the American Booksellers Association convention in Washington, D.C.

• Mayor Ed Koch dedicated Stonewall Place in New York City—the strip of Christopher Street where the Stonewall riots took place—to commemorate the twentieth anniversary of the event.

• The U.S. Post Office issued a lesbian and gay pride postmark, commemorating the twentieth anniversary of the Stonewall riots and featuring the artwork of gay artist Keith Haring.

• San Francisco's Maud's, "the world's oldest lesbian bar," closed after twenty-three years due in part to the rise of twelve-step recovery groups among lesbians and a subsequent decrease in patronage.

• Massachusetts became the second state to pass a gay civil rights law.

• Over five thousand ACT UP activists staged a massive protest in front of and inside New York's St. Patrick's Cathedral, rallying against the Catholic Church's negative policies on homosexuality and AIDS.

1990: Cincinnati Museum of Art director Dennis Barrie was charged and acquitted of obscenity for booking a traveling exhibit of homoerotic photographs by Robert Mapplethorpe.

• The American with Disabilities Act, which also prohibited AIDS-based discrimination, was signed into law.

• During President Bush's first major address on AIDS, National Gay and Lesbian Task Force executive director Urvashi Vaid interrupted his speech and protested his inactivity. She was escorted outside.

• Queer Nation—an in-your-face direct action group with the rallying cry, "We're here, we're queer, get used to it!"—was founded in New York City at a meeting at the Lesbian and Gay Community Services Center.

• The Astraea Foundation (founded in 1977) changed its name to the Astraea National Lesbian Action Foundation, becoming the first national foundation to fund lesbian cultural and social change projects exclusively.

• During Lesbian and Gay Pride weekend in June, the top of the Empire State Building was lit up in lavender for the first time.

• In an unprecedented move, National Endowment for the Arts chair John Frohnmayer revoked grants already awarded by a peer panel to four solo theater artists, Karen Finley, John Fleck, Holly Hughes, and Tim Miller. Frohnmayer cited as his rationale "political realities," but the artists (who became known as "The NEA Four") cried censorship, and their defunding became a cause célèbre in the lesbian and gay arts community. Three of the four were gay, and all created performance art dealing explicitly with sexuality. The investigation that led to the defunding was initiated by none other than Senator Jesse Helms, who said he wanted the public to know what filth their tax dollars were funding. The four artists brought a lawsuit against the NEA and in 1993 settled out of court for $252,000.

• Philip Morris—particularly its products, Miller Beer and Marlboro cigarettes—became the object of a national gay boycott, to protest the company's alleged funding of the campaign of virulently antigay senator Jesse Helms.

1991: The Minnesota Court of Appeals awarded guardianship of Sharon Kowalski, a lesbian severely injured in a car crash, to her lover, Karen Thompson over the objections of Kowalski's parents.

- Patricia Ireland, Executive Director of the National Organization for Women, admitted to having a female lover—in addition to a husband.
- *The Advocate* outed Department of Defense spokesperson Pete Williams.
- Lesbian poet, teacher, and activist Audre Lorde was named Poet Laureate of New York State.
- *Tongues Untied,* Marlon Riggs's documentary about African-American gay men, aired on PBS and drew complaints to the FCC from some homophobic viewers.
- Dr. Simon LeVay released a controversial study suggesting a biological influence for sexual orientation, widely referred to as "the gay brain."
- The first Black Gay and Lesbian Pride March was held in Washington, D.C.

1992: Aileen Wuornos, the first lesbian serial killer in the United States, was sentenced to death in Florida.
- Canadian country and pop star k.d. lang became the first major female recording artist to come out as a lesbian.
- Democratic candidate Bill Clinton, in his acceptance of his nomination for president, mentioned gay people in his speech—the first time a presidential candidate had done so at the convention.
- Roberta Achtenberg, a lesbian member of San Francisco's Board of Supervisors, Bob Hattoy, a member of Clinton's campaign staff and a gay man with AIDS, and Elizabeth Glaser, an HIV-positive heterosexual woman, addressed the Democratic National Convention in New York.
- The Republican National Convention in Miami was a gay-bashing travesty filled with the rhetoric of "family values." However, Mary Fisher, an HIV-positive woman, was permitted to address the convention.
- The first National Lesbian Conference, designed as a strategy-building meeting for lesbian liberation, drew 2,500 participants to Atlanta.
- Lesbian Avengers, International, a direct action group dedicated to fighting lesbian oppression, was launched by activists Anne Christine d'Adesky, Marie Honan, Anne Maguire, Sarah Schulman, Anna Maria Simo, and Maxine Wolfe at a meeting at the Lesbian and Gay Community Services Center in New York. Within two years, the direct action group had grown to thirty-five chapters in North America and Europe.
- The first U.S. governor to do so, William Weld of Massachusetts signed an executive order granting lesbian and gay state workers the same bereavement and family leave rights as heterosexual workers.
- The Canadian government released documents that show that the Canadian Mounted Police spied on gay men in Ottawa during the Cold War period, creating files against them and purging hundreds from government jobs.
- Antigay initiatives were introduced in Oregon and Colorado. After bitter fights, the Colorado initiative passed and the more harshly worded Oregon one was rejected. The passage of the Colorado initiative sparked a national boycott of Colorado by gay people and their supporters.

• Canada lifted its ban on lesbians and gays in the military.

• In a decision historic for all of North America, the Canadian immigration service granted immigrant status to an Irish lesbian whose lover was a Canadian citizen.

• The National Gay and Lesbian Task Force announced that almost 1,900 incidents of antigay assaults, murder, vandalism, and threats were reported in 1992, up 4 percent from 1991.

• The Canadian YMCA Board of Directors reluctantly extended family membership discounts to lesbian and gay couples.

• New Jersey, Vermont, and California enacted statewide bans on antigay discrimination.

• Louisiana governor Edwin Edwards issued an executive order banning antigay discrimination in state agencies, making his the first state in the southeast to do so.

1993: President Bill Clinton directed the Secretary of Defense to investigate the possibility of drafting an executive order to overturn the 1981 ban on gays in the military. However, encountering fierce opposition from Congress, Clinton settled for a "don't ask, don't tell" compromise, which did not significantly change the earlier ban.

• The March on Washington for Gay, Lesbian, and Bi Equal Rights attracted an estimated 750,000 participants to the capital.

• Organized by the Lesbian Avengers, the first International Dyke March was held the evening before the March on Washington.

• A federally funded survey by the Battelle Human Affairs Research Centers concluded that only 2.3 percent of U.S. men had sex with other men, and only 1.1 percent considered themselves exclusively homosexual. The Christian Right jumped on the findings to say that homosexuality was a "behavioral oddity" and that gays do not deserve "protected status."

• For the first time in a Canadian province, the Ontario Human Rights Commission ruled that a lesbian, Jan Waterman, was fired from her job because of her sexual orientation. She received $27,000 in compensation from National Life Assurance and two of its employees.

• Hawaii Supreme Court ruled that a lower court improperly dismissed a lawsuit challenging a state policy of denying marriage licenses to gay and lesbian couples. The court ruled that the prohibition of same-sex marriages constituted sex discrimination and was probably unconstitutional. The decision sparked hope that same-sex marriages would eventually be made legal in Hawaii.

• After months of futile negotiations with the Ancient Order of Hibernians, the Irish Lesbian and Gay Organization (ILGO) was once again excluded from New York's annual St. Patrick's Day Parade (their first attempt to participate was in the 1991 parade). In protest, both Mayor David Dinkins and Governor Mario Cuomo stayed away from the parade, as did thousands of others, making it the smallest St. Patrick's Day parade in the city's recent history. Over 200 people, including openly gay city councilman Tom Duane, were arrested when they staged an alternative parade on the same day.

- Voters in Cincinnati, Ohio; Portsmouth, New Hampshire; and Lewiston, Maine; approved antigay ballot measures.
- After a fierce struggle over a proposed multicultural, gay-tolerant curriculum (The Rainbow Curriculum) for New York City schools, the city Board of Education did not renew the contract of public schools chancellor Joseph Fernandez, who had backed the progressive curriculum.
- After a bitter debate in which Senator Jesse Helms called her a "damned lesbian," Roberta Achtenberg was approved by the Senate as assistant housing secretary, becoming the highest ranking out lesbian in the U.S. government.
- The commission of Cobb County, Georgia, set a dangerous precedent by voting unanimously to cease its arts-related funding for fear that it might be subsidizing lesbian and gay art and artists.
- A twenty-nine-cent stamp depicting a red ribbon and the words "AIDS Awareness" was issued by the U.S. Post Office.
- In a nationwide survey, 55 percent of all Canadians considered homosexuality "morally acceptable."
- Navy airman Terry Helvey was court-martialed for the brutal murder of a gay shipmate, Allen Schindler.
- After months of criticism from activists, President Clinton appointed the first "AIDS czar," Kristine Gebbie. She was widely criticized by AIDS activists for her low profile and lack of experience and was forced to resign the following year. In her place, Clinton named Patsy Fleming, an African-American woman with a gay son who considered herself an AIDS activist.

1994: A bill that would prohibit antigay employment discrimination was introduced into the U.S. House of Representatives.

- The Virginia Court of Appeals overturned a lower court ruling that stripped lesbian Sharon Bottoms of custody of her two-year-old son on the basis of her sexual orientation.
- The first Latina Lesbian Leadership and Self-Empowerment Conference was held in Tucson, Arizona.
- In Boston, organizers of the St. Patrick's Day Parade canceled the event rather than comply with a court order allowing the Irish-American Gay, Lesbian, and Bisexual Group to participate.
- Straight actor Tom Hanks won an Academy Award for Best Actor for his portrayal of a gay man with AIDS in *Philadelphia*.
- The United Nations revoked the consultative status granted the International Lesbian and Gay Association (ILGA) in 1993, on the grounds that some of its members were affiliated with pedophile groups, most notably the North American Man-Boy Love Association (NAMBLA).
- Openly gay choreographer Bill T. Jones and openly lesbian poet Adrienne Rich were recipients of MacArthur Foundation "genius" awards.
- Gay Games IV attracted approximately 15,000 participants in New York City.
- Stonewall 25 drew 1.1 million marchers in New York City, for the silver anniversary of the Stonewall Riots.

Members of the Lesbian Herstory Archives march in the Stonewall 25 Pride Parade, June 1994 *(Copyright © 1994 by Morgan Gwenwald)*

• The Tenth International Conference of AIDS convened in Yokohama, Japan, attracting fewer activists than in past years.

• In the national midterm elections, Republicans, with major backing from the homophobic Christian Right, took over the majority in both houses of the U.S. Congress and won gubernatorial elections in many large states, in a sweep that threatened the future of lesbian and gay civil rights in the United States.

• At the Virginia Slims women's tennis tournament in New York City, Martina Navratilova, nine-time Wimbledon singles champion and arguably the greatest woman tennis player of all time, played her last professional singles match, and lost to Gabriela Sabatini. The first woman (and out lesbian) to receive the honor, a banner with her name on it will be displayed at the Virginia Slims tournament each year at Madison Square Garden.

• The American Medical Association finally adopted a statement removing all references to "sexual orientation related disorders" from its official policy, which had been used for years to justify therapies for treating homosexuality. In handing down its new decision, the AMA acknowledged that antigay healthcare professionals needed to work on changing their attitude instead of their clients' sexual orientation.

• The National Association of Lesbian and Gay Community Centers was founded by the centers in New York, Los Angeles, Minneapolis, Denver, and Dallas.

1995: British actor Nigel Hawthorne, star of the film *The Madness of King*

George, became the first openly gay Best Actor nominee in the history of the Academy Awards.

• In what he claimed was an honest slip, Rep. Dick Armey (R-Tex.) publicly referred to openly gay Congressman Barney Frank (D-Mass.) as "Barney Fag." Armey was not reprimanded, denied responsibility, and would not acknowledge that using the epithet "fag" was injurious to gay people.

• Four-time Olympic gold medalist Greg Louganis, considered by many to be the greatest diver of all time, revealed in a television interview on *20/20* with Barbara Walters that he had AIDS. His announcement that he was HIV-positive when he hit his head on the diving board during the 1988 Olympics, drawing blood and requiring stitches, caused a flurry of indignation that he might have put other athletes and the doctor who stitched his wound at risk for HIV. The doctor, however, tested negative, and experts maintained that a few drops of blood in a chlorine-treated pool would not endanger anyone.

• Rhode Island became the ninth state to pass a statewide gay rights bill, protecting lesbians and gay men in housing, public employment, credit, and public accommodations.

• Wearing a red ribbon, Cherry Jones became the first out lesbian to win a Tony Award for Best Leading Actress in a Play, for her role in *The Heiress*.

CONGRESS MEMBERS WHO OPENLY DENOUNCED ARMEY'S SLUR

Reps. John Lewis (D-Ga.) and Nancy Pelosi (D-Calif.) led a press conference of seventeen representatives who denounced Richard Armey's slur against Barney Frank. The members appearing at the press conference included: John Baldacci (D-Maine), Rosa DeLauro (D-Conn.), Anna Eshoo (D-Calif.), Elizabeth Furse (D-Ore.), Nita Lowey (D-N.Y.), Jim McDermott (D-Wash.), Cynthia McKinney (D-Ga.), George Miller (D-Calif.), John Olver (D-Mass.), Lynn Rivers (D-Mich.), Tom Sawyer (D-Ohio), Chuck Schumer (D-N.Y.), Jose Serrano (D-N.Y.), Mike Ward (D-Ky.), and Lynn Woolsey (D-Calif.). Jerrold Nadler (D-N.Y.) issued a written statement.

REPOSITORIES OF LESBIAN AND GAY HISTORY

You don't have to be famous to leave your letters, photographs, and other personal documents to an archive to be preserved for posterity. Those letters that document your first love affair, the photos of you and your friends at the March on Washington, your collection of lesbian and gay buttons—all these items are valuable to lesbian and gay history archives. Lesbian and gay lives deserve to be remembered and chronicled. Here are just a few of the places that will welcome the artifacts of your own lesbian or gay history. Write or call first for their donation guidelines or for information on doing research in these collections.

Archives Gaies du Quebec
4067 St.-Laurent, Suite 202
Montreal, QC H2W 1Y7
Canada
Phone: 514/287-9987

Blanche Baker Memorial Library
　and Archives/ONE, Inc.
3340 Country Club Drive
Los Angeles, CA 90019
Phone: 213/735-5252

Canadian Gay Archives
P.O. Box 639, Station A
Toronto, Ontario M5W 1G2
Canada
Phone: 416/921-6310

Dallas Gay and Lesbian Historic
　Archives
2701 Reagan
Dallas, TX 75219
Phone: 214/528-4233

Douglas County Gay Archives
P.O. Box 942
Dillard, OR 97432-0942
Phone: 503/679-9913

Gay and Lesbian Archives of
　Washington, D.C.
P.O. Box 4218
Falls Church, VA 22044
Phone: 703/671-3930

Gay and Lesbian Historical Society
　of Northern California
P.O. Box 424280
San Francisco, CA 94142
Phone: 415/626-0980

Henry Gerber/Pearl M. Hart
　Library and Archives
Midwest Lesbian/Gay Resource
　Center
3352 N. Paulina Street
Chicago, IL 60657
Phone: 312/883-3003

Homosexual Information Center
115 Monroe Street
Bossier City, LA 71111
Phone: 318/742-4709

International Gay and Lesbian
　Archives
P.O. Box 38100
Los Angeles, CA 90038-0100
Phone: 310/854-0271

June Mazer Lesbian Collection
626 N. Robertson Blvd.
West Hollywood, CA 90069
Phone: 310/659-2478

Kentucky Collection of Lesbian
　Her-Story
P.O. Box 1701
Louisville, KY 40201

Lesbian and Gay Archives of San
   Diego
P.O. Box 40389
San Diego, CA 92164
Phone: 619/260-1522

Lesbian Herstory Archives
P.O. Box 1258
New York, NY 10116
Phone: 718/768-DYKE
Fax: 718/768-4663

National Museum & Archive of
   Lesbian and Gay History
Lesbian and Gay Community
   Services Center
208 West 13th Street

New York, NY 10011
Phone: 212/620-7310
Fax: 212/924-2657

New York Public Library
Division of Humanities, Social
   Sciences, and Special Collections
Fifth Avenue and 42nd Street
New York, NY 10018
Phone: 212/930-0584

Southeastern Lesbian Archives
Box 5502
Atlanta, GA 30307

Stonewall Library and Archives
330 SW 27th Street
Fort Lauderdale, FL 33315

THE NATIONAL MUSEUM & ARCHIVE OF LESBIAN AND GAY HISTORY

Its name may sound grandiose, but the National Museum & Archive of Lesbian and Gay History, a program of New York City's Lesbian and Gay Community Services Center, simply preserves the history of the daily lives and political struggles of lesbians and gay men.

The archive, one of the largest collections of its kind in the United States, is a repository for the personal papers, correspondence, artifacts, and publications of both individuals and organizations. Among the archive's current holdings are the papers of activist and singer Michael Callen, who died of AIDS in 1994; the records of the committee that organized the National March on Washington for Lesbian and Gay Rights in 1979; the FBI files on the Mattachine Society, the Gay Liberation Front, and the Gay Activists Alliance; and the records of the Christopher Street Liberation Day Committee from the 1970s.

The archive offers researchers the chance to piece together the pictures of a community that has been frequently overlooked or misrepresented. The collections of the archive are accessible on Thursday evenings from 8 to 10 P.M. and by appointment with the archivist, Rich Wandel. The archive welcomes donations of personal papers and artifacts. Here's your chance to be written into history. Call the archivist to find out how to make a donation, whether it's one photograph or a roomful.

The museum sponsors regular exhibitions of art and history. Its inaugural exhibition in 1988 featured portraits of lesbian and gay writers by photographer Robert Giard. Since then, other displays have included *"Keepin' On: Images of African-American Women from the Lesbian Herstory Archives," "A Memorial Dew Cloth: Celebrating 500 Years of Native American Survival,"* and *"Out on the Island: 60 Years of Lesbian and Gay Life on Fire Island."* To celebrate the twenty-fifth anniversary of the Stonewall Riots, the museum presented *"Windows on Gay Life,"* an art and archival exhibition in shop windows along Christopher Street near where the original Stonewall Inn was located.

The National Museum & Archive of Lesbian and Gay History
The Lesbian and Gay Community Services Center
208 West 13th Street, New York, NY 10011
Phone: 212/620-7310; Fax: 212/924-2657

LESBIAN HERSTORY ARCHIVES

Founded in 1973, the Lesbian Herstory Archives is the largest and oldest collection of lesbian material in the world. Until 1993, the archives were housed in the two-bedroom New York City apartment of one of its founders, Joan Nestle. With grassroots fund-raising and the renovation skills of volunteer lesbian carpenters, electricians, and painters, the archives moved to a beautiful three-story brownstone in the Park Slope ("Dyke Slope") region of Brooklyn. The new space includes comfortable spots to read and do research about lesbian lives, and the first floor is completely wheelchair accessible.

Included in the archives' holdings are over 10,000 books, 12,000 photographs, and 1,400 periodicals; hundreds of special collections, including the papers of the renowned poet, Audre Lorde; a steamy collection of lesbian pulp novels from the 1950s and 1960s; a clippings file on lesbian celebrities; a subject file on everything from butch-fem to lesbian theater; thousands of feet of film and videotape; and buttons, T-shirts, and other artifacts of the lesbian-feminist movement.

"All lesbian lives are important and welcome at the archives," is the official policy of the collective that runs the archives. "Every woman who has had the courage to touch another woman deserves to be remembered here, as do lesbians from all places, from every century, and from any political or sexual background. The archives aims to collect the full range of lesbian experience, not just the lives of the famous or the published."

The archives are open by appointment and usually one day of each weekend. (During their twenty-year history, the archives has been completely volunteer-run.)

Call to set up a time to visit and for directions to the brownstone. The archives also has a volunteer evening each Thursday, when women can come

The new home of the Lesbian Herstory Archives in Park Slope, Brooklyn, New York (*Copyright © LHEF, Inc., photo by Morgan Gwenwald*)

to help with the important work of cataloging the collection. If you have a research question but can't come to the archives in person, you can write or fax the question and a volunteer researcher will try to help you find the answer.

Lesbian Herstory Archives
Lesbian Herstory Educational Foundation, Inc.
P.O. Box 1258
New York, NY 10116
Phone: 718/768-DYKE; Fax: 718/768-4663

How the Canadian and United States Lesbian and Gay Liberation Movements Differ: An Interview with Gens Hellquist

Gens Hellquist has lived in Saskatoon, Saskatchewan, since he was five years old. "I'm the town fag. I stayed here because I believe if we are ever going to win the fight for equality, it will be won in small towns and communities."

Gens is a social worker, the current director of Gay and Lesbian Health Services, and the editor of *Perceptions,* the prairie lesbian and gay news magazine. He has been involved in the gay and lesbian liberation movement since 1971, when the movement "hit the prairies."

In addition to his gay civil rights work, he has also been instrumental in the formation of local AIDS organizations. Gens is particularly concerned with mental illness, suicide, substance abuse, and other serious self-esteem problems. "AIDS rates are going down," he notes, "but not among gay people with self-esteem issues."

In some ways, gays in Canada have made more progress than their sisters and brothers south of the border. The Charter of Rights and Freedoms, enacted in 1982, proclaimed basic human rights for all Canadians and encompassed sexual orientation. Eight of ten Canadian provinces already have legislative protection for lesbians and gay men; Alberta is the only major province without such protection. The Canadian government has promised since 1987 to pass formal national gay rights legislation, which is anticipated to be voted into law before 1997. This legislation will protect gay rights in all nationalized business—in the civil service as well as the transportation and communications industries.

"I don't mean to suggest all is perfect here," Gens says. "We're still in court a lot. We have censorship problems." Canadian customs officials are infamous for confiscating shipments of lesbian and gay material from the United States at the border. Until October 1994, depictions of anal sex were illegal in Canada. Gens points out the irony of the situation: "We could do it, but we couldn't read about it." Other depictions of lesbian and gay sexuality still continue to be censored. Currently, Little Sisters Bookstore in Vancouver is challenging Canada's censorship laws in court.

"I think the key difference between U.S. and Canadian life is that we're not as persecuted by the religious right here," Gens observes. "In our public opinion polls, people consistently and overwhelmingly favor gay rights, although public support breaks down as soon as children enter the picture."

Although the National Gay and Lesbian Rights Coalition was formed in Canada during the 1970s, the group became regionalized and broke apart. There are currently no national gay organizations in Canada, something that also marks a difference from the United States. "We tend not to work together well," Gens explains. "Quebec is always flirting with separation, a rift that trickles down to gay politics."

PART II

DON'T I KNOW YOU FROM SOMEWHERE?

A Guide to Notable North American Lesbians

SEXUALITY IS A tricky thing. This should not be read as a roster of "perfect 6s" on the Kinsey scale; sexuality is often much more fluid than that. No matter what label we give our identities—lesbian, bisexual, or straight—many of us have engaged in both homosexual and heterosexual relations over the course of our lives. Even though we may now claim a woman as lesbian by her sexual activity or by her emotional affinity with other women, she may not want to make this distinction. In fact, some women on this list are probably turning in their graves at being labeled lesbian. We ask, then, that you view this as a list of women who have, at some time in their lives, loved other women.

There are a lot of celebrities—particularly film and TV stars currently acting in Hollywood, but also writers, photographers, and other artists—who are either reputedly or known lesbians, but who adamantly refuse to come out of the closet. So far, only a few brave souls have ventured out, such as Amanda Bearse, one of the stars of *Married . . . with Children*, and singers k.d. lang and Melissa Etheridge. We have not intentionally outed any living celebrities here, but we wish we could add them to the next edition of this almanac.

Abbott, Berenice, 1898–1991: Photographer; known for her portraits of artists and writers in Paris in the 1920s; her book, *Changing New York*, chronicled the city's architecture before World War II.

Achtenberg, Roberta, b. 1951: Former member, San Francisco Board of Supervisors; first openly gay person ever confirmed by the U.S. Senate; resigned in April 1995 as assistant secretary of Housing and Urban Development to run for mayor of San Francisco.

Dorothy Allison
(*Photo by Jill
Posener. Courtesy
of Firebrand
Books.*)

Addams, Jane, 1860–1935: Social worker and activist; founder of Hull House in Chicago and cofounder of the American Civil Liberties Union; winner of Nobel Peace Prize in 1931.

Allen, Paula Gunn, b. 1939: Writer, professor, and activist; author of *The Sacred Hoop: Recovering the Feminine in American Indian Tradition* and the novel *The Woman Who Owned the Shadows.*

Allison, Dorothy, b. 1949: Writer and activist; works include *The Women Who Hate Me* (poems), *Trash* (stories), *Bastard Out of Carolina* (novel; finalist for National Book Award), and *Skin* (essays).

Anderson, Dame Judith, 1898–1992: Australian-born actor; films included *Rebecca, Laura, Salome, Cat on a Hot Tin Roof, Macbeth, A Man Called Horse.*

Anderson, Margaret, 1893–1973: Writer, editor, cofounder of the literary magazine, *The Little Review*, in 1920s Paris with her lover, Jane Heap.

Anthony, Katharine, 1877–1965: Teacher, writer, suffragist, peace activist; Wellesley College professor; longtime lover of **Elisabeth Irwin**.

Anthony, Susan B., 1820–1906: Reformer and suffragist; one of the organizers of the historic Seneca Falls Convention in 1848.

Anzaldúa, Gloria, b. 1942: Writer, editor, and activist; books include *Borderlands/La frontera*; coeditor of *This Bridge Called My Back: Writings by Radical Women of Color* and *Companeras.*

Apuzzo, Virginia: Activist and public official; longtime activist who at the 1980 Democratic National Convention coauthored the first lesbian and gay civil rights plank adopted by a major political party; former Executive Deputy Commissioner of the New York State Division of Housing and Community Renewal; currently serves as Commissioner of the New York State Civil Service.

Arnold, June, 1926–1982: Writer and publisher; novels included *The Cook and the Carpenter* and *Sister Gin;* cofounder of Daughters, Inc., a feminist press that was first to publish lesbian writers Bertha Harris, **Rita Mae Brown**, and Monique Wittig.

Arthur, Jean, 1905–1991: Actor; films included *The More the Merrier*, *Shane*, *Diamond Jim*, *Mr. Deeds Goes to Town*, *Mr. Smith Goes to Washington*, *You Can't Take It with You*, *The Devil and Miss Jones.*

Arzner, Dorothy, ca. 1900–1979: Film director; Hollywood credits from the 1920s and 1930s include *The Wild Party*, *Working Girls*, *Christopher Strong*, *The Bride Wore Red.*

Austin, Alice, 1866–1952: Photographer; chronicled her lesbian circle of friends on Staten Island at the turn of the century.

Baker, Josephine, 1906–1975: Singer and nightclub entertainer; achieved fame in Paris in 1920s; albums included *This Is Paris*, *Josephine Chante Paris*, and *Josephine Baker: Paris Mes Amours.*

Baker, Sara Josephine, 1873–1945: Physician; famous cross-dresser; worked for years for the New York City Department of Health.

Bankhead, Tallulah, 1903–1968: Actor; Broadway plays included *The Little Foxes*, *The Skin of Our Teeth*, *Private Lives;* films included *Lifeboat*, *Stage Door Canteen*, *Die! Die! My Darling.*

Bannon, Ann, b. 1932: Writer; works include classic lesbian pulp novels of the 1950s, *Odd Girl Out*, *I Am a Woman*, and *Beebo Brinker.*

Barcheeampe, 19th century: Crow nation "woman chief"; one of the most notable of all berdaches and the most famous war leader of the upper Missouri nations; she married several wives, and her bravery was honored in songs.

Barnes, Djuna, 1892–1982: Writer; works included *Nightwood* and *Ladies Almanack*, a satire about **Natalie Barney**'s Paris salon.

Barney, Natalie, 1876–1972: Writer and patron of the arts; best remembered as host of Parisian literary salon that included **Gertrude Stein**, André Gide, and Ezra Pound.

Bates, Katharine Lee, 1859–1929: Musician and teacher; composed the song "America the Beautiful" in 1893.

Batts, Deborah: Judge; former law professor at Fordham University Law School; first openly gay person to be appointed a federal judge.

Beach, Sylvia, 1887–1962: Publisher and intellectual; founder of famous Parisian bookstore, Shakespeare and Company, which stocked English and U.S. titles and served as a meeting place for the expatriate writers' community.

Bearse, Amanda, b. 1958: Actor; regular on TV series *Married . . . with Children.*

Bechdel, Alison, b. 1960: Cartoonist; creator of cartoon strip "Dykes to Watch Out For," which she has self-syndicated in lesbian and gay newspapers across the United States; has published numerous books (including *Dykes to Watch Out For*, *More Dykes to Watch Out For*, *Spawn of Dykes to Watch Out For*) and calendars featuring the characters of the cartoon strip.

Ben, Lisa, b. 1921: Singer, activist, writer and publisher of first known U.S. publication by and for lesbians, *Vice Versa*, in late 1940s.

Benedict, Ruth, 1887–1948: Anthropologist; mentor and lover of **Margaret Mead;** author of influential *Patterns of Culture.*

Bentley, Gladys, 1907–1960: Entertainer and singer during the Harlem Renaissance; famous also as cross-dresser.

Bernhard, Sandra, b. 1955: Actor and comedian; regular on TV series *Roseanne*; one-woman shows include *Without You I'm Nothing*, later made into a film.

Biren, Joan E. ("JEB"): Photographer and filmmaker; photo books include *Eye to Eye: Portraits of Lesbians* and *Making a Way: Lesbians Out Front*; documentaries include *A Simple Matter of Justice* and *For Love and for Life: The 1978 March on Washington for Lesbian and Gay Rights.*

Birtha, Becky, b. 1949: Writer; author of short story collections *Lover* and *For Nights Like This One* and poetry collection *The Forbidden Poems.*

Bishop, Elizabeth, 1911–1979: Poet; author of Pulitzer Prize–winning collections *North and South* and *Cold Spring.*

Blais, Marie-Claire, b. 1939: Writer; novels include *Tete Blanche*, *David Sterne*, *Le Loup*, *Les nuits de l'Underground*, and *Une Saison dans la vie d'Emmanuel*, winner of Canada's Prix Medicis.

Bogus, SDiane A.: Poet, writer, teacher; poetry collections include *I'm Off to See the Goddamn Wizard*, *Her Poems*, and *Sapphire Sampler.*

Bond, Pat, 1935–1990: Actor; best known for one-woman off-Broadway plays *Conversations with Pat Bond* and *Gerty Gerty Gerty Stein Is Back Back Back.*

Bottini, Ivy: Activist; a founding member of the first local chapter (New York) of

Becky Birtha
(*Courtesy of Seal Press*)

the National Organization for Women; created feminist consciousness-raising, which has been widely used in feminist organizations; was forced from office in NOW during the lesbian purges of 1970 (when Betty Friedan pronounced lesbians "the lavender menace").

Bowles, Jane, 1917–1973: Writer; works included the novel *Two Serious Ladies* and the play *In the Summer House*; married gay writer Paul Bowles.

Brant, Beth, b. 1941: Writer and editor; author of novels *Mohawk Trail* and *Food Spirits*, and editor of *A Gathering of Spirit: A Collection by North American Indian Women*.

Bright, Susie, b. 1958: Writer, editor, and sex activist; former editor of *On Our Backs* magazine; books include *Susie Bright's Sexual Reality* and the *Herotica* anthologies.

Brooks, Romaine, 1874–1970: Painter; known for her stylized portraits of celebrities such as Lady Una Troubridge, lover of Radclyffe Hall; longtime lover of **Natalie Barney**.

Brossard, Nicole, b. 1943: Writer, editor, and activist; author of novel *Mauve Desert* and poetry collections *Mecanique jongleuse* and *Double Impression*; cofounder of the Canadian journals *La Barre du Jour* and *La Nouvelle Barre du Jour*.

Broumas, Olga, b. 1949: Greek-born poet; most famous collection, *Beginning with O*.

Brown, Margaret Wise, 1910–1952: Writer; best known work is children's classic, *Goodnight Moon*.

Brown, Rita Mae, b. 1944: Writer; novels include *Rubyfruit Jungle*, the classic lesbian coming-of-age story (and one of the earliest lesbian novels to enjoy commercial success), *Six of One*, *In Her Day*, *Venus Envy*, *High Hearts*.

Bulkin, Elly, b. 1944: Writer and activist; cofounder of *Conditions* magazine; edited anthologies *Lesbian Fiction* and *Lesbian Poetry*; coauthored *Yours in Struggle* with **Minnie Bruce Pratt** and **Barbara Smith**.

Bunch, Charlotte, b. 1944: Writer and feminist activist; one of the founders of the lesbian-feminist Furies collective; editor of *Quest: A Feminist Journal*; author of *Passionate Politics: Feminist Theory in Action*; currently director of the Douglass College Center for Global Issues and Women's Leadership at Rutgers University.

Byington, Spring, 1886–1971: Actor; films included *You Can't Take It with You*, *Little Women*, *I'll Be Seeing You*, *Please Don't Eat the Daisies*; star of TV series *December Bride* and a regular on *Laramie*.

Califia, Pat, b. 1954: Writer; author of *Sapphistry*, *The Lesbian S/M Safety Manual*, *The Advocate Adviser*, *Doc and Fluff* (novel), and *Macho Sluts* (stories).

Cammermeyer, Margarethe, b. 1943: Activist and former servicewoman; a Bronze Star recipient discharged from Army National Guard after admitting her lesbianism.

Capucine, 1931–1990: French-born actor; films included *Walk on the Wild Side*, *The Pink Panther*, *What's New, Pussycat?*, and *Fellini Satyricon*.

Carangi, Gia, 1960–1986: Supermodel; posed for covers of *Cosmopolitan* and *Vogue* and for the collections of designers Dior and Armani; one of the first women to die of AIDS in United States.

Cather, Willa, 1876–1947: Writer; author of novels *My Antonia*, *O Pioneers*, *Death Comes for the Archbishop*; won 1923 Pulitzer Prize for *One of Ours*.

Chambers, Jane, 1937–1983: Playwright; most famous work, *Last Summer at Bluefish Cove*.

Chasnoff, Debra, b. 1958: Documentary filmmaker; best known films include *Choosing Children* and *Deadly Deception*, which won an Academy Award for best documentary (in her acceptance, she thanked her life partner and their son).

Chrystos, b. 1947: Poet and writer; poetry collections include *Not Vanishing*, *Dream On*, *In Her I Am*.

Clark, Karen: State legislator; has served fourteen years as a Minnesota Representative, making her the longest-serving openly gay public official in the United States.

Clarke, Cheryl, b. 1947: Poet, editor, and essayist; author of poetry collections *Living as a Lesbian*, *Narratives*, *Humid Pitch*, *Experimental Love*; former editor of *Conditions* magazine.

Chrystos (l.) at the 1993 March on Washington for Lesbian, Gay, and Bisexual Rights (*Copyright © Morgan Gwenwald*)

Cheryl Clarke
(*Photo by George Ganges. Courtesy of Firebrand Books.*)

Cliff, Michelle: Jamaican-born writer and editor; books include *Claiming an Identity They Taught Me to Despise* (poems), and novels *Abeng, No Telephone to Heaven,* and *Free Enterprise*; former editor (with **Adrienne Rich**) of *Sinister Wisdom* magazine.

Clinton, Kate, b. 1951: Writer and stand-up comedian; has made guest appearances on *The Arsenio Hall Show, Good Morning America,* and *Nightline* and has hosted the gay variety show *In the Life*; starred in one-woman off-Broadway show *Out Is In.*

Colbert, Claudette, b. 1903: Actor; films included *It Happened One Night, Cleopatra, Imitation of Life, Drums Along the Mohawk, Since You Went Away, The Egg and I.*

Cook, Blanche Wiesen, b. 1941: Historian and professor; author of the controversial biography, *Eleanor Roosevelt,* which discusses the former First Lady's lesbian experiences.

Corinne, Tee: Artist, editor, and writer; published the classic books of erotic line drawings, *Cunt Coloring Book* and *Labiaflowers*; editor of several collections of erotica, including *Intricate Passions* and *The Poetry of Sex*; author of novels *The Sparkling Lavender Dust of Lust* and *Dreams of the Woman Who Loved Sex.*

Cornell, Katharine, 1893–1974: Actor; in the early twentieth century, known as "The First Lady of the American Theater."

Kate Clinton
(*Photo by Susan Wilson*)

Cushman, Charlotte, 1816–1876: Actor and patron of the arts.

Daly, Mary, b. 1928: Writer, theologian, and philosopher; author of *Beyond God the Father, Gyn/Ecology,* and *Pure Lust.*

Davis, Ernestine ("Tiny"), b. 1907: Jazz musician; trumpet player who first appeared with the Harlem Playgirls and the International Sweethearts of Rhythm in the 1930s, and in 1947 formed her own all-woman six-piece band, The Hell Divers. One of the members of the band was Ruby Lucas, Davis's lover.

Deitch, Donna: Film director; credits include *Desert Hearts* and TV movie *Women of Brewster Place.*

Blanche Wiesen Cook (*Photo by Colleen McKay*)

Deborah Edel (l.), one of the cofounders of the Lesbian Herstory Archives, and Storme DeLarverie *(Copyright © Morgan Gwenwald)*

de la Pena, Terri, b. 1947: Writer; author of novels *Margins* and *Latin Satins*, plus short stories, which have appeared in numerous anthologies.

DeLaria, Lea: Stand-up comedian; has made guest appearances on *The Arsenio Hall Show, Matlock, The John Laroquette Show*, and *20/20*.

DeLarverie, Storme, b. 1922: Entertainer; emcee—who performed in drag—of the "Jewel Box Revue," the famous male drag show of the 1950s and 1960s.

Deming, Barbara, 1917–: Writer and peace activist; author of *Prison Notes, Wash Us and Comb Us, Remembering Who We Are, We Cannot Live Without Our Lives*, and *Revolution and Equilibrium*.

Dennis, Sandy, 1937-1992: Actor; films included *Up the Down Staircase, The Fox, The Out-of-Towners*, and *Who's Afraid of Virginia Woolf?* for which she won an Academy Award.

de Wolfe, Elsie, 1865–1950: World's first interior designer; projects included the Colony Club in New York, the first private club for women; wrote nonfiction book on design, *The House in Good Taste*.

Dickinson, Emily, 1830–1886: Poet; her hand-bound notebooks of poems were found after her death; the subject of many of her homoerotic poems was her sister-in-law, Sue Gilbert.

Melissa Etheridge (l.) and Candace Gingrich (*Courtesy Gay and Lesbian Alliance Against Defamation*)

Didrickson Zaharias, Babe, 1914–1956: All-around athlete; set world records in javelin throw and eighty-meter hurdles in 1938 Olympics; cofounded Ladies Professional Golf Association.

Dietrich, Marlene, 1901–1992: Actor; films included *The Blue Angel, Blonde Venus, Shanghai Express.*

DiMassa, Diane: Cartoonist; creator of cartoon strip, "Hothead Paisan."

Dlugasz, Judy: Women's music producer; one of the cofounders of the pioneering women's record company, Olivia Records, in 1973; she still serves as its president.

Doolittle, Hilda (H.D.), 1886–1961: Poet; longtime lover of British novelist, Bryher (Winifred Ellerman); best-known collection, *Sea Garden.*

Dunbar-Nelson, Alice Moore, 1875–1935: Poet, activist, and journalist.

Etheridge, Melissa, b. 1961: Rock singer; recordings include *Brave and Crazy, Yes, I Am,* and *Never Enough.*

Faderman, Lillian: Writer and teacher; author of *Surpassing the Love of Women: Romantic Friendship and Love between Women from the Renaissance to the Present, Scotch Verdict,* and *Odd Girls and Twilight Lovers: A History of Lesbian Life in Twentieth-Century America.*

Leslie Feinberg
(*Photo by Bill Hackwell. Courtesy of Firebrand Books.*)

Faye, Frances, 1912–1991: Entertainer and singer; popular nightclub singer of the 1940s and 1950s.

Feinberg, Leslie, b. 1949: Writer and transgender activist; author of novel *Stone Butch Blues.*

Ferber, Edna, 1885–1968: Writer; novels included *Giant, Cimarron, Show Boat, Saratoga Trunk,* and *Ice Palace,* all of which were made into successful Hollywood films.

Flanner, Janet, 1892–1978: Writer; famous for articles written as "Genet" for the New Yorker in the 1920s and 1930s (later published as *Paris Was Yesterday*); author of novel, *The Cubicle City.*

Forrest, Katherine V., b. 1939: Writer; mystery novels include *Curious Wine, Amateur City,* and *Murder at the Nightwood Bar.*

Francis, Kay, 1903–1968: Actor; in the 1930s, one of Hollywood's most glamorous and highly paid stars; films included *Ladies' Man, Cynara, Mandalay, The White Angel, First Lady, My Bill, Little Men.*

Fuller, Margaret, 1810–1850: Writer, editor, and feminist; author of *Woman in the Nineteenth Century*; reporter for the *New York Tribune.*

Garbo, Greta, 1905–1990: Swedish-born actor; films included *Anna Karenina, Anna Christie, Ninotchka, Camille*; awarded a special Academy Award for "her unforgettable screen performances" in 1954.

Gish, Lillian, 1896–1993: Actor; called "The First Lady of the Silent Screen"; silent films included *Broken Blossoms, Orphans of the Storm, The Scarlet Let-*

Jewelle Gomez
(Photo by Val Willmer.
Courtesy of
Firebrand Books.)

ter, *The Birth of a Nation, Intolerance, La Boheme*; in 1930s starred in Broadway plays *Uncle Vanya, Camille, Hamlet*; in 1980s made a comeback in films
Sweet Liberty and *The Whales of August*.

Gomez, Jewelle, b. 1949: Poet, novelist, editor, and essayist; author of poetry collections *Flamingoes and Bears* and *The Lipstick Papers*; novel *The Gilda Sto-*
ries; and essay collection *Forty-Three Septembers*; former editor of *Conditions*
magazine.

Grahn, Judy, b. 1940: Poet and writer; works include poetry collections *The*
Queen of Swords and *The Work of a Common Woman*, and the nonfiction *An-*
other Mother Tongue: Gay Words, Gay Worlds.

Grier, Barbara: Editor and publisher; cofounder (with partner Donna McBride)
of Naiad Press, oldest existing lesbian publishing company in the United States.

Grimke, Angelina Weld, 1880–1958: Poet and writer of the Harlem Renaissance; best known for her poems "Rosabel," "Autumn," "Under the Days," and
"El Beso."

Grumbach, Doris, b. 1924: Writer and critic; works include novels *Chamber*
Music, The Ladies, and *The Magician's Girl*, and memoir *Coming into the End*
Zone.

Hacker, Marilyn, b. 1943: Poet and editor; author of poetry collections *Love,*
Death, and the Changing of the Seasons; Winter Numbers; Taking Notice; As-
sumptions; and the winner of the National Book Award and the Lamont Poetry
Award, *Presentation Piece*; former editor of the *Kenyon Review*.

Hall, Murray, c. 1830–1901: Politician; "passing woman" who played an active
role in the Tammany Hall (New York) political machine of the late nineteenth
century; her sex was discovered only after her death.

Hansberry, Lorraine, 1930–1965: Playwright; most famous work, *A Raisin in the*
Sun.

Harper, Frances E. W., 1825–1911: Writer and abolitionist; best known for her
novel *Iola Leroy: Or Shadows Uplifted*.

Hart, Alberta Lucille (Alan L.), 1892–?: Physician; famous cross-dresser; wrote
numerous books on science, including *These Mysterious Rays*.

Head, Edith, 1907–1981: Hollywood costume designer; film credits included *She Done Him Wrong*, *The Ten Commandments*, *Sweet Charity*, *Butch Cassidy and the Sundance Kid*; won Academy Awards for *All about Eve*, *A Place in the Sun*, *Sabrina*, and *The Sting*.

Henson, Brenda and Wanda, b. 1945 and 1954: Activists; founders of Camp Sister Spirit, a feminist center that has been repeatedly threatened with violence by the neigboring community of Ovett, Mississippi; dedicate themselves to women's education, culture, and literacy.

Hickock, Lorena, 1893–1968: Journalist; reporter for Associated Press; intimate friend and lover of **Eleanor Roosevelt**.

Highsmith, Patricia, 1921–1995: Writer; novels include *Strangers on a Train*, *The Talented Mr. Ripley*, *Ripley Underground*, and, under the pseudonym Claire Morgan, the classic lesbian novel *The Price of Salt*.

Holiday, Billie, 1915–1959: Jazz singer; most famous songs include "God Bless the Child," "My Man," "Billie's Blues," and "Don't Explain."

Hollibaugh, Amber, b. 1947: Writer, filmmaker, and activist; films include *The Heart of the Matter*, about women and AIDS; currently heads the Lesbian AIDS Project of GMHC.

Holliday, Judy, 1922–1965: Actor; films included *The Marrying Kind*, *It Should Happen to You*, and *Born Yesterday*, for which she won an Academy Award.

Hosmer, Harriet, 1830–1908: Neoclassical sculptor; subjects included women such as Medusa, Queen Zenobia, and Beatrice Cenci, who was executed for killing her abusive father.

Hughes, Holly: Playwright and performance artist; plays include *The Well of Horniness*, *Dress Suits to Hire*, *The Lady Dick*; one of the famous NEA Four, defunded by Chair John Frohnmayer in 1990 for the explicit sexual nature of their work (see page 141).

Hull, Helen R., 1888–1971: Writer and English professor; novels included *Labyrinth*, *Quest*, *Islanders*.

Hunter, Alberta, 1895–1984: Songwriter, entertainer, and blues singer of the 1920s and 1930s.

Ian, Janice, b. 1951: Singer and songwriter; hit singles include "At Seventeen" and "Jesse."

Ireland, Patricia, b. 1945: Current president of the National Organization for Women.

Irwin, Elisabeth, 1880–1942: Psychologist, progressive educator; founding director of the Little Red School House in New York City; longtime lover of **Katharine Anthony**.

Jackson, Bessie: Blues singer and entertainer; known for singing "B.D. [Bulldagger] Woman's Blues."

Jay, Karla: Writer, activist, editor, teacher; coedited (with Allen Young) classic anthologies *Out of the Closets: Voices of Gay Liberation*, *After You're Out*, and *Lavender Culture*; coeditor (with Joanne Glasgow) of anthology *Lesbian Texts and Contexts*; editor of anthology *Lesbian Passages*; author of *The Amazon and the Page: Natalie Clifford Barney and Renee Vivien*.

Jean, Lorri L.: Activist and lawyer; as deputy regional director of the Federal

Emergency Management Agency, she was the highest ranking openly gay federal employee of the Reagan/Bush era; currently executive director of the Los Angeles Gay and Lesbian Community Services Center, the world's largest gay center.

Jewett, Sarah Orne, 1849–1909: Writer and feminist; novels included *The Country of Pointed Firs* and *Deephaven*; partner in a Boston marriage with literary hostess, Annie Fields.

Johnston, Jill: Writer and activist; author of nonfiction books *Lesbian Nation* and *Marmalade Me*; former columnist for *The Village Voice*.

Joplin, Janis, 1943–1970: Rock singer; albums included *I Got Dem Ol' Kozmic Blues Again Mama!* and *Pearl*.

Jordan, June, b. 1936: Poet, essayist, activist; works include the nonfiction *Technical Difficulties* and *Naming Our Destiny*, and *haruko/love poems*.

Kelly, Patsy, 1910–1981: Actor; films included *Nobody's Baby*, *Hit Parade of 1941*, *Topper Returns*, *Broadway Limited*, *Please Don't Eat the Daisies*, *Rosemary's Baby*.

Kim, Willyce: Writer; author of novel *Dancer Dawkins and the California Kid*.

King, Billie Jean, b. 1943: Tennis champion.

Klepfisz, Irena, b. 1941: Poet and essayist; cofounder of *Conditions* magazine; poetry collections include *A Few Words in the Mother Tongue*, *Keeper of Accounts*, and *Dreams of an Insomniac*; coedited *A Tribe of Dina: A Jewish Woman's Anthology* and *A Jewish Woman's Call for Peace*.

Klumpke, Anna, 19th century: Artist; lover and biographer of French artist, Rosa Bonheur.

Kuehl, Sheila James, b. 1941: Actor, lawyer, and politician; played Zelda in the 1960s TV series *The Many Loves of Dobie Gillis*; elected in 1994 to be the first openly gay California assembly member.

Kulp, Nancy, 1921–1991: Actor; best known as Miss Hathaway on the 1960s TV series, *The Beverly Hillbillies*.

Lane, Alycee, b. 1967: Editor; recently launched *Black Lace* magazine, the first erotic quarterly magazine for black lesbians.

lang, k.d., b. 1961: Singer, composer, and actor; recordings include *Angel with a Lariat*, *Absolute Torch and Twang*, *Shadowland*, *Ingenue*, *Even Cowgirls Get the Blues*; winner of three Grammy Awards; played lead role in movie *Salmonberries*.

Larsen, Nella, 1891–1964: Writer; active during the Harlem Renaissance; novels included *Passing* and *Quicksand*.

Le Gallienne, Eva, 1899–1991: British-born stage actor; founder of the Civic Repertory Theater of New York.

LeGuin, Ursula K., b. 1929: Science fiction writer; most famous novels include *The Farthest Shore*, *The Dispossessed*, *The Left Hand of Darkness*.

Levin, Jenifer: Writer; author of novels *Water Dancer*, *Snow*, *Shimoni's Lover*, *The Sea of Light*; former U.S. Masters swimmer.

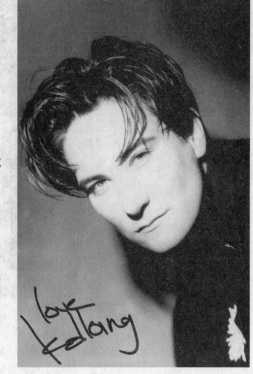

k.d. lang

Lewis, Edmonia, 1845–1909: Artist and sculptor; one of the few students of color enrolled at Oberlin College before the Civil War, she sculpted busts of Maria Weston Chapman, an abolitionist, and Robert Gould Shaw, an African-American Civil War leader; later known for her paintings of Native Americans.

Lillie, Beatrice, 1898–1989: Canadian-born singer and entertainer; made famous Noel Coward's song "Mad Dogs and Englishmen."

Lorde, Audre, 1934–1992: Poet and writer; works included the nonfiction *The Cancer Journals* and *A Burst of Light*; *Zami: A New Spelling of My Name* (biomythography); and *The Marvelous Arithmetic of Distance* (poems); cofounder with Barbara Smith of Kitchen Table: Women of Color Press.

Loulan, Joann: Writer, sex activist, and psychotherapist; author of *Lesbian Sex*, *Lesbian Passion*, and *The Lesbian Erotic Dance*.

Lowell, Amy, 1874–1925: Poet; works included *Sword Blades*, *Pictures of the Floating World*, *Ballads for Sale*, and the Pulitzer Prize–winning *What's O'Clock*.

Lyon, Phyllis: Activist; with her lover **Del Martin** (they've been together since 1950) and six other women, cofounded the Daughters of Bilitis in San Francisco in 1953, the first lesbian organization in the United States; with Martin, coauthored the classic memoir *Lesbian/Woman* about growing up lesbian and beginning their partnership.

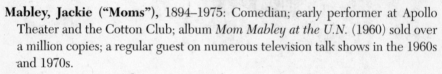

Audre Lorde
(*Courtesy of Firebrand Books*)

Mabley, Jackie ("Moms"), 1894–1975: Comedian; early performer at Apollo Theater and the Cotton Club; album *Mom Mabley at the U.N.* (1960) sold over a million copies; a regular guest on numerous television talk shows in the 1960s and 1970s.

McCorvey, Norma (aka Jane Roe), b. 1947: Plaintiff in the landmark U.S. Supreme Court case on abortion, *Roe v. Wade*; author of *I Am Roe*.

McCullers, Carson, 1917–1967: Writer; novels included *The Heart Is a Lonely Hunter, Reflections in a Golden Eye, Ballad of the Sad Cafe*.

McDaniel, Judith: Writer; cofounder with Maureen Brady of Spinsters Ink, a feminist publishing house; author of novel *Just Say Yes* and nonfiction *Metamorphosis* and *Sanctuary*.

Main, Marjorie, 1890–1975: Actor; films included *Dead End, Stella Dallas*, plus a series of Ma and Pa Kettle films, in which she played Ma.

Martin, Del: Activist; with her lover **Phyllis Lyon** (they've been together since 1950) and six other women, cofounded the Daughters of Bilitis in San Francisco in 1953, the first lesbian organization in the United States; with Lyon, coauthored the classic memoir *Lesbian/Woman* about growing up lesbian and beginning their partnership.

Martin, Mary, 1913–1990: Actor; Broadway musicals included *South Pacific; Peter Pan; The Sound of Music; I Do, I Do*; films included *Birth of the Blues, Star Spangled Rhythm, Night and Day*; the filmed version of her stage performance as Peter Pan was a TV perennial in the 1960s.

Martinac, Paula, b. 1954: Writer, editor, and activist; books include novels *Out of Time* and *Home Movies* and young adult biography *k.d. lang*; editor of anthology *The One You Call Sister: New Women's Fiction*; former editor of *Conditions* magazine.

Mead, Margaret, 1901–1978: Anthropologist; author of *Coming of Age in Samoa*.

Mercer, Mabel, c. 1900–1984: British-born singer and entertainer; albums included *Mabel Mercer Sings Cole Porter* and *Midnight at Mabel Mercer's*.

Millay, Edna St. Vincent, 1892–1950: Poet; works included *A Few Figs from Thistles, Renascence*, and the Pulitzer Prize–winning *The Ballad of the Harp-Weaver and Other Poems*.

Miller, Isabel (Alma Routsong), b. 1924: Writer; most famous novel, *Patience and Sarah*.

Millett, Kate, b. 1934: Writer, feminist theorist, and sculptor; author of nonfiction *Sexual Politics, Flying*, and *The Loony-Bin Trip*, and the novel *Sita*.

Miner, Valerie: Writer; author of novels *Blood Sisters, Murder in the English Department, All Good Women*, and the short story collection *Trespassing and Other Stories*; coeditor (with Helen Longino) of nonfiction anthology, *Competition: A Feminist Taboo?*

Moore, Marianne, 1887–1972: Poet; works included *The Arctic Ox, O to Be a Dragon*, and the Pulitzer Prize–winning *Collected Poems*.

Moorehead, Agnes, 1900–1974: Actor; films included *Citizen Kane; The Magnificent Ambersons; Hush, Hush, Sweet Charlotte*; best remembered for her role as Endora on 1960s TV show, *Bewitched*.

Moraga, Cherríe, b. 1952: Writer and editor; works include *Loving in the War Years*; coedited the anthology *This Bridge Called My Back: Writings by Radical Women of Color* with **Gloria Anzaldúa**.

Morgan, Robin, b. 1941: Writer, editor, and feminist activist; longtime (until 1993) editor of *Ms.* magazine; editor of anthologies *Sisterhood Is Powerful* and *Sisterhood Is Global*.

Navratilova, Martina, b. 1956: Czech-born tennis champion; nine-time Wimbledon women's singles champion.

Nazimova, Alla, 1879–1945: Russian-born actor and film producer; leading interpreter of Ibsen on the stage; silent films that she produced and starred in included *A Doll's House, Salome, The Red Lantern*.

NdegeOcello, Me'shell: Singer and songwriter; debut album is *Plantation Lullabies*.

Near, Holly, b. 1949: Singer and songwriter; albums include *Hang in There, Imagine My Surprise, Fire in the Rain, Don't Hold Back*.

Negron-Muntaner, Frances: Puerto Rican–born writer and filmmaker; films include *AIDS in the Barrio: Eso no me pasa a mi* and *Brincando el charco*; editor of *Beyond Nationalism and Colonialism: Rethinking the Puerto Rican Political Imagery*.

Nestle, Joan, b. 1940: Writer, editor, and feminist activist; author of *A Restricted Country*; editor of *The Persistent Desire: A Butch-Femme Reader*, the *Women on Women* series of anthologies (with Naomi Holoch), and *Sister and Brother* (with John Preston); cofounder with Deborah Edel of the Lesbian Herstory Archives in New York City.

Suzanne Pharr
(Copyright ©
Morgan
Gwenwald)

Newman, Lesléa: Writer; author of *Good Enough to Eat* (novel), *A Letter to Harvey Milk* (short stories), *Write from the Heart* (writing exercises), and a series of children's books on gay themes, including *Heather Has Two Mommies* and *Gloria Goes to Gay Pride*; her children's books stirred a controversy that made national headlines when they were included in a proposed Rainbow Curriculum for New York City public schools in 1993 (see pages 183–184).

Northrop, Ann: Activist, journalist, and AIDS educator; former producer of CBS News and freelance writer for *Good Morning America*; dynamic member of ACT UP and a commentator for DYKE-TV; former AIDS educator at New York's Harvey Milk School for lesbian and gay teenagers.

Oliver, Edna May, 1883–1942: Actor; films included *Little Women, David Copperfield, Romeo and Juliet, Drums Along the Mohawk, A Tale of Two Cities.*

Oliver, Mary, b. 1935: Poet; poetry volumes include *Dream Work, House of Light* (which won a Pulitzer Prize), *Twelve Moons, American Primitive,* and *New and Selected Poems* (which won a National Book Award).

Osborn, Torie: Writer and activist; women's music producer in the 1970s; former executive director of the Los Angeles Gay and Lesbian Community Services Center; former executive director of the National Gay and Lesbian Task Force.

Paglia, Camille, b. 1947: Writer, professor, and cultural critic; author of *Sexual Personae* and *Vamps and Tramps.*

Minnie Bruce
Pratt (*Photo by
Doug Lawson.
Courtesy of
Firebrand Books.*)

Parker, Pat, 1944–1989: Poet; author of *Jonestown and Other Madness* and
Movement in Black.

Parmar, Pratibha: Writer, activist, and filmmaker; coedited anthology *Many
Voices, One Chant: Black Feminist Perspectives*; films include *Emergence, Re-
framing AIDS,* and *Warrior Marks: Female Genital Mutilation and the Sexual
Blinding of Women* (with Alice Walker; also a book by the same name).

Patton, Cindy: Writer and AIDS activist; former managing editor of *Gay Community News*; cofounder of *Bad Attitude* magazine; author of *Sex and Germs,
Inventing AIDS,* and *Women and Children Last?: Gendering the HIV Pandemic*.

Pharr, Suzanne: Writer and activist; author of *Homophobia: Weapon of Sexism*;
one of the leaders of the No on Nine campaign in Oregon in 1990 and a leading Fight the Right activist and trainer.

Pratt, Minnie Bruce, b. 1946: Poet and essayist; author of *Crime Against Nature,*
winner of the Lamont Prize for Poetry; coauthor of *Yours in Struggle* with **Elly
Bulkin** and **Barbara Smith**.

Rainey, Ma, 1886–1939: Blues singer and entertainer; wrote the openly lesbian "Prove It on Me Blues"; popularly called the "Mother of the Blues."

Randall, Margaret, b. 1936: Writer, editor, translator, and photographer; author of *Women in Cuba, Sandino's Daughters, This Is about Incest, Memory Says Yes.*

Rich, Adrienne, b. 1929: Poet and essayist; works include poetry collections *A Change of the World, Diving into the Wreck, Dream of a Common Language,* and *A Wild Patience Has Taken Me This Far,* and the nonfiction *On Lies, Secrets, and Silences* and *Of Woman Born.*

Romo-Carmona, Mariana, b. 1952: Chilean-born writer, editor, and activist; former editor of *Conditions* magazine; coeditor of *Cuentos: Stories by Lesbians* and *Queer City: The Portable Lower East Side;* editor of people of color magazine, *Color Life.*

Roosevelt, Eleanor, 1884–1962: Pubic figure and journalist; the first activist First Lady of the United States, from 1932 to 1945; later, U.S. delegate to the United Nations and chair of the Commission on Human Rights.

Rukeyser, Muriel, 1913–1980: Poet and activist; works include *Theory of Flight, Breaking Open, The Gates, Mazes,* and *The Outer Banks.*

Rule, Jane, b. 1931: Writer; novels include *Desert of the Heart, Contract with the World, Memory Board,* and *After the Fire.*

Russ, Joanna, b. 1937: Science fiction writer; novels include *On Strike Against God* and *The Female Man.*

Sahaykwisa, c. 1850–c. 1895: Healer and shaman from the Mohave nation, who wore men's clothing and had several female wives.

Sapphire, b. 1950: Poet; widely anthologized in such works as *Women on Women, High Risk 2,* and *Queer City: The Portable Lower East Side;* author of poetry collection, *American Dream.*

Sarton, May, b. 1912–1995: Writer; works include novels *Mrs. Stevens Hears the Mermaids Singing* and *The Education of Harriet Hatfield,* and the memoirs *Journal of Solitude* and *At Seventy: A Journal.*

Schulman, Sarah, b. 1958: Writer and activist; cofounder of Lesbian Avengers; novels include *The Sophie Horowitz Story; Girls, Visions, and Everything; After Delores; People in Trouble, Empathy;* author of nonfiction collection *My American History.*

Shimizu, Jenny: Model; first Asian-American to achieve supermodel status.

Shockley, Ann Allen, b. 1927: Writer and editor; author of novels *Say Jesus and Come to Me* and *Loving Her,* and nonfiction *The Black and White of It;* editor of the anthology, *Afro-American Women Writers, 1746–1933.*

Silvera, Makeda: Writer, publisher, and activist; cofounder of SisterVision Press, the only women of color press in Canada; editor of *Piece of My Heart: A Lesbian of Color Anthology;* author of *Her Head a Village and Other Stories.*

Sischy, Ingrid: Journalist; editor-in-chief of *Interview* magazine.

Smith, Barbara, b. 1946: Writer, activist, and editor; cofounder with **Audre Lorde** of Kitchen Table: Women of Color Press; editor of *Home Girls: A Black Feminist Anthology* and *But Some of Us Are Brave: Black Women's Studies;*

Sapphire

coauthored *Yours in Struggle* with **Minnie Bruce Pratt** and **Elly Bulkin**; author of a forthcoming history on African-American lesbians and gay men.

Smith, Bessie, 1894–1937: Blues singer and entertainer; recorded over 160 "race records," among them "Down Hearted Blues," "St. Louis Blues," "Careless Love," and "Nobody Knows When You're Down and Out"; popularly called the "Empress of the Blues."

Sontag, Susan, b. 1933: Writer; books include nonfiction *On Photography*, *Illness as Metaphor*, and *AIDS and Its Metaphors*; fiction *The Volcano Lover*; and play *Alice in Bed: A Play in Eight Scenes*.

Stanwyck, Barbara, 1907–1990: Actor; films included *Stella Dallas*; *Sorry, Wrong Number*; *Double Indemnity*; *Walk on the Wild Side*; star of TV show *The Big Valley*.

Stebbins, Emma, 1815–?: Sculptor; member of "lesbian circle" of actor **Charlotte Cushman**.

Stein, Gertrude, 1874–1946: Writer; works included *Three Lives*, *Tender Buttons*, *The Autobiography of Alice B. Toklas*; longtime lover of Alice B. Toklas.

Stimpson, Catharine R.: Writer, editor, and educator; former graduate dean, Rutgers University; current director of the MacArthur Foundation; founding editor of *Signs* magazine; author of novel *Class Notes* and essay collection *Where the Meanings Are*.

Streicher, Rikki, 1926–1994: Activist and bar owner; in 1966 opened Maud's in San Francisco, the oldest lesbian bar in continuous operation (closed 1989); also owned and operated Amelia's, another San Francisco women's bar.

Swallow, Jean, 1953–1995: Editor; edited anthologies *Out from Under* and *The Next Step*, about lesbians and sobriety.

Swenson, May, b. 1919: Poet; books include *Another Animal, Poems to Solve, Half Sun Half Sleep*.

Taylor, Kathleen de Vere, 1873–1949: Stockbroker who managed branch in New York City designed for women customers; member of Heterodoxy, feminist women's club.

Teasdale, Sara, 1884–1933: Poet; works included *Sonnets to Duse* and the Pulitzer Prize–winning *Love Songs*.

Thomas, M. Carey, 1857–1935: Feminist and educator; first woman president of Bryn Mawr College.

Thompson, Dorothy, 1893–1961: Journalist and foreign correspondent.

Tipton, Billy, 1914–1989: Jazz musician; passing woman whose birth sex was discovered at time of death.

Tiptree, James, Jr. (born Alice Sheldon), early twentieth century: Science fiction writer; novels included *Houston, Houston, Do You Read?* and *The Girl Who Was Plugged In*; writing combined tough narrative voice with a feminist sensibility.

Tomlin, Lily, b. 1939: Actor, writer, comedian; regular on 1960s TV series *Laugh-*

Lily Tomlin
(*Courtesy the Gay and Lesbian Alliance Against Defamation*)

Urvashi Vaid
(*Copyright ©*
Morgan
Gwenwald)

In; developed (with partner Jane Wagner) and starred in the Broadway hit *Search for Signs of Intelligent Life in the Universe*; films include *Nashville, Moment by Moment, 9 to 5, The Incredible Shrinking Woman, Big Business, Shadows and Fog, Short Cuts, The Beverly Hillbillies*, and *And the Band Played On*.

Troche, Rose: Filmmaker; cowrote (with Guinevere Turner) and directed small-budget, black and white lesbian film *Go Fish*, which was bought by the Samuel Goldwyn Company and went on to gross over two million dollars after its release in 1994.

Tsui, Kitty: Poet; author of *The Words of a Woman Who Breathes Fire*.

Vaid, Urvashi, b. 1959: Writer and activist; former executive director of the National Gay and Lesbian Task Force; author of *Virtual Equality: The Mainstreaming of Gay and Lesbian Liberation*.

Vance, Danitra, 1959–1994: Actor; first black woman to join the regular cast of *Saturday Night Live*.

Vazquez, Carmen: Activist; founding director of the San Francisco Women's Building; former coordinator of lesbian and gay health services, the San Francisco Department of Health; current Director of Public Policy, the New York Lesbian and Gay Community Services Center.

Villarosa, Linda, b. 1959: Journalist; executive editor of *Essence* magazine; editor of *Body & Soul: The Black Woman's Guide to Physical Health and Emotional Well-Being*.

Wald, Lillian D., 1867–1940: Nurse, social worker, and peace activist; founder of the Henry Street Settlement in New York City.

Walker, Mary Edwards, 1823–1919: Physician; famous cross-dresser; joined Union Army during the Civil War and was awarded the Congressional Medal of Honor in 1866.

Barbara Wilson
(*Photo by Timo Pylvanainen Pressfoto. Courtesy of Seal Press.*)

Warren, Patricia Nell, b. 1936: Writer; most famous works include *Harlan's Race* and *The Front Runner*, which made history by cracking the *New York Times* best-seller list.

Waters, Ethel, 1896–1977: Jazz singer and actor; films included *Pinky* and *The Member of the Wedding*; starred in early 1950s TV series *Beulah*.

Weaver, Lois: Actor and writer; with longtime lover Peggy Shaw, pioneered lesbian theater in the United States, founding the Split Britches theater company and the WOW Cafe for lesbian drama and performance in New York City; their plays include *Split Britches*, *Belle Reprieve*, and *Patience and Sarah*; also starred in movie *She Must Be Seeing Things*.

Wilhelm, Gale, 1908–1991: Writer; novels included *We Too Are Drifting* and *Torchlight to Valhalla*.

Wilson, Barbara, b. 1950: Writer, editor, and publisher; cofounder of Seal Press; novels include *Murder in the Collective*, *Sisters of the Road*, *The Dog Collar Murders*, *Gaudi Afternoon*, *Trouble in Transylvania*.

Woo, Merle: Writer and educator; author of *Yellow Woman Speaks: Selected*

Poems; her work has been anthologized in *This Bridge Called My Back: Writing by Radical Women of Color* and *Tilting the Tower: Lesbian and Gay Studies*; in a much-publicized legal battle in the early 1980s, Woo brought and won a discrimination suit against University of California, Berkeley (on the basis of race, sex, sexual orientation, and political ideology) after she was fired from the Asian-American Studies Department.

Woodson, Jacqueline, b. 1963: Writer; author of numerous young adult novels (including *Last Summer with Maizon* and *The Dear One*) that tackle such issues as lesbianism, alcoholism, and racism, usually believed to be unsuitable for children; also of the adult novel, *Autobiography of a Family Photo*.

Woolley, Mary, 1863–1947: Writer and academic; former president of Mount Holyoke College; only female member of 1932 Geneva Arms Conference.

PART III

SAY WHAT?

Quotable Quotes by and About Lesbians

I WANT YOUR SEX

I would like to enter a woman the way any man can, and to be entered—to leave and to be left—to be hot and hard and soft all at the same time in the cause of our loving.

—AUDRE LORDE, Author of *Zami, A New Spelling of My Name*, 1982

Without a doubt, the greatest thing about sex is vaginas. Looking at one is like looking into the face of God. Whenever I do, I speak in tongues.

—LEA DELARIA, comedian, 1994

After seeing Michael Douglas's ass in Basic Instinct, *most of us never wanted to think about sex again as long as we lived.*

—LOIS BROMFIELD, television writer, 1994

I didn't want all the lesbian buy-a-house shit. I just wanted to fuck around. I believed that the best way to get to know a woman was to go to bed with her. The second best way was to take her by the throat and see what she did. So pretty much everywhere I've lived I've had a real bad reputation. But it has gotten me a lot of interesting dates.

—DOROTHY ALLISON, author, 1993

I have lived and slept in the same bed with English countesses and Prussian farm women . . . no woman has excited passions among women more than I have.

—FLORENCE NIGHTINGALE

When people are laughing together, it's like women coming together. You make sounds you wouldn't ordinarily make. You gasp for air. You rock back and forth. There's soft moaning afterward. And if you're lucky, your face hurts.

—KATE CLINTON, comedian, 1993

The most radical contribution the gay movement has made to society is the idea that pleasure justifies sexuality at least as much as reproduction.

—PAT CALIFIA, author, sex radical

You younger generation of lesbians have a much freer attitude about sex. I like to say that we worked our fingers to the bone—literally!—so you wouldn't have to suffer like we did.

—JOANN LOULAN, sex educator, author, therapist

Sexuality is what people keep wanting to clean up and pretend doesn't happen— desexualize lesbians and make them okay. But sexuality is a defining bottom line. . . . I mean, we're persecuted because we're sexual, not because we're nice little old ladies who like other women.

—TEE CORINNE, visual artist, editor, writer

The popular misconception that Lesbians wish to be men is so pervasive that a Lesbian herself may believe it. . . . Later she discovers that a woman who wants a woman usually wants a woman.

—DEL MARTIN and PHYLIS LYON, cofounders of Daughters of Bilitis, 1972

Extreme heterosexuality is a perversion.

—MARGARET MEAD, bisexual anthropologist

If cruising were music, then lesbian cruising would be Muzak.

—LIZ TRACEY, 1989

I WANT YOUR LOVE

Hick darling . . . I couldn't say je t'aime et je t'adore as I longed to do, but always remember I am saying it, that I go to sleep thinking of you.

—ELEANOR ROOSEVELT, in a letter to American journalist Lorena Hickok

In loving me she of necessity thought first. And so did I. How prettily we swim. Not in water. Not on land. But in love.

—GERTRUDE STEIN, 1953

I found out I was gay when I was in about the third grade at Our Lady of the Elms Elementary School. I was "married" to Debbie Evans for about two years. We were very much in love and we had a little ceremony. Everybody loved us; we

were very popular. We stayed overnight at each other's houses and kissed and watched "77 Sunset Strip" together.

—JEAN O'LEARY, activist

I love, & only love, the fairer sex & thus beloved by them in turn, my heart revolts from any other love than theirs.

—ANNE LISTER, diary entry for January 29, 1821

I chose a white school because I thought that would nip any interests in women in the bud. But I discovered women were women, I don't care what color they are. I was falling in love with white women. That was really wild.

—CAROLYN MOBLEY, pastor

PASSION AND FIDELITY

No, I am in no muddles . . . Dorothy I have not seen. Louise, no muddles (either Genoux or Loraine), Vera, no muddles. Lady Hillingdon, no muddles; don't know her; don't want to. Violet [Trefusis], no muddles; don't even know where she is; don't want to get into touch, thank you. Virginia [Woolf]—not a muddle exactly; she is a busy and sensible woman. But she does love me, and I did sleep with her at Rodmell. That does not constitute a muddle though.

—VITA SACKVILLE-WEST, in a 1926 letter to her husband Harold Nicolson

At the time we were with other women. I remember walking in and seeing her at the bar and thinking to myself, Goddamn! Perfect! *Then I met her and realized,* I am going to get in trouble with this woman. Somehow, somewhere, I will definitely get in trouble with this woman.

—ZANDRA JOHNSON-ROLON, activist

A woman: take her or leave her, but do not take her and leave her.

—NATALIE BARNEY, 1910

Natalie, my husband kisses your hands, and I the rest.

—COLETTE, in a note to Natalie Barney

Darling, you're divine. I've had an affair with your husband. You'll be next.

—TALLULAH BANKHEAD to Joan Crawford

BUTCH/FEMME

Girls Will/Be Boys/You Know.

—Message on a postcard from the 1920s

Butch-femme relationships, as I experienced them, were complex erotic state-ments, not phony heterosexual replicas. They were filled with a deeply Lesbian language of stance, dress, gesture, loving, courage and autonomy.

—JOAN NESTLE, 1987

Well honey, when I went to [Greenwich Village in the early 1960s], there was les-bians in the streets in droves. Women that looked like men, men that looked like women. Women with their hair slicked back, the femmes with the beehives . . . I found myself a girlfriend; she was a femme type. And I loved it . . .

—RED JORDAN AROBATEAU, 1988

. . . the femme woman has been the most ambiguous figure in lesbian history; she is often described as the nonlesbian lesbian, the duped wife of the passing woman, the lesbian who marries.

—JOAN NESTLE, 1992

I thought I was a butch top, until I slept with one.

—STEPHANIE GRANT, writer

Studs as a result of having attained the ultimate in homosexuality (as is perceived by members of this group) are therefore privileged with a higher status within the subculture than that which is accorded the fish, who on the other hand enjoyed the situation of marginality.

—ETHEL SAWYER, of studs (butches) and fish (femmes), 1965

Miss Butler is tall and masculine, she wears always a riding habit, hangs her hat with the air of a sportsman in the hall, and appears in all respects as a young man if we except the petticoats which she still retains. Miss Ponsonby, on the contrary, is polite so effeminate, fair and beautiful.

—of Eleanor Butler and Sarah Ponsonby (also known as the Ladies of Llan-geollen) in the *General Evening Post*, July 24, 1790

SEPARATION AND SEPARATING

I hope for you so much and feel so eager for you, feel that I cannot wait, feel that now I must have you—that the expectation once more to see your face again, makes me feel hot and feverish, and my heart beats too fast . . .

—EMILY DICKINSON, in a letter to Sue Gilbert, 1852

For sixteen nights I have listened expectantly for the opening of my door, for the whispered "Lushka!" as you entered my room, and tonight I am alone. How can I sleep? This can't go on. We must once and for all take courage in both hands and go away together.

—VIOLET TREFUSIS, in a letter to Vita Sackville-West, 1918

When Nancy Leberman and I split up and I paid her some money, Judy [Nelson] said, "Oh, you have given her too much money. She doesn't deserve any of it." Nancy did a whole lot more for me than Judy ever did. When Judy and I split up, I said, "Judy, what about Nancy? You said she shouldn't have gotten all that money!" And she said, "This is different." It's not different. But it's different because it's her.

—MARTINA NAVRATILOVA, 1994

I cannot grow reconciled to the thought of being away from you. Even a day or two is hard . . . Dearest, my dearest, it is hard not to have your good-night kiss . . . God in His Providence has given me this love when I most need it, when I am about to take up crushing responsibilities. . . .

—MARY WOOLLEY, in a letter to Jeanette Marks, written just before Woolley became president of Mount Holyoke College in January 1901

Every woman I have ever loved has left her print upon me, where I loved some invaluable piece of myself apart from me—so different that I had to stretch and grow in order to recognize her. And in that growing, we came to separation, that place where work begins.

—AUDRE LORDE, author of *Zami, A New Spelling of My Name*, 1982

ON THE DEATH OF A LOVER

I wish to God we had gone together as I always so fatuously thought we would— a bomb—a shipwreck—just anything but this.

—ALICE B. TOKLAS (1877–1967), in a letter written to friend a little more than a year after Gertrude Stein's death

Ah Alice what can I send you now? No words can match such a loss, and what consolation can be found amongst Gertrude's things—without so vivifying a pres-

ence? Perhaps her works, which you will continue later on, may bring a feeling of accomplishing those duties which you have always filled to the utmost.

　　—NATALIE BARNEY in a letter to Alice B. Toklas, on the death of Gertrude
　　Stein

This isn't just pain, it is torture. . . . My God, if it weren't for a stubborn instructive [instinctive?] holding to a faith that is in me . . . that we shall, we must meet again, I wouldn't endure this thing another hour. . . .

　　—LADY UNA TROUBRIDGE (1887–1963), in her diary, after the death of
　　Radclyffe Hall

THE PERSONAL IS STILL POLITICAL

When I dare to be powerful—to use my strength in the service of my vision, then it becomes less and less important whether I am afraid.

　　　　　　　　　　　　　　　　　　　　　　　—AUDRE LORDE, author

Dan White may have pulled the trigger, but Anita Bryant and John Briggs loaded the gun.

　　　　　　　　　　　　　　　　　　　　　　　—ROBIN TYLER, comedian

As a lesbian and a Jew, I have had to live with the fear for my physical safety and that of my people. Leaders like George Bush have scapegoated people like me— and families like mine—by charging that we are destroying America. What is destroying America is lack of opportunity, the abandonment of justice, and the harangues of false prophets.

　　　　　　　　　　　　　　　　　　　　—ROBERTA ACHTENBERG, politician

I go in with what is, in fact, a radically different point of view, which is my own normalcy. Don't tolerate me as different. Accept me as part of the spectrum of normalcy. That turns out to be a radical point of view, but one that is very exciting to most people.

　　　　　　　　　　　　　　　　　　—ANN NORTHROP, journalist, activist

This is why work is important: Its power doesn't lie in the me that lives in the words as much as in the heart's blood pumping behind the eye that is reading, the muscle behind the desire that is sparked by the work—hope as a living state that propels us, open-eyed and fearful, into all the battles of our lives. And some of those battles we do not win. And some we do.

　　　　　　　　　　　　　　　　　　　　　　　—AUDRE LORDE, author

I became an activist to reconcile myself, to give voice to experiences of oppression, and to resist the slow death of silence and inaction.

　　　　　　　　　　　　　　　　　　　　　—CARMEN VAZQUEZ, activist

Are we the gay wing of the women's movement, or the women's wing of the gay movement?

> —TORIE OSBORN, activist, former executive director of NGLTF, summarizing the dilemma faced by lesbians, who often feel disenfranchised by both movements

People were hung from trees for being Black. Today, people are beaten up and murdered for being gay and lesbian. Any Black person who can't equate being gay with being Black is essentially denying that gay and lesbian Black people exist.

> —MANDY CARTER, activist

If you can't raise consciousness, at least raise hell.

> —RITA MAE BROWN, novelist

This is what it's going to take: the creation of a multi-racial/multi-sexuality feminist coalition for radical economic change: revolutionary integration.

> —MERLE WOO, educator

I don't fight to live in the lesbian community. I fight to live in the whole world.

> —URVASHI VAID, activist

The racism took different forms in the gay community, but perhaps the most blatant kinds I encountered during those years were the exclusionary policies at the gay clubs, at places like Studio One. If you were black, you could only get in on a certain night. We used to call it "Plantation Night."

> —DEBORAH JOHNSON-ROLON, activist

I had this sense that we had earned this moment—step by step, death by death, fight by fight. There was a definite sense that our time had come.

> —TORIE OSBORN, activist, former executive director of the NGLTF, regarding the April 1993 meeting between community activists and President Bill Clinton

Many boards of education are filled with spineless, cowardly, gutless individuals who at the slightest criticism fall apart at the seams. If they could just get it into their heads that public education serves all children, then they would want to protect all children.

> —VIRGINIA URIBE, founder of Project 10, an on-campus program aimed at keeping lesbian and gay kids in school, off drugs, and sexually responsible

I became an activist by accident. I stood up for Sharon's rights, and as a result began to make connections to issues far bigger than the two of us.

> —KAREN THOMPSON, activist

I believe there is justice, I believe there is truth. Nothing in life is free; there is a price we have to pay for everything. The question then becomes—are you willing to pay the price? In my case, I was raised to be a Maccabee. It is not a matter of courage, but of conscience.

—JANIS IAN, singer/songwriter

Over the years, I think, people have remembered the drag queens and the bar, but they don't remember that the drag queens were black and Puerto Rican. People of color have a legacy here that we absolutely cannot let others forget or rewrite.

—MANDY CARTER, activist

Talk is cheap, AIDS funding is not.

—sign held by former NGLTF executive director URVASHI VAID who joined other AIDS activists invited to attend President George Bush's first speech on AIDS since taking office fourteen months before; Vaid was escorted out of the auditorium by police

It was thrilling. You knew you were doing something momentous. People would stare at you. They had never seen self-declared homosexuals parading with signs.

—BARBARA GIDDINGS, member of The Daughters of Bilitis, who picketed Independence Hall in Philadelphia and the White House in 1965.

LIFTING THE BAN

Apple pie, motherhood, and the American flag will not fall. We're already in the military.

—MIRIAM BEN-SHALOM, 1992

The fight to end military discrimination proves one fact: Until we stop confusing access to the political system with real power in it, we will be in compromising positions.

—URVASHI VAID, former executive director of NGLTF, 1993

It's my most fervent hope that nobody has to go through a witch-hunt or this sort of ordeal and exposure ever again. If we're the last ones, then it will have been worth going through it.

—MARGARETHE CAMMERMEYER, former U.S. Army colonel

I was more comfortable with lesbians. Lesbians tend to be rougher, tougher, tomboyish types. I came across good heterosexual marines, but the majority were a bunch of little makeup-wearing prissies. With lesbians, I could swear up a storm, drink beer, burp.

—BARBARA BAUM, a former marine who was court-martialed for having lesbian sex and served six months in prison; Baum has said she is not a lesbian; 1989

LESBIAN FEMINISM

Considering the centrality of lesbianism to the Women's Movement it should now seem absurd to persist in associating lesbian women with the male homosexual movement. Lesbians are feminists, not homosexuals.

—JILL JOHNSTON, writer

I have met many, many feminists who are not Lesbians, but I never met a Lesbian who was not a feminist.

MARTHA SHELLEY, writer, 1970

Lesbianism is to feminism what the Communist Party was to the trade-union movement.

—TI-GRACE ATKINSON, writer, 1974

A lesbian is the rage of all women condensed to the point of exploding.

—RADICALESBIANS, 1972

Women's love for women has been represented almost entirely through silence and lies.

—ADRIENNE RICH, feminist, poet

Women who love their own sex love the sameness in the other. They become both subject and object to each other. That makes two subjects and two objects.

—JILL JOHNSTON, 1973

Men fear Lesbians because they are less dependent, and because their hostility is less controlled. Straight women fear Lesbians because of the Lesbian inside them, because we represent an alternative.

—MARTHA SHELLEY, 1970

Whatever their physical type, education level, temperament or mentality, all homosexual women are one in their rejection of bondage to the male. They refuse to be the second sex.

—CHARLOTTE WOLFF, 1973

Modern woman is no longer satisfied to be the beloved of a man; she looks for understanding, comradeship; she wants to be treated as a human being and not simply as an object for sexual gratification. And since man in many cases cannot offer her this, she turns to her sisters.

—EMMA GOLDMAN, 1923

ART AND SENSIBILITY

If I hear one more solo singer-songwriter who is earnest and politically correct, I'm gonna scream. If the only reason that these artists are being invited to perform at festivals is because they're lesbian, then that's just not enough for me.

—KATHY KORNILOFF, singer, member of Two Nice Girls, 1993

I like perhaps a quarter of my books. If I really had a choice, I'd read only about an eighth. But the criticisms of Naiad Press take for granted that all lesbians are well-educated and already know everything there is to know in the world, which is a crock of crap.

—BARBARA GRIER, publisher of Naiad Press

To me the great pride, the miracle really, is the gay and lesbian community. We're the only community that takes in all color and creed, all races. It is so important to me as a writer to try to convey that in my work, the diversity and the power of all these various elements.

—KATHERINE V. FORREST, novelist

I love having a cryptic sexuality. I was always most intrigued by people who were mysterious in that aspect. Androgyny is a natural thing for me, but it's also that I don't want to sell my music through sexuality.

—K.D. LANG, singer/songwriter

I try to write really complicated and dangerous characters that leave you with a contradiction. I write to save my own life, and so that young people will have hope.

—DOROTHY ALLISON, author

I have never, for any reason, in any book of mine, falsified anything deliberately which I knew or believed to be true. One can at least desire the truth; and it is inconceivable to me how anyone deliberately betrays it.

—MARY RENAULT, author

I don't fool myself into thinking that if people experience love one night in a concert with me, that that's going to change their lives. It would be great if I could just open my mouth and people would be like, "Oh Toshi, I'm converted—I love women, I love big, black, queer women."

—TOSHI REAGON, singer/songwriter, 1994

Jews and homosexuals are the outstanding creative minorities in contemporary urban culture. Creative, that is, in the truest sense: they are creators of sensibilities. The two pioneering forces of modern sensibility are Jewish moral seriousness and homosexual aesthetics and irony.

—SUSAN SONTAG, 1969

On Being a Lesbian

You can't type what a lesbian is. We're anything and everything. The one thing in common is that we make love to other women. So give up trying to limit us.

—AMANDA BEARSE, actor, 1993

I might be inclined to join the group if the gay community got back to being a bit like it was in the '20s and '30s, when it was more varied and more about being intellectual and sophisticated and about doing great things like playing bridge or going on fabulous trips to Paris and sitting around cafés being brilliant.

—SANDRA BERNHARD, 1993

You're so afraid to be who you are in the lesbian community. There are so many guidelines you have to follow to be "a real lesbian." It's discouraging.

—LYNN POPMEY, openly lesbian member of Fem2Fem, 1994

I dream of a day when your sexuality doesn't have to be your career.

—MARGA GOMEZ, actor/comedian, 1993

Oh, you mean I'm a homosexual! Of course I am, and heterosexual too. But what's that got to do with my headache?

—EDNA ST. VINCENT MILLAY, poet, in response to a doctor who hinted that her severe recurring headaches might be due to repressed lesbian impulses

She was the friend of men and lover of women, which for people full of ardor and drive is better than the other way round.

—NATALIE BARNEY's idea for her epitaph, 1920

I resent like hell that I was maybe eighteen before I ever heard the "L" word. It would have made all the difference for me had I grown up knowing that the reason I didn't fit in was because they hadn't told me there were more categories to fit into.

—MICHELLE SHOCKED, singer/songwriter

On Coming Out

Coming out was funny. It was like finally registering your car. And when it's not registered, you're always worried that every cop, every policeman is going to get you. You've got that weight on your shoulders, and you're always looking behind you.

—MELISSA ETHRIDGE, rock star, 1993

I'm still friends with all of the women I've dated, and they're extremely private. If I talked about them, I'd be outing them. Besides, it would be bad karma.

—SALLY HERSHBERGER, fashion photographer, 1994

Coming out wasn't a choice that I had. The choice I had was to survive or not to survive. As soon as I found out, I came out . . . for me that was a survival tool. I think I probably would have died if I hadn't come out. I really do.

—PHRANC, folksinger

I think it was tiresome being the only out lesbian in Canada.

—JANE RULE, novelist, 1993

I decided to come out after going to that dance [at the Firehouse in Greenwich Village]. It was either kill myself or come out.

—JOYCE HUNTER, activist, gay and lesbian youth advocate

ON STAYING IN

We don't do bed checks. Just watch the golf.

—Golfing official, when asked about lesbianism and the Ladies Professional Golf Association Tour, 1993

LESBIAN CHIC

We're like the Evian water of the '90s. Everybody wants to know a lesbian or to be with a lesbian or just to dress like one.

—SUZANNE WESTENHOEFER, comic, 1993

You used to have to go hide in a booth in Denny's to be a dyke. Now everyone wants to be one.

—LOIS BROMFIELD, comedian and scriptwriter for Roseanne, 1994

Why should I be faithful? Roseanne cheated on me with Carol Burnett.

—MARIEL HEMINGWAY, after kissing Lea DeLaria so hard that the lesbian comic fell facedown on stage at the GLAAD L.A. Media Awards; Roseanne and Burnett had enjoyed a passionate clinch during the People's Choice Awards a few days earlier

You know what they say—every time two lesbians kiss, an angel in heaven gets her wings.

—ROSEANNE, on the television show of the same name, 1992

All of my sexual experiences when I was young were with girls. I mean, we didn't have those sleep-over parties for nothing. I think that's really normal; same-sex experimentation.

—MADONNA, rock star, 1991

Sometimes I think it's the year of the woman squared. It's sort of like the year of the woman loving woman.

—KATE CLINTON, comedian, 1993

Every man should own at least one dress—and so should lesbians.

—JANE ADAMS SPAHR, activist

ON GROWING OLDER

At approximately the age of fifty I became a "pioneer," a "classic," a "mother" or a "grandmother" of avant-garde or lesbian film, depending on who was relating to me. I noticed more deference in attitude, more respect, more acclaim from almost everyone, younger women and men, as well as curators and collectors. It came as a surprise at first and really was what marked my age to myself. The other, so to speak, told me I was now old or nearly old.

—BARBARA HAMMER, filmmaker

SOURCES

The Advocate, Los Angeles, CA.

BLK, Los Angeles, CA.

Marcus, Eric. *Making History: The Struggle for Gay and Lesbian Equal Rights, 1945–1990.* HarperCollins, 1992.

Out magazine, New York, NY.

Rutledge, Leigh W. *The Gay Decades, From Stonewall to the Present: The People and Events That Shaped Gay Lives.* Plume, 1992.

Sherman, Phillip, and Samuel Bernstein. *Uncommon Heroes: A Celebration of Heroes and Role Models for Gay and Lesbian Americans.* Fletcher Press, 1994.

Silva, Rosemary. *Lesbian Quotations.* Alyson Publications, 1993.

PART IV

I WONDER WHAT *THAT* MEANS

A Glossary of Sayings, Slang, Signs,
and Symbols for Lesbians

LESBIANS HAVE, OVER time, developed a language all their own: words and phrases that pertain to their culture, experiences, sexual behavior, and history. Some phrases, like *closet* and *coming out*, have infiltrated general usage, though with different meanings from the original. The following is a list of terms and sayings that are or have been common in lesbian lives, though not all of them are exclusive to lesbians.

Note: Many slang terms specific to lesbians in Quebec are anglicisms—une butch, for example—and have been omitted from this list.

ac/dc: An adjective that originated in the 1960s to describe a person who had sex with either men or women; bisexual. The term came from the abbreviations for two types of electrical currents, alternating current and direct current.

Activist: One who actively engages in efforts to change the existing social or political order.

Alternative insemination (AI): Any method, other than sexual intercourse, of injecting sperm into the uterus in order to bring about pregnancy. More commonly called artificial insemination by the general public, a term that was rejected by many lesbians in the late 1980s as too heterosexist, since it implied that any insemination other than via heterosexual intercourse was not *real*. One AI method often used by lesbians before AIDS was at home via turkey basters, injecting the sperm of gay male friends. Now, clinics and sperm banks that screen donors and sperm are often used by those who can afford the high cost of the injections. Also called *donor insemination*.

Amazon: A strong, aggressive woman, particularly a lesbian. In the 1920s, Natalie Barney was reputedly the first to employ this term for lesbians; it became commonly used by lesbian-feminists during the 1970s. In Greek mythology, the Amazons were a nation of stately and powerful warrior women who reputedly lived (without men) near the Black Sea in Scythia in about the twelfth century B.C.

Androgyny: From the combined Greek words for man and woman. It was once used to denote the state of having both male and female attributes—for example, butches in the 1940s and 1950s, who, according to Gayle Rubin, "combined highly masculine signals with detectably female bodies." Its current usage is to denote a form of self-presentation somewhere between butch and femme.

Anilingus: To tongue the anus. *See* **Rim.**

Anonymous sex: Sex between consenting adults who don't know each other and never exchange full names.

Baby butch: A young lesbian, particularly of high school or college age, who acts and looks tough and masculine.

Back room: A dark room at the back of a bar or club designated for sex. During the sexually experimental 1970s, gay men's bars initiated the use of back rooms for anonymous sex. Inspired by gay male sexual openness, lesbian clubs in cities such as New York and San Francisco began to feature back rooms in the early 1990s. In the age of AIDS, back rooms come equipped with safer sex items, such as condoms, dental dams, and latex gloves.

Baiting: The verbal attacking, insulting, taunting, or criticizing of lesbians and gay men on the basis of their sexual orientation.

Bar dyke: A lesbian who frequents women's bars.

Bashing: Physical assault of lesbians and gay men because of their sexual orientation; also commonly called queer bashing and fag bashing. *See* **Bias crime.**

B & D: Bondage and discipline; a form of sexual play in which one partner is tied up and the other (or others) "discipline" her or him, verbally and/or physically. *See* **S/M.**

Beard: A person of the opposite sex, either heterosexual or homosexual, who knowingly dates or marries a closeted lesbian or gay man to provide him or her with a heterosexual disguise, usually for family or career purposes. Beard has been in use since the first half of this century and originally applied only to a straight woman who provided cover for a gay man. In his classic gay novel of 1948, *The City and the Pillar*, Gore Vidal wrote: "A number of women acted as outriders to the beautiful legion, and they were often called upon to be public escorts. They were known as 'beards.'" *See also* **Front marriage.**

Bed death: The period of time, usually a few years into a lesbian relationship, when sexual desire between partners lessens and sex becomes infrequent, until it sometimes ceases to occur at all. Lesbian sexologist Joann Loulan and others have attributed bed death to a variety of causes related to the complexity of female sexuality, including the tendency of committed lesbian partners to experience fusion or merging.

Berdache: In approximately 130 Native American cultures, a man or woman who was unable or unwilling to fit into the role assigned to his/her gender. The word is a French colonialist one (meaning *slave boy*), first used by explorers who observed and wrote about North American Indian men-women as early as the seventeenth century. Native American languages had their own words for these gender benders, who were allowed to occupy a place somewhere between male and female and were often honored as healers and shamans. Male berdaches specialized in traditional women's skills, and female berdaches sometimes became recognized warriors and guides.

Bias crime: A crime perpetrated on a person because of the victim's minority status in society, most often due to race or sexual orientation. Also called a *hate crime. See also* **Bashing.**

Bisexual/bi: A person who has sexual and emotional relationships with both women and men, though not necessarily at the same time.

Black triangle: A symbol in the shape of an inverted triangle adopted by lesbian culture in remembrance of the lesbians who were killed by the Nazis in Europe. Between 1933 and 1945, the Nazis rounded up and arrested millions of individuals whom they perceived as threats to their power and incarcerated them in concentration camps. Each category of prisoner had its own identifying triangle or symbol. Included with Jews, homosexuals, and gypsies were thousands of prostitutes, antisocials, and misfits, who were required to wear an inverted black triangle sewn onto their clothing. Though the Nazis had no specific category for lesbians, it is believed that lesbians may have been included in the antisocial category. Women who wore the black triangle were often forced to have sex with male camp personnel, which may have been viewed as a way to cure lesbians.

Boston marriage: Used primarily in nineteenth-century New England to refer to two women who set up a household together for an extended period of time. Some Boston marriages were undoubtedly lesbian in nature, but others were probably platonic, based on the women's mutual desire to pursue careers, a goal that would have been impeded if they married and followed the traditionally prescribed roles of wife and mother. *See also* **Romantic friendship.**

Bottom: An erotic sex role; the passive recipient in sex. *See* **Top.**

Breeders: Before the lesbian baby boom of the late 1980s and early 1990s, a derogatory term for heterosexuals, especially those who glorified childbearing and childrearing. A popular lesbian button of the early 1980s read, "Non-Breeder."

Bring out: To aid and abet the coming-out process, as in "She brought me out"; usually refers to an experienced lesbian initiating a sexual relationship with a woman who has never had sex with another woman.

Buffet flat: An after-hours partying spot in Harlem of the 1920s, usually in someone's apartment, which was a common place for African-American lesbians and gay men to socialize. Buffet referred to a smorgasbord of sexual possibilities: straight, gay, group sex, etc.

Bulldyke/bulldagger: Since the early twentieth century, a butch lesbian; derogatory when used by straight people, but also occasionally used by lesbians to indicate toughness. Judy Grahn says in her book, *Another Mother Tongue,* that *bulldyke* comes from Boudica, a warrior queen of the Celtic people. Also called *boon-dagger.*

Bush: Pubic hair.

Butch: 1. A lesbian who prefers masculine dress, style, expression, or identity. Though there have been butch lesbians throughout history, the term was probably first used in the United States in the 1940s. Butch was formerly a common nickname for a young boy and also the name of a severe men's haircut. 2. A gay man who is traditionally virile or masculine in speech, dress, and sexual behavior.

Butch-femme: According to Joan Nestle, an erotic lesbian partnership between a butch and a femme that was part social rebellion and part intimate exploration of women's sexuality. Butch-femme as a code of lesbian behavior and style was prominent from the 1940s to the 1960s. During the second wave of feminism in the 1970s, butch-femme relationships became regarded as embarrassing by many younger lesbians who perceived them as an Uncle Tom mimicry of straight society, rather than as an elaborate erotic communication between women.

Butt plug: Small sex toy shaped to be inserted into the anus.

Camp: A style of humor or satire based on exaggeration, artifice, and androgyny. Within the lesbian and gay community, the term most often refers to gay men assuming a comically exaggerated feminine manner in order to entertain; but there is also a tradition of lesbian camp. *High camp* is over the top. The word also appears as a verb, as in *to camp it up,* and an adjective, *campy.* According to Judy Grahn (*Another Mother Tongue*), *camp* comes from the British term *camping,* which was the practice of young men wearing women's clothing in a play and which in turn came from the French *campagne,* the outdoor space where medieval minstrels performed.

Cherry Grove: A summer beach resort community on Fire Island founded in the late nineteenth century. Though originally frequented by middle-class heterosexual families, Cherry Grove became a predominantly gay or bohemian community in the 1930s and has remained so ever since. Today, it attracts more lesbians and people of color than its sister community, Fire Island Pines, an upscale, mostly white gay male colony founded a mile up the beach from Cherry Grove in the 1950s.

Clit: Shorthand for clitoris.

Clit-tease: A flirt; a woman who sexually arouses another woman with no intention of having sex with her; one who doesn't put out. A humorous twist on the traditional straight man's complaint about a flirtatious woman, or cock-tease.

Closet: The confining state of being secretive about one's homosexuality. According to historian George Chauncey, the word *closet* cannot be found in lesbian and gay literature before the 1960s and probably was not used until then.

Closet case/closeted: One who does not admit her/his homosexuality and who often actively denies it.

Coalition politics: Type of political analysis and action that recognizes the interconnectedness of oppressions (e.g., racism, sexism, homophobia) and establishes bridges across differences to a common goal of social and political change.

Collective: In leftist politics of the 1960s and then in second-wave feminist politics, a nonhierarchical group or organization in which each member (ostensibly) had an equal voice. Decisions affecting the whole were made by group consensus. Some lesbian-feminist collectives still function, but many had passed out of existence by the early 1990s, as lesbians became more involved in coalition politics with gay men.

Colors historically associated with homosexuality: *Green:* United States, 1930s to 1950s. *Red:* United States, late nineteenth and early twentieth century. *Pink:* Nazi Germany. *Scarlet:* Imperial Rome. *Violet:* Imperial Rome. *Blue:* present-day Russia. *Lavender:* throughout history and in present-day United States. *Rainbow:* present-day United States.

Comadres: In Chicano/Chicana communities of the American Southwest, two unmarried women who live together in a close relationship, as in Boston marriage or romantic friendship; in English translation, comothers.

Come/cum: (*v*) To achieve orgasm. (*n*) Semen.

Come out: To acknowledge one's homosexuality, either to oneself or to others; most often a public declaration of being lesbian or gay.

Coming-out story: An individual's personal story about one of the following: 1. Realizing she/he is gay for the first time. 2. Having lesbian or gay sex for the first time. 3. Telling family, friends, or colleagues she/he is gay. 4. Being discovered involuntarily as gay by family, friends, or colleagues. Most lesbians and gay men have more than one story (Aren't we *always* having to come out?), and they are usually a mixture of humor and pathos.

Commitment ceremony: Any ritual, religious or secular, for honoring the union of lesbian or gay male couples in marriage. Since same-sex marriages are not yet legally recognized in the United States or Canada, although they are, in fact, legal in the progressive Scandinavian countries of Denmark and Norway, lesbian and gay couples sometimes hold commitment ceremonies (a term coined in the 1980s), usually with friends and families present, to venerate their decision to stay together "for better or for worse."

Compulsory heterosexuality: Term coined by poet/activist Adrienne Rich in the 1970s to describe the social conditioning of women to believe that marriage and sexual coupling with men are inevitable for them.

Consciousness raising (CR): A formalized, intragroup educational discussion process, created by the feminist movement of the 1960s. In CR, small groups of women discussed their personal experiences, starting from the assumption that all women's experiences are political in nature (the personal is political). In doing so, women could understand and analyze the roles allotted to them in society. CR became one of the primary tools of the women's liberation movement of the 1960s and 1970s, and its methods were later adopted by other political groups and organizations as a means of politicizing their members.

Cream: (*n*) Creamy, white vaginal fluid. (*v*) To become sexually aroused and therefore wet. (She creamed herself watching Maria dance.)

Crime against nature: Term used especially by religious fundamentalists to describe homosexuality, taken from wording in the Old Testament. Homosexual sex is described as being against nature because it does not lead to the procreation of children, the supposed natural use of sexual organs.

Crone: A derogatory term for an old, witchlike woman, similar to *hag*. *Crone* and *hag* were reclaimed by 1970s feminists as proud names for older lesbians.

Cross-dressing: The practice of dressing in clothes traditionally assigned to the opposite gender; also called *transvestism* or *drag*.

Cruise/cruising: To look for sexual partners; to flirt with the intention of finding a sexual partner.

Cunnilingus: Oral stimulation of a woman's clitoris or vulva.

Cunt: Vulva. Originally (and still) used by men as a derogatory word for uppity or bitchy women, it has been reclaimed by lesbians for erotic usage.

Day without Art: December 1 (World AIDS Day), when many cultural institutions, museums, and galleries either close their doors, drape works of art, or offer special programs in memory of those who have died of AIDS. The project started in 1989 in New York City and has since spread around the world.

Dental dam: In safer sex, a square sheet of thin latex (approximately 6" x 6") used to cover a woman's clitoris and vulva during cunnilingus to prevent the transmission of bodily fluids. Its name comes from its original use by dentists to keep teeth dry during root canal, fillings, or other dental work.

Diesel dyke: A rough, tough, butch lesbian; used primarily in the 1950s. Also, sometimes called *truck driver.*

Dildo: A sex toy shaped somewhat like an erect penis, which can be inserted into the vagina, anus, or mouth. When worn with a harness, it is sometimes referred to as a *strap-on.*

Direct action: A form of activism in which participants become directly, physically involved in trying to disrupt or change the social or political order. ACT UP, Queer Nation, and Lesbian Avengers are examples of direct-action groups. *See also* **Zap/zap action.**

Dish: (*n*) Gossip, hearsay, or buzz, often critical (What's the dish on Alice?). (*v*) To engage in gossip. (We dished for hours.)

Domestic partnership: An official recognition of partners (either homosexual or heterosexual) who are not legally married but who cohabit and share a committed, spousal relationship. In about a dozen U.S. cities and one state, government employees are eligible to receive health benefits for their domestic partners, and a number of private corporations extend similar domestic partnership benefits.

Drag: Cross-dressing, assuming both the dress and mannerisms of the opposite gender. *See* **Cross-dressing.**

Drag king: A lesbian who dresses in full male attire, sometimes passing as a man. *See* **Cross-dressing.**

Dyke: A derogatory term for a lesbian, particularly a butch. The word *dyke* was reclaimed by lesbians in the 1970s as slang, and many lesbians now refer to themselves as dykes. When used by heterosexuals, the term remains pejorative. According to Bruce Rodgers (*Gay Talk*), *dyke* was a distortion of the *-dite* in *hermaphrodite*; Judy Grahn (*Another Mother Tongue*) says it was a shortened version of *bulldyke*, which derived from the Celtic queen Boudica.

Eat/eat out: To perform oral sex.

Elective lesbian: A woman who experiences her lesbianism as chosen or elected, rather than as innate.

Erotophobia: A fear of eroticism or sexual play. Coined during the sex wars of the early 1980s to refer to lesbians and feminists who sought to censor different kinds of lesbian sexual expression (such as butch-femme and S/M).

Essentialism: The theory that lesbianism is biologically determined and is a permanent, immutable characteristic incapable of being reversed or changed. Essentialists hold that there have always been lesbians, even before the term came into existence and even before it was possible for women to live as lesbians. *See*, in contrast, **Social constructionism.**

Etre aux femmes: French-Canadian; in English translation, to be lesbian.

Fag hag: A straight woman who actively seeks out friendships with gay men.

Fairy lady: In the mid-1900s, a lesbian bottom.

Femme: A lesbian who prefers feminine dress, style, expression, or identity. The term was probably first used in the United States in the 1940s, as a counterpoint to *butch*, and comes from the French word for woman.

Une femme aux femmes: French-Canadian for a lesbian.

Finger cot: In safer sex, a small latex condom that fits over individual fingers and prevents the transmission of bodily fluids through cuts on the hands.

Finger fuck: To insert one or more fingers into the vagina or anus.

Fire Island: A barrier island off the coast of Long Island, New York, known for its two gay beach resorts, Cherry Grove and Fire Island Pines.

Fist fuck: To insert all or most of the hand into the vagina or anus.

Fluff: In the 1950s, another word for femme.

Frig: In lesbian sex, to finger fuck or stroke a woman's genitals; from *friction*.

Front marriage: A marriage between a lesbian and a gay man for the purpose of passing, at work and/or with family. *See also* **Beard.**

Freedom rings: Necklace created by David Spada, a New York designer, in 1991, comprised of anodized aluminum rings in the colors of the rainbow flag and worn loose on a chain. Freedom rings, signifying gay pride and unity, have since been incorporated into numerous kinds of gay jewelry, including earrings, rings, and bracelets; sometimes colored aluminum triangles are substituted for circles.

Fuck buddy: A casual sex partner, usually a friend with whom one has infrequent sex without commitment.

Fusion: In lesbian love relationships, an intense intimacy between the two partners that causes them to be overinvolved with each other. The result is that the differences between the two seem to be lessened, and each partner's ability to maintain an independent identity is weakened. Often blamed for lesbian bed death, or loss of sexual desire. Also called *merging*.

Gangster woman/gangster dyke: Among African-Americans, a young, tough, butch, street lesbian.

Gay: Homosexual. The term refers to both men and women, though many gay women now prefer to call themselves lesbians. According to historian George Chauncey, it was in the seventeenth century that the word *gay*, which had always connoted pleasurable things, began to indicate a life of immoral pleasures. Later, when applied to women in the nineteenth century, *gay* meant *prostitute*. By the early 1900s, homosexuals appropriated the term as a camp word to refer not only to themselves, but to promiscuity, flamboyance, and lack of restraint. Since the 1940s, *gay* has been the preferred term used by homosexuals to refer to themselves.

Gaydar: The uncanny and seemingly innate ability lesbians and gay men have to recognize and detect one another; from *gay* and *radar*.

Gay vote: In electoral politics, the tendency of lesbians and gays to vote in a particular way, or as a bloc, reflecting their needs and desires as a minority group. Political candidates who recognize this tendency and seek to take advantage of it are said to court the gay vote. Lesbians and gay men have been found in local and national elections to vote overwhelmingly for Democratic candidates.

Gender bender: One who blurs gender lines, usually by dressing or acting in a way traditionally assigned to the opposite sex.

Gender fuck: Gender bending, with an attitude.

Glamour dyke: A lesbian for whom fashion, elegance, and glamour are important aspects of personal style and expression.

Go down on: To perform oral sex on.

Golden shower: Urination used for sexual or erotic play; also called *water sports*.

Une gouine: French-Canadian for a lesbian.

Granola lesbian: An overly wholesome, health-conscious lesbian.

Harness: Beltlike device, usually made of leather, strapped over the hips and crotch to hold a dildo in place for vaginal or anal sex.

Hermaphrodite: A person born with both male and female sexual organs.

Herstory: The history of women and/or lesbians left out of traditional historical accounts. The term was coined in the 1970s by lesbian feminists to take the patriarchal *his* out of history. Most famous example: the Lesbian Herstory Archives, founded in New York City in 1974.

He-she: Used before Stonewall for a woman whose gender expression was primarily male and who therefore blurred the traditional lines of gender.

Heterosexism: A bias toward heterosexuality, to the exclusion of homosexuality.

Homoerotic: An erotic presentation that is suggestively homosexual in nature. For example, commercial ads or billboards that show two women or two men together in a suggestively erotic pose are said to be homoerotic.

Homophile: Term used from the beginning of the twentieth century until just before the Stonewall rebellion for a homosexual.

Homophobe: One who is actively homophobic.

Homophobia: Literally, the fear of homosexuals and homosexuality, sometimes merely implied, but often taken to the point where biased statements are made or biased actions are taken against lesbians and gay men. Homophobia can be societal, external, or internalized.

Homosexual panic: Conscious fear of one's own possible homosexuality. Homosexual panic implies that a woman will take whatever steps are necessary—open denial, heterosexual marriage and motherhood, etc.—to prove to herself and others that she is not really a lesbian.

Honeypot: A woman's genitals.

Hwame: Pima Indian for lesbian medicine woman.

Identity politics: Identifying and allying for political reasons with a minority group to which one belongs—for example, along lines of ethnicity, race, gender, age, or sexual orientation.

Internalized homophobia: The unconscious fear and hatred of homosexuality as experienced by lesbians and gay men. Because society is so riddled with blatant homophobia, gay people often turn hatred of homosexuality back against themselves. In one example, when a lesbian does not come out to her parents, stating that it would hurt or kill them, she internalizes the notion that being gay is bad.

In the life: In the African-American lesbian and gay community of the 1920s and later, the term commonly used for being gay (So-and-so is in the life).

Invert: Pseudoscientific term used by psychologists and doctors from the late nineteenth century until the 1940s for a lesbian or gay man. Homosexuality was referred to as inversion or the inverted sexual instinct because it was viewed as a reversal of normal, straight sexuality.

Jack and Jill party: In the late 1980s, a circle jerk (group masturbation party) that welcomed gay men and lesbians, who occasionally had sex with one another.

Jam: Mid–twentieth century slang for straight people.

Kiki: used in the 1940s and 1950s for a woman who could not decide if she was butch or femme. The term could also refer to two butches or two femmes who were lovers and thus confused the structured butch-femme social world.

Kinsey 6: One whose sexual experience and identification is exclusively homosexual. In the Kinsey Institute's landmark studies of male and female sexuality (1948 and 1953, respectively), researchers set up a simple numerical scale to classify human sexuality. A 1 indicated exclusive heterosexuality, a 6 indicated exclusive homosexuality, with a range of options in between. It was the Kinsey study of male sexuality that first established (to the shock of straight people and the delight of gays) that one man in ten is homosexual, a statistic that has been hotly debated ever since.

Koskalaka: Lakota (Sioux) Indian lesbian medicine woman; in English translation, *young man* or *woman who doesn't want to marry.*

Labrys: Double-sided axe used as a symbol of lesbian power and self-sufficiency, particularly in jewelry. In ancient, matriarchal societies, the labrys was used as both a weapon and a harvesting tool. The Greeks often pictured it in their art as the weapon of choice of the Amazons.

Lambda: Used internationally as a symbol of being gay, the lambda is both the eleventh letter of the Greek alphabet and the symbol in physics of kinetic energy. The Gay Activists Alliance first adopted the lambda in 1970 as a symbol of the energy of the nascent gay movement.

Lavender: Throughout western history, the color most commonly associated with being gay. Lavender is the mixture of blue (male now, but formerly female) with pink (female now, but formerly male).

Lavender law: The specialized study or practice of lesbian and gay legal issues and concerns.

Lavender menace: Since 1970, a phrase attributed to Betty Friedan, one of the founders of the modern feminist movement, for feisty, outspoken lesbians whose radical (and hence unpalatable) demands for lesbian liberation supposedly jeopardized feminist attempts to gain equality for women. Friedan actually used the term "lavender herring," but lesbians revised her slur and used it proudly for themselves.

Leather dyke: A lesbian whose personal style and expression includes the heavy use of leather clothing and accoutrements, usually with the implication that she is interested in S/M.

Lesberado: Combination of *lesbian* and *desperado*.

Lesbian: A female homosexual. The term literally means a resident of the Isle of Lesbos, a Greek island where the ancient lyric poet Sappho, whose verse celebrated love between women, lived.

Lesbian and gay studies: The burgeoning interdisciplinary, academic study of lesbian and gay lives, culture, thought, and history.

Lesbian baby boom: Since the late 1980s, the sudden sharp increase in the number of lesbians conceiving and bearing or adopting children, either alone or with a lesbian partner.

Lesbian chic: Beginning in 1992, the discovery of and interest in lesbians and lesbian culture by the mainstream media, where lesbians have traditionally been invisible. This new interest has resulted in cover stories on lesbian lives in *Newsweek* and *New York* magazines, a proliferation of books from mainstream publishers on lesbian topics, and increasingly positive portrayals of lesbians in movies and on television. Unfortunately, the term *chic* implies a faddish fashionability that could easily reverse.

Lesbian continuum: The range of woman-identified experience that may or may not include actual or desired genital sexual experience with other women; the spectrum of sexual experience between homosexuality and heterosexuality.

Lesbian feminist: Beginning with the second wave of feminism in the late 1960s, a woman who derived her identity from her feminist political beliefs as well as from her sexual orientation.

Lesbian invisibility: 1. The omission of lesbian lives and issues from public discussions and media presentations of homosexuality. 2. The conflation of homosexuality with gay men, to the exclusion of lesbians. 3. The tendency in heterosexual society to obscure the fact that lesbianism exists.

Lesbian liberation: The goal of radical social change that would permit the free expression of lesbianism without stigma or oppression.

Lesbian Nation: Term taken from the title of a 1973 collection of newspaper articles by writer Jill Johnston to describe the global linking of lesbians through alternative social and community structures and distinct ways of thinking about women, patriarchy, and language.

Lesbian thought police: Extreme political correctness, based on the idea that there is one certain way that all lesbians should think. A lesbian who feels guilt about her S/M sexual fantasies, for example, might joke that she is going to be hunted down by the lesbian thought police.

Leviticus: The passages in the Old Testament used by the Christian Right to justify homophobia and antigay discrimination. See pages 358–359 for the exact wording of the passages.

Lifestyle: Term used primarily by heterosexuals to describe lesbian and gay lives, tending to depreciate homosexuality as a style or fad.

Lipstick lesbian: Since the 1980s, a lesbian whose gender expression is feminine, including the traditional aspects of women's dress—makeup, nail polish, short skirts, high heels—eschewed by 1970s lesbian-feminism.

"Love that dares not speak its name": Phrase used by poet Lord Alfred Douglas (lover of Oscar Wilde) for homosexual love and desire.

Lube: Lubricant for anal or vaginal sex.

Luppies: Lesbian yuppies.

Mannish woman: In the early twentieth century, the code word used by heterosexuals for butch lesbians.

Marimacha: Spanish slang for lesbian, roughly equivalent to *dyke*.

Matriarchy: A social system in which descent is traced through mothers, as opposed to patriarchy, which traces lineage through fathers.

Ménage à trois: Sexual encounter involving three partners of any combination of genders.

Merged women's symbols: The universal symbol for woman is a circle with a cross at the bottom, said to be the mirror of the goddess. In the 1970s, lesbians joined two or more women's symbols in different configurations to indicate lesbianism, or women together. Today, when two joined men's symbols are linked with two joined women's symbols, it signifies lesbian and gay community or solidarity.

Merging: *see* **Fusion.**

Michigan: Shorthand for the Michigan Womyn's Music Festival, the oldest continuing cultural festival for lesbians in the United States, which takes place annually on women-owned land in Michigan and is one of the few remaining bastions of lesbian separatism in the country.

Monogamy/nonmonogamy: The ultimate question in most love relationships: to have sex only with each other (monogamy), or to have an open relationship in which partners are free to have sex with numerous people besides each other (nonmonogamy).

Muff dive/muff diving: Cunnilingus.

Nature or nurture: The debate over whether homosexuality is a result of biology (nature) or socialization (nurture).

Nipple clamps: Sex toys that attach to nipples to heighten sexual pleasure.

Out: To be out of the closet.

Outing: The controversial practice of publicly revealing the sexual orientation of a gay celebrity or public figure against her or his wishes. The gay magazine *OutWeek*, and reporter Michaelangelo Signorile in particular, introduced the technique in 1989–1990 and referred to it as "equalizing." Heterosexuals and homosexuals, Signorile said, were treated by the mainstream media in different ways; notably, homosexuality was seen as a matter of privacy that should not be broached. This hands-off approach, Signorile maintained, implied that homosexuality was bad or shameful, and his goal was to equalize the way heterosexuality and homosexuality were dealt with by the media. *Time* magazine coined the term "outing" to describe the technique. Recently, outing has taken on a broader meaning, signifying any type of unwanted, unwilling exposure.

Packing: In butch erotic presentation, wearing a dildo, sock, or some other padding in one's underwear to create a bulge suggestive of a penis or dildo.

Pancake: Among African-American lesbians in the 1950s, a butch who allowed herself to be flipped (from "top" to "bottom").

Pass/passing: The pretense of acting or appearing to be heterosexual, when one is in fact lesbian or gay.

Passing woman: Especially in the nineteenth and early twentieth centuries, a woman who dressed, acted, and lived as a man, often living with and marrying a traditionally feminine woman.

Patriarchy: Technically, a social system in which lineage is traced through the fathers, patriarchy has come to mean much more than that in late twentieth-century feminism. Patriarchy is now synonymous with the entire male-dominated social system of institutions, laws, and customs through which women have been held in lesser and unequal roles in government, economics, culture, etc., over the course of time. *See also* **Matriarchy.**

Phone sex: Sexual play over the telephone, usually involving mutual masturbation. Phone sex became extremely popular as a form of safer sex early in the AIDS pandemic, and phone services and networks specializing in sex sprouted up for lesbians and gay men.

Pink triangle: A symbol in the shape of an inverted triangle adopted by lesbian and gay culture in remembrance of the homosexuals who were killed by the Nazis in Europe. From 1933 to 1945, the Nazis arrested between twenty and fifty thousand gay men for the crime of homosexuality (along with millions of Jews, gypsies, and other criminals) and placed them in concentration camps. Homosexual men were identified in the camps by an inverted pink triangle sewn onto their clothing—pink to suggest that they were like women. Most of the gay prisoners did not survive the work camps; many died from the barbaric conditions, and thousands were executed. *See also* **Black triangle.**

Political dyke: A lesbian activist, especially one who is involved in one or more community organizations or political groups.

Power dyke: A lesbian who has risen to a position of high visibility and/or influence within the lesbian and gay community, based on activism, connections, or economic standing.

Postop: A person who has recently undergone sex reassignment surgery and has changed his/her birth sex. *See* **Transsexual (TS).**

Preop: A person preparing for sex reassignment surgery by taking hormones and receiving counseling.

Pride march: A public procession or parade of lesbians and gay men to proclaim the pride, solidarity, and unity of gay people. The biggest pride march takes place the last weekend in June in New York City, in commemoration of the Stonewall rebellion, but numerous other cities and towns around the world also celebrate the birth of the modern gay movement with pride marches and festivities.

Primary lesbian: A woman who experiences her lesbianism as innate or biologically determined, rather than as chosen or elected. *See* **Elective lesbian.**

Provincetown (P-town): Lesbian and gay resort at the tip of Cape Cod in Massachusetts, with a wealth of gay accommodations, businesses, clubs, and restaurants. Provincetown was the original landing site of the Pilgrims in 1620, and for years functioned primarily as a quiet fishing village. It became an artists' mecca in the early 1900s, and gradually—given the number of gay people in the arts—evolved into a gay haven.

Public sex: Sex in a public setting where others can observe or join in, as in a back room.

Pussy: Vagina.

Queer: Since the early twentieth century, a derogatory term for homosexual. *Queer* was reclaimed by radical lesbian, gay, and bisexual activists in the 1980s as a proud name for themselves. ("We're here, we're queer, get used to it!") *Queer* blurs both gender and sexual orientation and is regarded as more inclusive of difference than *lesbian* or *gay.*

Queer studies: An offshoot of lesbian and gay studies that tends to be more theoretical in nature, questioning accepted ideas about community and identity, and more inclusive of different types of people: lesbian, gay, bisexual, transgender, and straight people who somehow don't fit society's norm.

Rainbow flag: Designed in 1978 in San Francisco by artist Gilbert Baker as a symbol of lesbian and gay pride. Originally, there were eight colors in the flag: pink for sexuality, red for light, orange for healing, yellow for the sun, green for natural serenity, turquoise for art, indigo for harmony, and violet for spirit. In 1979, the flag was modified to its current six-stripe format (pink was omitted, blue was substituted for turquoise and indigo, and violet became a rich purple), signifying the diversity and unity of the lesbian and gay movement.

Red ribbon: A loop of ribbon fastened to the lapel or shirt with a small safety pin, indicating AIDS awareness and solidarity against the epidemic. Conceived by artist Frank Moore in 1991, who envisioned it as a symbol of compassion for PWAs and their lovers and families, just as yellow ribbons had been used during the Iran hostage crisis. The language of ribbons has been extended to many different colors that indicate various diseases. For example, a pink ribbon signifies solidarity in the fight against breast cancer; pink and red together indicate both AIDS and breast cancer.

Rent parties: In 1920s Harlem, house parties at which guests paid a fee to help their host raise money for the rent. Usually a mix of heterosexuals and homosexuals, rent parties were a safe way for African-American lesbians and gay men to socialize away from the speakeasies.

Rim: To tongue the anus; also called *anilingus.*

Ring on pinky: Wearing a ring on the little finger of the left hand has for much of the twentieth century been a code for homosexual.

Roles: Opposite functions played out by sexual partners, such as top or bottom, butch or femme; also, fantasy characters played by sexual partners in a scene.

Romantic friendship: In the late nineteenth and early twentieth centuries, an intimate companionship between two unmarried women that was socially approved and recognized. Two women could share a bond "no less sacred than the tie of marriage," according to author William Cullen Bryant, which was broken only if an eligible man stepped into the picture. Outwardly, there was allowed to be no erotic element to their relationship, but the language of their commitment to each other was often laced with love and romance. Whether or not these relationships were actually sexual is not known. *See* **Boston marriage.**

Rubber: A condom.

Rug-muncher: A lesbian.

Russian River: An area north of San Francisco in California's Sonoma County that has become a popular lesbian and gay resort spot. The town of Guerneville is at the center of lesbian and gay activity there.

Safer sex: An array of sexual practices that can decrease the risk of HIV infection by preventing the transmission of bodily fluids during sex. Some of the tools of lesbian safer sex are condoms, finger cots, dental dams, and latex gloves; some other forms of safer sex are kissing, mutual masturbation, rubbing, and the use of individual sex toys.

Sapphic/sapphistry: Having to do with lesbians and lesbian love; from the lesbian Greek lyric poet, Sappho. This term was especially popular in the early twentieth century, before *lesbian* became a common way of referring to gay women.

Scene: In sexual play, a mutually agreed-upon fantasy scenario in which partners assume roles.

Sergeant: In the mid-1900s, a butch lesbian.

Second-parent adoption: The legal adoption of a child, who already has one legal parent, by a second parent of the same gender. Also called coparent adoption.

Separatism: Voluntary withdrawal of women from men and male-dominated society. In the 1970s, separatism became a prominent lesbian-feminist philosophy, seen as a way for women both to avoid men's intolerable and frustrating sexism and to understand and define womanhood for themselves. Since, practically, it was hard for many women to withdraw completely from society, women-only spaces were often established as places where women would not have to deal with men. In the age of AIDS, with the increased political collaboration between and socializing of lesbians and gay men in the 1980s, separatism as a philosophy and practice became less and less adhered to.

Sex reassignment: The surgical alteration of a person's birth sex. *See* **Transsexual (TS).**

Sexual orientation: Sexual identification, defined as primarily homosexual, heterosexual, or bisexual, depending on a person's sexual relationships or affinity. This term is currently favored by many gay people over *sexual preference,* because it indicates an identity that cannot be changed or cast aside lightly, like a preference.

Sex positive: To be open to and accepting of all types of sexual expression and practice. The opposite—sex negative—means being closed to these things.

Sex wars: In the early 1980s, a volatile discussion among feminists about sexuality and women's sexual expression. One major issue was pornography and violence against women. Some feminists wanted to eliminate all types of pornographic expression because it was demeaning to women and decried S/M as violence against women. Others asserted that women's desires and fantasies could not fit into neat compartments and that many women wanted to incorporate pornography, erotica, and/or S/M into their sexual play and should be free to do so.

Significant other: One's chosen romantic partner. Because U.S. society is so weighted toward heterosexual marriage, there is no one term to signify the relationship of partners (homosexual or heterosexual) who are outside the bounds of legal wedlock. Some popular variants in the lesbian community are: lover, girlfriend, amiga, partner, life partner, domestic partner, wife, spouse.

Sisterhood: The vast, amorphous community of lesbians.

Sixty-nine: Mutual, simultaneous oral sex.

S/M: Sadomasochism. A form of consensual sexual play involving the exploration of power and (sometimes) pain. S/M can include a range of activities: everything from domination and submission fantasies and scenes to whipping, spanking, and cutting.

Smash: A young woman's crush on another woman. The term was used in late nineteenth-century and early twentieth-century women's colleges.

Social constructionism: The theory that lesbianism is not innate, but that specific social conditions allow it to occur. In contrast to the essentialists, social constructionists believe that Western society evolved in such a way as to make it possible for women to live as lesbians—for example, through urbanization; through the creation of institutions where women could meet; through increased sexual freedom and more open discussion of sexuality; and through economic self-sufficiency for women that allowed them to live without men. Therefore, social constructionism holds that lesbianism was not possible or viable until the twentieth century and therefore did not exist as we know it. *See* **Essentialism.**

Sodomy: Any one of a number of sexual acts. 1. Sex between two men. 2. Sex between two women. 3. Anal sex between a man and either another man or a woman. The name comes from the city of Sodom in the Old Testament, where men supposedly performed unspeakably wicked acts that incurred the wrath of God and brought about the destruction of the city. Modern interpreters of the Bible, however, believe that the only sin of the Sodomites alluded to in the story was that of inhospitality. Sodomy, which was punishable by death in many of the American colonies (*see* Part I), is still a felony or misdemeanor on the books of half of the United States, though it is no longer illegal in Canada.

Spinster: Formerly, a woman who remained unmarried; sometimes used as a euphemism or code word for *lesbian*

Stirring the bean curd: English translation of Chinese term for the lesbian sexual act of finger fucking.

Stone butch: A butch lesbian who does not want to be touched during sex, but whose sexual pleasure derives from giving pleasure to her partner.

Stonewall Rebellion: The riots that took place on the streets of Greenwich Village in New York City in June of 1969, when patrons of a gay bar called the Stonewall Inn on Christopher Street fought back against a police raid of the bar. Stonewall has come to signal the birth of the modern lesbian and gay rights movement.

Strap-on: A dildo when used with a harness.

Stud: In the 1940s and 1950s, an alternate term for butch, used primarily among African-Americans.

Style wars: In the early 1980s, an explosive debate among lesbians about women's clothing and presentation. For some, androgyny (a watered-down carryover form of butch presentation) was correct because it exemplified a feminist mode of dressing that eschewed the traditional and restrictive feminine appearance women had been forced into for centuries. For others, lesbians had to be free to choose their own style of self-expression and not be dictated to by a pre-dominantly white middle-class lesbian aesthetic.

Subculture: The culture of a minority group in society; any group other than the white, heterosexual majority.

Take back the night: A feminist political action, usually a night march, in protest against the violence perpetrated on women by men, often at night.

Une tchomme: French-Canadian for a lesbian.

Third sex: Formerly, homosexuals. The first sex meant heterosexual men, the second sex indicated heterosexual women, and the third sex meant those who fell in between.

Las Tías: In Chicano/Chicana communities of the American Southwest, two unmarried women who live together in a close relationship, as in Boston marriage or romantic friendship; in English, *the aunts*.

Tomboy: A young girl who acts and dresses like a boy or displays boyish gender expression. While many lesbians were tomboys as children, tomboy is also seen as a stage of female development that does not necessarily carry the stigma of lesbian, since a stage may be outgrown.

Tongue: To go down on; to use the tongue in any way that gives sexual pleasure.

Top: An erotic sex role; the active participant in sex. *See* **Bottom.**

Tortillera: Spanish slang for a lesbian, roughly equivalent to *dyke*. The term suggests tribadism, or two *tortillas* rubbing together.

Transgender: An umbrella term for those gender outlaws who blur the lines of traditional gender expression. Transgendered people include or have been referred to as transvestites, transsexuals, drag queens and kings, cross-dressers, and berdaches, to name just a few.

Transsexual (TS): A person who has undergone or is preparing to undergo sex reassignment surgery. Transsexuals can be either MTF (male-to-female) or FTM (female-to-male), homosexual, heterosexual, or bisexual.

Transvestite (TV): A person who dresses in the clothes of and assumes the gender expression of the opposite sex.

Tribadism: In lesbian sex, rhythmic rubbing of the genitals against a partner's thigh to achieve sexual arousal and/or orgasm.

Trick: A casual sexual partner, usually for just one brief interlude.

Turkey baster baby: *See* **Alternative insemination (AI).**

Vanilla sex: Conventional sex, with the connotation that it is boring, and that it does not incorporate any S/M fantasy or sexual play.

Vibrator: An electric or battery-powered sex toy for stimulating the genitals and other erogenous zones.

Violet: A color and a flower long associated with lesbians. Sappho, the Greek lesbian poet, and a woman-lover, supposedly wore garlands of violets, and in sixteenth-century England, men and women wore violets to indicate that they had no plans to marry. Edouard Bourdet, a French playwright, used violets as a symbol of lesbian love in his play *The Captive* (1926), one of the first plays on Broadway to contain a lesbian theme.

Vulva hands: A gesture used in lesbian gatherings during the 1980s, probably originating in the women's peace camp at Greenham Common in England and continuing at the Seneca Women's Peace Encampment in upstate New York, and indicating the strength of lesbian sexuality. The two forefingers and thumbs were placed together to form a triangle, and then the hands were held over the head in the air. Some lesbian jewelry still employs the image of vulva hands.

Water sports: *See* **Golden shower.**

Woman-identified woman: Term coined by the lesbian-feminist collective Radicalesbians in 1970, equating sexual orientation with feminist politics. Formerly used as a synonym or euphemism for lesbianism, this term fell out of use as the sex wars of the 1980s drove a wedge between traditional feminism's stance against pornography and the actual sexual preferences of lesbians.

Women's music: Music from the American folk tradition that incorporates lesbian sexuality and identity and often feminist politics into its lyrics. Because lesbian experience was excluded from mainstream music, women musicians in the early 1970s began creating their own recording labels (Olivia Records was the best known), producing songs that spoke directly to predominantly white lesbian experience. Names such as Holly Near, Cris Williamson, Alix Dobkin, Margie Adam, and Meg Christian have been preeminent in women's music.

Womon/womyn/wimmin: Alternative lesbian-feminist spellings of *woman* and *women*. (*Womon* is singular; the other two are plural.) In the 1970s and 1980s, many lesbian-feminists (particularly separatists) replaced the traditional spellings of these words in order to avoid the patriarchal root words, *man* and *men*. The political spellings are still occasionally used—for example, the separatist Michigan Womyn's Music Festival continues to use the spelling it adopted twenty years ago.

Zap/zap action: A form of direct action intended to be loud, quick, and showy, to capture media attention.

'Zine: Since the late 1980s, a small, low-budget magazine on a specific topic, produced by either one person or just a few people. The first 'zines were primarily devoted to sex. When a 'zine is dedicated to exploring the life and work of a celebrity (for example, *Highway Twelve*, a 'zine about the singer k.d. lang), it's called a fanzine.

Please see pages 444–447 for a separate dictionary of AIDS-related terms.

SOURCES

The Alyson Almanac, 1994–95 Edition. Alyson Publications, 1994.

Duberman, Martin, Martha Vicinus, and George Chauncey, eds. *Hidden from History: Reclaiming the Gay and Lesbian Past*. New American Library, 1989.

Dynes, Wayne, ed. *The Encyclopedia of Homosexuality*. 2 vols. Garland Publishing, Inc., 1990.

Faderman, Lillian. *Odd Girls and Twilight Lovers: A History of Lesbian Life in Twentieth-Century America*. Columbia University Press, 1991.

Fletcher, Lynne Yamaguchi. *The First Gay Pope and Other Records*. Alyson Publications, 1992.

Grahn, Judy. *Another Mother Tongue: Gay Words, Gay Worlds*. Beacon, 1984, 1990.

Katz, Jonathan Ned. *Gay/Lesbian Almanac: A New Documentary*. Carroll & Graf, 1994.

Spears, Richard. *Slang and Euphemism*. Second revised edition. Signet, 1991.

Stewart, William. *Cassell's Queer Companion*. Cassell, 1995.

PART V

WE ARE (LITERALLY) EVERYWHERE

Statistics on Lesbians and Gay Men

LESBIANS AND GAY men have been largely invisible in mainstream surveys and polls. The portrait of a typical American, as painted by U.S. Census Bureau stats, does not include a separate category for gay people, even though we work, pay taxes, have children, own homes, and are represented in different ethnic and racial groups. The only time we are counted is in surveys on sex and sexual practices, which (as with heterosexuals) is only one aspect of our identity.

Some gay research firms have begun to do exploratory surveys of lesbians and gay men for marketing purposes, to help clients test print ads, refine product concepts, and assess needs. The surveys turn up interesting, if necessarily sketchy and limited, information about lesbians and gays. Also, gay and lesbian organizations and magazines periodically conduct surveys on various aspects of our lives, from religious beliefs to dating practices to the discriminatory violence we face every day because of sexual orientation. The following section highlights some of the existing—and very preliminary—findings in the area of lesbian and gay demographics and statistics.

WHERE WE LIVE

FIFTEEN LARGEST CONCENTRATIONS OF LESBIANS AND GAYS IN THE UNITED STATES

1. Manhattan
2. San Francisco
3. Boston/Cambridge
4. Seattle

5. Oakland/Berkeley
6. Washington, D.C.
7. Chicago/Evanston
8. Atlanta

 9. Minneapolis   13. Portland, Oregon
10. Marin County, California   14. San Diego
11. Los Angeles   15. Pittsburgh
12. Santa Monica Bay

SOURCE: Raymond G. McLeod, "Gay Market as a Potential Goldmine." *San Francisco Chronicle*, August 27, 1991. Reprinted by permission.

Gay adults under the age of thirty-five change their place of residence more than once every other year.

SOURCE: Overlooked Opinions, Inc., Chicago, Illinois, 1995

QUALITY OF LIFE ISSUES

Overlooked Opinions, Inc., was formed in 1989 in Chicago as a market research and opinion polling firm specializing in the gay, lesbian, and bisexual market. The following are results of a 1992 survey of queer lives. However, the survey has severe limitations and looks at only one segment of the gay and lesbian population.[1] For more information, contact Overlooked Opinions, 3162 North Broadway, Chicago, IL 60657; Phone: 800/473-3405.

[1]Sample size: 7,500 gay men and lesbians. Median age: men, 37; women, 35. Race/ethnic background: 84.3 percent white men, 78.9 percent white women; 9.5 percent Latino men, 11.7 percent Latino women; 4 percent African-American men, 5.8 percent African-American women; 1.2 percent Asian/Pacific Islander men, 2 percent Asian/Pacific Islander women; 1 percent Native American men, 1.6 percent Native American women. Self-identification: 57.5 percent identified as gay men, 4.2 percent as gay women, 78.8 percent as lesbians, 32.2 percent as homosexual men, 5.2 percent as homosexual women, 4.7 percent as bisexual men, 7.8 percent as bisexual women.

EDUCATION

	LESBIANS	GAY MEN
Median years of education	15.7	15.7
High school only	16.4%	16.9%
Some college	18.7%	18.5%
Associate degree	7.3%	6.4%
Undergraduate degree	32.0%	31.5%
Graduate degree	25.6%	26.8%

FAMILY SIZE

Average household size	1.9	1.7
Households with children under 18	10.2%	4.8%
In relationship	71.2%	55.5%
Live with partner	52.0%	37.0%

	LESBIANS	GAY MEN
Of those in relationships are monogamous	81.2%	51.8%
Median years in relationship	3.5	3.7

INCOME

Median annual household income	$36,072	$42,689

OCCUPATION

	LESBIANS	GAY MEN
Management	10.9%	13.4%
Health care	16.0%	10.0%
Education	11.7%	9.9%
Sales/marketing	8.1%	9.2%
Technical	5.6%	8.3%
Clerical	7.3%	5.7%
Financial	4.0%	5.6%
Literature/library science	5.0%	4.3%
The arts	3.1%	4.5%
Law	3.3%	3.9%
Entrepreneur	3.0%	3.6%
Science	3.3%	2.3%
Food service	1.9%	2.7%
Public safety	2.5%	1.4%
Other	14.1%	15.1%

Over 45 percent of lesbians and gay men have been promoted at work at least once in the past three years.

Over 8 percent of lesbians and gay men report that they have experienced some sort of employment discrimination—being fired, verbal abuse, denial of promotions—in the past six months.

SOURCE: Overlooked Opinions, Inc., Chicago, Illinois, 1995. Reprinted by permission.

RESIDENCE

	LESBIANS	GAY MEN
Home owners	43.1%	47.7%
Median years at present address	2.4	3.0
Urban dwellers	45.1%	52.7%
Suburban dwellers	33.1%	31.7%
Reside in small town	15.0%	11.6%
Reside in rural area	6.8%	4.0%

GRAB BAG OF STATS

- Lesbians and gay men bought almost six million home computers between 1988 and 1991.
- Lesbians and gay men took more than 162 million trips in 1991, 78 percent of which were for business.
- 63.5 percent of lesbians consider themselves politically active.
- 79.3 percent of lesbians and gay men buy based on gay media advertising.
- 89.3 percent of lesbians and gay men dine out on a regular basis.
- 65.3 percent of lesbians go camping.
- 23.6 percent of gay men do aerobics.
- 15.6 percent of lesbians have four or more pets (cats and dogs).
- 37.8 percent of lesbians and gay men play board games.
- 39.1 percent of lesbians and gay men traveled outside the United States in the last year.

RELIGION AND SPIRITUALITY

The now-defunct magazine *OUT/LOOK* did a survey of its readership in late 1991 to examine how important religion and spirituality are in lesbian and gay lives. The results from 648 readers (among whom gender differences were negligible) were as follows:

How important is organized religion in your life?

Very important	28%
Somewhat important	24%
Not important	48%
No answer	0.2%

How important is spirituality in your life?

Very important	58%
Somewhat important	26%
Not important	16%
No answer	0.8%

How important is spirituality in your life? (by age group)

AGE 21–29

Very important	50%
Somewhat important	34%
Not important	15%

AGE 30–39

Very important	60%
Somewhat important	26%
Not important	13%

AGE 40–49

Very important	67%
Somewhat important	19%
Not important	14%

AGE 50+

Very important	49%
Somewhat important	18%
Not important	32%

Do you believe in God, or in some transcendent spiritual form?

Yes	66.2%
No	20.5%
Don't know	12.5%
No answer	0.8%

Do you believe that people can contact spirits?

Yes	43%
No	27%
Don't know	28%
No answer	1%

Do you believe in reincarnation?

Yes	29%
No	37%
Don't know	33%
No answer	1%

Do you believe in astrology?

Yes	26%
No	50%
Don't know	24%
No answer	1%

Do you believe that nature has its own wisdom/consciousness?

Yes	57%
No	25%
Don't know	18%
No answer	1%

Current religious affiliations/identities of respondents (if any)

Protestant/other Christian	22%
Recovery program members	14%
Alternative/other religions	14%

Gay Christian (for example, Metropolitan Community Church)	12%
Roman Catholic	6%
Jewish	6%
Buddhist	2%
Fundamentalist/evangelical	0.7%
Hindu	0.6%
Muslim	0.5%

How supportive is your particular religious community of homosexuality?

Extremely supportive	41%
Very supportive	18%
Somewhat supportive	14%
Not very	12%
Not at all	12%

SOURCE: *OUT/LOOK* magazine, Issue 14, Fall 1991

WHAT STRAIGHTS THINK ABOUT LESBIANS AND GAYS

In the spring of 1993, at the height of the controversy about lesbians and gays in the military, the mainstream magazine *U.S. News & World Report* did a poll of 1,000 straight registered voters and came up with the following results (margin of error plus or minus 3.1 percent; where percentages don't add up to 100 percent, it is because some respondents said, "I don't know."):

FAMILIARITY

Personally know someone who is gay and this familiarity makes them think more favorably about gay rights	53%
Do not think they know any gay people and oppose gay rights	46%

FAMILY LIFE

Oppose recognizing "legal partnerships" for homosexuals	60%
Approve of gay partnerships	35%
Oppose allowing gays to adopt	70%
Support allowing gays to adopt	24%

MEDIA IMAGES

Worry that media portrayals of gays have had a negative influence on society	56%
Say media images have had a positive influence	33%

PRESIDENT CLINTON'S FOCUS

Clinton has spent too much time on gay rights issues	56%
Clinton has spent about the right amount of time	29%

AIDS CRISIS

Made them less sympathetic to gays	39%
Made them more sympathetic (the largest group of those whose sympathy grew was African-Americans)	35%

SEX EDUCATION

Oppose teaching about gay orientation in sex education classes in public schools (strong opposition comes from those with school children)	52%
Favor it	44%

ANTI-BIAS LAW

Gays suffer from discrimination	50%
Want to ensure equal rights for gay people, but	65%
Oppose extending civil rights laws to cover homosexuals	50%

THE CAUSE

Believe that homosexuals choose to be gay or lesbian (this group tends to oppose civil rights for gays. However, 32% think that gays are born that way.)	46%

OPINION CUES (TOP-RANKING INFLUENCES ON VOTERS' ATTITUDES ON HOMOSEXUALITY)

Say religious organizations (of those, 79% oppose gay rights)	29%
Say gay acquaintances (of those, 66% support gay rights)	18%

Say the media (of those, 44% oppose gay rights)	17%
Say family (of those, 47% oppose gay rights)	15%

PATTERNS

VOTERS LEAST LIKELY TO KNOW A HOMOSEXUAL	DO NOT KNOW ANYONE GAY OR LESBIAN
South Central U.S. region	55%
Homemakers	55%
Retirees	67%
Those with less than a high school education	63%
Those in small towns	54%

THOSE MOST LIKELY TO KNOW A HOMOSEXUAL	KNOW SOMEONE GAY OR LESBIAN
Mountain states residents	64%
Suburbanites	58%
College graduates	63%
Those between the ages of 35 and 64	58%

SOURCE: *U.S. News & World Report*, July 5, 1993. Reprinted by permission.

SEX SURVEYS

Various sex surveys have been conducted over the years that have given some hints as to how many self-identified lesbians and gay men there are in the United States. The following are the results of the first and the most recent studies, which are also the most famous and controversial.

KINSEY REPORT

In 1948, the Kinsey Institute published a groundbreaking study of sexual behavior in 5,300 American men. The celebrated Kinsey scale outlined a significant amount of fluctuation in sexual activity, from 1 (exclusively heterosexual) to 6 (exclusively homosexual). Kinsey's findings shook the heterosexual world and helped foster a sense of community and self-acceptance among homosexuals. In 1953, the Kinsey Institute published its findings on sexual behavior among 5,940 American women.

	MEN	WOMEN
Reported being more or less exclusively homosexual for at least 3 years between the ages of 16 and 55	10%	
Reported being more or less exclusively lesbian between the ages of 20 and 35		2-6%
Had some homosexual or lesbian experience that resulted in orgasm	37%	13%
Responded erotically to others of the same sex	50%	28%

"SEX IN AMERICA" REPORT

Conducted through the National Opinion Research Center at the University of Chicago, the "Sex in America" survey was originally conceived in 1987 by federal AIDS researchers frustrated with the lack of data about sexual practices. The federal government was to fund the study of 20,000 Americans, both heterosexual and homosexual. Congress pulled the plug on funding four years later, and the scaled-down survey interviewed only 3,400 Americans. Researchers completed the study in late 1994, drawing some conclusions that impact on lesbians and gay men. The numbers of men (10.2 percent) and women (8.6 percent) exhibiting same-gender sexuality are significantly larger than those men (2.8 percent) and women (1.4 percent) who actually identify as lesbian or gay; but overall, the numbers are much smaller than when the Kinsey Institute undertook its study.

ANTILESBIAN/GAY VIOLENCE

Incidents of antilesbian/gay violence rose 2 percent overall around the country in 1994, according to a national report coordinated by the New York City Gay and Lesbian Anti-Violence Project (NYC-AVP). Nationally, antilesbian/gay violence is becoming increasingly brutal and is being perpetrated by very young people. NYC-AVP and eight other victim assistance programs around the country released the statistics in early 1995, reflecting complete data for 1993 and 1994 from nine cities—Boston; Chicago; Columbus, Ohio; Denver; Detroit; Minneapolis/St. Paul; New York City; Portland, Oregon; and San Francisco—and data for 1994 from eight other cities and states. Copies of the complete seventy-page report are available for $2 from the New York City Gay and Lesbian Anti-Violence Project, 647 Hudson Street, New York, NY 10014. To add your name or organization to their mailing list, call 212/807-6761.

INCIDENTS OF ANTILESBIAN/GAY VIOLENCE REPORTED TO VICTIM ASSISTANCE ORGANIZATIONS

	1993	1994
BOSTON		
Harassment	143	203
Threats or menacing	44	49
Bomb threats	1	1
Physical assaults/thrown objects	60	61
Police verbal/physical abuse	11	8
Vandalism	9	24
Arson	0	0
Murder	0	0
Sexual assault	2	0
Kidnapping, extortion, other	0	0

	1993	1994
Robbery	0	5
Total offenses	270	351
Total incidents reported	187	234
Offenses per incident	1.44	1.50
CHICAGO		
Harassment	114	136
Threats or menacing	54	37
Bomb threats	1	0
Physical assaults/thrown objects	59	62
Police verbal/physical abuse	29	26
Vandalism	9	19
Arson	1	3
Murder	3	2
Sexual assault	16	18
Kidnapping, extortion, other	0	0
Robbery	5	6
Total offenses	291	309
Total incidents reported	204	177
Offenses per incident	1.43	1.75
COLUMBUS, OHIO		
Harassment	50	41
Threats or menacing	17	20
Bomb threats	0	0
Physical assaults/thrown objects	41	47
Police verbal/physical abuse	6	5
Vandalism	16	27
Arson	0	7
Murder	1	1
Sexual assault	14	12
Kidnapping, extortion, other	0	0
Robbery	0	18
Total offenses	145	178
Total incidents reported	140	149
Offenses per incident	1.04	1.19
DENVER		
Harassment	118	84
Threats or menacing	21	58
Bomb threats	4	0
Physical assaults/thrown objects	35	108
Police verbal/physical abuse	5	18
Vandalism	54	20
Arson	0	0
Murder	2	2
Sexual assault	3	12
Kidnapping, extortion, other	14	44

	1993	1994
Robbery	11	26
Total offenses	267	372
Total incidents reported	211	156
Offenses per incident	1.27	2.38

DETROIT

Harassment	40	45
Threats or menacing	9	13
Bomb threats	0	0
Physical assaults/thrown objects	11	15
Police verbal/physical abuse	15	9
Vandalism	15	13
Arson	0	0
Murder	3	3
Sexual assault	2	1
Kidnapping, extortion, other	11	9
Robbery	0	0
Total offenses	106	108
Total incidents reported	84	96
Offenses per incident	1.26	1.13

MINNEAPOLIS/ST. PAUL

Harassment	442	225
Threats or menacing	34	40
Bomb threats	3	3
Physical assaults/thrown objects	30	33
Police verbal/physical abuse	10	23
Vandalism	13	11
Arson	1	1
Murder	5	2
Sexual assault	1	3
Kidnapping, extortion, other	3	4
Robbery	7	1
Total offenses	549	346
Total incidents reported	153	190
Offenses per incident	3.59	1.82

NEW YORK CITY

Harassment	627	653
Threats or menacing	289	288
Bomb threats	2	3
Physical assaults/thrown objects	227	334
Police verbal/physical abuse	83	129
Vandalism	31	51
Arson	3	1
Murder	15	9
Sexual assault	5	23
Kidnapping, extortion, other	79	65

	1993	1994
Robbery	36	42
Total offenses	1,397	1,598
Total incidents reported	587	632
Offenses per incident	2.38	2.53

PORTLAND, OREGON

	1993	1994
Harassment	99	100
Threats or menacing	66	56
Bomb threats	0	1
Physical assaults/thrown objects	26	21
Police verbal/physical abuse	8	0
Vandalism	18	46
Arson	0	0
Murder	0	0
Sexual assault	0	0
Kidnapping, extortion, other	0	1
Robbery	5	3
Total offenses	222	228
Total incidents reported	99	106
Offenses per incident	2.24	2.15

SAN FRANCISCO

	1993	1994
Harassment	262	376
Threats or menacing	122	73
Bomb threats	3	0
Physical assaults/thrown objects	260	160
Police verbal/physical abuse	23	20
Vandalism	39	25
Arson	1	1
Murder	0	3
Sexual assault	12	12
Kidnapping, extortion, other	0	35
Robbery	2	0
Total offenses	724	705
Total incidents reported	366	324
Offenses per incident	1.98	2.18

NATIONAL VICTIM PROFILE

Gender

	1993	1994
Women	624	833
Men	1,578	1,674
Unknown or Institution	113	232

Race

	1993	1994
African-American	159	171
Asian/Pacific Islander	24	39
Latina/Latino	182	180
Native American	13	10
White/European	1,207	1,398

	1993	1994
Unknown	382	595
Other	72	70
Age		
Under 18		51
18-29		592
30-44		759
45-64		146
Unknown		614

NATIONAL OFFENDER PROFILE
Race

African-American	522
Asian/Pacific Islander	40
Latina/Latino	374
Native American	3
White/European	884
Unknown	1,016
Other	44
Age	
Under 18	488
18–29	741
30–44	361
45–64	118
Unknown	1,175

SOURCE: "Anti-Gay/Lesbian Violence in 1994: National Trends, Analysis and Incident Summaries." New York City Gay and Lesbian Anti-Violence Project, 1995. Reprinted with permission.

PART VI

WE HAVE LIVES, NOT LIFESTYLES

Just About Everything You Wanted to Know About Lesbian Lives

I. LESBIAN ACTIVISM

For a woman to be a lesbian in a male-supremacist, capitalist, misogynist, racist, homophobic, imperialist culture, such as that of North America, is an act of resistance.

—CHERYL CLARKE, poet and writer

Activism requires a constant leap of faith in myself and others, and the openness to change and be changed. Personal and political transformation is about reflection and action—about keeping my heart and mind on what I believe and on whom I love.

—KATHERINE ACEY, Executive Director, Astraea Foundation

You may think that lesbian and gay activism started with Stonewall, but gay people in the United States have been organizing for their rights since the early twentieth century. The very first homosexual organization in the United States, the Society for Human Rights, was founded in Illinois in 1924. Though it lasted only a few months, the society also published two issues of *Friendship and Freedom*, the first gay liberation magazine in the country.

Other pioneers of lesbian activism include Lisa Ben, who started the first lesbian magazine, *Vice Versa*, in 1947, and Del Martin and Phyllis Lyons, who co-founded the Daughters of Bilitis in 1955.

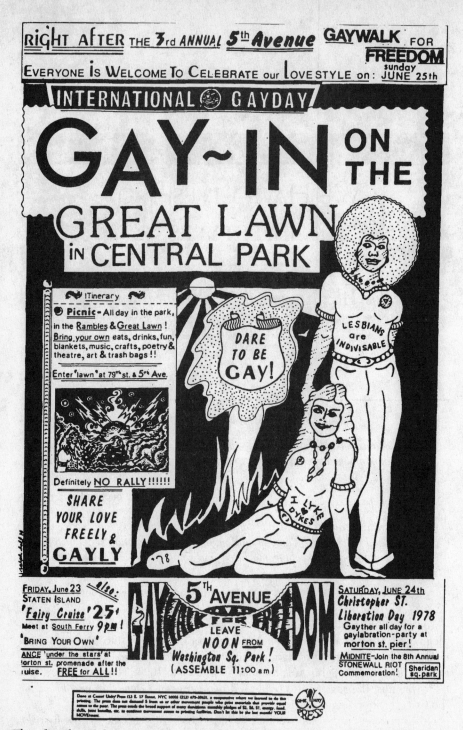

Flyer for Christopher Street Liberation Day celebration, 1978. (*Collection of the National Museum & Archive of Lesbian and Gay History*)

DEMAND YOUR RIGHTS!

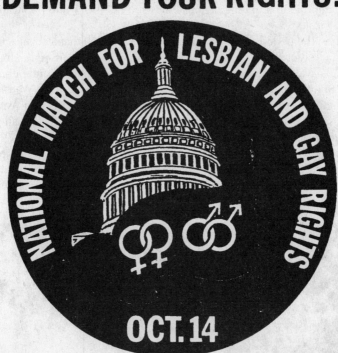

NATIONAL MARCH FOR LESBIAN AND GAY RIGHTS

OCT. 14

MARCH ON WASHINGTON

**TO CONTACT ORGANIZERS IN YOUR AREA
AND GET TRAVEL INFORMATION
CALL TOLL FREE**

800 528-7382

**NATIONAL THIRD WORLD LESBIAN/GAY
CONFERENCE OCT. 12—15
FOR INFORMATION CALL (301) 596-5865
OR CALL (202) 789-1070**

Flyer for first National March on Washington for Lesbian and Gay Rights, 1979
(Collection of the National Museum & Archive of Lesbian and Gay History)

Lesbians have always been in the forefront of the feminist movement, with nineteenth-century pioneers like Susan B. Anthony leading the way to women's rights. In the second wave of feminism, which started in the mid-1960s, lesbians played a vital role in founding organizations such as NOW and publications such as *Ms.* magazine.

But it is in the period since the Stonewall riots of 1969 that lesbian activism has taken off in full force. In the last quarter century, we've witnessed the founding of lesbian and gay community centers, organizations, newspapers, and publishers, all designed to unite and strengthen the lesbian and gay community. We've seen the blossoming of an exciting direct action group for lesbians, Lesbian Avengers, in cities across the United States. And the AIDS crisis has realigned lesbian-feminists with gay male activists to safeguard our rights and save our lives.

But our activism doesn't always mean being on the front lines of a protest or starting a new lesbian organization. Activism can have many faces: writing a letter to a congressional representative, marching in a gay pride parade, or coming out

Katherine Acey (l.), executive director of ASTRAEA National Lesbian Action Foundation, and Urvashi Vaid, former executive director of the National Gay and Lesbian Task Force

to someone on National Coming Out Day. Any action that makes lesbians more visible is a form of activism.

LESBIAN ACTIVISM 101: A BIBLIOGRAPHY[1]

[1]Compiled by Polly Thistlethwaite and Lucinda Zoe; courtesy the Lesbian Herstory Archives

BOOKS AND ARTICLES

Abbott, Sidney, and Barbara Love, eds. *Sappho Was a Right-On Woman: A Liberated View of Lesbianism.* Stein & Day, 1972.

ACT UP NY Women & AIDS Book Group. *Women, AIDS & Activism.* South End Press, 1990.

Adam, Barry. *The Rise of a Gay and Lesbian Movement.* Twayne, 1987.

Altman, Dennis. *Homosexual Oppression and Liberation.* Outerbridge & Dienstfrey, 1971.

Bowles, Sheila. "Active Lesbianism," *Lesbian Ethics*, 2:1 (Spring 1986), 87–8.

Brack, Amy. "Out in the Open: Ten Years in the Gay Movement," *Spare Rib*, 84 (July 1979) 42–46.

Bullough, Vern. *Homosexuality: A History.* Meridian, 1979.

Bunch, Charlotte. *Passionate Politics: Feminist Theory in Action.* St. Martin's Press, 1987.

Cant, Bob, and Susan Hemmings, eds. *Radical Records: Thirty Years of Lesbian and Gay History.* Routledge, 1988.

Come Out: Selections from the Radical Gay Liberation Newspaper. Times Change Press, 1970

"Chronicle—the Lesbian Movement, 1970–1976," *Lesbian Tide*, 6 (1), 24+, (July–Aug. 1976).

Delacoste, Frederique, and Felice Newman, eds. *Fight Back! Feminist Resistance to Male Violence.* Cleis Press, 1981.

Duberman, Martin. *About Time: Exploring the Gay Past.* Gay Presses of New York, 1986.

Echols, Alice. *Daring to Be Bad: Radical Feminism in America 1967–1975.* University of Minnesota Press, 1989.

Epstein, Barbara. "Direct Action: Lesbians Lead the Movement." *OUT/LOOK*, 1:2 (Summer 1988), 26–32.

Faderman, Lillian. *Odd Girls and Twilight Lovers: A History of Lesbian Life in Twentieth-Century America.* Columbia University Press, 1991.

———. *Surpassing the Love of Men.* Morrow, 1981.

Giddings, Paula. *When and Where I Enter: The Impact of Black Women on Race and Sex in America.* William Morrow, 1984.

Grier, Barbara, and Coletta Reid, eds. *The Lavender Herring: Lesbian Essays from* The Ladder. Diana Press, 1976.

Hoagland, Sarah, and Julia Penelope, eds. *For Lesbians Only: A Separatist Anthology*. Onlywomen Press, 1988.

Humphreys, Laud. *Out of the Closets: The Sociology of Homosexual Liberation*. Prentice-Hall, 1972.

International Lesbian and Gay Association (ILGA). *Second Pink Book: A Global View of Lesbian and Gay Liberation and Oppression*. ILGA, 1988.

Jay, Karla, and Allen Young. *Out of the Closets: Voices of Gay Liberation*. Harcourt, 1972.

Kaye Kantrowitz, Melanie, and Irena Klepfisz, eds. *The Tribe of Dina: A Jewish Women's Anthology*. Sinister Wisdom Books, 1986.

Klaich, Dolores. *Women + Women: Attitudes Toward Lesbianism*. William Morrow, 1974.

Koedt, Anne, Ellen Levine, and Anita Rapone, eds. *Radical Feminism*. Quadrangle Books, 1973.

"Lesbian Activism," *Connexions*, 29 (1989).

Marotta, Toby. *The Politics of Homosexuality: How Lesbians and Gay Men Have Made Themselves a Political and Social Force in Modern America*. Houghton Mifflin, 1981.

Martin, Del, and Phyllis Lyon. *Lesbian/Woman*. Glide Publications, 1972.

Moraga, Cherríe, and Gloria Anzaldúa, eds. *The Bridge Called My Back: Writings by Radical Women of Color*. Kitchen Table: Women of Color Press, 1981.

Myron, Nancy, and Charlotte Bunch, eds. *Lesbianism and the Women's Movement*. Diana Press, 1975.

Nestle, Joan. *A Restricted Country*. Firebrand Books, 1987.

Peck, Abe. *Uncovering the Sixties: The Life and Times of the Underground Press*. Pantheon, 1985.

Radicalesbian. "Sister Love," *Off Our Backs* 1:9, 10 (July 31, 1970): 3.

Ramos, Juanita, ed. *Companeras: Latina Lesbians*. Latina Lesbian History Project, 1987.

Ruzek, Sheryl. *The Women's Health Movement: Feminist Alternatives to Medical Control*. Praeger, 1978.

Schulman, Sarah. *My American History: Lesbian and Gay Life During the Reagan/Bush Years*. Routledge, 1994.

Smith, Barbara, ed. *Home Girls: A Black Feminist Anthology*. Kitchen Table: Women of Color Press, 1983.

Thayer Sweet, Roxana. *Political and Social Action in Homophile Organizations*. Arno, 1975.

Teal, Donn. *The Gay Militants*. Stein and Day, 1971.

Tobin, Kay, and Randy Wicker. *The Gay Crusaders*. Arno, 1972.

Vaid, Urvashi. "We Have a Blueprint; Now We Need Tools," *OUT/LOOK*, 5 (summer 1989), 59–60.

FILE UNDER: KNOW YOUR ENEMIES!

The following is a short list, supplied by P-FLAG, of "family values" hate groups that have declared open season on the rights of lesbians and gay men. Unfortunately, there are many more.

AMERICAN FAMILY ASSOCIATION

Objects to homosexuality, pornography, profanity, anti-Christian bigotry, liberal media. Has been influential on National Endowment for the Arts (NEA) funding and public school curricula. There are 600,000 members in 640 chapters. Donald Wildmon, P.O. Box 2440, Tupelo, MS 38803.

CONCERNED WOMEN OF AMERICA

Antigay, antiabortion, profamily. Grassroots organizing and Congressional lobbying. Sponsors "prayer chains," i.e., pressures elected officials via local groups. Has 600,000 members in 800 U.S. chapters. Beverly LaHaye, 370 L'Enfant Promenade SW, #800, Washington, DC 20024.

EAGLE FORUM

Women's organization powerful in national and Republican party politics. Opposes AIDS education, sex education, day care, family leave, abortion, and NEA funding. Has 80,000 members. Phyllis Schlafly, Box 618, Alton, IL 62002.

FAMILY RESEARCH COUNCIL

Opposes gay/lesbian/bisexual rights, reproductive freedom, government-funded health care, child care, and equal protection laws for women in the workplace. Believes allowing gay men in the military will cause drastic increase in AIDS incidence. Split from Focus on the Family in 1992. Gary Bauer, 700 Thirteenth St. NW, Ste. 500, Washington, DC 20005.

FOCUS ON THE FAMILY

This organization controls 1,550 radio stations worldwide, with almost 1,000 employees. Major player in passage of Colorado Amendment 2 to disallow equal rights for lesbians and gay men. National training seminars to involve believers in political process. James Dobson, P.O. Box 35500, Colorado Springs, CO 80935; 719/531-3400. Press contact: Paul Hetric.

TRADITIONAL VALUES COALITION

Opposes gay rights, reproductive rights, teaching evolution, and sex education other than abstinence. Organizes antigay ballot initiatives. Helped repeal lesbian rights in California municipalities. Advocates AIDS quarantine. Involves 25,000 churches across the country. Rev. Lou Sheldon, 100 S. Anaheim Blvd., Ste. 320, Anaheim, CA 92805; Washington, DC contact: Kelly Mullins, 202/547-8570.

FREE CONGRESS FOUNDATION

Research and education organization that created National Empowerment Television (NET) to mobilize the right. Four television programs, one to college campuses, another addressed to African-American conservatives. Paul Weyrich, 717 Second St. NW, Washington, DC 20002.

OPERATION RESCUE

Well-known for violent disruption of abortion clinics and the harassment, intimidation, and terrorization of women and health care providers. It added the opposition of gay rights to its agenda when the military ban issue came to prominence. There are more than 35,000 members. Randall Terry, P.O. Box 1180, Binghamton, NY 13902.

NATIONAL ASSOCIATION OF CHRISTIAN EDUCATORS/CITIZENS FOR EXCELLENCE IN EDUCATION

Primarily attacks public school curricula, textbooks, and school board members in order to bring public education under Christian control. Has 1,250 chapters. Dr. Robert L. Simonds, P.O. Box 3200, Costa Mesa, CA 92628.

OTHERS WE CAN'T AFFORD TO IGNORE

Chalcedon. Major think tank; center of the Christian Reconstruction Movement. Establishes Christian legal organizations. Has publications, speakers bureau, and sponsors seminars.

Christian Coalition, Chesapeake, VA; 804/424-2630. Contact: Michael Russell.
Oregon and Idaho Citizens Alliances.
Colorado for Family Values.

RIGHT-WING WATCHDOG GROUPS

The following groups keep track of what the right wing is up to:
People for the American Way, Washington, DC; 202/467-4999.
Institute for First Amendment Studies, Great Barrington, MA. Contact: Skip Portius, 413/274-3786.

KEY LESBIAN AND GAY RIGHTS ISSUES

- Marriage
- Foster parenting and adoption
- Child custody and visitation
- Second-parent adoption
- Housing
- Tax equity
- Immigration
- Public services and accommodations
- Sodomy laws
- AIDS-related discrimination (employment, testing, privacy rights)
- Military ban
- Employment and benefits
- Freedom of speech/expression
- Antigay initiatives

ACTIVISM OPPORTUNITY

According to the Gay and Lesbian Alliance Against Defamation (GLAAD), companies that advertise in gay and lesbian publications frequently fall victim to attacks from the right wing. These courageous advertisers have indicated that their advertising support of queer publications will continue as long as there is positive response from the gay market. Pay attention to these advertisers, purchase their products, and write and thank them for their support.

ARMCHAIR ACTIVISM: ORGANIZING ON-LINE

The Internet—the most revolutionary catalyst of gay and lesbian community organizing and communicating since the invention of the gay bar a century ago. . . . Gay liberation is thriving in cyberspace like nowhere else on earth.

—GABRIEL ROTELLO, *New York Newsday* columnist

Lesbian and Gay Community Services Center—New York is now on the Worldwide Web, linking activists to information about the programs and work of the center and providing a path to other gay community organizations around the country. The center can be accessed at: http://www.panix.com/~dhuppert/gay/center/center.html.

Gay and Lesbian Victory Fund, a network of donors who contribute $100 or more to join and pledge to contribute at least $100 to two or more gay or lesbian candidates for public office of the member's choice from Victory Fund's recommended list can be accessed on American Online (member: VictoryF); Internet (victoryf@aol.com); the Victory Fund BBS. For more information, contact Van Do, 202/842-8679.

National Gay and Lesbian Task Force (NGLTF) is on-line in the Gay and Lesbian Community Forum of America Online. NGLTF's Legislative Alert outlines homophobic amendments and describes alternative amendments that representatives should be encouraged to support. To be added to the Legislative Alert E-mail distribution list, send E-mail address to: Tanya Domi, NGLTF Legislative Director (tldngltf@aol.com) or Beth Barrett, NGLTF Public Information Assistant (babngltf@aol.com).

Queer Resources Directory can be accessed by E-mail at: qrd2vector.casti.com.

GayNet Digest: You can subscribe by sending E-mail to: majordomo2queer-net.org; type the message: subscribe gaynet-digest.

Lesbian and gay action alert E-mail list. To be added to the distribution list, send E-mail to: majordomo@vector.casti.com and type the message: subscribe action alert. To send an action alert message, E-mail to: actionalert@vector.casti.com.

Culture Wars is an on-line information clearinghouse on the radical right. For information, contact: AlterNet, 77 Federal St., San Francisco, CA 94107; *Fax:* 415/284-1414, *E-mail:* 71362,27 CompuServe.

Digital Queers, San Francisco. *E-mail:* digiqueers@aol.com. *Phone*: 415/252-6282. Promotes gay and lesbian workplace rights via the development of a lesbian and gay high-tech computer infrastructure. Computer industry queers offer training in use of the computer as an organizing tool.

THE LESBIAN AVENGERS—DIRECT ACTION DYKES

LESBIAN AVENGERS MANIFESTO

The Lesbian Avengers are a direct action group focused on issues vital to Lesbian survival and visibility.

Lesbian Avengers believe in creative activism: loud, bold, sexy, silly, fierce, tasty, and dramatic. Arrest is optional.

Lesbian Avengers think that demonstrations are a good time and a great place to cruise for women.

Lesbian Avengers don't have patience for polite politics and are bored with the boys.

Lesbian Avengers believe confrontation fosters growth and strong bones.

Lesbian Avengers don't believe in the feminization of poverty. We demand universal insurance and housing.

Lesbian Avengers plan to infiltrate the Christian right.

Lesbian Avengers think actions must be local, regional, national, global, cosmic.

Lesbian Avengers think closeted lesbians, queer boys, and sympathetic straights should send us money.

Lesbian Avengers believe it's time to organize and incite—get together and fight!

SOME SIGNIFICANT DATES

May 28, 1992: Founding meeting of the Lesbian Avengers in New York.

July 8, 1992: First public meeting of the Lesbian Avengers in New York.

October 30–November 3, 1992: New York Avengers shrine to Hattie Mae Cohens and Brian Mock. Fire-eating tradition begins.

January 6, 1993: Durham Avengers founded.

January 28, 1993: Los Angeles Avengers founded.

January 31, 1993: Austin Avengers founded.

Lesbian Avengers action in Tampa, Florida *(Copyright © Morgan Gwenwald)*

February 1, 1993: Atlanta Avengers founded.
February 25, 1993: Minneapolis Avengers founded.

New York Lesbian Avengers' Valentine's Day action, 1993—erecting a papier-mâché sculpture of Alice B. Toklas beside the statue of Gertrude Stein in Bryant Park *(Copyright © 1993 by Morgan Gwenwald)*

April 25, 1993: First Annual Dyke March, Washington, D.C.

April 26, 1993: Lesbian and Gay March on Washington; New York. Avengers stinkbomb House of Representatives/National Health Care Action.

April 29, 1993: Tampa Avengers founded.

May 20, 1993: Memphis Avengers founded.

May 31, 1993: San Francisco Avengers founded.

June 18, 1993: San Francisco Dyke March.

June 30, 1993: New Orleans Avengers founded.

June 26, 1993: First Annual New York City Dyke March.

July 12, 1993: Colorado Springs Avengers founded.

August 17, 1993: Portland, Oregon Avengers founded.

August 18, 1993: Denver Avengers founded.

August 30, 1993: Boston Avengers founded.

September 3, 1993: Cincinnati Avengers founded.

September 18, 1993: March in Gulfport, Mississippi, protesting right wing's attempt to close lesbian and gay community center.

September 29, 1993: Lansing, Michigan, Avengers founded.

September 20, 1993: Detroit Avengers founded.

October 12, 1993: Freedom Ride Action at State School Board, Albany, New York.

1992 Lesbian and Gay Pride March, New York City (*Photo by Harry Stevens*)

October 13, 1993: Freedom Ride Action in Syracuse, New York.
October 14, 1993: Freedom Ride Action in Burlington, Vermont.
October 15, 1993: Freedom Ride Action in Lewiston, Maine.
October 9, 1993: Freedom Ride Action in Boston.

LESBIAN AVENGERS PREACTION CHECKLIST

If I'm not scared before an action, it's not worth doing."

—PHYLLIS LUTSKY, New York Lesbian Avenger

1. Do you have a clear message, dramatic visuals?
2. Have you gotten the word out (through posters, mailings, parties, phone trees)?
3. Have you leaked information to the media? Timely press releases and follow-up calls are absolutely essential.
4. Have you arranged for transportation?
5. Do you have a fact sheet?
6. Do you have a video person?
7. If you expect trouble, do you have marshals, police liaisons, legal observers, and support people ready?
8. Do you have bail money in case of arrest?

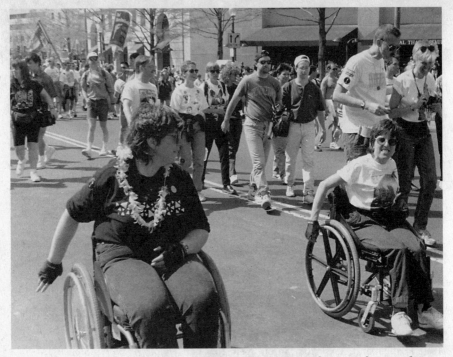

Janet Weinberg and Judge Rosalyn Richter at the 1993 March on Washington for Lesbian, Gay, and Bisexual Rights *(Photo by Dave LeFave)*

For a copy of the fifty-five-minute documentary of the Lesbian Avengers' first year, *The Lesbian Avengers Eat Fire, Too*, contact The Lesbian Avengers, c/o the Lesbian and Gay Community Services Center, 208 W. 13th St., New York, NY 10011; or call: 212/967-7711, ext. 3204.

OTHER NATIONAL LESBIAN AND GAY DIRECT ACTION AND ADVOCACY ORGANIZATIONS

ACT-UP (AIDS Coalition to Unleash Power)

A direct action group that works for AIDS funding, research, and visibility.

135 W. 29th St., 10th floor
New York, NY 10001
Phone: 212/564-2437
Fax: 212/989-1797

QUEER NATION

A multicultural, direct-action group dedicated to fighting homophobia, queer invisibility, and all forms of oppression.

c/o Lesbian and Gay Community Services Center
208 W. 13th St.
New York, NY 10011
Phone: 212/260-6156

GAY AND LESBIAN ALLIANCE AGAINST DEFAMATION (GLAAD)

A national organization, founded in 1985, that advocates for fair, accurate, and inclusive portrayals of lesbian, gay, and bisexual lives in all forms of the media.

New York Office
150 W. 26th St., Suite 503
New York, NY 10001
Phone: 212/807-1700
Fax: 212/807-1806

Los Angeles Office
8455 Beverly Blvd., #305
Los Angeles, CA 90048
English hot line: 213/U R GLAAD
Spanish hot line: 213/658-6074
Phone: 213/658-6775
Fax: 213/658-6776

National Field Office, Portland
Donna Red Wing, Director
Phone: 503/224-5285
Fax: 503/224-5480

Atlanta
Phone: 404/876-1398
Fax: 404/876-4051

Chicago
Phone: 312/871-7633
Fax: 312/338-5482

Dallas
Phone: 214/521-5342, ext. 816
Fax: 214/522-4604

Denver
Phone: 303/331-2773
Fax: 303/494-7216

Kansas City
Phone: 816/374-5927
Fax: 816/756-1760

San Diego
Phone: 619/688-0094
Fax: 619/294-4814

San Francisco Bay Area
Phone: 415/861-2244
Fax: 415/861-4893

Washington, D.C.
Phone: 202/429-9500
Fax: 202/857-0077

HUMAN RIGHTS CAMPAIGN

The nation's largest political organization fighting for the rights, health, safety, and dignity of lesbians, gay men, and bisexuals. Established in 1980, it now has 80,000 members and a staff of forty. Lobbies Congress on issues that affect the lesbian and gay community, fights antigay state ballot initiatives, and supports candidates who believe that discrimination based on sexual orientation is wrong. Has Political Action Committee (PAC) supporting candidates working to end antigay discrimination, supporting AIDS funding, and promoting women's health and choice. HRCF's SPEAK OUT program allows gay and Lesbian input into Congressional decision making through overnight mail. Sponsors annual National Coming Out

Day on October 11. Lobbies Congress, supports candidates, and mobilizes grass-roots political support for equal rights for Lesbian, gay, and bisexual Americans.

P.O. Box 1396
Washington, DC 20013

1104 14th St. NW, Suite 200
Washington, DC 20005
Phone: 202/628-4160

NATIONAL CENTER FOR LESBIAN RIGHTS (NCLR)

National Office
870 Market St., Suite 570
San Francisco, CA 94102
Phone: 415/392-6257
Fax: 415/392-8442

PUBLIC POLICY PROJECT

NCLR is the only national Lesbian and gay rights organization run by and for women. Founded in 1977, it is the only national public interest law center dedicated to achieving full civil and human rights for all lesbians through a program of litigation, public policy advocacy, community education, resource publications, and judicial training.

462 Broadway, Suite 500A
New York, NY 10013
Phone: 212/343-9589
Fax: 212/343-9687

NATIONAL GAY AND LESBIAN TASK FORCE (NGLTF)

Lobbies, organizes, educates, and advocates for gay and lesbian civil rights and for responsible AIDS policies.

NGLTF's Fight the Right Project provides lobbying, media, fund-raising, computer activism, and other training to local activists. Long-term, grassroots, multiracial, multicultural movement building directly in the field.

2320 Seventeenth St. NW
Washington, DC 20009
Phone: 202/332-6483
Fax: 202/332-0207
TTY: 202/332-6219
E-mail: ngltf@aol.com

LAMBDA LEGAL DEFENSE AND EDUCATION FUND

A national organization committee to achieve full recognition of the civil rights of lesbians, gay men, and people with HIV/AIDS, through impact litigation, education, and public policy work. Founded in 1973.

National Headquarters
666 Broadway, Suite 1200
New York, NY 10012
Phone: 212/995-8585
Fax: 212/995-2306

Midwest Regional Office
17 E. Monroe, Suite 212
Chicago, IL 60603
Phone: 312/759-8110
Fax: 312/641-1921

Western Regional Office
6030 Wilshire Blvd., Suite 200
Los Angeles, CA 90036
Phone: 213/937-2728
Fax: 213/937-0601

GAY AND LESBIAN VICTORY FUND

Dedicated to electing openly gay politicians. Founded in 1991 as a political action committee (OPAC) assisting only openly gay and lesbian candidates. Helped elect fourteen such municipal and state candidates during the 1994 elections, including the first openly gay officials elected to the Missouri and Arizona legislatures, the Washington State Senate, and the California State Assembly.

1012 Fourteenth Street NW, #707
Washington, DC 20005
Phone: 202/842-8679
Fax: 202/638-0243

PRIDE AT WORK: THE NATIONAL GAY, LESBIAN, BI, AND TRANSGENDER LABOR ORGANIZATION

Funded by the American Federation of State, County, and Municipal Employees (AFSCME) and eleven other unions, this group, formed during the Stonewall 25 celebration, welcomed more than 300 representatives of unions and gay labor groups at its first conference.

P.O. Box 9605
North Amherst, MA 01059
Phone: 413/549-5972

1992 Lesbian and Gay Pride March, New York City *(Photo by Harry Stevens)*

A Very Personal Activism: Ten Tips for Coming Out to Parents

Coming out to anyone is a form of activism, and coming out to parents is one of the hardest things to do. Most of us reach the point where we can no longer hide and want our families to understand us more fully. Even though you're very happy being a lesbian, there's no predicting how your parents will react. Here are some things to keep in mind as you get ready to break the news to your parents.

1. Be prepared to be emotional, even if you feel calm beforehand or rarely cry. Many of us have found that the intense relief of coming out has brought on a flood of tears. Breathe deeply and remember that there are millions of lesbians in the world—you aren't the only one.
2. Be prepared for your parents to be emotional. Even if your parents suspected what you were going to tell them, they may cry when they actually hear you say the words.
3. It's better to consider what you're going to say before you say it. Although you may be very comfortable with your sexual orientation because you've known about it for years, your parents may have a lot of questions that you don't have responses to on the spur of the moment. Think about your answers to obvious questions, like "How long have you known?" or "But what about that boyfriend

you had in college?" Be positive and affirming. Your parents aren't made of glass, and being a lesbian isn't something to hide or be ashamed of.

4. If you plan to come out to them in person, ask a supportive sibling to come with you.

5. If it isn't possible to have a sibling with you, have a supportive friend, lover, or sibling waiting for you who can help you afterward if your parents have a bad response or who can celebrate with you if your parents' reaction is supportive.

6. If you live with your parents, have a place to go after you tell them—to a friend's or an older sibling's house—to give you and them some time apart to breathe.

7. If you live in another city, consider writing your parents a letter. You can get all your thoughts down clearly and give them time to absorb the announcement before you actually see or talk to them.

8. Don't set up a coming out scenario that leaves no breathing room for you or your parents. One young woman told her parents at the beginning of a cross-country plane trip. Her parents weren't happy about the announcement, and it made for a very long trip for everyone.

9. Request the pamphlet "Can We Understand?" from your local P-FLAG chapter (Parents and Friends of Lesbians and Gay Men National Office, P.O. Box 27605, Washington, DC 20038; Phone: 202/638-4200). The booklet is a guide to help parents understand and accept their children's sexual orientation by answering some of the most common questions parents have. Read it yourself, then take it to your parents or send it to them after you visit. Give them the address and phone number of the nearest P-FLAG chapter, in case they want help accepting your news.

10. Do something gay for yourself in the next day or two after you come out. Buy yourself a present at the lesbian and gay bookstore, go to a lesbian or gay event. Remember that bringing your secret out of the closet is ultimately the best present you could give to yourself.

NEW YORK CITY YOUTH ACTIVISM TIME LINE

Before the Stonewall Riots, Gay Youth of New York was founded to combat the oppression of gay youth. Their slogan was "Youth Organized, Youth Run."

Over the next decade, the organization evolved into Gay and Lesbian Youth of New York (GLYNY). When the Lesbian and Gay Community Services Center was formed in 1983, it welcomed GLYNY, providing the organization with free meeting space and a mailbox.

In 1989, the center launched its own youth program, Youth Enrichment Services (Y.E.S.), a creative arts based substance and alcohol abuse prevention and intervention program. The program's third director, Barbara Bickart, founded its theater component, the Alternate Visions Theater Group.

During the 1992–1993 year, GLYNY changed its name to Bisexual, Gay and Lesbian Youth of New York (BiGLYNY), and Y.E.S. began providing leadership development training for members of BiGLYNY, creating a formal working relationship between the two youth groups. BiGLYNY, now a multiservice support and social group, holds rap sessions every Saturday. The organization sponsors an outreach program to high schools and holds many social events. It is the oldest independent, ongoing gay organization in New York City.

In 1992, Y.E.S. and members of BiGLYNY began production of *OutYouth Newsmagazine,* currently published twice a year and distributed to young lesbians and gay people across the United States and to youth groups abroad.

PROFILE

CARMEN VAZQUEZ

Carmen Vazquez spent the first five years of her life on a farm in the hills of Puerto Rico, living for the most part with her grandparents while her parents got a start in New York City. Her introduction to New York was in the parks and backyards of Manhattan's Lower East Side, fighting immigrant Italian and Jewish kids who teased her because she didn't speak English. "I thought they were stupid because they didn't speak Spanish," she recalled. "We had lots of fights."

She lived in a one-room apartment with her parents, brother, and three sisters as her father, injured during World War II combat in the Pacific, grew increasingly disabled and unable to work. The family existed on welfare, but in 1957, when Carmen was in third grade, they were accepted for residence in the projects in Harlem. "We couldn't believe how great the apartment was—it had bedrooms and hallways!" she said.

"We moved from a neighborhood of European immigrants to one where we were light-skinned Puerto Ricans in a predominantly African-American setting. Again, it was a whole new world, and I didn't know what was going on. I'd known dark-skinned Puerto Ricans, but these people were Americans speaking English. This meant, in short, more fights. The taunts would fly—'Act your age, not your color,' 'Get back on the boat,' 'Fight, fight, nigger and a white.' They called us white, but we weren't white, we were Puerto Rican—whatever we were, we were not what they called us."

Carmen spent fourteen years in Harlem, attending Catholic school. "Faith, passion, mysticism, mystery, repression, guilt, idealism—all these elements of Catholicism were influential in my spiritual development," she said. "I was imbued at an early age with a sense of valuing the good parts of the Christian ethic—taking care of people, believing in right and wrong, and that the common good is more important than the individual. This is still operative in me.

"I still call myself Catholic even though I don't practice the religion. It framed my spiritual values, my belief in faith, in something better than now, in a sense of responsibility for humanity. It is really responsible for my belief in my connection to everyone else because we all have a soul."

Carmen came out at fifteen, when she had her first sexual experience with a woman, prompting her to abandon her early plans to be a nun, a missionary helping the poor. "I realized the power of desire and pleasure, which I was not about to give up!" she said. "But the desire to serve and feel connected to other human beings is very much a part of what is at the basis of my activism.

"It would never occur to me not to participate in political activity that would further social change, to make things better for everyone, because—whether or not it has anything to do with the jobs I've had—that's my life's work," Carmen continued. "And the range of my activism has been determined by the different pieces of who I am. Racism, sexism, homophobia, and poverty—these are issues I have a visceral, immediate reaction to because they are all a part of my personal experience."

In the late 1960s and early 1970s, while she was in college, her activism revolved around black and Puerto Rican youth empowerment issues such as the establishment of black and Puerto Rican studies departments and students having a voice in university governance. Then, in 1975, she moved to San Francisco and began to grapple with being a lesbian on a sociopolitical level.

"I was responding to the whole women's liberation/radical feminist stuff, which I'd been isolated from," she said. "I felt unwelcome in that movement because I did not accept that sexism was the root of all oppression. You just can't say that, if you've experienced racism, poverty, and U.S. imperialism. Also, I was butch, in a '70s fashion—you know, more denim. This was wrong in the feminist community, because it was identified with the patriarchy. Eventually, I did come to understand the women's movement as something that related to me, and sexism as something I could identify in my own experience."

During the late 1970s and early 1980s, Carmen focused on the lesbian feminist movement and the broader lesbian and gay community in the Bay Area. During this period, she was the founding director of the San Francisco Women's Building, and continued to serve on its board through 1991.

Her broad professional and volunteer activist experience also includes efforts on behalf of the Community United Against Violence, the San Francisco Human Rights Commission, the Lavender Youth Recreation and Information Center, Somos Hermanas (a Central American women's solidarity network), and the National Network for Immigrant and Refugee Rights. She now serves on the Board of Directors of the OUT Fund for Lesbian and Gay Liberation, a project of the Funding Exchange, and Astraea National Lesbian Action Foundation.

From 1984 to 1988, she focused her activist energy around Central American political issues and solidarity work. She met her lover of ten years, Marcia Gallo, when they were both part of a delegation to Nicaragua. "It was terribly romantic, in the middle of a war," she recollected.

In 1988, she returned to work with the lesbian and gay community, joining the Lesbian Agenda for Action, seeking to empower lesbians and make them more visible in the political arena. The group, which existed for four years, was very helpful to the candidacies of women such as Roberta Achtenberg, Donna Hitchens, and Carol Migden.

Carmen became Coordinator of Lesbian and Gay Health Services for the City of San Francisco, a position she held for six years. "It was a shift, moving from nonprofit, community-based organizing and advocacy work to work inside the system. That job was where I learned about policy making, and became more sophisticated about how to present messages, how to organize politically, how to deal with the media. I did a lot of educational work on homosexuality and homophobia, and began to develop an interest in doing more outside the Bay Area."

In 1991, Carmen joined the Board of the National Gay and Lesbian Task Force. "My national lesbian and gay organizing began there. I also developed a feel for the tensions that existed between lesbian and gay rights organizing workers and our national organizations, which seemed not to be too in touch with local organizers and their efforts."

Currently, in her position as Director of Public Policy for the Lesbian and Gay Community Services Center in New York, Carmen perceives an opportunity to do more rigorous intellectual work on the issues of race, sexuality, class, and gender. "Intellectual and theoretical work have become separate from activism, and it's essential that it not be so. Movements don't succeed without a very clear political framework that can guide activism, and we don't have one. That's largely because it's hard to devote ourselves to the intellectual rigor of writing and reading and analyzing, and at the same time be effective organizers.

"We need an accessible, popular understanding of the economic basis for the use of sexual repression. This is where our oppression IS. It's not simply a matter of other people's bad attitudes. We represent a challenge to the established family structure. The forward march of capitalism means that we must move in the direction of the individual as the basic economic unit in society, not the husband-wife-kids paradigm that's been long employed. It's no longer functional. If we don't understand this, we can't develop effective strategies to fight the right. When we ignore the economic basis for our sexual oppression, we're hurting ourselves, because we've lost sight of why and how they beat us down and beat us back. If we don't look at this economic stratification within our community, we don't create ways to involve all of us, and we obscure the incredible diversity of our culture.

"We also need an intergenerational life, with children, teens, old folks, and young and middle-age adults experiencing community together—social events, organizing, spiritual celebration.

"It's all about expanding to include all of us. We've got to stop seeking to be mirror images of each other. Because that's not a community. That's a problem."

---

2. LESBIAN ART AND DESIGN

In a sense the [lesbian] art [being made today] both reflects and contributes to ever shifting definitions of lesbian identity, and can be seen to mirror both the desexualization of lesbian feminism in the '70s and early '80s, and the exploration of lesbian fantasy and desire in the late '80s and '90s, which reasserts sexuality as central to lesbian identity.

—HARMONY HAMMOND, lesbian artist

It's hard to imagine the American artistic legacy without the photographs of lesbian artist Berenice Abbott, the paintings of bisexual artists Georgia O'Keeffe and

Portraits by Grace Graupe-Pillard hanging in the office of the New York City Lesbian and Gay Community Services Center, as part of its 1989 art exhibition, The Center Show *(Photo by Roberta Raeburn)*

Frida Kahlo, the contributions of the lesbian-feminist artists of the 1970s to the present. Elsie de Wolfe (1865–1950), a lesbian, was the first professional interior designer. As in other creative fields, lesbians have distinguished themselves in many areas of visual arts and design, and in this section we give an overview of some of their wonderful accomplishments over the course of American history.

Throughout much of history, the artistic work of women has received little attention or visibility. It wasn't until the women's movement of the 1960s and 1970s that art by women (both straight and lesbian) drew more attention. The first feminist art history course was started in 1969, and shortly after, Judy Chicago taught the first feminist studio arts class. This class expanded into the innovative and influential Feminist Art Program (FAP), which Chicago taught at the California Institute of the Arts from 1971 to 1973. Among other projects, FAP sponsored the historic exhibition, "Womanhouse," in 1972 and produced the book, *Anonymous Was a Woman* in 1974.

Much of the women's art movement of the 1970s was motivated by feminist principles, which male critics used to denigrate it. Female genitalia were the image of choice. In the 1980s, subject matter for women artists expanded and lesbian concerns emerged full-fledged. The Guerrilla Girls—the conscience of the art world—continued the assault on sexism in the arts with an updated, activist twist. Finally, by the 1990s, a range of women's experiences could be represented, and what was hot shifted from "Womanhouse" to "Bad Girls," from vaginas to self-portraits of body piercings.

As we move closer to the twenty-first century, the increased visibility, acceptance, and recognition of openly lesbian and gay artists and subject matter are sure to proliferate, as are the attempts to censor them. Certain doors have been opened to lesbian artists and their work, and there are more and more closets that will never be opened again.

SOME FAMOUS LESBIAN ARTISTS OF THE PAST

Romaine Brooks, 1874–1970: An American painter living in Paris (lovers with Natalie Barney for 55 years).

Harriet Hosmer, 1830–1908: Lesbian neoclassical sculptor, very successful in her day. In order to visit art collections in monasteries that were closed to women, Harriet Hosmer would dress in men's clothes and pass with her friend Robert Browning.

Anna Elizabeth Klumpke, 19th c.: Painter and lovers with French painter Rosa Bonheur.

Mary Edmonia Lewis, 1843–1909: Black Native American sculptor and painter.

Emma Stebbins, b. 1815: Sculptor and a lover of actress and art patron, Charlotte Cushman.

Mary Ann Willson, b. ca. 1820: Painter in the primitive style.

SOME RECLAIMED ARTISTS WHO HAD LESBIAN IMAGERY IN THEIR WORK

Frida Kahlo, 1907–1954: Surrealist painter who had a troubled marriage to painter Diego Rivera; she had affairs with women; paintings such as *Two Nudes in a Forest* (1939) reflect her love for women.

Georgia O'Keeffe, 1887–1986: O'Keeffe's paintings of flowers (beginning in the 1920s) are a sexualized and erotic evocation of female genitalia that puts much of the feminist cunt art of the 1970s to shame; she was bisexual, and sometimes she and her husband Alfred Stieglitz had affairs with the same woman, such as Rebecca Strand.

Tamara de Lempicka, 1898–1980: Polish-born, American-made painter. If not a true lesbian, certainly a marvelous ambiguous role model. She once said, "I live on the fringe of society, and the rules of normal society have no currency for those on the fringe." She was a legend in her time and came to represent the age between the two world wars. The *New York Times* called her the "steely-eyed goddess of the automobile age." Her painting, *The Two Friends*, (1923, oil on canvas, 130 x 160 cm; Musée d'Art Moderne, Geneva) is a luscious rendition of two female nudes casually and erotically leaning against and into each other. Among others, Tamara had a scandal-ridden affair with Romaine Brooks.

NOTABLE LESBIANS PAINTED/PHOTOGRAPHED BY FAMOUS ARTISTS

Gertrude Stein portrait painted by Pablo Picasso.
Marlene Dietrich in top hat holding a cigarette photographed by Eisenstadt.
Janet Flanner photographed by Bernice Abbott.
Lady Una Troubridge, posing in a tuxedo and monocle, portrait painted by Romaine Brooks.

SELECTED LIST OF CONTEMPORARY LESBIAN AND BISEXUAL ARTISTS

Nancy Azara
Gaye Chan
Judy Chicago
Tee Corinne
Nicole Eisenman
Louise Fishman
Nancy Grossman
Harmony Hammond
Ester Hernandez
Eva Hesse

Roni Horn
Rosalyn Jacobs
Frida Kahlo
Deborah Kass
Zoe Leonard
Catherine Opie
Eve Sander
May Stevens
Nicola Tyson
Carrie Yamaoka

(See many others below.)

LESBIAN PHOTOGRAPHERS OF THE PAST

Alice Austen, 1866–1945: You can visit the Alice Austen House (it's a public museum) at 2 Hylan Boulevard, Staten Island, New York, to get a first-hand glimpse of some of her photographs, which exhibit her "playful mockery of Victorian middle-class mores, her tombstone irreverence" according to curator Vivienne Shaffer. Her longtime companion was Gertrude Tate, whom she called Trude. For further information, see the biography *Alice's World* by Ann Novotny (Old Greenwich, CT: The Chatham Press, 1976).

Bernice Abbott, 1898–1991: Her famous book was *Changing New York*; her longtime partner was essayist Elizabeth McCausland.

   • Other lesbian photographers listed in the introduction to JEB's *Eye to Eye* by Judith Schwartz:

Emma Jane Gay, b. 1830
Frances Benjamin Johnston, b. 1864
Sarah Holcomb, b. 1846

SOME LESBIAN PHOTOGRAPHY BOOKS REPRESENTATIVE OF THEIR DECADE

1970s: *Eye to Eye: Portraits of Lesbians*, by Joan E. Biren
1980s: *Drawing the Line*, photography by Susan Stewart in collaboration with Persimmon Blackbridge and Lizard Jones
1990s: *Stolen Glances: Lesbians Take Photographs*, edited by Tessa Boffin and Jean Fraser

CONTEMPORARY LESBIAN ARTISTS FEATURED IN *ART IN AMERICA* MAGAZINE FOR THE TWENTY-FIFTH ANNIVERSARY OF STONEWALL

Nicole Eisenman (b. 1963)   Zoe Leonard (b. 1961)
Louise Fishman (b. 1939)   Ellen B. Neipris (b. 1961)
Deborah Kass (b. 1952)

SOME GALLERIES WHERE LESBIAN ARTISTS HAVE HAD SOLO SHOWS

Barbara Krakow Gallery, Boston (Deborah Kass, 1994)
Jose Freire Fine Art, New York (Deborah Kass, 1995)
Robert Miller Gallery, New York (Louise Fishman, 1993)
Paula Cooper Gallery, New York (Zoe Leonard, 1995)
Jack Tilton Gallery, New York (Nicole Eisenman, 1994)
Synchronicity, New York (Rosalyn Jacobs, 1992, 1994, 1995)
Gavin Brown's Enterprise Gallery, New York (Catherine Opie, 1995)
The Drawing Center, New York (various artists)
Trial Balloon Gallery, New York (various artists)

THE NEW STANDARD FOR LESBIAN/GAY ART EXHIBITIONS

"In a Different Light," University Art Museum, at the University of California at Berkeley, January 11–April 9, 1995, was an extensive exhibition unprecedented in its theoretical concerns and in the sheer volume of material presented. With more than 200 catalogued pieces, the show was presented in nine groupings: "Void," "Self," "Drag," "Other," "Couple," "Family," "Orgy," "World," and "Utopia." For those who were unable to attend, be sure to pick up the catalogue for the exhibition, *In a Different Light*, copublished by City Lights Books and the University Art

Museum/Pacific Film Archive, and edited by Nayland Blake, Lawrence Rinder, and Amy Scholder.

Following is just a sampling of the gay and lesbian artists and works represented:

Romaine Brooks, *Peter, a Young English Girl*, 1923–1924, oil on canvas

Judy Chicago, *Female Rejection Drawing*, 1974, prismacolor on rag paper

Nicole Eisenman, *Alive with Pleasure*, 1992–1994, mixed media installation

Harmony Hammond, *Flesh Journals*, 1993, latex rubber, ink, and acrylic with incised text

Eva Hesse, *Test Piece*, 1968, mixed media

Zoe Leonard, *Washington, D.C.*, 1989, gelatin silver print

Catherine Opie, *Self-Portrait*, 1994, chromogenic print

Nicola Tyson, *Group #5*, 1994, graphite on paper

SOME FAMOUS LESBIAN/FEMINIST ART EXHIBITS

"Womanhouse," a collaborative site installation created in an abandoned L.A. mansion in 1972 by students of Judy Chicago at CalArts. (The accompanying art book, *Womanhouse*, documents this project of the Feminist Art Program at the California Institute of the Arts, which Chicago and Miriam Schapiro directed in the early seventies.)

"The Dinner Party," a feminist collaboration work, coordinated by Judy Chicago, at the San Francisco Museum of Modern Art, 1979.

"Homo Video: Where We Are in the 1980s" (December 1986–February 1987) at the New Museum of Contemporary Art (gay and lesbian).

"Drawing the Line" from three female artists known as Kiss and Tell, an interactive exhibit and traveling show (from 1988 on) that explored issues of censorship and sexuality. The Kiss and Tell collective (photography by Susan Stewart in collaboration with Persimmon Blackbridge and Lizard Jones) exhibits 100 black-and-white photographs of lesbian imagery and asks viewers to write their commentary directly on the gallery walls. (Also available as a book, *Drawing the Line*, from Press Gang Publishers in Canada.)

"Where Are the Women?" (November 1990) exhibition of work by lesbian artists shown at National Museum of Lesbian and Gay History at the Lesbian and Gay Community Services Center in New York City.

"Bad Girls," Los Angeles County Museum and the New Museum of Contemporary Art in New York City, 1994.

ART AND RACISM EXHIBITION BY LESBIANS

"The Dynamics of Color" Art Exhibition in San Francisco in 1989 featured lesbian artists' work on racism and was conceived to promote lesbian visibility in the fight against racism and to promote dialogue. Entries were juried by three San Francisco Bay Area artists, Wendy Cadden, Ester Hernandez, and Orlanda Uffre. The exhibit was shown at the Sargent Johnson Gallery of the Western Addition Cultural Center and was part of the 1989 conference, "Dynamics of Color—Building a Stronger Lesbian Community, Combating Racism, Honoring Diversity." The exhibit was conceived and coordinated by lesbian artist Happy/L. A. Hyder. Below are selected artists and titles of their pieces that were in the show:

Julie Potratz, *Mrs. & Mrs.*, photograph of two Asian women in wedding gowns
Tee A. Corinne, *Willyce Kim*, photo collage of Asian woman
Julia Youngblood, *Silent Shards*, poem and photo collage
Catalina Govea, *Quinceniera at A.P.U.M.E.C. Hall, Oakland*, photo of older woman dancing with bride during the dollar dance
Juana Maria de la Caridad, *Las Amigas*, woodcut of biracial lesbian couple
Terese Armstrong, *Untitled*, photograph of black and white women's hands holding
Jean Weisinger, *Domestic Violence*, painting with female images and text
Victoria Fontana, *today we will not be invisible nor silent*, poem and photograph of Native Americans
Ester Hernandez, *Weaving of the Disappeared/Tejido de los Desaparecidos*, weaving with painted bloodstains
Kevyn Lutton, *We all, everyone of us*, painting of five portraits

---

Art Exhibitions at the National Museum and Archive of Lesbian and Gay History, a Program of the New York City Lesbian and Gay Community Services Center

Founded in the winter of 1988, the center's National Museum and Archive of Lesbian and Gay History preserves lesbian and gay heritage and makes it accessible through regular exhibits, publications, and scholarly research activities. The center's museum and archive is one of the country's major collections of lesbian and gay history; its goal is to gain a clearer understanding of our community's past and present, as well as insight into our future, through the work of our artists and historians.

The first exhibition of the museum was in the fall of 1988. Since then, the museum has presented several exhibitions each year and has coordinated the center's observances of A Day Without Art, held on December 1 of each year to commemorate World AIDS Day.

In 1994, in honor of the twenty-fifth anniversary of the Stonewall Rebellion, the museum produced "Windows on Gay Life," a site-specific exhibit in the storefront windows of more than thirty businesses along and adjacent to Christopher Street. Curated by Joe E. Jeffreys, the exhibit emphasized both the history of the gay liberation movement and the culture of the community, while recognizing the significance of the Christopher Street neighborhood in lesbian and gay life.

"Windows on Gay Life" used photographs, objects, artifacts, and text to cover topics such as erotica, night and street life, business, performance, activism, families, AIDS, and homophobia.

Other exhibits in 1994 included "OUT Houses," an exhibit of works from Big Dicks Make Me Sweat Productions, a militant dadaist gay men's art collective, and Fierce Pussy, a lesbian activist public art collective. The works were installed in the center's newly renovated ground floor bathroom from February through March.

Still on view throughout the center are most of the site-specific installations created by more than fifty artists for "The Center Show" in June 1989, in celebration of the twentieth anniversary of Stonewall. Among the many highlights of this exhibition is the mural created by Keith Haring in the second-floor men's room.

CENTER MUSEUM EXHIBITS

"Portraits of Gay & Lesbian Writers: An Exhibition of Photographs by Robert Giard," 1988

"For Love and For Life: Photo-Documentary Exhibit by Marilyn Humphries," 1989

"The Center Show," Rick Barnett and Barbara Sahlman, curators, 1989

"A Hundred Legends," Don Ruddy, curator, 1989

"Imagining Stonewall," Mark Johnson, curator, 1989

"Mariette Allen Transformations: Cross-Dressers and Those Who Love Them," 1989

"Works by Lesbian Artists," Lesbians About Visual Arts (LAVA), curators, 1990; this show coincided with The Women's Caucus for Art Conference which was also held at the center

"The Cartoon Show," Jennifer Camper, Burton Clarke, Howard Cruse, Mark Johnson, curators, 1990

"Prejudice & Pride," 1990

"Where Are the Women?" Cheryl Gross, curator, 1990

"Images from the Front: Photography Challenging AIDS," Morgan Gwenwald, Mark Johnson, Tracey Litt, Robert Mignott, Robert Vazquez, jury, 1990–1991; artists include: John Lesnick, Y. Nagasaki, Henry Baker, Tom McKitterick, Tom McGovern, Michael Transue, Joe Ziolkowski, among others

"Keepin' On: Images of Afro-American Women from the Lesbian Herstory Archives," Lesbian Herstory Archives, curator (Morgan Gwenwald, Georgia Brooks, and Paula Grant), 1991

"New York in June: A History of the Lesbian & Gay Pride March," 1991

"Lasting Impressions: Women with Tattoos," Cheryl Gross, curator, 1991

"Graphic Facts: AIDS Posters from Around the World," Joe E. Jeffries, curator, 1991–1992

"Out and Exposed: Young Lesbian & Gay Artists, New Work," 1992

"Coming of Age: BiGLYNY, 1969–1992," Steven Cohen, producer, 1992

"A Memorial Dew Cloth: Celebrating 500 Years of Native American Survival,"
    Rich Wandel, producer; We Wah & Bar Chee Ampee Native Two Spirits in New
    York City, curator, 1992
"Body Parts: Visions from the Inside," Seth Gurvitz, producer; Barbara Bickart,
    Bridget Hughes, Lisa Jacobsen, curators, 1992
"Center Kids & AIDS: How Our Children See AIDS," Center Kids, curator, 1992
"Marked Men: Photographs of Seth Gurvitz," Joe E. Jeffries, producer, 1993
"Out on the Island: Gay and Lesbian Life on Fire Island," Steve Cohen, producer;
    Ester Newton, Steve Weinstein, curators, 1993
"OUT Houses," Seth Gurvitz, curator, 1994
"Windows on Gay Life," Joe E. Jeffries, curator, 1994
"Nuestras Vidas, Nuestras Familias, Nuestras Comunidad," Las Buenas Amigas,
    curator, 1995

CENTER COOPERATIVE ART EXHIBITS WITH THE 24 HOURS FOR LIFE GALLERY

"Eclipse del Alma" by Javier Cintron, December 7, 1993
"Santo Nino Incarnate" by Paul Pfeiffer, March 3, 1994
"Pride in Our Diversity: A Group Photo Exhibition," June 14, 1994

ART INSTRUCTION IN A LESBIAN/FEMINIST CONTEXT

The first feminist art history course was at Vassar, created and taught by Linda
Nochlin in 1969.

The first feminist art class was organized and created by Judy Chicago at California State University at Fresno in 1970; consciousness-raising methods were
used to create art.

That first feminist art class was the basis for the innovative and influential Feminist Art Program (FAP) that Judy Chicago taught at the California Institute of the
Arts (aka, CalArts) from 1971 to 1973. The FAP sponsored the collaborative exhibition/installation "Womanhouse" and the "West Coast Conference of Women
Artists" in 1972. FAP also produced the books *Anonymous Was a Woman*, in 1974
and *Art: A Woman's Sensibility*, in 1975.

The Feminist Art Institute, an educational program focusing on visual arts from
a feminist perspective, opened in New York City in 1979.

THE FIRST ALL-WOMAN EXHIBITION IN A MAJOR CULTURAL INSTITUTION

"Women Choose Women" was organized by the newly formed New York City–

based Women in the Arts, and was displayed at the New York Cultural Center in 1973.

NOTABLE COOPERATIVE WOMEN'S GALLERIES INITIATED IN THE MID-SEVENTIES

A.I.R., New York
Artemesia, Chicago
Women's Interart Gallery of the Women's Interart Center, New York
Atlantic Gallery, Brooklyn
Hera, Wakefield, Rhode Island
Muse, Philadelphia

NOTABLE WOMEN'S ART MAGAZINES LAUNCHED IN THE MID-SEVENTIES

Heresies: A Feminist Publication on Art and Politics, New York, NY
Chrysalis, Los Angeles, CA
Feminist Art Journal, New York, NY
Women Artists Newsletter, New York, NY
Womanart, New York

OTHER LESBIAN ART MAGAZINES

Calyx: A Journal of Art and Literature by Women
FAN (Feminist Art News)
Hot Wire: The Journal of Women's Music and Culture
Masques

A HAVEN OF FEMINIST ART AND CULTURE

The Woman's Building, a center for women's art and culture, opened in 1973 in Los Angeles. Among its members were Womanspace, the first women's exhibition space on the West Coast; and the Feminist Studio Workshop, an experimental program in women's art education, with its subsidiaries, the Women's Graphic Center and Center for Feminist Art Historical Studies.

The Guerrilla Girls

The Guerrilla Girls are New York–based artists/activists who, in their roles as the Conscience of the Art World, wear gorilla suits, making protests and statements regarding the secondary status of women in the arts. This anonymous group of women in the arts began posting statistics about art world sexism on the streets of New York in 1985. They can be contacted at:

Guerrilla Girls
P.O. Box 1056, Cooper Station
New York, NY 10276

The Advantages of Being a Woman Artist, by The Guerrilla Girls (Conscience of the Art World)

Working without the pressure of success
Not having to be in shows with men
Having an escape from the art world in your four freelance jobs
Knowing your career might pick up after you're eighty
Being reassured that whatever kind of art you make, it will be labeled feminine
Not being stuck in a tenured teaching position
Seeing your ideas live on in the work of others
Having the opportunity to choose between career and motherhood
Not having to choke on those big cigars or paint in Italian suits
Having more time to work after your mate dumps you for someone younger
Being included in revised versions of art history
Not having to undergo the embarrassment of being called a genius
Getting your picture in the art magazines wearing a gorilla suit

The above list was first published by *FAN* (Feminist Art News), P.O. Box CR8, Leeds LS7 4TD, England.

Women's Art Stats

51.2 percent of all artists in the United States are women.
30.7 percent of all photographers are women.
90 percent of all artists' models are women.
67 percent of bachelor degrees in fine arts go to women.
46 percent of bachelor degrees in photography go to women.
65 percent of bachelor degrees in painting go to women.
60 percent of M.F.A.'s in fine arts go to women.
55 percent of M.F.A.'s in painting go to women.
47 percent of M.F.A.'s in photography go to women.
59 percent of Ph.D.'s in fine arts go to women.
66.5 percent of Ph.D.'s in art history go to women.

59 percent of trained artists and art historians are women.

33 percent of art faculty are women.

5 percent of works in museums are by women.

17 percent of works in galleries are by women.

26 percent of artists reviewed in art periodicals are women.

Women artists' income is 30 percent that of male artists.

30 percent of Guggenheim grants go to women.

42 percent of $5,000 NEA grants go to women.

33 percent of $10,000 NEA grants go to women.

29 percent of $15,000 NEA grants go to women.

25 percent of $25,000 NEA grants go to women.

Of the art commissioned by the Department of Cultural Affairs Percent for Art Program in New York City, 70 percent have been artists of color, 41 percent women, and 39 percent of the 41 percent women of color. Of the 1992 New York Foundation of the Arts awards given, women received 53.4 percent, men received 46.6 percent. Of the world's top 200 collectors, approximately 128 are male, 52 are male-female couples, and 20 are female. Seven out of thirty-six one-person museum exhibitions in the 1991–1992 New York season were by women.

SOURCE: *WAC Stats*. Published by Women's Action Coalition, P.O. Box 1862, Chelsea Station, New York, NY 10011

GAY/LESBIAN ART AND CENSORSHIP

Art hath an enemy called Ignorance.

—BEN JOHNSON

In the late 1980s and early 1990s, a great debate about art and censorship arose in the United States. There were primarily three scandals that brought this topic to national prominence: Senator Jesse Helms's (R-North Carolina) outcry about a Robert Mapplethorpe retrospective, which included homoerotic and S/M photographs; NEA funding of an exhibition that included Andres Serrano's work, *Piss Christ*, a large photograph of a crucifix submerged in a yellow liquid identified as urine; and the funding, followed by the defunding, and later court-ordered refunding, of the so-called NEA Four—four performance artists whose work became controversial after right-wing Christians began a smear campaign against them. Three of these artists (John Fleck, Holly Hughes, and Tim Miller) were openly gay and included lesbian and gay material in their work.

Christina Orr-Cahall was director of the Corcoran Gallery in Washington, D.C., who canceled the Robert Mapplethorpe retrospective scheduled there in 1989 after the uproar from Jesse Helms. She canceled the show in order to avoid controversy—a few of the photographs depicted homoerotic and S/M activity—but instead drew the ire of the art and gay communities. She resigned a few months afterward.

Mapplethorpe's work was the center of another controversy, this time in Cincinnati in 1990 when the local sheriff arrested Dennis Barrie, director of the Cincinnati Contemporary Arts Center, on obscenity charges. Barrie was acquitted, but the five photographs in question, which were of homoerotic sex or of children's genitals, became the focus of a nationwide debate on art and obscenity.

ARTISTIC FREEDOM UNDER ATTACK

The People for the American Way, a 300,000-member nonpartisan constitutional liberties organization, published *Artistic Freedom Under Attack*, Volume 2, in 1994. According to the introduction, this publication provides "a nationwide snapshot of challenges to artistic free expression in America during 1992 and 1993." Not surprisingly, the study found lesbian and gay issues to be a significant portion of the art attacked: "The types of objections raised about art reflected deep divisions in American society around hot-button issues of sexuality, religion, race, sexual orientation, and gender. The most common type of objections to artistic works (with some statistical overlap) include: nudity and/or sexual material (50%); alleged anti-religious content (16%); homosexuality (13%); content alleged to be sexually harassing (6%)."

The study noted the censorship of community productions of two plays that touched on gay themes: John Guare's *Six Degrees of Separation* and Terrence McNally's *Lips Together, Teeth Apart*. The latter production in Cobb County, Georgia, sparked such controversy that the County Commission approved a general antigay resolution and voted to end the county's public arts funding.

In a section called "Battles over Art Reflect Cultural and Social Tensions," the study has this to say: "The increased visibility of [lesbians and gay men], and gay artists, in American society is leading to a rash of attacks on artistic freedom that reflects the culture's lingering discomfort with homosexuality. Parents in Duluth, Minnesota, attacked a dance performance by an all-male troupe, which was scheduled to perform for local schoolchildren, because of unfounded fears concerning homosexual content. And in Danville, Virginia, administrators at Averett College canceled a planned screening of the film *Henry and June* because the film's homosexual content allegedly conflicted with the religious college's 'Christian heritage and values.'"

The study contains hundreds of documented cases of art censorship and their outcomes. It is available from: People for the American Way, 2000 M Street NW, Suite 400, Washington, DC 20036.

A SELECTED HISTORY OF ANTIGAY CENSORSHIP

Comstock censorship: Self-proclaimed morals crusader Anthony Comstock (1844–1915) was the head of the New York Society for the Suppression of Vice and was responsible for the destruction of 160 tons of literature and pictures. Since homosexual activity and images were practically synonymous with vice, it does not take much of a stretch of imagination to deduce that a substantial portion of this censorship was aimed at eradicating such images and written depictions. Comstock also spearheaded the push for strong censorship legislation.

Postal censorship: Restrictions on the mailing of obscenities was particularly detrimental on published materials dealing with homosexuality. This was not amended until 1954 when the gay publication, *ONE*, won a Supreme Court decision to be distributed through the mail.

Broadway censorship: In the early part of the century, entire casts of scandalous drama were arrested, including those of the lesbian-themed *The Captive* in 1926. In 1927, the New York State Wade "Padlock" Law went into effect, preventing Broadway plays from overtly portraying lesbians and gay men. The statute was removed from the books only in 1967.

Hollywood censorship: From 1930 until 1956, the movie industry committed self-censorship under the Motion Picture Production Code, also known as the Hays Code. In addition to adding a morals code into actors' contracts, the code also mandated that lesbians and gay men either not be included in films or be shown in a negative light on the rare occasions they were allowed to be included.

Some of the Seventeen Openly Gay and Lesbian Artists in the 1995 Whitney Biennial: This very gay, very postmodern, very political show was assembled by the Whitney Museum's openly gay curator, Klaus Kertess.

David Armstrong	Nan Goldin
Lyle Ashton Harris	David McDermott
Catherine Opie	Peter McGough
Lari Pittman	Frances Negron-Mutaner
Nicole Eisenman	Jack Pierson

(and, basically, the entire third floor)

Some Lesbian Cartoonists

Alison Bechdel	Roberta Gregory
Jennifer Camper	Kris Kovick
Diane DiMassa	Andrea Natalie

Alison Bechdel
(*Photo by Amey Radcliffe*)

LESBIAN AND GAY COMIC BOOK AND CARTOON CHARACTERS

The first comic strips as we know them in modern times appeared in the Sunday supplements of Hearst newspapers in 1897 as a circulation-boosting tactic. The first commercial pulp book appeared in 1934 during the Depression. These works generally avoided all explicit indications of sex or alternative culture.

Of note is the *Batman* and *Wonder Woman* books, which were early mainstream series interpreted by gay men and lesbians to suggest their desires and power.

The earliest predecessor to actual gay comics are the illustrated stories of Blade (Carlyle Kneeland Bate, 1917–1989) in the late 1940s.

However, the social revolutions taking place in the 1960s, in conjunction with dismantled censorship laws, first allowed the exploration of once-taboo subjects.

One of the first explicitly gay comic characters ran in 1964 in *Drum*, a Philadelphia gay monthly newspaper: "Harry Chess," drawn by Al Shapiro, aka, A. Jay.

In the 1970s, more sexually explicit characters were drawn by such artists as Bill Ward, Sean, and Stephen. *The Advocate* ran a regular one-panel series by Joe

Johnson called "Miss Thing." *Christopher Street* also published a series of cartoons.

In the early 1980s, Howard Cruse began *Gay Comix*, a series of pulp books, which included comics by both men and women.

Also, in the early 1980s, Alison Bechdel began to run a series of plates called "Dykes to Watch Out For" in the New York City newspaper, *Womanews*. Later, she began expanding the idea in a regular cartoon strip, which is now syndicated in lesbian and gay newspapers and magazines across the country.

Today, several lesbian and gay cartoons run regularly in the lesbian and gay media. There are also lesbian and gay characters in strips drawn by straight artists and syndicated in mainstream venues. Below is a selected survey of both types:

Northstar, gay comic book hero in straight comic

Shadow Hawk, a mainstream superhero with AIDS (who died in Issue #18)

Andy Lippincott, a "Doonesbury" character, drawn by Gary Trudeau, came out on February 10, 1976

Akbar & Jeff, from "Life in Hell," drawn by Matt Groening

Homer Simpsons's male secretary, from the animated TV show *The Simpsons*, also created by Matt Groening (the voice was provided by Harvey Fierstein)

Captain Maggie Sawyer, comic book hero from "Metropolis S.C.U.," from DC Comics

Maggie and Hopie, from "Love and Rockets," by Jaime Hernandez

Hothead Paisan: Homocidal Lesbian Terrorist, comic book cult classic, by Diane Dimassa

Lawrence Poirier, from "For Better or for Worse," drawn by Lynn Johnston (gay teenager who came out and was thrown out of his home by his parents), 1993

"Outland"

Bert and Ernie on *Sesame Street* (In June of 1994, fundamentalists outed the muppet couple, saying that they "live together in a one-bedroom house, never do anything without each other and exhibit feminine characteristics." In a press release, the Children's Television Workshop, which produces the show, flatly denied that Bert and Ernie were a gay couple. You can make up your own mind, regardless of the political context.)

For more information, see *Gay Comics*, Robert Triptow, New York: New American Library, 1989.

DESIGN CONFERENCES

"Queer by Design," a working conference for lesbian and gay graphic designers, art directors, photographers, illustrators, and other communication professionals, was held in 1991 in San Francisco.

"Design Pride '94," held June 1994 at Cooper Union in New York City and sponsored by the Organization of Lesbian and Gay Architects and Designers, was the first-ever international conference for lesbian and gay architects, interior designers, landscape architects, and product designers. Participants met to talk about the history of lesbian and gay design and discuss issues in the workplace.

PROFILE

MABEL MANEY

Perhaps better known for her series of lesbian parodies of girl detective Nancy Drew, Mabel Maney's first career and creative anchor is as a visual artist. The Nancy Clue novels from Cleis Press (*The Case of the Not-So-Nice Nurse* and *The Case of the Good-For-Nothing Girlfriend*) have made her a household name in camp-appreciating circles, but Mabel's visual art is the springboard and touchstone of her creative life.

Entertainingly sketchy about the details of her childhood, Mabel printed this tale of her youth in the "About the Author" page in both her handmade and trade paperback books: "After her parents were lost at sea, Mabel took up residence with her Great Aunts Maude and Mavis Maney, who had as young women earned their living as bareback riders in a traveling circus before settling in the farm town of Appleton to write their memoirs, *Circus Queens*." Mabel was actually born in Appleton, Wisconsin, in 1958, but the aunts are a figment of her imagination and her parents are very much alive. In fact, she is one of four siblings from a working-class Irish Catholic family, and she grew up in Ohio.

Mabel received a Bachelor in Fine Arts from Ohio State University in 1985, concentrating on photography and film. In 1991, she received a Masters in Fine Arts from San Francisco State University, with an emphasis in book arts. Mabel has been a resident of San Francisco ever since she moved there from Ohio in the late 1980s.

Mabel has shown her work throughout the Midwest and San Francisco, artwork that has consisted of beautifully crafted and politically charged handmade books. Her "Nancy Clue/Cherry Aimless" and "Hardly Boys" handmade art books were included in the prominent group exhibition, "Bad Girls," shown at the New Museum of Contemporary Art in New York and the Los Angeles County Museum. Other examples of her *books* (a shorthand term for mixed media pieces that incorporate both image and text) have been exhibited at the San Francisco Camera Works, the San Francisco Art Institute, the Eye Gallery in San Francisco, and the San Francisco Arts Commission Gallery. In helping to define the label of *book* for her work, Mabel states that her art pieces are experiments in image/text combinations, materials, narrative form, and voice. "My art pieces all have that same relationship to the formation of a book, although they take totally different forms. Essentially, they are mixed-media pieces combining image and text, and occasionally they end up looking like real, honest-to-goodness, bookshelf books."

Cleis's publisher, Frederique Delacoste, saw a showing of Maney's work and liked the art books so much that she asked Maney if she could develop one into a full-length novel. The result was *The Case of the Not-So-Nice Nurse*, published in

Mabel Maney

1993, which marked the beginning of Mabel's career as a novelist and expert satirist. Even though her novels are created in a different medium than her visual work, many of the same themes and concerns run throughout both.

"My primary concern," explains Mabel, "is to examine the role of The Girl within the confines of the institution of the home and the limitations of cultural gender roles." She does this by drawing upon her personal experiences as a girl growing up in the 1960s and 1970s, and by positioning that personal experience within a cultural context. "The thrust of my work is really a critique of the idea of the nuclear family as the perfect unit," she states. "Creating female heros is what all the book-work is about."

Mabel's books have been as large as forty feet long, made out of linen and curtain fabric from the 1950s, and as small as one-inch boxes. Regarding the former, she used the fabric as the page of her book because of the unmistakable femaleness and the domestic quality associated with fabric. "Fabric reads as female no matter who works it," she explains. "And a lot of the undercurrents in my work are about the undercurrents of the terror in the home. In that piece, the fabric page symbolized the home, and the story between the lines of the text placed upon the fabric points to the terror there." Mabel notes that she is also concerned with issues of nostalgia in her work, particularly surrounding post–World War II and middle-class culture.

"My early work was very small," she says. "It was all family stories told from a little girl's point of view. I used real books and retold my story on top of it, juxtaposing an old image and old text with a new image and new text, and offsetting the cultural story with the real story."

But some of Mabel's stories just couldn't be told in the small, diminutive spaces of books (no matter how creatively altered), and hence she began explorations into room-sized, installation books. For instance, she created a giant one-day installation at San Francisco State University called "The Amnesia Victim," which consisted of wall-sized pages of a pseudopsychiatric text of a woman's amnesia problem. "The look of the piece is quite innocent," she states, "but the story is very scary." "The Amnesia Victim" was the first part of a large-scale project Mabel planned called "The Family Museum." It was to be the story of the nuclear family, with each member to get his/her own story told in gripping reality. Exposing the story of the mother, "The Amnesia Victim" was the only part ever completed, and Mabel has subsequently translated it into a limited-edition offset book.

"That project was how I got into the Nancy Drew books," Mabel explains. "Nancy didn't have a mother, and I am very interested in the notion of the missing mother—whether literally or figuratively."

Regarding her art, Mabel states, "The images don't illustrate the text, they provide the environment for it. The images and the material of the pages are really the whole world that collapses and gets put away. It's all about the World of Girls." And this is exactly the name Mabel gave her publishing company when she self-published the handmade artist books about Nancy Clue and the Hardly Boys: World O' Girls Books. (These works are still available in art bookstores such as Printed Matter in New York City and Artist Space in Washington, D.C.)

Mabel's most recent project is the third novel in the Nancy Clue series, entitled *The Hardly Boys in a Ghost in the Closet*. It features a twist on the Hardy Boys, Joe and Frank Hardly, and looks to capture a gay male following the way Nancy and Cherry have captivated lesbians. At the time of this writing the book is scheduled for publication in late 1995, about the same time that Mabel plans to move to Columbus, Ohio, to set up shop in a more affordable area and concentrate again on her visual art.

PROFILE

AMY SHOCK

One of the up-and-coming stars of theater design is Amy Shock, a recent NEA Design Fellow based in New York City, who has worked all over the country.

Amy was born in Willmington, Delaware, in 1959 and received her bachelor of arts in architecture at Cornell University in 1982. For the next eight years, she worked for an architectural firm in Ithaca, New York, mostly doing residential work and designing houses. She began painting in her spare time, and eventually had exhibitions of her work, including a show at the Sloan Gallery in Santa Fe, New Mexico, and shows with the Pastel Society of America.

"But as I started spending more time painting," Amy explains, "I began to feel more and more isolated, and I decided I wanted to work more collaboratively." Her solution was to start working in theater (a notoriously collaborative art form).

"My first theater job was with Holly Hughes," Amy recalls. "She was performing in her play *The Lady Dick*, directed by Lisa Kron, in Ithaca, and I signed up to be the set designer. I hadn't designed a set before, but I had done so many things that are artistically related to the task that my previous experience was all very relevant." Amy loved her first taste of collaborative theater work and design, and the experience prompted her to go back to school. "I wanted to learn more about the craft," she says, "and I didn't have much of a literary/drama background."

Around this same time, in 1989, Amy met Jill Moon, a set designer in Santa Fe (where Amy had moved to enhance her painting career), and Amy became her assistant. Moon had received a master of fine arts in theater design from the University of California at San Diego, and she encouraged Amy to go there, too. Amy did, receiving an M.F.A. from the UCSD theater department in 1993, and began what has quickly turned out to be a very promising new career as a set designer.

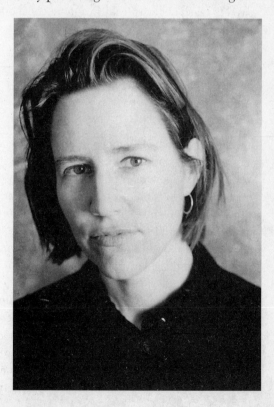

Amy Shock (*Photo by Mary Ward*)

A quick survey of some of the highlights of her two-year career make the point: Her most recent project has been designing sets and costumes for the Joanne Akalaitis production of *Prisoner of Love*, written by Jean Genet, with music by Philip Glass, at the New York Theatre Workshop (which opened in June 1995). She was also named an NEA Design Fellow (winning a highly competitive design fellowship jointly from the National Endowment for the Arts and the Theatre Communications Group), which allows her to observe theater projects all over the world. This spring she was an observer at the Metropolitan Opera in New York City, and currently Amy is traveling in Europe (specifically Berlin; Amsterdam; and Orange, France) to observe productions there.

In addition to her set designing career, Amy is also a cofounder of Fresh Dish Productions in San Diego, a company that presents lesbian and gay performance and music in various venues. "We just did our fortieth show," she notes. "It was a concert by BETTY [a performing group composed of twins Amy and Bitsy, and Allyson]."

Working with the gay and especially lesbian community is a commitment Amy, thirty-six, has long cherished. "The lesbian community is very important to my work," she says. "The first theater people I ever met were Holly Hughes and Lisa Kron, and I thought the inspiration behind their work was so smart and politically motivated. Because I felt the content of their work was so interesting, I was inspired to reach out artistically in a more collaborative way and to become a part of that process and a part of that world."

MINI PROFILES

NICOLE EISENMAN

Born in 1963, Nicole Eisenman is one of the rising young stars of the postmodern, gay-friendly art world. In 1994, she had a solo show at the Jack Tilton Gallery in New York, and a few years before that, a solo show at The Drawing Center in New York. In 1995, you could catch her eclectic work in such high-profile exhibitions as the Whitney Biennial at the Whitney Museum for American Art in New York, and the "In a Different Light" exhibition at the University Art Museum in Berkeley, where she showed a mixed-media installation, *Alive with Pleasure*, 1992–1994.

This is what the gallery program booklet from the "In a Different Light" exhibit had to say about her work:

"Nicole Eisenman's installations consist of hundreds of drawings and other elements that endlessly shuffle styles and voices. Eisenman's work runs from starstruck mooning to pure raunch to mythologizing to pungent self-mockery— sometimes all in the same drawing. She borrows visual stylings from 1920s Neo-Classicism, WPA murals, and underground comics. Through all of it, her work alludes to a new kind of queer subjectivity: angry, horny, raucous, and smart."

CATHERINE OPIE

Like her colleague, Nicole Eisenman, Catherine Opie is currently a provocative figure in the art world, and her work was also in the 1995 Whitney Biennial and the "In a Different Light" exhibition. Moreover, Opie had a solo exhibition in 1995 at Gavin Brown's Enterprise Gallery in New York City.

In its May 1995 issue, *Out* magazine said of her, "Catherine Opie is one of the hottest artists in Los Angeles, a photographer whose lush, color-saturated portraits document her friends from the leather and transsexual scenes."

In the "In a Different Light" exhibition, Opie exhibited her *Self-Portrait*, 1994, a chromogenic print that showed her encased in leather with a bleeding outline of two stick-figure girls in front of a happy home carved on her back. She also featured similar photographs at the Whitney Biennial, along with portraits of friends and colleagues in the leather and TV/TS/TG communities, such as Idexa and Justin Bond.

SUGGESTED FURTHER READING

Boffin, Tess, and Jean Fraser, eds. *Stolen Glances: Lesbians Take Photographs.* Pandora, 1991.

Broude, Norma, and Mary D. Garrard, eds. *The Power of Feminist Art: The American Movement of the 1970s, History and Impact.* Harry N. Abrams, 1994.

Frueh, Joanna, Cassandra L. Langer, and Arlene Raven, eds. *Feminist Art Criticism: An Anthology,* Icon/HarperCollins, 1991.

———*New Feminist Criticism: Art, Identity, Action.* Icon/HarperCollins, 1994.

Johnston, Jill. *Secret Lives in Art: Essays on Art, Literature, and Performance.* Chicago Review Press, 1994.

Kiss and Tell Collective. *Drawing the Line: Lesbian Sexual Politics on the Wall.* Press Gang Publishers, 1991.

"Lesbian Art and Artists." *Heresies* magazine, no. 3 (1977).

"Twelve Years." *Heresies* magazine, no. 24 (1989).

---

3. LESBIAN BUSINESS AND INDUSTRY

Often [lesbians and gays are] less willing to leave jobs—they're comfortable there, how do they know they'll be comfortable in the next place? Do they even want to go through coming out all over again?

—JUDITH LANSKY, career consultant, quoted in *Victory!* magazine

Some of us are fortunate to work in lesbian and gay organizations or to be in business for ourselves, but many lesbians have faced homophobia in the mainstream business world and found it difficult or impossible to come out in the one area where they spend most of their waking hours. Having to hide in the closet at work can sap both our energy and our creativity. How many times have we avoided divulging anything about our personal lives, when everyone around us was talking about the hubby and kids?

Fortunately, lesbian and gay employee associations and union groups are sprouting up across corporate America, lobbying for gay employees' rights and domestic partner benefits. Many major companies have already instituted progressive policies for their lesbian and gay employees. The following is a guide to some of the groundbreaking work that is being done to make more workplaces gay friendly.

How to Come Out in the Workplace

Coming out on the job can be an awkward experience, but it doesn't have to be, especially if you heed the following suggestions for dispelling coworkers' confusion and easing any misgivings of your own:

- *Come out to workplace friends first.* Building a support system of trusted coworkers who respect you and your sexual identity is an important first step toward fully coming out.
- *Make coming out to the boss your next priority.* Choose an environment in which you feel comfortable. The occasion need not be formal or the statement overt; casually mentioning the name of a girlfriend or partner while sharing a cab to a meeting or over a drink after work should be sufficient notification.
- *Initiate lesbian and gay awareness in the workplace.* Start or support existing programs that are homo-friendly. Something as simple as asking coworkers to sponsor you for a fundraising event with a lesbian and or gay theme can boost employee consciousness and possibly alert other lesbians to your identity.

Visibility in the workplace is important; it can foster heightened sensitivity among non-lesbian and gay employees and help other lesbians and gays feel more relaxed about coming out.

When Gay-Friendly Isn't Friendly Enough

Lesbians looking for a gay-friendly workplace should not only consider the sexuality issue, but whether the environment they are going to is hospitable to women. C. Arthur Bain, publisher of *The Gay/Lesbian/Bisexual Corporate Letter*, wrote in a business column appearing in the October 4, 1994 issue of *The Advocate*, "During interviews at Microsoft I found that lesbians and bisexual women consistently described the working environment as sexist and male-oriented, while gay and bisexual men were uniformly glowing in their assessments of the company. It was almost as if the two sexes worked for different employers."

News Brief: Cop in Transit

"Typically in the past, [transsexuals] have left their lives and jobs and have had to pick up and make new lives somewhere else," says thirty-nine-year-old Stephanie Thorne. "I see no reason why I should have to do that." Thorne, an openly lesbian San Francisco police officer, quoted in a news item in *The Advocate*, plans to undergo a sex-change operation, perhaps making her San Francisco's first openly transsexual cop. Thorne is a fourteen-year veteran officer who has spent ten years on the San Francisco force.

SOURCE: *The Advocate*, June 14, 1994

Queer Labor Notes from Here and There

- The first regional chapter of the U.S. Department of Agriculture's Gay, Lesbian, and Bisexual Employee's Organization (USDA GLOBE) was formed in Northern California in May 1995. USDA GLOBE was informally organized in December 1993 and was officially recognized by the USDA on March 25, 1994. It has 118 members stationed around the nation.
- In mid-1994, the Service Employees International Union (SEIU) added two gay groups to its shop roster: the Human Rights Campaign Fund (HRCF) and the San Francisco AIDS Foundation.
- In March 1995, gay, lesbian, and unmarried heterosexual municipal employees in Denver won a victory in gaining permission to take sick leave to care for their domestic partners under a policy change approved four to one by the city personnel board.
- The first-ever gay newspaper to unionize was the *San Francisco Bay Times*, whose five full-time employees became affiliated with the Northern California Newspaper Guild in March 1995.
- In 1994, Capital Cities/ABC Inc., which has about 20,000 employees, became the only one of the four major television studios to extend spousal benefits to the domestic partners of gay and lesbian employees.

SOURCES: *Washington Blade*, 5/26/95; *The Advocate*, 5/31/94; 10/10/94; 4/18/95

Labor Highs and Lows in the Nation's Capital

The phrase *Lavender Hill Mob* took on new meaning in May 1994, when the Lesbian and Gay Congressional Staff Association became an officially registered staff organization on Capitol Hill. The group's cofounder, Mark Agrast, senior legislative assistant to openly gay representative Gerry Studds (D-Mass.), explained the purpose of the group by observing that "the working environment on Capitol Hill varies sharply from one office to the next. Our goal is to improve the quality of life for lesbian and gay congressional employees."

Nothing is ever that simple and straightforward in Washington. As of mid-1995, activities of this kind by federal employees have come under direct attack from two bills introduced by—who else?—Senator Jesse Helms (R-North Carolina). One bill would ban the use of federal funds to carry out progay programs for federal employees, initiatives just like the Lesbian and Gay Congressional Staff Association. The bill could prevent gay employee groups from meeting in federal offices, posting notices on bulletin boards, or using interoffice mail for communications. The second bill would give special exemption from workplace nondiscrimination policies to government employees who voice prejudice against lesbian and gay coworkers.

SOURCES: *Washington Blade*, 5/26/95; *The Advocate*, 4/18/95

GROUNDBREAKING UNIONS

• The first union involvement in gay and lesbian issues came in 1973, when the leadership of the American Federation of Labor and Congress of Industrial Organizations responded to firings of gay members of the American Federation of Teachers by publicly stating its support for gay rights.

• In 1982, the gay and lesbian union caucus at *The Village Voice* was the first ever to win domestic-partnership benefits.

• In the mid-1980s the Service Employees International Union (SEIU), which has thousands of members in over twenty Lavender Caucuses, and the American Federation of State, County, and Municipal Employees (AFSCME) negotiated full domestic-partnership benefits in Seattle and other cities, years ahead of gay-friendly corporate America.

• The Stonewall 25 celebration in New York City saw the formation of *Pride at Work: The National Gay, Lesbian, Bi, and Transgender Labor Organization*. Funded by AFSCME and eleven other unions, the organization's founding conference brought together more than 300 representatives of twenty-five unions and local and regional gay and lesbian union groups.

BUSINESS-RELATED QUOTATIONS

"We need a listing of all the gay people in San Francisco."

—SAN FRANCISCO BUSINESS, compilation of the zaniest questions and requests received by the city's Chambers of Commerce in 1993

In American life, business and politics are two sides of the same coin—and that's a good reason for gays and lesbians to keep an eye on the business world. . . . Whether we function as consumers, activists, or entrepreneurs, one thing is certain: Taking care of business is a great way to make changes.

—THE ADVOCATE, special report on gay money/gay power, 4/18/95

*Many single gay and lesbian employees—as well as those with domestic part-
ners—now see [domestic-partner benefits] as a simple matter of equal pay for
equal work. Extensions of equal benefits has become a tangible symbol that their
employer pays and values them as much as it does their heterosexual colleagues.*

　　—C. ARTHUR BAIN, "How Do I Find a Gay-Friendly Employer?" *The Advo-
　　　cate*, 10/4/94

*So how do you get [domestic-partnership benefits]? My standard motto is, "Don't
ask, don't get."*

　　　　　　　　　　　　　　—ED MIKENS, *The Advocate*, 2/22/94

BUSINESS QUICK FACTS

- Half of the Fortune 1000 companies have nondiscrimination policies protecting their gay and lesbian employees.[1]
- More than 20 federal agencies currently have nondiscrimination policies that include sexual orientation.[2]
- More than 60 American companies have lesbian, gay, and bisexual employee groups—many officially recognized and funded by the company—and new groups are forming all the time.[3]
- When Vermont became the first state to provide domestic partner health benefits to its state employees in August of 1994, of the 136 unmarried couples claiming the benefit, 119 were heterosexual, while only 17 same-sex couples applied. This ratio is typical of companies offering these benefits throughout the nation.[4]
- Multinational corporations often do not require their foreign subsidiaries to apply the same nondiscrimination policies that their U.S. offices follow.[5]
- It is estimated that gay men and lesbians spend as much as $500 billion annually in the U.S.[6]

[1]Elizabeth Birch, executive director of the Human Rights Campaign Fund, as quoted in *The Advocate*, 4/18/95, p. 40.
[2]"Federal Employees Under Siege," *The Advocate*, p. 40; 4/18/95.
[3]"How Do I Find a Gay-Friendly Employer?" *The Advocate*, C. Arthur Bain, p. 49, 10/4/94.
[4]"Straight Couples Come Out," *The Advocate*, p. 49, 10/4/94.
[5]"How Do I Find a Gay-Friendly Employer?" *The Advocate*, C. Arthur Bain, p. 50, 10/4/94.
[6]"Ikea's Gay Gamble," *The Advocate*, John Gallagher, p. 25, 5/3/94.

STATES THAT FORBID ANTIGAY DISCRIMINATION IN EMPLOYMENT AS OF MAY, 1995

California	Hawaii
Connecticut	Massachusetts

Minnesota	Vermont
New Jersey	Wisconsin
Rhode Island	

LESBIAN AND GAY BUSINESS TRAVEL

A recent special advertising section in *The Advocate* featured a how-to guide for the queer business traveler. Although most of us associate gay travel with a vacation, the fact is that most gay people—like most Americans—also travel for business purposes. Surveys assessing the size of all travel done by gay men and lesbians—a volume estimated to be as high as $17 billion annually—find that a large percentage of this travel is business-related. A number of mainstream travel companies are now seeking to attract this substantial gay and lesbian consumer base through gay-focused marketing and making policy changes that address the needs and concerns of gay business travelers. Herewith is a brief listing of travel companies rated by *The Advocate* (using information culled from *Out & About*, the gay and lesbian travel newsletter) as "exceptional," "gay-friendly," or "antigay."

EXCEPTIONAL POLICIES OR PRACTICES

American Airlines	National Car Rental
Northwest Airlines	Hyatt Hotels
Virgin Airlines	American Express Credit Card
Avis Car Rental	

GAY-FRIENDLY POLICIES OR PRACTICES

| Continental Airlines | Lufthansa Airlines |
| Kiwi Airlines | Alamo Car Rental |

ANTIGAY POLICIES OR PRACTICES

| TWA Airlines | Hertz Car Rental |

SOME MAJOR (RECENT) QUEER MOMENTS IN "PUSHING PRODUCT"

- In the public service arena, Melissa Etheridge posed nude with her (also nude) girlfriend on behalf of People for the Ethical Treatment of Animals.
- Minneapolis-based Dayton Hudson Corporations, one of the nation's largest retailers, began test marketing gay-themed greeting cards at two of its Marshall Field's Department stores in Chicago and a Dayton's department store in Min-

neapolis. The cards are created and distributed by Cardthartic, a Chicago firm that describes themselves as "Hallmark-like."

- RuPaul recently became the featured "covergirl" for M.A.C. Cosmetics' "Who's That M.A.C. girl?" ad campaign, which included posters throughout New York City.
- In 1995, Nike began airing a television commercial featuring Ric Muñoz, a media darling of last year's Gay Games IV, with captions reading: "80 miles every week—10 marathons every year—HIV Positive—Just Do It." (William Burroughs, *Naked Lunch* author, cyber/queer literary forefather and famed heroin addict, was also featured on a Nike TV ad that aired in 1994.)
- A recent addition to the ongoing, oh-so-Britishly acerbic ad series for Tanqueray gin featured the regularly appearing Mr. Jenkins character alongside the following copy: "Mr. Jenkins hopes to see you riding in front of him in the California AIDS Ride 2 as the view from behind Mr. Jenkins may not be too flattering." In addition to selling gin, the ad promoted the annual May California AIDS Ride. Tanqueray also underwrote and promoted the 1995 Boston–New York AIDS Ride.

SOURCES: *Out*, 5/95; *The Advocate*, 4/5/94

THE BEST AND THE WORST COMPANIES FOR GAYS AND LESBIANS

Cracking the Corporate Closet, a gay and lesbian guidebook on the best and worst companies to work for, buy from, and invest in, uses three major criteria for assessing how gay-positive or gay-friendly a given company is. The first is fundamental: Is sexual orientation included in the company's antidiscrimination policy? Any company lacking such a policy automatically received a low ranking. Here are a few of the winners and losers on the antidiscrimination policy litmus test:

TWENTY LOSERS—A SAMPLING OF COMPANIES THAT DO NOT INCLUDE SEXUAL ORIENTATION IN THEIR ANTIDISCRIMINATION POLICIES*

American Home Products	Marriott
Burger King	Mobil
Corning	Motorola
Hill and Knowlton	PBS
Hilton	Pepsico
Hoffman-La Roche	Phillips
Home Depot	Reynolds Metal
JC Penney	Rite Aid
Lands' End	The Gap
Lockheed	Toys "R" Us

*As of July 1994

Twenty Winners—A Sampling of Companies That Do Include Sexual Orientation in Their Antidiscrimination Policies

Allstate	General Motors
Apple Computers	Harley-Davidson
AT&T	Hewlett-Packard
Bankers Trust	McGraw Hill
Ben & Jerry's	Procter & Gamble
Burroughs Wellcome	RJR Nabisco
CBS	Seagram
Citicorp	Sprint
Disney	Tambrands
Eastman Kodak	Xerox

The second criteria is whether the company goes beyond basic antidiscrimination protections and extends domestic partnership benefits to its employees. This is important, since according to the U.S. Chamber of Commerce, nearly 40 percent of the average American worker's earnings are received in benefits. Since extending domestic-partner benefits costs the company money, the number of corporations extending such benefits to their lesbian and gay employees is signficantly smaller than those providing basic antidiscrimination protections. Here's a list of ten companies that do extend such benefits:

Apple Computer	Lotus
Ben & Jerry's	MCA (Universal)
Boston Globe	Microsoft
Charles Schwab	Quark
Fannie Mae	Viacom
Levi Strauss & Co.	Village Voice

Interestingly, according to a study by *Human Resources Focus* (January 1994), the four top reasons cited by companies that do not offer domestic partnership benefits are: fear of rising benefits expenditures; too few employee requests, lack of senior-management support, and anxiety over moving into uncharted waters.

The third method used in *Cracking the Corporate Closet* for making overall determinations of how corporations ranked in terms of doing well by their gay and lesbian employees was conducting interviews with present and former employees of the companies under consideration and searching through press reports of corporate behavior on relevant issues. Based on these three criteria, *Cracking the Corporate Closet* provides the following rankings on the best and worst American companies for gay male and lesbian employees.

The Twelve Best Companies for Gay and Lesbian Employees

1. Apple Computer	3. Boston Globe
2. Ben & Jerry's	4. Charles Schwab

5. Fannie Mae
6. Levi Strauss & Co.
7. Lotus
8. MCA (Universal)

9. Pacific Gas and Electric
10. Quark
11. Viacom
12. Ziff-Davis

THE THIRTEEN WORST COMPANIES FOR GAY AND LESBIAN EMPLOYEES

1. Abbott Laboratories
2. American Home Products Corp.
3. Circle K Corporation
4. Coastal Corporation
5. Cracker Barrel Old Country Store
6. Delta
7. First Interstate Bank

8. General Electric
9. Great Republic Insurance Co.
10. Guardian Life Insurance Corp.
11. H & H Music Company
12. HealthAmerica Corp.
13. Milliken & Company

SOURCE: *Cracking the Corporate Closet*, by Dan Baker and Sean Strub, HarperCollins, 1995

GAY AND LESBIAN EMPLOYEE GROUPS

When conducting extensive research on the level of gay-friendliness in America's corporate world, the authors of *Cracking the Corporate Closet* (from which the selected listing below is taken) found that active, vocal lesbian and gay employee groups are a key factor in effecting change within a corporation. They point out that very few corporations have adopted domestic partnership benefits, antigay discrimination clauses, and related policies without pressure from such groups. Often beginning as informal social networks, these employee groups eventually took the step of announcing their existence publicly, soliciting new members, and advocating for improved work environments for lesbians and gay men.

AT&T

LEAGUE—Lesbian, Bisexual, and
Gay United Employees at AT&T
4 Campus Drive
Parsippany, NJ 07054
Contact: Ms. Kathleen Dermody,
908/658-6013

COORS

LAGER—Lesbian and Gay Employee
Resource
Mail Stop #NH420
Coors Brewing Co.
Golden, CO 80401
Contact: Mr. Earl Nissen,
303/277-5309

THE WALT DISNEY CO.

LEAGUE
500 South Buena Vista St.
Burbank, CA 91521-5209
Contact: Mr. Garrett Hicks,
818/560-1000

HEWLETT-PACKARD

GLEN—Gay, Lesbian and Bisexual
Employee Network
P.O. Box 700542
San Jose, CA 95170
Contact: Mr. Kim Harris,
415/857-7771 or Mr. Greg Gloss
415/447-6123

JOHNSON & JOHNSON

RWJPRI
700 Route 200
Raritan, NJ 08869
Contact: Ms. Cheryl Vitow,
    908/704-5607

LEVI STRAUSS & CO.

Lesbian and Gay Employee
    Association
1155 Battery St.
San Francisco, CA 94111
Contact: Ms. Michele Dryden,
    415/544-7103

LOCKHEED MISSILES AND SPACE

GLOBAL—Gay, Lesbian, or Bisexual
    at Lockheed
LMSC Management Assn.—Bay Area
    Chapter
Dept. 27-62, Building 599
P.O. Box 3504
Sunnyvale, CA 95088-3504
Contact: Mr. Frederick Parsons,
    408/255-4936 or Mr. Patrick Miller,
    408/369-1713

MICROSOFT

GLEAM—Gay, Lesbian & Bisexual
    Employees at Microsoft
1 Microsoft Way
Redmond, WA 98052
Contact: Mr. Jeff Howard,
    206/936-5581

NEW YORK TIMES CO.

Gay & Lesbian Caucus
229 W. 43rd St.
New York, NY 10036
Contact: Mr. David Dunlap,
    212/556-7082

POLAROID

Polaroid Gay, Lesbian & Bisexual
    Association
585 Technology Square-4
Cambridge, MA 02139

PRUDENTIAL

EAGLES—Employee Association of
    Gay Men and Lesbians
P.O. Box 1566
Minneapolis, MN 55440-1566
Contact: Ms. Cathy Perkins,
    612/557-7918

UNITED AIRLINES

GLUE Coalition—Gay & Lesbian
    United Employees
2261 Market St., #293
San Francisco, CA 94114
Contact: Mr. Tom Cross, 800/999-3448

THE VILLAGE VOICE

Lesbian & Gay Caucus
36 Cooper Square
New York, NY 10003
Contact: Mr. Richard Goldstein,
    212/475-3300

WELLS FARGO

Mail Stop #MAC 0188-133
111 Sutter St., 13th Fl.
San Francisco, CA 94104
Contact: Ms. Barbara Zoloth,
    415/396-2767

XEROX

GALAXE—Gays and Lesbians at
    Xerox
P.O. Box 25382
Rochester, NY 14625
Contact: Mr. David Frishkorn,
    716/423-5090

EXCERPTS AS SUBMITTED from
Cracking the Corporate Closet by
Daniel B. Baker and Sean O. Strub.
Copyright © 1995 by Daniel B. Baker,
Sean O'Brien Strub, and Bill Henning.
Reprinted by permission of Harper-
Collins Publishers, Inc.

OTHER RESOURCES

NEWSLETTERS/MAGAZINES

Gay/Lesbian/Bisexual Corporate Letter
Art Bain
P.O. Box 602
Murray Hill Station, NY 10156-0601
Phone: 212/447-7328
Internet address: corpletter@aol.com
$20 for four quarterly issues

Aimed at gay, lesbian, and bisexual employees, corporate human resources departments, and others concerned with gay issues in the workplace.

Working It Out: The Newsletter for
  Gay and Lesbian Employment
  Issues
Ed Mickens
P.O. Box 2079
New York, NY 10108
Phone: 212/769-2384
Fax: 212/721-2680
$60 for four quarterly issues

Victory!
1500 W. El Camino Avenue,
Suite 526
Sacramento, CA 95833
Phone: 916/444-6894

Written by, for, and about gays and lesbians working for themselves. Aimed at corporate human resource departments, management, and others concerned with gay issues in the workplace.

WORKPLACE-RELATED—LEGAL

These groups can provide information regarding domestic-partner benefits and discuss the laws that pertain to sexual orientation, AIDS, transgenderism, and other work-related issues.

American Civil Liberties Union
  (ACLU)
National Gay and Lesbian
  Rights Project
132 West 43rd St.
New York, NY 10036
Phone: 212/944-9800, ext. 545

Gay and Lesbian Advocates and
  Defenders (GLAD)
P.O. Box 218
Boston, MA 02112
Phone: 617/426-1350

Lambda Legal Defense and Education
  Fund
666 Broadway
New York, NY 10012
Phone: 212/995-8585

National Center for Lesbian Rights
1663 Mission Street, Suite 550
San Francisco, CA 94103
Phone: 415/392-6257

National Lesbian and Gay Law
  Association
Box 77130, National Capital Station
Washington, DC 20014
Phone: 202/389-0161

WORKPLACE-RELATED—POLITICAL

These organizations coordinate national civil rights efforts or are specifically devoted to work-related issues. They can provide information about what other corporations are doing, provide model nondiscrimination policies, information of legislation, and other resources.

Hollywood Supports
6430 Sunset Blvd., Suite 102
Los Angeles, CA 90028
Phone: 213/962-3023

Human Rights Campaign Fund
1012 Fourteenth St. NW
Washington, DC 20005
Phone: 202/628-4160

Interfaith Center on Corporate
  Responsibility
475 Riverside Dr., Rm. 566
New York, NY 10115
Phone: 212/870-2296

National Gay and Lesbian Task Force
  (NGLTF)
1734 Fourteenth St. NW
Washington, DC 20009-4309
Phone: 202/332-6483

The NGLTF has a network of grassroots organizing teams that include workplace issues among their areas of focus. NGLTF also provides several materials on workplace issues, including a list of companies with lesbian and gay employee groups (with contact names and numbers); a list of companies that include sexual orientation in the EEO statements; a list of companies that provide domestic partnership coverage; and a how-to guide on starting lesbian/gay employee groups. They also distribute a publication produced by Pride at Work on gay and lesbian labor union organizing. All of these materials are available at minimal cost.

Wall Street Project/Community Lesbian and Gay Rights Institute
217 E. 85th St., Suite 162
New York, NY 10028

WORKPLACE-RELATED—UNION

Pride at Work: The National Gay, Lesbian, Bi, and Transgender Labor
  Organization

P.O. Box 9605
North Amherst, MA 01059-9605
Phone: 413/549-5972

BOOKS

Baker, Dan, and Sean Strub. *Cracking the Corporate Closet*. HarperCollins, 1995.

Beer, Chris, et al. *Gay Workers: Trade Unions and the Law*. State Mutual Books, 1983.

Frank, Miriam, and Desma Holcomb. *Pride at Work: Organizing for Lesbian and Gay Rights in Unions*. Lesbian and Gay Labor Network, P.O. Box 1159, Peter Stuyvesant Station, New York, NY 10009.

Harbeck, Karen M., ed. *Coming Out of the Classroom Closet: Gay and Lesbian Students, Teachers, and Curricula*. Harrington Park Press, 1992.

Hunter, Nan, Sherryl Michaelson, and Thomas Stoddard. *The Rights of Lesbians and Gay Men: The Basic ACLU Guide to a Gay Person's Rights*. Southern University Press.

McNaught, Brian. *Gay Issues in the Workplace*. St. Martin's Press, 1993.

Mickens, Ed. *The 100 Best Companies for Gay Men and Lesbians*. Pocket Books, 1994.

Stone, Susan Carol, and Anthony Patrick Carnevale. *Our Diverse Work Force: A Survey of Issues and a Practical Guide*. U.S. Dept. of Labor and the American Society of Training and Development, 1993.

Woods, James D., and Jay H. Lucas. *The Corporate Closet: The Professional Lives of Gay Men in America*. The Free Press, 1993.

VIDEOS

Gay Issues in the Workplace: Gay, Lesbian and Bisexual Employees Speak for Themselves with Brian McNaught, 1993 (TRB Productions, P.O. Box 2362, Boston, MA 02107).

BROKERING RESOURCES

The *Gales Investment Letter* is an investment advisory newsletter devoted to gay-friendly growth stocks. Wesley Hicks is the publisher, and can be reached at 800/226-9245.

Howard Tharsing, an independent broker, is also the director of Progressive Asset Management's Lavender Screen Project, which uses a five-point scale in evaluating companies on their level of gay-friendliness. A leading participant in NGLTF workplace activities, Tharsing provides competitively priced brokerage services and can be reached in Oakland, California, at 800/786-2998.

PROFILE

TOWER PRESS

Lesbian-owned and operated Tower Press celebrated its twentieth anniversary last year. Founded in New York City in 1975 by Susan Horowitz and Lisa Szer at a time when female printers were virtually unheard of, the business is now run by Robin Imandt and Barbara Pfanz, a couple whose lives intertwine on both the personal and professional fronts.

Robin Imandt told us a bit about the genesis of Tower Press: Susan Horowitz was taught the printing trade by an older African-American man who knew all too well about the restrictions and limitations that minorities faced in the printing business. He knew that if it had been a struggle for him, it would also be hard for women, and he was committed to mentoring her. Susan and Lisa were in their early twenties when they started the business and were full of youthful exuberance. For the first ten years, they hired all lesbians and invested a great deal of time and equipment in training so that these women could enter the male-dominated printing trade.

Robin joined Tower in 1978. She had another business at the time—as a women's music producer—and was sharing space on Tower's premises. In exchange for her rent, she answered the telephone there. In time, Robin found herself drawn to the printing business, and decided to learn typesetting at Tower because it seemed like a good, flexible skill to have. She started as a typesetter in 1981, and in 1984 was made a partner in the business. In 1989, Susan Horowitz left Tower to move into the world of desktop publishing (among her other activities, Susan is the publisher of the *New York City Lesbian and Gay Pride Guide*). Upon Susan's departure, Robin became the full owner (she is now coowner with Barbara Pfanz, who joined the press in 1987 as production manager). Cofounder Lisa Szer had left the press back in 1978.

As Tower started to grow in the mid-1980s, more skilled people were needed, so word went out through the various printing channels, and after a decade as a lesbian-only press, Tower hired its first man, a gay male bookkeeper. Some straight male printers followed. "Everyone got along well," Robin says. "Working with women who were not sexually available to them seemed to create a nice camaraderie between the straight men and the lesbians." In fact, Robin muses, the only on-the-job romances at Tower were lesbian trysts. She recalls giving two lesbian employees a lecture on why they couldn't make out in the press room, and having them respond by asking, "Not even when things are slow?"

Throughout the late 1970s and early 1980s, with its focus on doing print work for gay, lesbian, and woman-identified causes, Tower found itself doing lots of free printing for hard-pressed grassroots groups throughout New York City. "Then the recession hit and we learned the hard way that you have to make choices," Robin says. "We went through some hard times and survived. In 1988 we went from being a print shop to being printing brokers because the industry was changing tremendously as a result of the growth in technology and the computerization of printing equipment. Keeping up with that would have cost millions of dollars in investments. So we became brokers—we have the experience to buy printing and do so for our clients. We put together the whole package using trade sources that work just with ad agencies and print brokers like us."

Today, Tower has three to four full-time employees, plus freelancers. Most of the work they do is for corporate clients, many of whom are gay or lesbian. They continue to work on major jobs within the community (GMHC's now-infamous lesbian safer sex handbook was a recent project, the *New York City Lesbian and Gay Pride Guide* another), and have maintained their community spirit by occasionally issuing grants for printing. "Like many other lesbian and gay businesses," says Robin, "Tower has become more professional and more out. That's a long way from where we started, because back then we were an oddity. People would line up at our door to look at the women working on the printing machines—but at the same time they respected what we did."

---

4. LESBIAN CULTURE

Lesbianism is the culture through which we can politically question heterosexual society on its sexual categories, on the meaning of its institutions of domination in general, and in particular on the meaning of that institution of personal dependence, marriage, imposed on women.

—MONIQUE WITTIG, lesbian theorist

It would be impossible to define or confine lesbian culture—we're too diverse a community, composed of women of many ages, nationalities, races, and economic backgrounds. Ideas about who lesbians are and how they define themselves have changed drastically over the years. Yet certain themes have resonated across our differences—from passing to butch-femme to particular lesbian styles. Here is a grab bag of lesbian culture across two centuries.

A PASSING LOOK AT SOME PASSING WOMEN

JEANNE BONNET, 1849–1876

The most notorious passing woman in San Francisco, a newspaper report from that time described her as "hastening down the broad road to moral destruction. She became imbued with the spirit of heroism and cursed the day she was born a female instead of a male." As a very young woman, Jeanne organized a gang of boys, whose thievery and other crimes were "seldom equalled by even the more daring men of her class for their boldness of execution." One news report described her as a man-hater with "short cropped hair, an unwomanly voice, and a masculine face which harmonized excellently with her customary suit of boys' clothes, including a jaunty hat which she wore with all the grace of an experienced hoodlum."

"Getting ready for the dance" *(Copyright © 1986 by Morgan Gwenwald)*

At twenty-six, Jeanne began visiting San Francisco brothels, where she organized an all-woman gang of prostitutes. Giving up prostitution, the gang members supported themselves by petty thievery and shoplifting. Jeanne's special friend was gang member Blanche Buneau.

On September 14, 1876, at the San Miguel Saloon, Jeanne was lying in bed, waiting for Blanche, when she was shot through the window and killed. The murder was never solved.

BABE BEAN, 1877–1936

In August 1897, the police in Stockton, California, detained a twenty-year-old woman for masquerading in men's clothing. She explained that she had lost her speech in an accident, and, writing out her story for the police, informed them that her real name was Babe Bean, though most people called her Jack. "I have been wearing men's clothing off and on for five years," she wrote, "for as a man, I can travel freely, feel protected, and find work."

An oddity, Babe Bean was front-page news in the Stockton papers for months, and word of the "Trousered Puzzle" reached all the way to Boston. Later, a "small man" named Jack Garland served as a lieutenant during the Spanish-American War, then moved to San Francisco, where in 1906 he served as a male nurse during the earthquake and fire.

Until his death in 1936, Jack Garland (aka Babe Bean) lived in San Francisco rooming houses and acted as a kind of freelance social worker, aiding homeless and hungry people. On his death, it was discovered that Uncle Jack, as he was affectionately known, had been born Elvira Virginia Mugarrieta, the daughter of José Marcos Mugarrieta, founder of the Mexican consulate in San Francisco, and Eliza Alice Garland, reportedly the daughter of a Louisiana Supreme Court Justice.

MURRAY HALL, D. 1901

Murray Hall was a well-known and respected New York City political organizer, part of the infamous Tammany Hall political machine. Married twice, a heavy drinker, and a poker player who enjoyed big black cigars, Hall was discovered at his death to have been born a woman. The story of the politician's passing for twenty-five years garnered headlines in the *New York Tribune* and the *New York Times*, such as "Murray Hall Fooled Many Shrewd Men."

SOURCES: *Gay American History: Lesbians and Gay Men in the U.S.A.*, Jonathan Ned Katz; and "'She Even Chewed Tobacco': A Pictorial Narrative of Passing Women in America," by the San Francisco Lesbian and Gay History Project, in *Hidden from History: Reclaiming the Gay and Lesbian Past*

THE LESBIAN HOUSE PARTY SCENE OF THE HARLEM RENAISSANCE, 1920–1935

RENT PARTY

A party held at an individual's apartment, at which guests paid a small fee to help their host raise money for the rent. Usually a mix of heterosexuals and homosexuals, rent parties were a safe way for African-American lesbians and gay men to socialize away from the speakeasies.

BUFFET FLAT

An after-hours party held in someone's apartment, which was a common place for African-American lesbians and gay men to socialize. *Buffet* referred to the smorgasbord of sexual possibilities: straight, gay, group sex, etc. Buffet flats, as with other parties, might last several days or an entire weekend.

ELEMENTS OF LESBIAN STYLE, THEN AND NOW

THE ELEMENTS OF STYLE—IF YOU WERE BUTCH—IN THE 1940s, 1950s, AND EARLY 1960s

Hair: Slicked back; D.A.–style; crew cuts; short

Shirts: Heavily starched shirts; T-shirts (worn backward); button-downs; western shirts; tuxedo shirts

The western look *(Copyright © 1993 by Micha Kwiatkowska)*

Sweaters: V-neck; cardigan; collegiate-style pullovers

Pants: Men's dress pants (sharply creased); dungarees; khakis; chinos, tapered at the bottom

Jackets: Sport jackets

Shoes: Wing tips, oxfords, penny loafers (accompanied by argyle socks), Florsheim dress shoes (accompanied by dark nylon socks); low-cut men's dress boots; cowboy boots

Accoutrements: Pinkie rings, tattoos, cuff links, neckties, thin belts

THE ELEMENTS OF STYLE—IF YOU WERE FEM—IN THE 1940S, 1950S, AND EARLY 1960S

Sweaters: The sweater-girl look (form-fitting Orlon and Banlon sweaters)

Dresses: Strapless, low cut

Pants: Women's slacks; toreador pants

Hair: Curls, bouffant, straightened and then curled

And to complete the look: nylon and dacron sheer stockings, high heels, gloves, fashionable women's hats (with or without veils), purses, perfume, makeup

THE ELEMENTS OF STYLE—HERE AND NOW

Select from among the following menu items depending on your mood, the day of the week, and/or who you're trying to attract: baggy pants; flannel shirts (with or without sleeves); overall shorts; combat boots; black leather motorcycle jackets; miniskirts; Wonder bras (with or without anything on top); black latex shorts; multiple ear piercings; leather vests; Doc Martens; corporate drag (women's suits, pumps, etc.); jean jackets; softball uniforms; spandex pants or tube dresses; lipstick and eye makeup; Obsession perfume for women (or for men); work boots; high heels; wing tips; Calvin Klein men's underwear as beach wear; porkpie caps; suspenders; baseball caps; Keds sneakers (high tops or low); pierced nose, nipple, lip, eyebrow, tongue, or navel; Levi's 501s; political buttons; Madras shorts; pocket watches; tattoos; Lesbian Avengers T-shirts; Birkenstocks; boxer shorts; muscle Ts; short leather skirts; down vests; red plaid hunting caps (with earflaps); summer dresses; latex gloves (in bed and out); long key chains; cowboy boots; bolo ties; bandanna head scarves; men's pajama tops; bicycle pants; fishnet stockings; and pretty much anything else, separately or in combination.

DYKE ICONS AND HEARTTHROBS (NOT NECESSARILY LESBIAN, RELATIVELY RANDOM, AND IN NO PARTICULAR ORDER)

Marlene Dietrich	Audre Lorde
Kristy McNichol	Annie Lennox
Frida Kahlo	Queen Latifah
Gertrude Stein	Madonna
Geraldine Ferraro	Angela Davis
Martina Navratilova	Jenny Shimizu
Grace Jones	Susan Sontag
Sandra Bernhard	Phranc
k.d. lang	Ellen DeGeneres
Anna Deveare Smith	Marianne Faithfull
Sue Simmons	Sappho
Sigourney Weaver	Emma Goldman
Tina Turner	Jodie Foster
Agnes Moorehead	Alice Walker

Billie Jean King   Greta Garbo
Me'Shell NdegeOcello   Susan Sarandon
Ingrid Casares   Danitra Vance

THE LESBIAN SOCIAL SCENE TODAY

Lesbian social life and culture have come an awfully long way from the days when bars and house parties were the primary—and often the only—vehicles for public socializing. Today, lesbian culture and community consists of many overlapping networks, formal and informal, organized around an almost infinite variety of interests. From spiritual/religious meetings to virtual lesbianism on-line, skydiving clubs to dog owners' associations, book groups to art collectives, lesbian social and cultural life have evolved dramatically from the smoke-filled bar and backyard potluck (two fine institutions that will, with luck, endure).

A small sampling of the groups and organizations that meet at the Lesbian and Gay Community Services Center in New York City offers a glimpse at the thriving eclecticism that is the lesbian social scene today:

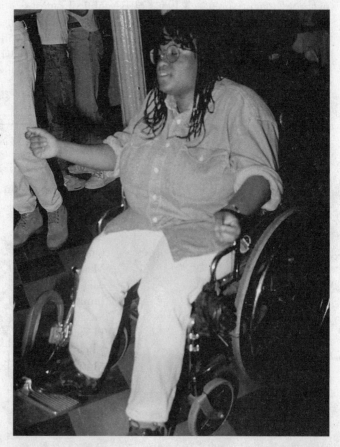

Dancing at a New York City Lesbian and Gay Community Services Center women's dance *(Copyright © 1993 by Micha Kwiatkowska)*

African Ancestral Lesbians United for Social Change

Art Group for Gay and Lesbian Artists

Bisexual Women of All Colors

Butch/Femme Society

Conference for Catholic Lesbians

Fat is a Lesbian Issue

Lesbian and Gay Firefighters

Gay and Lesbian Educators

Gay and Lesbian Italians

Gay and Lesbian Reading Group

Gejaro, Lesbian and Gay Esperanto Language Club

Irish Lesbian and Gay Organization

Las Buenas Amigas

Lavender Bytes—Lesbians in Computers

Lavender Light: The Black and People of All Colors Lesbian and Gay Gospel Choir

Lesbian Avengers

Meditation for Gays, Lesbians, and Bisexuals

Lesbian and Gay Naturalists of New York

Organization of Lesbian + Gay Architects + Designers

Radical Women

Scrabble-Players Club

Sirens Motorcycle Club

Social Activities for Lesbians

Southerners: Lesbians and Gay Men in New York

Support Group for Single Lesbians

Times Squares (square dancing group)

WHAM! Women's Health Action & Mobilization

Women Playwrights Collective

FEATURE

WHERE THE GRRLS ARE: A LESBIAN GUIDE TO THE INTERNET

BY JENNIFER L. COSTLEY (JLCOSTLEY@AOL.COM)

INTRODUCTION

When I first cruised the Net over ten years ago, the only place for lesbians to meet was a somewhat obscure news group called alt.motss (*motss* means *members of the same sex*). While motss news groups are still alive and well (242 at last count), the number of watering holes and way stations has multiplied enormously. Today, in addition to news groups and mailing lists, there are lesbian and gay forums on all of the major on-line services, gay and feminist Web pages, and many other points of interest to net-surfing lesbians.

The following is a brief introduction to some of these locations. The Net is a dynamic world; I have tried to provide some relatively stable Web sites that should provide links to the latest action. For up-to-date information on Net locations, you can also pick up *NetGuide Magazine* (at your local newsstand or contact 800/829-0421 or http://techweb.cmp.com/net). A practical, gay-friendly guide to exploring the Internet, each issue contains listings of sites by topic and useful articles on all aspects of Net culture.

A word of warning: Many Net sites are not moderated, and it is common for

Panel members at a celebration of butch-femme identities at the New York City Lesbian and Gay Community Services Center (Front row, from left: Joan Nestle, Val Tavai, Jewelle Gomez; back row, from left: Jill Harris, Lisa Winters, Sue Hyde) *(Copyright © 1990 by Morgan Gwenwald)*

Contingent at the 1992 Lesbian and Gay Pride March, New York City *(Photo by Harry Stevens)*

people to assume alternative identities while cruising forums and discussion groups (you may find yourself indulging in a fantasy alter ego as well). It is wise to assume that you may be engaged in a hot discussion with anyone—far-right fanatic or FBI agent—and not to discuss illegal activities or give your real identity.

ON-LINE SERVICES

On-line services such as Prodigy, America Online, and CompuServe are some of the easiest and most popular ways to get on-line. In addition, they provide access to the Internet through built-in Web browsers and gophers. Typical of these services is America Online, which has the "Gay and Lesbian Forum" (go to keyword LESBIAN). The Forum includes:

- "Heart to Heart": Meet someone special in the "Lesbian Personals" folders of this message board area.
- "Lambda Lounge": A live chat area, this lounge reminds me of a small-town gay bar. Mostly men, often crowded, but private rooms are sometimes available.
- "Resource Library": Articles on gay and lesbian legal and political topics are available for download. Where else can you find the complete text of the Colorado gay rights decision, or an article on how to set up a living trust?
- "Community Organizations": Local and national organizations have folders set up here. Since anyone can post, this area is a mixed lot of useful info and "does anyone know . . ." queries.

QUEER RESOURCES DIRECTORY (QRD)

(gopher english-server.hss.cmu.edu,select QUEER RESOURCES DIRECTORY or http://www.casti.com:80/QRD/ is the first place to look for lesbian information and current listings of Internet resources. The self-described "electronic research library specifically dedicated to sexual minorities" is also frequently found as a path to other home pages of interest.

NEWS GROUPS

Venerable but still going strong, news groups provide the most democratic form of access to the Net and content sometimes suffers as a result. Still active is USENET's soc.motss, a social forum for lesbians and gay men to discuss anything and everything. Lesbian-only news groups are few—an AOL search turned up only four—only soc.women.lesbian-and-bi is of more than topical interest. Avoid soc.women, unless you are interested in listening to straight women complain about men. Also avoid alt.feminism, unless you are interested in hearing women complain about each other. soc.feminism is moderated, making it tamer but more focused than some of the other women's forums. More interesting forums include alt.country/western, with ongoing discussion of Mary Chapin Carpenter (MCC here) and alt.homosexual, a more politically aware version of soc.motss.

GOPHERS

Gophers are essentially listings of available databases on remote Net sites. Some of the more interesting gophers include:

Women's Wire Gopher (gopher GOPHER.WWIRE.NET:8101): Women and politics, women's professional organizations, and more.

Women's Health Issues (gopher GOPHER.UIUC.EDU/11/UI/CSF/HEALTH/HEAINFO/WOMEN).

Feminist Studies (gopher english.hss.cmu.edu; select FEMINISM): Lots of links to other resources listed here, comprehensive coverage of the range of feminist studies today. Plus a terrific paper on deconstructing Madonna. How can you miss?

WEB SITES

The World Wide Web is a colorful, easily accessible on-line world in which each page, or location, can be linked to any other, making it easy to move freely through cyberspace. By clicking on the hyperlinks imbedded in the home pages at the center of the organization's (or individual's) Web site, you can go deeper or move sideways, or take a detour. Since all of the major on-line services now have Web browser access, the most difficult task for you is making sure you type all those http's and html's correctly. Here are some of my favorite lesbian-friendly home pages:

Women's Resources (http://sunsite.unc.edu/cheryb/women/wresources.html): Links to women's forums, Web sites, gophers, etc. (a women-oriented version of QRD)

Lesbian Homepage (http://www.best.com/~agoodloe/queer.html)

Women's Studies Database (http://info.umd.edu:86/educational_resources/academicresour cesbytopic/womensstudies): Politically correct grrl talk

Cybergrrl! (http://www.cybergrrl.com): One of my two favorite Web sites, Cybrgrrl! presents an open-ended adventure to the politically aware Net explorer: links to Breast Cancer Awareness, Webgrrls (home pages by women, surf with Cybergrrl, and more). Try it!

Virtual Sisterhood (http://www.igc.apc.org/vsister/vsister.html): Home page for Virtual Sisterhood, a global women's electronic support network

Geekgirl (http://www.next.com.au/spyfood/geekgirl/): My second favorite Web site, Geekgirl is a feminist cyber-magazine that provides news and articles on women in cyberspace.

FOR FURTHER READING ON LESBIAN CULTURE

Duberman, Martin, Martha Vicinus, and George Chauncey, eds. *Hidden from History: Reclaiming the Gay and Lesbian Past*. New American Library, 1989.

Faderman, Lillian. *Odd Girls and Twilight Lovers: A History of Lesbian Life in Twentieth-Century America*. Columbia University Press, 1991.

Gibbs, Liz, ed. *Daring to Dissent: Lesbian Culture from Margin to Mainstream*. Cassell, 1994.

Jay, Karla, ed. *Dyke Lives: From Growing Up to Growing Old, A Celebration of the Lesbian Experience*. BasicBooks, 1995.

Katz, Jonathan. *Gay American History*. Avon, 1976, 1992.

Kennedy, Elizabeth Lapovsky, and Madeline D. Davis. *Boots of Leather, Slippers of Gold: A History of a Lesbian Community*. Routledge, 1993.

Nestle, Joan, ed. *The Persistent Desire: A Femme-Butch Reader*. Alyson Publications, 1992.

Ramos, Juanita, ed. *Companeras: Latina Lesbians: An Anthology*. Routledge, 1994.

Smith, Barbara, ed. *Home Girls: A Black Feminist Anthology*. Kitchen Table: Women of Color Press, 1983.

Stein, Arlene, ed. *Sisters, Sexperts, Queers: Beyond the Lesbian Nation*. Plume, 1993.

Trujillo, Carla, ed. *Chicana Lesbians: The Girls Our Mothers Warned Us About*. Third Woman Press, 1991.

---

5. LESBIANS AND EDUCATION

You do not have to explain about sex for children to understand that two people can love each other. Young children understand mothers' and fathers' love for each other without knowing about heterosexual sex. Yes, two men or two women can love each other and want to live together. They also sometimes raise children together.

> —Children of the Rainbow activist, as quoted in "Sexuality, Multicultural Education, and the New York City Public Schools," *Radical Teacher*, no. 45, winter 1994, p. 15

The institution of education offers both hope and disappointment for lesbian students and teachers. At the college and university level, great strides have been made. Lesbian and gay studies courses have been appearing in college catalogs, and the first lesbian and gay studies conference took place at Yale University in 1989. Subsequent conferences have been held at Harvard, Rutgers/Princeton, and most recently at the University of Iowa. In both classes and at conferences, discussion is no longer dominated by coming out, but has evolved into a truly interdisciplinary dialogue.

University presses such as Minnesota, Duke, NYU, Columbia, and Temple now publish a variety of lesbian and gay scholarly titles. The Center for Lesbian and Gay

Studies (CLAGS) at the City University of New York, the first institution of its kind in the country, awards research grants to both affiliated and independent scholars.

Still, compared to other academic fields, there is very little funding for students and professors working in the area of lesbian and gay studies. There is also evidence that some funding agencies are biased against lesbian and gay research proposals. Although there have been more job openings in academia recently for queer scholars, they have mostly been in the areas of English and women's studies, departments that are already glutted with qualified candidates, and rarely are positions advertised in history or the social sciences.

At the grade school and high school level, lesbian and gay studies are virtually nonexistent. Conservative school districts (see the story of New York's Rainbow Curriculum on page 183) stifle efforts to integrate lesbian and gay experience into the curriculum. Add to that the fact that it is even harder for lesbian and gay teachers to come out in many schools for fear of losing their jobs. The prevailing cultural belief that homosexuality is a perversion convinces misinformed parents that lesbian and gay teachers might sexually abuse their children or recruit them to their lifestyle.

To fill in the gaps, lesbians and gay men have created such institutions as the Harvey Milk High School for lesbian and gay high school students and professional organizations such as the Lesbian and Gay Teachers Association (LGTA) in New York. Unfortunately, though LGTA estimates that there are probably 5,000 lesbian and gay teachers in the city, their current membership is only 200 teachers.

Time Line of Firsts

1956: ONE Institute in Los Angeles was founded as an educational institute. In 1981, it became the first gay graduate school when it was recognized as such by the state of California. It offers a Ph.D. in homophile studies and has so far awarded two, as well as four master's degrees and four honorary doctorates.

1966: The Student Homophile League at Columbia University was founded by a bisexual undergraduate, Robert A. Martin, making it the first (and eventually the oldest) gay campus organization. Its first formal program was held on October 28, 1966. The group was then officially recognized as a campus organization on April 19, 1967. Martin, now known as Stephen Donaldson, went on to help establish chapters at New York University (chaired by Rita Mae Brown) and Cornell (chaired by Gerald Moldenhauer). The Columbia group, though having gone through many name changes, is still going.

1969: The first college-level homosexual dance was the First NYC All-College Gay Mixer, sponsored by the New York University and Columbia University chapters of the Student Homophile League. The dance was held in the parish hall of the Church of the Holy Apostles and drew several hundred people.

• The Supreme Court of California ruled in the case of *Morrison v. State Board of Education* that the state could not revoke the teaching license of a homosexual teacher unless it could demonstrate unfitness to teach with factual evidence rather than with a presumption of immorality.

1970: The first gay studies course was taught at the University of Nebraska. It was an interdisciplinary course through the anthropology, sociology, and English departments, and was taught by Louis Compton. The course focused on the civil rights of homosexuals and included a critique of the sickness theory.

1972: The District of Columbia school board, at the urging of the local Gay Activists Alliance, enacted a resolution prohibiting discrimination in any aspect of the D.C. school system's hiring practices and thus became the first school board to ban antigay discrimination.

1973: George Washington High School in Manhattan and the Bronx High School of Science became the first high schools to officially recognize gay student groups. Both groups were formed after representatives from the Gay Activists Alliance's Agitprop Committee spoke at classes and assemblies at each school.

1974: Lavender U: A University for Gay Women and Gay Men, offered its first classes in San Francisco. Classes were taught out of private homes or public facilities and had titles like "Gay Greek Literature I and II," "The Bath Experience," "Opera Appreciation," and "A Rose Is a Rose Is a Rose." Founded by seven gay men and two lesbians, Lavender U is considered the first gay university and had an enrollment of about 200 people from its first catalogue.

   • The National Education Association, the nation's largest organization of public school employees, added "sexual orientation" to its resolution on nondiscriminatory personnel policies and practices that it urges its members' employers to follow.

1977: Santa Barbara, California, became the first school district to ban discrimination against gay students. The board of education voted to broaden its policy of nondiscrimination against teachers and other gay school employees to include gay students while also establishing a grievance procedure for handling cases of discrimination against employees or students.

1982: Bryton High, in Philadelphia, was founded as the first gay high school. The school was started for gay teens as an alternative to the public high school system. The class of 1983, its first graduates, consisted of three male students and one female.

1988: Lambda Delta Lambda won official recognition from the University of California, Los Angeles, making it the first lesbian sorority.

1990: The first college ban on ROTC in protest of the military's antigay policies was approved at Pitzer College in Claremont, California.

1991: The Center for Lesbian and Gay Studies (CLAGS) under the direction of historian Martin Duberman at the City University of New York became the first university-affiliated research center in the United States devoted exclusively to the study of gay and lesbian subjects.

FACTS AND STATISTICS

A survey of Americans in 1993 found that 52 percent were opposed to teaching about lesbian and gay orientation in sex education classes in public schools.

Since 1982, more than 1,600 school districts have adopted sex education curricula that presents sexual abstinence and monogamy within heterosexual marriage as the only sexual choices available to teenagers.

In a psychological test that predicts the success of teachers in the classroom, which was administered to seventy-four gay and lesbian and sixty-six heterosexual teachers in 1990, there were no differences in scores between the two groups.

Eight out of ten prospective teachers and nearly two-thirds of guidance counselors expressed negative feelings about homosexuality and about lesbians and gay men, said a study conducted by the South Carolina Guidance Counselors' association in 1987.

Citizens for Excellence in Education, a right-wing group based in Costa Mesa, California, says that more than two thousand of its members have been elected to school boards across the United States.

Forty-five percent of gay males and 20 percent of lesbians experience physical or verbal assault in high school. Twenty-eight percent of these young people feel forced to drop out of school due to harassment problems based on sexual orientation.

In 1988, there were no gay/straight school alliances in private high schools. By 1993, at least sixteen independent schools had such alliances, and seventeen had at least one openly gay teacher.

As of 1993, there were more than one hundred lesbian and gay support groups in high schools across the nation.

As of January 1992, 15 U.S. colleges and universities had lesbian/gay/bisexual task forces or offices, 248 have nondiscrimination policies that include sexual orientation, and at least 43 offer some sort of lesbian, gay, and bisexual courses.

LESBIAN AND GAY EDUCATION BIBLIOGRAPHY

Bull, Chris. "Why Johnny Can't Learn About Condoms: How the Religious Right Censors Sex Education across the U.S.," *The Advocate*, December 15, 1992.

Dorning, Mike. "Schools' Support Groups Helping Gay Teens to Cope," *Chicago Tribune*, November 30, 1993.

"Factfile: Lesbian, Gay, and Bisexual Youth." Hetrick-Martin Institute, 1992 and 1993.

Garber, Linda, ed. *Tilting the Tower*. Routledge, 1994.

Haggerty, George, and Bonnie Zimmerman, eds. *Professions of Desire*. The Modern Language Association of America, 1990.

Harbeck, Karen M., ed. *Coming Out of the Classroom Closet: Gay and Lesbian Students, Teachers and Curricula*. Harrington Park, 1992.

Hooks, Bell. *Teaching to Transgress*. Routledge, 1994.

Jennings, Kevin, ed. *Becoming Visible: A Reader in Lesbian and Gay History for High School and College Students*. Alyson, 1994.

Khayatt, Madiha Didi. *Lesbian Teachers: An Invisible Presence*. State University of New York Press, 1992.

Lesbian/Gay/Queer Studies issue. *Radical Teacher*, no. 45, winter 1994.

Levine, David, and Robert Lowe. *Rethinking Schools: An Agenda for Change*. The New Press, 1995.

McConnell-Celi, Sue. *Twenty-First Century Challenge: Lesbians and Gays in Education: Bridging the Gap*. Lavender Crystal Press, 1993.

McLaughlin, Daniel, and William G. Tierney, eds. *Naming the Silenced Lives: Personal Narratives and the Process of Educational Change*. Routledge, 1992.

Malinowitz, Harriet. *Textual Orientations: Lesbian and Gay Students and the Making of Discourse Communities*. Boynton/Cook, 1995.

Martin, M. "Gay, Lesbian, and Heterosexual Teachers: Acceptance of Self, Acceptance of Others," unpublished report, 1990.

Shapiro, Joseph, et al., "Straight Talk about Gays," *U.S. News and World Report*, July 5, 1993.

Singer, Bennet L., and David Deschamps, eds. *Gay and Lesbian Stats*. The New Press, 1994.

Woog, Dan. *School's Out: The Impact of Gay and Lesbian Issues on America's Schools*. Alyson, 1995.

Yamaguchi Fletcher, Lynne. *The First Gay Pope and Other Records*. Alyson, 1992.

FIRST ANNUAL LESBIAN, GAY, AND BISEXUAL HISTORY MONTH ESSAY AND VISUAL ARTS COMPETITIONS

Sponsored by the Gay, Lesbian, and Straight Teachers Network (GLSTN), the first Lesbian, Gay, and Bisexual History Month Essay and Visual Arts Competitions were held in the spring of 1995, to focus young people's attention on the contributions of lesbians, gay men, and bisexuals to the development of the United States. Open to youth age twenty-two and under, the essay competition asked participants to address—in 750 words or less—the subject, "Why it's important to know lesbian, gay, and bisexual history." The visual arts competition for the same age group requested entries of logos for Lesbian, Gay, and Bisexual History Month, suitable for use on T-shirts and posters. The winner in each category received a $250 prize.

For information on the 1996 competition, write to: Lesbian, Gay, and Bisexual History Month Competition, c/o Gay, Lesbian, and Straight Teachers Network, Box 390526, Cambridge, MA 02139-0006. Or send E-mail requests to: GLSTN@aol.com.

GRANTS AVAILABLE TO LESBIAN STUDENTS

ASTRAEA NATIONAL LESBIAN ACTION FOUNDATION

Astraea, the first nationwide lesbian foundation, was begun in 1977 by a multiracial and multicultural group of feminist activists to empower women and girls through financial and organizational support. Astraea makes grants and awards to community organizations, film/video projects, and emerging lesbian writers. Astraea provides technical assistance to community organizations and supports the development of lesbian leadership and activism.

MARGOT KARLE SCHOLARSHIP

Margot Karle was an activist for social and political justice. As a lesbian attorney and the president of Lambda Legal Defense and Education Fund, Margot Karle made enormous contributions to the struggle for human rights and social justice.

The Astraea Foundation makes the Margot Karle Scholarship available to full-time students in the City University of New York undergraduate system who have demonstrated both financial need and a high degree of community involvement.

Two scholarships are awarded each year. All awards are for one academic year. Scholarship recipients may not reapply for renewal.

For more information contact: Astraea National Lesbian Action Foundation, 116 E. 16th Street, 7th Floor, New York, NY 10003.

Application deadlines are August 15 and December 15.

AN UNCOMMON LEGACY FOUNDATION, INC.

The mission of Legacy is to provide financial support for projects that address the social, cultural, and educational needs of lesbians as well as promote the civil rights and well-being of all lesbians in today's society and future generations.

Each year, Legacy will reach out to the educational community for outstanding lesbian students to be the recipients of $1,000 grants. Applicants must be undergraduate or graduate students of an accredited college or university. Consideration will be given to the following factors: academic performance, honors, personal/financial hardship, and especially, service to the lesbian/gay community.

For more information contact: Scholarship Committee, Legacy Foundation, 150 West 26th Street, Suite 503, New York, NY 10001; Phone: 212/366-6507; Fax: 212/366-6509.

Application deadline is May 1.

NEW YORK CITY LESBIAN AND GAY COMMUNITY SERVICES CENTER

PAUL RAPOPORT MEMORIAL SCHOLARSHIP

The scholarship honors the memory of Paul Rapoport, a founder of the Lesbian and Gay Community Services Center, NYC. His commitment to educational achievement and his efforts to encourage lesbian and gay youth to obtain a higher education is acknowledged in the awarding of these scholarships every year during Lesbian and Gay Pride Month.

Paul Rapoport received his education at Cornell University, A.B., LL.B. and New York University, LL.M.—Taxation. The students of these institutions are especially encouraged to apply.

The scholarship, funded by the Paul Rapoport Foundation, is awarded at the center's annual garden party in June, enabling lesbian and gay students to begin or continue their college and graduate school studies.

For more information, call the New York Lesbian and Gay Community Services Center (212/620-7310) or write: The Lesbian and Gay Community Services Center, re: Paul Rapoport Memorial Scholarship, 208 West 13th Street, New York, NY 10011.

Application deadline is April 21.

CENTER FOR LESBIAN AND GAY STUDIES (CLAGS)

ROCKEFELLER RESIDENCY FELLOWSHIP IN THE HUMANITIES

Amount: Fellows will receive $35,000, plus a $2,000 travel and relocation stipend for residency from September 1 to June 1.

Eligibility: Open to all academic scholars in the humanities and related areas who have shown a genuine commitment to lesbian and gay studies. Activists, junior faculty, and independant scholars are especially encouraged to apply. *Dissertation proposals will not be considered.*

Deadline is February 15.

1993–1994 winners: Carra Leah Hood and Charles I. Nero
1994–1995 winners: Allan Berube and Janice Irvine

KEN DAWSON AWARD

Amount: $5,000.

Eligibilty: Anyone working in the field of gay and lesbian history. Preference will be given to proposals in the media of print. No university affiliation is required.

Deadline is March 15.

1994 winner: Jonathan Ned Katz

CONSTANCE JORDAN AWARD

Amount: One $4,000 award per year for each of the academic years 1995–1996, 1996–1997, and 1997–1998. The winner of the first year may reapply once.

Eligibility: CUNY doctoral students working on the topic of gay and lesbian literary studies with historical content.

Deadline is May 1.

CUNY STUDENT PAPER AWARDS

Amount: First prize: $250; second prize: $150.

Eligibility: CUNY graduate students on master's or doctoral levels with papers on a topic related to lesbian and gay studies in any academic discipline or professional program.

Deadline is May 15.

1994 Winners: Ira Elliott and Tracy Morgan

OPEN MEADOWS FOUNDATION AWARD

Amount: A one-time award of $2,000 for work in lesbian scholarship.

Eligibility: Restricted to unaffiliated scholars; students working on a thesis toward an advancing degree are not eligible.

Deadline is May 15.

SCHOLARLY GRANTS-IN-AID

CUNY graduate students may apply to CLAGS for up to $500 to assist in their work in lesbian and gay studies. The fund may be used to cover such expenses as travel to libraries, conferences, or professional society meetings, and costs of translations or photocopying.

Application deadlines are October 15 for the fall semester and March 1 for the spring semester. Emergency situations will be considered between the two dates.

An application consists of:

1. Purpose of request
2. Time, date, and place
3. Itemized budget
4. Statement of how this request relates to the individual's academic/career plans

For more information on any of these grants or for application forms, call the CLAGS office at 212/642-2924 or write: Center for Lesbian and Gay Studies, The Graduate School and University Center of the City of New York, 33 West 42nd Street, Room 404N, New York, NY 10036-8099.

PROFILE

Center for Lesbian and Gay Studies

The Center for Lesbian and Gay Studies (CLAGS) was formally established in April 1991, after five years of planning, at the Graduate School of the City University of New York. CLAGS is the first university-affiliated research center in the United States devoted exclusively to the study of gay and lesbian subjects. From the start, CLAGS has operated under the principles of gender parity, ethnic and racial diversity, and the participation of unaffiliated scholars.

CLAGS, its staff, scholars, and students gather, disseminate, and encourage research on the lives of gay men and lesbians from multicultural, multiracial, and feminist perspectives.

CLAGS also serves as a national clearinghouse for scholarly research through the publication of a biannual newsletter and through a nationwide directory of lesbian and gay scholars.

CLAGS offers financial support for research and awards for outstanding work in the field, including the first Rockefeller Humanities Fellowships ever given to a gay or lesbian institution, and the David R. Kessler endowed lectureship for a noteworthy contribution to gay and lesbian life.

CLAGS has begun to examine curriculum reform at all grade levels and is preparing pilot studies syllabi for those seeking help in offering gay and lesbian courses. Assistance has been given in response to inquiries from all over the United States, as well as from China, New Zealand, Europe, and Latin America.

CLAGS offers symposia, conferences, and regular public programs on issues of scholarly and general interest such "AIDS and Public Policy," "The Brain and Homosexuality," "Latin American Perspectives on Homosexuality," "Homa/Economics: Market and Community in Lesbian and Gay Life," "Sissies and Tomboys," and "Black Nations/Queer Nations?"

CLAGS is under the direction of Distinguished Professor of History Martin Duberman.

SOURCE: Preface of CLAGS's *Directory of Lesbian and Gay Studies. Reprinted with permission.*

FEATURE

The Rainbow Curriculum

In New York City in 1989, a plan to introduce non-European, women's, and gay and lesbian history and culture into every stage of education, from kindergarten through high school, was mandated by the central Board of Education. This multicultural curriculum, specifically the first-grade portion, "Children of the Rainbow," caused an uproar with local school board conservatives and made New York the first city with a nonwhite majority targeted by the religious right. The organizers against the Rainbow Curriculum used the empowerment of parents of color as a goal that could only be reached by disempowering gays and lesbians throughout the school system. This battle hit its peak in spring of 1993, just before the school board elections.

"Through old-fashioned, grass roots organizing and savvy media work, they [the religious right] made homophobia more socially acceptable in the city where the contemporary gay and lesbian movement began," wrote Donna Minkowitz in her *Nation* article, "Wrong Side of the Rainbow."

Mary Cummins, president of the Queens School Board 24, said, "I will not demean our legitimate minorities, such as blacks, Hispanics and Asians, by lumping them together with homosexuals in that curriculum." She was responsible for kicking off the fight against the multicultural curriculum by refusing to have it taught in her school district.

According to Minkowitz, "Many in the media have portrayed the anti-Rainbow movement as a spontaneous outpouring of parental outrage. In reality, it was anything but spontaneous. For over a year, conservative evangelicals and Catholics organized in Latino, white, and a few African-American neighborhoods, telling parents that the gay-inclusive curriculum was a plot by a 'Manhattan elite' of gays and lesbians to gain control of schools so they could 'recruit' and 'brainwash' children into becoming gay," as anti-Rainbow organizer Dolores Ayling put it.

Religious right organizers tried to tie together race and sexuality in order to pit one against the other. Leaflets said things like, "The Rainbow program is not a program against racial discrimination, it has nothing to do with color, it has to do with homosexuals and lesbians." But the Rainbow Curriculum had plenty to do with race. The majority of the first-grade plan teaches children about the different holidays, art forms, and histories of people of various ethnic backgrounds. In a curriculum that totals over four hundred pages, references to gay and lesbian families appear on only three pages. The children's books, *Heather Has Two Mommies* and *Daddy's Roommate*, which were widely criticized, appeared only on a suggested reading list for teachers and were not part of the mandated curriculum.

Some activists suspected that the right's obsessive focus on those three pages and on the books stemmed from a desire to derail the entire multicultural curriculum, said Minkowitz. Opponents of the Rainbow Curriculum implied that lessons depicting lesbian and gay families are inherently dirty and corrupting. While local school boards, especially District 24, were working hard to dismantle the Rainbow Curriculum, they were neglecting some fundamental problems within their own districts. The right needed people of color to defeat the multicultural plan, so they picked battlegrounds, or school districts, where large populations of working-class and poor people of color coexisted with mostly white communities of lesbians and gay men and other progressives. This backfired somewhat on the religious right, and there is evidence to show that lesbians and gay men in the three battleground districts voted in higher numbers and greater unity in this 1993 school board election than they had in any previous New York election.

In numerical terms, the election proved to be a win for gays and progressives, with openly lesbian and gay candidates being the leading vote-getters in the most heavily contested districts. But for the Rainbow Curriculum, it is another story. Recently, the curriculum was finally dismantled, and all references to homosexuality were removed.

SOURCE: The information from this section was taken primarily from Donna Minkowitz's article, "Wrong Side of the Rainbow: The Religious Right Hits N.Y.C.," in the June 28, 1993, issue of *The Nation*, and has been quoted at length with her permission.

PROFILE

Linda Levy

Linda Levy has spent a lifetime in the New York City public school system. Not only did she attend public schools from kindergarten through twelfth grade, she has taught in them for the past thirty-two years. Linda is fifty-two years old and has lived most of her life in New York City, only recently moving upstate to the Hudson Valley. Health and physical education are what Linda has taught "pretty consistently" in both junior high and high schools in Queens, Brooklyn, and the Bronx.

Linda has been at her present school in the Bronx for eight years. "I'm in a school now which is a member of the Coalition of Essential Schools, which are moving more and more towards being generalists. So while I still teach some specific physical education stuff like swimming and Project Adventure, I'm also in the classroom most of the time, dealing with students on all subject areas." Linda teaches with a partner teacher, and they are responsible for about forty high school students all day, every day. Their style of teaching is to encourage students to use their minds fully, instead of learning by rote memorization.

"I am completely out at school," says Linda. "I didn't come out until I was thirty, and I was married for ten years before that. I was going through huge changes in my life. I got divorced, and moved myself and my three young children in with my lover and her three children." But Linda says that once she was out to herself, she came out in all other areas of her life, too. She and her lover, Ilene Weidler, have been together for two and a half years.

"What I do with school [is] I establish myself first as a teacher and then come out in some appropriate way. Usually it is within the curriculum, and since I teach health and human sexuality, there are plenty opportunities to address the subject.

"The first time I came out was back in 1978. I was on television with my lover on a CBS program called 'Eye On . . . Lesbians Without Rights.'" First, Linda agreed to be on the program, and then went to her principal with her decision. The principal worried about parental response, but Linda reminded her that the issue was not about her sexuality, but about being a good teacher.

After coming out on television, Linda came out to her students in casual conversations and in the classroom. Eventually, on the first day of any school year, she would introduce herself to her students and mention her partner. "That way, they get to deal with the issue right off . . . and be comfortable with each other."

Linda and her lover go to school events together, including the prom. "Everything is much more open than twenty years ago." When she talks to her students about her sexuality, the kinds of questions they ask are: "How do your kids feel?"; "How did your family react?"; and "Are you afraid you are going to lose your job?". Linda says, "The kids are very concerned about job issues. They don't realize the extent of discrimination. They don't realize that gay people are losing their jobs for being gay in areas of the country not as liberal as New York.

After recently applying for a teaching job in Arizona, Linda shared with her students the fact that, if she got the job, she probably wouldn't be able to be as out as a lesbian, if at all. "They just couldn't understand. The kids said that they would have to go over to Arizona and 'straighten them out.'"

The classes at Linda's school are heterogeneous: all ages, all learning levels, and all abilities. "It is a school built upon respect. The students are predominantly African-American and Latino, but there is a mix within that. There is no fighting, as in other schools, like Puerto Rican versus Dominican versus West Indian. In my small school, the whole culture of the school is about diversity and acceptance. I have no problem whatsoever being out here. The most I've ever heard any teacher saying is that they still have some questions about it." As far the school administration and policy is concerned, they will not allow negative statements to be made about an individual or group of people.

"During the controversy over the Children of the Rainbow curriculum, we would have great conversations among the students. No matter how they felt about homosexuality, they would have varying opinions about whether it should be mentioned or taught in terms of family issues to first graders. I was able to point out to them that there are lots of kids with gay parents—just look at my kids—and why shouldn't their families be represented? We are not talking about sex, we're talking about family composition." There are kids in Linda's class who have gay parents, but they are only out to her, not publicly.

"I feel that the homophobia has always been in the school system, but it was having to confront it in the Rainbow Curriculum that brought it out into the open. It became virulent. You could see how much of an issue it really is. For many teachers homosexuality wasn't a problem if they didn't have to address it; once it was going to have to be taught, the real negativity came out. It really made people have to take a stance."

Since she is out at school, do all the gay kids on campus flock to Linda's door? "I certainly have had a series of students coming to me with questions like 'How do you know who you are?' Mostly girls tend to come to me. Sometimes they will come back after they have finished school and talk about being gay. Usually they will say that they knew about me and it was helpful having me around, but they couldn't talk about it at the time. The guys tend to find the gay guys in school, even though they may not be out. Sometimes kids will come and say, 'Let's get together a group,' and want me to help. I say, 'Well, you organize it and I'll be behind you,' but nothing has ever really come to fruition. Maybe they are just too unsure or not quite ready; I really leave it up to them.

"I've been disappointed by that, but it's not my job to push it. They have me to talk to, and come to for literature to find out where they can go." Linda doesn't hand out literature about being gay in class; she wants it to be there without forcing it on anyone. "I'm not interested in being accused by anybody of pushing something on the kids."

Also an activist, Linda has been a part of Lesbian and Gay Teachers Association for almost twenty years. LGTA is "a small organization with a loud voice," which started as a support group in 1974. Mark Rubin and Meryl Friedman put a notice in the *Village Voice* that attracted almost 40 people to their first meeting. Two decades later, there are approximately 200 members, which bespeaks how closeted teachers still are. LGTA estimates that there are a minimum of at least 5000 lesbian and gay teachers in New York City alone. It wasn't long before the group became active with the teachers' unions and the Board of Education to get their causes heard. The union has always been supportive of lesbians and gay men as teachers, but in terms of issues with curriculum, union backing has not been so strong.

Linda was busy in LGTA during the suit for domestic partnership benefits against the Board of Education, but now that she has moved away from the city, she's slowing down a bit on the activist front. She has been busy doing a lot within her school, attending educational conferences, and, with Ilene, making a home and friends in their new area, while also thinking about leaving city life altogether. But, she says, "I will not have a job where I can't be out, especially as a teacher. Staying in the closet is a barrier between me and my kids and my colleagues."

PROFILE

Vera Miao

Vera Miao just finished her sophomore year at Barnard, the women's college of Columbia University, in New York City. And what a full year it was. At nineteen, she is not only one of the founding members of the student organization Queers of Color, she is also involved in at least five other political groups, works in the Barnard Women's Studies Department, and at the New York City Lesbian and Gay Community Services Center. If you think this sounds like a full plate, she also has edited her own magazine, attended many Queer Studies conferences, gets arrested on occasion, and manages to fit a full-time class schedule in there somewhere while maintaining a 3.9 grade point average.

Born in Guam, Vera spent the eleven years before college living with her parents and older brother in Long Island while making frequent forays into Manhattan. Her family is the only area of her life where she is not out. Vera came out to herself freshman year of college. "Before I was out to myself, people had thought that I was queer." She got together with a woman she met at school: "In comparison to other coming out narratives, mine was relatively painless."

"College definitely provided the right environment," says Vera about discovering her sexuality, "being away from home was a catalyst. The distinction between home and college isn't necessarily het to homo, it was like asexual/desexual to sexual. I always knew that I wanted to go to a women's college, but I specifically chose Barnard because it wasn't isolated."

Though Vera didn't really identify herself as a feminist before college, "I really solidified a specific set of politics once I got to college. I took a lot of Women's Studies courses. I don't know if I would slap on the label of Women's Studies to what I would specialize in, but to a certain extent it is a useful tool because it is really interdisciplinary. Women's Studies can function with its hands in Queer Studies, Cultural Studies, social theory, post-colonialism.

"At Columbia and Barnard, there is no possibility to either major or minor in Queer Studies. Even though this is New York City, Columbia is an incredibly conservative, white male institution." Women's Studies is Vera's major, with a concentration in Asian Studies. Another field of study in which there are no available degrees is Asian-American studies. "There is no Asian-American studies program, which has been an ongoing battle at Columbia for several years." Columbia isn't the only school where that battle is taking place. "All over the country right now students are demanding Asian-American studies be included: at Northwestern students went on a hunger strike, at Princeton students occupied the office of the university's president.

"Women's studies has provided so much for me. At Barnard and Columbia, Women's Studies has an independent department, but teachers come from their area of expertise. Since Women's Studies doesn't get a lot of money, the departments are usually very small and have only a few specific faculty." As far as what kind of Lesbian and Gay Studies courses are available at Columbia/Barnard, Vera says there aren't that many. Another problem is that there are only two out lesbian professors on campus, one at Columbia and one at Barnard.

As a part of Queers of Color, Vera has helped organize a number of events. Queers of Color was conceptualized during spring semester 1993, but it didn't function as an organization until fall 1994, and was officially sanctioned as a campus group in spring 1995. The group's members are both undergraduate and graduate students from Columbia and Barnard. The general meetings and planning sessions are attended by about thirty members, but their events are attended by many more. Because they hand out a lot of flyers, Vera says that they "always get this really wide spectrum of different people."

Queers of Color have organized a two-night film festival, which included films and appearances by Stephen Winter, Catherine Saalfield, and Jacqueline Woodson. Another event that was a success was when Prathiba Parmar flew in from London to speak and screen a short film she had done. Other speakers this past semester included Judith Halberstam, Ricki Anne Wilchins, José Muños, and Richard Fung. Queers of Color networks with graduate groups like Asian-American Graduates Association and the Lesbian and Gay Studies Group.

Vera was coeditor of a school-based queer magazine called *Token*, and was also involved in another recently formed group, API-PAC (Asian Pacific Islanders Political Action Committee). It is a noncollege-based coalitional group of different New York Asian/Pacific Islander activists and organizations. API-PAC was formed in direct response to the Contract "On" America (as Vera likes to call it), and how it will affect Asian-American people.

In spring 1995, Vera was arrested along with 184 other people at a demonstration protesting police brutality and anti-Asian violence. "April 25 was the Day of Unanimous Protest that had been planned for about five months. In conjunction with four advertised protests, there were four covert civil disobediences that were planned that day. I was a part of the one led primarily by the Committee Against Anti-Asian Violence (CAAV). The National Congress for Puerto Rican Rights joined up, and we blocked the entrance to the Manhattan Bridge during rush-hour traffic. That day, the four different civil disobediences blocked two bridges and two tunnels during rush-hour traffic, all within a twenty-minute window of each other. The official report said that we caused gridlock in New York for over an hour."

Conferences are another passion in Vera's life. "I love conferences. I went to the sixth annual North American Queer Studies Conference in Iowa City, Iowa, and panel hopped." To go, Vera petitioned groups to get help and "worked my ass off." Though she had a good time and heard some interesting things, "the conference was problematic as all conferences are." Some of those problems stem from the lack of diversity among not just the panelists, but the conference-goers as well. "It was really white in terms of conference-goers, but who can have the money to fly out to Iowa? Also a lot of people of color don't go because they know what the situation will be like. Queer Studies, as it becomes institutionalized and commodified, is quickly very much a white canon, there is this tension going on in a big way all the time. Overall, it was interesting, and I met really good people, mostly Asian-Americans from the West Coast."

She has also attended several conferences at the Center for Lesbian and Gay Studies (CLAGS) in New York, including "Black Nations/Queer Nations" and "Sissies and Tomboys." "Conferences have been, more so than not, valuable to me."

"My long-term goal is to finish up undergrad work, go to grad school, get my Ph.D., and end up as a professor." She is thinking about venturing to the West Coast after finishing school at Barnard.

PROFILE

Harvey Milk School

The Harvey Milk School is an alternative public high school established in 1985 in a unique collaboration between the Hetrick-Martin Institute (HMI) and the New York City Public Schools. The school was founded because the staff of HMI, a social service agency for lesbian, gay, and bisexual youth, recognized that these young people often met with violence and intolerance in school, and that many had dropped out. Some, under the immense pressure of hiding their real identities, leave both school and home. In addition, the children of gay or lesbian parents also suffer painful harassment.

The Hetrick-Martin Institute was founded in 1979 in response to the difficulties that lesbian, gay, and bisexual youth experience as they are growing up. After serving only a handful of people in the beginning, HMI now serves at least 1,500 clients. When the institute's social workers first determined that many of their clients were not going to school, they sought to bring these disaffected young people back into the school system. Working with the New York City Public Schools, they employed a school system policy that provides for a teacher to be assigned to any social agency with at least twenty-two clients who are not attending school. Today, the Harvey Milk School reopens the door to school for lesbian and gay youth, and offers them an education in an environment that is safe and supportive. Whenever possible, Harvey Milk School students are mainstreamed back into their community high schools.

The Harvey Milk School enrolls a maximum of thirty youth per year and is one of twenty-five alternative city high school programs. The students range in age from fourteen to twenty-one. Currently, 80 percent of the students are African-American and Latino.

Young people enter the school with varying backgrounds. Individualized programs are developed to enable students to meet graduation requirements and to take the New York State Regents examination.

Group classes such as Literature, Math for Living, Art, Law, and Health take place two periods per day, and for other subjects, students study independently and at their own pace with the assistance of their teachers.

Because of the stigmatism they face, lesbian, gay, and bisexual youth confront many complicated issues that make adolescence a particularly difficult time. Students of the Harvey Milk School have access to the institute's extensive counseling services to help them address emotional concerns as well as academic issues. Students are also encouraged to participate in several other programs at the institute.

HMI's after-school Drop-In Center is a safe place for lesbian, gay, and bisexual youth to socialize and participate in arts and educational activities. Through peer educator training and a mentoring program, the institute helps youth reach their academic and career goals in a place where they can be open about who they are. HIV/AIDS prevention education is provided in all of the institute's programs. Through direct service, education, and advocacy, the Hetrick-Martin Institute is committed to creating a world where lesbian, gay, and bisexual youth can grow successfully into adulthood and find understanding and respect from the larger society.

For more information on the Hetrick-Martin Institute and the Harvey Milk School, call 212/674-2400; TTY: 212/674-8695; or write: Hetrick-Martin Institute, 2 Astor Place, New York, NY 10003-6998.

SOURCE: "The Harvey Milk School: A Program of the HMI and the New York City Board of Ed"

A SHORT READING COURSE

When Lesbian and Gay Studies first emerged, works in and pertaining to the field could have been contained in a rather brief bibliography. Today, however, it would be impossible to concisely list the texts and essays available to anyone interested in the field. An unprecedented outpouring of new work has coincided with the increasing acceptance of Lesbian and Gay Studies. Listed below are a few popular texts under traditional liberal arts headings. There are, of course, many other relevant works; the bibliographies in those mentioned here should be useful for further suggestions. Also, the specific areas of study are not absolute, as the field itself tends to be interdisciplinary. The canon is not by any means fixed, nor should it be, for new and exciting work is appearing all the time.

GENERAL ANTHOLOGIES

Abelove, Henry, Michele Aina Barale, and David Halperin, eds. *The Lesbian and Gay Studies Reader.* Routledge, 1993.

Fuss, Diana, ed. *Inside/Out.* Routledge, 1991.

Moraga, Cherríe, and Gloria Anzaldua, eds. *This Bridge Called My Back: Writings by Radical Women of Color.* Persephone Press, 1981; reprinted by Kitchen Table: Women of Color Press.

HISTORY

Duberman, Martin, Martha Vicinus, and George Chauncey, eds. *Hidden from History.* Meridian, 1989.

Faderman, Lillian. *Odd Girls and Twilight Lovers: A History of Lesbian Life in Twentieth-Century America.* Columbia University Press, 1991.

Katz, Jonathan Ned, and Thomas Y. Crowell. *Gay American History.* 1976; revised, 1992.

LITERATURE

Dollimore, Jonathan. *Sexual Dissidence.* Clarendon Press, 1991.

Haggerty, George, and Bonnie Zimmerman, eds. *Professions of Desire.* MLA, 1995.

McKinley, Catherine E., and L. Joyce Delaney, eds. *Afrekete: An Anthology of Black Lesbian Writing.* Anchor, 1995.

Sedgwick, Eve Kosofsky. *Epistemology of the Closet.* University of California Press, 1990.

POLITICS/CULTURE

Beam, Joseph, ed. *In the Life.* Alyson, 1986.

Browning, Frank. *The Culture of Desire: Paradox and Perversity in Gay Lives Today.* Crown, 1993.

Jay, Karla, and Allen Young, eds. *Out of the Closets: Voices of Gay Liberation.* New York University Press, 1972; revised, 1992.

Nestle, Joan, ed. *The Persistent Desire: A Femme-Butch Reader.* Alyson, 1992.

AIDS

Crimp, Douglas, ed. *AIDS: Cultural Analysis/Cultural Activism.* MIT Press, 1988.

Patton, Cindy. *Inventing AIDS.* Routledge, 1990.

Stoller, Nancy, and Beth Schneider, eds. *Women Resisting AIDS: Feminist Strategies of Empowerment.* Temple University Press, 1995.

Watney, Simon. *Policing Desire.* University of Minnesota Press, 1987.

QUEER THEORY

de Laurentis, Teresa. *The Practice of Love: Lesbian Sexuality and Perverse Desire.* University of Indiana Press, 1994.

Foucault, Michel. *History of Sexuality, vol. 1.* Vintage Books, 1978.

Weeks, Jeffrey. *Sexuality and Its Discontents.* Routledge, 1985.

OTHER

Film: Gever, Martha, John Greyson, and Pratibha Parmar, eds. *Queer Looks.* Routledge, 1993.

Cross-dressing: Garber, Marjorie. *Vested Interests.* Routledge, 1992.

Music: Koestenbaum, Wayne. *The Queen's Throat.* Vintage Books, 1993. Brett, Philip, Elizabeth Wood, and Gary C. Thomas, eds. *Queering the Pitch: The New Gay and Lesbian Musicology.* Routledge, 1994.

RESOURCE GUIDE FOR QUEER STUDENTS

There is an important and interesting book that all lesbians and gay men considering college should take a look at. Though surveyed from a somewhat narrow perspective, *The Gay, Lesbian and Bisexual Students' Guide to Colleges, Universities, and Graduate Schools,* by Jan-Mitchell Sherrill and Craig A. Hardesty (NYU Press, 1994), gives *students'* perspectives about how homo-friendly their schools are. Everything from actual school policy to homophobia on campus, to what types (if any) of lesbian and gay studies courses are available. The students even tell if they would recommend their school to another lesbian or gay student. Almost 200 colleges are listed, making the book a good starting point of reference.

QUEER MLA

The following were listed as calls for papers for the 1995 Modern Language Association Convention in Chicago:

Buying "Out": Consumer Culture and Queer Identity in Literature and Mass Media. This interdisciplinary panel will address both appropriation of "the homosexual" within consumer culture and representations of gay men and lesbian women as particular kinds of consumers.

GJM Seeks Lesbian and Gay Studies Work on 17th- and 18th-Century English, French, American (Other European?) Literature. Turn-ons: eggheads with communications skills. Turnoffs: theoryheads into big words (verbal size queens), reflex social constructionism.

Lesbianism and Orality. Orality as a determining trope in figurations of lesbianism. Orality and narrative, speech and writing, oral erotics, and notions of the "pre" (presexual, preoedipal, precultural). Deconstructive and psychoanalytic perspectives especially welcome.

Queer Autobiography. Possible topics: Representing the queer body; queering gender or genre difference; outlaw subjects; figuring queer space (borderlands, home, the closet); questions of passing and reading.

Queering the Sixties. Any lesbian, gay, bisexual, transsexual, transvestite, or otherwise queer aspect of British, American, or other anglophone literary, artistic, or cultural production during the 1960s.

Queer Montaigne. Topics might include the (homo)erotics of melancholia or of influence and citation; friendship, freedom, and voluntary servitude; sex, heterosex, and impotence; Montaigne in/and translation; Montaigne and a homosexual literary tradition.

Queer Primitivism(s). How have fantasies of the "primitive" influenced the imagining of queer identities? Does the "primitive" continue to exert a pull on the queer imagination?

Tutti Frutti: Gender Studies on Outrageous Performers Who Have Become Cultural Icons of the Modern Era (Liberace, Carmen Miranda, etc.).

SOURCE: *MLA Newsletter*, Spring 1995, Vol. 27, No. 1. Reprinted by permission of the Modern Language Association of America from "Call for Papers for the 1995 Convention in Chicago."

INQUEERY, INTHEORY, INDEED

"InQueery, InTheory, InDeed," the sixth annual North American Lesbian, Gay, Bisexual Studies Conference, was held at the University of Iowa in November 1994, and over one thousand students, faculty, and activists attended. Topics for papers ranged from the serious to the sublime. The following are a list of presentations and panels recorded in the conference program.

"Beyond Binary: Queer Family Values and the Primal Cream"—keynote address by Lani Ka'ahumanu

"Your Blues Ain't Like Mine: Black Demogogues and the Politics of Homophobia"

"The Dialectics of Dominance and Submission: Emmanuel Levinas as Butch/Top"

"Is There Heterosexuality in the Bible?"

"Bisexuality in a Gender Container: The Tupperware Theory"

"Butch Rage: Daggers, Dykes, and Daddies"—panel

"Harder, Pussycat, More, More!"

"Teutonic Sexuality"

"Buckling Down or Knuckling Under: Discipline or Punish in Lesbian and Gay Studies"

"The Erect Penis: Can We Top It? A Visual and Theoretical Interrogation of Imagery for Active Female Desire"—workshop

"Unspecified Details: Banishing the Specter of Female Homoeroticism in 19th-Century Anti-Masturbatory Writing"

"Clits in Court: Lesbians and the Law"—panel

"Moving the Pink Agenda into the Ivory Tower"

"Trans(homo)sexuality? Double Inversion, Psychiatric Confusion, and Hetero-Hegemony"

"Anals of History"—panel

"Sex Between Men in the Hebrew Bible and Rabbinical Culture I and II"—panel

"Rectal Foreign Bodies: A Review of the Medical Literature"

"G.I. Joes in Barbie Land: Recontextualizing the Meaning of Butch in Lesbian Culture"

"The Sexism-Homophobia Connection: A Model"

"Fruitcakes at Christmas"

"Save Our Children: Queer Activism and the Youth Public Sphere"—presentation

"Lesbian, Gay, and Bisexual Curriculum Inclusion Advocacy at the k–12 Level"—presentation

---

6. Lesbians In Film, Video, and Television

Eliminate in Reel 5D: Scene of Miss Julie holding Olivia in close embrace and kissing her on the mouth. Reason: Immoral, would tend to corrupt morals.

> —notation of censor regarding the movie *The Pit of Loneliness*, 1954

There are probably all of three lesbian killers in the entire country, and they're all in Basic Instinct. *America's twelve million lesbians are not pathetic creatures. We have wonderful, diverse lives. It's Hollywood's responsibility to show what's really going on in this country.*

> —ELLEN CARTON, former executive director of the Gay and Lesbian Alliance Against Defamation (GLAAD), quoted in *Glamour* magazine, 1992

Lesbians have always been hungry for images of themselves, but a strict Hollywood censorship code, in effect from 1930 until 1968, made lesbians virtually invisible on the big screen. When they appeared as characters in movies at all, lesbians were stereotyped as everything from lonely, unfulfilled spinsters to man-hating, icepick-wielding killers to tragic, pathetic suicides. Even in very recent years, when novels about lesbians—such as *The Color Purple* and *Fried Green Tomatoes*—were adapted for Hollywood, their lesbian content was watered down to the point of obliteration.

Network television's record has been even worse. Until very recently, lesbians have rarely surfaced on the tube, except as the brunt of bad sitcom jokes. When a woman-to-woman kiss was written into the script of *L.A. Law* during the 1990–1991 season, neither character was allowed to be a lesbian: one was stereotyped as a freewheeling, "anything-that-moves" bisexual, the other as a "confused" straight woman.

For honest representations of our lives, we've had to rely on videos and films made by independent lesbian artists and distributed for viewing at lesbian and gay

Forbidden Love:
The Unashamed
Stories of Lesbian
Lives (*Courtesy
Women Make
Movies*)

film festivals. In 1994, independent filmmaker Rose Troche hit pay dirt when her
low-budget black-and-white film, *Go Fish*, was purchased by the Samuel Goldwyn
Company and went on to gross over two million dollars—proving that lesbians on
the big screen can and do sell tickets.

It was mainly through the activist efforts of the Gay and Lesbian Alliance
Against Defamation (GLAAD), a watchdog organization founded in 1985 to make
mainstream media and Hollywood aware of and receptive to lesbian and gay concerns, that Hollywood film and television studios began to attempt more accurate
depictions of lesbian lives. GLAAD turned the heat up on the Hollywood studios
for two vicious portrayals of gay people, in the films *Silence of the Lambs* and *Basic
Instinct*. Director Jonathan Demme's next movie after *Silence of the Lambs* was
the big-budget, gay-positive *Philadelphia*.

What we know as "lesbian chic"—the interest of the mainstream film industry
and media in lesbians and lesbian culture since the election of Bill Clinton—has
managed to open some doors on lesbian experience in Hollywood film and television. Oscar winner Whoopi Goldberg has turned up as a lesbian character in *Boys
on the Side*, also the first movie to touch the subject of women and HIV. Positive

lesbian characters are featured in two other studio films, Robert Altman's *Ready to Wear* and John Singleton's *Higher Learning*. Conservative Hollywood studios have courted producers such as Lauren Lloyd, an out lesbian, to work on lesbian-themed projects. Her upcoming comedy for Disney, *Chicks in White Satin*, will center around a lesbian commitment ceremony.

TV actor Roseanne (who has a gay brother and a lesbian sister) has probably done more to boost the appearance of lesbians and gay men on television than anyone else. Besides featuring two regular gay characters on her popular weekly show, in a spring 1994 episode, her character Roseanne Connor was kissed by a woman at a gay bar and the world didn't stop spinning. After that, television witnessed an explosion of lesbian and gay characters and themes on other major sitcoms and dramas, including *Frasier*, the short-lived *Daddy's Girls*, *Friends*, *Sisters*, and *Melrose Place*.

Sadly, though, lesbians have never had an out movie star to call their own, though the question of who's gay in Hollywood has been a topic of lesbian and gay gossip for decades. Such respected actors as Greta Garbo, Marlene Dietrich, and Sandy Dennis never felt free enough to reveal their sexual orientation, and today, lesbian movie and television actors still dodge the question of sexuality in interviews. Only Amanda Bearse, one of the stars of Fox-TV's *Married . . . with Children*, has publicly acknowledged being a lesbian. If Hollywood retains its interest in "lesbian chic," maybe more actors will find a safe atmosphere for coming out of the closet.

SOURCES FOR FURTHER READING

"Hollywood Power: The Industry Comes Out." *Out* magazine Special Issue, November 1994.

Murray, Raymond. *Images in the Dark: An Encyclopedia of Gay and Lesbian Film and Video*. Philadelphia: TLA Publications, 1994.

Russo, Vito. *The Celluloid Closet*. New York: Harper & Row, 1987, 1981.

Weiss, Andrea. *Vampires and Violets: Lesbians in Film*. New York: Penguin Books, 1994.

SEE ALSO

Dry Kisses Only (1989), a documentary by Jane Cottis and Kaucylia, which provides humorous commentary on lesbian subtext in famous Hollywood movies.

YES, VIRGINIA, SOME OF YOUR FAVORITE FILM ACTORS WERE LESBIANS

Anderson, Dame Judith, 1898–1992: Films included *Rebecca, Laura, Salome, Cat on a Hot Tin Roof, Macbeth, A Man Called Horse*.

Arthur, Jean, 1905–1991: Films included *The More the Merrier, Shane, Diamond*

EXCERPTS FROM MOVIE PRODUCTION CODE OF 1930

"No picture shall be produced which will lower the standards of those who see it. Hence the sympathy of the audience should never be thrown to crime, wrong-doing, evil or sin."

"Sex perversion or any inference to it is forbidden."

"The sanctity of the institution of marriage and the home shall be upheld. Pictures shall not infer that low forms of sex relationships are the accepted or common thing."

Jim, Mr. Deeds Goes to Town, Mr. Smith Goes to Washington, You Can't Take It with You, The Devil and Miss Jones.

Bankhead, Tallulah, 1903–1968: Films included *Lifeboat, Stage Door Canteen, Die! Die! My Darling.*

Colbert, Claudette, b. 1903: Films included *It Happened One Night, Cleopatra, Imitation of Life, Drums Along the Mohawk, Since You Went Away, The Egg and I.*

Dennis, Sandy, 1937–1992: Films included *Up the Down Staircase, The Fox, The Out-of-Towners,* and *Who's Afraid of Virginia Woolf?* for which she won an Academy Award.

Dietrich, Marlene, 1901–1992: Films included *The Blue Angel, Blonde Venus, Shanghai Express.*

Francis, Kay, 1903–1968: Films included *Ladies' Man, Cynara, Mandalay, The White Angel, First Lady, My Bill, Little Men.*

Garbo, Greta, 1905–1990: Films included *Anna Karenina, Anna Christie, Ninotchka, Camille;* awarded a special Academy Award for "her unforgettable screen performances" in 1954.

Gish, Lillian, 1896–1993: Dubbed "The First Lady of the Silent Screen"; silent films included *Broken Blossoms, Orphans of the Storm, The Scarlet Letter, The Birth of a Nation, Intolerance, La Boheme;* in 1980s made a comeback in films *Sweet Liberty* and *The Whales of August.*

Holliday, Judy, 1922–1965: Films included *The Marrying Kind, It Should Happen to You,* and *Born Yesterday,* for which she won an Academy Award.

Kelly, Patsy, 1910–1981: Films included *Nobody's Baby, Hit Parade of 1941, Topper Returns, Broadway Limited, Please Don't Eat the Daisies, Rosemary's Baby.*

Main, Marjorie, 1890–1975: Films included *Dead End, Stella Dallas;* plus a series of Ma and Pa Kettle films, in which she played Ma.

Oliver, Edna May, 1883–1942: Films included *Little Women, David Copperfield, Romeo and Juliet, Drums Along the Mohawk, A Tale of Two Cities.*

Stanwyck, Barbara, 1907–1990: Films included *Stella Dallas; Sorry, Wrong Number; Double Indemnity; Walk on the Wild Side;* star of TV show *The Big Valley.*

Images of Lesbians in Mainstream Films: The Silent Era to the Present

Lesbian Schoolgirls

Mädchen in Uniform (1931; remakes, 1950, 1958): Based on a play, "Yesterday and Today," by lesbian poet Christa Winsloe (one-time lover of journalist Dorothy Thompson). The earnest dyke-in-the-making Manuela develops an attachment to her teacher, Fraulein von Bernbourg. In the 1958 remake, Romy Schneider made her screen debut as Manuela.

The Wild Party (1929): Clara Bow as a flighty student in an all-girl dormitory with an undercurrent of lesbianism. Directed by Dorothy Arzner, a lesbian director.

Olivia (1951): A tender, sensual relationship between a schoolmistress (Edwige Feuillere) and a new student (Claire Olivia). Made in France, the film was released in the United States as *The Pit of Loneliness* with the tag line, "The daring drama of an unnatural love!"

Therese and Isabelle (1968): Another French schoolgirl film with some very explicit love scenes.

The Rainbow (1988): D. H. Lawrence's tale of Ursula (Sammi Davis) and her gym teacher (Amanda Donohue), whose relationship is just a sideline to "real" relationships with men.

Prison and Reformatory Girls

Caged (1950): Eleanor Parker is at the mercy of rough, tough prison matron Hope Emerson.

Reform School Girl (1957): Sally Kellerman made her film debut as a naive teenager sent to prison who has several run-ins with tough women in the joint.

Born Innocent (1974): Linda Blair is sent to a detention center, where she is raped with a broom handle by lesbians.

Scrubbers (1983): Not the usual women-in-prison exploitation film, but an intense drama notable for featuring a black lesbian couple.

Chained Heat (1983): Violent and sexually explicit exploitation film featuring—once again—Linda Blair.

Red Heat (1985): Linda Blair just can't get her fill of prison movies! This one is set in an unnamed Communist country.

Reform School Girls (1986): Linda Carol is the innocent victim of the sadistic warden, Pat Ast.

Chained Heat 2 (1993): Brigitte Nielsen is the warden with a taste for pretty girls.

Girls in Prison (1994): Ione Skye is the inmate who has "always liked girls."

VAMPIRES

Many mainstream horror movies gave society's stereotype of the predatory lesbian a literal meaning. Though the lesbian vampire movie made its first appearance in 1936 with *Dracula's Daughter*, the genre reached its height in the 1960s and early 1970s. Probably the best-known in this genre is *The Hunger* (1983), starring Catherine Deneuve as the elegant vampire Miriam and Susan Sarandon as her willing prey, Sara. Some popular lesbian vampire movies include:

Dracula's Daughter (1936)
Black Sunday (1960)
Blood and Roses (1960)
Castle of Blood (1963)
Le Viol du Vampire (1967)
La Vampire Nue (1969)
Vampire Lovers (1970)
Le Frisson des Vampires (1970)
Daughters of the Darkness (1970)
Vierge et Vampire (1971)
Twins of Evil (1971)

Vampyros Lesbos (1971)
Lust for a Vampire (1971)
Countess Dracula (1971)
The Blood-Spattered Bride (1972)
Vampyres (1974)
The Hunger (1980)
Mark of Lilith (1986)
Because the Dawn (1988)
The Lair of the White Worm (1988)
Carmilla (1989)

CROSS-DRESSERS

A Florida Enchantment (1914): Edith Storey swallows a seed that turns her into a man.

Beggars of Life (1928): Louise Brooks makes a handsome boy.

Christopher Strong (1933): Katharine Hepburn dresses as a man.

Sylvia Scarlett (1935): Katharine Hepburn masquerades as a boy trying to help her criminal father leave the country.

Morocco (1930) and *Blonde Venus* (1932): Marlene Dietrich appears both times in drag as a cabaret performer.

Viktor und Viktoria (Germany, 1933; its English remake, *First a Girl*, 1935; and the U.S. remake, *Victor/Victoria*, 1982): The story of a woman passing as a homosexual man, wearing lesbian-signifying drag.

Queen Christina (1933): Greta Garbo is the cross-dressing Swedish queen.

Blood Money (1933): Sandra Shaw in tuxedo with monocle.

Girls Will Be Boys (1934): Dolly Haas sings and dances in drag.

Calamity Jane (1953): Doris Day in cowboy drag.

Something Special (1986): Pamela Segal plays teenager Milly Niceman who gets her wish when she wakes up with "a guy's thing down there."

Vera (1987): Ana Beatriz Nogueria plays a female-to-male transsexual mistaken for a lesbian.

She Must Be Seeing Things (1988): Agatha (Sheila Dabney) dons men's clothing to spy on lover Jo (Lois Weaver).

The Ballad of Little Jo (1993): A frontierswoman decides it's safer and easier to live life as a man.

Orlando (1993): Virginia Woolf's androgyne Orlando makes it to the screen, played by Tilda Swinton.

LESBIANS WHO RECRUIT

Pandora's Box (1928): Countess Geshwitz, played by Alice Roberts.

Walk on the Wild Side (1962): Jo, played by Barbara Stanwyck, madam of a New Orleans brothel.

The Balcony (1963): Shelley Winters plays a predatory madam.

Who Killed Teddy Bear? (1965): Lesbian club owner Elaine Stritch puts the moves on hostess Juliet Prowse.

Puzzle of a Downfall Child (1970): Fashion photographer Viveca Lindfors preys on innocent Faye Dunaway.

From Russia with Love (1963): Colonel Rosa Klebb, played by Lotte Lenya, tries to seduce a young blonde agent who is in love with James Bond.

Les Biches (1968): Stephane Audran plays a villainous seductress.

The Legend of Lylah Clare (1968): Rosella Falk plays a dyke drug addict with the hots for Kim Novak.

The Last Emperor (1991): The calculating, predatory Eastern Jewel (Maggie Han) seduces Wam Jung (Joan Chen), addicts her to opium, then sends her away in disgrace.

LESBIANS WHO DIE BY THE END OF THE MOVIE

Note bene: Often many of the "Lesbians Who Recruit" also "Die by the End of the Movie."

Pandora's Box (1929): Countess Geshwitz (Alice Roberts) is beaten to death.

Madchen in Uniform (1931): Manuela (Hertha Thiele) jumps out a window to her death.

Dracula's Daughter (1936): Countess Alesca (Gloria Holden) gets a stake through her vampire's heart.

Caged (1950): Evelyn Harper (Hope Emerson) is stabbed to death.

The Children's Hour (1962): Martha Dobie (Shirley MacLaine) hangs herself.

Walk on the Wild Side (1962): Hallie (Capucine) is murdered.

From Russia with Love (1963): Colonel Rosa Klebb (Lotte Lenya) is shot by the girl she tries to seduce.

Who Killed Teddy Bear? (1965): Lesbian club owner Elaine Stritch is strangled by psychotic busboy Sal Mineo.

The Fox (1968): Jill (Sandy Dennis) commits suicide by jumping out of a tree and lands with a phallic branch between her legs.

Cleopatra Jones (1973): Mommy (Shelley Winters) is shot to death.

The Bell Jar (1979): in an "Ivy League loony bin," lesbian Joan befriends Esther, then hangs herself when Esther rejects her advances.

Single White Female (1992): Jennifer Jason Leigh plays a sociopath who is obsessed with her hetero roommate Bridget Fonda; Fonda prevails.

Bitter Moon (1993): Voluptuous Mimi (Emmanuelle Seigner) is murdered by her husband (Peter Coyote) while in bed with a woman he encouraged her to sleep with.

LESBIANS WHO JUST NEED TO MEET THE RIGHT MAN

Goldfinger (1964): Pussy Galore (Honor Blackman) is conquered by James Bond (Sean Connery).

Lilith (1964): Lilith (Jean Seberg) is a mental patient who is cured by Warren Beatty, a hospital trainee who makes love to her after discovering her with another woman.

Personal Best (1982): Chris (Mariel Hemingway) inexplicably chooses a man over the sexy Tori (Patrice Donnelly).

The Bostonians (1984): Vanessa Redgrave and Christopher Reeve in a struggle for the love of the young Madeleine Potter, with Reeve winning out. From Henry James's novel.

The Rainbow (1988): D. H. Lawrence's tale of Ursula (Sammi Davis) and her female gym teacher (Amanda Donohue), whose relationship is just a sideline to "real" relationships with men.

Three of Hearts (1993): Kelly Lynch's heart is broken by Sherilyn Fenn, who falls for male hustler William Baldwin.

LESBIANS WHO DON'T KNOW THEY ARE LESBIANS (UNCONSCIOUS LESBIANS)

Night of the Iguana (1964): Heterosexual Maxine (Ava Gardner) has to tell the repressed Miss Fellowes (Grayson Hall) that she is a dyke.

Seven Women (1966): Margaret Leighton plays a repressed missionary with feelings for young Sue Lyon.

Rachel, Rachel (1968): Calla Mackie (Estelle Parsons) is a lonely schoolteacher who finds out she's a lesbian when she kisses the local spinster (Joanne Woodward).

A Wedding (1978): Geraldine Chaplin as "the bride lady" discovers her true self when she kisses the bride.

KILLER DYKES

Faster, Pussycat! Kill! Kill! (1966): Tura Satana stars as Varla, the proto-lesbian killer and leader of a wild girl-gang.

The Girl with the Hungry Eyes (1967): Cathy Crowfoot plays the man-hating Tigercat who goes after all of her bisexual girlfriend Kitty's suitors, male and female.

They Only Kill Their Masters (1972): A jealous June Allyson murders her female lover.

Windows (1980): Elizabeth Ashley plays an unhinged lesbian who goes on a killing spree.

Black Widow (1987): Theresa Russell's husbands don't last long.

Basic Instinct (1992): Sharon Stone plays the omniverous, ice-pick-wielding lesbian.

Night Rhythms (1992): Bridget (Delia Sheppard) is a jealous, murdering lesbian who makes Sharon Stone look like an angel.

AND NOW FOR THE *POSITIVE* (OR BEARABLE) LESBIAN CHARACTERS

Club de Femmes (The Women's Club) (1936): Set in Paris in an all-women's hotel, it features Josette Day as a lesbian with an unrequited crush on Elize Argal.

The L-Shaped Room (1962): Cicely Courtneidge plays a sweet old lesbian vaudevillian who lives upstairs from Leslie Caron.

The Group (1966): Candace Bergen as Lakey, who returns from Europe with a butch female lover.

Girlfriends (1978): A lesbian roommate takes the heat of the intense friendship between Melanie Mayron and her best friend.

Manhattan (1979): Meryl Streep plays Woody Allen's ex-wife who has left him for a woman.

Silkwood (1983): Dolly (Cher) is in love with Karen (Meryl Streep), but Karen does not love Dolly.

A Perfect Couple (1979): Heather MacRae and Tomi-Lee Bradley play a happy lesbian couple in Robert Altman's film.

By Design (1981): Patty Duke and Sara Botsford play lesbian-mom-wannabes in this Canadian film.

I've Heard the Mermaids Singing (1987): The French-Canadian curator, Gabrielle, and her young lover, Mary, are the focus of Polly Vandersmee's (Sheila McCarthy) romantic voyeurism.

The Handmaid's Tale (1990): Elizabeth McGovern plays lesbian Moira, taken by the authorities for "gender treachery."

Strangers in Good Company (1990): Mary Meigs as Mary, a seventy-year-old lesbian painter.

Daughters of the Dust (1992): A black lesbian and her "companion" at a family reunion in the South Carolina barrier islands.

Chantilly Lace (1993): At a girls-only getaway in Colorado, lesbian Ally Sheedy confesses her love for one of her straight gal pals, played by Martha Plimpton.

Even Cowgirls Get the Blues (1994): In an otherwise horrible movie, a lesbian affair between Sissy Hankshaw (Uma Thurman) and Bonanza Jellybean (Rain Phoenix).

Ready-to-Wear (1994): Lili Taylor plays a lesbian photographer in a role that was written for Lily Tomlin.

Higher Learning (1994): Kristy Swanson is a college freshman from Orange County who is just coming out.

Boys on the Side (1995): Whoopi Goldberg as lesbian Jane falls for straight Mary-Louise Parker, who is dying of AIDS.

FILMS WITH FAMOUS SMOOCHES

Manslaughter (1922): A brief orgy scene showed two women locked in a passionate embrace.

Morocco (1930): Marlene Dietrich, performing in a club in top hat and tuxedo, kisses a female spectator.

Queen Christina (1933): Garbo in the title role kisses her lady in waiting, Countess Ebba; the script was written by lesbian Salka Viertel, who had an affair with Garbo.

The Balcony (1963): Shelley Winters plays a madam who hits on her bookkeeper, Lee Grant. Their smooch earned the character the description "lesbian letch" in a *Variety* review.

Black Widow (1987): Theresa Russell, a sophisticated husband-killer, plants a wet one on Debra Winger, the FBI agent obsessed with tracking her down.

Thelma and Louise (1991): Susan Sarandon kisses Geena Davis just before they plunge to their deaths.

Poison Ivy (1992): Husband-stealing Drew Barrymore kisses Sara Gilbert, then plummets to her death.

FILMS WITH LESBIAN SEX SCENES

Therese and Isabelle (1968)

The Killing of Sister George (1968)

Emmanuelle (1974)

Personal Best (1982)

Lianna (1983)

Desert Hearts (1986)

Oranges Are Not the Only Fruit (1989)

Henry and June (1991)

Claire of the Moon (1993)

FILMS THAT SHOULD HAVE HAD
LESBIAN SEX SCENES BUT DIDN'T

Entre Nous (1984)

The Color Purple (1985)

Anne Trister (1986)

Waiting for the Moon (1987)

I, the Worst of All (1990)

Fried Green Tomatoes (1991)

Salmonberries (1991)

Switch (1991)

Three of Hearts (1993)

FILMS WITH OBVIOUS LESBIAN SUBTEXT

Rebecca (1940): Mrs. Danvers (Judith Anderson, a lesbian) is obsessed with the first Mrs. de Winter.

All About Eve (1950): After ruining Margo Channing's career, smarmy Eve (Anne Baxter) asks her new protégée Phoebe (Barbara Bates) to spend the night.

Young Man with a Horn (1950): Lauren Bacall leaves husband Kirk Douglas to tour Europe with a young female art student.

Johnny Guitar (1954): Mercedes McCambridge is Emma Small, uncomfortable with her attraction to saloonkeeper Vienna, played by Joan Crawford.

The Goddess (1958): Nurse Haywood (Elizabeth Wilson) "kind of loves" her charge, a doomed Hollywood star played by Kim Stanley.

Touch of Evil (1958): Mercedes McCambridge is back as a butch lesbian who helps a gang of thugs rough up Janet Leigh.

The Haunting (1963): Claire Bloom as Theodora, a stylish lesbian who refers to herself as "nature's mistake," takes a liking to plain, nervous Eleanor (Julie Harris).

Julia (1977): Jane Fonda as Lillian Hellman is enamored of her childhood friend turned revolutionary, played by Vanessa Redgrave.

Little Darlings (1980): Kristy McNichol as baby butch and Tatum O'Neal as baby femme in this summer-camp comedy.

Black Widow (1987): Debra Winger is an FBI agent obsessed with her prey, the sexy, husband-killing Theresa Russell.

The House of the Spirits (1994): Glenn Close as Ferula, who keeps wanting to "feel the warmth" of sister-in-law Clara (Meryl Streep).

Heavenly Creatures (1994): Two young girlfriends who commit matricide in order to stay together.

LESBIAN-THEMED FAVORITES FROM LESBIAN PRODUCERS AND DIRECTORS

Desert Hearts (1985), directed by Donna Deitch

Claire of the Moon (1992), directed by Nicole Conn

Go Fish (1994), produced, directed, and cowritten (with Guinevere Turner) by Rose Troche

Bar Girls (1995), written and produced by Lauran Hoffman

The Incredibly True Adventure of Two Girls in Love (1995), directed by Maria Maggenti

A SAMPLING OF LESBIAN-MADE EROTICA

Fun with a Sausage/L'Ingenue (1985)   *BurLEZk Live!* (1987)

Erotic in Nature (1985)   *BurLEZk II Live!* (1988)

Where There's Smoke (1986)   *Dress Up for Daddy* (date unknown)
Hungry Hearts (1989)   *San Francisco Lesbians* (date unknown)
Bathroom Sluts (1991)   *Erotique* (1994)

SOME CLASSIC LESBIAN DOCUMENTARIES

Gertrude Stein: When You See This Remember Me (1970): A portrait of the celebrated writer.

In the Best Interests of the Children (1977): Lesbian parents threatened with loss of their children.

Choosing Children (1984): Academy Award–winning filmmaker Deborah Chasnoff's classic about women who decide to become parents after they come out as lesbians.

Before Stonewall (1985): A history of lesbian and gay life before Stonewall; won an Emmy award for codirectors Greta Schiller and Robbie Rosenberg.

Storme: The Lady of the Jewel Box (1987): A portrait of the lesbian who emceed the famous male drag show while in drag herself.

Tiny and Ruby: Hell-Divin' Women (1988): Two African-American musicians who had their own band and have been together over forty years.

Lesbian Tongues (1989): Interviews with out lesbians such as actors Peggy Shaw and Lois Weaver, writer Jewelle Gomez, and publishers Donna McBride and Barbara Grier.

Dry Kisses Only (1989): Humorous commentary on the lesbian subtext in many classic Hollywood movies.

West Coast Crones (1991): Proud older lesbians talk about everything from coming out to sex to approaching infirmity and death.

Forbidden Love: The Unashamed Stories of Lesbian Lives (1992): Gem about the important role of lesbian pulp novels in the lives of Canadian lesbians from the 1940s to the 1960s.

Framing Lesbian Fashion (1992): How apparel has shaped lesbian identity since the days of butch-femme.

Thank God I'm a Lesbian (1992): Canadian-made profile of out lesbians such as Sarah Schulman, Nicole Brossard, and Dionne Brand talking about everything from AIDS to outing to S/M.

Last Call at Maud's (1993): Profile of the classic San Francisco lesbian bar, Maud's Study, including its owner and various patrons over the twenty years it was in operation.

Cancer in Two Voices (1994): Barbara Rosenblum and her lover Sandra Butler courageously documented the last three years of their relationship before Barbara succumbed to breast cancer.

Chicks in White Satin (1994): A lesbian commitment ceremony; nominated for an Academy Award.

Cancer in Two Voices, a film by Lucy Massie Phenix (*Courtesy Women Make Movies*)

Long Time Comin' (1994): Profiles of two African-Canadian women, painter Grace Channer and singer Faith Nolan, talking about feminism, lesbianism, and being black.

Ballot Measure 9 (1994): The harrowing true story of the fight against Oregon's homophobic ballot initiative in 1992.

CLASSIC LESBIAN MOVIE LINES

I have no intention to, Chancellor; I shall die a bachelor.

—QUEEN CHRISTINA to the Chancellor who has warned her "You cannot die an old maid," in *Queen Christina* (1933)

How is it possible to endure the idea of sleeping with a man in the room?

—*Queen Christina* (1933)

You're so pretty . . . if I were a man, I'd really love you.

—JOSETTE DAY to Eliza Argal in *Club des Femmes* (1936)

She's too strong for you; you can't fight her.

> —DANNY (MRS. DANVERS) to the second Mrs. de Winter about the first Mrs. de Winter (Rebecca) in *Rebecca* (1940)

There's something in you, and you don't know anything about it because you don't know it's there. I couldn't call it by a name before, but I know now. It's there. It's been there ever since I first knew you.

> —MARTHA (SHIRLEY MACLAINE) trying to name her lesbianism to Karen (Audrey Hepburn) in *The Children's Hour* (1962)

You can turn off the charm. I'm immune.

> —PUSSY GALORE to James Bond in *Goldfinger* (1964)

CHILDIE: Not all girls are raving bloody lesbians, you know!

SISTER GEORGE: That's a misfortune of which I am perfectly well aware.

> —*The Killing of Sister George* (1968)

Guys are a pain in the ass.

> —KRISTY MCNICHOL as Angel in *Little Darlings* (1980)

Postmenopausal women should run the world.

> —A postmenopausal lesbian in *Forbidden Love: The Unashamed Stories of Lesbian Lives* (1992)

She looks like the angel of light, I want to climb into her bed, to feel the warmth of her skin, her gentle breathing.

> —FERULA (GLENN CLOSE) talking about her sister-in-law Clara (Meryl Streep) in *House of the Spirits* (1993)

We're going to grow old together, you and I.

> —DIANE (JUDY DAVIS) to Grethe (Glenn Close) in *Serving in Silence: The Margarethe Cammermeyer Story* (1995)

TEN THINGS MEN IN HOLLYWOOD SAY ABOUT WOMEN IN HOLLYWOOD

1. She's having her period.
2. She's a bitch.
3. She slept her way to the top.
4. She's sleeping her way to the top.
5. She's sleeping with the director.
6. She's not fuckable.
7. She needs to get fucked.
8. I fucked her.
9. She's fucked up.
10. She's a dyke.

SOURCE: *Movieline*, May 1992

INDEPENDENT LESBIAN FILMMAKERS

Friedrich, Sue, b. 1954: *The Ties That Bind* (1984); *Damned if You Don't* (1987); *Sink or Swim* (1990); *First Comes Love* (1991); *Rules of the Road* (1993); *The Lesbian Avengers Eat Fire, Too* (1993)

Chasnoff, Debra: *Choosing Children* (1984); *Deadly Deception* (1991), winner of an Academy Award

Gorris, Marleen, b. 1948: *A Question of Silence* (1983); *Broken Mirrors* (1984); *The Last Island* (1990)

Hammer, Barbara, b. 1939: *Menses* (1973); *Dyketactics* (1974); *Superdyke* (1975); *Double Strength* (1978); *Women I Love* (1979); *Our Trip* (1980); *Sync Touch* (1981); *Doll House* (1984); *No No Nooky, TV* (1987); *Sanctus* (1990); *Vital Signs* (1991); *Nitrate Kisses* (1992)

Oxenberg, Jan: *Home Movie* (1972); *I'm Not One of Them* (1974); *A Comedy in Six Unnatural Acts* (1975); *Thank You and Goodnight* (1991)

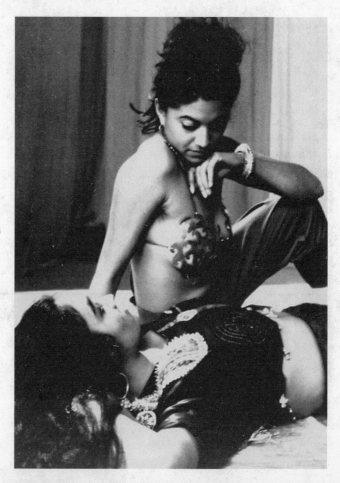

Khush, a film by Pratibha Parmar (*Courtesy Women Make Movies*)

International Sweethearts of Rhythm, a film by Greta Schiller and Andrea Weiss (*Courtesy Frameline*)

Parmar, Pratibha: *A Plague on You* (1987); *Reframing AIDS* (1988); *Memory Pictures* (1989); *Flesh and Paper* (1990); *Khush* (1991); *Warrior Marks* (1993)

Schiller, Greta: *Greta's Girls* (1977); *Before Stonewall* (1985); *The International Sweethearts of Rhythm* (1986); *Tiny and Ruby: Hell Divin' Women* (1988); *Waking Up: A Lesson in Love* (1988)

Treut, Monika, b. 1954: *Seduction: The Cruel Woman* (1985); *The Virgin Machine* (1988); *My Father Is Coming* (1991); *Dr. Paglia* (1992); *Erotique* (1994)

MADE-FOR-TELEVISION MOVIE LESBIANS

A Question of Love (1978): Jane Alexander and Gena Rowlands as lesbian parents struggling to keep custody of their children.

My Two Loves (1989): Mariette Hartley plays a widow torn between Lynn Redgrave and her male doctor.

The Women of Brewster Place (1989): Based on Gloria Naylor's novel, features a sophisticated African-American lesbian couple.

Portrait of a Marriage (1992): The love/hate relationship of Vita Sackville-West and Violet Trefusis. Originally aired in Britain, thirty-four minutes of sex scenes were cut when it was shown on PBS in the United States.

Other Mothers (1993): An after-school special about a young athlete and his two moms, played by Joanna Cassidy and Meredith Baxter.

Serving in Silence: The Margarethe Cammermeyer Story (1995): Glenn Close and Judy Davis light up the small screen as the discharged army colonel and her artist lover.

LESBIAN CHARACTERS ON TELEVISION SERIES

Heartbeat: Featured a lesbian nurse practitioner, Marilyn McGrath, played by Gail Strickland; the show was canceled after one season.

All My Children: Lesbian character Lynn Carson, played by Donna Pescow, appeared briefly on the soap.

L.A. Law: C. J. (Amanda Donohue), a bisexual, participated in television's first-ever lesbian screen kiss.

Roseanne: Sandra Bernhard plays bisexual Nancy Bartlett Thomas. *Roseanne* also featured television's second-ever lesbian kiss when Mariel Hemingway smooched the series' star.

Northern Exposure: Lesbian lovers Cicely and Roslyn, the founders of the Alaskan town, appeared in a historical flashback episode.

Sisters: Nora Dunn plays Norma Lear, a lesbian television producer.

Friends: Carol, the lesbian mom-to-be, is played by Jane Sibbert.

FAVORITE LESBIAN OR BISEXUAL TV STARS

Bearse, Amanda, b. 1958: Marcy D'Arcy on *Married . . . with Children*

Bernhard, Sandra, b. 1955: Regular on *Roseanne*, playing Nancy, a bisexual character

Byington, Spring, 1886–1971: Star of *December Bride* and regular on *Laramie*

Kuehl, Sheila James, b. 1941: Zelda on *The Many Loves of Dobie Gillis*

Kulp, Nancy, 1921–1991: Miss Hathaway on the *The Beverly Hillbillies*

Moorehead, Agnes, 1900–1974: Endora on *Bewitched*

Stanwyck, Barbara, 1907–1990: Star of *The Big Valley*

Tomlin, Lily, b. 1930: Regular on *Laugh-In*, where she created the characters of Geraldine, the telephone operator, and Edith Ann, among others

Vance, Danitra, 1959–1994: Regular on *Saturday Night Live*

Waters, Ethel, 1896–1977: Star of *Beulah*

ADDRESSES OF THE MAJOR AND MINOR TV NETWORKS

If you see something on TV that you like or dislike, you can make your opinion heard by writing to the powers-that-be at the various networks.

ABC
Audience Information
77 W. 66th St.
New York, NY 10023-6298

CBS
Audience Services
51 W. 52nd St.
New York, NY 10019

FOX
P.O. Box 900
Beverly Hills, CA 90213

NBC
Audience Services
30 Rockefeller Plaza
New York, NY 10112

PBS
1320 Braddock Place
Alexandria, VA 22314-1698

AMC (American Movie Classics)
150 Crossways Park West
Woodbury, NY 11797

A&E (Arts & Entertainment Network)
235 East 45th St.
New York, NY 10017

BET (Black Entertainment Television)
1232 31st St. NW
Washington, DC 20007

CNN (Cable News Network) and
  TBS, TNT (Turner Network
  Television)
One CNN Center
Box 105366
Atlanta, GA 30348-5366

CBN ("Family Channel")
100 Centerville Turnpike
Virginia Beach, VA 23463

MAX (Cinemax)
200 Avenue of the Americas
New York, NY 10036

C-Span
400 N. Capitol Street NW
Suite 412
Washington, DC 20001

TDC (The Discovery Channel)
7700 Wisconsin Avenue
Bethesda, MD 20814-3522

DIS (The Disney Channel)
3800 W. Alameda Ave.
Burbank, CA 91505

E! (Entertainment Television)
1800 N. Vine St., 3rd Floor
Hollywood, CA 90028

ENC (Encore)
4643 South Ulster St., Suite 300
Denver, CO 80237

ESPN (Entertainment and Sports
  Programming Network)
ESPN Plaza
Bristol, CT 06010

Galavision
2121 Avenue of the Stars, Suite 2300
Los Angeles, CA 90067

HBO (Home Box Office)
1100 Avenue of the Americas
New York, NY 10036

LIFE (Lifetime)
36-12 35th Ave.
Astoria, NY 11106

TMC (The Movie Channel),
1633 Broadway
New York, NY 10019

MTV (Music Television)
1515 Broadway
New York, NY 10036

TNN (The Nashville Network)
2806 Opryland Drive
Nashville, TN 37214

NICK (Nickelodeon)
1515 Broadway
New York, NY 10036

SHOW (Showtime)
1633 Broadway
New York, NY 10019

USA (USA Network)
1230 Avenue of the Americas
New York, NY 10020

FEATURE

Queer TV Celebrities

On National Coming Out Day, October 11, 1994, talk-show host Marilu Henner (*Marilu*, CBS, 9 A.M. weekdays) welcomed four openly gay celebrities to her show to discuss coming out personally and on the job. The four guests were actor Amanda Bearse, who plays neighbor Marcy D'Arcy on *Married . . . with Children*; Dan Butler, the macho sportscaster Bulldog on *Frasier*; stand-up comedian Suzanne Westenhoefer, who recently starred in her own HBO special; and *Entertainment Tonight* reporter Garrett Glaser. The following are excerpts from their discussion of coming out in the entertainment business:

AMANDA BEARSE: I came out professionally a little over a year ago. And that was a decision that I knew was inevitable, given the amount of success that I was reaching in my career. It was a decision that I gave a lot of thought to. It wasn't a difficult decision, it was just an important one. . . . Being in someone's home every week or every day, now that *Married . . . with Children*'s in syndication . . . it gives it [coming out] more power. It makes a more powerful statement to say, "You're used to me, you've known me for many, many years, now you know this about me."

DAN BUTLER: I never really hid it [being gay], because it was just a part of me, it was natural. This year I professionally came out. I'm doing a one-man show that I've written called "The Only Thing Worse You Could Have Told Me," which comes from a conversation I had with my dad when talking about it. But it was a natural step. You know, people ask me, "Well, did you go through a lot of trauma or thought?" . . . I didn't think about it that much. . . . It was just something I was clear I wanted to do.

SUZANNE WESTENHOEFER: I came out four years ago onstage. . . . You know, comedy is about honesty. Most people you see who are comics are telling you all these personal stories about their lives. I didn't want to be standing up there going, "And then my g-g-boy-girl-boyfriend."

GARRETT GLASER: I think . . . people are becoming used to hearing about gay people, and the more of us who say, "Yeah, I'm gay," "I'm lesbian," the more it becomes a nonissue.

AMANDA BEARSE: Everybody that takes that step to come out, it's a baby step for our community. And you're not going to get giant steps without those baby steps. And so everybody who makes the decision to do that fights the discrimination.

PROFILE

I Want My DYKE-TV

Founded in 1993 by a trio of activist/artists, DYKE-TV produces national documentary television programming by and for lesbians that enhances lesbian visibility and empowerment. It is the brainchild of Ana Maria Simo, playwright and cofounder of the Lesbian Avengers; Linda Chapman, theater director and producer, formerly of The Wooster Group; and Mary Patierno, independent film and videomaker. DYKE-TV is grassroots lesbian media activism to incite, subvert, organize, and provoke: a blueprint for a national lesbian television network in the United States.

DYKE-TV comes to your living room in a stylish and dynamic weekly half-hour magazine format TV show that mixes news, arts, sports, political commentary, health coverage, and more. Currently cable cast in twenty-two cities, with a steady rate of expansion, DYKE-TV reaches more than 6.5 million households and is the second most widely distributed lesbian or gay television program in the United States. Tapes of the weekly show are available through bookstores and individual subscriptions.

Weekly features on DYKE-TV include:

News: A five-minute news segment covers current stories relevant to lesbian lives as seen from a lesbian perspective.

Eyewitness: An in-depth look at issues of particular interest to the lesbian community. Topics have included the Dyke March to the White House; the action protesting the firebombing of the home of an HIV-positive lesbian activist in Tampa, Florida; lesbians in the military; domestic partnership; lesbians in prison; and antigay, antilesbian activities of the radical right.

Arts: Interviews with lesbian artists showcase examples of their work. Featured artists have included filmmakers Cheryl Dunye and Barbara Hammer; performers Phranc, Reno, Holly Hughes, and The Five Lesbian Brothers; the bands Girls in the Nose and Disappear Fear; choreographers Jennifer Monson and Elizabeth Streb; writers Jewelle Gomez and Dorothy Allison; and comedian Kate Clinton.

I Was a Lesbian Child: Home movies revisited, or: why you always wore that cowboy suit.

Other recurring features include: *Ann Northrop Mouths Off* (political commentary by a former debutante turned activist); *From the Archives* (on lesbian herstory); *Workplace* (we're everywhere); *Lesbian Health*; *Dyke Dish* (gossip); *Jocklife* (sports); *Street Squad* (revealing guerrilla interviews); *Fab Girls Fix-It* (a how-to with a lesbo-comic twist); and *Dyke Calendar* (weekly events not to be missed).

DYKE-TV may come to a city near you. Airdates and locations:

CITY	WHERE	WHEN
Atlanta GA	Channel 12	Monday, 9:30 P.M.
Austin, TX	Channel 10	Sunday, 11:00 P.M.
Bronx, NY	Channel 70	Thursday, 9:00 P.M.
Brooklyn, NY	Channel 34/67	Tuesday, 10:30 P.M.
Cambridge, MA	Channel 19	Wednesday, 10:00 P.M.
Dallas, TX	Channel 23B	Monday, 11:30 P.M.
Denver, CO	Channel 12	Thursday, 11:00 P.M.
Los Angeles, CA	Channel 3	Tuesday, 9:30 P.M.
Madison, WI	Channel 4	Monday, 8:30 P.M.
Manhattan, NYC	Channel 34	Tuesday, 8:00 P.M.
New Orleans, LA	Channel 49	See local listings
Newton, MA	Channel 13	Tuesday, 10:00 P.M.
Northampton, MA	Channel 2	Monday, 10:30 P.M.
Philadelphia, PA	Channel 54	Tuesday, 11:30 P.M.
San Antonio, TX	Channel 20	Saturday, midnight
San Francisco, CA	Channel 53	Friday, 6:00 P.M.
Seattle, WA	Channel 29	Thursday, 12:30 P.M.
The 90s at Nite		See local listing
Washington, DC	Channel 25	Wednesday, 9:00 P.M.

THE 90s CHANNEL

Baltimore, MD	Los Angeles, CA, county & e. valley
Boulder, CO	Santa Cruz, CA
Denver, CO, suburbs	Vernon, CT
Detroit, MI, suburbs	

7. LESBIAN HEALTH

Battling racism, battling heterosexism, and battling apartheid share the same urgency inside me as battling cancer.

—AUDRE LORDE

In the last century, we've come a long way in the medical establishment's treatment of lesbians. Lesbians were once subjected to medical "cures" ranging from hypnosis to clitorectomy to lobotomy. Neither the American Psychiatric Association nor the American Medical Association consider lesbianism a disease anymore, but we still have a long way to go to understand the specific health concerns that lesbians face.

Are lesbians more at risk for breast, uterine, and ovarian cancer than hetero-

New York Lesbian Health Fair, 1992 *(Photo by Morgan Gwenwald)*

sexual women? Do they consume more alcohol and smoke more cigarettes, placing them at higher risk for heart attacks and strokes? How significant is it that lesbians have fewer babies than heterosexual women? Data on lesbian health issues are still spotty and inconclusive, because lesbians have not been demographically profiled for health concerns. Often, lesbians confronting homophobic physicians elect not to come out to their healthcare providers.

The Women's Health Initiative, a federally funded eight-to-fifteen-year study of 163,000 women covering diet, exercise, hormones, bone density, and heart disease, recently agreed to add a question on sexual orientation to its survey, allowing a lesbian health profile to emerge. In addition, the Nurses Health Study, an ongoing project studying 21,000 nurses, has decided to add sexual orientation to its considerations. These two studies combined should add important information to our understanding of what lesbian health problems are and how we can best combat them.

Please note that this section is meant only to offer suggestions and guidance about where to go if you have a health or medical problem. Please consult a doctor or health care professional with questions and concerns about your health.

PRESCRIBED MEDICAL "CURES" FOR LESBIANISM
OVER THE YEARS

Until 1973, the American Psychiatric Association viewed lesbianism as a mental disorder to be cured. Not until late 1994 did the American Medical Association remove all references to "sexual orientation related disorders" from its official policy, which was used for years to justify therapies for treating lesbianism. Since the late 1800s, lesbians were subjected to everything from cold baths to shock therapy as the medical establishment attempted to find a cure for lesbianism.

The following are some of the cures prescribed for lesbians over the years:

1. Removal of the ovaries (1880s)
2. Removal of the clitoris (1890s)
3. Hypnosis (1890s to 1960s)
4. Lobotomy (early 1900s to 1950s)
5. Analysis (1920s to 1970s)
6. Institutionalization or hospitalization (1920s to 1970s)
7. Aversion therapy, inducing nausea through drugs or electroshock (to the 1970s)
8. Abstinence (1890s to present; still advocated by some organized religions)

AN EXAMPLE: THE "WISDOM" OF DR. LA FOREST POTTER, 1933

In his book, *Strange Loves: A Study in Sexual Abnormalities*, Dr. Potter, a New York City psychoanalyst, proposed this therapeutic path:

> It merely requires that the *right* instruction, the *right* environment, the *right* opportunities be afforded, and thousands of women and girls, who now follow lesbian practices might once more become normal individuals. They might even become happy wives and mothers, if only their mental condition could be corrected by therapeutic or normal suggestion, and their endocrine system toned up by administration of such extracts as would enhance their feminine characteristics and reactions.
>
> In brief, the lesbian, in her attitude of hopelessness and her protestations of incurability, is self-deluded. She is making a gesture, which creates in her inverted mind some similitude of the heroic, the martyred, the harried power of nature—an attitude which, in an enormous number of cases, is totally unwarranted.
>
> For there is much that medical science and psychology has to offer these women, if only they will accept this help.
>
> Where the *will to be normal* is overpoweringly strong; where there exists the fullest cooperation; marriage may help marvelously in restoring normal mental and physical equilibrium.

SOURCE: Jonathan Ned Katz, *Gay American History: Lesbians and Gay Men in the U.S.A.*, revised edition, 1992

FINDING A LESBIAN PHYSICIAN

How many times have you been stung by a doctor's homophobia or sexism? Tired of being asked what kind of birth control you use? Not getting the care you need because you're afraid to come out to your doctor? The Gay and Lesbian Medical Association can refer you to 1,600 practicing lesbian or gay doctors across North America. For names of the doctors nearest you, write to GLMA, 273 Church Street, San Francisco, CA 94114; or call 415/255-4547.

FINDING A LESBIAN OR GAY THERAPIST

The Committee on Gay and Lesbian Concerns of the American Psychological Association publishes a Therapist Roster, listing the names, addresses, specialties, and interests of individual therapists across the United States. Write to: Committee on Gay and Lesbian Concerns, American Psychological Association, 1200 Seventeenth Street NW, Washington, DC 20036; or call the APA at 202/336-5500.

For referrals, you can also contact the Association of Lesbian and Gay Psychiatrists, 1439 Pineville Road, New Hope, PA 18938.

INTERVIEWING A PROSPECTIVE THERAPIST

Before choosing a therapist, think about the following questions:

1. Would you feel most comfortable talking to a woman or to a man?
2. Would you feel most comfortable talking to someone your own age, or someone older or younger than you?
3. Is it important that you know if your therapist is lesbian or gay?

There are different types of therapists, and the following list may help you sort out the array of practitioners available:

Clinical or counseling psychologist: Has completed postgraduate study in psychology with a degree of Ph.D., Psy.D., or Ed.D. Training includes psychological testing and psychotherapy.

Psychiatrist: A medical doctor who specializes in psychiatry, or the prevention, causes, and diagnosis/treatment of mental, emotional, and behavioral disorders. Can prescribe medication.

Social worker: Has completed a graduate degree in social work (M.S.W.) and has received specialized training in individual, group, or community work. Some insurance companies will not reimburse for this type of therapy unless the social worker has passed a state certification process and achieved the rank of C.S.W.

Pastoral counselor: A theological counselor with graduate study in a related field, possessing experience in both pastoral counseling and ministry.

You can also get referrals from your medical doctor, from friends in the medical field, or from the therapists of friends. It's a good idea to interview several therapists before choosing one you feel you can work with, though most therapists charge for these sessions. In the interview (it's best to do it face to face, to test your comfort level), you can ask the following questions to help you make your decision:

1. What is the therapist's training? Is the therapist licensed? Does she or he fall into a particular school of thought (e.g., Jungian, Freudian)? How many years of experience does the therapist have?
2. Has the therapist counseled people with issues similar to yours (e.g., couples, sexual abuse, work-related issues, substance abuse, family issues, chronic illness, bereavement)?
3. Does the therapist feel comfortable counseling lesbians? Has she or he counseled other lesbians or gay men? (If you feel you only want to work with a lesbian therapist, you should make that clear.)
4. What type of treatment approaches does the therapist use (e.g., behavior modification, hypnosis, group therapy, medication, psychoanalysis)? Does she or he work primarily in short-term or long-term counseling? How does the therapist feel about medications?
5. What are the therapists' fees? Are they insurance reimbursable? What method of payment does the therapist accept? Does the therapist charge for missed appointments?
6. Where will the appointments be held and how often? How long will they last?
7. Is the therapist available for emergencies between sessions? What is the therapist's policy about receiving calls from clients outside of scheduled appointments?

Remember, you don't have to be in crisis to start therapy. Most people wait until they are in pain, but therapy can aid in preventing crises, as well as in achieving self-knowledge, self-esteem, and personal growth.

Thanks to Dr. Barbara Warren for her help in compiling this section.

RESOURCES FOR LESBIAN HEALTH

BOOKS

For sources on HIV/AIDS, see pp. 425–426.

GENERAL

The Boston Women's Health Collective. *The New Our Bodies, Ourselves, Updated and Expanded for the Nineties.* (1992)

Evelyn White, author
of *The Black
Women's Health
Book* (*Photo by Liz
Hafalia, San
Francisco Chronicle.
Courtesy of Seal
Press.*)

Federation of Feminist Women's Health Centers. *How to Stay Out of the Gyne-
cologist's Office.* (1991)
————. *A New View of a Woman's Body.* (1991)
Hepturn and Gutirrez. *Alive and Well: A Lesbian Health Guide.* (1988)
Northrup, Christiane. *Women's Bodies, Women's Wisdom.* (1994)
Ruzek, Sheryl. *The Women's Health Movement: Feminist Alternatives to Medical
Control.* (1978)
Santa Cruz Women's Health Collective. *Lesbian Health Matters.* (1979)
Steward, Felicia, et al. *Understanding Your Body: Every Woman's Guide to Gy-
necology and Health.* (1987)
Villarosa, Linda, ed. *Body and Soul: The Black Women's Guide to Physical Health
and Emotional Well-Being.* (1995)
White, Evelyn. *The Black Women's Health Book: Speaking for Ourselves.* (1990)

BREAST CARE

Love, Susan. *The Breast Book.* (1990)

CANCER

Brady, Judith. *One in Three: Women with Cancer Confront an Epidemic*. (1991)
Butler, Sandra, and Barbara Rosenblum. *Cancer in Two Voices*. (1991)
Lorde, Audre. *The Cancer Journals*. (1980)
Stocker, Midge. *Cancer as a Woman's Issue*. (1991)

MENSTRUATION

Lark, Susan. *PMS Self-Help Book*. (1984)
Taylor, Dena. *The Red Flower: Rethinking Menstruation*. (1988)

NUTRITION

Adams, Carol. *The Sexual Politics of Meat: A Feminist-Vegetarian Critical Theory*. (1990)
Colbin, Annemarie. *Food and Healing*. (1988)

OTHER HEALTH CONCERNS

Ballweg, Mary Lou, and the Endometriosis Association. *Overcoming Endometriosis*. (1987)
Chalker, Rebecca, and Kristene Whitmore. *Overcoming Bladder Disorders*. (1990)

OVER FORTY

Doress, Paula Brown, Diana Laskin Siegal, et al. *Ourselves, Growing Older*. (1994)
Greenwood, Sadja. *Menopause, Naturally: Preparing for the Second Half of Life*. (1989)

PSYCHOLOGY

The Boston Lesbian Psychologies Collective. *Lesbian Psychologies: Explorations and Challenges*. (1987)
Lerner, Harriet Goldhor. *The Dance of Intimacy: A Woman's Guide to Courageous Acts of Change in Key Relationships*. (1989)
_____. *The Dance of Anger: A Woman's Guide to Changing the Patterns of Intimate Relationships*. (1985)
Sanford, Linda T., and Mary Ellen Donovan. *Women & Self-Esteem: Understanding and Improving the Way We Think and Feel about Ourselves*. (1986)

RECOVERY

Al-Anon Family Group Headquarters, Inc. Staff.
The Courage to Change: One Day at a Time in Al-Anon. (1992)
McDaniel, Judith. *Metamorphosis: Reflections on Recovery*. (1989)
Swallow, Jean, ed. *Out from Under: Sober Dykes and Our Friends*. (1983)

SEXUAL ABUSE

Bass, Ellen, and Laura Davis. *The Courage to Heal: A Guide for Women Survivors of Child Sexual Abuse.* (1989)

Davis, Laura. *Allies in Healing: When the Person You Love Was Sexually Abused as a Child.* (1991)

Maltz, Wendy. *The Sexual Healing Journey.* (1991)

ORGANIZATIONS AND NEWSLETTERS

For sources on HIV/AIDS, see pages 449–454.

GENERAL

Hikane
P.O. Box 841
Great Barr, MA 01230
Disabled lesbian news and health

Lesbian Health News
P.O. Box 12121
Columbus, OH 43212

National Lesbian and Gay Health
 Association
1407 S Street NW
Washington, DC 20009
Phone: 202/939-7880
 Fax: 202/797-3504

National Women's Health Network
224 7th Street SE
Washington, DC 20003

BREAST CANCER

Strang Cancer Prevention Center
National High Risk Registry
428 East 72nd Street
New York, NY 10021
Phone: 212/794-4900
A free national program to determine your risk for breast cancer

CANCER

Lesbian Community Cancer Project
Pat Parker Place
1902 W. Montrose Avenue
Chicago, IL 60613
Phone: 312/561-4662

Mary Helen Mautner Project for
 Lesbians with Cancer
1707 L Street NW
Washington, DC 20036
Phone: 202/332-5536

Whitman-Walker Clinic
1407 South Street, NW
Washington, DC 20009
Phone: 202/797-3585
 Fax: 202/797-3504

Women's Cancer Resource Center
3023 Shattuck Avenue
Berkeley, CA 94705
Phone: 510/548-9272

New York Lesbian Health Fair, 1993 *(Photo by Morgan Gwenwald)*

Women's Community Cancer Project
Women's Center
46 Pleasant Street
Cambridge, MA 02139
Phone: 617/354-9888

MENSTRUATION

Dixie PMS Center
2161 Newmarket Parkway, Suite 222
Marietta, GA 30067
Phone: 800/767-9232

Menstrual Health Foundation
104 Petaluma Avenue
Sebastopol, CA 95472
Phone: 707/829-2744

RECOVERY

International Advisory Council for
   Homosexual Men and Women in AA
P.O. Box 90
Washington, DC 20044-0090

Pride Institute
14400 Martin Drive
Eden Prairie, MN 55344
Phone: 800/54-PRIDE

Project Connect
Lesbian and Gay Community Services
   Center
208 West 13th Street
New York, NY 10011
Phone: 212/620-7310

Spencer Recovery Center
343 West Foothill Boulevard
Monrovia, CA 91016
Phone: 800/232-5484 or 818/358-3662

SEXUAL ABUSE

The Healing Woman
P.O. Box 3038
Moss Beach, CA 94038
Phone: 415/728-0339

LESBIAN-FRIENDLY HEALTH CARE CLINICS

See also pages 466–487 for a listing of community centers and the services provided. Some of the larger ones offer health care.

CANADA

Hassle-Free Clinic
556 Church Street, 2nd floor
Toronto, Ontario M4Y 2E3
Phone: 613/922-0566

UNITED STATES

Beach Area Community Health
  Center
3705 Mission Boulevard
San Diego, CA 92109
Phone: 619/488-0644

Hartford Gay and Lesbian Health
  Collective
P.O. Box 2094
Hartford, CT 06145-2094
Phone: 203/236-1959

Women's Health Services
911 State Street
New Haven, CT 06511
Phone: 203/777-4781

Whitman Walker Clinic
1407 S Street NW
Washington, DC 20009
Phone: 202/797-3500

Feminist Women's Health Center
580 14th Street NW
Atlanta, GA 30318
Phone: 800/877-6013

Chicago Women's Health Center
3435 N. Sheffield Avenue
Chicago, IL 60657
Phone: 312/935-6126

Chase-Brexton Clinic
101 West Read Street #211
Baltimore, MD 21201
Phone: 410/837-2050

Fenway Community Health Center
7 Haviland Street
Boston, MA 02115
Phone: 617/267-0900

Community Health Project
Lesbian and Gay Community Services
  Center
208 West 13th Street
New York, NY 10011
Phone: 212/675-3559; TTY: 800/662-
  1220

St. Mark's Health Collective
9 Second Avenue
New York, NY
Mailing address:
P.O. Box A-711
Grand Central Station
New York, NY 10163-0711
Phone: 212/228-7482

Elizabeth Blackwell Health Center for
  Women
1124 Walnut Street
Philadelphia, PA 19107
Phone: 215/923-7577

Vermont Women's Health Center
P.O. Box 29
Burlington, VT 05402
Phone: 802/863-1386

Madison Naturopathic Clinic
1812 East Madison, #205
Seattle, WA 98122
Phone: 206/329-1237

THE BASICS OF BREAST SELF-EXAMINATION

1. Remove your shirt and bra. In front of a mirror, look for anything unusual about your breasts: discharge, dimpling, puckering. Gently squeeze each nipple to check for discharge.
2. Raise your right arm. With the fingers of your left hand, explore your right breast, starting at the outer edge and moving in small circles slowly around the breast. Make sure you check the armpit, too. Feel for any lumps or abnormalities under the skin. Lower your arm.
3. Raise your left arm and repeat the procedure for the left breast.
4. Lie down, with your right arm behind your head on a pillow. Repeat step 2 in this position. Lower your arm.
5. Still lying down, place your left arm behind your head and repeat step 3.

The best way to examine your breasts is in the shower, where the water and soap make your fingers glide more easily over them. Another method is using an invention called a Sensor Pad, a soft, pliable plastic pad that makes examination easier. Ask your health care provider about it or write to Inventive Products, 1450 East North Street, Decatur, IL 62521, for information on obtaining the Sensor Pad.

THE KEGEL EXERCISE

The Kegel exercise is used to strengthen and tone the pelvic floor muscles supporting the bladder, urethra, vagina, uterus, and rectum. Toning these essential muscles can increase sexual pleasure, aid in labor, and guard against urinary incontinence. Studies show that 8 percent of all women ages twenty-four to sixty-three and 15 percent of women over sixty-four will experience incontinence.

Just follow these two simple steps:

1. Contract your pelvic muscles.
2. Count to ten quickly and then release.

Do as many a day as you can to improve muscle tone.

SOURCE: *NYC Lesbian Health Fair Journal*, 1994

AWARDS AND SCHOLARSHIPS IN THE AREA OF LESBIAN HEALTH

Annual Lesbian Psychologies Unpublished Manuscripts Award: One award is given annually for scholarship on the psychology of lesbians. Unpublished manuscripts up to 100 pages in length focusing on any aspect of lesbian psychology may be submitted. Both sole and jointly authored papers are eligible. The prize of up to $250—donated by the Boston Lesbian Psychologies Collective, editors of *Lesbian Psychologies*, from their royalties—helps pay for travel to the annual Association for Women in Psychology conference. The deadline is May of each year. For more information: Association for Women in Psychology, c/o Jo Ruprecht, Satoru Associates, 703 North Reymond, Las Cruces, NM 88005-2135; Phone: 505/526-6481.

Barbara Rosenblum Fellowship for the Study of Women and Cancer: Named for Barbara Rosenblum, a lesbian and the coauthor of *Cancer in Two Voices*, this fellowship is open to feminist women doctoral students who are interested in studying breast cancer and its impact on women from diverse social classes and cultural backgrounds. The research may be conducted in the areas of sociology, anthropology, psychology, or related fields dealing with women's experiences of breast cancer and the prevention of breast cancer. Priority is given to research with practical applications that can be presented to lay audiences as well as to social scientists. One grant of $1,500 is awarded annually; the deadline is June. For more information: Sociologists for Women in Society, c/o Virginia Olsen, 158 Funston, San Francisco, CA 94118; Phone: 415/476-2453.

The Lesbian Health Fund: This project of the Gay and Lesbian Medical Association establishes grants for research and education addressing lesbian health issues (medical and mental health). For information contact: Lesbian Health Fund, 273 Church Street, San Francisco, CA 94114; Phone: 415/255-4547.

QUICK FACTS ABOUT LESBIAN HEALTH

In the National Lesbian Health Survey of 1987 of 1,600 lesbians, 80 percent said they regularly used seat belts, only 20 percent smoked, and 38 percent did aerobic exercise three or more times a week.

In a 1988 study of lesbians' relationships with their health care providers, 72 percent recounted negative experiences.

A 1988 study of 529 African-American lesbians and bisexual women showed that only 33 percent had revealed their sexual orientation to their health care provider.

A Midwest nursing school faculty survey published in 1989 revealed that half of the teachers thought lesbianism was unnatural and disgusting. Almost one-fifth believed that lesbians molest children.

A 1994 survey of members of the Gay and Lesbian Medical Association (GLMA) indicated that more than half of the GLMA physicians observed their heterosexual colleagues providing substandard care to lesbian and gay clients.

It is estimated that one in three lesbians is at risk for breast cancer.

In 1993, Women, Inc., a San Francisco–based organization serving battered women, reported that domestic violence occurs in one-fourth of all lesbian relationships, about the same as for heterosexual relationships.

SOURCE: *Gay and Lesbian Stats*, edited by Bennet T. L. Singer and David Deschamps

---

MAKING SENSE OF HEALTH INSURANCE

If you're self-employed, your employer doesn't provide medical benefits, or your workplace makes available a number of health care options, it's often a challenge to determine which health care plan would work best for you. There are basically three types of health insurance available.

HEALTH MAINTENANCE ORGANIZATIONS (HMOS)

Health maintenance organizations represent prepaid insurance plans in which individuals or their employers pay a fixed monthly fee for services, instead of a separate charge for each visit or service. The monthly fees remain the same, regardless of the types or levels of services provided. Services are provided by physicians who are employed by or under contract with the HMO. HMOs vary in design. Depending on the type of HMO, services may be provided in a central facility or in a physician's own office. *Independent practice associations (IPAs)* are similar to HMOs, except that individuals receive care in a physician's own office, rather than in an HMO facility.

In general, HMOs are designed for people in good health, who need only basic preventive care coverage and who don't have any specific or chronic health concerns. They are also not available in some areas of the country.

INDEMNITY HEALTH PLAN

Indemnity health insurance plans are also called fee-for-service. These are the types of plans that primarily existed before the rise of HMOs, IPAs, and PPOs (preferred provider organizations). With indemnity plans, the individual pays a predetermined percentage of the cost of health care services, and the insurance company (or self-insured employer) pays the other percentage. For example, an individual might pay 20 percent for services and the insurance company pays 80 percent. The fees for services are defined by the providers and vary from physician to physician. Indemnity health plans offer individuals the freedom to choose their health care professionals.

PREFERRED PROVIDER ORGANIZATION (PPO)

With PPOs, you or your employer receive discounted rates if you use doctors from a preselected group. If you use a physician outside the PPO plan, you must pay more for the medical care. PPOs differ from HMOs because the physicians are only affiliated with the PPO, not employed by it.

The following questions may help you decide among the three types of plans:

What services does the plan cover?

What, if any, are the deductibles? Are they one-time or yearly?

What preventive health services are covered? How many preventive visits are covered?

What is the maximum lifetime dollar limit that the policy will pay? What are the limits for chronic conditions? (This question is especially important where illnesses such as breast cancer or HIV/AIDS are an issue.)

What is the maximum out-of-pocket expenses you are likely to incur in a given year?

Are mental health services included? Alternative forms of health care, such as chiropractic and acupuncture? What are the limits of coverage on these services?

Are treatments for substance abuse covered?

What are the policy's restrictions on preexisting conditions?

What are the restrictions on inpatient and outpatient care?

What maternity services are covered?

What is the average turnaround time on claims?

Will the policy cover medical emergencies when you travel?

Do you have the freedom to choose a physician? If it is an HMO, can you change physicians within the health care facility? Must you choose a physician from among those specified? Can you see a list of physicians before making your choice? Can you find out which, if any, have dealt with your particular health concerns? Are the physicians board certified? How can you change physicians if you choose one you don't like? Are there physicians within your geographic area?

Can you choose the hospital of preference if you require inpatient care?

DOMESTIC PARTNER HEALTH BENEFITS

The National Lesbian and Gay Journalists Association has just produced an eight-page booklet called "News Media Executive's Guide to Domestic Partner Benefits." The booklet is aimed at the news industry, but it could be given to any employer to show that offering health insurance to the domestic partners of employees is affordable, feasible, and fair. For a copy, send a $2 check (tax deductible) made out to NLGJA to: NLGJA, 874 Gravenstein Highway South, Suite 4, Sebastopol, CA 95472; Phone: 707/823-2193; Fax: 707/823-4176. NLGJA also publishes a list (constantly updated) of U.S. employers offering domestic partner benefits, available at the same address for $2.70.

COMPANIES WITH DOMESTIC PARTNER HEALTH BENEFITS

Apple Computers
Ben & Jerry's Ice Cream
Borland International
The Boston Globe
Capital Cities/ABC
Adolph Coors Co.
FNMA (Fannie Mae)
Frame Technology
International Data Group
KQED-TV and Radio
  (San Francisco)
Levi Strauss & Co.
Lotus Development Corp.
MCA/Universal Studios
Microsoft Corp.
Minnesota Communications
  Group/MN Public Radio

Montefiore Medical Center
  (New York City)
National Public Radio
Charles Schwab
The Seattle Times
Silicon Graphics
Starbucks Coffee
Sun Microsystems
Time-Warner Inc. (including
  many of its divisions: HBO,
  Time Inc., Warner Brothers
  Pictures, and Atlantic Pictures)
Viacom
The Village Voice
WGBH-TV (Boston)
Ziff-Davis Publications

INSURANCE COMPANIES THAT HAVE PROVIDED (OR ARE WILLING TO PROVIDE) DOMESTIC PARTNER HEALTH BENEFITS

Aetna
Blue Cross
Bridgeway
Cigna

Consumers United
Fireman's Insurance Co.
Foundation Health Plan
George Washington University HMO

Great West Life

Group Health Cooperative
of Puget Sound

Group Health Insurance of
New York

Harvard Community Health Plan

Kaiser Permanente

Liberty Mutual

Mass Mutual

Pacific Care

Pacific Health

Prudential

Qualmed

Vision Service Plan

SOURCE: "Domestic Partner Benefits: At What Cost?" National Lesbian and Gay Journalists Association, 1994

MYTHS AND FACTS ABOUT THE DISABLED

Myth: Gay disabled people are not sexual.

Fact: Disabled people have the same sexual and emotional needs as everyone else. We are sexual, we can give and receive love, and we can establish relationships. Many disabled gays and lesbians are in loving, adult relationships.

Myth: The disabled are deformed and unattractive.

Fact: Many of us do not have visible signs of disability and not all visible disabilities are unattractive. Beauty is in the eye of the beholder.

Myth: There are no disabled gay men or women.

Fact: Ten percent of the population is gay and lesbian. Therefore, it is common sense to assume a percentage is physically disabled.

Myth: Disabled lesbians and gays isolate themselves by choice.

Fact: Isolation is rarely a matter of choice. Physical barriers and society's prejudices can cause isolation and withdrawal.

Myth: The disabled are unable to make their own choices or decisions.

Fact: Disabled individuals are often not asked what they want; it is assumed their dependencies are across the board. Just because someone cannot do what they want does not mean they don't know what they want.

Myth: The disabled are an embarrassment.

Fact: The public response to the disabled is often one of embarrassment and discomfort. We are an embarrassment of riches and have the same variety of skills and talents as everyone else. Disabled does not mean un-abled.

Myth: The disabled have nothing to offer and cannot be helpful.

Fact: Many disabled people hold valuable positions in all walks of life regardless of our balance and posture.

SOURCE: EDGE (Education in a Disabled Gay Environment).

PROFILE

Project Connect

The New York City Lesbian and Gay Community Services Center is home to an award-winning addiction prevention and intervention program called Project Connect. Established in 1987, it has become a model for similar drug and alcohol programs across the country. Project Connect provides information, counseling, support groups, and referrals to gay-affirmative treatment to all those interested in pursuing recovery from substance abuse and to family members, friends, and lovers of problem drinkers and drug users. Under the guidance of Dr. Barbara Warren, the center's director of mental health and social services, Project Connect has served more than three thousand lesbians and gay men throughout the five boroughs of New York.

Project Connect is the only gay- and lesbian-identified program of its kind on the East Coast and is the winner of numerous awards, including the Outstanding Community Health Promotion Program Award from the U.S. Secretary of Health and Human Services.

Essential to Project Connect's mission of serving gay and lesbian substance abusers is its commitment to training and educating mainstream treatment facilities about the needs of their lesbian and gay clients. Project Connect has provided more than 250 diversity trainings, which make the linkages, for client and staff alike, between the recovery process and issues surrounding lesbian and gay identity and between the recovery process and issues surrounding race and gender.

In 1993, a contract under the Ryan White Emergency Care Act enabled Project Connect to offer more enhanced services, including relapse prevention counseling for individuals and groups and recovery readiness programming for HIV-positive men and women.

Project Connect has also initiated numerous off-site groups for lesbians and bisexual women, including an ongoing group at the Single Parent Resource Center, a four-week group at Damon House, a long-term residential drug and alcohol program in Brooklyn, and a seminar for women in a work-release program at Rikers Island incarceration unit. All of these groups and seminars addressed issues of identity, sexuality, HIV, and recovery.

Project Connect
Lesbian and Gay Community Services Center
208 West 13th Street
New York, NY 10011
Phone: 212/620-7310; Fax: 212/924-2657

PROFILE

National Lesbian and Gay Health Association

In June 1994, eleven lesbian and gay community health centers from around the United States joined together with a network of 20,000 lesbian and gay health care providers to form the National Lesbian and Gay Health Association. NLGHA is now the only national lesbian and gay organization headquartered in the nation's capital that focuses solely on improving our community's health.

NLGHA resulted from the merger of the National Alliance of Lesbian and Gay Health Clinics and the National Lesbian and Gay Health Foundation. The National Alliance of Lesbian and Gay Health Clinics was founded in 1992 to facilitate communication among clinics and to foster a national lesbian and gay health care agenda. The National Lesbian and Gay Health Foundation, started in 1978, sponsored an annual conference for sixteen years, which was the first conference to feature an international forum on HIV/AIDS.

Currently, NLGHA has two full-time staffers and more than twenty members on the board of directors. The association is dedicated to enhancing the quality of health care for lesbians and gay men through education, policy development, advocacy, and the facilitation of health care delivery.

The association holds a contract with the U.S Public Health Service to provide technical assistance, training materials, and educational initiatives to health care institutions, organizations, and providers. The particular emphasis is on sensitizing health care professionals to lesbian and gay health needs.

Other projects of the association include establishing a national research institute on lesbian and gay health; setting up a resource center on lesbian and gay health issues; undertaking the annual publication of a white paper on lesbian and gay health; and linking current lesbian and gay health organizations, centers, and providers for information sharing and networking. There are also numerous projects currently being handled by undergraduate and graduate interns and volunteers, including compiling a press list, developing a newsletter, creating an electronic network, and tracking legislation related to lesbian and gay health concerns.

National Lesbian and Gay Health Association
1407 S Street NW
Washington, DC 20009
Phone: 202/939-7880; Fax: 202/797-3504

8. Lesbian Homes and Families

Good parents are good parents—regardless of their sexual orientation. It's clear that the sexual orientation of parents has nothing to do with the sexual orientation or outlook of their children.

—Joycelyn Elders, former U.S. Surgeon General

We're here, we're queer, we're redefining the term *family*.

In a 1992 study of the United States, 55 percent of gay men and 71 percent of lesbians were in what they considered to be committed or steady relationships. Still, as of this writing, both the United States and Canada continue to deny lesbians and gay men the right to marry and the legal benefits that a marriage certificate brings, though an important court case pending in the state of Hawaii may soon change that by setting a legal precedent for same-sex marriage. Until then, lesbians and gay men continue to create their own weddings and commitment ceremonies, the largest of which was the 3,000-couple mass wedding that took place during the third March on Washington for Lesbian, Gay, and Bisexual Rights in April 1993.

In the last decade, some inroads have been made for domestic partners (couples who live together in relationships without being legally married). In thirteen U.S. cities and one state (Vermont), for example, government employees have been afforded health care benefits for their same-sex domestic partners. And sev-

At the 1993 Lesbian and Gay Pride March, New York City *(Photo by Harry Stevens)*

At the 1992 Lesbian and Gay Pride March, New York City *(Photo by Harry Stevens)*

eral dozen private-sector companies and organizations have also begun to recognize same-sex relationships in their employee benefits programs.

A 1993 study indicated that, in the United States, there were between three and eight million lesbian and gay parents, raising between six and fourteen million children. Most of these children live with parents who were formerly in heterosexual marriages or relationships and then came out as lesbian or gay, but a growing number of lesbians and gay men in the last decade have opted to become parents.

The term *lesbian baby boom* refers to the sudden sharp increase in the number of lesbians who, since the mid-1980s, have made the decision to have children—sometimes on their own but usually with a lesbian partner; occasionally with a gay male friend as sperm donor, but more often using the services of sperm banks. These are women from the postwar baby boom of 1945–1960 and later, who came of age with the feminist and gay rights movements with a greater knowledge of reproductive rights and alternatives. Gay men have enjoyed a parenting boom all their own, relying on adoptions and surrogacy arrangements to create their new families.

In a few areas of the United States, particularly California, second-parent adoption—the legal adoption of a child, who already has one legal parent, by a second parent of the same gender—has been possible for dozens of these lesbian parents.

To respond to the growing need, advocacy organizations and groups have sprung up for lesbian and gay parents and their children. Programs such as Center Kids at New York's Lesbian and Gay Community Services Center provide support not only for parents and children, but for those gay people contemplating parenthood.

Despite the myth that lesbians and gay men do not make fit parents, and that children must be protected from gay people, psychologists' studies continue to show that the children of lesbian and gay parents are neither emotionally nor psychologically disadvantaged simply by having same-sex parents, nor do they necessarily grow up to be gay themselves.

It is young lesbians and gays, often stigmatized by their peers and rejected by their families, who continue to be the ones in jeopardy. Gay teens are among those at highest risk for alcoholism, drug abuse, suicide, and HIV infection and are in desperate need of positive role models and risk-prevention programs that will help them make it to adulthood.

Some of us are lucky—our parents accept us, even if they don't always understand us. Supportive parents formed their own organization in the early 1980s, Parents and Friends of Lesbians and Gays (P-FLAG), which is still going strong. Their mission is to not only support each other and their children, but to also raise the consciousness of the general population to the fact that gay people are healthy human beings who are part of families everywhere.

SOME STATISTICS

There were between three and eight million lesbian and gay parents in the United States in 1993, raising between six and fourteen million children.

A 1987 government survey reported that there were approximately 11,000 physicians in the United States performing alternative inseminations, and about 37 percent (roughly 4,000) of them were willing to inseminate lesbians.

A 1988 newspaper article reported 1,000 surrogacy births in the prior ten years. Other experts believe 2,000 to be a more accurate number.

Two states, Florida and New Hampshire, expressly forbid lesbian and gay adoption. As of 1993, more than 200 second-parent adoptions had been granted in eight jurisdictions: Alabama, California, Minnesota, New York, Oregon, Vermont, Washington, and Washington, D.C.

A TIME LINE OF LESBIAN AND GAY FAMILY ISSUES

1953: *ONE* magazine began publication, the first openly gay magazine to achieve wide circulation. The U.S. Post Office claimed articles about homosexuality were obscene, specifically an article on gay marriages.

1962: A study by Dr. Irving Bieber concluded that homosexuality is largely caused by seductive mothers and hostile fathers.

1970: Jack Baker, student at the University of Minnesota, unsuccessfully applied for a marriage license with his lover, Jim McConnell. They did, however, manage to file joint tax returns in 1972 and 1973.

FROM THE MOUTHS OF ACADEMIC RESEARCHERS

"All the studies agree that when lesbian couples choose to become parents together, they most often strive for, and often achieve, a near 50/50 sharing of all aspects of family life: decision-making, child care, household tasks.

"Our study was also consistent with the others in showing that, in most couples, both partners had not only a strong measurable involvement in parenting, but also a profound subjective sense of themselves as parents.

"On the basis of our data, we suggested that planned lesbian families present a viable model of an effectively functioning family in contemporary America."

—Drs. Valory Mitchell and Diane Wilson, Institute for the Psychology of Women, California School of Professional Psychology, Alameda, California, in an ongoing study of planned lesbian families

1972: Camille Mitchell is the first open lesbian to be awarded custody of her children in a divorce case. The judge restricted the arrangement by precluding Ms. Mitchell's lover from moving in with her and the children.

• A made-for-TV film about a fourteen-year-old boy who discovers his father is gay, "That Certain Summer," aired on ABC. This is one of the first TV dramas to portray homosexual issues in a relatively nonhomophobic way, and was generally well reviewed.

1973: Controversial gay minister Rev. Ray Broshears married three WAC couples in San Francisco, generating much publicity in the process. Two of the women, Gail Bates and Valerie Randolph, were discharged from the military.

1977: Two lesbians won custody cases. In Michigan, Jacqueline Stamper won joint custody rights for her two children in spite of her ex-husband's charge that she was morally unfit because she was a lesbian. In Denver, Donna Levy won custody of her deceased former lover's daughter, against opposition by the child's aunt and uncle.

1979: Seventeen-year-old Randy Rohl of Sioux Falls, South Dakota, took a male date to the prom. A year later, Rhode Island high school student Aaron Fricke took a gay date to his prom, following a court order forcing school administrators to relax their refusal.

1981: New Kinsey study reports neither parental nor societal influences have much effect on sexual orientation.

• Parents and Friends of Lesbians and Gays formed in Los Angeles.

1983: Karen Thompson's eight-year struggle for legal guardianship of her lover, Sharon Kowalski, began when a drunk driver collided with Sharon's vehicle, placing her in a coma for several months and leaving her quadriplegic and severely brain damaged. Despite Sharon's wishes to be cared for by Karen, Sharon's parents refused Karen full access or input into her care. Karen Thompson became a key spokesperson for lesbian and gay couples' rights. Karen's case was won in 1991.

1984: Gay, lesbian, and unmarried heterosexual couples can receive the same benefits as married couples in areas such as health care and bereavement leave in Berkeley, California, the first U.S. city to pass a domestic partners law for municipal employees.

1985: Following the loss of a highly publicized lawsuit filed by two gay men who had been evicted from Disneyland for dancing together, the amusement park announced that it would allow same-sex couples to dance together, stating the rule was changed to accommodate teenage girls who came without dates and wanted to dance.

1987: Approximately 2,000 same-sex couples were "married" in a mass wedding on the steps of the Internal Revenue Service in Washington, D.C., on October 10. The ceremony was part of the 1987 March on Washington activities, dramatizing the tax benefits for married people that lesbian and gay couples are denied.

1989: A New York State court ruled that a gay couple could be considered family for purposes of rent-controlled apartments. The California Bar Association urged that lesbian and gay marriage be legally recognized, and in Seattle, San Francisco, and other cities, partners regulations extending certain protections and rights to unmarried couples—straight and gay—were adopted.

1989: The New York State Court of Appeals declared that a lesbian or gay couple living together for at least ten years could be considered a family for purposes of rent control protection, the first time a state's highest court ruled that a gay couple could be called a family. On the same day in July, a recent ordinance giving limited protections to same-sex couples in San Francisco was suspended after opponents gathered enough signatures on petitions to place the issue on the November ballot. The ordinance lost that vote by only a 1 percent margin.

1989: Center Kids, the family project of the Lesbian and Gay Community Services Center, was founded in New York to provide support and networking opportunities for lesbian and gay parents and their children.

1990: For the first time, the U.S. census included a question that more or less identified gay couples. It found 88,200 gay male couples with an average household income of $56,863, and 69,200 lesbian couples with an average household income of $44,793.

1991: *Pediatrics* magazine reported nearly half of the lesbian and gay teenagers interviewed for a study say they have attempted suicide.

1992: Domestic partners of employees of Levi Strauss & Co. were granted full medical benefits.

    • The province of Ontario, Canada, extended spousal benefits to same-sex partners of government workers.

    • William Weld, Governor of Massachusetts, signed an executive order granting lesbian and gay state workers the same bereavement and family leave rights as heterosexual workers.

    • A proposed multicultural curriculum for first graders that includes references to lesbian and gay parents resulted in heated debate, demonstrations, threats of violence toward gay parents, the forced resignation of the New York City school chancellor, and the largest turnout for a school board election in the city's history. The curriculum was revised to delete virtually all mention of lesbian and gay families.

1993: Hawaii Supreme Court ruled that a lower court improperly dismissed a lawsuit challenging a state policy of denying marriage licenses to gay and lesbian couples. The court ruled that the prohibition of same-sex marriages constitutes sex discrimination and is probably unconstitutional.

 • Lesbian mother Roberta Achtenberg was confirmed by the U.S. Senate to become the assistant secretary for fair housing and equal opportunity at the Department of Housing and Urban Development, the first time an openly gay person had ever been confirmed by the Senate for a high-level government position.

1994: The Virginia Court of Appeals overturned a lower court ruling stripping lesbian mother Sharon Bottoms of custody of her son based on her sexual orientation.

 • A resolution was passed at the convention of the Oregon PTA that read: "Resolved that the Oregon PTA rejects prejudice, harassment, discrimination or intolerance directed against students, parents, teachers or staff members as a result of their sexual orientation; and be it further resolved that the Oregon PTA opposes all legislative attempts to suppress discussion of family diversity and sexual orientation."

 • Portland, Oregon, allowed nonmarried city employees' domestic partners to be eligible for full spousal benefits.

 • On July 9, what would have been the most comprehensive domestic partner law in North America, equalizing seventy-nine statutes that use the word *spouse* to include lesbian and gay couples, was defeated by the Ontario Parliament due to a stalemate on the ever-controversial issue of gay and lesbian adoption. Following the vote, 5,000 lesbians and gay men marched on Parliament chanting "Equal Taxes, Equal Rights!"

BIBLIOGRAPHY

LESBIAN AND GAY PARENTING

Alpert, Harriet, ed. *We Are Everywhere: Writings by and about Lesbian Mothers.* Crossing Press, 1988.

Bozett, Frederick W., ed. *Gay and Lesbian Parents.* Praeger, 1987.

Burke, Phyllis. *Family Values: Two Moms and Their Son.* Random House, 1993.

Corley, Rip. *The Final Closet: The Gay Parents' Guide for Coming Out to Their Children.* Editech Press, 1990.

Curry, Hayden, and Denis Clifford. *A Legal Guide for Lesbians and Gay Couples.* Nolo Press, 1991.

de Lamadrid, Maria Gill, ed. *Lesbians Choosing Motherhood: Legal Implications of Donor Insemination and Co-Parenting.* National Center for Lesbian Rights, 1991.

Hanscombe, Gillian E., and Jackie Forster. *Rocking the Cradle: Lesbian Mothers, A Challenge in Family Living*. Alyson Publications, 1981.

MacPike, Loralee, ed. *There's Something I've Been Meaning to Tell You: An Anthology about Lesbians and Gay Men Coming Out to Their Children*. Naiad Press, 1989.

Martin, April. *Lesbian and Gay Parenting Handbook: Creating and Raising Our Families*. HarperCollins, 1993.

Noble, Elizabeth. *Having Your Baby by Donor Insemination*. Houghton Mifflin, 1987.

Pies, Cheri. *Considering Parenthood: A Workbook for Lesbians*. Spinsters Ink/Aunt Lute, 1985.

Pollack, Sandra, and Jean Vaughn, eds. *Politics of the Heart: A Lesbian Parenting Anthology*. Firebrand Books, 1987.

Pratt, Minnie Bruce. *Crime Against Nature*. Firebrand Books, 1990.

Rafkin, Louise, ed. *Different Mothers: Sons and Daughters of Lesbians Talk About Their Lives*. Cleis Press, 1990.

Rizzo, Cindy, et al., eds. *All the Ways Home: Parenting and Children in the Lesbian and Gay Community—A Collection of Short Fiction*. New Victoria Publishers, 1995.

Robinson, Susan, and H. F. Pizer. *Having a Baby Without a Man: A Woman's Guide to Alternative Insemination*. Simon and Schuster, Inc., 1987.

Robson, Ruthann. *Cecile*. Firebrand Books, 1991.

Schulenberg, Joy. *Gay Parenting: A Complete Guide for Gay Men and Lesbians with Children*. Doubleday/Anchor, 1985.

LESBIAN AND GAY PARENTING NEWSLETTERS

The Family Next Door. Next Door Publishing, Ltd., P.O. Box 21580, Oakland, CA 94620; 510/482-5778. Provides lesbian and gay parents, their families, and friends with a forum for communication and support. Published 6 times a year.

Gay Fathers of Los Angeles. GFLA, 7985 Santa Monica Blvd., Suite 90046, Los Angeles, CA 90046; 213/654-0307 or 213/654-0307.

Love Makes a Family. P.O. Box 11694, Portland, OR 97211; 503/228-3892.

News Updates. Gay Fathers of Toronto (GFT), Box 187, Station F, Toronto, Ontario M4Y 2L5; 416/975-1680 or 800/663-5016.

Triangles and Hearts. Houston Gay and Lesbian Parents (HGLP), P.O. Box 35709-0262, Houston, TX 77235-5709; Glenda Redworth, editor, 713/666-8256.

CHILDREN OF LESBIAN AND GAY PARENTS

Homosexuality is now the number one topic for censorship, especially if the books are for children.

—Ros Udow, National Coalition Against Censorship

Alden, Joan. *A Boy's Best Friend*. Alyson Publications, Boston, 1992. Ages 5–8. Will, who suffers from asthma, can't have a real dog. But his two moms come up with a birthday solution to his problem.

Elwin, Rosamund, and Michele Paulse. *Asha's Mums*. Women's Press, 1990. Ages 4–7. African-Canadian moms and their daughter.

Homes, Norma. *Breaking Up*. Macmillan, 1989. Teenage girl learns her mother is a lesbian; custody issues.

Newman, Lesléa. *Saturday is Pattyday*. Alyson Publications, 1993. A child of separated lesbian moms.

———. *Belinda's Bouquet*. Alyson Publications, 1991. Ages 4–8. Daniel's lesbian mom helps his best friend, Belinda, toward self-acceptance as she struggles with weight issues.

———. *Gloria Goes to Gay Pride*. Alyson Publications, 1991. Ages 3–7. She goes with her lesbian moms.

———. *Heather Has Two Mommies*. Alyson Publications, 1989. Ages 3–8. Explains alternative insemination.

Schaffer, Patricia. *How Babies and Families Are Made: There Is More Than One Way*. Tabor Sarah Books, 1988. Includes discussion of alternative insemination.

Severance, Jan. *Lots of Mommies*. Lollipop Power, 1983. Ages 3–6. A little girl with four mothers; an unusual account of a child living in a women's collective.

———. *When Megan Went Away*. Lollipop Power, 1983. Ages 4–7. A little girl and her mother feel sad and angry when her mom's lover moves out of their home.

PARENTS OF LESBIAN AND GAY CHILDREN

Fairchild, Betty, and Nancy Howard. *Now that You Know: What Every Parent Should Know About Homosexuality*. Harcourt, Brace, Jovanovich, 1978.

Griffin, Carolyn, Marian Wirth, and Arthur Wirth. *Beyond Acceptance: Parents of Lesbians and Gays Talk About Their Experiences*. St. Martin's Press, New York, 1986.

Rafkin, Louise. *Different Daughters: A Book by Mothers of Lesbians*. Cleis Press, 1987.

LESBIAN AND GAY YOUTH

Alyson, Sasha, ed. *Young, Gay and Proud*. Alyson Publications, 1991.

Garden, Nancy. *Annie on My Mind*. Farrar, Straus and Giroux, 1982.

Grima, Tony. *Not the Only One*. Alyson Publications, 1995.

Heron, Ann, ed. *Two Teenagers in Twenty: Writings about Lesbian and Gay Youth*. Alyson Publications, 1994.

Rench, Janice E. *Understanding Sexual Identity: A Book for Gay Teens and Their Friends*. Lerner, 1990.

LESBIAN AND GAY COUPLES

Ayers, Tess, and Paul Brown. *The Essential Guide to Gay and Lesbian Weddings.* HarperSanFrancisco, 1994.

Berzon, Betty. *Permanent Partners: Building Gay and Lesbian Relationships.* New American Library, 1990.

Butler, Becky. *Ceremonies of the Heart: Celebrating Lesbian Unions.* Seal Press, 1990.

Clunis, D. Merilee, and G. Dorsey Green. *Lesbian Couples: Creating Healthy Relationships for the Nineties.* Seal Press, 1993.

Curry, Hayden, Dennis Clifford, and Robin Leonard. *A Legal Guide for Lesbian and Gay Couples.* 8th ed. Nolo Press, 1992.

Mendola, Mary. *The Mendola Report: A New Look at Gay Couples.* Crown Publishers, 1980.

VIDEOTAPES

Alternative Conceptions, by Christina Sunley and Vicky Funari. 1985, video, 36 minutes.

Lesbian Motherhood via Donor Insemination. Available from: Women Make Movies, 225 Lafayette St., New York, NY 10012; 212/925-0606.

Both of My Moms' Names Are Judy: Children of Lesbians and Gays Speak Out, produced by Camomile Bortman, Lisa Rudman, Dwayne Schanz, and Diane Livia. Handouts accompanying the video include a pamphlet of myths and realities about lesbian and gay parents, articles by young people with gay friends or family members, suggestions for how to handle harassment and ways to include the issue in the classroom, a bibliography and resource list. Available from: Lesbian/Gay Parents Association (LGPA), 6705 California St., Apt. 1, San Francisco, CA 94121.

Choosing Children, by Debra Chasnoff and Kim Klausner. 16mm film, 1984, 45 minutes.

Lesbians Becoming Parents. Available from: Cambridge Documentary Films, P.O. Box 385, Cambridge, MA 02139; 617/354-3677.

In the Best Interests of the Children: A Film About Lesbian Mothers and Child Custody, by Frances Reid, Elizabeth Stevens, and Cathy Zheutlin. 16mm film, 53 minutes, 1977. Available from: Women Make Movies, 225 Lafayette St., New York, NY 10012; 212/925-0606.

Labor More Than Once, by Liz Mersky. 1983, video, 52 minutes. Lesbian mother's custody battle. Available from: Women Make Movies, 225 Lafayette St., New York, NY 10012; 212/925-0606.

Not All Parents Are Straight, by Kevin White. 1987, 16mm or video, 58 minutes. Family profiles of lesbian and gay parents and their children. Available from: Cinema Guild, Suite 802, 1697 Broadway, New York, NY 10019; 212/246-5522.

A Question of Love (made-for-TV movie), with Jane Alexander and Gena Rowlands as lesbians fighting for child custody. 1978. Available from: Lambda Rising, 1625 Connecticut Ave. NW, Washington, DC 20009; 212/462-6969.

Sandy and Madeleine's Family, by Sharrie Farrell. 1974, 16mm film, 30 minutes. Available from: Multi-Focus, Inc., 1525 Franklin St., San Francisco, CA 94109; 415/673-5100.

We Are Family, by Amee Sands and Dasal Banks. 1987, 3/4" video. Legal and social implications of gay and lesbian parenting explored through three families. Available from: WGBH-TV, 125 Western Ave., Alston, MA 02134; 617/492-2777.

SOME FAMOUS NORTH AMERICAN LESBIAN/GAY/BISEXUAL PARENTS

Roberta Achtenberg
Dorothy Allison
Joan Baez
Josephine Baker
Ann Bannon
Amanda Bearse
Leonard Bernstein
Susie Bright
Margarethe Cammermeyer
John Cheever
Aaron Copeland
Samuel Delaney
Lillian Faderman
Malcolm Forbes
Stephen Foster
Paul Goodman

Harry Hay
James Hormel
Audre Lorde
JoAnn Loulan
Thomas Mann
Del Martin and Phyllis Lyon
Rod McKuen
Herman Melville
Robin Morgan
Rev. Troy Perry
Minnie Bruce Pratt
Adrienne Rich
Mariana Romo-Carmona
Eleanor Roosevelt
Dr. Tom Waddell

JURISDICTIONS WHERE SECOND-PARENT ADOPTIONS HAVE BEEN GRANTED

Alaska
California
District of Columbia
Illinois
Massachusetts (statewide)
Michigan
Minnesota
New Jersey

New York
Ohio
Oregon
Pennsylvania
Rhode Island
Texas
Vermont (statewide)
Washington

SOURCE: GLPCI Network, Summer 1994

RESOURCES

GENERAL

Lambda Legal Defense and Education
  Fund
666 Broadway, 12th Fl.
New York, NY 10012
Phone: 212/995-8585
One of the oldest (1973) and largest
  gay legal organizations. Advocates
  for the rights of lesbian and gay
  people.

National Center for Lesbian Rights
  (NCLR)
1663 Mission St., 5th Fl.
San Francisco, CA 94103
Phone: 415/621-0674
  Fax: 415/621-6744
Founded in 1977. Legal
  representation and advocacy, advice
  and counseling, technical assistance,
  and education.

PARENTS OF LESBIANS AND GAY MEN

Federation of Parents and Friends of
  Lesbians and Gays, Inc.
1012 14th St. NW, #700
Washington, DC 20005
or
Box 27605
Washington, DC, 20038
Phone: 202/638-0243 or 202/638-4200
To help parents and friends of gay
  men and lesbians understand
  homosexuality through education
  and support, to educate the larger
  community on the issue, and to
  advocate for lesbian and gay civil
  rights.

National Federation of Parents and
  Friends of Gays
8020 Eastern Avenue, NW
Washington, DC 20012
Phone: 202/726-3223
Provides educational materials to
  anyone searching for understanding
  of human sexuality issues.

Parents and Friends of Integrity
Box 19561
Washington, DC 20036
For relatives and friends of gay
  people, with ties to the Episcopal
  church.

LESBIAN AND GAY PARENTS (NATIONAL)

Custody Action for Lesbian Moms
Narberth, PA 19072
Phone: 215/667-7508
Litigation support service for lesbian
  mothers.

Gay and Lesbian Parents Coalition
  International (GLPCI)
P.O. Box 50360
Washington, DC 20091
Phone: 202/583-8029

Coalition of gay parenting groups
  across the country. Sponsors annual
  national conference of lesbian and
  gay parents and their children.
  Newsletter, bibliographies.

Lavender Families (formerly Lesbian
  Mothers National Defense Fund)
P.O. Box 21567
Seattle, WA 98111
Phone: 206/325-2643

Attorney referrals, legal information, personal support for lesbians and gay men involved in custody disputes.

The Lyon-Martin Women's Health Clinic
1748 Market St., Suite 201
San Francisco, CA 94102
Phone: 415/565-7674

Momazons: Lesbians Choosing Children
P.O. Box 02069
Columbus, OH
Phone: 614/267-0193
National organization for lesbian mothers and lesbians who want kids in their lives.

LOCAL LESBIAN AND GAY PARENTING ORGANIZATIONS (BY STATE)

Gay and Lesbian Parent Support Network
P.O. Box 66823
Phoenix, AZ 85082-6823
Phone: 602/256-9173

Lesbian Mothers Group of Long Beach
2017 E. Routh St.
Long Beach, CA 90814
Phone: 310/424-4455

Outreach for Couples
405 W. Washington St., #86
San Diego, CA 92103

Gay and Lesbian Parents of Los Angeles
7985 Santa Monica, Suite 109-346
West Hollywood, CA 90046
Phone: 213/654-0307

Gay and Lesbian Parents—Denver
P.O. Box Drawer E
Denver, CO 80218
Phone: 303/937-3625

GLPCI Central Florida Chapter
P.O. Box 561-504
Orlando, FL 32856-1504
Attn: Chris Alexander
Phone: 407/420-2191

Evansville GLPC
P.O. Box 8341
Evansville, IN 47716

Gay and Lesbian Parents—Indiana
P.O. Box 831
Indianapolis, IN 46206
Phone: 317/926-9741
Attn: Craig or Terry

Gay and Lesbian Parenting Coalition of Metropolitan Washington
14908 Piney Grove Ct.
North Potomac, MD 20878
Phone: 301/762-4828

Lesbians Choosing Children Network
P.O. Box 393
Arlington, MA 02174
Phone: 508/458-0740

Lesbian/Gay Family and Parenting Services
Fenway Community Health Center
7 Haviland St.
Boston, MA 02115
Phone: 617/267-0900, ext. 282

Gay and Lesbian Parents Association—Detroit
P.O. Box 2694
Southfield, MI 48037-2694
Phone: 313/891-7292 or 313/790-2440

New Hampshire Gay Parents
P.O. Box 5981
Manchester, NH 03108
Phone: 603/527-1082

Center Kids contingent at the 1993 Lesbian and Gay Pride March, New York City
(Photo by Harry Stevens)

Center Kids, The Family Project of
    the Lesbian and Gay Community
    Services Center
208 W. 13th St.
New York, NY 10011
Phone: 212/620-7310
Fax: 212/924-2657

Lesmos W.A.C.C.
669 Woodfield Rd.
West Hempstead, NY 11522

GLP/Queen City—Charlotte
4417-F Sharon Chase Dr.
Charlotte, NC 28215

Gay and Lesbian Parenting Group of
    Central Ohio
P.O. Box 16235
Columbus, OH 43216

CALM, Inc. (Custody Action for
    Lesbian Mothers)
P.O. Box 281
Narberth, PA 19072
Phone: 215/667-7508

Houston Gay and Lesbian Parents
    Support
1301 Richmond, #T10
Houston, TX 77006
Phone: 713/522-6766

SAGL Parents
P.O. Box 15094
San Antonio, TX 78212
Attn: Rob O. Blanch
Phone: 512/828-4092

Gay and Lesbian League of Parents
    (GALLOP)
P.O. Box 64736
Burlington, VT 05406

National network providing variety of resources relevant to lesbian and gay parents.

Gay and Lesbian Parents Coalition of Milwaukee
P.O. Box 93503
Milwaukee, WI 53203

ADOPTIVE PARENTS (BY STATE)

Chain of Life
P.O. Box 8081
Berkeley, CA 94707
Janine Baer, ed. Gay/lesbian/feminist adoption newsletter.

Gay and Lesbian Adolescent Social Services (GLASS)
89012 Melrose Ave., Suite 202
Los Angeles, CA 90069-5605
Phone: 213/653-3496
Primarily services to adolescents, but has placed lesbian and gay youth in foster homes and in families for adoption.

AASK America (Aid to Adoption of Special Kids)
450 Sansome St., Suite 210
San Francisco, CA 94111
Phone: 415/781-4112
Chapters and cooperative agencies throughout the country. Places children with disabilities, sibling groups, children of color and racially mixed children, those born with drug dependencies, and babies with HIV/AIDS. The national board has an explicit nondiscrimination policy on the basis of sexual orientation.

The Triangle Project
1296 North Fairfax Ave.
West Hollywood, CA 90046
Phone: 213/656-5005
Lesbian and gay social service agency for gay youth, actively recruits prospective foster parents.

International Concerns Committee for Children
Report on Foreign Adoption
911 Cypress Drive
Boulder, CO 80303
Phone: 303/494-8333
Publishes annual listing of U.S. agencies handling international placements.

Americans for African Adoptions, Inc.
8910 Timberwood Dr.
Indianapolis, IN 46234
Sheryl Carter Shotts, Managing Director
Phone: 317/271-4567
Will accept applications from singles. Has openly sought lesbian and gay families.

Committee for Single Adoptive Parents
P.O. Box 15084
Chevy Chase, MD 20815
For U.S. and Canadian singles; domestic and foreign adoptions.

National Adoption Information Clearinghouse
11426 Rockville Pike, Suite 410
Rockville, MD 20852
Phone: 301/231-6512
Provides information about adoption nationwide. Maintains active search of resources and information. Can do computer searches on topics, i.e., lesbian and gay adoption.

Resolve, Inc.
5 Water St.
Arlington, MA 02174
Phone: 617/643-2424
Education and support for infertility; adoption information.

Adoptive Families of America, Inc.
Ours Magazine
Suite 203
2207 Highway 100 North
Minneapolis, MN 55422
Phone: 612/535-4829
National support, advocacy, and education for adoptive and preadoptive parents.

North American Council on Adoptable Children (NACAC)
970 Raymond Ave., Suite 106
St. Paul, MN 55114-1149
Phone: 612/644-3036
National advocacy organization. Nationwide resources/referrals.

North American Council on Adoptable Children
1821 University Avenue
Suite S-275
St. Paul, MN 55104
Phone: 612/644-3036
Focuses on needs of waiting U.S. and Canadian children.

Little Flower Children's Services
186 Remsen St.
Brooklyn, NY 11201
Phone: 718/260-8840
Full service agency offering public adoptions. Has made placements in gay and lesbian homes.

Family Focus Adoption Services
54-40 Little Neck Parkway, Suite 3
Little Neck, NY 11362
Phone: 718/224-1919
Handles hard to place children; gives referrals to social workers for home

studies for private adoptions. Has international adoption resources. Comfortable with lesbians and gay men.

Lutheran Community Services, Inc.
27 Park Place
New York, NY 10007
Phone: 212/406-9110
Full service adoption agency offering public adoptions. Has made placements in gay and lesbian homes.

New Life Adoption Agency, Inc.
117 South State St.
Syracuse, NY 13202-1103
Phone: 315/422-7300
New York State authorized and approved private adoption agency, social, legal, and medical professionals. Foster care, adoption. Can assist with international adoptions from China and Eastern Europe. Have nondiscrimination policy as part of their mission statement.

Family Service of Westchester, Inc.
One Summit Ave.
White Plains, NY 10606
Phone: 914/948-8004
Works with pre- and postadoption families as well as pregnant women. Adoption counseling, home study, placements. Willing to work with lesbian and gay families.

Adoption Information Services
901-B East Willow Grove Ave.
Lyndmoor, PA 19038
Phone: 215/233-1380
Counseling and education on adoption, with specific help for gay men and lesbians.

Three Rivers Adoption Council
307 Fourth Ave., Suite 710
Pittsburgh, PA 15222
Phone: 412/471-8722
Counseling, support services, parent
  education, referral to agencies,
  resource publications, and an
  adoption exchange. Contacts in
  western Pennsylvania, eastern Ohio,
  and West Virginia. Maintains lists of
  waiting families and waiting
  children of special needs adoptions.
  Very willing to work with lesbian
  and gay families.

Friends in Adoption
Box 7270,
Buxton Ave.
Middletown Springs, VT 05757
Phone: 802/235-2312
Works with those interested in
adopting and with those considering
placing their children. Open to
lesbians and gay men.

American Adoption Congress
1000 Connecticut Ave. NW, Suite 9
Washington, DC 20035
Umbrella organization for hundreds of
  local search and support
  organizations in U.S. Most are
  searching adult adoptees and birth
  parents.

National Adoption Information
  Clearinghouse
1400 I St., NW, Suite 600
Washington, DC 20005
Phone: 202/842-1919
Information and referrals. Directory of
  adoption agencies and support
  groups.

CHILDREN OF LESBIAN AND GAY PARENTS

Children of Lesbians and Gays Everywhere (COLAGE)
2300 Market St., #165
San Francisco, CA 94114
Phone: 415/206-1930
or
Box 187, Station F
Toronto, ON M4Y 2L5
Canada
Outgrowth of Gay and Lesbian Parents Coalition International, run by and for
children of gay parents. Publishes *Just for Us*, a monthly newsletter, pen pal
connection service, annual two-day conference for people age thirteen and up.

LESBIAN AND GAY YOUNG PEOPLE

Bisexual, Gay and Lesbian Youth of
  New York (BiGLYNY)
c/o The Center
208 W. 13th St.
New York, NY 10011
Phone: 212/620-7310
Peer-run social and support network
open to anyone twenty-two years
and under.

Hetrick-Martin Institute for Lesbian
  and Gay Youth
2 Astor Place
New York, NY 10003

Phone: 212/674-2400

Fax: 212/674-8650

Social service, education, and advocacy organization for lesbian, gay, and bisexual adolescents, homeless/runaway youth, and youth with HIV. Home of Harvey Milk High School, an alternative public school for gay and lesbian students.

The Neutral Zone
162 Christopher St.
New York, NY 10014
Phone: 212/924-3294
Substance/violence free center open late for lesbian, gay, and bisexual teens.

Youth Enrichment Services (Y.E.S.)
The Youth Program of the Lesbian and Gay Community Services Center
208 W. 13th St.
New York, NY 10011
Phone: 212/620-7310
Creative arts–based youth empowerment and substance and alcohol abuse prevention and HIV prevention program for lesbian, gay, and bisexual youth ages thirteen to twenty-two.

LESBIAN AND GAY SENIORS

Senior Action in a Gay Environment (SAGE)
208 W. 13th St.
New York, NY 10011
Phone: 212/741-2247
Homebound program, support groups, counseling, drop-in center, women's events, AIDS and seniors programs, education, community outreach.

BiGLYNY contingent at the 1993 Lesbian and Gay Pride March, New York City (*Photo by Harry Stevens*)

LESBIAN AND GAY COUPLES

Partners
P.O. Box 9685
Seattle, WA 98109
Phone: 206/784-1519
Information, support, and advocacy for same-sex couples, asserting that gay and lesbian couples are families. Newsletter.

SPERM BANKS (BY STATE)

This is a partial list of human cryobanks. There are dozens more throughout the country. Mention here does not constitute endorsement, except where noted.

California Cryobank
1019 Gayley Avenue
Los Angeles, CA 90024
Founded in 1977. Cappy Rothman, M.D. and Charles A. Sims, M.D., Medical Directors; Latrice Allen, Client Representative.

Procreative Technologies
1321 No. Mission Rd.
Los Angeles, CA 90033
Phone: 213/343-9967
Contact: Melonee Evans.

SAGE bus at the 1993 Lesbian and Gay Pride March, New York City (*Photo by Harry Stevens*)

The Sperm Bank of California
Telegraph Hill Medical Plaza
3007 Telegraph Avenue, Suite 2
Oakland, CA 04609-3205
Phone: 510/444-2014
Fax: 510/465-3187
Established in 1982. Services include
   donor semen, donor insemination,
   health education, support groups,
   long- and short-term semen storage,
   designated donor screening, semen
   analysis, sperm washing. Feminist
   orientation, lesbian positive. This
   bank is one of a very few offering
   identity-release donors, those who
   agree to be identified to their
   offspring after the children reach
   age eighteen. Will deliver semen to
   doctors across the country.

Pacific Reproductive Services
444 DeHaro, Suite 222
San Francisco, CA 94107
Phone: 415/487-2288
Contact: Emily

Zygen Laboratories
16742 Stagg St., Suite 105
Van Nuys, CA 91406
Phone: 800/255-7242
Contact: Carnie

Fenway Community Health Center
Lesbian-Gay Family and Parenting
   Services
7 Haviland St.
Boston, MA 02115
Phone: 617/267-0900, ext. 282
Alternative insemination since 1983.
   Provides education, support, and
   advocacy for gay families.
   Newsletter.

New England Sperm Bank
2014 Washington St.
Newton, MA 02152
Phone: 617/332-1228
Contact: Ken

Livingston Fertility
176 W. Mt. Pleasant Ave.
Livingston, NJ 07039
Phone: 201/994-1515

Biogenetics Corp.
1130 Rt. 22 W.
Mountainside, NJ 07092
Phone: 908/654-8836 or 201/399-8228
Contact: Sandy

UMDNJ Newark
185 S. Orange Ave.
Newark, NJ 07103
Phone: 201/456-6480

Idant Labs
350 Fifth Ave.
New York, NY 10118
Phone: 212/244-0555
Contact: Nancy

Repro Labs
336 E. 30th St.
New York, NY 10016
Phone: 212/779-3988
Contact: Natalie

Park Avenue Fertility Ltd.
67-55A Woodhaven Blvd.
Rego Park, NY, 11374
Phone: 718/459-2063 or 800/464-6390
Fax: 718/459-2213 or 800/540-6752

Rochester Regional Cryobank
919 Westfall Rd., Bldg. C, #224
Rochester, NY 14618

Fairfax Cryobank
3015 Williams Dr., #110
Fairfax, VA 22031
Phone: 703/698-3976

SURROGACY

The following are surrogate mother matching services, all of which have worked successfully with gay clients.

Center for Reproductive
   Alternatives—Southern California
Kathryn Wyckoff
727 Via Otono
San Clemente, CA 92672
Phone: 714/492-2161

Infertility Center of America
Noel Keane, J.D.
14 E. 60th St., Suite 309
New York, NY 10022
Phone: 212/371-0811
or

2601 Fortune Circle East, Suite 102B
Indianapolis, IN 46241
Phone: 317/243-8793
or
101 Larkspur Landing Circle,
   Suite 318
Larkspur, CA 94939
Phone: 415/925-9020

Surrogate Mothers, Inc.
Steven Litz, J.D.
P.O. Box 216
Monrovia, IN 46157
Phone: 317/996-2000

SURROGATE MOTHER GROUPS

Surrogate Mothers, Inc.
P.O. Box 216
Monrovia, IN 46157
Phone: 800/228-9066
Steven C. Litz, Director

The Surrogate Mother Program, Inc.
640 West End Ave., Suite 3D
New York, NY 10024
Phone: 212/496-1070
Dr. Betsy P. Aigen, Director

PROFILE

Center Kids

Children raised in lesbian and gay households are the youngest members of the lesbian and gay community. Center Kids, the family project of New York's Lesbian and Gay Community Services Center, provides children from gay homes in the New York area with frequent play opportunities with children from families like their own. Children in Center Kids have ongoing opportunities to befriend dozens of others who come from same-sex parents, while their parents have a chance to meet and socialize for support.

Founded in 1988 by a small group of new gay parents who gathered in Central Park to share their stories and garner support, Center Kids now has a mailing list of 1,800 lesbian and gay households.

Those contemplating parenthood may choose from Center Kids support groups on adoption, alternative insemination, and other options for biological parent-

The Census Bureau reported in 1991 that only 26 percent of U.S. households fit the conventional definition of a family: a married couple with at least one child. That misses the essence of the American family, which is a unit joined by love and support. Homophobia, not homosexuality, constitutes a threat to this family.

According to a National Gay and Lesbian Task Force study, gay and lesbian youth are two to three times more likely to attempt suicide than their heterosexual peers. Twenty-six percent of gay and lesbian youth are forced to leave home due to family complications over their sexual orientations.

When such conditions cease, and when lesbian and gay parents are no longer denied custody or access to their own children, the American family will be a lot stronger. In a period when the strife and violence in our world are reflected within many families, it is important to recognize that a supportive home in which children are truly wanted is a valuable contribution to society and is more crucial than the sexual orientation or marital status of the parents.

What some people forget is that all lesbians and gay men were once children who suffered from thinking that no one they knew or admired was like them. As adults, we affirm our right to let children know that their homosexual feelings are part of what it means to be human, and that a healthy set of values includes respect for one's own uniqueness.

SOURCE: Gay and Lesbian Alliance Against Defamation (GLAAD)/NY

hood. A support group exists for parents separated from their children by gay "divorce." Center Kids sponsors forums and panels throughout the year on topics such as legal concerns for lesbian and gay families, child development issues in single sex households, and how to explain bigotry and prejudice to children. In addition, discussion groups are held throughout the year, covering subjects ranging from "Dealing with Family Occasions" to "Answering Kids' Difficult Questions" to "Known vs. Unknown Donors."

Kids' Talk, the Center Kids monthly newsletter, contains a calendar of family-related events and information on gay and lesbian family issues, and is available to the households on the program's mailing list.

The Center Kids contingent in the Lesbian and Gay Pride March is reliably one of the largest and, with young and old alike in cherry-red Center Kids T-shirts and balloons festooning strollers, one of the most colorful and engaging. It is a symbol of the profound joy of lesbian and gay parents who come by their families through long consideration, effort, and an abiding belief in their often disputed right and ability to raise healthy, happy children.

For more information on lesbian and gay parenting issues and on Center Kids' advocacy, education, and social support efforts, contact Center Kids, Lesbian and Gay Community Services Center, 208 W. 13th St., New York, NY 10011; 212/620-7310, or fax the program at 212/924-2657.

PROFILE

Jeanne Manford

"In 1972, when my son Morty came out to me and to my husband, we didn't really understand about homosexuality, but my first words were, 'I love you. You are the same person today as you were yesterday,'" said Jeanne Manford, the founding mother of Parents and Friends of Lesbians and Gays.

But Jeanne herself was not ever to be the same. When Morty and other gay activists were beaten in a public forum, she wrote an outraged letter to the New York *Post* complaining that her gay son was attacked while the police looked on and did nothing. "People were flabbergasted that I would admit that I had a gay son in the newspaper," she said. The letter led to a guest spot on New York radio talk show host Barry Farber's program, and a television appearance in Boston. When Morty asked her to march with him in the Lesbian and Gay Pride March the same year, she did so with a sign proclaiming her love and support for her gay son: "Parents of gays unite in support of our children," it read. "This created quite a stir," Jeanne recollected quietly. "People ran up to kiss me, and they asked me to speak to their parents on their behalf. And Morty himself felt so angry that so many of his friends couldn't tell their parents. So Morty put up fliers in bars and other places, announcing our first parents' support meeting. That was in 1973. There were about twenty of us there." And Parents, Families and Friends of Lesbians and Gays (Parents-FLAG, or P-FLAG) was born.

Today, P-FLAG has more than 30,000 member households in chapters throughout the United States and around the world, including England, Holland, Canada, and Israel. The group advocates and educates on behalf of their lesbian and gay loved ones, and members offer each other support.

Although Morty died of AIDS in 1993, and she lost her husband in 1982, Jeanne's work on behalf of lesbian and gay children continues. She recently spearheaded the formation of a Queens, New York, chapter of P-FLAG. And this July, she'll become a great-grandmother.

"Looking back, everyone kept saying how brave I was, and it seems to me as if I did nothing. I loved my son, and supported him. That's all." To the gay and lesbian children of straight parents, that's everything.

9. Lesbian Legal Issues

This section was prepared almost exclusively from *The Lambda Update*, a triannual newsletter, and *The Lambda* 1994 Annual Report, which are publications of Lambda Legal Defense and Education Fund. For information on Lambda, see page 268.

Antigay Initiative Campaigns

The radical right's hostility toward lesbians and gay men is expressed most clearly in antigay ballot initiatives. These referenda attempt to write gay and lesbian people out of state and local constitutions by preventing the passage of legislation protecting our rights, by curtailing our ability to petition our government for civil rights, and by diminishing our political clout as a community.

Antigay initiatives invite the general public to vote on whether lesbians and gay men are entitled to the same civil rights as other Americans. These referenda, which mimic a rash of ballot measures targeted at African-American civil rights in the 1960s and 1970s, threaten all communities not in the majority.

Legal organizations fighting the radical right work to prevent antigay initiatives from reaching the ballot through preemptive legal challenges. When preventive efforts fail, activists work to educate the public about the antidemocratic nature of antigay initiatives. If antigay initiatives are ultimately approved by a majority of voters (as they have been in Colorado and Cincinnati, Ohio, for example) legal activists pursue litigation to invalidate antigay initiatives on the grounds that they are unconstitutional.

So far, a broad coalition of community organizations, legal activists, and political organizers have come together to defeat the voter-approved initiatives of Colorado and Cincinnati in the courts. Similar coalitions have also been effective in thwarting other initiatives in a variety of ways.

Arizona: The radical right did not gather enough signatures to place an antigay initiative on the ballot in November 1994.

Florida: A statewide antigay measure was struck from the ballot in March 1994.

Idaho: An antigay measure was voted down by an informed electorate in November 1994.

Michigan: The radical right did not gather enough signatures to place an antigay initiative on the ballot in November 1994.

Missouri: The radical right did not gather enough signatures to place an antigay initiative on the ballot in November 1994.

Nevada: The radical right did not gather enough signatures to place an antigay initiative on the ballot in November 1994.

Ohio: The radical right promised a statewide antigay initiative campaign, but did not follow through in 1994.

The Honorable Rosalyn Richter (1.) and The Honorable Marcy Kahn, openly lesbian judges

Oregon: An antigay measure was voted down by an informed electorate in November 1994.

Washington: The radical right did not gather enough signatures to place an antigay initiative on the ballot in November 1994.

©1995 Lambda Legal Defense and Education Fund, Inc.

CASE HISTORY

EVANS ET AL. V. ROMER AND NORTON

On October 11, 1994, the Colorado Supreme Court upheld the district court's ruling that the antigay initiative known as Amendment 2 violates the United States Constitution. The court soundly rejected each of the six justifications offered by the state for Amendment 2. The ruling followed the Colorado Supreme Court's previous ruling in this case in July 1993 when it found that the measure infringed on the fundamental constitutional rights of lesbians, gay men, and bisexuals and upheld the preliminary injunction against the measure's enforcement.

Amendment 2 would prohibit all branches of state government in Colorado (including cities, school districts, and courts) from passing legislation or adopting policies to protect lesbians, gay men, and bisexuals from discrimination based on their sexual orientation. Although approved by Colorado voters in 1992, Amendment 2 has never taken effect, thanks to the preliminary injunction.

Just over a month after the Colorado high court issued its ruling, the state filed a petition for review with the United States Supreme Court. The United States

Supreme Court heard oral argument in October 1995. Counsel for Evans et al. urged the court to uphold the Colorado Supreme Court's ruling that the amendment violates the U.S. Constitution. The challenge was brought by Lambda Legal Defense, the ACLU, and attorneys from the Colorado Legal Initiatives project. Counsel for Evans et al.—Lambda Legal Defense and Education Fund and Lambda cooperating attorney Clyde Wadsworth of Wilson, Sonsini, Goodrich & Rosati—filed a brief in January 1995 that opposed further review of the case.

The Colorado Supreme Court's invalidation of the amendment was based on a review of evidence introduced at a two-week trial in Denver in October 1993, at which the court heard testimony about a range of issues affecting lesbians and gay men, including discrimination and bias-motivated violence. This ruling is the first state supreme court decision to declare unconstitutional an antigay initiative passed by voters. The influence of this victory continues to be felt as others around the country work to block passage of similar amendments in their own communities.

©1995 Lambda Legal Defense and Education Fund, Inc.

COLORADO'S PERNICIOUS AMENDMENT 2

Neither the state of Colorado, through any of its branches or departments, nor any of its agencies, political subdivisions, municipalities, or school districts, shall enact, adopt, or enforce any statute, regulation, ordinance, or policy whereby homosexual, lesbian, or bisexual orientation, conduct, practices, or relationships shall constitute or otherwise be the basis of, or entitle any person or class of persons to have or claim any minority status, quota preferences, protected status, or claim of discrimination.

SODOMY LAW REFORM

Sodomy laws are used to make second-class citizens of gay people, to stigmatize sexual identity, and to justify many forms of discrimination against lesbians, gay men, and bisexuals. Since the U.S. Supreme Court's disappointing 1986 decision in *Bowers v. Hardwick* (in which the constitutionality of sodomy laws was upheld) lesbian and gay legal organizations have sought to challenge the sodomy statutes in state constitutions to secure the protection of private sexual intimacy for all people regardless of sexual orientation.

STATES WITH SODOMY LAWS

The following twenty-one states still have statutes on their books that outlaw consensual homosexual sex (termed sodomy, regardless of what variety of homosexual activity it is):

Alabama
Arkansas
Georgia
Kansas
Maryland
Minnesota
Missouri
North Carolina
Rhode Island
Texas
Virginia

Arizona
Florida
Idaho
Louisiana
Massachusetts
Mississippi
Montana
Oklahoma
South Carolina
Utah

SOURCE: *Out* magazine, June 1995

CASE HISTORY

ENGLAND V. CITY OF DALLAS

In 1993, an intermediate appellate court upheld the lower court victory of Mica England, who was denied employment as a police officer because she is a lesbian and thus in violation of the state sodomy law. The court affirmed the trial court's ruling that the Texas sodomy law, which singles out homosexual conduct, violates the state constitution, and struck it down. The court retained the judge's order that the police department not rely on the statute as a pretext for antigay discrimination.

In September 1994, the case was finally settled when the City of Dallas agreed to pay England $75,000 in damages. The Texas sodomy law remains off the books under the appellate court ruling despite the Texas Supreme Court's refusal in another case to strike down the sodomy law itself.

©1995 Lambda Legal Defense and Education Fund, Inc.

CASE HISTORY

BOWERS V. HARDWICK

In 1982 in Atlanta, twenty-eight-year-old Michael Hardwick was arrested and convicted of sodomy after police officers who were trying to serve a warrant for a minor traffic violation found him at home in his bed having mutual consensual oral sex with another man. Hardwick argued that the state sodomy law violated his right to privacy. The federal Court of Appeals agreed with him, ruling that Georgia's sodomy law was unconstitutional and that the right to privacy includes choices that are intimate and personal and central to personal dignity and autonomy. The State of Georgia then appealed to the Supreme Court. "It is the very act of homosexual sodomy that epitomizes moral delinquency," wrote Michael Bowers, the state attorney general, in his brief to the court.

In a five to four decision, the Supreme Court reversed the lower appellate court, rejecting that court's expansive view of the right to privacy. In his opinion, Justice Byron White concluded that the right to privacy does not extend to homosexuals, and for proof he invoked the Bible, stating, "Proscriptions against *that conduct* [emphasis added] have ancient roots." In a concurring opinion, Chief Justice Warren Burger wrote that "condemnation of *those practices* [emphasis added] is firmly rooted in Judeo-Christian moral and ethical standards."

In a dissenting opinion, Justice Harry Blackmun wrote, "I can only hope that
. . . the Court will reconsider its analysis and conclude that depriving individuals
of the right to choose for themselves how to conduct their intimate relationships
poses a far greater threat to the values most deeply rooted in our Nation's history
than tolerance of nonconformity could ever do. Because I think the Court betrays
those values, I dissent."

"The cop stood there for like . . . thirty-five seconds while I was engaged in
mutual oral sex. When I looked up and realized he was standing there, he
then identified himself. He said I was under arrest for sodomy. I said, 'What
are you doing in my bedroom?'"

—Michael Hardwick

EMPLOYMENT DISCRIMINATION

United States laws provide few protections for lesbian and gay workers. Only eight
statewide laws prohibit discrimination based on sexual orientation. None exist at
the federal level. In fact, discrimination against lesbians and gay men by some federal employers, like the military, is official policy.

The discrimination experienced by lesbian and gay people in the workplace can
be subtle or overt, motivated by private prejudice or sanctioned by company policy. Not limited to losing one's job or not being hired because one is gay, employment discrimination also takes the form of harassment, impeded advancement, and
unequal benefits. The closet is arguably the most ubiquitous and debilitating side-
effect of antigay employment discrimination, and a form of discrimination itself.

CASE HISTORY

BRIENZA V. UNITED PRESS INTERNATIONAL

Julie Brienza, a former Supreme Court reporter for United Press International,
has filed suit against UPI, WCVY, and Milwaukee-based religious broadcaster Vic
Eliason for unlawful job termination based on sexual orientation.

After Eliason learned that Brienza was a lesbian writing a freelance article for
the *Washington Blade,* the District of Columbia–based lesbian and gay newspaper,
he contacted other antigay notables and enlisted their help and that of his radio
listeners in organizing a campaign to have Brienza fired. UPI subsequently fired
Brienza, supposedly for minor professional infractions.

The Federal District Court has ruled that the District of Columbia Human
Rights Act did not apply to Eliason's acts, as they took place in Wisconsin, where
his radio station is located. The court also held that several Wisconsin statutes did

Julie Brienza, plaintiff in *Brienza v. United Press International (Courtesy of Lambda Legal Defense and Education Fund)*

not apply to the defendants' actions. However, the court maintained Brienza's claim that Eliason et al. tortiously interfered with her contract and invaded her privacy under District of Columbia law. Eliason and WCVY have appealed.

HOUSING DISCRIMINATION

Lesbians and gay men are frequently targets of sexual orientation discrimination by landlords, homeowners, or realtors who don't want to rent or sell to us. Fewer than ten states have laws prohibiting housing discrimination based on sexual orientation and there is no federal prohibition.

In the last ten years, combating housing discrimination has taken on a new urgency because of the AIDS epidemic. Surviving partners of people who die of AIDS are often discriminated against by landlords, co-op boards, homeowner's associations, and city and county taxing authorities whose rules protect only heterosexual spouses from displacement after the death of a life partner.

Lesbian and gay legal advocates pursue litigation to prevent housing discrimination against surviving lesbian or gay life partners and to assure that, at their time of greatest loss, gay people will not have to face the anxiety of total dislocation.

Lesbians and gay men do not all share the same burdens in terms of discrimination. Some of us are immediately identifiable as gay men or lesbians and therefore face quick and overt hostility; others of us do not. Many face additional forms of discrimination based on our race, our class, our health status, or our age. Litigation on our behalf must take into account all of the burdens faced by members of our community.

CASE HISTORY

HENRY PHIPPS PLAZA WEST V. GOMEZ

Alma Gomez, the surviving partner of Maria Rosas, has been given an interim lease in her own name to be followed by a permanent lease, after her landlord abandoned its attempt to evict her. Ms. Rosas was the tenant of record for the apartment that the couple shared as their primary residence for seven years. Before the settlement was reached, the landlord had argued that because Ms. Gomez was not a family member, she was not entitled to remain in the apartment after Maria's death. A hearing was held at the Department of Housing and Community Renewal in November 1991, and the settlement was negotiated in 1994 while both parties were awaiting the decision.

EQUAL MARRIAGE LAWS

In January 1995, after years of laying the groundwork for winning and keeping the right to marry, Lambda Legal Defense and Education Fund announced the formation of its Marriage Project.

The Marriage Project litigates Lambda's pioneering Hawaii case, *Baehr v. Lewin,* indisputably the most promising challenge to unequal marriage laws in the country, a suit brought by two lesbian couples and one gay male couple. The project also works to mobilize the lesbian and gay movement and our allies to secure this most basic civil right.

To ensure that other states and the federal government recognize marriages validly contracted in Hawaii, Lambda's Marriage Project is preparing for the federal and state-by-state litigation that will follow a victory in *Baehr v. Lewin.* The project is developing a network of volunteer attorneys, law professors, and law students to research the legal arguments available against backlash and in favor of recognition. Working with other organizations, the Marriage Project will serve as a national coordinator and clearinghouse for the analysis and materials developed.

To help promote the recognition of equal marriage rights and to build a national coalition, the project has developed the Marriage Resolution and is asking community members, organizations, and allies to adopt and promote the resolution:

Because marriage is a basic human and an individual, personal choice,

RESOLVED, the State should not interfere with same-gender couples who choose to marry and share fully and equally in the rights, responsibilities and commitment of civil marriage.

Genora Dancel
and Ninia Baehr,
plaintiffs in *Baehr
v. Lewin*, the
Hawaiian
marriage suit
(*Courtesy
Lambda Legal
Defense and
Education Fund*)

CASE HISTORY

BAEHR V. LEWIN

On May 5, 1993, the Hawaii Supreme Court took a giant step toward allowing lesbians and gay men to marry. The court's ruling in *Baehr v. Lewin* held that the refusal to issue marriage licenses to same-sex couples appeared to violate the state constitutional right to equal protection and ordered a trial in which the state would either have to present compelling reasons for continuing to discriminate against gay and lesbian couples who want to marry, or stop discriminating.

Since the ruling, there has been significant political and legislative ferment in Hawaii around the issue, with momentum building toward acceptance of equal marriage rights in the face of a heavy right-wing attack. Both of the state's largest newspapers have editorialized in support of equal marriage laws, and the new governor campaigned in favor of equality, while the legislature has passed a law reaffirming its desire to discriminate on the basis of gender in precisely the manner the court held unconstitutional.

POLITICAL ASYLUM AND IMMIGRATION

Gay men, lesbians, and people with HIV are seeking safe haven in the United States. In many countries, members of our community are singled out for government-sanctioned persecution in varying degrees of severity. In one country, the penalty for consensual same-sex relations is death.

On June 19, 1994, Attorney General Janet Reno designated as precedent a Board of Immigration Appeals decision finding that gay men or lesbians who are persecuted by their governments may be eligible for relief from deportation. Since then, advocacy efforts have been aimed toward strengthening this policy and pressing for reasonable standards by which lesbian and gay people can demonstrate their fear of persecution, especially in countries where there is scant documentation of antigay violence.

WHAT A POTENTIAL IMMIGRANT NEEDS TO KNOW

Currently, there are three ways to immigrate legally to the United States: 1. family sponsorship; 2. sponsorship through employment or profession; and 3. asylum. One should consult with an immigration lawyer or specialist before attempting any of the three avenues.

It is not yet possible for U.S. citizens to sponsor their gay or lesbian lovers; the Immigration and Naturalization Service (INS) does not currently recognize the validity of such unions. This is true even if the ceremony was held in one of the few countries that recognize gay and lesbian marriage (Denmark and Sweden). The Lesbian and Gay Immigration Rights Task Force advocates for changes in the INS's discriminatory policies with regard to lesbians, gay men, and people with HIV.

Gay men and lesbians are no longer excludable or deportable from the United States based solely on sexual orientation, although INS officers often harass people perceived as gay or lesbian.

Despite national efforts to have the restriction removed, infection with HIV currently remains a ground for exclusion. Some people may qualify for a waiver of the exclusion. Never assume that HIV infection will irretrievably doom an immigration application.

Immigration procedures and forms can be misleading—especially those related to family sponsorship. Many people run afoul of the INS because they make innocent errors on the documents. In preparing to immigrate, any applicant should consult an immigration lawyer or specialist.

Arrests, prior immigration difficulties, receipt of public assistance of any kind, and certain health conditions are serious complications. If a potential immigrant has ever had any of these problems, he or she should not attempt to process a case without legal assistance.

Applicants should never argue with, insult, or visibly lose their temper with an INS officer. If problems arise, applicants should note the officer's badge number and pursue options after leaving the officer's presence.

Asylum cases are politically sensitive and extremely complex. Anyone attempting to claim asylum in the United States should seek a qualified immigration law practitioner to handle the case.

CASE HISTORY

IN RE PITCHERSKAIA

The asylum application of Alla Pitcherskaia, a Russian lesbian, was denied in June 1994 by an immigration judge in San Francisco. The decision acknowledged that persecution based on one's sexual orientation is a ground for political asylum; however, the judge decided that the evidence presented to demonstrate the arrests, imprisonment, and physical violence suffered by Alla did not constitute persecution. An appeal is under way.

©1995 Lambda Legal Defense and Education Fund, Inc.

AIDS

Legal advocates working in the AIDS arena must address the broad spectrum of public policy issues raised by the HIV pandemic. Generally speaking, AIDS-related cases fall into two categories: discrimination and access to health care. Thus far, precedent-setting cases have challenged discrimination in employment, housing, public accommodations, medical treatment, and provision of benefits. Because medical intervention can prolong the lives of people with HIV, the fight for access to basic health care, as well as access to essential treatments refused by insurers as experimental, has become paramount. Legal advocates challenge discrimination and deficiencies in the health care system, as it affects both providers and consumers, and work toward winning access to sound treatment for people with HIV.

At the same time, activists and lawyers continue to identify areas of unmet need and to advocate vigorously for members of our community whose voices have been denied or ignored: victims of HIV-related bias crimes, the incarcerated, individuals caught in or kept out of the foster care and adoption systems, and others whose survival often hinges on the cooperation of hostile bureaucracies.

CASE HISTORY

S. P. V. SULLIVAN

In 1993, the Centers for Disease Control (CDC) announced new regulations governing disability benefits for people with HIV infection. These changes addressed virtually all of the concerns raised by a lawsuit challenging the Social Security Administration's (SSA) reliance on a grossly inadequate definition of AIDS from the CDC for awarding Social Security benefits. The new regulations add the predominant manifestations of HIV in women, drug users, and low income people as criteria by which HIV-infected individuals can qualify for disability.

Previously, the SSA regulations required people suffering from aggressive and recurrent infections such as pneumonia, sepsis, endocarditis, and meningitis to meet extremely stringent functional tests while persons suffering from disease contained in the CDC's definition of AIDS could qualify on the basis of medical evidence alone. Additionally, the new regulations list disabling conditions common in women such as pelvic inflammatory disease, which did not appear at all in the earlier standards.

CASE HISTORY

STATE OF MISSISSIPPI V. MARVIN MCCLENDON

On October 8, 1994, two unarmed gay men, Robert Walters and Joseph Shoemake, were shot to death in Laurel, Mississippi. A local teenager, Marvin McClendon, was arrested and confessed to the murders. McClendon alleged that the victims had tried to sexually assault him and he acted in self-defense.

Lambda Legal Defense and Education Fund became involved in the case when the defendant's attorney moved that the victims' blood be tested for HIV, arguing that had the victims been HIV positive, McClendon would have been justified in killing them.

Lambda submitted a brief that the local district attorney used in its entirety to support his motion to block the use of HIV serostatus as evidence. The brief argued that the HIV status of the two victims was irrelevant to the case and that disclosure would violate Mississippi law, and would serve to encourage and justify attacks on people with HIV or other disabilities.

Ultimately, the judge allowed the HIV serostatus to be entered as evidence. Despite the defense attorney's attempt to stoke prejudice and fear, and despite the trial judge's apparent collusion, the jury found McClendon guilty of two counts of murder.

©1995 Lambda Legal Defense and Education Fund, Inc.

CASE HISTORY

SCOLES V. MERCY HEALTH CORPORATION OF SOUTHEASTERN PENNSYLVANIA

Dr. Paul Scoles, an orthopedic surgeon, was denied admitting privileges at Mercy Health Corporation of Southeastern Pennsylvania after he disclosed his HIV status. Mercy Health officials sent 1,050 letters informing former patients about Scoles's HIV status, removed his name from a list of orthopedic consultants, and suspended his surgical privileges. The hospital later modified its policy and decided to allow Dr. Scoles to continue performing surgery, but only under the condition that he inform all patients of his HIV status.

Scoles's lawsuit successfully argued that Mercy Health's actions violated both the Rehabilitation Act of 1973, and the provisions of the Americans with Disabilities Act, which prohibit discrimination against employees with HIV unless there is a "direct threat to the health or safety of other individuals in the workplace."

Scoles and Mercy Health reached a satisfactory settlement in February 1995.

©1995 Lambda Legal Defense and Education Fund, Inc.

FAMILY LAW

For those accustomed to legal recognition of their families, it is often hard to imagine the difficulties presented by living in a family configuration not sanctioned by the state.

Lesbian and gay couples have long struggled with the indignities and inequities of such a limitation, from being denied insurance coverage as spouses or family members, to being denied access to the hospital room of a dying partner, to being refused the promise of burial in a family plot. When our families include children, this lack of legal recognition has even more sinister implications.

Legal advocates are working to gain fair treatment for lesbian and gay couples in many contexts, to protect the rights of all gay and lesbian parents, to insure the adoption and foster parent privileges of gay men and lesbians, and to expand marriage law to recognize same-sex unions.

Like other marginalized communities, the gay and lesbian community has a long history of creating family configurations—both with and without children—that support and nurture its members. And like others not in the majority, our family forms often have been met with fear and hostility from the mainstream.

Family law advocates work not only to assure the rights of lesbian and gay couples and families, but to expand our country's notion of family itself—from single mothers to coparents to extended networks of parents, partners, and caregivers—so that the ideal more accurately reflects the complex reality of American lives.

CASE HISTORY

ADOPTION OF TAMMY

The Supreme Judicial Court of Massachusetts permitted the lesbian partner of a child's biological mother to adopt as a second parent.

Previously, the trial court judge had granted the adoption of the three-year-old girl by her nonbiological mother. However, before allowing the adoption to be finalized, the judge, in a surprising move, asked the Massachusetts Appeals Court whether state law allows such adoptions, which the court weighed in favorably on September 10.

©1995 Lambda Legal Defense and Education Fund, Inc.

MILITARY

For information about important legal cases affecting gays in the military, see pages 318–320.

Supreme Court Decisions That Have Affected Lesbians and Gays

1958: In *ONE Inc. v. Olesen*, the Supreme Court overturned a California district court that had banned the mailing of *ONE* magazine, one of the first gay publications.

1967: In *Boutilier v. Immigration and Naturalization Service*, the Supreme Court voted six to three that the INS could prevent homosexuals from entering the United States.

1976: In *Doe v. Commonwealth's Attorney*, the Court upheld a Virginia court's ruling that there is no constitutional right to engage in private homosexual acts.

  • In *Enslin v. North Carolina*, the Court upheld the conviction of a man sentenced to one year in jail for having consensual oral sex with a man in his own home.

1986: In *Bowers v. Hardwick*, the Court voted five to four to uphold Georgia's sodomy law.

1995: The Court will determine whether or not Colorado's Amendment 2 is unconstitutional. (See AntiGay Initiative Campaigns on page 254.)

SOURCE: Leigh Rutledge, *The Gay Fireside Companion*. Alyson Publications, 1989

Profile

National Center for Lesbian Rights

The National Center for Lesbian Rights (NCLR) is a lesbian, feminist, multicultural, legal resource center committed to creating a world where all lesbians can live life fully without fear of discrimination.

NCLR works to change discriminatory laws and to create new laws benefiting lesbians in the areas of civil rights, employment, housing, immigration, partner benefits, child custody, donor insemination, adoption, foster parenting, lesbian health, and youth rights.

NCLR's Lesbians of Color Project provides legal assistance to lesbians of color, develops analyses of how racism and homophobia affect lesbians of color, designs educational programs, provides technical assistance to lesbians of color organizations, and forms alliances with lesbian and gay civil rights groups nationally and internationally.

NCLR's Public Policy Project drafts and advocates for policies that meet the needs of lesbians, develops lesbian-centered analyses of issues such as health care and employment discrimination, and represents lesbian perspectives when lesbian and gay issues are being discussed in national forums.

NCLR's Youth Project works on behalf of lesbian, gay, bisexual, and transgender youth who have been adversely affected by the mental health system, the child welfare system, the criminal justice system, and the educational system. The project provides legal representation, advocacy, and information and referral.

NCLR's workshops, videos, and publications help lesbians learn about parenting options, emergency health care documents, employment rights, and a host of other issues vital to our communities.

NCLR was founded in 1977 by Donna Hitchens, who is now a superior court judge in San Francisco. The second executive director was Roberta Achtenberg, former assistant secretary of housing and urban development in Washington, D.C., who resigned in April 1995 to run for mayor of San Francisco. Liz Hendrickson, a noted civil rights attorney specializing in family law, has been executive director since 1991. NCLR remains based in San Francisco, with the Public Policy Project office located in New York. NCLR serves lesbians and gay men in all fifty states each year through litigation, community education, advocacy for legal and policy reform, judicial and other professional training, and the production of a range of legal resource publications. NCLR is the only legal organization in the country that focuses on the civil rights of lesbians, and it is also the only legal organization with a program designed specifically to serve lesbians of color.

Over the past eighteen years, NCLR has steadily grown from a regional project to a national center. At its founding in 1977, NCLR was called the Lesbian Rights Project and was part of another public interest law firm, Equal Rights Advocates (ERA). NCLR incorporated separately in 1989 and has experienced remarkable growth since then, going from an annual budget in 1989 of $200,000 to a current budget of $600,000.

PROFILE

Gay and Lesbian Advocates and Defenders (GLAD)

In 1978, Boston's gay community found itself under siege. During a reelection bid, Suffolk County District Attorney Garret Byrne inflamed antigay hysteria by setting up an anonymous hot line to gather tips on gay men having sex with minors, in the midst of what was called the Revere Sex Ring Scandal. Plainclothes Boston police officers entrapped and arrested more than 100 individuals for acts of public lewdness in the Boston Public Library.

Feeling vulnerable and unprotected, the gay community called for a local organization to help people facing antigay harassment or discrimination and to advocate for advances in gay/lesbian rights. Led by attorney John Ward, activists met at the Old West Church to organize such a group, and Gay and Lesbian Advocates and Defenders was born. Ward became the first executive director and Richard Burns became the first president of the board of directors.

For the last fifteen years, GLAD has litigated or participated in thousands of cases. At the forefront of virtually every area of lesbian and gay legal rights in New England, GLAD has pursued both local issues, such as securing the right of the Irish-American Gay, Lesbian and Bisexual Group of Boston (GLIB) to march in Boston's St. Patrick's Day Parade (a decision overturned by the U.S. Supreme

Court in June 1995), and test-case litigation with national implications, including the landmark second-parent adoption case *Adoption of Tammy* (see page 265).

GLAD's list of organizational alumni reads like a virtual Who's Who of lesbian and gay activism:

Richard Burns, GLAD's first board president, is now executive director of the Lesbian and Gay Community Services Center of New York.

Kevin Cathcart, executive director, 1984–1992, is now executive director of Lambda Legal Defense and Education Fund.

Linda Giles, former litigation committee member, became the first openly lesbian judge in Massachusetts in 1992, also serving on the Boston Municipal Court.

Emily Hewitt, former board member, was named by President Clinton as general counsel to the General Services Administration in 1993.

Tim McFeeley, former board member and development committee chair, went on to become the executive director of the Human Rights Campaign Fund in Washington, D.C.

Denise McWilliams, former AIDS Law Project Director, is now Director of Legal Programs for JRI Health in Boston.

Dermot Meagher, former board member, became the first openly gay judge in Massachusetts in 1989, and still serves on the Boston Municipal Court.

Neil Miller, former board member, is now the author of *In Search of Gay America, Out in the World,* and *Out of the Past.*

Cindy Rizzo, former board president, is now associate director of development for Fenway Community Health Center in Boston.

Urvashi Vaid, GLAD's first legal intern, served as executive director of the National Gay and Lesbian Task Force in Washington, D.C., from 1989 to 1992.

©1995 Lambda Legal Defense and Education Fund, Inc.

PROFILE

Lambda Legal Defense and Education Fund

Lambda Legal Defense and Education Fund is a national organization committed to achieving full recognition of the civil rights of lesbians, gay men, and people with HIV through impact litigation, education, and public policy work.

Lambda Legal Defense and Education Fund, Inc., logo

Founded in 1973, Lambda challenges discrimination in employment, in housing, in public services and accommodations, and in the military; Lambda advocates for parenting rights, for domestic partner benefits, and for equal marriage rights; and Lambda works to protect privacy, equal protection, and first amendment rights.

HISTORY

In 1972, a New York court denied Lambda's application for incorporation on the grounds that Lambda's "stated purposes are on their face neither benevolent nor charitable, nor, in any event, is there a demonstrated need for this corporation." New York's highest court overturned the ruling in 1973, and Lambda was born. In its early years, Lambda was an *entirely* volunteer organization, with legal work provided by William Thom, who had filed the initial suit, and a network of supporting attorneys. In 1977, Lambda began to change from a volunteer organization into one with a governing board of directors and a paid executive director. Lambda opened its first offices, housed at the New York Civil Liberties office, in 1979. By 1982, its offices had doubled in size and its board of directors was transforming from a local board to a national one, with almost half of its members from outside New York City.

Lambda fought and won the nation's first AIDS discrimination lawsuit in 1983. Lambda and cooperating attorney Bill Hibsher represented Dr. Joseph Sonnabend, whose co-op board tried to evict him and his medical practice because he was treating patients with AIDS. Since then, Lambda has become the nation's premier legal organization advocating for the rights of people with HIV/AIDS.

In 1987, Lambda moved its offices to their present site at 666 Broadway. Now in its twenty-first year, Lambda Legal Defense and Education Fund is the country's oldest and largest legal organization working to advance the civil rights of lesbians, gay men, and people with HIV. With offices in New York, Los Angeles, and Chicago, Lambda's impact is felt nationwide: its staff attorneys work in cooperation with a network of more than 400 volunteer attorneys across the country; its legal services are provided without charge to clients.

LEGAL RESOURCES

UNITED STATES

Calm, Inc. (Custody Action of Lesbian Mothers)
P.O. Box 281
Narberth, PA 19702
Phone: 215/667-7508

Gay and Lesbian Advocates and Defenders (GLAD)
P.O. Box 218
Boston, MA 02112
Phone: 617/426-1350

Lambda Legal Defense and Education
    Fund
National Headquarters
666 Broadway, 12th Floor
New York, NY 10012
Phone: 212/995-8585
Test case litigation only.

LeGaL: Lesbian and Gay Law
    Association
799 Broadway #340
New York, NY 10003
Membership: 212/353-9118,
Fax: 212/353-2970

Referral Service: 212/459-4873,
E-mail: le-gal@interport.net

National Center for Lesbian Rights
1663 Mission Street, 5th Floor
San Francisco, CA 94103
Phone: 415/392-6257

National Lesbian and Gay Law
    Association
Box 77130, National Capital Station
Washington, DC 20014
Phone: 202/389-0161

CANADA

EGALE (Equality for Gays and Lesbians Everywhere)
P.O. Box 2891, Stn D
Ottawa, ON K1P 5W9
Phone: 613/230-4391

---

10. LESBIANS IN LITERATURE

The Lesbian is one of the least-known members of our culture. Less is known about her—and less accurately—than the Newfoundland dog. In the 1960s, two books on the Lesbian appeared. Both were written by men, and both were liberal attempts to deal with the worst stereotypes about Lesbians—which says they are men trapped in women's bodies. Both failed to destroy the stereotype, since they only described behavior and since the authors were largely unable or unwilling to deal with the Lesbian's emotional life.

    —from *Sappho Was a Right-On Woman,* by Sidney Abbott and Barbara Love
    (1972); writing about Frank S. Caprio's *Female Homosexuality* (1967) and
    Donald Webster Cory's *The Lesbian in America* (1965)

Before 1969, lesbians appeared in literature, but they looked very different from today. Apart from a handful of positive and happy depictions, such as Claire Morgan's (Patricia Highsmith) *The Price of Salt* (1950) and Jane Rule's *Desert of the Heart* (1964), lesbian literary characters tended to fall into a few preordained stereotypes. They might be self-hating inverts, like Stephen Gordon in *The Well of Loneliness* (1928), or effete sapphists, as in Compton Mackenzie's *Extraordi-*

Audre Lorde *(Photo by Morgan Gwenwald)*

nary Women (1928). Often, they were merely unfulfilled spinsters. Or lesbians might appear, as they did in dozens of pulp novels written by both men and women (see page 273), as sexual predators waiting to pounce on naive women and convert them to their wicked ways. The moral of many of these novels—lesbian pulp fiction usually ended with the naive woman finding true love with a man, while the lesbian was left alone—was that lesbianism was a sad, pathetic road that was only for the sick or inverted.

Contemporary lesbian literature owes a lot to Alma Routsong (aka Isabel Miller) and Rita Mae Brown, who wrote and published two of the earliest post-Stonewall lesbian-themed novels. Miller's *Patience and Sarah* (1972) (originally self-published as *A Place for Us*) depicted a warm, loving relationship—based on a true story—of two women in nineteenth-century New York State, who left their families to make a home and a life together. Brown's classic *Rubyfruit Jungle* (1973) made growing up a lesbian spitfire a source of pride rather than a cause for shame.

But mainstream publishers weren't about to rush lesbian literature into print in the volume that lesbians wanted to read it. Publishing to this day is still controlled largely by straight white men. In the early 1970s, feminist and lesbian publishers began setting up shop, realizing that in order for lesbian stories to be published, lesbians themselves would have to publish them. Daughters, Inc., Diana Press, and Persephone Press were a few notable pioneers in lesbian publishing, though they all had closed shop by the early 1980s. Still thriving today are lesbian and feminist publishers such as Naiad Press, Seal Press, Spinsters/Aunt Lute, Cleis

Press, Firebrand Books, and Kitchen Table: Women of Color Press, who have all shown an unwavering commitment to lesbian literature. Writers such as Rita Mae Brown, Dorothy Allison, and Sarah Schulman, who have since published successfully with mainstream presses, all got their start with lesbian publishers.

Hand in hand with the publishers has been a network of women's bookstores to distribute the books we have most wanted to read. Unfortunately, in these days of large book chains offering customers attractive discounts and comfortable coffee bars, many women's bookstores have been unable to compete and have gone out of business. In early 1995, even New York City, with its large, visible lesbian population, lost its only women's bookstore, Judith's Room, to rising expenses and decreasing sales.

Today, there are an impressive number of lesbian novelists, poets, nonfiction writers, children's book authors, and biographers publishing with both small women's presses and with large mainstream publishers. We not only have our own presses, we have our own awards, our own writing colonies, our own funding sources, our own workshops, and our own reading series. Out of the shaky heritage of *The Well of Loneliness*, lesbians have built a proud literary tradition for themselves.

Sources for Further Reading

Foster, Jeanette. *Sex Variant Women in Literature*. Vantage Press, 1956; reprint, Naiad Press, 1985.

Zimmerman, Bonnie. *The Safe Sea of Women: Lesbian Fiction, 1969–1989*. Beacon Press, 1990.

A Dozen Pre-Stonewall Novels by Lesbian Authors with Lesbian Characters or Content

1. Barnes, Djuna. *Ladies Almanack*. (1928)
2. Barnes, Djuna. *Nightwood*. (1937)
3. Colette. *Claudine at School*. (1903; first published in U.S. in 1930)
4. Hall, Radclyffe. *The Well of Loneliness*. (1928)
5. Hull, Helen R. *Labyrinth*. (1922)
6. Morgan, Claire (Patricia Highsmith). *The Price of Salt*. (1950)
7. Renault, Mary. *The Friendly Young Ladies*. (1944; published in the U.S. as *The Middle Mist*)
8. Rule, Jane. *Desert of the Heart*. (1964)
9. Sinclair, Jo. *Wasteland*. (1946)
10. Vivien, Renee. *A Woman Appeared to Me*. (1904)
11. Wilhelm, Gale. *We Too Are Drifting*. (1935)
12. Wilhelm, Gale. *Torchlight to Valhalla*. (1938)

Ann Bannon, lesbian pulp novel pioneer *(Photo by Tee Corinne. Courtesy of Naiad Press.)*

LESBIAN PULP FICTION FROM THE 1940S TO THE 1960S

In 1939, the paperback book industry started in the United States. Few books with lesbian content were published in the very early years, but after World War II, the boom in pulp fiction, so-called because of the cheap, grainy paper on which it was printed, exploded. Publishers such as Fawcett Books specialized in inexpensive and mass-produced novels, particularly in the genres of westerns, mysteries, and sex and romance, including lesbian sex.

Some of these lesbian-themed novels were written by men for straight male voyeur readers, but many were written by women like Ann Bannon and Vin Packer, with a lesbian audience in mind. Joan Nestle of the Lesbian Herstory Archives calls lesbian pulp novels "survival fiction," because they helped lesbians to realize they were not alone in a hostile world.

Most lesbian pulp novels were formulaic. Girl meets girl, girl gets girl, girl loses girl to boy or tragedy. The strict tenor of the 1950s dictated moral endings, in which lesbians were put in their place—either with men, or out in the cold. Claire Morgan's (aka Patricia Highsmith) *The Price of Salt*, published in 1950, was unusual for its happy ending.

Pulps reached a peak in the early 1960s, then went out of fashion with the sexual revolution and the women's and gay liberation movements. But in the early 1980s, Naiad Press began reissuing Ann Bannon's Beebo Brinker novels from the 1950s. Naiad has since continued the tradition of publishing lesbian romance fiction by contemporary lesbian authors.

You can find out more about lesbian pulp fiction at the Lesbian Herstory Archives in New York City (718/768-DYKE), which has an extensive collection, or in the 1993 Canadian documentary, *Forbidden Love: The Unashamed Stories of Lesbian Lives*.

SOME POPULAR LESBIAN PULP TITLES

Women Without Men (one of
the top ten best-selling
paperbacks of 1957)
21 Gay Street
Strange Sisters
Warped Women
The Price of Salt
Odd Girl Out
I Am a Woman
Women in the Shadows
Journey to a Woman

Women's Barracks
How Dark My Love
Spring Fire
Private School
The Outcast
The Twisted Ones
Guerrilla Girls
The Savage Salome
Queer Patterns
The Sex Between

A DOZEN STANDARDS OF EARLY LESBIAN-FEMINIST LITERATURE, 1972–1983

1. Allen, Paula Gunn. *The Woman Who Owned the Shadows*. (1983)—novel
2. Arnold, June. *Sister Gin*. (1975)—novel
3. Brady, Maureen. *Folly*. (1982)—novel
4. Broumas, Olga. *Beginning with O*. (1977)—poetry
5. Brown, Rita Mae. *Rubyfruit Jungle*. (1973)—novel
6. Grahn, Judy. *The Work of a Common Woman*. (1978)—poetry
7. Guy, Rosa. *Ruby*. (1976)—novel
8. Harris, Bertha. *Lovers*. (1976)—novel
9. Lorde, Audre. *Zami: A New Spelling of My Name*. (1982)—biomythography
10. Miller, Isabel (Alma Routsong). *Patience and Sarah*. (1972)—novel
11. Rich, Adrienne. *The Dream of a Common Language: Poems, 1974–1978*. (1978)—poetry
12. Shockley, Ann Allen. *Loving Her*. (1974)—novel

AMERICAN LIBRARY ASSOCIATION GAY/ LESBIAN BOOK AWARD

Since 1971, the Gay/Lesbian Book Award of the American Library Association (ALA) has been given annually to English-language books of exceptional merit relating to the gay/lesbian experience. Awards are in two categories: literature and nonfiction. Nominations are accepted from the general public, librarians, members of the Gay/Lesbian Task Force of the AMA and the Gay/Lesbian Book Awards Committee of the AMA. Winners are chosen by the Book Awards Committee.

LESBIAN WINNERS

1971—Isabel Miller, *Patience and Sarah*

1972—Del Martin and Phyllis Lyon, *Lesbian/Woman*

1974—Jeanette Foster, *Sex Variant Women in Literature: A Historical and Quantitative Survey*

1978—Ginny Vida, ed., *Our Right to Love*

1979—Betty Fairchild and Nancy Howard, *Now That You Know: What Every Parent Should Know About Homosexuality*

1982—J. R. Roberts, *Black Lesbians: An Annotated Bibliography*

1982—Lillian Faderman, *Surpassing the Love of Men: Romantic Friendship and Love Between Women from the Renaissance to the Present*

1985—Judy Grahn, *Another Mother Tongue: Gay Words, Gay Worlds*

1986—Cindy Patton, *Sex and Germs: The Politics of AIDS*

1988—Joan Nestle, *A Restricted Country*

1989—Sarah Schulman, *After Delores*

1991—Minnie Bruce Pratt, *Crime Against Nature*

1992—Lillian Faderman, *Odd Girls and Twilight Lovers: A History of Lesbian Life in Twentieth Century America*

1993—Leslie Feinberg, *Stone Butch Blues*

LAMBDA LITERARY AWARDS

The Lambda Literary Awards are held each year on the eve of the American Booksellers Association's annual convention, cosponsored by the Publishing Triangle and Lambda Rising Bookstore. Since 1988, the Lammy has recognized excellence in gay and lesbian writing and publishing. Current categories include: fiction, poetry, lesbian studies, gay men's studies, mystery, biography/autobiography, anthologies/fiction, anthologies/nonfiction, humor, science fiction/fantasy, drama, children's/young adult books, and lesbian and gay small press books. Nominations can be made by the general public. Winners are chosen by a panel of seventy-five judges representing a broad cross section of the lesbian and gay literary community.

LESBIAN WINNERS, 1994

Rebecca Brown, *The Gifts of the Body,* fiction

Marilyn Hacker, *Winter Numbers,* poetry

Dorothy Allison, *Skin,* lesbian studies

Renate Stendhal, *Gertrude Stein in Words and Pictures,* biography/autobiography

Lillian Faderman, ed., *Chloe Plus Olivia,* anthologies/fiction

Joan Nestle and John Preston, eds., *Sister and Brother,* anthologies/nonfiction

Ellen Hart, *Small Sacrifice,* mystery

Melissa Scott, *Trouble and Her Friends,* science fiction/fantasy

Ellen Galford, *The Dyke and the Dybbuk,* humor

Book cover for *Out of Time*

Nancy Andrews, *Family,* photography/visual arts
Marion Dane Bauer, *Am I Blue?,* children's/young adult
Kiss & Tell Press Gang, *Her Tongue on My Theory,* small press

Lambda Literary Awards in Lesbian Fiction Since 1988

1988—Dorothy Allison, *Trash*
1989—Nisa Donnelly, *The Bar Stories*
1990—Paula Martinac, *Out of Time*
1991—Blanche McCrary Boyd, *Revolution of Little Girls* and Jewelle Gomez,
     Gilda Stories (tie)
1992—Judith Katz, *Running Fiercely Toward a High Thin Sound*
1993—Jeanette Winterson, *Written on the Body*

Lambda Literary Awards in Lesbian Poetry Since 1988

1988—Carl Morse and Joan Larkin, eds., *Gay and Lesbian Poetry in Our Time*
1990—Marilyn Hacker, *Going Back to the River*
1991—Adrienne Rich, *Atlas of the Difficult World: Poems: 1988–1991*
1992—Audre Lorde, *Undersong*
1993—Audre Lorde, *The Marvelous Arithmetics of Distance*

Judith Katz,
Lambda Literary
Award winner
(*Photo by Nan
Fulle. Courtesy
of Firebrand
Books.*)

PULITZER PRIZE–WINNING LESBIANS AND BISEXUAL WOMEN

1918—Sara Teasdale, poetry, *Love Songs*
1923—Willa Cather, fiction, *One of Ours*
1923—Edna St. Vincent Millay, poetry, *The Ballad of the Harp-Weaver and Other Poems*
1926—Amy Lowell, poetry, *What's O'Clock*
1952—Marianne Moore, poetry, *Collected Poems*
1956—Elizabeth Bishop, poetry, *Poems—North and South*
1961—Harper Lee, fiction, *To Kill a Mockingbird*
1983—Alice Walker, fiction, *The Color Purple*
1984—Mary Oliver, poetry, *House of Light*

LESBIAN WINNERS OF THE AMERICAN ACADEMY AND INSTITUTE OF ARTS AND LETTERS AWARD FOR LITERATURE

1943—Muriel Rukeyser, poetry
1943—Carson McCullers, fiction
1946—Marianne Moore, poetry
1951—Elizabeth Bishop, poetry
1960—Adrienne Rich, poetry
1960—May Swenson, poetry

OTHER LESBIAN WINNERS OF MAJOR LITERARY AWARDS

Elizabeth Bishop, 1970 National Book Award for *The Complete Poems*
Marie-Claire Blais (Canadian), 1966 Prix Medicis for *Une Saison dans la vie d'Emmanuel*

Olga Broumas, 1976 Yale Series of Younger Poets for *Beginning with O*

Judy Grahn, 1983 American Book Award for *Queen of Wands*

Marilyn Hacker, 1975 National Book Award for *Presentation Piece* and 1973, Lamont Poetry Selection for *Presentation Piece*

Ursula K. LeGuin, 1973 National Book Award for *The Farthest Shore* and Nebula Awards, 1970, 1975; Hugo Awards, 1970, 1973, 1974

Marianne Moore, 1952 National Book Award and 1968 National Medal for Literature

Cherríe Moraga and Gloria Anzaldúa, 1986 American Book Award for *This Bridge Called My Back: Writings by Radical Women of Color*

Mary Oliver, 1992 National Book Award for *New and Selected Poems*

Minnie Bruce Pratt, 1989 Lamont Poetry Selection for *Crime Against Nature*

Adrienne Rich, 1974 National Book Award for *Diving into the Wreck: Poems, 1971–1972*

Joanna Russ, 1973 Nebula Award for *When It Changed*

May Sarton, 1985 American Book Award for *At Seventy: A Journal*

May Swenson, 1979–1980 Bollingern Prize in Poetry and 1979 Fellowship of the Academy of American Poets

---

LITERARY CHARACTERS WE'VE ALWAYS WONDERED ABOUT

Jo March in *Little Women*
Scout Finch in *To Kill a Mockingbird*
Janie in *Their Eyes Were Watching God*
George in the Nancy Drew series

LESBIAN AND FEMINIST WRITERS AND PUBLICATIONS BANNED BY CANADIAN CUSTOMS

For years, Canadian customs officials have regularly seized, detained, and banned feminist, lesbian, and gay literature at the U.S.-Canada border. In 1990, Little Sister's Bookstore of Vancouver initiated a suit against Canadian Customs challenging this pernicious practice. Some of the writers whose works have been seized are:

Dorothy Allison   Katherine Forrest
Susie Bright   Bell Hooks
Pat Califia   Jane Rule
Deneuve magazine   Sarah Schulman

Katherine V. Forrest *(Photo by Maureen Kelly. Courtesy of Naiad Press.)*

LESBIAN/GAY LENDING LIBRARIES

Blanche Baker Memorial Library and Archives (ONE, Inc.)
3340 Country Club Drive
Los Angeles, CA 90019
Phone: 213/735-5252

Gerber/Hart Library and Archives
3352 N. Paulina Street
Chicago, IL 60657
Phone: 312/883-3003

Pat Parker/Vito Russo Center Library
Lesbian and Gay Community Services
  Center

208 West 13th Street
New York, NY 10011
Phone: 212/620-7310

Quatrefoil Library
1619 Dayton Avenue, #105-107
St. Paul, MN 55104
Phone: 612/641-0969

Stonewall Library and Archives
330 SW 27th Street
Fort Lauderdale, FL 33315

LESBIAN PUBLISHERS/LESBIAN-FRIENDLY SMALL PUBLISHERS/FEMINIST PUBLISHERS

Alyson Publications
40 Plympton Street
Boston, MA 02118
Phone: 617/542-5679

Primarily gay male, but also some lesbian erotica; Alyson Wonderland is an imprint for lesbian- and gay-themed children's books.

Calyx Books
Attn: Margarita Donnelly
P.O. Box B
Corvallis, OR 97339
Phone: 503/753-9384
Topical anthologies; also publishes
  Calyx, a journal of art and
  literature.

Cleis Press
Attn: Frederique Delacoste
P.O. Box 14684
San Francisco, CA 94114
Fiction, anthologies, essays, humor.

Eighth Mountain Press
Attn: Ruth Gundle
624 SE 29th Street
Portland, OR 97214
Poetry.

The Feminist Press at The City
  University of New York
Attn: Florence Howe
311 East 94th Street
New York, NY 10128
Phone: 212/360-5790
Memoirs, anthologies, reprints of out-
  of-print fiction, women's studies
  curriculum guides, children's books,
  travel books; also publishes *Women's
  Studies Quarterly*; no contemporary
  poetry or fiction.

Firebrand Books
Attn: Nancy Bereano
141 The Commons
Ithaca, NY 14850
Phone: 607/272-0000
Poetry, fiction, humor, essays.

Kitchen Table: Women of Color Press
Attn: A. Lockett
P.O. Box 40-4920
Brooklyn, NY 11240-4920
Phone: 718/935-1082
Anthologies, fiction, essays by women
  of color.

Naiad Press
Attn: Barbara Grier
P.O. Box 10543
Tallahassee, FL 32302
Phone: 800/533-1973
Mysteries, romance, adventure, other
  fiction.

New Victoria Publishers
Attn: Claudia Lamperti
P.O. Box 27
Norwich, VT 05055
Phone: 800/326-5297
Mysteries, romance, adventure, other
  fiction.

Seal Press
Attn: Faith Conlon
3131 Western Avenue, Suite 410
Seattle, WA 98121-1028
Phone: 206/283-7844
Fiction, some poetry, self-help,
  mysteries, anthologies.

Spinsters Ink/Aunt Lute
Attn: Joan Drury
P.O. Box 300170
Minneapolis, MN 55403
Phone: 612/377-0287
Fiction, anthologies, mysteries.

FUNDING OPPORTUNITIES FOR LESBIAN WRITERS

Astraea National Lesbian Action Foundation's Lesbian Writers Fund annually offers five grants of $11,000 to emerging lesbian poets and fiction writers. Write for grant guidelines and application: Astraea, 666 Broadway, Suite 520, New York, NY 10012.

Founded in 1975, the *Money for Women/Barbara Deming Memorial Fund* offers small grants of up to $1,000 to feminist and lesbian writers in the categories of fiction, nonfiction, and poetry. Deadlines are June 30 and December 31 of each year. For an application and guidelines, write to the Barbara Deming Memorial Fund, Inc., P.O. Box 40-1043, Brooklyn, NY 11240-1043.

LESBIAN/GAY WRITING AWARDS GIVEN BY THE PUBLISHING TRIANGLE

The Publishing Triangle is a dues-paying-membership organization dedicated to the furtherance of lesbian and gay writing and publishing. In addition to organizing regular forums on writing and publishing and cosponsoring the Lambda Literary Awards, PT also presents the following three prestigious annual awards to lesbian and gay writers:

The *Robert Chesley Playwrighting Award* is named for the first playwright to produce a full-length play on AIDS, Robert Chesley, who died of AIDS. This award acknowledges playwrighting that adds to lesbian and gay mythology. A cash prize of $1,000, one each to a lesbian and a gay man, is decided by internal nomination.

The *Ferro-Grumley Award* is named for novelists/lovers Robert Ferro and Michael Grumley, who both died of AIDS. This award recognizes excellence in lesbian and gay-themed writing. A cash prize of $1,000, one each to a lesbian and a gay man, is decided by internal nomination.

The *Bill Whitehead Prize* is named for the pioneering gay editor, Bill Whitehead, who died of AIDS. This prize honors lifetime achievement for a body of work with significant lesbian or gay content. A cash prize of $1,000, given in alternate years to a lesbian and a gay man, is decided by internal nomination.

For more information about The Publishing Triangle, write to them at P.O. Box 114, Prince Street Station, New York, NY 10012. A one-year membership, which includes a newsletter subscription, is $30.

LESBIAN AND FEMINIST WRITERS' RETREATS

Cottages at Hedgebrook is a writers' colony for women on Whidbey Island, just off the coast of Seattle. Founded by lesbian philanthropist Nancy Nordhoff and very lesbian friendly, Hedgebrook offers stays from three weeks to three months to women working in fiction, poetry, nonfiction, and drama. Write for guidelines and application: Cottages at Hedgebrook, 2197 East Millman Road, Langley, Washington 98260.

Norcroft: A Writing Retreat for Women was founded by lesbian philanthropist Joan Drury and, like Hedgebrook, it is open to all women writers working in fiction, poetry, nonfiction, and drama. The beautiful retreat is located on the north shore of Lake Superior. Write for guidelines: Norcroft, P.O. Box 300105, Minneapolis, MN 55403.

Women's Art Colony Tree Farm in Poughkeepsie, New York, is run every summer by writer/artist Kate Millett. Women writers can work a half day on a Christmas tree farm in exchange for studio time and space. The colony is in a beautiful country setting and provides writers with their own rooms and a communal life with other women artists. Seventy dollars a week is requested as a food contribution. For information, send a self-addressed stamped envelope to Kate Millett, 295 Bowery, New York, NY 10003.

Annual Lesbian Writing Conferences and Summer Workshops

OutWrite, the lesbian, gay, bisexual, and transgendered writers' conference, is produced annually in Boston the first weekend in March by the Bromfield Street Educational Foundation, the publisher of *Gay Community News*. Over two thousand writers, readers, booksellers, agents, and editors take part in sessions, workshops, readings, and roundtables. The 1995 conference featured keynote speakers Tony Kushner, Pulitzer Prize winner playwright, and Linda Villarosa, executive editor of *Essence* magazine. Cherríe Moraga delivered the Audre Lorde Memorial Lecture. For information on future conferences, contact: OutWrite, 25 West Street, Boston, MA 02111.

Since the early 1970s, the *Feminist Women's Writing Workshops* have taken place every July in the Finger Lakes region of upstate New York. Workshops and presentations cover everything from writing to editing to finding an agent. For information, send a self-addressed stamped envelope to FWWW, P.O. Box 6583, Ithaca, NY 14851.

Flight of the Mind writing workshops for women are held every year in late June to early July in a beautiful Pacific Northwest setting. In 1995, guest workshop leaders included Grace Paley, Ursula LeGuin, Evelyn C. White, and Judith Barrington. For a brochure, send a self-addressed stamped envelope to 622 SE 29th, Portland, OR 97214.

Profile

Kitchen Table: Women of Color Press

Kitchen Table: Women of Color Press was founded in 1981 by Audre Lorde and Barbara Smith. As both writers and feminists of color, these women sought to provide options for women of color who were denied access to both mainstream and feminist publishers, especially women whose class, politics, and/or sexual orientation made their work particularly vulnerable to silencing. Throughout the 1980s, Kitchen Table published such feminist classics as *This Bridge Called My Back: Writings by Radical Women of Color* and *Home Girls: A Black Feminist Anthology*. These texts have literally changed the shape of women's studies curricula over the past decade. Most importantly, Kitchen Table books articulated a point of view and made visible a community that heretofore had been marginalized by both the dominant culture and feminist movements.

More than a decade later, founding publisher Barbara Smith remains at the helm of Kitchen Table Press (New York State Poet Laureate Audre Lorde died of cancer in November 1992. Her final volume of poetry was nominated for a National Book Award.) Smith's guiding hand has created one of the nation's primary resources for women of color. More than an alternative press, Kitchen Table serves as an organizing hub for women of color seeking community, resources, and support. Each year, the press fields hundreds of unsolicited letters, manuscripts, and calls for help by women of color across the nation. Since its founding, Kitchen Table offers all of its books free upon request to women and men in prison or psychiatric institutions; the press also sends its titles on request to battered women's shelters, programs for the homeless, community libraries, and persons with AIDS.

Kitchen Table got its name, according to Smith, "because the kitchen is the center of the home, the place where women in particular work and communicate with each other and because we wanted to convey the fact that we are a kitchen-table, grassroots operation, begun and kept alive by women who cannot rely on inheritances or other benefits of class privilege to do the work we need to do."

In 1995, Kitchen Table Press moved from its Albany, New York, office in the home of Smith to offices in the Fort Greene section of Brooklyn, New York.

LANDMARK KITCHEN TABLE TITLES

Narratives: Poems in the Tradition of Black Women, Cheryl Clarke
Cuentos: Stories by Latinas, Alma Gómez, Cherríe Moraga, and Mariana Romo-Carmona, eds.
Home Girls: A Black Feminist Anthology, Barbara Smith, ed.
This Bridge Called My Back: Writings by Radical Women of Color, Cherríe Moraga and Gloria Anzaldúa, eds.
A Comrade Is as Precious as a Rice Seedling, Mila D. Aguilar
Camp Notes and Other Poems, Mitsuye Yamada
Seventeen Syllables and Other Stories, Hisaye Yamamoto
Healing Heart, Gloria T. Hull
The Combahee River Collective Statement: Black Feminist Organizing in the Seventies and Eighties, pamphlet
I Am Your Sister, Audre Lorde, pamphlet
Need: A Chorale for Black Woman Voices, Audre Lorde, pamphlet
Apartheid U.S.A., Audre Lorde, pamphlet
Our Common Enemy, Our Common Cause, Merle Woo, pamphlet

Violence Against Women and the Ongoing Challenge to Racism, Angela Y. Davis, pamphlet

It's a Family Affair, Barbara Omolade, pamphlet

FORTHCOMING FROM KITCHEN TABLE

The Third Wave: Feminist Perspectives on Racism, Jacqui Alexander, Lisa Albrecht, Sharon Day, Mab Segrest, and Norma Alarcón, eds.

Kitchen Table books are sent free upon request to persons in prison, persons in psychiatric institutions, and persons with AIDS. Write: P.O. Box 40-4920, Brooklyn, NY 11240-4920.

PROFILE

Jacqueline Woodson

Jacqueline Woodson began to consider becoming a writer when she was chosen to be the literary editor of a magazine in the fifth grade. What cinched it for Woodson was her discovery of three books: *The Bluest Eye* by Toni Morrison, *Daddy Was a Number Runner* by Louise Merriwether, and *Ruby* by Rosa Guy. In these books Woodson recognized parts of herself and her life; she realized that books could be about people like her; and she decided to write them.

Jacqueline Woodson

Jacqueline Woodson was born in Columbus, Ohio, in 1963 and grew up in Greenville, South Carolina, and Brooklyn, New York. The author of seven novels, six for young adults and one for adults, Woodson writes from the margins. "As a writer who is black and gay, but neither a black writer nor a gay writer, I do not feel as though I have a responsibility to only these two communities; but rather a responsibility to write beyond the systems of oppression in *all* marginal communities. I think as people who exist on the margins, we do have a better view of the world, and it is our responsibility to refocus."

Woodson writes about subjects once considered taboo for young adult fiction: alcoholism, racism, class tensions, lesbianism, death, and sexual abuse. She also writes compelling stories with complex characters. In other words, Woodson doesn't teach lessons with her fiction; kids hate that, she says. Woodson uses the difficult issues she writes about as "floaters" and "lets the story be the water that carries the issues." All of which has brought her rave reviews and a loyal readership.

YOUNG ADULT NOVELS

From the Notebooks of Melanin Sun, Scholastic Books, 1995
I Hadn't Meant to Tell You This, Delacorte, 1994
Between Madison and Palmetto, Delacorte, 1993
Maizon at Blue Hill, Delacorte, 1992
The Dear One, Delacorte, 1991
Last Summer with Maizon, Delacorte, 1990

FORTHCOMING YOUNG ADULT NOVELS

Staggerlee, Delacorte, 1996
Visiting Day, Scholastic 1997

ADULT NOVELS

Autobiography of a Family Photo, Dutton, 1995

AWARDS

Publishers Weekly, Best Book of 1994
Booklist Editor's Choice Award
Kenyon Review Award for Literary Excellence in Fiction
American Library Association Awards (2)
American Film Institute Award

PROFILE

Jane Rule

Jane Rule was born in Plainfield, New Jersey, in 1931. She discovered her love for women in her late teens and her love for literature at Mills College. Rule met her

Jane Rule *(Photo by Dave Morgan. Courtesy of Naiad Press.)*

partner of more than forty years, Helen Sonthoff, in a school for girls in Concord, Massachusetts, where they both taught. She and Helen moved to Vancouver in 1956 so that Rule could teach English literature at the University of British Columbia. Rule taught and wrote for ten years before her first book, *Desert of the Heart,* was published by Naiad Press.

Realistic rather than utopian, Jane Rule's dozen novels are recognized as standard bearers of excellence in lesbian fiction. For many, Rule's *Desert of the Heart* was the first book about lesbians they read that wasn't encoded. Gritty and honest, with complicated characters and subjects that reach beyond the lesbian community, Rule's fiction continues to generate interest, even now that she's stopped writing. Since the success of the 1985 film *Desert Hearts,* which was based on Rule's *Desert of the Heart,* her work has come under scrutiny in women's studies and literature classes. A second novel, *Memory Board,* has also been optioned for a film.

With her books still in print and still selling (*Desert of the Heart* sells some 2,000 copies a year), Rule herself has become the subject of two documentarians' work. Marilyn Schuster, professor of French and women's studies at Smith College, is writing a book about Rule's writing, and the filmmakers who produced *Forbidden*

Love (a documentary about Canadian lesbians in the 1950s and 1960s) are producing a film about Rule.

Rule's last book, *After the Fire*, was published in 1989, and since then she has stopped writing altogether.

"I realized an awful lot of the things I have to say, I have already said. Painters can do some of their best work when they're old, but writers rarely do. As you age a lot more of your day is spent keeping yourself nourished and comfortable."

Rule and Sonthoff have lived together on Galiano Island, a remote and rocky island off the coast of British Columbia, since 1976.

FICTION (ALL PUBLISHED BY NAIAD PRESS)

Desert of the Heart, 1964
This Is Not for You, 1970
Against the Season, 1971
Lesbian Images, 1975
Theme for Diverse Instruments,
   1975
The Young in One Another's Arms,
   1977

Contract with the World, 1980
Outlander, 1981
A Hot-Eyed Moderate, 1985
Inland Passage and Other Stories, 1985
Memory Board, 1987
After the Fire, 1989

PROFILE

Terri de la Pena

Born in 1947 in Santa Monica, California, where she still lives, Terri de la Pena is the Chicana daughter of a Mexican immigrant mother and a Mexican-American father. She is a self-taught writer who started writing fiction as an adolescent (her first stories were westerns), never went to college, and remained unpublished until after her fortieth birthday. De la Pena's fiction—written with bilingual dialogue—centers on the middle- and working-class urban Chicana experience in southern California, often contrasting differences that arise from age, class, and sexual orientation.

De la Pena is an avid reader who acknowledges the important influence lesbian-feminist writing has played on her work. In her search for lesbian-feminist titles, she found that very little published lesbian writing was Chicana focused. "I wrote *Margins*," she says of her first novel, "because I wanted to read it, because I couldn't find anything like it. . . . I never grew up in a barrio, I grew up in a beach town, and I felt like I could never find anybody like me in fiction." In addition to *Margins* and her second novel, *Latin Satins*, de la Pena's short stories and nonfiction have appeared in numerous anthologies and magazines.

"I like to think of my work," she says, "as being cross-cultural, entertaining while educating, using humor and passion to leap over the borders and barriers separating and dividing us. In both *Margins* and *Latin Satins* and also in my short stories,

Terri de la Pena *(Photo by
Tee Corinne)*

I place Chicana lesbians as main characters, providing them the freedom to be
themselves on the page—a freedom which, ironically, can be enviable and
ephemeral in reality."

NOVELS

Margins. The Seal Press, 1992.
Latin Satins. The Seal Press, 1994.

SHORT STORY COLLECTION

Territories. Third Woman Press, 1995.

SHORT STORIES

"A Saturday in August," in *Irvine Chicano Literary Prize, 1985–1987*. University
   of California, Irvine, 1988.
"Once a Friend," in *The One You Call Sister: New Women's Fiction*, Paula Mar-
   tinac, ed. Cleis Press, 1989.
"Tres Mujeres," in *Frontiers: A Journal of Women's Studies*, Vol. 11, No. 1, pp. 60-
   64.
"Mariposa," in *Lesbian Bedtime Stories*, Vol. 2, Terry Wolverton, ed. Tough Dove
   Books, 1990.
"Beyond El Camino Real," in *Chicana Lesbians: The Girls Our Mothers Warned
   Us About*, Carla Trujillo, ed. Third Woman Press, 1991.

"Frankie," in *Blood Whispers: L.A. Writers on AIDS,* Terry Wolverton, ed. Silverton Books and the Lesbian and Gay Community Services Center, 1991.

"Blue," in *Riding Desire,* Tee Corinne, ed. Banned Books, 1991.

"Desert Quartet," in *Lesbian Love Stories,* Vol. 2, Irene Zahava, ed. The Crossing Press, 1991.

"Tortilleras," in *Lesbian Culture: An Anthology,* Julia Penelope and Susan Wolfe, eds. The Crossing Press, 1993.

"Mujeres Morenas," in *Lavender Mansions: 40 Contemporary Lesbian and Gay Short Stories,* Irene Zahava, ed. Westview Press, 1994.

---

11. LESBIANS IN THE MEDIA

I had been out to my family since I was 20. I had even been out at other jobs. Somehow, when I got to Essence, *I slipped back in. . . . I finally came out because I got really tired of not talking about my personal life. . . . So one day . . . I just told everyone. I literally was going into people's office and saying, "Good morning, I'm a lesbian."*

—LINDA VILLAROSA, senior editor at *Essence* magazine, quoted in *New York* magazine

The lesbian and gay press has shaped and reflected the rise of gay and lesbian liberation. The proliferation of gay and lesbian newspapers, newsletters, and magazines in the United States has allowed us to weave a well-informed network of previously isolated individuals and communities, empowering and unifying gay and lesbian people.

In 1924, Chicago's Society for Human Rights published two issues of the journal *Friendship and Freedom* before organizers were arrested on obscenity charges. Sadly, no copies of this first U.S. gay publication are known to exist in any collection, but several earlier European gay and lesbian periodicals have survived. Lisa Ben's *Vice Versa* appeared in 1947 as a typewritten, carbon-copied, and retyped newsletter passed hand to hand—the first lesbian periodical in the United States.

In the 1950s, homophile groups—the Daughters of Bilitis, the Mattachine Society, and ONE—built themselves into national organizations by defying U.S. law that prohibited homosexual publications from being distributed by mail. Although the Comstock Act was changed with *ONE, Inc. vs. Olesen* in 1958, many gay and lesbian publications, especially those dealing directly with gay/lesbian sexuality, have continued to face censorship and harassment from the U.S. Postal Service, U.S. Customs, local government, and religious and political groups.

As a national gay and lesbian community became united, a gay liberation movement emerged, symbolized most often today by the New York City Stonewall riots in June 1969. The *Los Angeles Advocate* (now *The Advocate*), *Gay Community News,* and *Fag Rag* all date from these days of gay liberation. In the 1970s and 1980s, feminist publications began addressing lesbian concerns. During the 1980s and into the 1990s, gay and lesbian activism restructured to address the AIDS epidemic. Armed with a bold, life-affirming, sex-positive analysis, gay

Essence editor
Linda Villarosa

and lesbian publications promoted safer sex practices for "queers," countering homophobic mainstream admonitions to celibacy, blame, and self-loathing. With the rise of groups like ACT UP, a brazen sensibility ascended that changed the face of the gay/lesbian press, and also impacted the mainstream press as never before. The practice of "outing" homophobic public figures who are themselves gay or lesbian began with an article exposing entrepreneur Malcolm Forbes in New York's *OutWeek* magazine (which published from 1989 to 1991), prompting intense coverage in the mainstream media.

Another phenomenon in late-1980s/early-1990s gay/lesbian publishing is the fanzine craze. 'Zines, as they are popularly known, are homemade, some desktop published, comics-like productions that are uniformly creative, irreverent, outrageous, and usually sexually explicit. Underground 'zine favorites, sold in bookstores and by subscription, include *Thing, My Comrade/Sister, Lana's World, BimBox, Pansy Beat, Homocore, J.D.s,* and *Taste of Latex.*

Recent years have also seen the proliferation of newsletters and journals from gay and lesbian people of color within the United States, especially African-Americans and Asian-Americans. The airing of these voices of the previously silenced makes sure that the debate over gay and lesbian rights or liberation is no longer limited to whites.

Despite the growth of the computerized indexing industry, the gay and lesbian press is still routinely excluded from mainstream periodical indexes. While articles about outing from *Newsweek*, the *Village Voice*, and the *National Review* can be found on-line, on-disc, and with paper indexes, the original *OutWeek* article is not included in any periodical index. Similarly, critiques of HIV drugs and treatment programs in community-based gay/lesbian publications are ignored entirely by indexers, despite their undeniable value to doctors, researchers, students, the pharmaceutical industry, and HIV-positive people. Only one current periodical index, the *Alternative Press Index*, regularly includes a significant number of gay/lesbian titles. Under pressure from the American Library Association's Gay and Lesbian Task Force, however, Gale Research and Information Access Company began in 1991 to include five previously unindexed gay periodicals. Sadly, other publishers have refused to correct the bias in their indexing.

—Polly Thistlethwaite and Daniel C. Tsang

SOURCE: Reprinted with permission of R. R. Bowker, a Reed Reference Publishing Company, from "Magazines for Libraries," 7th edition, copyright © 1992, Reed Elsevier Inc. (pages 680 and 681).

HISTORIC GAY/LESBIAN PUBLICATIONS

Friendship and Freedom: Published by the Chicago Society for Human Rights, which only produced two issues in 1924 before being closed down by the police; produced by Henry Gerber.

Chanticleer: A mimeographed newsletter, started in 1934, again by Henry Gerber and Jacob Houser.

Vice Versa: The first American publication by and for lesbians, by Lisa Ben (an anagram of *lesbian*). In 1947–1948, Lisa Ben typed the magazine in her spare time at work, making four carbon copies of each of two originals, for a total of ten copies of each issue. These were circulated among friends and friends of friends. She published a total of nine issues, which included poetry; short stories; editorials; reviews of plays, books, and films; and an annotated bibliography of novels of interest to lesbians.

ONE Magazine: The Homosexual Viewpoint: Founded in 1952, it was the first gay magazine in the U.S. to reach a wide audience (5,000 readers at its peak). The U.S. Postal Service did not want to allow mailings of it, and in 1958, *ONE* won a decision from the U.S. Supreme Court to be allowed through the mails, thus opening a venue for all gay/lesbian magazines. It ended publication in 1972.

The Mattachine Review: More restrained in its gay activism than *ONE* and somewhat more scholarly, it started in 1955 and folded in the mid-1960s when newer publications more accurately reflected an increasingly militant community.

The Ladder: Started in 1956, a monthly publication of the Daughters of Bilitis, the first American organization for lesbians, it was purposely kept nonpolitical and aimed at "the lonely isolated lesbians away from big cities." It was the oldest continuously published gay periodical in the United States until it folded in 1972.

Vector: The magazine of the Society for Individual Rights, the leading gay advocacy group on the West Coast at the time, was started in 1964.

The Los Angeles Advocate: Now known as *The Advocate*, this publication was founded in 1966 by Dick Michaels in response to being at a gay bar during a routine police raid. It quickly became and still is the country's most prominent gay publication.

The 1970s saw the rise of magazines and newsletters for more specialized or specific gay and lesbian audiences, i.e., religion, politics, or professions. During this same period there was also the rise of scholarly publications, such as *Gay Books Bulletin* (1979–1985) and the *Journal of Homosexuality* (1974–present).

The Gay and Lesbian Press Association was established in the late 1970s, and the National Lesbian and Gay Journalists Association was established in the late 1980s. (To reach the NLGJA in New York, call 212/629-2045.)

In the late 1970s and increasingly in the 1980s and 1990s, there was a surge in culture magazines. For example, one of the first was published in 1976, *Christopher Street*, which had intentions of being the "gay *New Yorker.*" *Christopher Street* can be contacted by writing to P.O. Box 1475, Church Street Station, New York, NY 10008 or by calling 212/627-2120.

Today, in the mid-1990s, lesbian, gay, bisexual, and transgender/transsexual magazines, newspapers, and newsletters continue to proliferate both in North America and around the world at an unprecedented rate. As an example, the 1987 edition of the *International Directory of Gay and Lesbian Periodicals* listed 609 gay periodicals and 626 lesbian periodicals (please note that there is a great overlap between the two categories). Since that time, hundreds of new publications—from newsletters to 'zines to national glossies—have brought their lesbian, gay, bisexual, and transgendered perspective to the world.

THE MISSION STATEMENT FROM *VICE VERSA*, THE FIRST LESBIAN PERIODICAL

"Have you ever stopped to enumerate the many different publications to be found on the average newsstands? There are publications for a variety of races and creeds. A wide selection of fiction is available for those who like mysteries, westerns, science fiction or romantic stories. For those who prefer fact to fiction, a variety of publications on politics, world affairs, economics, and sports are available.

And newsstands fairly groan with the weight of hobby and miscellaneous publications devoted to subjects ranging from radio, engineering, gardening, home improvements, and sailing, to travel, fashion, and health.

"Yet, there is one kind of publication which would, I am sure, have a great appeal to a definite group. Such a publication has never appeared on the stands. Newsstands carrying the crudest kind of magazines or pictorial pamphlets appealing to the vulgar would find themselves severely censured were they to display this other type of publication. Why? Because *society* decrees it thus.

"Hence, the appearance of *Vice Versa*, a magazine dedicated, in all seriousness, to those of us who will never quite be able to adapt ourselves to the ironbound rules of convention."

SOURCE: *Vice Versa,* Vol. 1, No. 1, June 1947

LESBIAN PUBLICATIONS AFTER *THE LADDER*

According to Joan Nestle, "When *The Ladder* stopped publishing in 1972, a new lesbian cultural journal called *Amazon Quarterly*, a lesbian-feminist arts periodical, announced its intention to 'explore through its pages just what might be the female sensibility in the arts.' According to the editors, Gina and Laurel, lesbians, 'freed from male identification,' were to be the vanguard voice of this new cultural perspective."

Lesbian-feminist journal editors and poets (left to right): Susan Sherman (*IKON* magazine); Irena Klepfisz *(Conditions)*; Mi Ok Bruining *(Conditions) (Copyright © 1991 by Morgan Gwenwald)*

Nestle goes on to note that throughout the 1970s and 1980s, lesbian periodicals flourished, with their titles often suggesting their political and cultural take. Some examples (with their dates of founding) include:

Off Our Backs (1970)	*Feminary* (1976)
13th Moon (1973)	*Heresies* (1976)
Sinister Wisdom (1976)	*Azalea* (1978)
Conditions (1976)	*Common Lives/Lesbian Lives*
Quest (1976)	(1981)
Focus (1976)	*Lesbian Connection* (1982)
Chrysalis (1976)	

Nestle further notes, "Often produced by collectives, these publications were dedicated to being inclusive of all lesbian experience and to keeping their prices as low as possible. *Lesbian Connection,* a stapled multipage monthly, was and still is distributed free through a network of women's and gay bookstores as well as through a huge national mailing list. Contributions from a grateful community keep this publication alive. Embodying the lesbian feminist spirit of the seventies, these journals gave lesbian writers a chance to develop a community of sympathetic readers."

SOURCE: "Afterword" by Joan Nestle in *Women on Women: An Anthology of American Lesbian Short Fiction,* Joan Nestle and Naomi Holoch, eds. (New York: Plume, 1990)

LESBIAN NEWSPAPERS AND MAGAZINES (MOST NOW DEFUNCT)

Lesbian Tide (1970s)	*Dyke* (1970s)
Echo of Sappho (1970s)	*Leaping Lesbian* (1970s)
Sinister Wisdom (1970s–present)	*Lesbians Rising* (1970s)
Feminary (1970s)	*Lesbian Connection* (1980s–present)
Off Our Backs (1970s)	*Lesbian News* (1980s–present)
Herself (1970s)	*Womanews* (1979–1989)
Lavender Woman (1970s)	*Visibilities: The Lesbian Magazine* (1980s)
Big Mama Rag (1970s)	*Sappho's Isle* (1980s–present)
Quest (1970s)	

PERIODICALS BY LESBIANS OF COLOR

"In the United States, white lesbians have been publishing periodicals for over thirty years. Over a hundred titles since 1947. Of course, this has been a long, difficult process and not without struggle. But consider the fact that lesbians of color published their first periodical in 1976. The effects of racial oppression and homophobia in this country are devastating." J. R. Roberts, bibliographer and compiler of *Black Lesbians: An Annotated Bibliography,* published by the Naiad Press in 1981.

Azalea: A Magazine by Third World Lesbians
Brown Sister Magazine
Lesbians of Color Newsletter
Lesbians of Color Quarterly
Moja: Black and Gay
Third World Women's Gay-zette

SOME CURRENT PUBLICATIONS BY PEOPLE OF COLOR

ColorLife! (New York City)
Thing (Chicago)
BLK (Los Angeles)
BG (New York)
Black/Out (published by the National Coalition of Black Lesbians and Gays)
Other Countries (New York): literary/arts journal for black gay men
Asians & Friends/New York: (New York) (monthly magazine for Asian and Pacific Islander gay men)
Paz Y Liberacion: (Houston) (quarterly newsletter featuring lesbian and gay news about Latin America, Asia, Africa, and Middle East)

THE FIRST LESBIAN/GAY NEWSPAPER TO APPEAR IN NEW YORK AFTER THE STONEWALL REBELLION

Come Out! associated with the Gay Liberation Front, appeared in 1969.

FIRST LESBIAN/GAY NEWSWEEKLY TO RUN A COPY OF THE FIRST COVER OF *COME OUT!* ON ITS FIRST COVER

OutWeek: New York's Lesbian and Gay News Magazine, was a weekly magazine that began June 26, 1989, published by Gabriel Rotello.

LESBIAN SEX MAGAZINES

Bad Attitude: A Lesbian Sex Magazine (cofounded by Amy Hoffman and Cindy Patton in 1984); P.O. Box 390110, Cambridge, MA 02139; emphasis on S/M and B/D.

On Our Backs: Entertainment for the Adventurous Lesbian (founded in 1984 by

Susie Bright, aka Suzie Sexpert); 526 Castro St., San Francisco, CA 94114; Phone: 800/845-4617; bimonthly erotica with news, features, and fiction.

Outrageous Women: A Journal of Woman-to-Woman S/M
Yoni
Up Our Butts ('zine)
Eidos: Erotic Entertainment for Women
On Our Rag ('zine)
Yellow Silk: Journal of Erotic Arts (not strictly lesbian, but lesbian-friendly)
Ad Venture! (Your Passport to Erotic Pleasure)
Tits and Clits Comix

BISEXUAL MAGAZINES

Anything That Moves: Beyond the Myth of Bisexuality, a quarterly magazine (published by the Bay Area Bisexual Network); 2404 California St., #24, San Francisco, CA 94115; Phone: 415/564-2226

North Bi Northwest, a feminist bisexual women's newsletter
Bisexuality: The North American Journal: Phone: 213/597-2799
Bisexuality, P.O. Box 20917, Long Beach, CA 90801; Phone: 310/597-2799; bimonthly newsletter

---

MAGAZINE OF FEMALE-TO-MALE TRANSSEXUALS AND CROSS-DRESSERS

Rites of Passage, c/o S.G., P.O. Box 615, Tenafly, NJ 07670

HOW HAS JOURNALISTIC LANGUAGE CHANGED OVER TIME IN TALKING ABOUT HOMOSEXUALITY?

One of the major successes of the gay movement in the 1960s was the breakthrough into mainstream publications. Although hardly flattering, the stories at least began to break the silence and invisibility surrounding gay and lesbian lives. Here is a selected time line of homosexuality in the mainstream media:

1892: The word *lesbian* was first used in a newspaper article. It was the *New York Times,* and the article was entitled "Lesbian Love and Murder," about Alice Mitchell's murder of Freda Ward. (Mitchell and Ward were teenagers who had exchanged rings, and when their parents discovered their relationship, barred them from seeing each other. Mitchell claimed in court that the young lovers had made a pact to kill each other if they couldn't be together.)

1924: The *New York Times* first used the word *homosexual.* It was in a review of the book *The Doctor Looks at Love and Life* by Dr. Joseph Collins, which included a substantial chapter on homosexuality.

1948: *Life* magazine published an article entitled "Test by Portraits: Pictures of Pathological Types Help Diagnosis of Mental Illness." Of course, two of the sixteen photographs were that of homosexuals. The pictures included two types of each of the "major kinds of mental disturbances: the sadist, the homosexual, the hysteric, the depressive, the manic, the epileptic, the catatonic, and the paranoid." Oh, such company we keep!

1950s: The *New York Times* routinely used the word "perverts" to describe homosexuals. Actual headlines include "Federal Vigilance on Perverts Asked," "126 Perverts Discharged: State Department Reports Total Ousted Since Jan. 1, 1951," and "Perverts Called Government Peril."

1955: *People Today,* a national magazine, provided sympathetic coverage of a gay organization. This was the first instance of positive reporting about gay issues by a mainstream news source. It was an article on the group that published *ONE* magazine entitled "Third Sex Comes Out of Hiding."

1963: The *New York Times* published a large feature entitled "Growth of Overt Homosexuality Provokes Wide Concern: Condition Can Be Prevented or Cured, Many Experts Say; Conflicting Points of View Spur Discussion of Inverts." Although we're getting more press, the notion of respect still has a long way to go.

1964: *Life* magazine published an unprecedented look at gay life, entitled "Homosexuality in America." Although mostly negative in its take, it did try to explain the homosexual underground to the mainstream society.

1969: The *Los Angeles Times* was boycotted for refusing to allow the word *homosexual* to appear in any advertising. Today, the paper has many openly gay reporters and editors, as well as a gay caucus that meets weekly.

1970: On the first Gay Pride Parade in New York City after Stonewall, the *Daily News* reported the following on August 31, in an article entitled, "Cops Will Go 2 by 2 in the Dark of the City," where police commissioner Howard Leary directed that policemen will no longer walk city streets alone after dark. "More than 100 policemen were battling an unruly Greenwich Village crowd that included hundreds of homosexuals, hippies, and young militants. Seven policemen were hurt, including one who was knifed, and 18 persons were arrested. . . . The Greenwich Village ruckus followed a peaceful parade of some 350 homosexuals, members of the Gay Activists Alliance and the Gay Liberation Front, from Times Square to the Village."

1977: Harvey Milk was endorsed by the San Francisco *Chronicle,* a mainstream paper.

1978: *Time* magazine published a homophobic caricature of "Gay Bob," the world's first gay doll, showing him with false eyelashes, lipstick, rouge, and a limp wrist. They later apologized for reinforcing stereotypes.

1981: The first story to bring AIDS (though still unnamed as such) to the general public appears July 3 in the *New York Times*. It is entitled "Rare Cancer Seen in 41 Homosexuals."

1984: The *Wall Street Journal* begins using the word *gay* as an adjective.

1987: The *New York Times* begins using the word *gay* as an adjective.

1989: The *San Francisco Examiner* ran an unprecedented sixteen-day report entitled "Gay in America," detailing what it is like "to live as a gay or lesbian person in America 20 years after the Stonewall Riots knocked down the closet doors and forced the nation to confront its most virulently disliked minority." The *Examiner* interviewed thousands of people in the Bay Area and across the country to study gay and lesbian Americans, American society, and the often uneasy intersection between them.

1990: The *San Francisco Examiner* ran a long feature in its "Style" section on gay and lesbian dance clubs featuring The Box, which it reported "attracts a dance-mad collection of blacks, whites, straights, gays, Asians, Hispanics, and more."

1992: Publisher of the *New York Times,* Arthur Ochs Sulzberger, Jr., announced that diversity would be a priority at the paper of record. By the end of the year, the *Times* had become a leader on reporting gay and lesbian issues, which had significant influence on other media.

    • *Newsweek* ran a cover story entitled "Is This Child Gay? Born or Bred: The Origins of Homosexuality," which discussed recent studies on the possible biological origin of homosexuality (i.e., Dr. Simon LeVay and his study of hypothalamus sizes and the Bailey-Pillard study on gay male twins).

1993: *Newsweek* and *New York* magazine finally discovered lesbians, each running a cover story on so-called "lesbian chic."

THAT SPECIAL SEASON

In January 1993, the Inauguration of Bill Clinton and the quickly ensuing controversy over lifting the ban on gays in the military brought media attention on lesbian and gay issues to a new height. For a few weeks (if not months) we and some of our issues were on the lips of practically every newscaster, spin doctor, and dinner table expounder in the country.

In April 1993, again the media response to a gay and lesbian event was overwhelming. This time it was the 1993 March on Washington for Lesbian, Gay, and Bi Equal Rights and Liberation. One of the largest civil rights marches in history got the coverage it deserved with more than 100 mainstream papers featuring it on their covers the next day.

UNDERGROUND 'ZINE FAVORITES

Thing
My Comrade/Sister, edited by
   Les Simpson
Lana's World
BimBox
Pansy Beat

Homocore
J.D.'s (Juvenile Delinquents),
   edited by G. B. Jones and
   Bruce La Bruce
Taste of Latex

SOURCE: Polly Thistlethwait, Lesbian Herstory Archives

'ZINES, MAGAZINES, AND GRAPHICS EXHIBITED IN THE "A DIFFERENT LIGHT" ART EXHIBIT (UNIVERSITY ART MUSEUM, THE UNIVERSITY OF CALIFORNIA AT BERKELEY, 1995)

Brains, The Journal of Egghead Sexuality, Vol. 1, No. 1, Summer 1990 'zine)

Physique Pictorial, No. 40, June 1987 ('zine)

Bound & Gagged: Erotic Adventures in Male Bondage, No. 18, Sept./Oct. 1990 ('zine)

Hippie Dick!, No. 5, 1993 ('zine)

Bear, No. 6, 1988 ('zine)

Gay Power, Vol. 1, No. 1, September 1969 (magazine)

J.D.'s, No. 5, 1982 ('zine)

"Homosexuals Are Different," a poster by the Mattachine Society, 1966

ONE, October 1954, Mattachine Society magazine

Tantrum, Spring 1993 ('zine)

"Gay Liberation," 1970 poster

Homocore, No. 5, December 1990 ('zine)

Raw Vulva, No. 2, May 1993, ('zine)

Fizeek Art Quarterly, No. 8, circa 1963 ('zine)

Straight to Hell: The Manhattan Review of Unnatural Acts, No. 53, not dated ('zine)

Scream Box, No. 1, November 1990 ('zine)

The Ladder, Vol. 1, No. 8, May 1957, Daughters of Bilitis magazine

Heresies No. 3: Lesbian Art and Artists, 1977 (magazine)

On Our Rag, 1991 ('zine)

Pavement Surface, No. 4, March 1990 ('zine)

Stonewall Romances, 1979 (magazine)

Hothead Paison, No. 3, 1991 ('zine)

Homoture, No. 1, April 1990 ('zine)

LESBIAN/BISEXUAL JOURNALISTS OF THE PAST

Flanner, Janet, 1892–1978: Foreign correspondent who wrote a column for the *New Yorker* in the 1920s and 1930s under the name Genet. Her columns were later published in book form as *Paris Was Yesterday*.

Fuller, Margaret, 1810–1850: Bisexual; most prominent woman transcendentalist and author of *Woman in the Nineteenth Century*; journalist for the *New York Tribune*.

Gordon, Laura de Force, 1838–?: Journalist in California, petitioned Supreme Court to get acceptance to law school.

Hickok, Lorena, 1893–1968: Covered the White House for the Associated Press. She was involved with Eleanor Roosevelt.

Thompson, Dorothy, 1893–1961: One of the first women journalists to cover a foreign country for a major newspaper (she interviewed Adolf Hitler in 1931 for *Cosmopolitan,* and returned to the United States a celebrity when he later ordered her out of Germany). Married author Sinclair Lewis and later lived with Christa Winsloe, author of *Madchen in Uniform.*

SOURCE: *Lesbian Lists* by Dell Richards (Alyson, 1990)

SOME CONTEMPORARY LESBIAN JOURNALISTS AND EDITORS

Bettina Boxall, journalist, *Los Angeles Times*

Victoria Brownworth, syndicated columnist in many lesbian and gay newspapers/ magazines

C. Carr, critic for *Village Voice*

Anne-Christine D'Adesky, novelist, activist, and senior editor for *Out*

Liz Galst, writer for Boston *Phoenix,* an alternative weekly

Jewelle Gomez, contributing writer for *The Advocate*

Abby Haight, sports writer for the *Portland Oregonian*

Elise Harris, assistant editor for *Out*

Surina Khan, copublisher of *Metroline,* a gay and lesbian magazine in Hartford, Connecticut

Kate McCormick, *New York Newsday* editor

Sara Miles, contributing editor, *Out*

Donna Minkowitz, journalist for the *Village Voice;* columnist for *The Advocate*

Robin Morgan, former editor in chief of *Ms.* magazine

Ann Northrop, former producer of CBS News and freelance writer for "Good Morning America"; currently a commentator for DYKE-TV

Sarah Pettit, executive editor, *Out* magazine

Deb Price, in 1992 became the first syndicated weekly columnist on lesbian and gay issues in the *Detroit News;* her column was quickly picked up by other papers, including that pervasive colorful paper *USA Today*

B. Ruby Rich, film critic for the *Village Voice,* NYC

Ingrid Sischy, editor in chief of *Interview* magazine

Victoria Starr, radio journalist, WBAI

Frances Stevens, editor in chief of *Deneuve*

Robin Stevens, former managing editor of *OUT/LOOK*

Linda Villarosa, senior editor, *Essence,* mainstream black magazine

Helen Zia, former senior editor of *Ms.* magazine

THE NATIONAL LESBIAN AND GAY JOURNALISTS ASSOCIATION

Founded by Leroy F. Aarons, a former editor at the *Washington Post* and vice president of the Oakland *Tribune,* the NLGJA largely consists of lesbian and gay men who work in the straight media, although a growing number of members are lesbian and gay journalists from the gay and lesbian press. They hold regular conferences, publish a variety of informative pamphlets, and recently produced an employee guide to securing domestic partnership benefits at work. You can reach them at: National Lesbian/Gay Journalists Association, 874 Gravenstein Highway South, Suite 4, Sebastopol, California 95472; Phone: 707/823-2193. Fax: 707/823-4176.

CENSORSHIP IN THE CLASSIFIEDS

For many years, many daily newspapers, including major papers such as the *Los Angeles Times* and the *Washington Post,* refused to run ads that contained the word *homosexual* or later, *lesbian* and *gay*. Today, the situation is better, but there are still battles around the country away from the major cities.

In 1970, ads for the movie *The Boys in the Band* were rejected from major daily papers in Chicago, San Francisco, and Boston. Ads were initially rejected by the *Los Angeles Times* and the *New York Daily News* but later ran.

In 1987, the *Seattle Times* barred P-FLAG from publishing a meeting announcement unless it changed *lesbians and gay* to *homosexuals*.

In 1988, a Dallas newspaper refused to run a Coming Out Day ad. Finally, the *Dallas Morning News* ran the ad, after Coming Out Day was over, but blacked out all the names for fear that someone with a similar name would sue for libel.

In 1990, the *Wisconsin Green Bay Press-Gazette* refused to run ads for gay and lesbian resources and hand-painted sweatshirts for lesbians. The case was taken to court by Lambda Legal Defense and Education Fund but was lost on appeal.

ONLY MAGAZINE TO PUBLISH A LESBIAN EJACULATION ON ITS COVER

Rites, a Toronto lesbian and gay newspaper (in the early 1990s)

GAY AND LESBIAN PAPERS IN THE TWENTY-FIVE LARGEST U.S. CITIES

Atlanta, Georgia: *Etcetera, Southern Voice*
Baltimore, Maryland: *Baltimore Gay Paper, The Alternative, Woman's Express*
Boston, Massachusetts: *Bay Windows, The Guide, Sojourner, Gay Community News*
Chicago, Illinois: *Windy City Times, Outlines, Gay Chicago Magazine*
Cleveland, Ohio: *Gay People's Chronicle, Now Cleveland, What She Wants*
Columbus, Ohio: *Stonewall Union, Gaybeat*
Dallas, Texas: *Dallas Voice, This Week in Texas*
Denver, Colorado: *Quest, Outfront*
Detroit, Michigan: *Metro* magazine, *Cruise*
Houston, Texas: *The New Voice*
Indianapolis, Indiana: *Heartland, New Works News*
Kansas City, Missouri: *Alternative News*
Los Angeles, California: *Lesbian News, Frontiers, Edge*
Miami, Florida: *The Weekly News*
Milwaukee, Wisconsin: *The Wisconsin Light*
Minneapolis, Minnesota: *Twin Cities Gaze, Equal Time, GLC Voice*
New York, New York: *Sappho's Isle, HX (HomoExtra), Parlee Plus* (Long Island), *LGNY, New York Native*
Norfolk, Virginia: *Our Own Community Press, Out in Virginia*
Philadelphia, Pennsylvania: *Philadelphia Gay News, Au Courant*
Sacramento, California: *Mom, Guess What!*
St. Louis, Missouri: *St. Louis Lesbian and Gay News Telegraph*
San Diego, California: *San Diego Update, San Diego Gay Times, Bravo, The Lesbian Press*
San Francisco, California: *Bay Area Reporter, San Francisco Sentinel, Bay Times*
Seattle, Washington: *Seattle Gay News, LRC Community News*
Washington, D.C.: *The Washington Blade*

CURRENT NATIONAL GAY AND LESBIAN NEWS/CULTURE MAGAZINES

The Advocate
6922 Hollywood Blvd., 10th Floor
Los Angeles, CA 90028
Phone: 213/871-1225
Circulation: 200,000, first issue: 1967

Out
110 Greene St., Suite 800
New York, NY 10012
Phone: 212/334-9119
Circulation: 100,000+, first issue: Summer 1992

Ten Percent
54 Mint St., Suite 200
San Francisco, CA 94103
Phone: 415/905-8590
Circulation: 83,000, first issue:
  Winter 1992

Genre Magazine
8033 Sunset Blvd., #261
Los Angeles, CA 90046
Phone: 800/576-9933 (subscription)
213/467-8300 (editorial)
Circulation: 75,000, first issue: 1991

AMERICA'S BEST-SELLING LESBIAN MAGAZINE

Deneuve
2336 Market St., #15
San Francisco, CA 94114
Phone: 415/863-6538

FACTOID REGARDING INCLUSION

When *The Advocate* took out its classifieds (generally male and explicitly sexual), female readership jumped from 3 percent to 29 percent, and distribution expanded from the occasional big-city newsstand to the regular racks at every major chain bookstore in the country.

A LANDMARK IN MAINSTREAM TV JOURNALISM

Mike Wallace's CBS Report, "The Homosexuals," aired nationwide on March 7, 1967.

HIGHLIGHTS IN MEDIA ADVOCACY

In 1974, in response to outrageous stereotyping, the National Gay Task Force got the Television Review Board of the National Association of Broadcasters to mandate that The Television Code's injunction that "material with sexual connotations shall not be treated exploitatively or irresponsibly" applied to homosexuals.

In the 1970s, Newton Deiter's Gay Media Task Force monitored television scripts for the networks.

In 1987, the Gay and Lesbian Alliance Against Defamation was created, and it still organizes successful campaigns against stereotyping.

PROFILE

COLORLife!

COLORLife!: The Lesbian, Gay, Two Spirit and Bisexual People of Color Magazine published its premier issue in October 1992, featuring on its cover a profile of activist, mother, and visionary Sandy Lowe, and an activist response to the Quincentennial of the arrival of Columbus, "500 Years of Occupation."

COLORLife! is produced by a collective of people of color who came together in March 1992. Some members of the collective were also members of the Lesbian and Gay People of Color Steering Committee (LGPOCSC), a New York City–based coalition of lesbian and gay people of color and antiracist, progressive organizations. It quickly became apparent that a large majority of the LGPOCSC groups (between twenty-five and thirty) had their own newsletters and spent considerable resources in putting out their publications. Mariana Romo-Carmona, one of the founders of *COLORLife!* who was at the meeting, states, "We saw that there were many different smaller publications in the community because there really wasn't a central publication that met a broad range of people's needs. We decided our efforts would be more useful in producing one comprehensive newsletter or publication."

Mariana Romo-Carmona, former editor of *Conditions* magazine *(Copyright © 1991 by Morgan Gwenwald)*

This was the birth of The Cairos Project, which is the name of the collective that produces *COLORLife.* Mariana explains the origin of the name: "Karos is a Greek word which means 'a decisive moment in time,' and we were convinced as a group that this was certainly a decisive moment in time for people of color communities."

One of the primary reasons for creating a publication like *COLORLife!* was a fierce commitment that each contributor's work was going to be looked at with respect and consideration. "A lot of journalists of color do not receive a minimum standard of respect at mainstream gay publications, which have predominately white staffs," Mariana noted. "In these venues, traditionally there has been no real development or support of individual writers of color, nor has there been a building or progression surrounding our issues in terms of journalism. We started *COLORLife!* with the philosophy that journalists of color were going to get an equal ground. That is, writers of color were not only going to be nurtured, but editors were also not going to question what they were saying."

As part of this equal ground philosophy, *COLORLife!* presents a series of regular sections in each issue.

"Speaking for Ourselves" is a listing of all people of color organizations in the metropolitan tri-state area with descriptions written by those organizations, including an uncensored expansion or focus on a few groups in each issue.

"Role Model" is a personal feature that recognizes an individual's contribution to the community, from well-known role models such as Audre Lorde to the perhaps lesser-known ones such as activist attorney Angie Martel.

"International News" is a feature greatly appreciated by the diverse readership, since in the various communities served by *COLORLife!* readers have identities that encompass many different geopolitical borders.

In "Identity Politics," well-known and emerging writers alike (such as Beth Brant and Mona Oikawa) speak their minds on the politics of being a person of color, particularly regarding the intersection of sexual orientation and race.

"Commentary" is a series of critical articles analyzing political issues and situations of local, national, and international interest.

In addition to these regular sections (and letters and editorials), there are also art features and reviews of films, literature, dance, and music, as well as original poetry and fiction. In fact, *COLORLife!* has received and featured previously unpublished work by artists of stature such as Audre Lorde and Sapphire.

For a magazine that is officially based in New York City, *COLORLife!* has an exceptionally broad readership and support, drawing a national and international audience. Mariana notes, "We don't always have a consistent distribution internationally, but we know that it does get out there." For instance, during the 1994 Gay Games IV, people from all over the world were asking for copies of the publication at the people of color information booth. She adds, "The reason *COLORLife!* has a lot of international news, politics, and literature is that as lesbian and gay people of color we have something to say about the whole. And if one of our constituents says a subject is relevant to our communities, then we assume that it is." That's why, for instance, in the initial October 1992 issue, the collective ran a whole section on the 500 years of occupation, otherwise known as the Quincentennial; that is also why the magazine provides a forum for the progressive deeds of nongay activists.

Future plans for the magazine include expanding the length and further increasing the production values. For instance, the first issues of *COLORLife!* were printed on newsprint; it is now printed on a better quality paper that lasts longer and thus will ensure a longer archival life. However, the collective is committed to ensuring that the quality of the content is everything it can be before they go glossy. In the meantime, *COLORLife!* remains a quarterly publication, and one that is completely self-supporting (primarily through subscription and reader donations). Moreover, the collective has made a commitment not to accept advertising from tobacco and alcohol companies, since these products have ravaged so many lives in our various communities.

Another hallmark of *COLORLife!* is its production by a collective process. There is a commitment to gender parity in the collective, and Lidell Jackson and Mariana Romo-Carmona are the comanaging editors. The current editorial staff includes Vondora Corzen, Manny Torrijos, Adele Choo, Dale Ogaswara, and Lazerne. Art production is handled by Myrna Morales, and the production is handled by June Chan. "We are always open for people in the community to participate," states Mariana. "Anyone who wants to get involved is always welcome to come in and help."

For more information about getting involved with this publication or for subscriptions, which are $15.00 a year, write: *COLORLife!*, 301 Cathedral Parkway, Suite 287, Annex Building, New York, NY 10026.

To view all the issues of *COLORLife!*, you can check out your local university library (many around the country subscribe), or make appointments at the Lesbian Herstory Archives (in Brooklyn) or the Schomburg Center (in Harlem). The New York Public Library also subscribes to and catalogues *COLORLife!*.

PROFILE

Bettina Boxall

Bettina Boxall is a member of an increasingly numerous subgroup in the media workforce: the openly gay journalists in the mainstream newsroom. Bettina is currently a staff writer in the Metro department of one of the country's largest and most influential major metropolitan dailies, the *Los Angeles Times*, where she does both general assignments and stories on the gay beat.

Born in 1952 into a military family, Bettina moved around a lot but did the bulk of her growing up in Washington, D.C. Like many journalists, her career began with the high school newspaper, of which she was the editor. At the University of Maine in Orno, she majored in journalism because she wanted to do something interesting and rewarding as a career. However, she concentrated on photography rather than writing, and worked on the college yearbook not the paper.

After graduation, she took a job in Texas as a staff photographer for the *San Marcos Daily Record*. After several years in the Lone Star State, Bettina, in her late twenties, wanted to go back to New England. She took a job at the *Bennington Banner* in Vermont, which was looking for a reporter who also took photographs. Bettina quickly found the writing portion of her job more gratifying than her picture-taking duties, and she discovered that she was better at it.

In order to get ahead, journalists usually climb from smaller papers to larger ones, and within a few years Bettina's clippings got her a job at the well-respected, midsize daily, the *Record* of Hackensack, New Jersey (more commonly known as the *Bergen Record*). Her beat mainly consisted of the criminal and civil courts and the environment.

After five years at the *Bergen Record,* Bettina was looking to move on to a major newspaper. She was hired by the *Los Angeles Times* in 1987, starting off in a suburban bureau, covering cities in the southeast counties and the city government in Long Beach.

As part of Bettina's personal and professional development, she began attending the gay caucus meetings at the *L.A. Times.* About this time, she was promoted to the Metro section, where, coincidentally, the gay beat reporter (a straight man) was leaving. Because of Bettina's participation in gay caucus, her editor asked if she was interested in covering gay and lesbian stories, and she most definitely was.

Some of her journalism on lesbian and gay issues include reporting on the 1993 March on Washington; features on a gay teacher, harassed by his students, who ended up leaving that high school; some of the first-breaking stories on the gays in the military firestorm; the Oregon antigay initiative; a long piece on the Propaganda Wars between right-wing and gay activists, examining the messages that each side tries to put forward and how effective they are; and, most recently, gay marriage. In addition to her gay beat and Metro beat, Bettina has also written major pieces on domestic violence and police brutality.

While Bettina has happily participated as a speaker on GLAAD-sponsored panels on journalism and media, she is deliberately not active in gay organizations, except for the National Lesbian and Gay Journalists Association, a professional organization. "I feel it's important to observe that line between reporting and activism," Bettina says. "As long as I'm covering gay issues, I feel it's not appropriate to be a gay activist."

One of Bettina's long-term goals is to keep growing as a journalist; she also sees a place for development in gay journalism, as well. "I hope that the coverage of gay issues will move beyond the merely rhetorical stage," she says. "Too many times I've read journalists covering gay issues get stuck in a mode of 'this side says this and this side says that.' I think, as reporters, it's time we bring in the traditional task of analysis to gay issues. Ideally, as journalists, we should shed light on issues, not just endlessly repeat arguments from opposing sides."

PROFILE

Deb Price

On May 8, 1992, Deb Price began the first weekly column on gay issues in a mainstream newspaper, the *Detroit News.* The pioneering column—quickly recognized as a landmark in journalism—for the first time brought a gay voice regularly into

Deb Price

newspaper households. While news organizations have increased coverage of gay and lesbian issues in recent years, Price promised to offer readers something unique: life from a gay perspective.

Charting new territory in which many of her readers did not even know an openly gay person, Price chose a very personal style, inviting readers into her home life. The first column, for example, described how awkward it was for Price to try to introduce the woman she loves to her boss because no universal language exists to describe gay couples. "So tell me, America, how do I introduce Joyce?" The question invited responses from everyone, whether gay or straight, delighted or hateful, or just plain curious. And that invitation reflected Price's goal as a columnist: to bridge a gap between the gay and heterosexual communities, to get an open and honest dialogue started. To do that, she opened up her life and assured all readers she would present a completely new way of covering gay people and issues.

Her topics have been varied and thought-provoking and include gay rodeo; gay parents; Commercial Street in Provincetown, where lesbian and gay couples feel comfortable holding hands; gays in the military; and the selective use of the Bible throughout American history to support prejudice and discrimination.

Clearly filling a need, Deb Price's column was immediately picked up by other newspapers in the Gannett chain (to which the *Detroit News* belongs). The column has been published in dozens of diverse communities including Des Moines, Iowa; Niagara Falls, New York; Springfield, Missouri; Nashville, Tennessee; Muskogee, Oklahoma; Honolulu, Hawaii; and Guam. Media attention soon followed.

In addition to radio and television programs such as CNN's *Sonya Live* and the BBC's television special *Out in America,* Price has discussed her endeavor in numerous articles, including ones in the *New York Times,* the *Washington Post, Editor & Publisher,* the *Chicago Tribune,* and *People* magazine. The column is now available to non-Gannett newspapers through the Los Angeles Syndicate and appears in such standards as the *Minneapolis Star-Tribune,* the *San Francisco Examiner,* the *Atlanta Constitution,* and the *San Jose Mercury News.* The column also answered another question: Could it compete in mainstream journalism competitions? By winning first place in the annual Best of Gannett contest for metro columns, first place in the Michigan Associated Press Editorial Association awards, and numerous other writing awards, Deb Price's column proved that it could.

Price, thirty-seven, is formerly the news editor in the Washington Bureau of the *Detroit News.* Before arriving at the *Detroit News* in 1989, Price worked for the *Washington Post.* She has a B.A. and an M.A. in literature from Stanford University. She lives in the Washington, D.C., area with journalist Joyce Murdoch. Together, they have authored the book, *And Say Hi to Joyce: America's First Gay Column Comes Out,* containing the first twenty months of columns and the story of their impact, which was published by Doubleday in June 1995.

For further information or inquiries, you may contact Price at: *The Detroit News,* 1148 National Press Building, Washington, DC 20045.

---

12. Lesbians and the Military

If elected, I would reverse the ban on gays and lesbians serving in the United States Armed Forces. Every patriotic American should be allowed to serve their country, regardless of sexual orientation.

—Bill Clinton, presidential candidate, 1992

Clinton had the right idea, but unfortunately, he bowed to pressure from both the Pentagon and the U.S. Congress. His compromise measure, popularly referred to as "don't ask, don't tell," was nothing more than a continuation of the half-century-old ban against gays and lesbians in the military, with one new stipulation: commanding officers could not ask subordinates or recruits questions about their sexual orientation, and service members should not come out of the closet.

Lesbians have long served in the military of the United States and other countries, and served with distinction and honor. The military has provided an avenue
by which less privileged Americans could gain access to the education and job
training often unavailable to them in the civilian sector.

Lesbians have also been the most vulnerable to discharge, experiencing investigation and discharge three times more often than men. The armed forces remain
the bastion of manhood, and women who want to serve are sometimes immediately suspect.

The question is, shouldn't all service members, regardless of their sexual orientation, be allowed to serve *openly,* without fear of discharge based on status rather
than on conduct?

TIME LINE OF LESBIANS AND GAYS
IN THE U.S. MILITARY

1778: Baron Frederich von Steuben, one of Europe's greatest military minds and
a homosexual man, was engaged to train and discipline the disparate armies of
the thirteen rebellious American colonies.

   • After being discovered in bed with a private, Lieutenant Gotthold Frederick Enslin became the first known soldier to be dismissed from the U.S. military for homosexuality.

1916: Punishment of homosexual soldiers was first codified in American military
law. The Articles of War, which took effect the following year, include "assault
with the intent to commit sodomy" as a capital crime.

World War I: The Navy was the first branch of the armed forces to enlist women
who were not nurses. Ten thousand women served as yeomenettes, meaning
they typed and performed office work.

1919: A revision of the Articles of War of 1916 included the act of sodomy itself
as a felony.

   • Dispatching a squad of young enlisted men to act as decoys, the U.S.
Navy initiated a search for "sexual perverts" at the Newport (Rhode Island)
Naval Training Station. Based on information the plants gathered, twenty sailors
and sixteen civilians were arrested on morals charges by naval and municipal authorities. This was the first known attempt to purge homosexuals from the military.

1920s–1930s: Homosexuality continued to be treated as a criminal act, and thousands of gay soldiers and sailors were imprisoned. The military's move to trans-
form homosexuality from a crime to an illness did not take place until the
massive mobilization of World War II.

1941–1945: Each branch of the armed forces established a women's division. The
largest was the Women's Auxiliary Army Corps (which became just the Women's
Army Corps in 1943), with 140,000 women; the Navy WAVES were a close second with 100,000 women enlisted.

   • Nearly 10,000 enlisted people received dishonorable blue discharges for homosexuality from the armed forces, so called because they were typed on blue paper.

1942: The Armed Forces released the first regulations instructing military psychiatrists to discriminate between homosexual and heterosexual service members. Those who "habitually or occasionally engaged in homosexual or other perverse sexual practices" were deemed unsuitable for military service.

1943: Final regulations were issued banning homosexuals from all branches of military service. These have remained in effect for the last fifty years, with only slight modifications.

LOOKING FOR THE LESBIANS OF WORLD WAR II

A documentary and book entitled *Memories from the Women of World War II* is currently in production. This is the first time that the war will be seen from the experience of women worldwide, documenting the full range of wartime stories, straight and gay, civilian and veteran. The production is funded in part by the California Council for the Humanities and the North Carolina Humanities Council. To help document lesbian contributions to the war years, E-mail memories of those years and your part in them to ElShepard@aol.com.

1951: The U.S. Congress established the Uniform Code of Military Justice (UCMJ), which set down the basic policies, discharge procedures, and appeal channels for the disposition of homosexual service members.

1957: A 639-page navy report—called the Crittenden Report for the captain who headed the committee—concluded that there was no sound basis for the charge that homosexuals in the military posed a security risk. The Pentagon denied the existence of this report for nearly twenty years.

  • Federal courts ruled that military personnel may appeal military court decisions to civil courts. This allowed lesbians and gay men discharged for homosexuality to appeal to civil courts.

1966: Gay groups staged the first demonstrations protesting the treatment of lesbians and gays in the military.

1975: After being dismissed for homosexuality, Sergeant Leonard Matlovich sued the Air Force to be reinstated. Matlovich was thrust into national attention when he was featured on the cover of *Time* magazine with the headline: "'I Am a Homosexual': The Gay Drive for Acceptance." NBC subsequently made a TV movie of his story. His suit dragged on until 1980, when a federal judge ordered Matlovich reinstated. Instead of reentering the Air Force, Matlovich accepted a settlement of $160,000. Matlovich became a gay rights activist and died of AIDS in 1988.

1981: During the last week of the Carter administration, Deputy Secretary of Defense Graham Claytor issued a revision in his department's policy to state for the first time that "homosexuality is incompatible with military service." Though Claytor noted that this is not officially a change in policy, the revision is designed to make clear that homosexuality is grounds for discharge. The revision was implemented by the Reagan administration.

CLAYTOR'S LEGACY

The following three sentences constitute Deputy Defense Secretary Claytor's 1981 revision of the military policy on homosexuality.

Homosexuality is incompatible with military service. The presence in the military environment of persons who engage in homosexual conduct or who, by their statements, demonstrate a propensity to engage in homosexual conduct, seriously impairs the accomplishment of military mission. The presence of such members adversely affects the ability of the armed forces to maintain discipline, good order and morale; to foster mutual trust and confidence among service members; to insure the integrity of the system of rank and command; to facilitate assignment and worldwide deployment of service members who freuqently must live and work in close conditions affording minimal privacy; to recruit and retain members of the armed forces; to maintain the public acceptability of military service; and to prevent breaches of security.

1986: Discharged lesbian drill sergeant Miriam Ben-Shalom won a ten-year battle with the U.S. Army Reserves when a court ordered her reinstatement.

Apple pie, motherhood, and the American flag will not fall. We're already in the military.

—Miriam Ben-Shalom, 1992

1987: U.S. Naval Academy Midshipman Joseph Steffan, at the top of his class, was discharged six weeks prior to graduation because, when asked if he was gay, he answered honestly. Although a three-judge panel of the D.C. Circuit Court of Appeals ruled in Steffan's favor in 1994 and ordered his reinstatement, the government appealed the decision to a full panel of judges. In a major setback in early 1995, the full Court of Appeals upheld Steffan's dismissal.

1989: Members of Congress who supported lifting the military ban—including Gerry Studds (D-Mass.)—released draft copies of two internal Pentagon reports that found that homosexuals in the military pose no security risk and, in many cases, make better soldiers than heterosexuals.

1990: Sergeant Perry Watkins won a ten-year court battle against the Army, which discharged him in 1981 for homosexuality. The courts found that the Army inducted Watkins and allowed him to reenlist three times, knowing he was gay. Watkins eventually agreed to forgo reentry in return for $135,000 in back pay, an honorable discharge, and full retirement benefits. In the intervening years, Watkins has become an outspoken gay rights activist.

• ROTC cadet James Holobaugh was discharged from the corps on the grounds of homosexuality and ordered to repay his $25,000 scholarship.

1992: The General Accounting Office reported that almost 17,000 service men and women were discharged for homosexuality between 1981 and 1990, at a cost of $493,195,968 to replace them. GAO estimated that it would cost about $27 million to recruit and train replacements for the 1,000 discharged in 1990 alone. In addition, the GAO found that women were twice as likely to be investigated and dismissed as men.

• Presidential candidate Bill Clinton promised, if elected, to repeal the military's ban on gay and lesbian service members, because there is no legitimate justification for the exclusionary policy.

• The Navy Reserve Officers' Training Corps (ROTC) program created a policy requiring midshipmen to sign an affidavit stating that they agreed with the military's ban on homosexuals and would refund scholarship money if they were found to be gay.

1993: In January, President Clinton issued a Presidential Memorandum instructing Defense Secretary Les Aspin to develop by July of that year an "Executive Order ending discrimination on the basis of sexual orientation in determining who will serve in the Armed Forces." At the same time, Clinton issued an interim policy that preserved all existing restrictions on homosexuals in the military but ended the practice of questioning recruits about their sexual orientation.

• April: Secretary Aspin asked the Rand Corporation, a nonprofit research organization, to provide "information and analysis that would be useful in helping formulate the required draft executive order." Aspin also formed a fifty-member Defense Department Military Working Group to study the issue. Three weeks after its first meeting, the group recommended continuing the ban, with the sole change of instructing commanders not to ask soldiers or recruits about their sexual orientation.

• From March to July, the Senate Armed Forces Committee, headed by Senator Sam Nunn (D-Ga.), held public hearings to consider the ban.

• From May to July, the House Armed Services Committee also conducted hearings. At both House and Senate hearings, the overwhelming majority of those testifying were service members opposed to lifting the ban.

• In July, Secretary Aspin signed a directive adopting the April recommendation of the Military Working Group. One week later, the Senate and House Committees issued their findings. Both recommended codifying Aspin's directive.

• In August, Rand Corporation released its independent report, stating that "there is ample reason to believe that heterosexual and homosexual military personnel can work together effectively." The government buried the study.

- In September, the House and Senate both passed legislation discouraging homosexual enlistment in the military, the language of which was tougher than Clinton's "don't ask, don't tell." The legislation allowed a future defense secretary to reinstate questioning of recruits about their sexual orientation. Within days, Clinton signed the measure with no fanfare and little public notice.

RAND CORPORATION REPORT

In April 1993, Defense Secretary Aspin commissioned the Rand Corporation, an independent nonprofit research organization, to study the issue of gays in the military. Although the Rand Corporation could find no justification for discrimination against homosexuals in the military, the Pentagon suppressed the report. The printed study, *Sexual Orientation and U.S. Military Policy: Options and Assessment*, is now available for $16, plus shipping and handling. Prepayment is required by check or money order. For more ordering information, contact Rand Corporation, Customer Service, 1700 Main Street, P.O. Box 2138, Santa Monica, CA 90407-2138; Phone: 310/451-7002.

1994: In March, Lambda Legal Defense and Education Fund and the American Civil Liberties Union brought a lawsuit in federal court (*Able et al. v. USA*) on behalf of six lesbian and gay service members, the first direct constitutional challenge to the military's policy. The government immediately sought discharge proceedings against some of the plaintiffs.

- In April, Federal District Judge Eugene Nickerson granted the plaintiffs' preliminary injunction, preventing the military from initiating discharge proceedings while the case was active.

- In June, U.S. District Court Judge Thomas S. Zilly ordered the Army to reinstate Colonel Margarethe Cammermeyer to the National Guard. In his ruling, Zilly held unconstitutional the old version of the military ban barring service by lesbians and gay men. Colonel Cammermeyer, a twenty-seven-year veteran of the Army and National Guard, and Chief Nurse of the Washington State National Guard, was discharged from the military in June 1992 after she disclosed her sexual orientation during an interview for top security clearance.

1995: "Don't ask, don't tell" was challenged in a number of appeals courts, with some victories and some losses for lesbians and gays in the military.

- In January, a three-judge panel of the U.S. Court of Appeals upheld the preliminary injunction and directed the trial court to issue its ruling on *Able v. USA* by March 31, 1995.

- On March 13, the trial began for *Able v. USA*. On March 30, Judge Nickerson declared the military's "don't ask, don't tell" policy unconstitutional; the government promised to appeal.

• In June, a federal appeals court declined to block the discharge of Navy Lieutenant Paul Thomasson, who declared his homosexuality the day after the Clinton administration's "don't ask, don't tell" policy went into effect. The court cited that Thomasson refused "to rebut the presumption that he would . . . engage in homosexual conduct."

FOR FURTHER READING

Berube, Allan. *Coming Out Under Fire: The History of Gay Men and Women in World War II*. The Free Press, 1990.

Berube, Allan, and John D'Emilio. "The Military and Lesbians During the McCarthy Years." *Signs: Journal of Women in Culture and Society*. Summer 1984.

Cammermeyer, Margarethe, with Chris Fisher. *Serving in Silence*. Viking Press, 1994.

Dyer, Kate. *Gays in Uniform: The Pentagon's Secret Reports*. Alyson Publications, 1990.

Hippler, Mike. *Matlovich: The Good Soldier*. Alyson Publications, 1989.

Humphrey, Mary Ann. *My Country, My Right to Serve: Experiences of Gay Men and Women in the Military, World War II to the Present*. HarperCollins, 1990.

Murphy, Lawrence R. *Perverts by Official Order: The Campaign Against Homosexuals by the United States Navy*. The Haworth Press, 1988.

Shilts, Randy. *Conduct Unbecoming: Gays and Lesbians in the U.S. Military*. St. Martin's Press, 1993.

Steffan, Joseph. *Honor Bound: A Gay American Fights for the Right to Serve His Country*. Random House, 1992.

Webber, Winni S. *Lesbians in the Military Speak Out*. Madwoman Press, 1993.

Weinberg, Martin S., and Colin J. Williams. *Homosexuals and the Military: A Study of the Less Than Honorable Discharge*. Harper & Row, 1971.

Zeeland, Steven. *Barrack Buddies and Soldier Lovers: Dialogues with Gay Young Men in the U.S. Military*. Harrington Park Press, 1993.

SOURCE: Servicemembers Legal Defense Network

HOW TO SURVIVE A WITCH HUNT

If you're a service member being investigated for homosexuality, facing discharge, being threatened, or considering coming out, you aren't alone. There is confidential legal help available from the Servicemembers Legal Defense Network (SLDN). SLDN has issued the following guidelines for surviving a witch hunt if you are targeted by military investigators:

1. **Say nothing,** except to ask to speak to an attorney. Even if you want out of the service, saying the wrong thing could affect your discharge. Military investigators may say they are your friends, but they aren't.
2. **Sign nothing**. Even initialing something can waive your legal rights. Inform the investigators that you will show any papers they give you to your attorney, who can explain them to you.
3. **Get legal help**. SLDN (202/328-FAIR or SLDN1@aol.com) can assist you confidentially. A military defense attorney may also be able to help, but check to make sure if your conversations are covered by attorney-client privilege and if the attorney will keep what you say confidential. The Military Law Task Force can be reached at 619/233-1701.

Very important: Doctors, psychologists, chaplains, and friends sometimes do not keep secrets. Don't trust anyone but your defense attorney. E-mail and on-line communications are not secure and can be used against you.

SOURCE: Servicemembers Legal Defense Network

THE VOTE ON THE GAY MILITARY BAN IN CONGRESS, SEPTEMBER 1993

Passed in Senate, sixty-three to thirty-three.

	For Ban	Against Ban
Democrats	25	30
Republicans	38	3

Passed in House, 301 to 135.

	For Ban	Against Ban
Democrats	140	121
Republicans	161	13
Independent		1

TEXT OF CONGRESS'S MILITARY BAN

1. Section 8 of Article I of the Constitution of the United States commits exclusively to the Congress the powers to raise and support armies, provide and maintain a navy, and make rules for the government and regulation of the land and naval forces.
2. There is no constitutional right to serve in the Armed Forces.

3. Pursuant to the powers conferred by Section 8 of Article I of the Constitution of the United States, it lies within the discretion of the Congress to establish qualifications for and conditions of service in the armed forces.

4. The primary purpose of the armed forces is to prepare for and to prevail in combat should the need arise.

5. The conduct of military operations requires members of the armed forces to make extraordinary sacrifices, including the ultimate sacrifice, in order to provide for the common defense.

6. Success in combat requires military units that are characterized by high morale, good order and discipline, and unit cohesion.

7. One of the most crucial elements in combat capability is unit cohesion, that is, the bonds of trust among individual service members that make the combat effectiveness of a military unit greater than the sum of the combat effectiveness of the unit members.

8. Military life is fundamentally different from civilian life in that (a) The extraordinary responsibilities of the armed forces, the unique conditions of military service, and the critical role of unit cohesion require that the military community, while subject to civilian control, exist as a specialized society; and (b) The military society is characterized by its own laws, rules, customs, and traditions, including numerous restrictions on personal behavior, that would not be acceptable in civilian society.

9. The standards of conduct for members of the armed forces regulate a member's life for twenty-four hours each day beginning at the moment the member enters military status and not ending until that person is discharged or otherwise separated from the armed forces.

10. Those standards of conduct, including the Uniform Code of Military Justice, apply to a member of the armed forces at all times that the member has a military status, whether the member is on base or off base, and whether the member is on duty or off duty.

11. The pervasive application of the standards of conduct is necessary because members of the armed forces must be ready at all times for worldwide deployment to a combat environment.

12. The worldwide deployment of United States military forces, the international responsibilities of the United States, and the potential for involvement of the armed forces in actual combat routinely make it necessary for members of the armed forces involuntarily to accept living conditions and working conditions that are often spartan, primitive, and characterized by forced intimacy with little or no privacy.

13. The prohibition against homosexual conduct is a long-standing element of military law that continues to be necessary in the unique circumstances of military service.

14. The armed forces must maintain personnel policies that exclude persons whose presence in the armed forces would create an unacceptable risk to the armed forces' high standards of morale, good order and discipline, and unit cohesion that are the essence of military capability.

15. The presence in the armed forces of persons who demonstrate a propensity or intent to engage in homosexual acts would create an unacceptable risk to the high standards of morale, good order and discipline, and unit cohesion that are the essence of military capability.

QUICK FACTS ABOUT GAYS IN THE MILITARY

- Since 1943, approximately 100,000 gay men and lesbians have been discharged from the U.S. military.
- An estimated 35 percent of women in the military during the early 1980s were lesbians.
- In the 1980s, white women accounted for 6 percent of all personnel in the armed forces and 20 percent of all discharged for homosexuality.

Lesbians are especially hard hit by the military policy. Of all the discharges from the Marine Corps, for example, a woman is seven times more likely than a man to have been removed for homosexuality.

—*New York Times,* November 15, 1992

- There were more discharges for homosexuality in 1980 than at any other time since the McCarthy era.
- Canada lifted its ban on gays in the military in 1992, with no lowered troop morale or impaired unit cohesiveness.
- Of the sixteen members of NATO, only the United States and Great Britain ban lesbians and gay men from military service.

SOURCE: Gay and Lesbian Stats, edited by Bennett L. Singer and David Deschamps Copyright © 1994 Bennett L. Singer and David Deschamps. Reprinted by permission of The New Press.

IMPORTANT LEGAL CASES AFFECTING GAYS IN THE MILITARY

The United States military is the single largest employer in the country; it provides many people with the opportunity for jobs, education, and other benefits. For individuals from poor communities, the military offers one of the few doors to a better future. By closing that door to a select class of individuals, thereby excluding them from the many opportunities the military provides, the ban against lesbians and gay men in the military violates our country's most basic democratic principles, as well as our Constitution.

Despite efforts to package the latest version of the ban as a change in policy, "don't ask, don't tell" does not allow lesbians and gay men to serve openly or honestly in the military. In order to serve, lesbians and gay men must continue to deny their true identities, and, when found out, face expulsion.

The following case studies are excerpted from the *Lambda Update,* the triannual publication of Lambda Legal Defense and Education Fund.

CASE HISTORY

CAMMERMEYER V. U.S. ARMY

On June 1, 1994, U.S. District Court Judge Thomas S. Zilly ordered the Army to reinstate Colonel Margarethe Cammermeyer to the National Guard. In his ruling, Zilly held unconstitutional the old version of the military ban barring service by lesbians and gay men.

Colonel Cammermeyer, a twenty-seven-year veteran of the Army and National Guard, and Chief Nurse of the Washington State National Guard, had been discharged from the military in June 1992 because she was a lesbian. Cammermeyer disclosed her sexual orientation during an interview for top secret security clearance.

An administrative board comprised of fellow colonels concluded it was their "sad duty" to recommend her discharge based on the Army's regulation, despite her outstanding record. Among many other honors, Cammermeyer received a Bronze Star for her service in Vietnam and was selected as the 1985 Veterans Administration Nurse of the Year.

Colonel Margarethe Cammermeyer with Lambda Legal Defense development director, William Peters *(Photo by D. M. Reznik)*

The Army immediately appealed Judge Zilly's June 1994 decision and petitioned the Ninth Circuit Court of Appeals to stay Colonel Cammermeyer's reinstatement pending the results of the appeal. The Army's request for a stay was defeated and Cammermeyer has returned to work.

Cammermeyer's story is told in the book, *Serving in Silence,* cowritten by Cammermeyer and Chris Fisher, and published by Viking Press. Her successful struggle against the military ban was featured in a television movie produced by Barbra Streisand and starring Glenn Close as Cammermeyer and Judy Davis as Cammermeyer's lover, Diane.

CASE HISTORY

STEFFAN V. ASPIN

In early 1995, the D.C. Circuit Court of Appeals issued a ruling in sharp disagreement with a 1994 decision by a three-judge panel, which had articulated so beautifully the constitutional flaws of the military's ban on service by lesbians and gay men. The full court's ruling upheld the determination to deny Joseph Steffan his diploma and his commission as an officer because, six weeks before he was due to graduate from the Naval Academy, he answered honestly when asked whether he was gay.

The lengthy opinion, with which seven of the court's judges agreed and from which three dissented, employed the definitional twists and contortions that the government used to justify a ban on service by lesbians and gay men. In this manner, a case that is actually about a young midshipman who was asked about his sexual orientation was transformed by the court to be one about the military's right and ability to regulate the conduct of its soldiers. Because this case concerned the old version of the military ban, the decision will not be appealed. The battle against the government's discrimination against lesbians and gay men in the military will continue in the case known as *Able v. U.S.A.* in New York Federal Court.

COUNTERING MYTHS ABOUT GAY AND LESBIAN SERVICE MEMBERS

We've all heard them: the rumors, myths, and lies about the effect lifting the military ban against gay people would have on the armed forces. Here are some sample responses, which you can use to talk back to bigots.

Myth: Integration based on sexual orientation is not similar to integration based on race because race is a nonbehavioral characteristic while sexual orientation indicates a changeable behavior.

Answer: Whether or not sexual orientation is a biological or behavioral characteristic is a constant issue of scientific study, with several recent studies indicating that there may be a biological link. Regardless of the cause of sexual orientation, many of the arguments used in 1948 during the debate about integration by race were actually based on the ideas that African-Americans engaged in different behaviors than white Americans and that those behaviors would be disruptive to the effectiveness and morale of the military. The stereotypes invoked in 1948 were proven false and integration based on race was implemented. The stereotypes invoked in this argument are similarly false.

Myth: Military readiness would be hurt by allowing gays in the military.
Answer: Gay men and lesbians are already in the military—tens of thousands of them. They serve at all levels of the armed forces, including in the Pentagon. No one argues that they are not. They have even served bravely in Operation Desert Storm and are serving in Somalia. The military ban prevents them from serving their country openly.

Myth: Given the special environment of the military, the presence of openly gay and lesbian service members invades the privacy rights of heterosexuals in the foxholes, showers, and sleeping quarters.
Answer: These comments are based on the stereotype that gay people cannot control their sexuality. Gay and lesbian service members are in all those places today and are behaving themselves appropriately. The penalties for inappropriate sexual behavior, whether by gays or heterosexuals, are the same and are already in effect. Repealing the ban does not alter these regulations. The most similar civilian situation is that of fire and police departments, which must often sleep, live, and work in close quarters. The GAO study from June 1992 indicates that those agencies that have ended previous employment bans on gay officers "have not experienced any degradation of mission associated with these policies. Most department officials did not identify major problems related to retaining homosexuals in a work force."

Myth: Straight service members would have to fear sexual harassment and sexual overtures by openly gay and lesbian troops.
Answer: Sexual harassment is already prohibited through military codes of conduct. In recent years, we have seen that heterosexual service men have sexually harassed military women and violated many codes of conduct. The Tailhook incident shows that military leaders have often been slow to discipline troops who violate those codes. Instead of fearing the unsupported potential of sexual harassment and misbehavior from openly gay and lesbian troops, military leaders should enforce the current policies fairly, regardless of the sexual orientation of the perpetrators or the victims.

Myth: The presence of gay service members will increase AIDS in the military and make blood transfusions in combat highly risky.
Answer: AIDS is permeating all sectors of American society, and HIV does not discriminate. The spread of HIV among recruiting age American young men and women is growing rapidly as a result of failure to educate about the risks and self-protection measures involved with HIV. The Department of Defense already has a strict HIV testing and screening policy and bars new recruits with HIV. The number of service members with HIV has remained fairly level at about 500 from year to year.

Regarding blood transfusions, the reliance on battlefield transfusions has been historically very low. Instead, the military relies on blood that has been previously stored. Service members with HIV are not placed in deployable units.

Myth: Recent incidents indicate that violence against gay men and lesbians will increase in the military if the ban is lifted and they serve openly.
Answer: The Joint Chiefs of Staff and senior military leaders are responsible for the discipline and conduct of the troops. It should concern the U.S. public if military leaders cannot control the actions of their well-armed troops. If heterosexual service members act out their bigotry through violence against fellow gay service members, military leaders must swiftly discipline the offenders. The Joint Chiefs of Staff plus other senior military leadership must speak out as loudly against antigay violence by bigoted troops.

Myth: The military is no place for a social experiment, and we should respect heterosexual military members who don't want to serve with gays.
Answer: This is not a social experiment. In fact, gay men and lesbians already work, live, and even, in school and sports situations, shower side by side with heterosexuals throughout society. Gay men and lesbians are already in the military. Discrimination is wrong and the antigay policy should be repealed. The military is no place for bigoted service members who cannot cooperate and work with fellow Americans, gay or straight, who wish to serve their country.

Myth: The sexual practices of gay men and lesbians should not be permitted in the military.
Answer: Current military regulations prohibit many private sexual activities that heterosexuals engage in as frequently as gay men and lesbians. Those codes of conduct must be either revised to reflect the reality of individual sexual behavior or must be enforced across the board regardless of sexual orientation.

Myth: If the ban were lifted, men would dance with men in officers' clubs and women would hold hands with other women on bases.
Answer: The military already has regulations prohibiting open displays of affection while in uniform. This policy would not change if the ban were repealed, and gay and lesbian service members would be required to follow the same policies as heterosexuals. However, gay and lesbian service members would have the right to engage in behavior permissible for heterosexuals. Repealing the ban would end discrimination and allow gay and lesbian service members to serve their country openly and with honor.

Myth: Many other countries prohibit homosexuals from serving in the military.
Answer: Among NATO allies of the U.S., only Great Britain has an explicit policy barring gay and lesbian service members, as in the U.S. In 1992, both Canada and Australia successfully lifted their antigay bans. The world-renowned Israeli military doesn't ban gay and lesbian service members.

Myth: Even if the ban were lifted, gay and lesbian service members should be segregated from straight service members.
Answer: Segregated forces are unacceptable and unnecessary. Gay and lesbian

service members already do serve side by side with heterosexual troops. Enforcing current codes of conduct and instilling a sense of respect for fellow service members, regardless of sexual orientation, is what is necessary to maintain good order and discipline in the troops.

SOURCE: Adapted from information provided and reprinted by permission from the National Gay and Lesbian Task Force, Washington, DC

The Military Freedom Initiative of NGLTF challenges the antigay discriminatory policy of the U.S. Department of Defense. For further information, contact the Military Freedom Initiative at 202/332-6483.

It is time to shift the focus from status to misconduct. There are thousands of cases of sexual misconduct that have gone unresolved, while our military has spent nearly half a billion dollars separating 16,000 lesbians and gay men.

—SENATOR EDWARD KENNEDY (D-Mass.), 1993

NATIONAL ORGANIZATIONS DEALING WITH LESBIAN/GAY MILITARY ISSUES

American Federation of Veterans
Veterans Hall, Suite 811
346 Broadway
New York, NY 10013
Phone: 212/349-3455

Gay and Lesbian Military Freedom Project/National
 Gay and Lesbian Task Force
1734 14th Street
Washington, DC 20009
Phone: 202/332-6483

Lambda Legal Defense and Education Fund
666 Broadway, 12th Floor
New York, NY 10012
Phone: 212/995-8585

National Center for Lesbian Rights
1663 Mission Street, 5th Floor
San Francisco, CA 94103
Phone: 415/392-6257

13. LESBIANS IN THE PERFORMING ARTS

Androgyny to me is making your sexuality available, through your art, to every-one. Like Elvis, like Mick Jagger, like Annie Lennox or Marlene Dietrich—using the power of both male and female.

—K.D. LANG, pop singer

Ever since the first student of Sappho picked up a lyre, lesbians have been pace-setters in the realm of music and performance. From the Harlem Renaissance to the

Stand-up comic
Marga Gomez
(*Photo by Dave
LeFave*)

Stand-up comic Sara Cytron *(Copyright © 1993 by Micha Kwiatkowska)*

women's music scene of the 1970s to the crossover of artists like k.d. lang, lesbians have made their mark. Perhaps our draw to the performing arts comes from years of acting straight in a society that discourages a true performance of self. The Who's Who of the performing arts has always been a roster of who's queer in America.

In the last few decades, there has been a miniexplosion of openly lesbian performers who use lesbian and gay material. From drag king shows to HBO comedy specials, from disco to modern dance, from cabaret to classical compositions, lesbian performance continues to reach new audiences and achieve mainstream acceptance.

SOME CURRENT LESBIAN/BISEXUAL SINGERS AND PERFORMERS

BETTY (twins Amy and
  Bitsy, and Allyson)
Casselberry-Dupree
Melissa Etheridge
Girls in the Nose

Sophie B. Hawkins (prefers
  to be called omnisexual)
Janis Ian
Indigo Girls
k.d. lang

Deirdre McCalla
(*Copyright © Morgan Gwenwald*)

Deirdre McCalla
Me'Shell NdegoeOcello
Phranc
Toshi Reagon

Linda Tillery
Two Nice Girls (Kathy Korniloff,
    Laurie Freelove, and Gretchen Phillips
Cris Williamson

Where does the name BETTY come from?

It's a tribute to the Bettys they adore: Davis, Rubble, Boop, Cooper, and Friedan.

In Her Own Class

Janis Ian made waves with her 1970s hit singles "Society's Child" and "At Seventeen," then disappeared for many years. She came back (and out) with a vengeance in the early 1990s with her album, *Breaking the Silence*, and began writing a column for *The Advocate*. In 1995, she released a new album, *Revenge* (Beacon Records), which she says "is about survival. It is about outlasting the enemy." With her complex melodies and her haunting bluesy voice, Ian should outlast quite a few things.

The First Lesbian Camp Classic on Vinyl

PHRANC'S *I ENJOY BEING A GIRL*

Born Susie Gottlieb, Phranc is a self-styled average All-American Jewish lesbian folksinger with a flattop classic butch outfit of white T-shirt, blue jeans, and black boots. She originally toured as an opening act for The Smiths.

How Melissa Etheridge Spent 1994

- Taping an MTV Unplugged session
- Getting undressed in a PETA (People for the Ethical Treatment of Animals) ad against wearing fur with her girlfriend Julie Cypher
- Having two songs in the rock/pop Top Ten
- Selling out Madison Square Garden
- Performing at Woodstock '94
- Winning another Grammy

Some Lesbian Punk Rock Grrrl Bands

Bikini Kill   Lucy Stoners
Tribe 8   7 Year Bitch

Olivia Records Recording Artists and Some of Their Best Albums

Meg Christian, *I Know You Know* (1974); *Turning It Over* (1981)
Linda Tillery, *Linda Tillery* (1977)
Teresa Trull, *The Ways a Woman Can Be* (1977); *Let It Be Known* (1980)
Mary Watkins, *Something Moving: Mary Watkins* (1978)
Cris Williamson, *The Changer and the Changed* (1975); *Anniversary: Meg/Cris at Carnegie Hall* (1983)

Famous Lesbian/Bisexual Singers of the Harlem Renaissance

The Harlem Renaissance, taking place from approximately 1917 to 1937, was a period of profound artistic, literary, and intellectual activity centering around Harlem's black community. Many of the leaders of this movement were gay or bisexual.

Gladys Bentley, 1907–1960: She was a 250-pound singer and pianist who wore men's clothes, performed in a white tuxedo and top hat, and tried to marry a woman in Atlantic City. Later in her life she denounced her lesbian activities and image.

Mabel Hampton, 1902–1989: Dancer at Coney Island and Harlem's famed Lafayette Theatre (and later motivating spirit of the Lesbian Herstory Archives).

Alberta Hunter, 1895–1984: Blues star in the Harlem Renaissance who made a comeback in the 1970s, singing at the Carter White House and the Kennedy Center in 1978. Lovers with Lottie Tyler for many years.

Bessie Jackson: Blues singer in the 1920s and 1930s. Singer of "B.D. Woman's Blues" (B.D. means bull dagger), which had the following line: "B.D. women sure is rough; they drink up many a whiskey and they sure can strut their stuff."

Jackie "Moms" Mabley, 1897–1975: Blues singer in the Harlem Renaissance who later acheived crossover fame as a stand-up comedian in the 1960s.

Gertrude "Ma" Rainey, 1886–1939: The original Mother of the Blues, a "woman-lovin' woman" who sang the provocative "Prove It on Me Blues," where the narrator boasts of her preference for male dress and female companionship and dares the listener to prove it on her, as well as "Sissy Blues" where the narrator's husband has an affair with a queen named Miss Kate.

Bessie Smith, 1894–1937: Popularizer of black blues who can be seen in the film *St. Louis Blues*. In "Foolish Man Blues," Smith sings, "There's two things got me puzzled, there's two things I don't understand, that's a mannish-acting woman and a lisping, swishing, womanish-acting man." Often regarded as the greatest blues singer in history.

Ethel Waters, 1896–1977: Jazz singer during the Harlem Renaissance. Later became an actor, whose films included *Pinky* and *The Member of the Wedding*. She also starred in the early 1950s TV series *Beulah*.

Mabel Hampton (*Photo by Timothy Bissell*)

For a thorough look at this period, see Lilian Faderman's *Odd Girls and Twilight Lovers: A History of Lesbian Life in Twentieth-Century America,* pages 72–79; and "A Spectacle in Color: The Lesbian and Gay Subculture of Jazz Age Harlem" by Eric Garber in *Hidden from History: Reclaiming the Gay and Lesbian Past,* edited by Duberman, Vicinus, and Chauncey. For many of these songs, look for *AC/DC Blues: Gay Jazz Reissues* from Stash Records ST-106, which includes "BD Women" and "BD's Dream."

RECORDINGS OF BLACK LESBIAN BLUES MUSICIANS

AC/DC Blues: Gay Jazz Reissues (Stash Records, P.O. Box 1009, Mattituck, NY 11952)

Any Woman's Blues by The Women's Prison Concert Collective (Any Woman's Blues, UUSC, 78 Beacon St., Boston, MA 02108)

Mean Mothers, Piano Singer's Blues and *Boogie Blues,* where you can find Gladys Bentley's songs (among others) (Rosetta Records, 115 W. 16th St., Suite 267, New York, NY 10011).

RECLAIMED LESBIAN OR BISEXUAL PERFORMERS

Marlene Dietrich, 1901–1992: German singer, American-made movie star; she was always more or less open about her bisexuality.

Billy Tipton, d. 1989: Jazz musician and founder of the Billy Tipton Trio who passed her entire adult life as a man.

BISEXUAL PERFORMERS OF THE PAST

Isadora Duncan, 1877–1927: Pioneer of modern dance.

Loie Fuller, 1862–1928: Dancer, influenced Duncan.

Libby Holman: Actress/entertainer, popular during the 1920s and 1930s, had love affairs with other women including Josephine Baker.

Janis Joplin, 1943–1970: Rock singer.

Eva Le Gallienne, 1899–1991: Broadway actress who started the Civic Repertory Theater.

LESBIAN/BISEXUAL STAGE ACTRESSES

Tallulah Bankhead, 1902–1968: Stage and film goddess also known for outrageous wit.

Katharine Cornell, 1893–1974: Sometimes called the First Lady of the American Theater; married to a gay man, Gutherie McClintic.

Charlotte Cushman, 1816–1876: Expatriate in London and Rome, a superstar actress (called the greatest actress of her day), and lesbian patron of the arts.

Blythe Daly, early twentieth century: Pal of Eva Le Gallienne, and Tallulah Bankhead.

Nance O'Neill, early twentieth century: Lover of the infamous Lizzie Borden (who was acquitted of murdering her parents with an ax).

Ada Russell, early twentieth century: Also known as Ada Dwyer, lover of poet Amy Lowell.

FIRST TIME TWO ACTRESSES KISSED ON AN AMERICAN STAGE

In 1896, two actresses kissed each other onstage for the first time in the play, *A Florida Enchantment*. The play was not about lesbians, however, but a woman who changed into a man by magic. The meeting of lips caused an uproar, nonetheless.

Transsexual lesbian performance artist Kate Bornstein (*Copyright © 1994 by Morgan Gwenwald*)

First Play on American Stage to Feature Lesbian or Gay Characters

In 1922, *The God of Vengeance* by Sholom Asch focused on a lesbian relationship. Appropriately enough, it opened in Provincetown before it moved on to create a scandal on Broadway in 1923.

The First Anthology of Lesbian Plays

As sad and unbelievable as it may sound, the first anthology of lesbian plays was not published until 1985. *Places, Please!: The First Anthology of Lesbian Plays* was edited by Kate McDermott and published by the lesbian/feminist small press Spinsters/Aunt Lute. The plays and playwrights it contained were:

Dos Lesbos, by Terry Baum and Carolyn Myers
8 x 10 Glossy, by Sarah Dreher
Going Up, by Julia Willis
Immediate Family, by Terry Baum
Out of Bounds, by Mariah Burton Nelson
Ruby Christmas, by Sarah Dreher
Soup, by Ellen Gruber Garvey

The Lesbian Theater Project

The Lesbian Theater Project is a not-for-profit theater company by and for lesbian and bisexual playwrights, actors, producers, and directors. Their goal is to consistently produce quality pro-queer theater by lesbian and bisexual women artists without the tokenism that is often attached to representations of lesbians in the media.

The group has existed since April 1994 and officially incorporated in August of that year. The Board of Directors include Jill Dearman, Tracy Digesu, Mara Murphey, and Karen Small. Recent productions and readings have included works by Jill Dearman, Emma Donohue, Penny Perkins, and Sarah Schulman.

The project accepts submissions of both one-act pieces for upcoming festivals and full-length pieces for readings and productions. Contact: The Lesbian Theater Project, 77 Perry Street, #2B, New York, NY 10014; Phone/fax: 212/243-5770.

Pioneering theater troupe, Split Britches; from left: Lois Weaver, Peggy Shaw, and Deb Margolin

SELECTED HOTBEDS OF GAY AND LESBIAN PERFORMANCE THEATER

The Ridiculous Theatrical
   Company (New York City)
Theatre Rhinoceros (San Francisco)
Highways Performance Space
   (Los Angeles)
Alice B. Theatre (Seattle)

WOW Cafe (New York City)
Mark Taper Forum (Los Angeles)
Celebration Theatre (Los Angeles)
Perry Street Theatre (New York City)
Rainbow Repertory Theatre
   (New York City)

WOMEN'S MUSIC FESTIVALS

Campfest, the "comfortable womyn's music festival" in Pennsylvania; RR5, Box 185, Franklinville, NJ 08322; Phone: 609/694-2037. Campfest '95 (celebrating its twelfth year) featured the following performers: Sarah Cytron, Alix Dobkin, Derivative Duo, Diane Davidson, Ubaka Hill, and Justina & Joyce.

The first Michigan Womyn's Music Festival was held in 1976. Still going strong, it takes place in August in upper Michigan. For more information write: WWTMC, Box 22, Walhalla, MI 49458.

National Women's Music Festival (June, in Bloomington, Indiana): NWMF, Dept. LC, P.O. Box 1427, Indianapolis, IN 46206; Phone: 317/927-9355.

Rhythmfest (Labor Day weekend): Rhythmfest, 957 N. Highland Ave., Atlanta, GA 30306; Phone 404/873-1551.

Performance duet, Pura Fe *(Copyright © Morgan Gwenwald)*

PERFORMER RESOURCE

Booking Yourself, a comprehensive, step-by-step guide for artists and performers to book themselves, including a starter list of 300 names and contact numbers, is available in book form for $25 or on Mac (Microsoft Word) disk for $40. Contact: Sandy Ayala, 3929 Rhoda Ave., Oakland, CA 94602.

SOURCE: America Online

Virginia Women's Music Festival (May): INTOUCH, Rt. 2, Box 1096, Kent's Store, VA 23084; Phone: 804/589-6542.

West Coast Women's Music & Comedy Fest (Labor Day weekend, near Yosemite, California): Robin Tyler Prod., 15842 Chase St., North Hills, CA 91343; Phone: 818/893-4075; Fax: 818/893-1593.

MUST READING FOR THE LESBIAN CULTURE VULTURE

Hot Wire: The Journal of Women's Music and Culture
5210 N. Wayne
Chicago, IL 60640
Phone: 312/769-9009
First issue: November, 1984

RESOURCES: NATIONAL LESBIAN AND GAY GROUPS FOR PERFORMERS

Gay and Lesbian Association of Choruses
1617 East 22nd Street
Denver, CO 80205
Phone: 303/832-1526

Lambda Performing Arts Guild of America
P.O. Box 140131
Denver, CO 80214

LEND, International (Lesbian Exchange of New Drama)
559 Third Street
Brooklyn, NY 11215
Phone: 718/369-0075

Lesbian and Gay Bands of America
P.O. Box 57099
Washington, DC 20037-0099

Music Industry Network of Gays and Lesbians (MINGL)
P.O. Box 20357
Columbus Circle Station
New York, NY 10023
Phone: 718/858-8647

OUTMUSIC: Gay/Lesbian Musicians, Composers, and Lyricists
P.O. Box 1575
New York, NY 10013
Phone: 212/330-9197

The Purple Circuit, Artists Confronting AIDS
684½ Echo Park Avenue
Los Angeles, CA 90026
Phone: 213/250-1413

Theatre Rhinoceros
2926 16th Street, 16th Floor
San Francisco, CA 94103
Phone: 415/552-4100
Produces lesbian and gay theater

PROFILE

The Five Lesbian Brothers

The Five Lesbian Brothers are Moe Angelos, Babs Davy, Dominique Dibbell, Peg Healey, and Lisa Kron. They performed together in various combinations for many years at the Obie–award winning WOW Cafe Theatre before coming together as a company in 1989. The Brothers' work explores such dark themes as homophobia and sexism with devastating humor and occasional musical numbers.

The Five Lesbian Brothers are committed to creating provocative lesbian theater through collaboration. Their repertoire includes three full-length plays (*Voyage to Lesbos; Brave Smiles . . . Another Lesbian Tragedy*; and *The Secretaries*) and numerous event-specific acts (such as the garden party at the Lesbian and Gay Community Services Center in New York City in 1993, for which they wrote a rousing lesbionic song). They have performed in New York at the WOW Cafe Theatre, the New York Theatre Workshop, Downtown Arts Company, Performance Space 122, La Mama, Dixon Place, and Fez (where they recently showcased a trailer from their "maybe-someday-we'll-actually-write-it" musical entitled, *Sorrow, River to Shametown*). The campy crew has also performed in major cities throughout the United States, including Boston, Houston, San Diego, Los Angeles, San Francisco, and Seattle.

The Five Lesbian Brothers are recipients of a 1993 New York Dance and Performance Award (more popularly known as a Bessie) for outstanding creative achievement. They were also chosen Best Performance Group of 1991 by *New York Press*. The Brothers received a 1995 *Village Voice* Obie for their production of *The Secretaries* at the New York Theatre Workshop, produced in the fall of 1994.

Moe Angelos provided this further commentary on the Brothers' collective history:

"We all found ourselves at WOW—of course, coming there from our own personal various and sundry complicated routes—in the late 1980s. Peg, Lisa, and I had worked together the most. We really wanted to make our living performing— we were tired of having day jobs (and we still are tired of it), and we got the idea of having a small touring company. We thought about who would be natural to ask to join us, and Babs and Dom came immediately to mind. We all have a similar sense of humor and we all had—and have—a good sense of each other.

"We started working together as the Brothers and our first project—*Voyage to Lesbos*—just came together. At the time, we were all young and ambitious, wanted to work collaboratively, and didn't have a director. Although we still are committed to collaborative work, with *Brave Smiles* we began working with the incredibly talented and generous Kate Stafford. We also work with Susan Young on a regular basis as our costume designer, and Sama Blackwell is our manager.

"When we first started touring, we all had jobs, so we just went away for weekends, then long weekends, then the occasional 'sick day' tour. The next year we got longer gigs and touring dates, and some of us eventually quit our full-time work (supporting ourselves with temp work and part-time jobs). Last year we toured *The Secretaries* for four months, and rewrote it for the New York Theatre Workshop with the help of Sybille Pearson, our dramaturg."

For the future, there is a possible book deal in the works—"If everything goes according to schedule, there will be a lesbian humor trade paperback from the Brothers available for $8.95 in your local neighborhood mall chain bookstore," notes Moe. A finalized project is that their play, *Brave Smiles: Another Lesbian Tragedy,* is being published in an anthology of gay and lesbian plays coming out from Penguin and edited by Eric Lane. They also hope to begin writing a new full-length piece.

But what's the most important thing to remember about the Brothers? According to Moe, "The important piece is how we work together collaboratively. It is the most unique thing about the Brothers—and, truthfully, it's also the hardest."

---

14. Lesbians and Politics

While we have always been politically active, our power as a voting bloc has been recognized only recently. We have made progress, but we still have a long way to go. Although most Americans oppose job discrimination on the basis of sexual orientation, less than a majority find homosexuality to be an acceptable "life style."

— Ellen Carton, former executive director of the Gay and Lesbian Alliance
Against Defamation (GLAAD), 1992

One of the most exciting times in the history of electoral politics for lesbians and gay men in the United States may have been 1992. Mainstream politicians courted the gay vote, and Democratic presidential candidate Bill Clinton included gay people in his speech accepting his party's nomination and counted among his advisers an openly gay man, David Mixner. On the other hand, at the Republican Convention, candidate Patrick Buchanan exhibited such venomous public hatred of gay people that it alienated much of the electorate. To many, it looked like the dawn of a brighter era for gay citizens.

Though Clinton backed down from some of his promises to gay supporters once he was elected, the gay vote remains a force to be reckoned with, especially in areas with large lesbian and gay populations. The 1994 midterm elections saw openly lesbian and gay candidates running for more offices than ever. Some challengers won, like feminist attorney Sheila Kuehl, who became the first openly gay member of the California Assembly. Even more importantly, all openly lesbian and gay incumbents from the national to the local level retained their offices. Now, organizations like the Gay and Lesbian Victory Fund help train gay people who are interested in running for political office.

How important are electoral politics? Do our votes and our letters really count? The radical right has become expert at working the electoral system, helping the Republican Party take over the majority in both houses of Congress in 1994. The right actively registers people to vote and maintains an elaborate network of voters who write letters and make phone calls against such issues as lesbian and gay rights.

Mainstream politics is one means of working for lesbian rights. If we don't make our voices and opinions heard, we have no one to blame but ourselves.

Out Gay and Lesbian Officials in the Clinton Administration

Roberta Achtenberg, Assistant Secretary for Fair Housing and Opportunity, Department of Housing and Urban Development; highest ranking lesbian in the administration (resigned April 1995 to run for mayor of San Francisco)

Daniel Burkhardt, Special Assistant and Counsel to the Director, Office of Correspondence

Bob Chapman, Special Assistant to the Deputy Secretary for Drug Policy, Department of Defense

Bernie Delia, Counsel to the Executive Office for U.S. Attorneys, Department of Justice

Romy Diaz, Deputy Assistant Secretary for International Affairs, Department of Energy

Bob Hattoy, Special Assistant to the Deputy Secretary, Department of the Interior

Thomas Hehir, Director, Office of Special Education Programs, Department of Education

Mark Hunker, Special Assistant to Assistant Secretary for Administration and Management, Department of Labor

Nan Hunter, Deputy General Counsel, Department of Health and Human Services

Bruce Lehman, Assistant Secretary of Commerce and Commissioner of Patents and Trademarks

David Martin, Assistant to the Assistant Secretary, Office of Legislative and Intergovernmental Affairs, Department of Commerce

Zoon Nguyen, Special Assistant to the Assistant Secretary for Fair Housing and Opportunity, Department of Housing and Urban Development (resigned April 1995 to work on Roberta Achtenberg's campaign)

Patrick Nolan, Special Assistant to the Undersecretary, International Trade Administration, Department of Commerce

David Peterson, Confidential Assistant, Office of the General Counsel, Department of Commerce

Julian Potter, Special Assistant to the Assistant Secretary for Community Planning and Development, Department of Housing and Urban Development

Roberta Achtenberg (*Copyright © 1993 by Micha Kwiatkowska*)

R. Paul Richard, Executive Assistant to Commissioner Paul Steven Miller, Equal Employment Opportunity Commission

Martin Rouse, Special Assistant to the Assistant Secretary, Office of Fair Housing and Equal Opportunity, Department of Housing and Urban Development

Douglas S. Sheorn, Office of Presidential Personnel

Stephanie Smith, Special Assistant to Secretary Cisneros, Department of Housing and Urban Development

Richard Socarides, White House Liaison, Department of Labor

Jay Stowsky, Senior Economist, Council of Economic Advisors

Stan Strickland, Special Assistant, Office of Legislative Affairs, Department of Justice

Brian C. Thompson, White House Liaison, National Archives

David Tseng, Special Assistant to the Assistant Secretary, Pension and Welfare Benefits Administration, Department of Labor

Jesse White, Chair, Appalachian Commission

Victor Zonana, Deputy Assistant Secretary for Public Affairs, Department of Health and Human Services

SOURCE: *Out* magazine, March 1995. Reprinted with permission from *Out* magazine, February 1995. Copyright© 1995 by Out Publishing, Inc. All rights reserved. For subscription information, call 1-800-876-1199.

Openly Gay Candidates in the 1994 Elections

Challengers

STATEWIDE OFFICE

Karen Burstein (N.Y. Attorney General)
Tony Miller (Calif. Secretary of State)
Joseph Schreiner (Ill. Secretary of State)

STATE OFFICE

*Cal Anderson (D-Wash.)
Derek Belt (D-Mass.)
Chuck Carpenter (R-Ore.)
*Ken Cheuvront (D-Ariz.)
Scott Evertz (R-Wis.)
Brendan Hadash (D-Vt.)
James Harrison (R-Md.)
Denise Heap (D-Ariz.)

Jerry Keene (R-Ore.)
*Sheila Kuehl (D-Calif.)
Greg Nance (R-Utah)
Mike Pisaturo (D-R.I.)
Bruce Reeves (D-Tex.)
Mark Valverde (Libertarian-Calif.)
*Tim Van Zandt (D-Mo.)

LOCAL OFFICE

*Tom Ammiano (San Francisco
  Board of Supervisors)
Mark Brazil (San Luis Obispo, Calif.,
  City Council)
*Tom Chiola (Cook County, Ill.,
  circuit judge)
Sam Ciraulo (Robla, Calif.,
  school board)
*Bonnie Dumanis (San Diego
  Municipal Court)
John Fanning (D.C. school board)
Royce Gibson (D.C. school board)
Ron Gunzberger (Broward County,
  Fla., judge)

Arthur Jackson (San Francisco Board
  of Supervisors)
*Marcy Kahn (New York State Supreme
  Court)
*Leslie Katz (San Francisco Community
  College Board)
Vicky Kolakowski (AC Transit Board
  of Directors)
Kearse McGill (Sacramento Utility
  District)
*Teri Schwartz (Los Angeles Superior
  Court)
*Lawrence Wong (San Francisco
  Community College Board of Trustees)

Incumbents

FEDERAL OFFICE

*Rep. Barney Frank (D-Mass.)
*Rep. Steve Gunderson (R-Wis.)

*Rep. Gerry Studds (D-Mass.)

STATE OFFICE

*Rep. Tammy Baldwin (D-Wis.)
*Rep. Kate Brown (D-Ore.)

*Rep. Bill Lippert (D-Vt.)
*Rep. Glen Maxey (D-Tex.)

°Rep. Karen Clark (D-Minn.)　　°Rep. George Eighmey (D-Ore.)
°Sen. Dale McCormick (D-Maine)　°Rep. Gail Shibley (D-Ore.)
°Sen. Will Fitzpatrick (D-R.I.)　　°Rep. Cynthia Wooten (D-Ore.)
°Assemblymember
　Deborah Glick (D-N.Y.)

LOCAL OFFICE

°Susan Leal (San Francisco Board of Supervisors)
°Carol Migden (San Francisco Board of Supervisors)

°indicates candidate won race

SOURCE: *The Washington Blade,* November 11, 1994

LESBIAN AND GAY CANDIDATES

The Gay and Lesbian Victory Fund supports openly lesbian and gay candidates for office and provides an annual training for running a political campaign. For more information, contact the Victory Fund, 1012 Fourteenth Street NW, #707, Washington, DC 20005; Phone: 202/842-8679.

The National Gay and Lesbian Task Force (NGLTF) offers a number of publications and software packages via America Online useful in planning a political campaign, including congressional report cards (tracking how congress members voted on issues of concern to lesbians and gays) and a software program called Precinct Walker, which helps manage a local campaign. Contact NGLTF at 1734 Fourteenth Street NW, Washington, DC 20009; Phone: 202/332-6483.

The International Network of Lesbian and Gay Officials (INLGO) is a nonprofit organization incorporated in Minnesota that supports and encourages full participation in all aspects of society by openly gay men and lesbians. Its focus is on openly gay and lesbian elected and appointed officials. INLGO has held conferences annually since 1985, and the 1995 conference was held in Toronto, Canada. The group also maintains mailing lists and a newsletter and is working on a better system of electronic networking. For more information, check out INLGO's listing in the Queer Resources Directory on the Internet or send E-mail to INLGO@aol.com.

EMILY'S List (Early Money Is Like Yeast—it makes dough rise), founded in 1985 by lesbian political activist Ellen Malcolm, is the nation's largest financial resource for prochoice Democratic women candidates for the Senate, the House of Representatives, and for gubernatorial seats. Contact EMILY'S List at 1112 Sixteenth Street NW, Suite 750, Washington, DC 20036; Phone: 202/887-1957.

STATES, CITIES, AND COUNTIES WHOSE CIVIL RIGHTS LAWS, ORDINANCES, AND POLICIES BAR DISCRIMINATION BASED ON SEXUAL ORIENTATION AS OF MAY, 1995

SUMMARY OF CIVIL RIGHTS LAWS THAT INCLUDE SEXUAL ORIENTATION

Nine states in the U.S. have civil rights laws that include sexual orientation passed by the legislature and signed by the governor:

California—1992   New Jersey—1992
Connecticut—1991   Rhode Island—1995
Hawaii—1991   Vermont—1992
Massachusetts—1989   Wisconsin—1982
Minnesota—1993

At least eighteen states in the U.S. have executive orders barring discrimination based on sexual orientation.

At least eighty-seven cities or counties in the U.S. have civil rights ordinances barring discrimination based on sexual orientation.

At least thirty-nine cities/counties in the U.S. have council or mayoral proclamations banning discrimination based on sexual orientation in public employment.

State/City	Areas of Protection	Population
Alaska		
Anchorage	1	226,338
Arizona		
Phoenix	1	983,403
Tucson	1	405,390
California	1–4	29,760,021
Berkeley	1, 3–7	102,724
Cathedral City	1	30,085
Cupertino	1	39,967
Davis	1–3, 5–7	46,322
Hayward	1, 3–5	111,498
Laguna Beach	1–7	23,170
Long Beach	1, 3	423,433
Los Angeles	1–7	3,485,398
Mountain View	1	67,460
Oakland	1–7	372,242

State/City	Areas of Protection	Population
Palo Alto	4	55,900
Riverside	1	226,505
Sacramento	1–7	369,365
San Diego	1–7	1,110,549
San Francisco	1–7	723,959
San Jose	1	782,248
Santa Barbara	1, 4	85,571
Santa Cruz	1	49,711
Santa Monica	1–7	86,905
West Hollywood	1–7	36,118
Alameda County	Not Available	1,276,702
San Mateo County	1, 3, 5	649,623
Santa Barbara County	1	369,608
Santa Cruz County	1	229,734
Colorado		
Aspen	1–3, 5	5,049
Boulder	1–3	83,312
Denver	1–5, 7	467,610
Telluride	1–3, 5	1,309
Boulder County	1	225,339
Morgan County	1	21,939
Connecticut	1	3,287,116
Hartford	1–7	139,739
New Haven	1–7	130,474
Stamford	1–7	108,056
District of Columbia		
Washington	1–7	606,900
Florida		
Key West	1–3, 5–7	24,832
Miami Beach	1–3, 5	92,639
West Palm Beach	1	67,643
Alachua County	1–3, 5	181,596
Hillsborough County	2, 5	834,054
Palm Beach County	1–2, 5	863,518
Georgia		
Atlanta	1	394,017
Hawaii	1, 3	1,108,229
Honolulu	1	365,272
Illinois		
Champaign	1–3, 5–7	63,502
Chicago	1–4, 6	2,783,726
Evanston	1, 6	73,233
Oak Park	2, 5	53,648
Urbana	1–3, 4–5	36,344
Cook County	1–4, 6	5,105,067

State/City	Areas of Protection	Population
Indiana		
Bloomington	1–5	60,633
Lafayette	1–5	43,764
West Lafayette	1–5	23,138
Iowa		
Ames	1–7	47,198
Iowa City	1–3, 6, 7	59,738
Louisiana		
New Orleans	1–3, 5	496,938
Maine		
Portland	1–3, 4, 5	64,358
Maryland		
Baltimore	1–5	736,014
Gaithersburg	1, 3, 5–7	39,542
Rockville	1–7	44,835
Howard County	1–7	187,328
Montgomery County	1, 3, 5–7	757,027
Massachusetts	1–7	6,016,425
Amherst	1–7	35,228
Boston	1–4, 6, 7	574,283
Cambridge	1–7	95,802
Malden	1–6	53,884
Worcester	1–6	169,759
Michigan		
Ann Arbor	1–3, 5–7	109,392
Birmingham	5, 6	19,997
Detroit	1–7	1,027,974
East Lansing	1–3, 5–7	50,677
Flint	1–5, 7	140,762
Saginaw	4, 5	69,512
Ingham County	1	282,912
Minnesota	1–6	4,375,099
Marshall	1–3, 4, 5	12,023
Minneapolis	1–7	368,383
St. Paul	1–7	272,235
Hennepin County	1	1,032,431
Missouri		
Kansas City	1, 3, 5, 7	435,146
St. Louis	1–6	396,685
New Jersey	1–3, 4, 5	7,730,188
Essex County	1	778,204
New York		
Albany	1–3, 4, 5	101,082
Brighton	1	34,455
Buffalo	1	328,123
East Hampton	1–3	16,132

State/City	Areas of Protection	Population
Ithaca	1–7	29,541
New York	1–5, 7	7,322,564
Rochester	1	231,636
Syracuse	1–5	163,860
Troy	1	54,269
Watertown	1–6	29,429
Suffolk County	1	1,321,264
Tompkins County	1–7	94,097
North Carolina		
Chapel Hill	1	38,711
Durham	1	136,611
Raleigh	1	207,952
Ohio		
Columbus	1–6	632,910
Dayton	1	182,044
Yellow Springs	1–3, 5–7	3,973
Cayahoga County	1	1,412,140
Oregon		
Portland	1–3, 5	437,319
Pennsylvania		
Harrisburg	1–7	52,376
Lancaster	1–7	55,551
Philadelphia	1–3, 5–7	1,585,577
Pittsburgh	1–3, 5–7	369,879
York	1–3, 5	42,192
State College	5	40,949
Northampton County	1	247,305
Rhode Island	1, 2, 5, 6	947,154
South Carolina		
Columbia	1	98,052
South Dakota		
Minnehaha County	1	123,509
Texas		
Austin	1–3, 5–7	465,622
Dallas	1	1,852,810
Houston	1	1,630,553
Utah		
Salt Lake County	1	159,936
Vermont	1–7	562,758
Burlington	1, 3	39,127
Virginia		
Alexandria	1–6	111,283
Arlington County	1	170,936
Washington		
Olympia	1	33,840
Pullman	1, 5, 6	23,478

State/City	Areas of Protection	Population
Seattle	1, 3, 5–7	516,259
Clallam County	1	56,210
King County	5, 6	1,507,319
Wisconsin	1–7	4,891,769
Madison	1–3, 5–7	191,262
Milwaukee	1	628,088
Dane County	1	367,085

Key to areas of protection from discrimination based on sexual orientation:

1 = Public Employment
2 = Public Accommodations
3 = Private Employment
4 = Education
5 = Housing
6 = Credit
7 = Union Practices

Population figures are from the 1990 United States census.

This information is based upon newspaper articles and information sent to NGLTF by activists. Therefore, it is likely that there are cities and counties that have ordinances or proclamations that are not included in this chart. If you know of additions or corrections to this chart, please contact Karen Bullock-Jordan, Public Information & Fight the Right Association, NGLTF, 1734 Fourteenth St. NW, Washington, DC 20009; Phone: 202/332-6483, ext. 3206; Fax: 202/332-0207; kbjngltf@aol.com.

SAMPLE GAY RIGHTS ORDINANCE LANGUAGE

WASHINGTON, D.C.

Every individual shall have an equal opportunity to participate fully in the economic, cultural, and intellectual life of the district and to have an equal opportunity to participate in all aspects of life, including, but not limited to, in employment, in places of public accommodation, resort or amusement, in educational institutions, in public service, and in housing and commercial space accommodations.

It shall be an unlawful discriminatory practice to do any of the following acts, wholly or partially for a discriminatory reason based upon race, color, religion, national origin, sex, age, marital status, personal appearance, sexual orientation, family responsibilities, physical handicap, matriculation, or political affiliation, of any individual: to refuse to hire or to discharge; to fail to initiate or conduct any transaction in real property; to deny, directly or indirectly, any person the full and equal enjoyment of the goods, services, facilities, privileges, advantages, and accommodations of any place or public accommodation; to deny access to any of an educational institution's facilities and services.

That the proposed ordinance amending Chapter 34 of the Dallas City Code be amended by renumbering current Sections 21 through 28 as Sections 22 through 29 and adding a new Section 21 to read as follows:

SECTION 21. That Subsection (b) of Section 34–35, "Fair Employment Practices," of Article V, "Rules of Conduct," of CHAPTER 34, "PERSONNEL RULES," of the Dallas City Code, as amended, is amended to read as follows:

(b) MANAGEMENT RESPONSIBILITIES

(1) In keeping with the respect due each employee, city management is committed to:

(A)	provide effective and efficient delivery of services;
(B)	compensate employees fairly for work done;
(C)	provide safe, healthy work conditions in accordance with provisions of all applicable law;
(D)	adequately instruct and train employees in their duties;
(E)	supply necessary tools and equipment (except those customarily provided by employees);
(F)	provide reasonable opportunities for developmental experience and competitive advancement; and
(G)	actively engage in equal opportunity activities.

(2) City management may not discharge an individual, fail or refuse to hire an individual, or otherwise discriminate against an individual with respect to compensation, terms, conditions, or privileges of employment because of the individual's race, color, age, religion, sex, marital status, sexual orientation, national origin, disability, political opinions, or affiliations. Nothing in this paragraph extends any employee benefits, including but not limited to paid or unpaid leave, medical benefits, or pension benefits, to any individual who is ineligible for those benefits under any other provision of this chapter, the city's master health plan, the employees' retirement fund program, or the police and fire pension system or under any other city ordinance or resolution or state or federal law.

(3) City management may not limit, segregate, or classify employees or applicants for employment in a way that would deprive or tend to deprive an individual of employment opportunities or otherwise adversely affect an employee's status because of the individual's race, color, age, religion, sex, marital status, sexual orientation, national origin, disability, political opinions, or affiliations.

The following governmental agencies have employment policies that bar discrimination based on sexual orientation:

The Federal Bureau of
  Investigation
The Department of Housing
  and Urban Development
The Department of the Interior
The Department of Transportation

The Justice Department
The Office of Personnel
  Management
The White House
The State Department

JESSE HELMS'S HATE BILLS

Senator Jesse Helms (R-N.C.) introduced the following two bills into the 104th session of Congress during its first month, pursuing the antigay obsession on which he has focused for the last few years.

S.315   104TH CONGRESS

1ST SESSION

To protect the first amendment rights of employees of the Federal Government.

IN THE SENATE OF THE UNITED STATES

February 1 (legislative day, January 30), 1995

Mr. Helms introduced the following bill, which was read twice and referred to the Committee on Governmental Affairs

A BILL

to protect the first amendment rights of employees of the Federal Government.

Be it enacted by the Senate and House of Representatives of the United States of America in Congress assembled,

Section 1. Notwithstanding any other provision of law, no employee of the Federal Government shall be peremptorily removed without public hearings from his or her position because of remarks made during personal time in opposition to the Federal Government's policies, or proposed policies regarding homosexuals, and any such individual so removed prior to date of enactment of this Act shall be reinstated to his or her previous position.

S.317   104TH CONGRESS

1ST SESSION

To stop the waste of taxpayer funds on activities by Government agencies to encourage its employees or officials to accept homosexuality as a legitimate or normal lifestyle.

IN THE SENATE OF THE UNITED STATES

February 1 (legislative day, January 30), 1995

Mr. Helms introduced the following bill, which was read twice and referred to the Committee on Governmental Affairs

---

A BILL

to stop the waste of taxpayer funds on activities by Government agencies to encourage its employees or officials to accept homosexuality as a legitimate or normal lifestyle.

Be it enacted by the Senate and House of Representatives of the United States of America in Congress assembled,

Section 1. Limitation on use of appropriated funds. No funds appropriated out of the Treasury of the United States may be used by any entity to fund, promote, or carry out any seminar or program for employees of the Government, or to fund any position in the Government, the purpose of which is to compel, instruct, encourage, urge, or persuade employees or officials to—

(1) recruit, on the basis of sexual orientation, homosexuals for employment with the Government; or
(2) embrace, accept, condone, or celebrate homosexuality as a legitimate or normal lifestyle.

REGISTERING TO VOTE

By registering to vote and then casting votes on election day, lesbians and gay men make their voices heard and protect their interests and civil rights. Do you know which national candidates support a gay rights bill and vote for increased AIDS funding? Or which local school board candidates advocate for a tolerant, multicultural curriculum? We're the losers when we remain apathetic about voting; an informed lesbian and gay electorate is a powerful tool toward attaining civil rights. To find out more about the voting record of your congressperson, you can send for the "Congressional Report Card," which is available from the National Gay and Lesbian Task Force, 1734 Fourteenth Street NW, Washington, DC 20009; Phone: 202/332-6483.

To find out how to register to vote in your city or town or how to apply for an absentee ballot, contact your local Board of Elections. They're in the blue-pages section of the phone book, along with other offices of city government. You can also call the local office of the League of Women Voters for information on registering.

If your city has a gay and lesbian community center, check to see if the center registers voters. The New York Lesbian and Gay Community Services Center (208 West 13th Street, New York City), for example, has a voter registration project, and visitors to the building can register to vote on the spot at the lobby information desk.

LESBIAN VOTERS

In a 1992 survey of 7,500 lesbians and gay men, Overlooked Opinions, Inc., a gay/lesbian marketing research firm in Chicago, found the following results (based on data compiled in the thirty states that tabulate voters' party affiliations):

	LESBIANS	NATIONAL
Registered to vote (of those eligible)	90.0%	68.2%
Voted in the 1988 presidential election	82.0%	61.3%
Democrat	66.7%	48.7%°
Independent	21.3%	13.3%°
Republican	6.8%	33.8%°
Socialist	2.8%	NA
Libertarian	1.4%	NA
Other party affiliations	4.4%	4.2%°

Reprinted with permission from Overlooked Opinions, Chicago, and the Bureau of the Census, Washington, D.C. All rights reserved.

WRITING LETTERS

Writing a letter to a Congress member is a good way to make your voice heard. You may think your letter will get lost in the shuffle, but the number of responses for or against a particular policy or measure is tabulated. You will almost always get a letter in response, even if you are against a policy or bill. The radical right has an effective letter-writing campaign that floods Congress against issues such as abortion and gay rights. Let them hear from the other side.

To write to your Congress member, always use your name and address and type the letter if possible. Be direct and to the point; make your opinion clear. Avoid threats and demands. Show how you *as a voter* are affected by the policy or bill in question. If you're responding to a particular bill, refer to it by number or name. Letters can be addressed as follows:

Senator (fill in)   Representative (fill in)
Senate Office Building   House of Representatives Office Building
Washington, DC 20510   Washington, DC 20515

PROFILE

International Network of Lesbian and Gay Officials

Founded in 1985 by thirteen openly lesbian and gay political officials, INLGO is a network of elected and appointed officials, their partners, activists, and others interested in electoral politics. The nonprofit organization asserts in its mission statement: "We have a unique opportunity and responsibility to serve as teachers both within the institutions of government and to the larger community."

To that end, INLGO supports local, state, and national legislation in the following areas affecting the lives of lesbians and gay men: the outlawing of discrimination based on sexual orientation, race, religion, sex, marital status, disability status, national or ethnic origin, and age; the overturning of laws that prohibit consensual sexual activity between adults; domestic partnership; child custody, foster care, and adoption; protecting against AIDS and HIV-related discrimination; and increased services for people with AIDS and HIV and funding for research and education.

Each year in November, INLGO sponsors a conference that provides officials with a planning and support network of openly gay officials around the world. The conference is a springboard for ideas on political and social issues. Some topics of discussion include understanding polls, conflict resolution skills, national and local organizing, family issues, building bridges, and balancing public and private life. Limited grants and scholarships are available to those who need assistance with conference costs. Following each annual conference, participants are hooked up with more seasoned officials to provide a mentor relationship.

SCHEDULE OF CONFERENCES SINCE 1985

1985	West Hollywood, California	1991	Houston, Texas
1986	Washington, D.C.	1992	Chapel Hill, North Carolina
1987	Minneapolis, Minnesota	1993	Chicago, Illinois
1988	San Diego, California	1994	Seattle, Washington
1989	Madison, Wisconsin	1995	Toronto, Ontario
1990	Boston, Massachusetts	1996	West Hollywood, California

Openly gay New York City council member Tom Duane with Virginia Apuzzo, long-time lesbian activist and political figure *(Lesbian and Gay Community Services Center—New York)*

FOUNDERS OF INLGO, 1985

Harry Britt, Supervisor, San Francisco, California
Karen Clark, State Representative, Minnesota
Brian Coyle, City Council Member, Minneapolis, Minnesota
Robert Ebersole, Town Clerk, Tax Collector and Treasurer, Lunenburg, Massachusetts
Robert Gentry, City Council Member, Laguna Beach, California
John Heilman, Mayor, West Hollywood, California
John Laird, City Council Member, Santa Cruz, California
Kathleen Nichols, Supervisor, Dane County, Wisconsin
Steve Schulte, City Council Member, West Hollywood, California
David Scondras, City Council Member, Boston, Massachusetts
Allan Spear, State Senator, Minnesota
Valerie Terrigno, City Council Member, West Hollywood, California
Richard Wagner, Supervisor, Dane County, Wisconsin

STEERING COMMITTEE, 1994–1995

Cochairs:	Deborah Glick, New York, New York
	Kyle Rae, Toronto, Ontario
Secretary:	Kevin Vaughan, Philadelphia, Pennsylvania
Treasurer:	Tim Cole, Minneapolis, Minnesota
Elected Officials:	Tom Duane, New York, New York
	Will Fitzpatrick, Cranston, Rhode Island
	Deborah Glick, New York, New York
	Jill Harris, Brooklyn, New York
	Kyle Rae, Toronto, Ontario
Appointed Officials:	Tim Cole, Minneapolis, Minnesota
	Carlie Steen, Detroit, Michigan
	Kevin Vaughan, Philadelphia, Pennsylvania
At Large:	Dennis Amick, Laguna Beach, California
	Tanya Gulliver, Whitby, Ontario
	John Heilman, West Hollywood, California
Ex Officio:	Cal Anderson, Seattle, Washington

International Network of Lesbian and Gay Officials, 3801 Twenty-sixth Street East, Minneapolis, MN 55406-1857; E-mail: INLGO@aol.com.

15. LESBIANS, RELIGION, AND SPIRITUALITY

The Christian supremacists are wrong spiritually when they demonize us. They are wrong when they reduce the complexity and beauty of our spirit to a freak show. They are wrong spiritually because if we are the untouchables of America . . . then we are, as Mahatma Gandhi said, children of God.

—URVASHI VAID, former executive director of the National Gay and Lesbian Task Force, 1993

Across North America, lesbians are asserting their need and right to be spiritual—to take part in organized Eastern and Western religions; to establish their own churches; to create their own forms of spirituality, sometimes through eroticism; to revere pagan traditions; to honor the Two Spirit traditions of Native Americans; or to invoke the help of a Higher Power in twelve-step groups. In pursuing their spirituality, lesbians find the strength and pride they need to live and love in a homophobic society.

LESBIAN AND GAY RELIGION TIME LINE

BEFORE THE TWENTIETH CENTURY

1900 B.C.: According to the Book of Genesis, the cities of Sodom and Gomorrah are destroyed with fire and brimstone. This is interpreted by Philo of Alexandria centuries later, and then by religious writers, to have been a wrathful God's punishment for the homosexuality of the inhabitants. That interpretation, although common, hinges on an unlikely translation of the ambiguous Hebrew word meaning "to know." The term is used 943 times in the Old Testament: only 15 of those times is it a euphemism for sexual activity. According to many modern-day scholars, it is likely that the story of Sodom and Gomorrah did not involve homosexuality at all.

A.D. 60: Saint Paul wrote certain biblical passages, particularly Romans 1:26–27 and I Cor. 6–9, which are often used to prohibit/protest homosexuality. As twentieth-century scholar John Boswell indicates, this interpretation does not necessarily reflect Saint Paul's original meaning, which has been changed through translations.

380: St. Gregory of Nazianzus dismissed Sappho (610–580 B.C.)—usually called "the greatest love poet of the ancient world"—as "a lewd nymphomaniac" and ordered her books to be burned.

533: Homosexuality and blasphemy are proclaimed to be equally to blame for earthquakes, famines, and pestilences by Byzantine emperor Justinian I when he combines Roman law and Christian ethics. Castration is ordered for any lawbreaker.

1073: Pope Gregory VII ordered ecclesiastical authorities in Constantinople and Rome to burn what little of Sappho's works that were left. By the twelfth century, all that remained of her writings were two complete poems and a handful of fragments. In 1897, numerous ancient coffins lined with papier-mâché scraps of papyrus scrolls were found by archaeologists working in Egypt. The paper in the coffin turned out to be shredded fragments of Sappho's poetry, more of which was found wadded into the carcasses of mummified crocodiles and other animals at the same site. Out of twelve hundred lines that Sappho actually penned, we have only seven hundred.

1252: St. Thomas Aquinas begins his theological teaching. Aquinas pronounced that God created genitalia for no purpose other than reproduction and decreed that homosexual acts were unnatural and heretical. Though he did not originate these ideas, he had powerful influence with the church and the narrow-mindedness he espoused continues today.

1450–1453: The Spanish Inquisition is empowered by Pope Nicholas to investigate and punish homosexuality.

1620–1725: Approximately 350 persons were accused of witchcraft in colonial New England, of whom 78 percent were women and a number of those thought to have been lesbians. In total, thirty-five people were executed, twenty-eight of whom were women. More than half of the accusations, trials, and executions took place in the town of Salem, Massachusetts, from 1692–1693.

1641–1642: The Massachusetts Bay Colony became the first of several New England colonies to incorporate into its laws the language of Leviticus 20:13: "If a man lyeth with mankinde, as he lyeth with a woman, both of them have committed abomination, they both shall surely be put to death."

1656: Sexual relations between women became a capital offense in the colony of New Haven when the definition of sodomy was expanded to include lesbianism.

1682: A scandal arose in France surrounding the publishing of *Venus in the Cloister, or the Nun in her Smock,* a book about lesbian nuns written more for the excitement of the male reader than to document real life.

1700: Male confusion about lesbian sex reached a peak in Italy when Lodovico Maria Sinistrari, a Franciscan who attempted to codify appropriate punishments for sodomy in *Peccatum Mutum: The Secret Sin,* sought to enlighten the clergy about sexual practices between women.

    • Sinistrari rejected the ideas of other theologians that "if a woman gets upon a woman, and both fall to thrusting at one another mutually, it may happen that the seed of her on top may be injected into the natural vase of her lying under." Thus, the sodomy occurs only when the "seed" is received and, should the "seed" not be received "it is only pollution." He insisted that sodomy cannot be performed this way because "woman's seed cannot be injected."

    • Sinistrari also questioned theologians' definition of sodomy as penetration of one woman by the other with some form of dildo, with them both facing punishment or death for the act, because this sexual act would only leave one partner satisfied. Finally, Sinistrari offered his own definition of sodomy, which explains how both women receive gratification. He stated that some women have very large clitorises with which they can penetrate another woman, thus female sodomy consists only of this act and they cannot be absolved; any other act is pollution and can be absolved by the confessor.

1850: Suffragist Antoinette Brown Blackwell, romantic friend and sister-in-law of Lucy Stone, graduated from Oberlin college, making her the first woman divinity student in the United States.

THE TWENTIETH CENTURY

1916: The first gay church, an Anglican-derived Liberal Catholic Church, was founded in Sydney, Australia, by Charles Webster Leadbeater.

1946: George Hyde, a youth minister in the independent Catholic Movement, formed a church in Atlanta that is thought to have been the first American church organized primarily for homosexuals.

1956: The first documented gay church, The Church of ONE Brotherhood, was founded in Los Angeles by Chuck Rowland. It lasted only a year.

1957: The Catholic church in England, while emphasizing that it believed homosexuality to be a sin, recommended its decriminalization by endorsing the Wolfden Report. This report, published by the British government, recommended the legalization of homosexual acts between consenting adults. Three years later, after much debate nationwide, a proposal to adopt these recommendations was defeated by a two-to-one margin in the House of Commons.

1964: The Council on Religion and the Homosexual was founded in San Francisco by the Reverend Ted McIlvenna and other clergy members "to promote continuing dialogue between the church and the homosexual."

1967: The Glide Methodist Church and the Glide Foundation of San Francisco launched one of the first economic boycotts on behalf of gay rights by not only stating that they would not buy goods and services from companies that discriminated against homosexuals, but encouraging others to follow their lead.

1968: Rev. Troy Perry, a gay Pentecostal minister, conducted a service for twelve people gathered at a house in Huntington Park, California. This was the first meeting of what was to become the United Fellowship of Metropolitan Community Churches, a nondenominational Christian church for the gay community. Only two years later, MCC had over 500 members.

1969: The Church of Christ's Council on Christian Social Action adopted one of the first position statements on homosexuality, in which it called for the decriminalization of homosexual activities between consenting adults.

  • The first denominational religious organization for homosexuals began as a rap group for gay and lesbian Catholics in San Diego. After moving to Los Angeles, the first chapter of Dignity was founded in 1970.

1970s: There tended to be a spiritual separation between lesbian-feminists and lesbians who were part of the gay movement. Lesbian-feminists criticized the move of other lesbians to participate in mixed gay groups within established churches, Metropolitan Community Churches (MCC), or small groups within Judaism, saying that no matter what reforms were attempted in traditional organized religions, the churches and synagogues still perpetuated patriarchy. According to historian Lillian Faderman, lesbian-feminists didn't want their spirituality to be merely inner directed or a revision of Christianity. God the Father should not be traded for God the Mother, leaving the inherent power structure and other problems intact; rather, lesbian-feminists used spiritual models of ancient cultures where women had secular power as well as religious power.

1971–1985: Eighteen MCC churches experienced arson.

1971: Z. Budapest founded the first feminist coven, the Susan B. Anthony Coven #1, and explained the rebirth of witches: "Women lost their power through religion. We were determined to get it back again through a religion that had always belonged to women."

1972: Following a rap session at the Los Angeles Metropolitan Community Church, two gay men and two lesbians discovered they were all Jewish and decided to form their own temple. Beth Chayim Chadashim held their first service in July 1972 and were chartered on July 19,1974 by the Union of American Hebrew Congregations, making it not only the first gay and lesbian synagogue, but also the first gay religious organization of any kind to be officially recognized by a national body. In 1977, the congregation acquired its own building, dedicated in 1981.

  • The United Church of Christ in San Carlos, California, ordained William Johnson, making it the first Christian denomination to ordain an openly gay candidate. Johnson came out in 1970 while studying at the Pacific School of Religion in Berkeley, California.

1973: The first bisexual religious organization, The Committee of Friends on Bisexuality, was founded by Stephen Donaldson (aka Robert Martin) in Ithaca, New York. They issued the "Ithaca Statement on Bisexuality," during their first gathering in June 1972, which is thought to be the first statement on bisexuality—as well as condoning bisexuality—by any religious body. The committee ended in 1977.

 • The Unitarian Universalists became the first denomination to establish a lesbian and gay office. Three years earlier, a resolution was passed by the general assembly banning discrimination against gays in the church.

1975: Z. Budapest, a lesbian witch, was arrested for fortune-telling when she did a reading for an undercover policewoman. She claimed that not one law enforcement officer touched her during the arrest because she had threatened to hex the first person who did with nightmares. She was convicted of the offense, but tried to get her case appealed with the hope of seeing all U.S. laws against witchcraft—and the traditional ways witches make a living—revoked.

 • The "Covenant of the Goddess," a National Coalition of Covens, is founded. Among its founders were a number of open lesbians.

1977: Ellen Marie Barrett was ordained as an Episcopal priest in Manhattan, New York City, making her the first open lesbian to be ordained by a major Christian denomination.

1978: Rabbi Allen Bennet allowed himself to be outed in the *San Francisco Examiner*, making him the first openly gay rabbi. After becoming a rabbi in 1974, Bennet moved to San Francisco to continue his postgraduate studies and joined a gay synagogue, Congregation Sha'ar Zahav, where he then became the rabbi in 1979.

 • *Witchcraft and the Gay Counterculture*, by Arthur Evans, a historical view on heresy, gayness, and the witch hunts of Europe and England, is published.

1984: The Unitarian Universalists became the first modern Christian denomination to perform gay and lesbian union ceremonies.

1986: A fourteen-page letter issued by Pope John Paul II called gay people "intrinsically disordered" and stated that homosexuality could never be reconciled with church doctrine. From 1986 to 1991, fifty Dignity chapters nationwide were expelled from Roman Catholic Church property and had to find new places to meet when church officials complied with the order to withdraw all support from gay organizations.

1988: Catholic nun Sister Mary Kregar was ordered to pay damages of one million dollars to Steve Woolverton of Brownsville, Texas, for seducing his wife and destroying his marriage. Woolverton argued that his wife's joining the Brownsville Catholic Diocese choir apparently led to the breach. The church was also directed to pay five hundred thousand dollars for negligence, even though it had dismissed Kregar after learning of the affair. Kregar left the Franciscan order in August 1984 and became a social worker.

 • Mary Elizabeth Clark took vows of poverty, chastity, and obedience at an Episcopal church in San Clemente, California, making her the first transsexual nun, though the religious community she founded, Sisters of St. Elizabeth of Hungary, remains unsanctioned by the bishop of the Episcopal Church. A man named Michael Clark until 1974, Sister Mary Elizabeth is also the only person to serve in the military as both a male and a female.

1992: MCC's application for observer status within the National Council of Churches of Christ (NCC) was voted to not be acted upon. The debate regarding MCC's status caused some NCC member churches to side with MCC, including the United Church of Christ, the United Methodist Church, and the Swedenborgian Church. Several other groups indicated that they would pull out of the group if MCC's request were granted, particularly orthodox and predominantly black denominations.

• A four-page letter from the Vatican entitled "Some Considerations Concerning the Catholic Response to Legislative Proposals on the Non-Discrimination of Homosexual Persons" is issued to U.S. bishops. Basically, the letter stated the Vatican's opposition to such legislation and urged bishops to actively oppose gay civil rights laws. Bishops in Seattle, Honolulu, and other places made the surprising move of publicly dissenting.

OTHER STATISTICS AND FACTS

There are words in Greek for same-sex sexual activities, yet they never appear in the original text of the New Testament.

• "Joining a religious community from about 500 [A.D.] to about 1300 [A.D.] was probably the surest way of meeting other gay people [in Europe]," according to John Boswell in *Homosexuality and Religious Life: A Historical Approach*, written in 1989.

• The word *homosexual* did not appear in any translation of the Christian Bible until 1946.

• There are approximately 1 billion adherents of Christianity in the world and 142 million in the United States, including 79 million Protestants and 52 million Roman Catholics—equivalent to 60 percent of the United States' population. According to a public opinion survey in 1983, roughly 22 percent of the U.S. population age eighteen and older were Evangelical Christians. Of these, 88.7 percent expressed strong opposition to homosexuality.

• Buddhism is notable among world religions in that it does not condemn homosexuality. Also notably tolerant are Wicca and a number of native religions.

• The world's fastest growing religion, Islam, has more than six million followers in the United States. Islamic law punishes men and women found guilty of public homosexual behavior that is witnessed by four adult males, though the Koran does not condemn homosexuality per se.

• Pat Robertson's Christian Coalition, among whose primary objectives are to oppose homosexuality and restrict gay and lesbian rights, has over 250,000 members in forty-nine states.

• Père-Lachaise cemetery, in Paris, has been called "the world's gayest cemetery," with many notable lesbians, gays, and bisexuals buried there. The list includes Oscar Wilde, Gertrude Stein, Alice B. Toklas, Sarah Bernhardt, Marcel Proust, Isadora

Duncan, Jane Avril, Colette, and Anna de Noailles (the "French Sappho"). Rosa Bonheur, Natalie Micus, and Anna Klumpke are all buried together on the Micus family plot. Two nineteenth-century balloonists, Croce-Spinelli and Sivel, were buried together here after they were killed in 1875 in a ballooning accident in India. Their much-talked-about monument shows them lying naked under a sculpted sheet that covers them from the waist down, hand in hand, holding flowers.

• The Cathedral of Hope Metropolitan Community Church in Dallas, Texas, is the world's largest lesbian and gay congregation with 892 active members and 2,100 constituent members.

• There are currently 23,561 Roman Catholic churches, 200 Scientology churches, and 230 MCC churches in the United States. Worldwide, MCC has 42,000 voting members and nonvoting adherents in almost 300 churches in sixteen countries, with their congregations growing at a rate of approximately 10 percent a year.

• MCC's income of over $10 million in contributions annually and property holdings worth $50 million, makes it the largest nonprofit group serving lesbians and gay men.

• New York City's MCC passes out 1,500 bags of groceries to families every week and has six beds for the homeless.

• Dignity, an organization of Catholic lesbians and gay men working within the Roman Catholic Church, has over 6,000 dues-paying members and as many as 18,000 participating in its services and activities.

• Congregation Beth Simchat Torah (CBST) is the largest gay and lesbian synagogue in the world. With more than 1,000 members, it is also one of the largest synagogues in New York.

• During the High Holidays of Rosh Hashanah and Yom Kippur, CBST hosts some 2,500 people at a special service at New York City's Jacob K. Javits Convention Center.

• A conservative estimate of the percentage of homosexual men and women in the Catholic priesthood and religious life is around 30 percent, with approximately the same number in the rabbinate and the Protestant ministry.

THE MOST OFTEN QUOTED REFERENCES TO HOMOSEXUALITY IN THE BIBLE (KING JAMES VERSION)

LEVITICUS 18:22

"Thou shalt not lie with mankind, as with womankind: it is an abomination."

LEVITICUS 20:13

"If a man also lie with mankind, as he lieth with a woman, both of them have committed an abomination: they shall surely be put to death; their blood shall be upon them."

Romans 1:26–27

(This is the only place in the Bible that appears to include lesbian sexuality.)

"For this cause God gave them up unto vile affections: *for even their women did change the natural use into that which is against nature* [our emphasis]: And likewise also the men, leaving the natural use of the woman, burned in their lust towards one another; men with men working that which is unseemly, and receiving in themselves that recompense of the error which was met."

Corinthians 6:9–10

"Know ye not that the unrighteous shall not inherit the kingdom of God? Be not deceived: neither fornicators, nor idolaters, nor adulterers, nor effeminate, nor abusers of themselves with mankind, nor thieves, nor covetous, nor drunkards, nor revilers, nor extortioners shall inherit the kingdom of God."

Some Responses

This crucial issue of homophobia has to be addressed. The six allusions in the Old Testament and the three in the New, are often used as an attempt to justify hatred or even murder and killing of gay brothers and lesbian sisters. The fact that Jesus himself never mentions it [homosexuality], means that it was not as significant to him as it is seemingly to a whole host of other Christians. . . . What is going on is an attempt to use or mobilize the Bible as an authority to reinforce a certain sense of what it means to be Black in the latter part of the twentieth century. What it means to be Black is primarily: Imposing certain controls and regulations over women, over gays, over lesbians, and policing these regulations.

—Cornell West

If we are going to take the Levitical law, we are going to have to take the whole law. That means: to combine fabrics is against the Levitical law, to tattoo one's skin is against the Levitical law, to eat certain kinds of seafood, such as shrimp is against the Levitical law. And so our challenge to the mainstream church is: How much of this law are you going to exclude, and choose to include, in order to oppress people—specifically lesbian and gay people?

—Rev. Zachary Jones, Pastor of Unity Fellowship Church, Brooklyn, New York

---

Is Homosexuality a Sin? Where Religious Leaders Have Stood

This is one of the most difficult questions for Judeo-Christian religious people. Many religions teach that homosexuality is condemned. But *nowhere* in the Bible is there mention of those whose true nature is homosexual. Neither the Ten Commandments nor the Gospels mention homosexuality. Bible scholars tell us that the oft-quoted (out of context) proscriptions in Leviticus 18:22 and 20:13 and St. Paul's Epistles Rom. 1:26–27, refer to male prostitution in temples: sexual practices by *heterosexuals*.

CATHOLIC

Because of the diverse conditions of humans, it happens that some acts are virtuous to some people, as appropriate and suitable to them, while the same are immoral for others, as inappropriate to them."

—SAINT THOMAS AQUINAS, *Summa Theologica*

Homosexuality has nothing necessarily to do with sin, sickness or failure. It is a different way of fulfilling God's plan. . . . Supposedly, the sin for which God destroyed Sodom was homosexuality. That's the great myth. I discovered through scholarly research that it was not true. The sin of Sodom and Gomorrah was inhospitality to a stranger . . . In Matthew, Jesus says to his disciples: "Go out and preach the Gospel. If you come to any town and they don't receive you well, if they're inhospitable, shake the sand from your sandals and it will be worse for that town than it was for Sodom." . . . The four Gospels are totally silent on the issue of homosexuality.

—JOHN J. MCNEILL, S.J. in an interview with Charles Ortleb in the journal *Christopher Street*, Oct. 1976

PROTESTANT

Do I believe that homosexuality is a sin? . . . Homosexuality, quite like heterosexuality, is neither a virtue nor an accomplishment. Homosexual orientation is a mysterious gift of God's grace. . . . homosexuality is a gift, neither a virtue or a sin. What they *do [how about one does?] with their [one's or his/her?] homosexuality, however, is definitely their [one's] personal, moral and spiritual responsibility. Their behavior as homosexuals may be very sinful—brutal, exploitative, selfish, promiscuous, superficial. Their behavior as homosexuals, on the other hand, may be beautiful—tender, considerate, loyal, other-centered, profound.*

With this interpretation of the mystery that must be attributed to both heterosexual and homosexual orientations, I clearly do not believe that homosexuality is a sin.

—BISHOP MELVIN E. WHEATLY, JR., Methodist, retired, November 20, 1981

JEWISH

Above all else, Judaism has always stressed the importance and sanctity of the individual. The ancient rabbis likened each human life to the entire world. "Why did God create each human being different, not stamping us out like so many coins?" asked the rabbis. "To show us that each person is unique," they answered. Judaism has always gloried in the individuality of human life, and it has always cherished freedom as the vehicle through which each unique individual can develop his or her own potential.

It is for this reason, and because we Jews have learned first hand how stifling and destructive oppression is, that the Reform Jewish movement in all its branches has called for gay rights legislation and for loving acceptance of gay people. While all branches of Judaism do not agree, liberal Judaism recognizes that religious strictures against homosexuality were a product of their time and place, an ancient age in which existence itself depended upon each member of society having children to populate the frontier and the army. That was a long time ago, before modern science and psychiatry brought us new understanding of human nature. We Jews have always incorporated the latest knowledge in our Judaism—this adaptability is why we have survived, and why so many other Biblical prohibitions are disregarded. Thinking Jews today, indeed all thinking people, will refuse to invoke homophobic rules from these long-forgotten laws. After all, even the most Orthodox no longer stone disobedient children to death and fundamentalist Christians do not call for us to keep kosher, only two of the rules found in the Bible.

If we Jews, always being victimized for being different, are not accepting, who in God's name will be?

—Rabbi Charles D. Lippman, 1985

Source: Excerpted from "Can We Understand? A Guide for Parents," prepared by New York City Parents and Friends of Lesbians and Gays, 1983. Reprinted with permission.

Incredible Statements by Religious Homophobes

If homosexuality were the normal way, God would have made Adam and Bruce.

—Anita Bryant

There's a lot of talk these days about homosexuals coming out of the closet. I didn't know they'd been in the closet. I do know they've always been in the gutter.

—Rev. Jerry Falwell

Sweating is good for a boy and will help him avoid homosexual tendencies.

—Jack Hyles, Baptist minister

Homosexuals or lesbians cannot produce a baby, a family or a society. . . . There are no sexual preferences. The assumption that there are is in itself a defiance of nature, creation and God.

—American Council of Christian Churches

. . . those who behave in a homosexual fashion . . . shall not enter the kingdom of God.

—Pope John Paul II

They [homosexuals] should be killed through government means.

—DANIEL LOVELY, Baptist minister

Homosexuality makes God vomit.

—JAY GRIMSTEAD, fundamentalist

God made no one homosexual . . . God makes everyone heterosexual.

—WILLIAM CONSIGLIO

This is a socialist, antifamily political movement that encourages women to leave their husbands, kill their children, practice witchcraft, destroy capitalism, and become lesbians.

—PAT ROBERTSON

WHERE MAJOR JUDEO-CHRISTIAN RELIGIONS STAND ON HOMOSEXUALITY

Question: *In your opinion, does God regard homosexuality as a sin?*

Dr. Stayton (Baptist): "Absolutely not! There is nothing in the Bible or in my own theology that would lead me to believe that God regards homosexuality as sin. God is interested in our relationships with ourselves, others, the things in our lives, and with God."

Bishop Spong (Episcopalian): "Our prejudice rejects people or things outside our understanding. But the God of creation speaks and declares, 'I have looked out on everything I have made and behold it (is) very good.' (Gen. 1:31) The word of God in Christ says that we are loved, valued, redeemed and counted as precious no matter how we might be valued by a prejudiced world."

Bishop Olson (Lutheran): "Of course not. God could (not) care less about humanly devised categories that label and demean those who do not somehow fit into the norm of those in control. God made all of us and did not make all of us alike. Diversity is beautiful in creation. How we live our lives, in either affirming or destructive ways, is God's concern, but being either homosexually oriented or heterosexually oriented is neither a divine plus or minus."

Rabbi Marder (Judaism—Reform): "The God I worship endorses loving, committed, monogamous relationships, regardless of the gender of those involved."

Rabbi Dr. Teutsch (Judaism—Reconstructionist): "Homosexuality—as is true of heterosexuality—is a naturally occurring sexual orientation that can be expressed in more ethical and less ethical ways. In itself homosexual lovemaking is not sinful."

Dr. McGrath (Former Mormon): "I believe that the Creator of our natural erotic attractions, whether they are for opposite or same-sex persons, views our eroticism as an intrinsic and beautiful part of who God intended us to be. God did not intend that there would be one way of being sexual. Even among heterosexual people, there is no one 'right' way to be sexual. . . . I believe God is pleased when we respond to our unique form of sexuality in ways that are life-giving. I believe that it is life-giving when sexual relationships reflect a high degree of mutuality, love and justice."

Rev. Holfelder (Presbyterian): "No, I do not think that God regards homosexuality as a sin. I believe that one's sexual preference is first and foremost a matter of biology (creation) and only secondarily a matter of choice (responsibility). Since I also believe that all God creates is good, I conclude that human sexuality (not a matter of choice for anyone) is good, whether that sexual expression be heterosexual or homosexual."

Sister Gramick (Roman Catholic): "God has created people with romantic and physical attractions to the same sex, as well as those with attractions to the opposite sex. Many, if not most, people, we are now discovering, have both kinds of attractions in varying degrees. All of these feelings are natural and are considered good and blessed by God. These feelings and attractions are not sinful."

Dr. Nelson (United Church of Christ): "I am convinced that our sexuality and our sexual orientations, whatever they may be, are a gift from God. Sexual sin does not reside in our orientations, but rather in expressing our sexuality in ways that harm, oppress, or use others for our own selfish gratification. When we express ourselves sexually in ways that are loving and just, faithful and responsible, then I am convinced that God celebrates our sexuality, whatever our orientation may be."

Dr. Cobb (United Methodist): "Surely being attracted to persons of the same sex is not, as such, a sin. But of course how we act in our attractions, towards whichever sex, is often sinful. The ideal is to be responsible and faithful rather than self-indulgent. Unfortunately, society does not encourage responsible and faithful relations with persons of the same sex. That makes the situation of the homosexual very difficult."

Question: *In your opinion, do the Scriptures object to homosexuality?*

Dr. Stayton (Baptist): "There is *nothing* in the Bible regarding homosexual orientation. . . . I lead Bible study programs on this subject and am convinced that the Bible does not address the issue of a person's sexual orientation."

Rabbi Marder (Judaism—Reform): "I believe that the Hebrew Bible strongly condemns homosexuality. While it is part of my tradition, I do not regard all Biblical laws as binding on me. The Biblical condemnation of homosexuality is based on human ignorance, suspicion of those who are different, and an overwhelming concern for ensuring the survival of the people."

Rabbi Dr. Teutsch (Judaism—Reconstructionist): "The Scriptural references to homosexuality make no comment on lesbianism. They object to male homosexuality on three grounds: cultic prostitution, unnaturalness, and 'spilling seed' or Onanism. Gay men today are not involved in cultic acts. And the spilling of the seed through heterosexual, homosexual, or masturbatory acts is not an issue with me. Thus I take this prohibition no more seriously than many others, such as that against lending money at interest, that do not make sense in this time and place."

Bishop Olson (Lutheran): "Biblical scholars are busy restudying the few verses which have often been regarded as anti-homosexual. One thing is clear, these few verses do not refer to homosexuality as we understand and use that term today. . . . Here is a partial list of verses that has every right in being equally addressed to homosexual or heterosexual Christians: John 3:16; Galatians 3:27; Ephesians 2:8,9; Romans 3:21–24, Acts 10."

Sister Gramick (Roman Catholic): "When read at face value, the Scriptures have nothing positive to say about homogenital behavior. However, most Christians do not interpret the Bible literally; they try to understand the Scriptures in their historical and cultural context and see what meaning the Scriptures have for us today. . . . It is unfair of us to expect or impose a twentieth century mentality and understanding about equality of genders, races, and sexual orientations on the Biblical writers. We must be able to distinguish the eternal truths the Bible is meant to convey from the cultural forms and attitudes expressed there."

Dr. Schulz (Unitarian Universalist): "Most of the Old Testament is surely not an appropriate resource from which to obtain guidance regarding contemporary ethics! Turning to the New Testament, we discover that Jesus has nothing whatsoever to say regarding homosexuality. Inasmuch as he frequently condemned others of whose behavior he disapproved, it is significant that he makes no references to homosexuals or their practices."

Question: In your opinion, does God approve of two gay or lesbian individuals pledging their love to each other in a religious ceremony and raising children who may be born to them or adopted by them?

Dr. Stayton (Baptist): "Absolutely. God's concern must be that we are good and loving parents, whether gay or straight, and that we bring our children up to be independent of us, loving individuals with a value system that strives to accept, understand, and love all that is good."

Bishop Wood (Episcopalian): "Yes. The image of relationships God seeks for us is clear: self-giving, caring, faithful."

Rabbi Dr. Teutsch (Judaism—Reconstructionist): "Yes. The ideal religious way is one of long-term mutual commitment in a family setting. Those who have not obtained it deserve no condemnation; those who create permanent relationships and/or are raising children deserve our fullest support."

Bishop Olson (Lutheran): "Religious leaders are asked to invoke God's blessings on farms, homes, cemeteries, and people's pets. . . . What is so strange then about blessing the covenant of fidelity of two committed and loving persons who are gay or lesbian? If the home and family they seek to create is a place of love, sacrifice, fidelity and mutual respect it is surely a fit place for the raising of children."

Dr. McGrath (former Mormon): "God approves of all relationships that are life-giving. . . . My experience with gay couples and lesbian couples who have pledged their love to each other has taught me that they are no less capable than heterosexual couples in creating life-giving relationships into which children can be nurtured and loved."

Rev. Nugent (Roman Catholic): ". . . A religious ceremony would say clearly that the couple took their relationship with God seriously and would also [bear] witness to the social impact of their relationship on others of the faith community. Caring for children born of prior heterosexual unions, adopted or foster children by a same-gender couple would not only be 'approved' by God, but would be a serious religious obligation coming from one's belief in and commitment to God."

Dr. Nelson (United Church): "Yes, I believe God deeply approves of loving, committed, same-sex covenants, and the parenting for such children as may come to them. I rejoice in those churches and synagogues that now celebrate such unions, and I pray for the day when many more will do so."

Dr. Cobb (United Methodist): "I believe this pattern would be the one most pleasing to God of all the options available to gays and lesbians. Of course, the raising of children is not essential to a healthy relationship."

SOURCE: From "Is Homosexuality a Sin?" (1992), reprinted with permission of Parents, Families and Friends of Lesbians and Gays.

SOURCES FOR FURTHER READING

BOOKS AND ARTICLES

Anzaldúa, Gloria. "O.K. Momma, Who the Hell Am I?: An Interview with Luisa Teish," in *This Bridge Called My Back,* edited by Cherríe Moraga and Gloria Anzaldúa. Kitchen Table: Woman of Color Press, 1981, 1983.

Blumenfeld, Warren J., and Diane Raymond. *Looking at Gay and Lesbian Life.* Alyson, 1993.

Boswell, John. *Christianity, Social Tolerance, and Homosexuality.* University of Chicago Press, 1980.

———. "Homosexuality and Religious Life: A Historical Approach," in *Homosexuality, the Priesthood and the Religious Life,* Jeannine Gramick, ed. Crossroad, 1989.

———. *Same-Sex Unions in Pre-Modern Europe.* Villard, 1994.

Boyd, Malcolm, and Nancy Wilson, eds. *Amazing Grace, Stories of Lesbian and Gay Faith.* Crossing Press, 1991.

Brant, Beth. *Writing as Witness: Essay and Talk.* The Women's Press, 1994.

———, ed. *A Gathering of Spirit.* The Women's Press, 1989.

Budapest, Z. *The Holy Book of Women's Mysteries.* Wingbow Press, 1989.

Christ, Carol P., ed. *Diving Deep and Surfacing: Women Writers on a Spiritual Quest.* Beacon Press, 1980.

Commission on Social Justice. *The Catholic Church, Homosexuality and Social Justice: The Report by the Task Force on Gay and Lesbian Issues*. Archdiocese of San Francisco, 1982.

Comstock, Gary David. *Violence Against Lesbians and Gay Men*. Columbia University Press, 1991.

Curb, Rosemary. *Lesbian Nuns: Breaking the Silence*. Naiad Press, 1983.

D'Antonio, Michael. *Heaven on Earth: Dispatches from America's Spiritual Frontier*. Crown, 1992.

Dean, Amy. *Proud to Be: Daily Meditations for Lesbians and Gay Men*. Dutton, 1994.

Denman, Rosemary. *Let My People In: A Lesbian Minister Tells of Her Struggles to Live Openly and Maintain Her Ministry*. Morrow, 1990.

Dynes, Wayne R., ed. *Encyclopedia of Homosexuality*. Garland, 1990.

———., and Stephen Donaldson, eds. *Homosexuality and Religion and Philosophy*. Garland, 1992.

Faderman, Lillian. *Odd Girls and Twilight Lovers*. Columbia University Press, 1991.

———. *Surpassing the Love of Men*. Morrow, 1981.

Gallagher, John. "Is God Gay?," *The Advocate*, December 13, 1994.

Hageman, Alice L., ed. *Sexist Religion and Women in the Church: No More Silence!*. Harvard Divinity Press, 1974.

Harding, Rick. "Minneapolis Panel: Catholic Officials Violated Bias Law." *The Advocate*, January 1, 1991.

Helminiak, Daniel, *What the Bible Really Says About Homosexuality*. Alamo Square Press, 1994.

Hunter, James Davison. *American Evangelicalism*. Rutgers University Press, 1983.

McNeill, John J. *The Church and the Homosexual*. Farrar, Straus, Giroux, 1994.

Melton, J. Gordon. *The Churches Speak On: Homosexuality*. Gale Research, 1991.

O'Neill, Craig, and Kathleen Ritter. *Coming Out Within: Stories of Spiritual Awakening for Lesbians and Gay Men*. Harper, 1992.

O'Neill, John J. *Freedom, Glorious Freedom: The Spiritual Journey to the Fullness of Life for Gays, Lesbians, and Everybody Else*. Beacon, 1994.

Radford Ruether, Rosemary. *Religion & Sexism: Images of Women in the Jewish and Christian Traditions*. Simon & Schuster, 1974.

Richards, Dell. *Lesbian Lists*. Alyson, 1990.

Robinson, David J. "Troy Perry: Gay Advocate," in *Gay Speak: Gay Male and Lesbian Communication*. James W. Chesebro, ed. Pilgrim Press, 1981.

Schorr, Daniel. "Rise of the Religious Right." *The New Leader,* September 21, 1992.

Singer, Bennet L., and David Deschamps, eds. *Gay and Lesbian Stats: A Pocket Guide of Facts and Figures*. New Press, 1994.

Stone, Merlin. *When God Was a Woman*. HBJ/Harvest, 1976.

Stuart, Dr. Elizabeth. *Daring to Speak Love's Name: A Gay and Lesbian Prayer Book*. Hamish Hamilton/Penguin Group, 1992.

"The Universal Fellowship of Metropolitan Community Churches Fact Sheet."
   Universal Fellowship of Metropolitan Community Churches, 1993.
Villarosa, Linda, ed. *Body and Soul: The Black Woman's Guide to Physical Health
   and Emotional Well-Being*. HarperPerennial, 1994.
Williams, Robert. *Just as I Am: A Practical Guide to Being Out, Proud, and Chris-
   tian*. Crown, 1992.
Yamaguchi Fletcher, Lynne. *The First Gay Pope and Other Records*. Alyson, 1992.

NEWSLETTERS

Living Streams
P.O. Box 178
Concorde, CA 94522
Evangelical/charismatic publication
   providing a forum for Christian gays
   and lesbians

Malchus
6036 Richmond Highway, #301
Alexandria, VA 22303
Phone: 703/329-7896

Marilyn Medusa Gay-Pagan Journal
8701 NW 35th Street
Coral Springs, FL 33605

New Direction
1608 N. Cahuenga Blvd., #B-440
Los Angeles, CA 90028
Publication for gay and lesbian
   Mormons, relatives, and friends

Open Hands
3801 N. Keeler Ave.
Chicago, IL 60641
Phone: 312/736-5526; Fax: 312/736-
   5475
Resources for ministries affirming the
   diversity of human sexuality

The Second Stone
P.O. Box 8340
New Orleans, LA 70182
Phone: 504/891-7555
Religious news, information, features

Solitary
P.O. Box 6091
Madison, WI 53716
Phone: 608/244-0072
Quarterly journal for those practicing
   spiritual traditions alone while
   seeking dialogue with those who
   share a similar solitary pagan path

PUBLICATIONS SPECIFICALLY FOR WOMEN

*At the Crossroads: Feminism,
   Spirituality, and Science Exploring
   Earthly and Unearthly Reality*
P.O. Box 112
Saint Paul, AR 72760

Cauldron
P.O. Box 14779
Long Beach, CA 90803-1345

Daughters of Sarah
P.O. Box 411179
Chicago, IL 60641-1179
The magazine for Christian feminists

Woman of Power Magazine
P.O. Box 2785
Orleans, MA 02653
Phone: 508/240-7877
Feminism, spirituality, and politics

PROFILE

Sonia Ivette Roman/Singing Cow

"Singing Cow is my spiritual name. My mundane name is Sonia Ivette Roman." By day a customer service representative, Sonia is "out of the broom closet, so to speak. Everyone at work knows I'm a witch. Friends know. Family know." She is high priestess of Polyhymnia Coven in Queens, New York, and has taken quite a journey to get there.

"I was raised Roman Catholic. I was a *good* Catholic, my family were pretty good Catholics. We are Puerto Rican, so we also believed in spiritualism and Santeria. I had a very firm belief in the saints, we're talking from age five on, I used to carry around these little plastic images of saints that would come in this black vinyl holder with the saint on one side and a prayer on the other side. I had Theresa of the flowers, Theresa of Lucia, and my mom hated it because she was convinced I'd never marry. It was folklore, that you would never marry if you carried St. Theresa.

"I was a Catholic until I was twelve, then I met up with some born-again Christians and, along with my mom, became a born-again Christian. . . . Once I got into it, I was a *very* good born-again Christian, because that's just the way I was: no pants, no rock music, no makeup. I had a full-immersion water baptism at Rockaway Beach in October. It was freezing, but I loved it. They dunked me and, whoa! It was very pagan: You have the sand, the water, the dunking—it was wonderful.

"When I was fourteen I went to music and art high school and fell in love with my best friend, a woman. I came out to myself as bisexual and, knowing everything that I knew was in the Bible, I knew that this wasn't going to fly. So I left the church. This was very difficult to do because all of my friends were born-again Christians, except for my best friend who was Jewish. She was also a very avid feminist and she lent me books on feminism, which opened up my world a lot. We are still best friends after fifteen years.

"I drifted into Zen Buddhism, and loved it. I was a very good Buddhist. Pattern, pattern, pattern, I see a pattern emerging. I left Buddhism when I was eighteen, it was not in the body enough for me; there was a real negation of the body. I began to read some book about Wicca, and I actually found a coven that I studied with the summer before I went off to college at Oberlin in Ohio.

"In college I met a woman who I call my Goddess mother, because she was the one who really introduced me to *good* books about Wicca, as opposed to the trash I had been reading before. We formed a pagan students alliance. It was very loose, as pagans tend to be. Some of us were Wiccan and some of us were neopagans. One of our big events was bringing Starhawk over as a campus thing.

"While I had been in college, I was still kind of researching my cultural roots: the Santeria, and things like that. Once I left and moved to Boston, I started going to the Wyrd Sisters: A loose, eclectic group of people (I don't even know if I'd call it a coven) in which most of the people were gay or bisexual. It was through the

Wyrd Sisters that I started going to festivals, and it was at a festival called 'Rites of Spring' that I met Richard doing a queer ritual eight years ago."

Rich Wandel is the high priest to Sonia's priestess in their coven, Polyhymnia. Covens in New York, including theirs, tend to be apartment-sized covens. They meet roughly twice a month, and for the eight holidays or sabbaths that Wiccans usually celebrate. Their coven is open to both men and women, gay, straight, or bisexual.

Polyhymnia is a member of the Covenant of the Goddess (COG) the national organization of covens and solitary and individual witches. It is a church and is recognized as such under tax laws and things of that nature, but again there is no authority here, there is no dogma. Through COG, they help each other, support each other, work at dispelling false images of the craft, and help protect each other when the government or others try to shut groups down on the grounds of their religion. Things like this have been happening recently in Florida. "Both the coven we come out of, Kathexis, and Polyhymnia are very involved in COG, and I've been on the national board for the past three years."

Gardnerian witchcraft is a tradition that passes down the lineage through its third degree. The third degree denotes elder, or high priest and priestess, but the learning starts before then with the outer court. Training takes place in this circle, and that ultimately leads to initiation. In most traditions, witches are initiated.

The idea of Wicca in general, not just the Gardnerian tradition, is to empower people to do for themselves, to have their own personal contact with the divine, especially the Goddess. Wicca is not a religion, nor is theirs a coven, with the expectation that the high priest and priestess always do for the members.

Says Sonia, "Wicca is about doing it yourself, dispelling the notion that only certain people can do things. The priestess or priest isn't the only one with power. Everyone has the ability to create magic in their life, one just needs to know the things that can help achieve it." But with the magic, warns Sonia, comes a responsibility. Using magic to force the will of another person (also called black magic) is considered totally unethical in the Wiccan community.

"When you know that magic works, then you know that doing certain things are harmful. We do spell work for healing, and we generally talk a lot about magic before we do it. The idea should be clear as to why we are doing this, what is the motivation, is it the highest good for all involved, or do we have personal interest. We do a lot of soul searching before we do magic.

"It is so difficult to describe what Wicca means in my life. There is a real sense that the Goddess is always around. Looking at wood makes me think of Her. The real stereotypical things, the moon, trees, make me think of her, too. When the Goddess is everywhere, there is very little that is not ritual. I guess my job as a priestess is to point that out to people who are learning, that the Goddess is everywhere, you just need to be open to it.

If you are interested in more information about Polyhymnia, write a brief letter to Polyhymnia, P.O. Box 6208, Long Island City, NY 11106.

FEATURE

Native American Female Berdaches

The Native American lesbian and gay man is often referred to as *berdache*, a French term. Colonial French explorers were the first to use the word *berdache* to describe a male Indian who specialized in the work of women and formed emotional and sexual relationships with other men. But many tribes had female berdaches, too—women who took on men's work and married other women.

The Native words for such people vary within different tribal languages. The word *hermaphrodite* was repeatedly used by observers, without having any physical basis, to refer to an individual who would today be identified as a homosexual transvestite or transgendered individual.

Several reports suggest that homosexuals often performed religious and ceremonial functions among their people, and before Christianity, they generally occupied an institutionalized, important, and respected position within many Native groups. The berdache was often the tribe or band's doctor, medicine man/woman, leading scalp dancer, matchmaker, or storyteller. As well as these documented reports of lesbianism, many of the Native myths contain references to homosexuality, both male and female, as well as figures with a dual-sexed nature.

Many documents suggest that Native societies were very divided along sexual lines—a strict sexual division of labor, something that is said to be a key to understanding the character of homosexuality among Native Americans.

Some important female berdaches are described below.

WOMAN CHIEF (CROW)

Woman Chief, also known as Barcheeampe (Pine Leaf), is the most famous female war leader in the history of the upper Missouri tribes. At the age of ten, she was taken prisoner by the Crows. Her masculine habits were noted early on by the warrior to whom she belonged. Her foster father encouraged her in these pursuits partly to humor her and partly for his own comfort.

Woman Chief quickly learned the bow and arrow, and in later years carried a gun. She was a rival to any hunter with her shooting skill and riding expertise. She never dressed as a man, choosing to dress like the rest of the females except for her hunting arms. When her foster father was killed, she became both father and mother to his children.

Once during a negotiation with the Blackfeet tribe, she was the subject of an unprovoked attack. Woman Chief not only escaped unharmed, but killed two of the five attackers herself. This event won her much praise in the tribe, and the next year she headed her own war party against the Blackfeet. After many successful battles, she was elevated to a point of honor and respect that is not often reached even by male warriors. The elders of the tribe believed she led a charmed life, and she was soon the third ranking chief out of 160 lodges.

Ranking so high in the social spectrum, Woman Chief bought herself a wife to do the female work for her. She went through the traditional formula of Indian marriage, and finding it convenient to have a woman around the house, took three more wives in later years. Now she had all the things that equaled success in her tribe: fame, honor, standing, riches of women. For twenty years she lived the warrior/hunter's life. Then, in the summer of 1854, while on a friendly mission to another tribe, she was killed.

KAÚXUMA NÚPIKA (KUTENAI)

The Kutenai Indians had their home in western Montana and neighboring parts of Idaho and British Columbia. When the Kutenai berdache was a young woman, she was said to have been quite large and heavy boned. She wished to marry, but was rejected by the men in the tribe due to her size. She ran away with some white fur traders that were passing through the region, married one of their servants, and then disappeared for a year. She then returned to her people and told quite a tale. She said that her husband had operated on her and turned her into a man, and spoke of his supernatural power in order to convince them. She changed her name to Kaúxuma Núpika (Gone to the Spirits).

She then began to dress and behave as a man and decided that she wanted a wife. She encountered some problems in trying to get maidens to marry her and had to seek the company of divorced and widowed women. The women she courted seemed to be aware that she was a woman, and they were all made fun of openly within their communities. The Kutenai berdache was insecure and jealous of one of her lover's ex-husbands. She accused the lover of having an affair and began to physically abuse her. This cycle of courtship, love, jealousy, and abuse played itself out several times in her life.

The Kutenai berdache began to go on excursions with men, who soon discovered that she was really a woman and threatened to expose her. She eventually began to travel with another woman, described as her wife, and there are several accounts of them by white travelers. They were known as bold adventurous amazons and well-instructed cheats, who conned white people.

The Kutenai berdache and her companion dropped out of the historical record for many years. Then, on June 13, 1837, while serving as an intermediary in Flathead-Blackfoot peace negotiations, she was killed. It was said that all of the shots and knife cuts to her body healed themselves, and it was only when the tip of her heart was cut off that she finally died. No wild animals or birds disturbed her body, which gradually decayed.

SAHAYKWISA

Sahaykwisa, also known as Masahay Matkwisa (Girl's Shadow or Soul), was a full-blooded Mojave woman born around the middle of the nineteenth century. She was considered a Lesbian transvestite, formerly referred to as *hwame* and is thought to have gone through the initiation rite for female transvestites. She was known for being rich enough to wear real shoes. She occasionally prostituted herself to whites, but her main sources of success were from being a farmer and hunter and also a practicing shaman. She specialized in the treatment of venereal diseases, and this gave her the reputation of being lucky in love. She was easily able to find wives, though they often had trouble within the tribe of constantly being teased. People would ask her wives why they would want to be with a hwame, since she had no penis.

In secret, people called her Hithpan Kudhape (split vulva), which refers to one of the postures female homosexuals assume during coitus. When Sahaykwisa took her wife to dances, she sat with the men and her wife sat with the women. She had three wives in all, none of whom lasted very long. The third returned to her husband, who raped Sahaykwisa. After the rape, she became depressed and stopped courting women. Looking for a way to die, she boasted to the son and brother of a friend that she had bewitched their father's/brother's soul. They threw her into the Colorado River, where she drowned.

---

16. Lesbian Sex and Sexuality

Sex is the regenerative force of life . . . sex is life. It is birth and rebirth. Our sexuality gives us access to our power. Power over our own lives, our own sexuality.

—Betty Dodson, author of *Sex for One*

For centuries, women's sexuality has been erased, controlled, or objectified by men, and it has often intertwined with violence. In addition, lesbian sexuality has been virtually invisible, except when used to titillate straight men.

The actual term *lesbian* did not even exist until the late 1800s, when a medicalization of sex and sexual behavior created the category of the modern homosexual woman—an identity based exclusively on sexuality.

Lesbian-friendly sex researchers were instrumental in beginning to turn the tide of sickness associated with the new medical term of *lesbian*. In 1953, Alfred Kinsey documented that lesbian behavior was far more common than anyone suspected, which helped many gay women realize that they weren't alone in their desires.

In the twentieth century in America, the most significant events in liberating lesbian sexuality, according to historian Allan Berube, were the two world wars, which threw vast numbers of women together, either serving in the armed forces or doing munitions work in factories. After World War II especially, lesbians congregated in port cities and created the subculture and community identity that would eventually lead to the lesbian and gay liberation movement of the late 1960s.

Though lesbian sexuality is still often erased from mainstream consciousness, in recent years, the pioneering work of lesbian and bisexual activists and thinkers has helped break a lot of the silence surrounding it. Women who identify themselves as lesbian, bisexual, and queer have created many venues for erotic ex-

(Copyright © 1987 by Morgan Gwenwald)

pression and sexual transformation. Just look at the Clit Club in New York City, where a diverse community of women experiments with sexuality, and magazines such as the established *On Our Backs* and the newly launched *GirlFriends*, which includes a sexy monthly pin-up girl. Some of the best work being done on sexuality in the queer community reflects women's ability to embrace sexual complexity.

EARLY LESBIAN SEX RESEARCHERS

Havelock Ellis published *Studies in the Psychology of Sex* (several editions from 1896 to 1928) and wrote *Sexual Inversion* with John Addington Symonds in 1897, one of the first English-language books to argue for increased acceptance of homosexuality. His wife was a lesbian.

Alfred Kinsey wrote *Sexual Behavior in the Human Male* (1948) and *Sexual Behavior in the Human Female* (1953).

THE KINSEY REPORT

Although widely quoted as the source for the ever-popular figure that 10 percent of the American population is lesbian/gay, Kinsey's famous reports from the late 1940s and early 1950s never stated that. In fact, Kinsey's reports documented a far more complex world of sexual behavior than is even imagined by most people today.

Sexual Behavior in the Human Male, published in 1948, refuted the myth that homosexuals were rare. Alfred Kinsey found that 37 percent of adult men had had a homosexual experience in their adult lives, and that 4 percent were exclusively homosexual as adults.

In 1953, Kinsey followed up with a report on female sexuality, *Sexual Behavior in the Human Female,* finding that 2 percent of adult females were exclusively homosexual and 13 percent had had a homosexual experience as adults.

Kinsey used a continuous spectrum to measure sexual orientation, on a scale of 0 to 6, with 0 representing an exclusively heterosexual orientation/experience and 6 representing an exclusively homosexual orientation/experience. Almost all of the population fell in between the extremes. In other words, Kinsey found a continuous spectrum of sexuality, not a mutually exclusive polarity of homosexual or heterosexual.

A TIME LINE OF LESBIAN SEX IN THE TWENTIETH CENTURY

1900–1974: Catch as catch can. While gay men at least had the physique magazines of the 1950s and 1960s, sexually stimulating lesbian erotica (especially that made by women for women) was practically nonexistent. Although many of the pulp fiction books in the 1950s had sex scenes in them, many were written by men, and hardly any showed hot lesbian sex in a positive light. (That is, those women who actually enjoyed sex with other women were generally portrayed as evil perverts or got their just desserts in the end—they either died or went back to men.)

1975: Something was in the air. After three-quarters of a century of slim pickings, there was a virtual explosion of lesbian erotica by women for women with the publication of three books: *What Lesbians Do; Loving Women*; and Tee Corinne's now-classic *The Cunt Coloring Book.* According to Dell Richards, syndicated lesbian columnist and author of *Lesbian Lists,* "These three works radically altered the sexual landscape for lesbians by bringing sexuality out of the closet and into print." In addition to Tee Corinne, the pioneers behind these other books were Marilyn Gayle, Barbara Katherine, and the Nomadic Sisters of Sonora, California.

1976–1979: The snowball was rolling down the mountain of lesbian desire. Lesbian publications debated sexual topics (e.g., the penetration wars flared up), and in general, other voices were added to the growing cacophonous discussion of lesbian erotica and lesbian sexuality.

1979: Pat Califia published a study on lesbian sexuality in the *Journal of Homosexuality* (see below for results).

1980: Pat Califia burst onto the literary scene with the publication of her book *Sapphistry.* Today, along with JoAnn Loulan and Susie Bright (aka, Susie Sexpert), Califia is one of the best-known sex writers in the lesbian community.

1982: The Barnard Woman and Scholar Conference focused on sexuality, but certain feminists tried to define exactly what lesbian sexuality should be: no S/M, no butch-femme, no bad girl sex. The exclusion of diverse sexual experiences from the conferences started the sex wars of the 1980s and produced a more open (though usually volatile) discussion among lesbians about the nature of sex and sexuality.

1984: Something was in the air again. Two lesbian sex magazines burst upon the scene: *On Our Backs,* founded by Susie Bright, and *Bad Attitude,* cofounded by Cindy Patton and Amy Hoffman. Other magazines and journals—such as *Yoni* and *Outrageous Women*—(and in the 1990s, 'zines) soon followed.

1984: JoAnn Loulan, a lesbian sex therapist, pushed the lesbian sexuality envelope a little farther by advocating techniques to heal incest survivors and thus help untold numbers of lesbians reconnect to their sexuality. Her books *Lesbian Sex* and *Lesbian Passion* were the basis for a series of popular workshops and lectures throughout the late 1980s and early 1990s.

1987: Joan Nestle published *A Restricted Country* and shone a spotlight on a practically taboo subject of lesbian sexuality, the butch-femme past.

1988: Pat Califia did it again and published the instant classic, *Macho Sluts* (it came with a really cool button attached to the cover that said, "Macho Slut"). Some lesbians were critical of Califia's defense of sadomasochism, but at least the subject was being discussed.

1989: Sandra Bernhard and Madonna pretended to be girlfriends and Generation X lesbians all over the country got wet, masturbated, and generally felt better about their sexuality.

1990–1995: It just kept getting better. There was an explosion of 'zines, lipstick, piercings, back rooms, sex clubs for women, orgies, ménages, and sex panels at activist conferences. The Lust Conference in New York indicated that this was the decade of the increasingly sexually confident lesbian. Diversity and sex-positive power reigned, but at the same time breast and ovarian cancer, an epidemic of substance abuse, lesbian bed death, bisexual betrayal, and the specter of HIV transmission lingered in the background. Clearly, these were complicated times, and lesbian sex, lesbian erotica, and lesbian sexuality have grown exponentially in their own complexity.

PRELIMINARIES

Before you can have sex with a lesbian, you've got to find one first. Perhaps, then, the first step in lovemaking is lady-finding. Some popular mega-gatherings of lesbians include:

Dinah Shore Golf Weekend, Palm Springs, California (third weekend in March)

Michigan Women's Music Festival, Michigan (August)

Provincetown Women's Week, Provincetown (Cape Cod), Massachusetts (October)

Virginia Slims Tennis Tournament, New York City (November)

Gay Games: every 4 years; next one in 1998 in Amsterdam

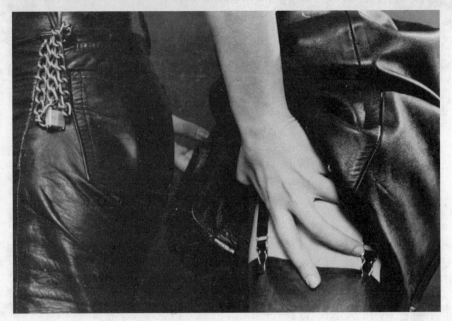

(Copyright © 1981 by Morgan Gwenwald)

OTHER SUGGESTED PLACES TO MEET LOVERS

Events at the local lesbian and gay community center: dances, readings, meetings,
    performances
Through a personal ad
Women's or lesbian/gay bookstores
Women's or lesbian and gay conferences
Volunteering for a local lesbian and gay group or organization
At a lesbian and gay pride march or rally
At a feminist meeting or rally

A BRIEF HISTORY OF PERSONAL ADS

In the early part of the century, mainstream newspapers in France and Germany
ran pieces by homosexuals in the personal columns that were "seeking friendship."
In the 1920s the nascent gay press in Germany began to run more sexually explicit
notices, but the rise of the Nazis in the early 1930s soon stamped this out. Nothing similar appeared in the United States until the 1960s, when the alternative and
counterculture press began to print sexually explicit descriptions in news stories.
These papers subsequently sought to increase revenue by running personal ads
specifically soliciting sexual partners. The post-Stonewall gay press copied this
practice, and the modern gay personal ad was born.

    Heavy on abbreviations, short on beating around the bush, the culture of per-
sonal ads has evolved over the last three decades.

THE PIONEER OF LESBIAN PERSONAL AD MAGAZINES

The Wishing Well, established in 1974, describes itself as a "beautiful, tender, loving alternative to *The Well of Loneliness.*" For an introductory copy ($5.00), write: *The Wishing Well,* P.O. Box 713090, Santee, CA 92072-3090.

LESBIAN SEX MAGAZINES

Bad Attitude: A Lesbian Sex Magazine
On Our Backs: Entertainment for the Adventurous Lesbian
Outrageous Women: A Journal of Woman-to-Woman S/M
Yoni
Up Our Butts ('zine)
Eidos: Erotic Entertainment for Women
On Our Rag ('zine)
Yellow Silk: Journal of Erotic Arts (not strictly lesbian, but lesbian-friendly)
Ad Venture! (Your Passport to Erotic Pleasure)
Tits and Clits Comix

BISEXUAL MAGAZINES

Anything That Moves: Beyond the Myth of Bisexuality, a quarterly magazine published by the Bay Area Bisexual Network
North Bi Northwest, a feminist bisexual women's newsletter
Bisexuality: The North American Journal (Phone: 213/597-2799)
Bisexuality (P.O. Box 20917, Long Beach, CA 90801; Phone: 310/597-2799), bimonthly newsletter
Slippery When Wet (Productions, P.O. Box 3101, Berkeley, CA 94703): their motto, "Don't sweat the petty things, pet the sweaty things."

SOME LESBIAN SEX WRITERS

Tee Corinne, *The Cunt Coloring Book* and *Dreams of the Woman Who Loved Sex*
JoAnn Loulan, sex therapist, author of *Lesbian Sex; Lesbian Passion*; and *The Lesbian Erotic Dance: Butch, Femme, Androgyny and Other Rhythms*
Susie Bright, founder of *On Our Backs* lesbian erotic magazine, and columnist as Suzie Sexpert; editor of *Herotica: A Collection of Women's Erotic Fiction* and author of *Suzie Sexpert's Lesbian Sex World*; and the 1995 release, *Susie Bright's Sexwise* (Cleis)
Pat Califia, author of *Sapphistry: The Book of Lesbian Sexuality; Macho Sluts; Doc and Fluff; Melting Point; PublicSex* (her most recent essay collection); and editor of *The Lesbian S/M Safety Manual*; she was also a long-time columnist in *The Advocate*

Bertha Harris and Emily Sisley, authors of *The Joy of Lesbian Sex*
Betty Dodson, *Sex for One: The Joy of Selfloving*
The Boston Women's Health Collective, *The New Our Bodies, Ourselves*

SEX SHOPS FOR WOMEN

As unbelievable as it sounds, for many years there were only two sex shops (sex toy shops) created by women for women. The first was Eve's Garden in New York City, opened by Dell Williams in 1974. Inspired by Eve's, Joani Blank opened Good Vibrations three years later in San Francisco. Both stores have mail order catalogues. More recently, two other shops owned and operated by lesbians have opened: Toys in Babeland in Seattle and Grand Opening in Boston.

Eve's Garden
119 West 57th St., Suite 420
New York, NY 10019
Phone: 212/757-8651
Open Tuesday to Saturday from 12 P.M. to 7 P.M.; send $1 for mail order
  catalogue.

Good Vibrations
Open Enterprises
1210 Valencia St., #OU
San Francisco, CA 94110
Phone: 415/974-8980
Send $2 for their catalogue of sex toys and books about sex, which they assure us
  is "friendly, feminist, and fun." Also available is their "Sexuality Library"
  catalogue, offering more than 200 books and videos from "enlightening
  advice" to "electrifying erotica."

LESBIAN-FRIENDLY CHAIN SEX SHOP

The Pleasure Chest has stores in New York; Philadelphia; Miami; Washington, D.C.; Chicago; and Los Angeles.

CATALOGUE

Stormy Leather
2339 Third St., Rm. 50, Dept. OUT
San Francisco, CA 94107
Send $4.00 for hot catalogue of leather, latex.

(Copyright © 1994 by Morgan Gwenwald)

FOR LEATHER ENTHUSIASTS

The Leather Journal, formerly a gay men's publication, now has a column "For Women, By Women."

THE *OUT/LOOK* SEX SURVEY

In *OUT/LOOK*'S issue number 8, published in the spring of 1990, more than 300 responses to a survey asking about the nature of friendships, the quality of relationships with best friends, and the dynamics between friendship and lover relationships were analyzed by Claremont College (California) sociologists Peter Nardi and Drury Sherrod. These were their general findings:

Gay men appear to have more sex with their casual and close friends than lesbians do. Lesbians, however, are more likely to be best friends with their ex-lovers than gay men are. They also were more likely to have been sexually attracted to their best friend in the past than gay men were.

Over time, it seems that sexual attractiveness, sexual activity, and romantic love with best friends fade. About 40 percent of the respondents have had some sexual experience with their same-sex gay or lesbian best friend in the past, but less than 5 percent currently do.

Some statistics: For 34 percent of the women who responded, their current best friend is a former lover; for men, the percentage was 11. For women, 38 percent had been in love with their current best friend in the past, and 27 percent had been sexually involved. For men, 37 percent had been in love with their best friend in the past, and 24 percent had been sexually involved.

THE *OUT/LOOK* SEX SURVEY REDUX

In issue number 12, in the spring of 1991, respondents were asked to rank the frequency with which they had achieved orgasm over the past twelve months by using various sexual techniques. Masturbation was the leading way orgasm was achieved for both men and women. It beat out oral-genital contact and homosexual intercourse, which were close seconds.

OTHER NAMES FOR THE DENTAL DAM

During the late 1980s and early 1990s, the issue of safe sex between women finally drew some much-needed attention. A hot topic for debate was the amount of concentration of HIV in vaginal fluids. Could women transmit HIV during oral sex? The debates raged and some AIDS activists began advocating the use of dental dams placed over the vagina and clitoris during oral sex. Since the term *dental dam* is—frankly—just not very sexy, lesbians in all their lingual cunningness were quick to rename it:

Love Lid	Eve Sleeve
Venus Veil	Box Top
Rubyfruit Suit	Rubber Dykie

A USEFUL VIDEO YOU CAN RENT

Well Sexy Women: A Lesbian Woman's Guide to Safer Sex (Greenwood/Cooper)

See pages 447–448 for advice on safer sex for lesbians.

SOME WOMEN'S SEX CONFERENCES AND FORUMS

"Women, Sex, and Censorship," February 1990: Women artists celebrated lust and liabilities in the age of Helms, including performances by Joan Nestle, Sapphire, and Annie Sprinkle.

The Lust Conference, New York City, 1992, is legendary not only for its myriad workshops, discussions, and how-to demonstrations, but also for its hot sex party afterward; cosponsored by the Lesbian and Gay Community Services Center of New York.

"A Celebration of Butch/Femme Identities" took place in December 1991 at the New York City Lesbian and Gay Community Services Center with panelists Joan Nestle, Val Tavai, Jewelle Gomez, Jill Harris, Lisa Winters, and Sue Hyde. The more than capacity crowd of nearly 500 women described this panel discussion "historic."

WHAT IS THAT ARC ON THE COVER?

In the early 1990s, the cover of *Rites,* a Toronto publication, featured a picture of a lesbian ejaculating. Consequently, the Canadian Magazine Publishers Association asked lawyers if they could be sued for distributing obscenity, although in the end, the magazine hit the stands without dire legal results.

THE ONLY LESBIAN "SODOMY" CASE EVER CHARGED IN CANADA

It did not occur until 1981, and because sodomy is about penises, the bewildered police finally charged them under the code forbidding gross indecency.

WHERE TO GET REAL ANSWERS AND NOT JUST THE MYTHS REGARDING TRANSSEXUALITY?

The New York City Lesbian and Gay Community Services Center sponsors the Gender Identity Program (under the auspices of its Project Connect) offering information, referrals, and peer counseling for the transgender community and for those with gender identity conflict. Gender Identity Project trained counselors discuss sex reassignment surgery, preoperative and postoperative sexual functioning, and the many myths surrounding transsexuality. Call the Center at 212/620-7310.

YOU KNOW IT'S TIME TO LEAVE YOUR GIRLFRIEND WHEN . . .

You don't know if dyke drama refers to lesbian theater or your relationship.
She'd rather sleep with her best gay boyfriend than you.
She'd rather sleep with her ex-husband than you.
You'd rather sleep with her ex-husband than her.
You'd rather she sleep with her ex-husband than you.

THE MOST MISUNDERSTOOD SEX WORKSHOP

"Why Women Should Have Sex in the Morning: The Politics of Night" was a sex workshop given by Penny Perkins and Mariana Romo-Carmona at the National Lesbian Conference in Atlanta, Georgia, in April, 1991. The confusion around this

(Copyright © Morgan Gwenwald)

workshop started with its listing in the program sheet in an abbreviated form as "Sex in the A.M." What many women mistakenly (and understandably) took to be a workshop about sex, was in actuality a theoretical and political analysis about what effect night and darkness has had on women, and women's sexuality, primarily in terms of control by fear and terror.

Once this misunderstanding was explained by the workshop's facilitators, most of the group of women left the workshop disappointed that a rousing discussion of hot lesbian sex in the morning was not to be had. The rumor quickly and erroneously spread that the workshop was about convincing women not to have sex at night—a dictum that was far beyond the facilitators' theoretical and political concerns (not to mention personal proclivities).

HANDY ADVICE FOR MAILING A LOVE LETTER

The Gay/Lesbian History Stamp Club suggests having your love letters canceled from a post office in a town with a romantic name. An article by Michael Greene lists places you can get a "love" postmark by sending your letter inside a larger envelope addressed to Postmaster of the town with a note inside explaining that you would like the enclosed letter postmarked from that post office:

Valentine, Texas 79854
Valentines, Virginia 23887
Lovejoy, Illinois 62059
Loving, New Mexico 88256

Lovelady, Texas 75851
Loveland, Ohio 45140
Heart Butte, Montana 59448

HONEY, THE MAIL'S HERE!

In 1993, an infamous chain letter circulated among lesbians: the panty chain letter. Instead of sending money (or—horrors!—recipes) recipients were instructed to send a pair of panties (new, thank you) to the next name on the list. The season's favorites: Calvin Klein men's brief boxers, wild-colored thongs, and that old standby, Jockey for Her.

HAVE A QUESTION NOT ANSWERED HERE?

You can always try the San Francisco Sex Information (SFSI) line, for free information and referral services. Call Monday to Friday, 3 P.M. to 9 P.M.: 415/621-7300.

Or you can also write or call the Sex Information and Educational Council of the U.S. (SIECUS), 130 W. 42nd St., Suite 2500, New York, NY 10012; Phone: 212/819-9770.

WHERE YOU CAN GET BOOKS AND VIDEOS ON LESBIAN SEX AND SEXUALITY

In addition to the women's sex stores mentioned on page 378, A Different Light bookstores are in New York (151 W. 19th St.), San Francisco (489 Castro St.), and West Hollywood, California (8853 Santa Monica Blvd.). They have mail order available to all areas of the country; call daily between 10 A.M. and midnight: 800/343-4002. Or mail your order to: A Different Light Mail Order, 153 West 19th St., New York, NY 10011.

FEATURE

The following faux academic study on a time-honored and confusing interaction—"What Is a Lesbian Date? Philosophical Musings on an Elusive Ritual"—was written by Penny Perkins for the Cleis Press anthology *Girlfriend Number One: Lesbian Life in the 90s,* edited by Robin Stevens, and is excerpted and reprinted with the permission of the author. Perkins, a freelance writer and veteran lesbian date survivor, is currently in the throes of writing her magnum opus, "What Is a Lesbian Relationship? Philosophical Complaints on the Inevitability of Lesbian Bed Death, or Honey, Did You Come?" She hopes to be done with her research before she gets carpal tunnel syndrome.

WHAT IS A LESBIAN DATE? PHILOSOPHICAL MUSINGS ON AN ELUSIVE RITUAL

PREAMBLE

There have long been three questions—one of which we shall examine here—dogging the sharp minds of the world's greatest philosophers. Specifically, throughout the lengthy annals of History, those three questions have been (in no particular order), 1) What is the meaning of Life?, 2) What is the largest prime number?, and 3) Just what exactly is a lesbian date?

While questions one and two have inspired volumes of scholarly tomes—and several mind-numbing religions to boot—question three has had far less attention, and, as a consequence, there has been even less success in the formulation of an acceptable answer. So, let us begin our exploration, difficult and messy as it may be, of the world's most elusive question: What is a lesbian date?

PART 1: GROUND RULES

What would a lesbian essay be without some initial ground rules?

First of all, I might hazard to postulate that a *lesbian date* is something that takes place between two (or, for the adventuresome, two or more) *lesbians*.

Given this fact—and further given that lesbians, and particularly lesbian feminists, tend to be sticklers for definition—one might expect that our first task would be to *define* what a *lesbian* is.

This, however, I wholly decline to do.

For it is not the *lesbian* part of *lesbian date* that I find so fascinating, but rather the *dating* part. Therefore, I am going to assume, for the sake of essentialist and constructivist argument alike, that one knows what a lesbian is, especially if it is one's objective to date her.

PART 2: CASE STUDIES

We are now in a position to proceed with specific case studies of lesbian dates. The following anecdotes are presented in *homosexus verité* (i.e., the individual style of each lesbian, who was orally interviewed).

[Note: case studies 1–3 excised]

CASE STUDY #4: TILDE IS SURE SHE ASKS SOMEONE OUT (IN RETROSPECT)

Ever on the lookout for more and divers subjects to interview, I attended a poetry reading. . . . One of the poets reading was . . . Tilde—who was wearing black motorcycle boots, a black leather sleeveless vest, and a black lace bra—was about five feet, four inches and had a tattoo of an anchor on her right shoulder. She seemed to be in her late twenties or early thirties and had grown up in New York City.

Using the sharpest of my anthropological field skills (not to mention a few flattering comments about her haikus), I not only secured an interview with Tilde, but I elicited the following story:

> There was this woman, Nicole, who had asked me out a few weeks ago. She said she just wanted to get together as "buddies," to cruise for other chicks, but I suspected she was just playing coy, that really, even if she didn't know yet herself, she wanted me. We had a nondescript first non-date and then an embarrassing encounter a few days later when I was out on a real date with someone else. You'd think after all these false starts I should call it quits. But for some reason I didn't.
>
> So, a couple of days later, I called her up and asked her to go to yet another lesbian literary event, and I didn't even mention cruising for other chicks.

A Lesbian Date Is Something that Sometimes Works Better the Second Time Around.

So I had a date scheduled, of sorts, with Nicole, although I didn't call what we were doing together a date. It was more like a "would you like to go with me to . . ." proposition. Nicole wasn't the only one who could play coy.

A Lesbian Date Is Something that Is Never Termed a "Date."

Well, the day came and we went to this event together; it was a fundraiser for a local queer writers' organization.

A Lesbian Date Is Something that Benefits the Entire Community.

We realized, belatedly, after we'd paid to get in, that there wasn't enough real food on the snack trays to sustain us. So, we decided to go downstairs (which was a restaurant) and have dinner together before returning to the party. We were having one of those nice, pseudo-intimate conversations (I found out why she dyed her hair blond last summer), but, during the main course, she bit into a pine nut at the wrong angle and cracked off a piece of a temporary crown that had just been installed that morning at the dentist's.

A Lesbian Date, Like Puritan Proscriptions against Masturbation, Is Something that Makes Your Teeth Fall Out.

I was properly sympathetic and ordered her a whiskey to help cut down on pain.

A Lesbian Date Is Something Where There Is Throbbing.

We finished our meal and I picked up the tab. She thanked me and mentioned something about picking up the next one.

A Lesbian Date Is Something that Contains a Hint of Reciprocity.

As we made our way up the stairs back to the party, I leaned into her, and asked, "Is that perfume you're wearing or just your own delicious body smell?" Her back was to me, but even so, I could see her blushing in the mirror that decorated the entrance to the party.

A Lesbian Date Is Something that Sometimes Takes Place Behind One's Back.

"It's a Gucci knock-off I got in Walgreen's," she finally said.
    I laughed, saying, "Whatever it is, Nicole, it smells great." Then I touched the small of her back, a gesture which I have found brings me much success in the ways of love, and which I repeated throughout the evening.
    As the night went on, Nicole and I made small talk with a variety of queer literati types, pushed our way to the bar fetching drinks for each other, and watched two editors from Naiad press up against each other on the dance floor.

A Lesbian Date Is Something that Makes You Face the Music.

"You ready to go soon?" Nicole asked.

I thought there was an interesting edge in her voice. Something about the way she said it made me look at her again. Hey, I thought, she is *cute* (even if she is taller than I usually like). And we seemed to have things in common: we liked going to community functions, we shared a love of literature, and, there was the clincher, we were both wearing the same kind of pants.

A Lesbian Date Is Something that Takes Place in Black Jeans.

"Yeah, I'm ready," I answered her. We smiled at each other. It felt like it meant something.

Once outside, we began a leisurely walk that seemed like it had a purpose, but I couldn't have told you where we were going. But I didn't have to wait too long for destiny to come to us: We turned a corner and bumped into a very surprised Liza and Sandra, who were out taking Otis for a walk.

A Lesbian Date Is Something that Participates in the Great Metaphorical Hairball.

We all shuffled our feet, avoided eye contact, and chatted for maybe a total of fifteen seconds. After we left them, and a certain amount of silence passed, I told Nicole that I thought she should know that I had once dated Sandra and I was currently dating Liza.

Nicole said that she wasn't surprised to hear that Liza and I were dating, that she had suspected as much from our encounter at the play.

"And besides," she said, "I've been dating Liza's ex, Polly."

At this point, I decided that Nicole and I were definitely *not* on a date, and I knew I would have to turn things around fast.

"'Hope is a thing with feathers,'" I said suddenly to her. She looked at me curiously. "It's a line from Emily Dickinson," I explained. "She's one of my favorite poets."

A Lesbian Date Is Something that Inspires Poetry.

"You know," she said, grinning, "it's still early. I'm not really ready to go home yet. Would you like to go for a cup of coffee?"

I quickly agreed to go for some coffee, and we ducked into the nearest greasy spoon. After we ordered, there was an awkward silence broken up with several goofy smiles. Thankfully, this ended when the waitress brought us our dessert and coffee. I made a mental note to leave a good tip.

A Lesbian Date Is Something that Boosts the Service Economy.

"So," I began, "What do you think of *Sex*?"

Startled, Nicole visibly jumped and ended up spilling her hot tea on my lap.

A Lesbian Date Is Something Where Hot Liquids Are Spilled on Thighs.

I was afraid she had ruined my 501s. This worry disappeared when she reached over with a napkin to help clean up the spill. When her hand touched my leg there was a disarming reaction in my stomach.

"No need to get so nervous," I laughed a little nervously, and finished cleaning up my own legs. "I just meant Madonna's book."

A Lesbian Date Is Something Where There is a Mandatory Mention of Jody, Martina, Madonna, or k.d.

For the remainder of our dinner session, Nicole and I discussed the merits of *Sex* (the book, not the act). We had finished every last crumb of the raspberry chocolate torte we had been sharing by the time the check came.

A Lesbian Date Is Something Where at Least the Check Comes.

"There it is," I thought in my sugar rush, "the bill, the tally, the symbol of the end of our encounter." I had prolonged this evening for about as long as possible.

But from here we would have to make some kind of decision: either go home together (and have sex, hopefully) or we would go to our separate tiny apartments alone (and still not know the status of our encounter).

A Lesbian Date Is Something that Presents a Certain Inevitable Fork in the Road.

Outside the diner, I decided to take a chance and offered to walk Nicole home. She seemed flattered at my chivalry and I thought I had scored big, but when we got to her place at the corner of Christopher and Gay, she took a step up the stoop without inviting me in, and my heart sank.

But, just as suddenly, Nicole moved back down, not one, but two steps, erasing the final barrier (of height) between us. We were now eye to eye, or at least lip to lip.

A Lesbian Date (like a Lesbian Essay) Is Something that Ends with a Kiss.

PROFILES

ONE-WOMAN SEX GURUS, PART I: JOANN LOULAN

JoAnn Loulan, M.S.W., a lesbian sex therapist, is one of several well-known lesbian authors on sex and sexuality. In 1984, she published the first of her books on lesbian sexuality, aptly and succinctly called *Lesbian Sex*. In this book and her follow-up, *Lesbian Passion: Loving Ourselves and Each Other*, she advocated, among other things, techniques to heal incest and sexual abuse survivors and has thus helped untold numbers of lesbians reconnect to their sexuality.

Lesbian Sex and *Lesbian Passion* are also the basis for a series of popular work-

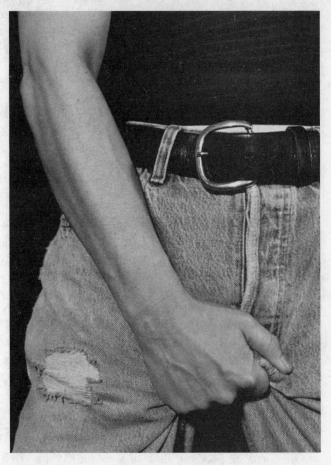

(Copyright © 1995 by Morgan Gwenwald)

shops and lectures on sexuality that Loulan led throughout the late 1980s and early 1990s. An example of one is "The Lesbian Erotic Workshop: Liberating Our Sexuality," an all-day workshop ($60). For this workshop, Loulan claims the following: "Through lecture, experiential exercises and group discussions, participants will explore: Secrets of Lesbian Sex; Likes and Dislikes; Issues Between Couples; The Impact of Roles/Rules on Sexuality; Dating; and Recovery and Sexuality."

Loulan is also the author of the more recent *The Lesbian Erotic Dance: Butch, Femme, Androgyny and Other Rhythms*. She writes a column for several lesbian newspapers, including the *Lesbian News* in southern California.

ONE-WOMAN SEX GURU, PART II: JOAN NESTLE

Joan Nestle, one of the founders and guiding spirits of the Lesbian Herstory Archives, has long been a powerful speaker and writer on the issues of lesbians, sex, and sexuality. Nestle, a pioneer in writing about lesbian sexuality, has been courageous enough to approach all aspects of lesbian sexuality—especially topics some lesbians haven't wanted to discuss. For example, in her classic reader on sexuality and the 1950s lesbian, *A Restricted Country,* Nestle was the first writer to discuss the butch/femme relationships of the past (and their relevance to the present) in a positive light; she also addressed lesbian attraction to men. She has edited several anthologies, including *The Persistent Desire: A Femme-Butch Reader* and the *Woman on Woman* series of lesbian fiction anthologies with Naomi Holoch.

In addition to her work as a writer and author, Nestle is also a celebrated speaker and has participated in hundreds of panels, workshops, conferences, presentations, and community forums. For example, she has spoken at several "Out-Write" conferences, the "LUST (Lesbians Undoing Sexual Taboos)" conference, several "Creating Change" conferences, and on many other specific occasions. As a member of the panel "Women, Sex, and Censorship," which took place in February 1990 and where women artists celebrated lust and liabilities in the age of Helms, Joan performed along with Sapphire and Annie Sprinkle. At "A Celebration of Butch/Femme Identities," a historic panel discussion in December 1991 at the New York City Lesbian and Gay Community Services Center, Joan spoke with panelists Val Tavai, Jewelle Gomez, Jill Harris, Lisa Winters, and Sue Hyde.

In 1994, along with John Preston, she edited *Sister and Brother: Lesbians and Gay Men Write about Their Lives Together*. Joan lives in New York City and can be contacted through the Lesbian Herstory Archives at 718/768-DYKE; or the Lesbian Herstory Education Foundation, P.O. Box 1258, New York, NY 10116.

One-Woman Sex Guru, Part III: Pat Califia

Pat Califia is a West Coast lesbian author and leather activist who also writes pornography, sex manuals, and theory. She is a self-proclaimed sexual outlaw and author of many sex standards including:

Sapphistry: The Book of Lesbian Sexuality (1980)—Dell Williams, founder of Eve's Garden, says this is "a comprehensive, positive and caring book that is both informative and practical in its approach to all aspects of lesbian sexuality and relationships."

Macho Sluts (1988)—According to Dell Williams again, "In her bold and courageous style, here is a collection of erotic short fiction, that, by its title, defies a machismo culture that violates women, and, by its content, dares to explore S/M fantasies that will either excite you, or cause your pubic hairs to stand on end!"

The Lesbian S/M Safety Manual, edited by Pat Califia, is a guide for women who want to be well-informed about how to play safe and remain healthy.

Of course, given the diversity of our community, not everyone appreciates her work. One lesbian feminist decided to read some of Califia's S/M science fiction to see what all the fuss was about and was less than turned on. "It was a story about women with funny names beating each other," she said. "I didn't get it—what is the point?"

For Pat, the point is that "sexual outlaws act as lightning rods," absorbing much of the criticism against the gay community from other groups. She takes our community to task for this, saying, "The lesbian and gay community is not comfortable in defending our sexuality in all its delightful variety. We're afraid of the cops and the state because they have the power to crush our community. We're still doing the same politics of appeasement we've been doing for the past twenty years." With advocates like Pat around, and with the sales of her books increasing, that is a situation that is sure to change as the gay nineties wear on.

Today, along with Susie Bright (aka, Susie Sexpert), Califia is one of the best-known sex writers in the lesbian community. In addition to the works mentioned above, Califia, forty, has also published erotic fiction, including *Doc and Fluff*, *Melting Point*, and *Public Sex*, her most recent essay collection. She was also a long-time columnist for *The Advocate*.

OTHER LESBIAN SEX GURUS

Susie Bright, best-known lesbian sex writer in America

Cathay Che, performance artist, activist, member of committee that coordinated New York City's 1992 "LUST (Lesbians Undoing Sexual Taboos)" conference; membership director of GLAAD-NY

Leslie Feinberg, author of *Stone Butch Blues*

Jewelle Gomez, author, activist, and speaker

Amber Hollibaugh, activist and sex writer

Jocelyn Taylor, cofounder of the notorious Clit Club, currently involved in DYKE-TV

Carmen Vazquez, activist and sex thinker, Director of Public Policy of the Lesbian and Gay Community Services Center—New York

Lisa Winters, founder of a New York City–area femme support group and BLUeS, Bronx Lesbian United in Sisterhood

---

17. LESBIANS AND SPORTS

Sport, with its physical empowerment and lesbian potential, is an inherently feminist act.

> —MARIAH BURTON NELSON, lesbian athlete

Until the present century, women were routinely excluded from sports. Society set up a code of exclusion, deeming sports and athletic training improper for girls and women. During the last twenty years, participation in women's high school and college sports increased 500 percent, thanks to the work of the feminist movement in securing the passage of Title IX in 1972, a landmark bill that provided funding for female athletics in schools.

The modern Olympic Games, begun in 1896 and based on the ancient Greek contests, barred women athletes from participation until 1928. Pierre de Coubertin, founder of the games, lobbied vigorously to keep women from participating, hoping the Olympics would foster manliness. Even as late as the 1984 Summer Olympics in Los Angeles, less than a quarter of the athletes were female.

Lesbian softball tournament, Park Slope, Brooklyn *(Copyright © 1992 by Morgan Gwenwald)*

To this day, the big three male team sports—professional baseball, basketball, and football—are closed to women. Members of women's pro teams command far less money and prestige than their male counterparts. In professional tennis and golf, women have had to fight to demand purses equal to men's.

On top of the sexism inherent in sports, female athletes have also had to face an enormous amount of homophobia. Many lesbians have been drawn to sports but have had to hide in the closet for fear of being ousted from a team, denied professional endorsements, or bullied by the press. The only professional female athletes ever to openly acknowledge their sexual orientation are Martina Navratilova in tennis, Mariah Burton Nelson in basketball, and Susan McGrievy in Olympic swimming. Navratilova remains the only player to come out in either amateur or professional sports in America while still active.

Outside of professional sports, though, lesbians have created their own support system. Lesbian softball teams have been in existence since the 1940s, often sponsored by lesbian bars. Many cities now have lesbian softball leagues and tournaments, providing an alternative way for lesbians to meet and socialize. As lesbian singer Alix Dobkin puts it, "Softball is the single greatest organizing force in lesbian society."

The Gay Games have also provided an outlet for lesbian athletics. Founded in 1982 by Dr. Tom Waddell, the Games occur every four years and feature everything from softball and billiards to more conventional events such as swimming and track. In 1994, fifteen thousand lesbian and gay athletes descended on New

York City to participate in the largest Gay Games ever. The Gay Games have grown from an idea in Tom Waddell's head to the most inclusive event in the world. Mariah Burton Nelson, former pro basketball player, has written of the first games, "It was a taste of what could be; a gathering at which everyone, regardless of skill, could pursue excellence, where competitors could encourage each other, and where athletes could be caring and demonstrative without hesitation."

SOURCES

Bull, Chris. "Disclosure," *The Advocate,* March 21, 1995.

Lenskyj, Helen. *Out of Bounds: Women, Sport, and Sexuality.* Women's Press, 1986.

Nelson, Mariah Burton. *Are We Winning Yet?* New York: Random House, 1991.

———. *The Stronger Women Get, the More Men Love Football: Sex and Sports in America,* Harcourt and Brace, 1994.

Reed, Susan. "Unlevel Playing Fields." *Out* magazine, June 1994.

Rogers, Susan Fox. *Sportsdykes.* St. Martin's Press, 1994.

Twin, Stephanie L. *Out of the Bleachers.* The Feminist Press, 1979.

Young, Perry Deane. *Lesbians and Gay Men in Sports.* Chelsea House, 1995.

Zipter, Yvonne. *Diamonds Are a Dyke's Best Friend.* Firebrand Books, 1988.

SPORTS TIME LINE

776 B.C.: The first Olympics were held in ancient Greece. Women were excluded from the games, and they competed in their own Heraea Games every four years.

393 A.D.: The end of the Greek Olympics, when the Christian Roman emperor Theodosius the Great banned the games and ordered all of the buildings at Olympia destroyed.

1636: A Jesuit missionary in North America observed Huron Indians playing a game with a hide-covered ball hurled from a curved stick with a pouch at the end. The Indians called the game bagataway, but the French dubbed it la crosse (the cross), because the stick resembled a cross.

From medieval times to the 1800s: Tennis was first played in monastic courtyards, but around the reign of Henry VIII, it became a royal sport played on the courts of Europe. It was exported to the United States in the nineteenth century, when the first official tennis court was built in Boston in 1876.

1823: Since American colonial days, men had been kicking around a pigskin. But in 1823, a new kind of football game—called rugby after the British school where it started—allowed players not just to kick the ball but to pick it up and run with it. In the United States, this new version of the sport was quickly adopted and transformed into its more violent modern counterpart.

1837: Although people had been swimming for at least two thousand years, in 1837 the first swimming competitions, using the breaststroke, were conducted in London.

1839: According to the Baseball Hall of Fame in Cooperstown, New York, baseball was invented there by Abner Doubleday. (Other versions of the stickball game had existed throughout the country and in Europe.)

1844: North American Indians won a 100-yard (91.4 meter) swimming contest in London, using an overarm stroke.

1845: The rules of baseball were formalized and the now-familiar diamond-shaped field was used at the New York Knickerbocker Club. Play ball.

1855: The first organized game of ice hockey was played in Kingston, Ontario.

Late 1800s: Swedish and German gymnasts began performing aerobatic and tumbling routines in swimming areas, developing the sport of diving.

• The game of soccer, which evolved from centuries of different ball games where participants were not allowed to use their hands, developed formal rules of play.

• The invention of bloomers (a type of legging for women that could replace ankle-length dresses) and the invention of the bicycle (which later constituted a cycling craze, an acceptable pastime for women) went a long way to liberate nineteenth-century women from confining Victorian mores.

1879: Even though it was still largely seen as inappropriate, teams of female baseball players traveled across the United States and Canada. Local morality police often leveled charges of prostitution at the athletes.

1880: The first diving competitions were held in England as a result of arguments among swimming clubs that claimed to have the best divers.

1881: The first American national tennis championships were held.

1886: The New York Athletic Club held the first track and field meet in the United States.

1887: A great moment in lesbian sports history: the softball was invented in November at Chicago's Farragut Boat Club by tying a boxing mitt tightly with twine into a ball. Within a few years, it spread across the country. Because the ball was softer and the bases were shorter, softball became one of the few acceptable physical exertions for women.

1891: Basketball was invented by James Naismith of the YMCA in Springfield, Massachusetts, as an indoor sport to play between football and baseball seasons. Women were encouraged to play.

1896: The modern Olympics games were revived, brought about by a Frenchman, Pierre de Coubertin. The first games were held in a restored stadium in Athens. They have been held every four years since, except during World War I and World War II when they were suspended.

1899: A separate set of rules for women's basketball was created to accommodate women's weaker constitutions.

1903: Early female athletes often breached the conventions of the times. For instance, the *Cincinnati Enquirer* reported on the following traveling female ball team: "A club of female ballplayers, claiming to be from Brooklyn, N.Y., were jailed at Ft. Worth [Texas] today [July 20] for persisting in playing a game with a club of young men, after being notified by the police that the city park could not be held for ballplaying purposes. The bloomer aggregation became 'brassy' and was run in. . . . In the corridors and cells the girls raised a 'rough house.'

They sang up-to-date 'topical' songs, roasted the jail officials and male prisoners, turned handsprings, stood on their heads, walked on their hands, did high kicking, wide splits, and other startling performances." [Quoted in *Diamonds Are a Dyke's Best Friend* by Yvonne Zipter]

World War I: While the men were away, the women were allowed to work . . . and play. . . . Men at the front meant that women got a larger toehold into society, including sports.

1928: Women were allowed to participate in the Olympics.

The Great Depression: With the crash of the stock market, the decade of relaxed social constraints and women's nascent flapper freedom came crashing down, too. A conservative and restricting tone ruled the country until the next great war.

1931: Jackie Mitchell, a seventeen-year-old female pitcher, made baseball history by playing with the Chattanooga Lookouts, a Class A team. In an exhibition game against the New York Yankees, she struck out Lou Gehrig and Babe Ruth.

World War II: Again, the massive need for man power at the front allowed women to take over jobs and social roles at home. Further inroads were made in society and in the arena.

1943: Philip Wrigley, owner of the Chicago Cubs and founder of the Wrigley Chewing Gum Company, conceived and created an all-girl ball league as alternative entertainment, fearing that World War II would create another manpower shortage in sports as well as in the manufacturing world. The All-American Girls Professional Baseball League (AAGPBL) was born. It began with four pro teams, and at its height had as many as ten.

1943–1954: The life span of the AAGPBL, which until the early 1990s was the longest-lived of any women's professional athletic league. The women who played in this league were true pioneers in the world of women's sport.

1952: In practice, women were always excluded from playing men's professional baseball, but that standard was formalized in baseball rules this year.

1967: Suspicious of improvements in women's performance times, the International Olympic Committee required all women athletes from any nation in any sport to take the so-called sex test—chromosomal testing that determined the sex of a competitor. The test was designed to get rid of speculation.

1972: The Education Act of 1972 was passed, which contained Title IX, prohibiting gender discrimination in educational institutions that received federal funds. For the first time, any institution receiving federal funds was required to equally allocate its resources to boys and girls.

1975: The Education Act of 1972 was applied to sports, and made an enormous impact on the lives of girls and women. For instance, in 1972 there were virtually no athletic scholarships for women in colleges; today there are more than 12,000 in twenty-two different college sports.

• Reporter Lynn Rosellini writes a groundbreaking series of articles on homosexual athletes, "Gays in Sports," in the *Washington Star*. She can find no athlete who would talk openly about his or her sexuality until former NFL running back David Kopay agreed to speak.

1975–1979: Billie Jean King, along with others, founded the International

---

The Importance of Title IX

Title IX is the name of an act that has had and continues to have enormous impact on women athletes and women in general. Title IX is a stipulation of the Education Act of 1972 that simply states, "No person in the U.S. shall, on the basis of sex, be excluded from the participation in, be denied the benefits of, or be subjected to discrimination under any education program or activity receiving federal financial assistance." In 1975, feminist advocates got this to apply to sports as well as textbooks. (It was gutted in 1984 by Reagan, but reinstated by an act of Congress in 1988.)

Women's Professional Softball League (IWPSL). However, it was an idea whose time had already come (and gone), and the league folded after only four years.

1982: The AAGPBL held its first reunion and was rediscovered by feminists and historians. Between 1954, when the league folded, and this reunion, the league had been all but forgotten by history. The movie *A League of Their Own*, directed by Penny Marshall, was made about the AAGPBL in 1992.

• Dr. Tom Waddell founded the Gay Games, a version of the Olympics for lesbian and gay athletes. He was prevented by the Supreme Court from calling them Olympic games.

• Pam Parsons, coach of the undefeated and number-two ranked women's basketball team at the University of Southern California, and one of her players, Tina Buck, were implicated in a love affair reported in *Sports Illustrated*. They sued for libel, denying their relationship, but were later sentenced to jail for perjury.

• The disappointing and homophobic movie *Personal Best* opened. Mariel Hemingway starred as a lesbian (for a little while) athlete, who had a romance with another female track star. End of story homophobia: Mariel ended up with her male coach.

1984: At the Caesar's World Cup, the largest female bodybuilding competition with the largest purse, judges decided that the body bulk of an Australian competitor, Bev Francis, was too unfeminine. Though she was expected to win, she placed eighth instead because, as one competitor said, "the judges were afraid of her." In fact, Francis was heterosexual.

1991: Rene Portland, the coach of the top-ranked Penn State women's basketball team, the Lady Lions, made public statements that lesbians would have no place on her team. The university reaffirmed its antidiscrimination policies only after much protest from gay and lesbian activists.

1993: Barry Meisel wrote a series of newspaper articles on gay athletes for the *New York Daily News*, which was widely syndicated and published in papers throughout the country. He found that attitudes had changed very little since the time of Rosellini's investigation.

• Louise Swoopes brought her daughter Sheryl home from the University of Texas's tryouts for the Lady Longhorns because of rumors of lesbians on the team. She later told the *Austin American-Statesman* that lesbian members of the team had made sexual advances toward her daughter. The coach, Jody Conradt, refused to be intimidated by the homophobia and reaffirmed the university's policy against sexual orientation discrimination.

1994: Gay Games IV were held in New York City, coinciding with the twenty-fifth anniversary of Stonewall. More than 15,000 athletes participated and 500,000 spectators watched the biggest Games ever.

1995: Greg Louganis, gold medal Olympian diver, came out as being HIV-positive and gay.

ABOUT SOFTBALL

Softball is a popular American sport. According to a *Sports Illustrated* poll taken in 1986, softball is the number-one team sport played by women. It is especially popular with lesbians. Historian Lillian Faderman, in her book *Odd Girls and Twilight Lovers,* demonstrates that the popularity of softball among lesbians dramatically rose in the 1950s and 1960s as an alternative to dangerous, police-raided bars that were for decades one of the only places where lesbians could find and meet each other.

"To most lesbians, softball is more than just a game," writes Yvonne Zipter in *Diamonds Are a Dyke's Best Friend*. "It is a social event. It is a test of endurance

Lesbian softball tournament, Park Slope, Brooklyn (*Copyright © 1992 by Morgan Gwenwald*)

and skill. It is the incubator for an extended family. It is a way of fitting in, of making friends. It is a statement of independence, of courage, of commitment. It is the sheer joy of outdoor physical activity. In short, it is the beauty of distinctly different parts coming together to form a whole; for some, it is almost a mystical experience."

BROOKLYN'S LARGEST EXPLICITLY LESBIAN OUTDOOR GATHERING

The Annual Center Lesbian Softball Tournament and Picnic, sponsored by the New York City Lesbian and Gay Community Services Center, is held each September in Brooklyn's Prospect Park. Both a fund-raiser for the center and an outdoor celebration of lesbian culture and visibility, the tournament brings competitive and recreational teams from New York's women's softball leagues as well as from lesbian and gay organizations and businesses.

Trophies are awarded to the top teams in three divisions: modified fast pitch, fast pitch, and recreational. The center group, Women and Friends, recently took over the organization of the tournament, which brings out more than 200 players and scores of spectators each year.

EARLY NAMES FOR SOFTBALL

Diamondball	Lineball
Indoor baseball	Mushball
Kittenball	

THREE THINGS THAT COULD GET YOU KICKED OUT OF THE INTERNATIONAL WOMEN'S PROFESSIONAL SOFTBALL LEAGUE IN THE MID-1970s FOR DEMONSTRATING OVERT LESBIAN BEHAVIOR

Having unshaven legs
Reading a copy of *Lesbian Images* (a nonfiction book by Jane Rule) in
    public
Massaging another woman's temples

ALL-AMERICAN GIRLS PROFESSIONAL BASEBALL LEAGUE (AAGPBL)

In 1943, Philip Wrigley, owner of the Chicago Cubs and founder of the Wrigley Chewing Gum Company, conceived the idea of an all-girl ball league as alternative entertainment, since World War II had created a manpower shortage in sports as well as in the manufacturing world. The All-American Girls Professional Baseball League (AAGPBL) was born. It began with four pro teams, and at its height had as many as ten. The league lasted until 1954, when societal pressures were forcing women out of the public sphere and back into the home.

AAGPBL players were required to go to charm school for feminizing in addition to long hours of sweaty practice and games. The schools were run by none other than Helena Rubinstein, who insisted the girls wear high heels at night after their games. All this trouble was taken because the league was deathly afraid of the women being perceived as too masculine, the euphemism for lesbian. According to Lois Browne, who wrote about the league in *The Girls of Summer* (which inspired the 1992 movie *A League of Their Own*), many of the best players were rejected because of their masculine demeanor. Even the whiff of rumor regarding lesbian relationships or masculine behavior of any kind was enough to ban a woman from the league. Perry Deane Young, author of *Lesbian and Gays and Sports,* records that a total of 550 women played in the league during its eleven-year life span.

PLAYERS

Dorothy "Dottie" Kamenshek, the league's best all around player, who was given an offer (later rescinded) to play on a men's professional team
Lavonne "Pepper" Paine, one of the best players in the league
Sophie Kury
Eleanor Engle
Dottie Schroeder
Shirley Jameson

THE FOUR ORIGINAL TEAMS

Racine Belles (Wisconsin)   Kenosha Comets (Wisconsin)
Rockford Peaches (Illinois)   South Bend Blue Sox (Indiana)

A GAY GAMES RETROSPECTIVE

The Gay Games define us as a coherent, diverse population, asserting our right to celebrate ourselves—not ask for someone else's approval. It is the ultimate manifestation of self-esteem.

—ANN NORTHROP, AIDS and lesbian activist, and board member of Gay Games IV and Cultural Festival

GAY GAMES I

Opening Day: August 28, 1982
San Francisco, California
Attendance: 1,700–1,800 athletes; 10,000 spectators
Masters of Ceremony: Rita Mae Brown and Armistead Maupin
Festivities and events: art exhibitions, music and comedy performances

The opening ceremonies included Susan McGrievy, on the 1956 U.S. Olympic swimming team, and George Frenn, on the 1972 U.S. Olympic track team, carrying a torch that had been carried across country from the Stonewall Inn in New York City, site of the Stonewall Riots in 1969.

GAY GAMES II

August 9–17, 1986
San Francisco, California
Attendance: 3,500 athletes; 10,000–15,000 spectators
Official Slogan: Something Wonderful Will Happen . . . For the Second Time
Master of Ceremonies: Rita Mae Brown
Festivities and events: Sports (seventeen events): basketball, bowling, boxing, cycling, golf marathon, physique, powerlifting, pool (billiards), racquetball, soccer, softball, swimming and diving, tennis, track and field, triathlon, volleyball, men's wrestling

GAY GAMES III

August 4–11, 1990
Vancouver, British Columbia
Attendance: 7,000 athletes; 20,000 spectators
Money the Games brought to the host city: $30 million
Festivities and events: Cultural festival including readings, exhibits, and workshops; Sports (twenty-eight sporting events): basketball, powerlifting, volleyball, racquetball, swimming, water polo, equestrian, golf, billiards, cycling, tennis, softball, race walking, croquet, martial arts, physique, soccer, bowling, squash, diving,

Team New York Aquatics relay action at Gay Games IV, June 1994 *(Photo by Alphones P. Guardino)*

badminton, touch/flag football, triathlon, marathon, wrestling, track and field, curling, ice hockey

GAY GAMES IV

June 18–25, 1994
New York, New York
Attendance: 15,000 athletes; 500,000 spectators
Official Slogan: Games Can Change the World
Money the Games brought to the host city: $100 million
Festivities and events: Cultural festival: 130 different exhibits/performances, including readings, exhibits, a Carnegie Hall gay choir performance, a Madison Square Garden gay and lesbian band performance, a comedy extravaganza at Town Hall, opening ceremonies at Columbia University's Wien Stadium, and closing ceremonies at Shea Stadium; Sports: (twenty-nine sporting events): basketball, powerlifting, volleyball, racquetball, swimming, water polo, equestrian, golf, billiards, cycling, tennis, softball, race walking, croquet, martial arts, physique, soccer, bowling, squash, diving, badminton, touch/flag football, triathlon, marathon, wrestling, track and field, curling, ice hockey, figure skating

---

A FEW STARS OF GAY GAMES IV
(PROFILED IN *OUT* MAGAZINE, JUNE 1994):

Robin Rothhammer, thirty-five, ranked in the top ten in the Eastern Tennis Association's listing for women of all ages. Identifies as a bisexual who lives a monogamous, heterosexual life.

Juanita Harvey, thirty-nine, African-American grandmother and lesbian wrestler from Brooklyn, who loves the strength wrestling brings, as well as the mental, emotional, and spiritual aspects.

Nancy Stevens, thirty-four, blind track and field competitor and former ski star; she won two downhill gold medals at the 1988 Nationals for the Blind and three silver medals at Ridder Renet, Norway's annual sporting event for the disabled.

Susan Greene, thirty-two, ranked in the top fifteen in the nation by the United States Squash Rackets Association; organized the Gay Games IV squash tournament; competed in the 1993 Maccabiah Games, held every four years in Tel Aviv since 1957.

GAY GAMES V (1998)

Scheduled to be held in Amsterdam, the Netherlands

WORLD RECORDS SET AT A GAY GAMES

So far, there has been just one: the 100-meter butterfly, for age group 50–54, by Michael Mealiffe in 1990.

POLITICS AND SPORTS

The U.S. Olympic Committee took the Gay Games to court in order to prevent the games from being called the *Gay Olympics*. In 1987 the U.S. Supreme Court ruled in a five-to-four vote to forbid the use of the term *Gay Olympics*. However, according to the book *Lavender Lists,* there are thirteen other events that have been allowed the use of the word *Olympic* in their titles:

Special Olympics	Wheelchair Olympics
Bridge Olympics	Eskimo Olympics
International Police Olympics	Junior Olympics
Rat Olympics	Crab Cooking Olympics
Armenian Olympics	Explorer Scout Olympics
K-9 Olympics	Armchair Olympics
Senior Olympics	

Excerpt from Lavender Lists by Lynne Yamaguchi Fletcher and Adrion Saks, © 1990 by Alyson Publications. Used by permission of the publisher.

LESBIAN OR GAY ATHLETE WHO HAS COMPETED AT AN OLYMPICS AS OPENLY GAY

None

WOMEN OF GAY GAMES IV CALENDAR

In addition to twelve hot women in action at the games, this calendar also lists the dates of lesbian and gay national and international sporting events as well as women's Division 1 college and pro tournaments. Order from Realsports Productions. Call 910/292-3663.

SPORTS ON-LINE

America Online has a category for the Gay Games under "Leisure Interests" in the Gay and Lesbian Community Forum. There are also numerous folders for different sporting activities, everything from bowling to softball to rodeo to kayaking.

Rich Quigley and Kile Ozier have produced a forty-five-minute video of the opening and closing ceremonies of Gay Games IV. It is available for $8 plus $2.90 for mailing. You can order by E-mail at KileO@aol.com.

INTERNATIONAL GAY RODEO ASSOCIATION (IGRA)

In his book, *Lesbians and Gays and Sports,* Perry Deane Young states, "Surely the most unexpected and most successful of the gay alternatives to straight sporting events is the most macho of all American activities of any sort, the rodeo. The first gay rodeo was staged in Reno, Nevada, in 1975. From fairly small beginnings, the International Gay Rodeo Association has now expanded to include rodeos in six different cities every year. The 1993 schedule took the show to the East Coast for its first rodeo in the nation's capital, Washington, D.C." Also, unlike the straight rodeos, all events and competitions in the gay rodeos are open to women.

IGRA currently has twenty member associations representing twenty-five states, the District of Columbia, and two Canadian provinces. A full season of regional rodeos concludes with international finals in Denver. For more information about IGRA or upcoming rodeo seasons, contact IGRA Executive Office, 900 East Colfax Avenue, Denver, CO 80218; Phone: 303/832-IGRA.

CITIES THAT HAVE HOSTED RODEOS OF THE INTERNATIONAL GAY RODEO ASOCIATION

Albuquerque, NM
Atlanta, GA
Bethesda, MD
Chicago, IL
Colorado Springs, CO
Denver, CO
Detroit, MI
Kansas City, MO
Little Rock, AR

Los Angeles, CA
Minneapolis, MN
Oklahoma City, OK
Phoenix, AZ
San Diego, CA
San Francisco, CA
Seattle, WA
Tucson, AZ
Wichita, KS

OTHER LESBIAN COWGIRLS

The 1995 Atlanta Gay Rodeo held in Atlanta, Georgia on April 28–30, included such spectacles as The Wild Drag Race, the Goat Dressing, and The Calf Scramble, in addition to the more traditional bull riding, bareback bronco riding, and others. The event was sponsored by SEGRA (South East Gay Rodeo Association).

THE FIRST ANNUAL BOSTON–NEW YORK AIDS RIDE

On September 15–17, 1995, the first annual Boston–New York AIDS Ride took place. Underwritten by Tanqueray, the three-day, noncompetitive bicycle ride from Boston to New York City registered nearly 3,000 riders who tackled the 250 miles as a fund-raiser against AIDS. Each rider was asked to raise $1,200, which will go to three beneficiaries who provide services to people with HIV and AIDS: the Fenway Community Health Project in Boston, the Community Health Project in New York, and the New York City Lesbian and Gay Community Services Center. This was an event of community participation, with the riders being ordinary people from all walks of life who felt they wanted to make a personal commitment to do something about AIDS. The ride itself was accompanied by opening ceremonies in Boston and closing festivities in New York. For information about future AIDS rides, contact the NYC Lesbian and Gay Community Services Center, 208 West 13th Street, New York, NY 10011; Phone: 212/620-7310.

LESBIANS AND GOLF

DINAH SHORE TOURNAMENT

The Dinah Shore Weekend occurs every third weekend in March in Palm

Springs. Lesbians and golf-lovers flock to this city for the LPGA (Ladies Professional Golf Association, founded by lesbian Babe Didrickson Zaharias) tournament to which the former big-band singer lent her name in 1972. With 25,000 women arriving annually, it is the largest gathering of lesbians in the world, "a surreal land of the Amazons," according to reporter Tracie Cone (*San Jose Mercury News*). Parties for women, sponsored by major corporations, outdraw the golf tournament. The week provides many lesbians who live outside major cities to escape hometowns where they may not be able to be openly gay. And it is an economic windfall for the host town—their most lucrative week of tourism all year.

LESBIAN GOLF STATS

Players in the Ladies Professional Golf Association estimate that 30 to 40 percent of the women playing professional golf are lesbians. However, none of the currently top-ranked 144 players are out.

I WAS A LESBIAN SEX SLUT AT THE DINAH SHORE GOLF CLASSIC

Angela Darling,

Greetings from sunny Palm Springs, California!

I am *over* the East Village/New York scene. I don't care if I ever again hear acid house music, eat Ukrainian food, search for love in the Outweek, oh excuse me, hunt personals, or try to figure out if it's the right night for Girl World, Clit Club or Shescape. Angela, I've had more sex in the last six days than I did in six months on Avenue B. Here at the Dinah Shore Golf Classic, every night is for women, and every day too. It's a nonstop 24-hour party for all kinds of bush bumpers, and it feels like home to me. I feel wonderful, and my skin has cleared up too.

I admit it was a bit of a culture shock at first. It was much too hot for my new Patricia Field jacket, so I left it in the hotel room and headed straight for the cafeteria. I pushed open the swinging doors and there was this huge banner, "Palm Springs Welcomes Dinah Shore Golf Classic Friends." Could that be me? I hate the sun, I hate golf, but Angela, as you well know, I *adore* jocks, and the room was a veritable sea of sportswomen.

Well, my entrance had not gone unnoticed. Maybe they had never seen a Wigstock T-shirt before, or maybe my knee-high Dr. Martens were a little de trop for the green. I don't know. I can't say I was impressed with *their* fashion sense. This was a roomful of women who wouldn't know a Mizrahi from a Mitsubishi. It was either madras, or combos of pink and forest green.

I couldn't move. Ang, I probably would have been frozen in front of the stringbeans forever if this gorgeous woman hadn't tapped me on the shoulder. "First time?" she asked. I nodded. Her name was Samantha and she led me to a table. All around, women were laughing, talking and greeting each other.

"Everyone's here this year," said one. "Except Jane, but I think Lily made it." Another woman took a bite of orange jello and said, "As long as they keep Rita and Martina far apart, there won't be any problems."

"Oh, that's *old*, Betty," a third woman snorted. "That's even older than Jody and what's-her-name and no one cares about that anymore." She turned to me and asked, "So honey, you came to *play*?"

"I don't think so," I mumbled. "I mean I used to play putt-putt in high school, but that's about it."

The women at my table thought I was joking because they screamed with laughter. Betty was laughing so hard she dropped a spoonful of Jell-O. Samantha noticed how embarrassed I was and she reached under the table and put her hand on my trembling leg. She ran her fingers up and down my thigh and smiled at me. "Don't worry, honey, I'm sure you know how to play just fine." And as I soon discovered, "playing" at the Dinah Shore Golf Classic does not necessarily have anything to do with golf. . . .

It started that night. After a few cups of spiked Gatorade, I had loosened up enough to join a group of women in the hot tub for an orgy that lasted for six hours. I only took one break, and that was to run up to my room to get those novelty dildos I bought at the Pink Pussycat. The Minnie Mouse was a real favorite, although the Susan Sontag ran a close second. And before you start lecturing me, Angela, there were endless supplies of condoms and dental dams and these girls knew how to use them.

When the orgy at the hot tub started slowing down, I had a moment of panic. This can't end yet, I thought, I'm just warming up. I guess my desperation was pretty obvious, because Gladys, one of the finest toe suckers I've ever known, stopped what she was doing and took my hand. "It's alright, honey. This hotel has 237 rooms and every room has a party. And that doesn't even include the banquet hall."

So Angela, I spent the next six days and nights moving from one party to the next, delighting in the sensual imaginations of my Sapphic sisters. It was all remarkably good-natured, no tension, no attitude. Well, that's not entirely true. Muffy Jenkins accused my new friend Marge of stealing her prized day-glo golf ball collection and using them as Ben-wa balls. Marge denied it, but Muffy went on a rampage and I had to hide Marge in my room for a few hours until someone could calm her down. (Muffy was one of the few women who actually came to play golf, and was not well-liked.)

Marge and I used the time to compare notes. Marge, a three-time Classic veteran, had a complicated rating system for different women which I didn't entirely follow, as it was based on golf terms: under par, caddy, birdy, hole in one, sandtrap. We both gave highest scores to Doris from Martinez, California. My nickname for Doris had been "200% Polyester" because of her taste for synthetics, but undressed, Doris was a tiger.

The Classic ended with a banquet and dance and it was actually fun to put on clothes for a change. Loretta Johnson kept dropping ice cubes down dresses and offering to find them again. Muriel and Sandy started a mini-tryst by the fruit bowl and created new uses for the tangelos, while Henrietta passed out the fresh whipped butter tubs to all interested. It was the kind of night where anything could happen.

Angela, as I looked around the ballroom at all my new-found friends I felt positively sentimental. How could I ever go back to my drab East Village existence? I ran to the ladies room to collect my thoughts, to stop the morbid fears of what the end of this week would mean for me. At the sink was a woman humming a little tune as she dried her hands with a paper towel. She was an older woman, full of energy and radiating self-confidence. It was Dinah Shore! "Having a good time, sweetie?" she asked.

"Oh yes," I replied. "The best."

"That's great. Be sure to try the chicken breasts, mmmm. We woman athletes have to stick together."

Angela, it was at that moment I made a decision. I called a travel agent, and was able to cash in the return portion of my plane ticket in exchange for a bus ticket to Gary, Indiana. Angela, I know you won't mind feeding Nooshka for another two weeks. (There's more kitty litter in the cabinet under the kitchen sink.) I'm off with Marge to the Professional Women's Bowling Tournament. Marge swears it's the hottest action around, and I can't wait!

Love
Tanya

—Katy Krocodile

SOURCE: Reprinted with permission from *My Comrade/Sister*, Winter, 1991.

NATIONAL WOMEN'S MARTIAL ARTS FEDERATION

This nonprofit agency promotes women in the martial arts, runs regional and national competitions for all styles and experience levels, and provides networking opportunities across the country. Contact: NWMAF, P.O. Box 820, King's Park, NY 11754.

INTERNATIONAL ASSOCIATION OF GAY AND LESBIAN MARTIAL ARTISTS

A voting member of the Federation of Gay Games, and founded in 1990 after the Vancouver Games, IAGLMA helps martial artists of all styles network within the lesbian and gay community. A $20 membership fee to this nonprofit organization gets you a quarterly newsletter and information about upcoming events, seminars, and competitions. For more information, E-mail at IAGLMA@aol.com or write: IAGLMA, P.O. Box 590601, San Francisco, CA 94159; Phone: 610/940-1434.

THE LARGEST WOMEN'S FLAG FOOTBALL TOURNAMENT IN THE NATION

The Third Annual (1994) Key West Women's Flag Football League Ferrari National Kick-Off offered $2,000 in prizes and subscriptions to *Girljock* magazine.

LESBIAN ATHLETE WHO WAS FIRED FROM THE (SHORT-LIVED) WOMEN'S PRO BASKETBALL LEAGUE FOR BEING TOO AGGRESSIVE OFF THE COURT, AND BASICALLY BEING A LESBIAN SPOTTED AT A GAY PRIDE PARADE

Mariah Burton Nelson

THE LARGEST LESBIAN/GAY SPORTS GROUP

The International Gay Bowling Organization

LESBIAN ATHLETES' AUTOBIOGRAPHIES

Navratilova, Martina, with George Vecsey. *Martina.* Alfred Knopf, 1985.
King, Billie Jean, with Kim Chapin. *Billie Jean,* Harper & Row, 1974. (prelesbian scandal)
King, Billie Jean, with Frank Deford. *Billie Jean.* Viking, 1982. (postlesbian scandal)
Nelson, Mariah Burton. *Are We Winning Yet?* Random House, 1991

PROFILE

A Martina Navratilova Time Line

Late 1940s: Soviets invaded Czechoslovakia; wealthy families, like Martina's, lost their estates and property.

Martina
Navratilova
(*Copyright ©
1994 by Morgan
Gwenwald*)

1956: Martina is born on October 18 in Prague, then the capital city of Czecho-slovakia.

1968: Martina was eleven when the Czech people rebelled against the Communist government; in August, the Russians quelled the rebellion and the country lost its morale.

1969: A rising young tennis star at the age of thirteen, Martina was allowed out of the country for the first time to compete in a tournament in West Germany.

1973: Martina played tennis for the first time in the United States.

1975: She applied for and received political asylum in the United States.

1978: She won her first Wimbledon championship; the WTA ranked her as the number-one women's player in the world, replacing Chris Everet who had held that position for four years.

1979: Martina met Rita Mae Brown after a tournament in Virginia. Within a year they became lovers and lived together on a nine-acre estate in Charlottesville, Virginia.

1980: After a match in Florida, Martina met Nancy Lieberman, a professional women's basketball player, who promised to help her get into tip-top physical shape.

1981: Billie Jean King's palimony suit appeared in all the newspapers, and Martina worried that her own sexual orientation would be disclosed, ruining her chances for citizenship.

  • Martina applied for U.S. citizenship in California in the hopes of more tolerant attitudes toward sexuality.

  • Martina was granted U.S. citizenship.

  • The *New York Daily News* publishes an interview with Martina about her relationship with Rita Mae, thus making Martina the only major athlete to publicly come out while still competing.

1984: Martina and Judy Nelson fall in love and are "married" in a Methodist church in Brisbane, Australia.

1985: Martina publishes her autobiography, which discloses her relationships with women but identifies her as bisexual. Until she is sued for galimony in 1991, the topic of her homosexuality is rarely discussed outside lesbian circles and she herself downplays it.

  • Martina leaves Nancy and moves to Aspen, Colorado, with her new "spouse," Judy Nelson.

1991: The relationship with Judy ends, and Martina is sued for galimony.

1992: Colorado voters pass Amendment 2, which allows discrimination against lesbians and gay men. After years of silence, Martina decides to speak out against antigay bigotry in Colorado and across the country.

1993: Martina is a featured speaker at the massive March on Washington for lesbian and gay rights; she is the most quoted speaker.

  • A lesbian and gay tribute to Martina is held at Madison Square Garden in New York City as a fund-raiser for the upcoming Gay Games IV. The event raises more than $250,000 and Billie Jean King appears with Martina.

1994: Martina is the chief spokesperson and official poster girl for the Gay Games IV.

  • At age thirty-eight, Martina retires from tennis, having won more major singles titles than any other female player in history.

PROFILE

Susan Greene

For a good example of the boundless energy of athletes, one need look no further than nationally ranked squash player Susan Greene.

Susan maintains her status as one of the top fifty squash players in the nation by playing in tournaments most weekends out of the year, but she still finds time for a variety of community-related activities, including volunteering at New York City's Lesbian and Gay Switchboard and the Pat Parker/Vito Russo library at the New York City Lesbian and Gay Community Services Center. She also helped to organize a gay and lesbian alumni group for her alma mater and acted as chairperson of the squash tournament/events for the 1994 Gay Games IV (where she also competed and won a medal).

"The 1994 Gay Games were the first games I had been involved with," Susan says. "I knew someone who was involved with the organizing of the games, and she tapped me to run the squash events after the first person didn't work out. I signed up because I didn't want to see the squash events not happen."

A long-time squash enthusiast, Susan had never run a tournament before, but that didn't stop her from organizing several different rounds, including events in women's A, B, C, and D levels and men's events according to age group. Susan was kept extremely busy, both running the tournament and playing in it, winning a bronze medal in the women's A level. "I didn't see one other sport the whole week," she confesses. "I began every morning at eight A.M. and got home at midnight for a week." Her workplace was very supportive about her involvement in the Gay Games and gave her a week off.

Susan also has another distinction to her credit as an athlete: she is a two-time participant in the international Maccabiah Games (also known as the Jewish Olympics, she says). She tried out for the U.S. squash teams in 1989 and 1993 and made it both times, a feat that entitled her to free trips to Israel for three weeks for the competitions. In 1993, the U.S. squash team of which she was part won the silver team medal.

The experience of competing with other Jewish athletes in front of thousands of spectators was exhilarating, she notes. "But even though I was in the midst of all these other Jewish athletes, I still felt separated from them," she stated, because of her sexual orientation. In 1989, Susan did not feel comfortable enough to be out at the Maccabiah Games, but by 1993 she was a lone pioneer, the only out gay athlete on the entire 500-member U.S. team.

"It has really been an exciting and educational experience to have been in two international competitions that are so different from each other," the thirty-two-year-old athlete said, speaking of both the Gay and Jewish competitions.

Born in 1962 in Rochester, New York, Susan grew up outside Philadelphia and went to Abbington Friends School (a small Quaker school with only seventy-seven in its graduating class), where she played tennis both in school and in junior tournaments.

"Sports were always encouraged at home," Susan relates. "I would go out and throw a football with my dad while my mother cooked—to her credit she never called me in to help. I am an only child, and I was lucky that they could spend the time to practice with me and come see my matches or take me to the skating rink."

She continued her athletic ways at Trinity College in Hartford, Connecticut, where she was a political science major, playing four years of tennis, two seasons of squash, a season of basketball, and time as a field hockey goalie. By her senior year, she made the varsity squash team and was voted most improved player.

After graduating college in 1984, Susan ended up in the publishing world in New York City, working at a foreign affairs magazine until 1989. Since then, she has worked at a stock photo agency, which represents photographers and sells their images to textbooks, newspapers, and so on.

When she arrived in New York to join the working world, she also joined a squash club and quickly started playing in tournaments. She started as a B player, but after only a few years became an A player, essentially teaching herself. "I've spent a lot of time on squash road trips," she states, "and it's somewhat reminiscent of college. In fact, one of the reasons I play squash is for the social aspect. It's a lesson my folks taught me: that an athletic skill is useful for meeting people and for developing camaraderie." But make no mistake; Susan takes her game seriously, too: "It's a fact that I like competing."

On the whole, you could say that Susan Greene has been good for squash (the Gay Games IV tournaments would not have taken place without her), but squash has also been good to Susan Greene. "In fact"—she smiles—"I met my main relationship in a squash club. One of the great things about the relationship was that we could go to squash games together and share that interest."

In addition to her other volunteer activities, Susan also founded an informal squash group in Manhattan—initially to get volunteers for the 1994 Games— which she dubbed the New York Nicks ("nicks" is a squash term designating a ball that hits the bottom of the floor and the wall and dies). "As chairperson of the 1994 Games squash events, I got a call from the Boston gay squash group who wanted to play the New York group. Unfortunately, a New York group didn't exist. I named it on the spot and started making phone calls. Currently, we have a list of about forty to fifty names, with about thirty-five men, which is really nice because gay male squash players tend to be more isolated than lesbian squash players." A few months ago, the New York Nicks had a small round robin; there are plans for a full-fledged gay squash tournament in the fall of 1995.

In addition to her other work and volunteer activities, Susan also is on the board of the Metro Squash and Racket Association (the New York City–wide squash association) and acts as chairperson of the league, overseeing the tournaments. "What can I say?" she asks good-naturedly. "I just love squash."

---

18. Lesbians and Travel

No matter what your travel interests or financial considerations, it's great to get away from it all—either camping on the cheap with your sweetie or friends or being pampered at a Victorian bed-and-breakfast in Provincetown.

While this chapter isn't meant to be a definitive lesbian travel guide (there are plenty of those already out there), it's designed as a guidepost to finding the resources and information you'll need to plan that much-needed time away with your lover or your friends. Have a great vacation—and send us a postcard.

Lesbian Travel Resources

Books and Magazines

The resources listed below are available at most gay-friendly bookstores or newsstands, in addition to the direct numbers provided. Also, the International Gay

Travel Association (800/448-8550) provides contact information for its member travel agencies, guest houses, and tour operators.

Damron guides are known for their male-oriented sexual focus, but the company also publishes the *Women's Traveler*. Filled with information that has a women/lesbian focus, these books are available by calling 800/462-6654.

Detour's guides are written for the more mainstream GUPPIE contingent, with information for the traveler who has a fairly healthy budget. The general tourist listings of accommodations, bars, etc. are peppered with historical and neighborhood information. Their guides are currently available for New York; New England; Miami; Southern California; Washington, D.C.; Amsterdam; London; and Paris. To purchase a guide, call 800/888-2052, ext. 62.

Ferrari publishes guides such as *Places of Interest for Women*, by Marianne Ferrari, which has a unique local perspective on gay-specific destinations. Ms. Ferrari has the editors of local papers in each destination choose points of interest specifically for the lesbian traveler. The guide also includes comprehensive cruise and tour listings. Another Ferrari guidebook, *InnPlaces,* is a source of both lesbian and gay and lesbian/gay-friendly accommodations worldwide. The book consists of entirely of paid advertisements, yet as a reference for anyone considering alternative accommodations, it is a must. To order a Ferrari publication, call 602/863-2408.

Our World was started in 1986, and it is the first gay travel magazine. It is known for being one of the first gay publications to not accept sexually oriented advertising. Its listings, editorials, and photos can be helpful planning tools for your vacation; just be aware of all the advertising and reprinted press releases. To subscribe to *Our World,* call 904/441-5367.

Out & About has only been in existence for two years, but it is a favorite among gay travelers. It describes itself as "a privately published newsletter providing travel information free from advertising bias for lesbian and gay travelers and their travel agents." It is full of information and locations ranging from traditional to hold-onto-your-hat adventures. Monthly issues contain articles on travel from a gay perspective, up-to-date city information, tour and cruise announcements, and bed and breakfast reviews. If you can't find it at your newsstand, write to: Out & About Inc., 8 West 19th Street, Suite 401, New York, NY 10011; or call 800/929-2268.

Following are more travel guides that might be helpful:

Adventures in Good Company: The Complete Guide to Women's Tours and Outdoor Trips (1994), Thalia Zepatos; Eighth Mountain Press, Portland

A Journey of One's Own: Uncommon Adventures for the Independent Woman Traveler (1992), Thalia Zepatos; Eighth Mountain Press, Portland

Women's Travel Guides to San Francisco/Amsterdam/Paris/New York; all published by Virago Press, London

Betty and Pansy's Severe Queer Review of New York/San Francisco/Washington, D.C.,; published by Bedpan Productions, 584 Castro Street, Suite 410, San Francisco, CA 94114-2588

Australia for Women (1994), by Susan Hawthorne and Renate Klein; published by The Feminist Press at The City University of New York, 311 East 94th Street, New York, NY 10128. (Forthcoming guides in same series: *China for Women, Italy for Women, Greece for Women*)

SELECTED TRAVEL LITERATURE BOOKS

Barnes Djuna. *New York* (1989 reprint)

Hersey, John. *Key West Tales* (1993)

Keith, June. *Postcards from Paradise: Romancing Key West* (1995)

Lane, Michael, and Jim Crotty. *Mad Monks on the Road: A 47,000 Hour Dashboard Adventure—From Paradise, California to Royal, Arkansas and Up the New Jersey Turnpike* (1993). (Also available: *Monk Magazine* by the same authors. You can be sure it is filled with just as much wacky travel stuff as the book, with articles like "Portland Kicks Butt," etc.) Write: 175 Fifth Avenue, Suite 2322, New York, NY 10010; or call 212/465-3231

Miller, John, ed. *San Francisco Street* (1990)

Newton, Esther. *Cherry Grove, Fire Island: Sixty Years in America's First Gay and Lesbian Town* (1993)

Trebay, Guy, with photographs by Sylvia Plachy. *In the Place to Be: Guy Trebay's New York* (1994)

Van Gelder, Linsey, and Pamela Brandt. *Are You Two . . . Together?* (1991)—a guide to western Europe, part literature, part travel information

LESBIAN/GAY TRAVEL ORGANIZATIONS

Gay Hospitality Exchange International
P.O. Box 612, Station C
Montreal, QC H2L 4K5

Gayroute: Tour Gay Canada
Box 314-G, Station deLorimier
Montreal, QC H2H 2N7

International Gay Travel Association
P.O. Box 4974
Key West, FL 33041
Phone: 800/448-8550

Olivia Cruises
4400 Market Street
Oakland, CA 94608
Phone: 510/655-0364 or 800/631-6277

BARBARA AND BRIDGET'S GUIDE TO CAMPING FOR FIRST-TIMERS

BY BARBARA BICKART AND BRIDGET HUGHES

We have been camping together for five years now and we've got a good thing going, but our advice to new campers or women who are camping together for the

Bridget Hughes (l.) and Barbara Bickart on a camping trip in Sedona, Arizona

first time is to figure out what camping means to you first. We had a few really good fights on this topic.

For instance: the Bridget Hughes Way to Camp is all about settling in and making yourself at home in the woods. You get to know the trails that lead to your tent and you slowly fall in love with the view from your fireside and the very specific trees in your site. You must get the best campsite, hang a clothesline, and pitch your tent before dusk. Then put the cooler on the plastic tablecloth, make a plate of Triscuits and hickory smoked cheese, light the citronella candles, and sit back listening to John Denver and the Supremes singing softly above the sound of crickets. Then you carve your personal roasting stick, drink from tin cups, and make s'mores under the stars and sparks. It's a truly beautiful vision of camping, perfected by different Hughes relatives, and made magical by childhood memories.

Not that childhood memories haven't shaped the Barbara Bickart Way to Camp. Indeed, they have. That's why the Barbara Bickart Way to Camp is the only right way to camp, because it's the way the Bickarts do it. They have no real affection for the site or any interest in things suggesting domesticity in the woods—things like clotheslines. Bickarts are minimalists, purists in the purest sense of the word. They don't unpack. They open the hatchback where the cooler sits ready for easy access, it never has to come out of the car. Neither does anything else, really. You only need to bring out the tent and a sleeping bag. You get up at the crack of dawn, because someone is hollering, "We're burning daylight!" So then you are too tired in the evening to stay up past dark. Campsites are for sleeping; that's all. You move around a lot. That's the point. You cover a lot of ground and see everything, you travel light and feel the thrill of needing nothing but water in your bag and a small can of asparagus or peanuts and raisins for a snack. A favorite Bickart pastime is to play Roots & Herbs with the campfire at night, adding pine cones and grasses that throw delicious camping aromas into the air.

Whatever camping means to you, just be sure to figure it out first, discuss it, and plan together what you want to do.

OUR ADVICE ON WHAT TO BRING

Swiss army knife (each person should have her very own)
Tent (with an external frame, we recommend Ureka for the brand)
Lantern (Coleman)
A big cooler (with a tray to keep some stuff from getting soggy)
Flashlights and candles
Sleeping bags (the kind that zip together and make a two-person bag)
Foam mattress, especially if you are past your twenties (We recommend the Thermarest self-inflating kind. Even Bickarts use the mattresses. It's okay.)
Waterproof matches
Rope (twenty feet, for a clothesline and emergencies)
A nest of cooking pots
Coleman stove and/or a hibachi with coals
Little folding chairs
Water bottles (two per person for long hikes; get Nalgene widemouthed quart bottles)
Wool socks and hiking boots
A day pack

THINGS TO GET AT THE GROCERY STORE NEAR YOUR CAMPSITE

Aluminum foil
Toilet paper
Baby wipes (for cleaning up your hands)
A big water jug

Charcoal and lighter fluid
Garlic and onions
Some canned goods and pasta
Graham crackers, marshmallows, and Hershey bars

SOME FUN CAMPING RECIPES

S'mores: roast the marshmallow, put it on a graham cracker with chocolate, like a sandwich.
Corn: you can cook it in the husk over the fire; it will steam itself.
Famous WOW Retreat Veggie Pockets: cut up raw vegetables (whatever kind you like) into little chunks or slices and add cloves of garlic. Sprinkle with salt and pepper and drizzle with olive oil. Put a handful or two on tinfoil, wrap it up, and seal it around the edges. Put it near the fire and it will cook in about a half hour.

It needs some moisture to steam itself, so you can add a little water or marinate the vegetables first.

PLACES TO GO

Cape Hatteras National Seashore, North Carolina: camp on the beach.

Grand Canyon, Arizona: The North Rim is less populated and really beautiful, though the view of the canyon from the rim is not as extensive. The famous views are from the South Rim, but who cares about fame when you can have solitude.

Algonquin Provincial Park, Whitney, Ontario, Canada: Fly in a water taxi, with a rented canoe and all your gear twelve miles up into the main lake and then explore for days on end canoeing along the network of inland waterways from campsite to campsite.

Glacier National Park, Montana

North of Highlands Campground, North Truro, Massachusetts: ten-minute ride to Provincetown, on Cape Cod. This is a private campground, where the trees have been left in place and where there is plenty of room between campsites, so you don't have to listen to your neighbors snoring.

Long Lake, New York: A couple of hours from Lake George, only much more remote and quiet. Rent a canoe for as many days as you need, fill it with all of your stuff. Paddle out to one of the islands that has a campsite on it. Set up your tent. Swim, pick fresh water mussels, and listen to the loons at night.

Yosemite National Park, California

Great Smoky Mountains National Park in North Carolina

Juniper Springs Campground in the Ocala National Forest, Florida

Oak Creek Canyon, Arizona

Zion National Park, Utah: Hike to Angels Landing; tube in the river

Arches National Park, Moab, Utah

Canyonlands National Park, Utah

Badlands National Park, North Dakota

Acadia National Park, near Bar Harbor, Maine

Swans Island, Maine: This is off the coast of Acadia and worth going to and renting a cabin for a week. There is no camping available, but it's gorgeous and quiet. Get lots of reading and nooky done. Socialize with each other because there's not really anyone else to do it with, except when buying milk and groceries at the general store and lobsters from Norman, the lobsterman, who lives in the white house at the end of the road, up on the hill. That's Norman, the son, not the father.

Lilly Bay State Park, Greenville, Maine: Gorgeous and rustic on Moosehead Lake

Note: Make calls and reservations for campsites ahead of time if you are going in the spring and summer, especially to national parks and North of Highlands in North Truro on Cape Cod. If you are ever desperate for a good, clean, hot shower, look for a KOA (Kampgrounds of America). They are usually really sparse and ugly and full of trailers, concrete, and pinball games, but they have good bathrooms.

WOMEN'S FESTIVAL SCHEDULE FOR 1995

This list first appeared in *Lesbian Connection*, the free nationwide forum of news and ideas for lesbians. For more info or to get on *LC*'s mailing list, write to: *LC*, c/o Ambitious Amazons, P.O. Box 811, East Lansing, MI 48826.

Women's International Square Dance
  Event
Early March in Denver, Colorado
Sugar & Spice Sister Squares
P.O. Box 480122
Denver, CO 80248
Phone: 303/433-4948
Hotel: 800/800-8000

Gulf Coast Womyn's Festival
Mid-April at Camp Sister Spirit
GCWF
P.O. Box 12
Ovett, MS 39464
Phone: 601/344-2005

Virginia Women's Music Festival
Mid-May
INTOUCH
Rt. 2, Box 1096
Kent's Store, VA 23084
Phone: 804/589-6542

In Gaia's Lap, The Maryland Womyn's
  Gathering
Mid-May
21300 Heathcote Rd.
Freeland, MD 21053
Phone: 410/329-6708

Campfest
Late May (Memorial Day weekend)
Campfest
R.R. 5, Box 185
Franklinville, NJ 08322
Phone: 609/694-2037
TTY: 301/598-9035 (eves.)

WiminFest
Late May (Memorial Day weekend)
WiminFest
P.O. Box 80204

Albuquerque, NM 87198-0204
Phone: 505/265-3297

National Women's Music Festival
Early June in Bloomington, IN
NWMF
Dept. LC
P.O. Box 1427
Indianapolis, IN 46206
Phone: 317/927-9355

Womongathering
Festival of Womyn's Spirituality
Mid June in the Poconos
R.R. 5, Box 185
Franklinville, NJ 08322
Phone: 609/694-2037

Northampton Lesbian Festival
Mid-July
WOW Productions
160 Main St.
Northampton, MA 01060
Phone: 413/586-8251

20th Michigan Womyn's Music
  Festival
Mid August
Near Hart, Michigan
WWTMC
Box 22
Walhalla, MI 49458
Phone: 616/757-4766
Sept.–May:
Box 7430
Berkeley, CA 94707
Phone: 510/652-5441

West Coast Women's Music &
  Comedy Fest
(Labor Day weekend)
Near Yosemite, California

Robin Tyler Prod.
15842 Chase St.
North Hills, CA 91343
Phone: 818/893-4075
Fax: 818/893-1593

Rhythmfest
Labor Day weekend
Rhythmfest
957 N. Highland Ave.
Atlanta, GA 30306
Phone: 404/873-1551

Ohio Lesbian Festival
Early Sept.
Near Columbus, Ohio
LBA
P.O. Box 02086
Columbus, OH 43202
Phone: 614/267-DYKE (267-3953)

Sisterspace Pocono Weekend
Early Sept.
In Pennsylvania's Poconos Mountains
 (2½ hrs. from NYC & Philly)

Sisterspace of the Delaware Valley
 (SODV)
542A S. 48th St.
Philadelphia, PA 19143
Phone: 215/747-7565 or 215/476-8856

Wild Western Women's Weekend
Late September
INTOUCH
Rt. 2, Box 1096
Kent's Store, VA 23084
Phone: 804/589-6542

Heart of the West Fest
Early November
In Las Vegas, Nevada
Plus Prod.
P.O. Box 103
Lakeside, CA 92040
Phone: 800/GET-PLUS
Fax: 619/390-9830

TRAVEL ON-LINE

A new guide and resource called *The Gay Traveler: An Online Lesbian and Gay Travel Resource* opened in May 1995 on America Online under the Gay and Lesbian Community Forum. The new service includes such information as lists of lesbian and gay tour operators and cruise companies; libraries of travel brochures and booklets that you can download; a calendar of lesbian and gay travel events; a directory of people and places; profiles of popular lesbian and gay resorts such as Provincetown, Palm Springs, and Key West; and travel tips for every part of the globe, from North America to the Pacific Rim.

The Gay Traveler also features a "Friday Letter" every week, chock-full of interesting travel information, and a "Travel Conference" live every Wednesday night from 9 to 10 P.M. EST in the GLCF Community Conference Room.

Don't miss this information-packed resource guide that's waiting for you on your computer.

NATIONAL CAR RENTAL: THEY REALLY DO TRY HARDER

Renting a car anywhere in the United States? In late 1994, National Car Rental became the first major car rental agency to recognize domestic part- ners when accepting additional drivers on car rental contracts. All other companies charge unmarried couples an additional $5 per day when they add a second driver, while legally married couples can add another driver at no cost, a policy that clearly discriminates against lesbians and gays. Na- tional has also pledged to donate to lesbian and gay charities 5 percent of the gross receipts of cars reserved through travel agents affiliated with the International Gay Travel Association (IGTA).

Lesbian and gay travelers interested in reserving National rental cars should contact their local IGTA travel agent or call National directly at 800/328-4567.

SOURCE: "The Gay Traveler Friday Letter," May 26, 1995, America Online

---

PROFILE

Cherry Grove

If San Francisco was America's gay capital in terms of political clout, the Grove was its summer capital, the pleasure island of gay imagination. The resort's lack of formal power was no indication of what its rumored existence represented in hope and possibility.

—ESTHER NEWTON

It was exactly that hope and possibility that would draw lesbians to Cherry Grove on Fire Island and keep lesbians in Cherry Grove, quietly fighting to have their own in a town that they helped create.

Geographically, Fire Island is a barrier island that buffers the southern edge of Long Island, New York, from the Atlantic Ocean. Until the 1850s, according to legend, the beach was considered dangerous to visit because of pirates, ghosts, and murdering Indians. Cherry Grove, created in 1869 and getting its name from the wild black cherry trees that cover the area, is the oldest and continuously inhab- ited resort on Fire Island.

Gay people stared coming to Cherry Grove from New York City in the 1920s and 1930s. Most of them were affiliated with the theater in some way. "Gay the- ater people's migration to Cherry Grove is one of the clearest proofs we have that sexual preference was becoming the basis for a complete social identity," says Es- ther Newton in her history of Cherry Grove. Then, after being devastated by a hurricane in 1938, gay men and some lesbians found a place they could afford, and began buying property that no one else would.

Cherry Grove was the first, and for years the only, gay-controlled area in the United States. Many gay vacation spots like Provincetown, Massachusetts; Key West, Florida; and Cherry Grove were (and to a large degree, still are) the *only* public resort places lesbians and gay men could gather and be social without being subjected to the same level of pressure and hostility they would receive from straight society in other communities. "Of these resorts," says Newton, "the Grove was the only one with such a substantial gay majority, and so it was the safest."

It is important to recognize that the place where lesbians and gays were first able to be openly together was a resort. Cherry Grove was considered a private sphere as opposed to the public sphere of the city. So, though gay people could be open about their sexuality while on the island, this was clearly a case of keeping all sexuality in the private sphere. Cherry Grove was the proverbial bedroom in which gay people were to keep their sexual business.

Gay people in Cherry Grove eventually became very visible not only to each other, but to the outside world. This visibility has created what Newton describes as "the false idea that gay is synonymous with young, white, male, promiscuous, artistically inclined, and middle class." [In reality] An important part of the Grove's history has included other gay people that do not fit these stereotypes, and their fight to be recognized, both on the island and off.

One must realize that Cherry Grove was not a fantasy island that gay people necessarily chose because they wanted to, but it was a place where they retreated due to the lack of tolerance and choices available within a straight society. It was a matter of settling for certain possibilities.

Many of the Grove's first lesbians were white women with their own incomes, either from jobs or family money. They had high standing within professional and social circles. On the island they were lesbians tried and true, with lovers and dyke drama that would rival today's standards. But in the outside world, many of these women maintained husbands (often gay men) and families for cover in straight society. This first period of lesbian presence, from the 1930s to the late 1950s, is what Newton refers to as the "country club era." These Grove ladies got along well with the other men on the island, were not excluded from the cultural realm, and were rarely discriminated against.

From the 1960s to the 1980s, a new group of women, many of them Jewish and Italian from working-class and middle-class backgrounds, came to the Grove and fought for their place against quite a bit of resistance. The ladies of the country club era saw them as brash and uncultured, and the men saw them as spaces taken up that could have been filled by other men.

Throughout both these periods, women tended to socialize differently than most of the men on the island. There were the bars that stayed mixed, but women tended to have gatherings and theme parties at their houses while men played more in the bars or at drag shows and spent their time cruising and having outdoor sex.

If women had such a hard time, why would they want to be in the Grove? Their options were even more limited than those of gay men, and because of the power gay men had in the Grove, women could also enjoy the same freedom of a publicly open sexuality while remaining relatively safe from the advances and violence of straight men.

When AIDS hit hard during the 1980s, male predominance in the Grove weakened. This fact, accompanied by an increase in some women's discretionary income and a softening of the lesbian separatist ideas of the 1970s, brought the largest influx of women to the Grove since its inception. Many second-generation dykes (those from the 1960s), were glad to see more women in the Grove, but there was a rift in the way the two groups viewed things on the island.

Older lesbians who had to fight for their place in the Grove felt lucky to be able to exist in what they saw as a male community and wanted the newcomers to do the same. The new lesbians, having more of a feminist sensibility, were not tied to the old (male) ways of the island and would voice their opinions among themselves about the sexist male attitudes they felt were infringing upon their rights. Old-timers of both sexes really weren't ready for the lesbian baby boom, still seeing the Grove as a place of exile and fantasy. Marriage and families were *adult* things that most gay people of the first two generations thought they would never have; hence, the Grove had always been a place where gay women and men could be young indefinitely. Seeing lesbians with children shattered the dream world, and many felt that children had no place on the island.

Toward the 1990s, lesbians were almost half of all renters, though they owned only 15 percent of the 275 homes many dreamed of buying. Today, Cherry Grove is known as the lesbian part of Fire Island, and it is still as beautiful and wonderful as one might imagine it was in its early bohemian days.

SOURCE: Esther Newton, *Cherry Grove, Fire Island: Sixty Years in America's First Gay and Lesbian Town* (Beacon, 1993)

HOW TO GET TO CHERRY GROVE

Cherry Grove is accessible via the Long Island Railroad (for schedules, phone 718/217-5477) from Penn Station, New York, to Sayville (fare: $17.50 round-trip peak, $12 round-trip off peak; you'll transfer at either Babylon or Jamaica). When you exit at Sayville, shuttle buses (fare: $2 each way) will be waiting to take you to the ferry (for departure times, phone 516/589-0810; fare: $10 round-trip). The entire trip will take approximately two hours.

PROFILE

Provincetown

As the heat of summer settles over the cities of the northeastern United States, the thoughts of lesbians and gay men turn to the gay resort at the tip of Cape Cod, affectionately known as P'town.

For many years a quiet fishing village, Provincetown was the site where the first British settlers landed in the early 1600s. It is now "the definitive gay resort," according to the lesbian and gay travel magazine, *Out & About,* with accommodations, businesses, bars, and restaurants catering to lesbian and gay clientele.

Memorial Day weekend marks the beginning of the ten-week season for this New England resort town. Traditional summer holidays like Memorial Day, July Fourth, and Labor Day mean big crowds and a tight market for accommodations. The carnival held each August is another time when the town fills to overflowing, as is Women's Weekend in October. But with nearly fifty hotels and guest houses, Provincetown almost always has room for a couple more.

On the other hand, it's best not to just drop in to Provincetown in the summer without reservations. During the season, most of the better resorts have a five-day minimum stay. While there may always be room at the inn, it may not be exactly the inn you envisioned on those hot sweltering days at home. Early planning pays off in P'town. The town has a wide variety of hotels, bed-and-breakfasts, and quaint inns, some predominantly lesbian, some mixed lesbian and gay men. You can also rent cottages and condos if you're planning a longer stay.

No cars are necessary in Provincetown. In fact, make sure your inn has free parking, or a car can be a bit of a hindrance. Everything you need—from restaurants to shops to dancing—is accessible by foot along Provincetown's main thoroughfare, Commercial Street.

Summer is chock-full of entertainment, and the local clubs book many nationally known lesbian and gay performers. You can catch comedian Kate Clinton's act or run into her shopping on Commercial Street: she's a year-round resident of P'town.

HANDY NUMBERS FOR PLANNING YOUR P'TOWN VACATION

In Town Reservation: 800/67P'TOWN (accommodations)
Provincetown Reservations System: 800/648-0364 (accommodations)
Provincetown Business Guild: 800/637-8696 (offers a free guide to the town)

E-MAIL ADDRESSES FOR PLANNING YOUR P'TOWN VACATION

P Banner1@aol.com: *Provincetown Banner* (local newspaper)
Idilu@aol.com: timeshare information
AKHalles@aol.com: apartment and cottage rental
CrazyCJ@aol.com: a P'town specialist offering information on the best resorts, clubs, etc., by mail
  Make sure you include your mailing address.

SOURCE: "The Gay Travelers," Gay and Lesbian Community Forum, America Online

PART VII

⚜

AN AIDS PRIMER

INTRODUCTION: LESBIANS AND HIV/AIDS

Since 1981, when it first began ravaging the gay community, this four-letter acronym for acquired immunodeficiency syndrome has torn many of our lives apart, and lesbians have been in the forefront of AIDS activism. The lesbian and gay community has constructed health and treatment networks, clinics, and national organizations to care for our own. We've taken to the streets of Washington and our state capitals for needed funding. We've sponsored bereavement programs to deal with the realities of grief and multiple loss. We've created films, art, music, and literature on the political and personal faces of the pandemic, trying to make sense out of our pain.

Do lesbians get HIV disease? The answer is yes. The data on woman-to-woman transmission is inconclusive, but many lesbian-identified women have been infected through other means, including sex with men and injection drug use. This makes it important for lesbians to be up-front with their sexual partners and to follow specific guidelines for keeping safe.

In this section, we'll briefly outline the AIDS pandemic, define some of its most frequently used terms, and look at the responses our community has had to the health crisis within it and without.

SOURCES FOR FURTHER READING

See also the list of newsletters and magazines on pages 453–454.

ACT UP/NY Women and AIDS Book Group. *Women, AIDS, and Activism*. South End Press, 1990.

d'Adesky, Anne-Christine, and Achy Obejas. "Female Figures." *Out* magazine, April 1994.

Madansky, Cynthia, and Julie Tolentino Wood. "Safer Sex Handbook for Lesbians." Lesbian AIDS Project/Gay Men's Health Crisis, Inc., 1993.

Patton, Cindy, and Janis Kelly. *Making It: A Woman's Guide to Sex in the Age of AIDS*. Firebrand Books, 1987.

Solomon, Nancy. "Risky Business: Should Lesbians Practice Safer Sex?" *OUT/LOOK* magazine, Spring 1992.

Vazquez, Carmen. "The Myth of Invulnerability: Lesbians and HIV Disease." *Focus: A Guide to AIDS Research and Counseling*, Vol. 8, No. 9, September 1994.

A Time Line of the AIDS Pandemic

1959: A twenty-five-year-old British man died of a mysterious disease in Manchester. His doctor stored samples of his tissues for future research, and since 1990, many scientists believed that he was the first recorded person to die of AIDS.

1977: A Danish woman surgeon in Zaire died of Pneumocystis carinii pneumonia (PCP) at the age of forty-seven.

1981: An article headlined "Rare Cancer Seen in 41 Homosexuals" appeared on a back page of the *New York Times* on July 3. The cancer was Kaposi's sarcoma (KS), and this was the first major reporting on what would later become known as AIDS.

• A Canadian nun who spent thirty years in Haiti rehabilitating prostitutes died of PCP. She was reported to have had one male sexual partner while in Haiti and no other known risk factors.

• The Centers for Disease Control (CDC) released information about the growing number of cases of Pneumocystis carinii pneumonia (PCP) among gay men. Researchers tried to make a connection between the mysterious disease and the use of the drug amyl nitrite (poppers) among gay men.

• Researchers began to link the outbreaks of KS and PCP among gay men. In an inaccurate and stigmatizing choice of names, a scientist dubbed the new disease gay-related immune disorder (GRID).

• By the end of the year, the disease had begun to show up among intravenous drug users.

1982: At the beginning of the year, the CDC reported that 250 Americans had developed GRID, and 99 of them had died.

• Writers Larry Kramer and Edmund White and four other men founded the Gay Men's Health Crisis (GMHC), a nonprofit organization based in New York City to confront "gay cancer" by raising money for research. GMHC also trained volunteers to staff a hot line for the community's questions and concerns about the disease.

• The *Miami Herald* reported that the "gay plague" had begun to show up among heterosexual Haitian refugees in the form of PCP and toxoplasmosis, a brain infection.

• Lab tests on gay men at St. Luke's–Roosevelt Hospital in New York City showed a connection with cytomegalovirus (CMV) and GRID and also indicated a serious depletion of the T-4 (helper) cells in the men's blood, suggesting a breakdown of their immune systems.

• The first reported cases of GRID among hemophiliacs appeared.

• Because GRID continued to show up in heterosexuals, researchers looked for other more accurate acronyms for the disease. Among those suggested were ACIDS (acquired community immune deficiency syndrome) and CAIDS (community acquired immune deficiency syndrome). Finally, they settled on the new name of AIDS (acquired immunodeficiency syndrome), which was sexually neutral.

• *CBS Nightly News* with Dan Rather broadcast one of the first network news pieces about AIDS.

• One of the first links between AIDS and blood transfusions was made at Bellevue Hospital in New York City, where a heterosexual Latino, who had not used IV drugs but had had massive blood transfusions, came down with PCP.

• The American Red Cross advised lesbians and gay men not to give blood.

• The Centers for Disease Control (CDC) reported cases of immunodeficiency and opportunistic infection in infants born to mothers at risk in New York, New Jersey, and California.

• The CDC reported that 6 percent of the total AIDS cases were women.

1983: In January, the *Morbidity and Mortality Weekly Report (MMWR)* on AIDS established the last major risk group for the disease: female sexual partners of male persons with AIDS (PWAs).

• Two years into the epidemic, the *New York Times* did its first cover story on AIDS.

• U.S. scientists started to look for the beginnings of AIDS, and their findings took them back to Africa, where a Danish woman surgeon living in Zaire had died of PCP in the early 1970s.

• The phrase "innocent victims" begins to be applied to children and blood-transfusion recipients, while other PWAs are stigmatized by "aberrant" sexual and drug-use behavior.

• In New York's gay newspaper, *The Native*, a March 7 cover story by Larry Kramer, "1,112 and Counting," not only indicted the CDC, the *New York Times*, and the New York City Health Commissioner for lack of response to the AIDS crisis, it also lashed out at apathetic gay men who continued to have "careless sex" in the middle of an epidemic.

• Reverend Jerry Falwell, founder of the Moral Majority, told his followers in Lynchburg, Virginia, that AIDS is "the judgment of God."

• A news release of the American Medical Association reported findings (later discredited) that AIDS could be transmitted through casual contact, causing a rash of AIDS hysteria stories in the press.

• The CDC reported immunodeficiency among female sexual partners of men with AIDS.

• *Ms.* is the first women's magazine to mention AIDS in an article by lesbian writer Linsey Van Gelder, though the article does not specifically mention the risk to women.

• The CDC reported that almost 7 percent of all AIDS cases were women.

• Dr. Mervyn Silverman, San Francisco's public health director, ordered the city's gay bathhouses to display warning posters against promiscuous sex and recreational drug use. He threatened to close any bathhouses that did not comply.

- By Gay Pride weekend in 1983, 17,000 people had been diagnosed with AIDS in the United States, and 750 of those had died.
- The CDC defined a new phenomenon called AIDS-related complex (ARC), in which people showed clinical conditions that seemed to precede AIDS.
- In Geneva, Switzerland, AIDS experts from around the world convened at the World Health Organization headquarters for the first meeting on the international implications of the epidemic. The disease had been reported in thirty-three countries on five continents.
- CDC researchers determined that the incubation period for AIDS is somewhere between five and eleven years.

1984: Dr. Robert Gallo, a National Cancer Institute researcher, informed the director of the National Health Institutes that he had isolated the virus that causes AIDS, a variant of the human T cell leukemia virus (HTLV) family that he discovered in 1980. He called it HTLV-III. Days later, researchers at the Pasteur Institute in Paris showed proof that they had discovered the AIDS virus, which they call LAV (lymphadenopathy-associated virus). In subsequent tests, it became clear that both Gallo and the French had isolated the same microbe.

- The Shanti Project, a community clinic in San Francisco since 1974, turned its focus exclusively to AIDS and HIV treatment.
- By early 1984, 35,000 people in the United States were diagnosed with AIDS, of whom 15,000 had died.
- The San Francisco AIDS Foundation received a grant from the State Department of Health to develop a pilot program on women and AIDS, the first such study to focus on women.
- *Mademoiselle* published one of the first articles addressing women's risk of AIDS.
- With the announcement of the isolation of the AIDS virus, researchers pushed to develop a blood test and began talk about an AIDS vaccine.
- After repeated reports about unsafe sexual practices in San Francisco bathhouses, Dr. Mervyn Silverman ordered their closing. "These fourteen establishments," he announced, "are not fostering gay liberation. They are fostering disease and death." Only months later, Silverman resigned his position as public health commissioner.

1985: The Food and Drug Administration (FDA) approved the first HTLV blood test, which tested for the presence of antibodies to the AIDS virus in the bloodstream.

- Blood banks began testing their blood supplies for the presence of antibodies to HTLV.
- By midyear, the CDC reported that 11,000 Americans had contracted AIDS and of those, 5,400 had died.
- After repeated denials, movie and television actor Rock Hudson issued a public statement that he had AIDS, and three months later he died.
- Following San Francisco's lead, public health officials in New York City and Los Angeles closed gay bathhouses in their cities. The New York City Health

Department also closed the Mineshaft, a famous gay bar, after undercover inspectors reported on the sexual acts taking place there.

1986: Amid competition between the National Cancer Institute and the Pasteur Institute over which could claim discovery of the AIDS virus, an international committee renamed it the human immunodeficiency virus, or HIV.

• U.S. Surgeon General C. Everett Koop cited the growing threat of AIDS as the reason for much-needed sex education in secondary schools on both heterosexual and homosexual relationships.

1987: President Reagan underwent testing for HIV when he became concerned about the blood transfusions he received when he was shot in 1981. According to a White House spokesperson, he tested negative.

• The AIDS Coalition to Unleash Power (ACT UP) was founded by writer Larry Kramer and others at a public forum at New York's Lesbian and Gay Community Services Center. The direct action group staged its first protest in the financial district of the city, demanding that the Reagan administration stop dragging its feet on the approval of new drugs to help people with AIDS.

• Mandatory testing of pregnant women and marriage applicants was put in place in some states.

• The *Journal of the American Medical Association* published one of the first medical accounts of women and AIDS.

• President Reagan gave his first speech on AIDS, in which he called for more HIV testing. By this time, 36,000 Americans had been diagnosed with AIDS and almost 21,000 had died.

• U.S. Attorney General Edwin Meese announced two new administration policies on AIDS: that all federal prisoners would receive mandatory HIV testing; and that immigrants and refugees known to be HIV-positive would be denied entry to the country.

• AZT (zidovudine) became the first FDA-licensed antiviral in the fight against AIDS. AZT slows down the replication of HIV within healthy cells and helps prevent the onset of opportunistic infections, but it often has negative side effects, ranging from nausea to serious liver problems.

• The Names Project AIDS Memorial Quilt was displayed for the first time on the mall in front of the U.S. Capitol during the second March on Washington for Lesbian and Gay Rights.

• San Francisco reporter Randy Shilts's book *And the Band Played On*, which chronicled and criticized the Reagan administration's blatant disregard of the AIDS pandemic, was published.

1988: The World Health Organization (WHO) decreed the first World AIDS Day. Delegates to the Southern Baptist Convention pass a resolution blaming gay men for AIDS and condemning homosexuality as "an abomination."

• Studies reported that antigay violence was on a rise, with AIDS phobia a factor in many reported instances.

• President Reagan's newly founded National AIDS Commission released a report, with over 500 recommendations for addressing the epidemic. A presidential adviser reduced the list to 10 items.

• AIDS is the fifteenth leading cause of death among Americans, according to the National Center for Health Statistics.

1989: The first Advanced Immune Discoveries Symposium was held, centering on holistic and natural therapies for combating AIDS.

• The FDA approved the antiviral ddI (dideoxyinosine), which slows down the replication of HIV in healthy cells. Like AZT, though, ddI was shown to have side effects ranging from neuropathy to diarrhea to pancreatitis.

• Over 5,000 activists staged a massive protest in front of New York's St. Patrick's Cathedral, rallying against the Catholic Church's negative policies on homosexuality and AIDS. A half dozen of the protestors chained themselves to pews inside the cathedral and were arrested. This was the largest AIDS demonstration in the United States at that time.

• A report from the National Association of State Boards of Education revealed that only twenty-four states in the United States required HIV/AIDS education in public schools, and of those, only three directed teachers to discuss condom use.

1990: The third antiviral for the treatment of HIV/AIDS, dideoxycytidine (ddC), became available.

• The movie *Longtime Companion,* the first major Hollywood film about AIDS, opened in theaters.

• According to the CDC, the number of deaths from AIDS in the United States topped 100,000, with approximately 1,100 AIDS deaths every week.

1991: ACT UP led a massive demonstration at the Centers for Disease Control in Atlanta to protest the agency's underestimating of the number of women with AIDS.

• The first clinical trials for the Salk immunogen vaccine, designed by polio vaccine pioneer Dr. Jonas Salk, took place in Philadelphia. The Salk vaccine was for those already infected with HIV, to stop the erosion of their immune systems.

• A number of alarming studies across the United States showed that unprotected anal intercourse was on the rise among gay and bisexual men, resulting in a new wave of HIV infections.

• After protest demonstrations by lesbian health activists, Gay Men's Health Crisis added lesbians to their mission statement. The following year, GMHC's Lesbian AIDS Project was founded, and Amber Hollibaugh became its first coordinator.

• Professional basketball star Earvin "Magic" Johnson publicly announced that he had tested positive for HIV. As when Rock Hudson revealed he had AIDS in 1985, the media rushed to cover AIDS issues that had held little interest for them before. Johnson was promptly appointed to the National Commission on AIDS by President Bush.

1992: For the first time at both the Democratic and Republican national conventions, HIV-positive speakers presented the concerns and needs of people with AIDS—the human face of AIDS. At the Democratic convention, Bob Hattoy, an adviser to Bill Clinton, and Elizabeth Glaser, a pediatric AIDS activist, took the podium. At the Republican convention, Mary Fisher, the daughter of a prominent Republican fund-raiser, addressed the delegates.

• The National Commission on AIDS, established late in the Reagan administration, said, "President Bush and the Department of Health and Human Services have failed to meet fully their responsibility in leading the national response" to the epidemic. Magic Johnson, a highly visible member of the commission, resigned to protest the president's inaction.

• The Centers for Disease Control initiated Business Responds to AIDS, an HIV prevention program encouraging businesses to take an active role in providing HIV/AIDS education to their employees.

1993: The Centers for Disease Control once again expanded their definition of full-blown AIDS, increasing the number of indicator diseases that spelled the onset of immunosuppression to include more of the opportunistic infections that attack women with AIDS. This far-reaching move nearly doubled the number of people with AIDS across the country and was the most dramatic change in the CDC definition since the start of the pandemic.

• William Roper, head of the CDC and an opponent of sexually explicit content in federally funded AIDS education programs, was dismissed. The Clinton administration maintained that AIDS prevention programs must address sexual behavior as well as IV drug use.

• At the Ninth International Conference on AIDS in Berlin, scientists reported that the ways in which HIV destroyed the immune system were far more complex than previously thought, thus dimming the hope for a vaccine or magic bullet drug.

• President Clinton appointed Kristine Gebbie, the former Washington State health department director, to be his first AIDS czar. AIDS activists viewed this as a weak and disappointing choice, since Gebbie had shown no commitment to the AIDS fight or experience in AIDS issues.

• AIDS became the leading killer of American men between the ages of twenty-five and forty-four and the fourth leading killer of women in the same age group.

• The U.S. Congress boosted spending for AIDS research in fiscal 1994 to the highest it had ever been—a full 27 percent over fiscal 1993.

• Tuberculosis began to spread at an alarming rate across the United States, posing a new threat to PWAs.

1994: The CDC reported that in 1993 heterosexually acquired cases of AIDS rose 130 percent over the previous year, while cases attributed to homosexual sex rose 87 percent.

• The first HIV Prevention Summit was held in Dallas, Texas, in an attempt to address the problem of the breakdown of safer sex and the resulting rise of new HIV infections, the second wave of HIV.

• The Concorde Project, a British-French study of AZT, concluded that the antiviral does not delay the onset of AIDS symptoms in those who are HIV positive, though it may prolong life in people with AIDS.

• Canada began a two-year inquiry into charges that health officials allowed HIV-infected blood products to be distributed there after the HIV-antibody test had been developed.

• AIDS czar Kristine Gebbie, widely criticized by AIDS activists for her low profile, lack of experience, and ineffectiveness, resigned from office. In her place, Clinton named Patsy Fleming, an African-American woman with a gay son, who considered herself an AIDS activist.

• Recognizing that the search for traditional drug and vaccine therapies for AIDS was ineffectual, the National Institute of Allergy and Infectious Diseases awarded a twenty-five-million-dollar grant for research in alternative treatments for AIDS.

1995: New findings on the replication and mutation of HIV showed that the immune system wages a fierce battle against the virus from the very beginning of infection, losing just a little ground each day until the virus eventually wins and immunosuppression sets in. Research, scientists concluded, should focus on finding ways to boost the immune system's powers so it does not lose the battle.

• Olympic gold medalist Greg Louganis, considered by many to be the greatest diver of all time, announced in a television interview on *20/20* with Barbara Walters that he had AIDS. His announcement that he was HIV-positive when he hit his head on the diving board during the 1988 Olympics, drawing blood and requiring stitches, caused a flurry of indignation that he might have put other athletes and the doctor who stitched his wound at risk for HIV. The doctor, however, tested negative, and experts maintained that a few drops of blood in a chlorine-treated pool would not endanger anyone.

• The Centers for Disease Control reported that 50 percent of all new HIV infections were among women, with the disease being transmitted fastest among black and Latina women. In 1994, the number of AIDS cases increased 151 percent for women, compared with 105 percent for men.

• Congressman Robert Dornan (R-Calif.) introduced a measure into the House of Representatives that would discharge all HIV-positive people from the U.S. Armed Forces. Although HIV-positive people were not allowed to enlist in the military, Pentagon officials said there is no reason to dismiss those who become HIV positive during their service, as long as their health remains good.

SOURCES: *The Advocate; And the Band Played On,* by Randy Shilts; *Invisible Epidemic,* by Gena Corea

---

If KS [Kaposi's sarcoma] were a new form of cancer attacking straight people, it would be receiving constant media attention, and pressure from every side would be so great upon the cancer-funding institutions that research would be proceeding with great intensity.

—LARRY KRAMER, 1981

[Kaposi's sarcoma] afflicts members of one of the nation's most stigmatized and discriminated against minorities. . . . Legionnaire's Disease affected fewer people and proved less likely to be fatal. What society judged was not the severity of the disease but the social acceptability of the individuals affected with it. . . .

—CONGRESSMAN HENRY WAXMAN (D-Calif.), 1982

Rare Cancer Seen in 41 Homosexuals
Outbreak Occurs Among Men in New York and California
—8 Died Inside 2 Years

BY LAWRENCE K. ALTMAN

Doctors in New York and California have diagnosed among homosexual men 41 cases of a rare and often rapidly fatal form of cancer. Eight of the victims died less than 24 months after the diagnosis was made.

The cause of the outbreak is yet unknown, and there is as yet no evidence of contagion. But the doctors who have made the diagnoses, mostly in New York City and the San Francisco Bay area, are alerting other physicians who treat large numbers of homosexual men to the problem in an effort to help identify more cases and to reduce the delay in offering chemotherapy treatment.

The sudden appearance of the cancer, called Kaposi's Sarcoma, has prompted a medical investigation that experts say could have as much scientific as public health importance because of what it may teach about determining the causes of more common types of cancer.

1,112 and Counting

BY LARRY KRAMER

If this article doesn't scare the shit out of you we're in real trouble. If this article doesn't rouse you to anger, fury, rage and action, gay men may have no future on this earth. . . . Unless we fight for our lives we shall die. In all the history of homosexuality we have never been so close to death and extinction before. Many of us are dying or dead already.

. . . I am sick of guys who moan that giving up careless sex until this thing blows over is worse than death. How can they value life so little and cocks and asses so much?

The poor homosexuals—they have declared war upon nature, and now nature is exacting an awful retribution.

—PATRICK BUCHANAN, May 1983

AIDS DISEASE COULD ENDANGER GENERAL POPULATION

CHICAGO (AP)—A study showing children may catch the deadly immune deficiency disease AIDS from their families could mean the general population is at greater risk from the illness than previously believed, a medical journal reported today.

If "routine" personal contact among family members in a household is enough to spread the illness, "then AIDS takes on an entirely new dimension," said Dr. Anthony Fauci of the National Institutes of Health in Bethesda, Maryland.

SOURCE: Associated Press May 6, 1983. Reprinted by permission.

Tragically, funding levels for AIDS investigations have been dictated by political considerations rather than by the professional judgments of scientists and public health officials who are waging the battle against the epidemic. The inadequacy of funding, coupled with inexcusable delays in research activity, leads me to question the Federal Government's preparedness for national health emergencies, as well as this Administration's commitment to an urgent resolution to the AIDS crisis.

—CONGRESSMAN TED WEISS (D-N.Y.), 1984

We must conquer AIDS before it affects the heterosexual population.
—U.S. Secretary of Health and Human Services MARGARET HECKLER, April 1985

HOLLYWOOD (UPI)—Actor Rock Hudson, last of the traditional square-jawed, romantic leading men, known recently for his roles on "McMillan and Wife" and "Dynasty," is suffering from inoperable liver cancer possibly linked to AIDS, it was disclosed Tuesday.

SOURCE: United Press International, July 23, 1985

You get the feeling you're in Beirut or on the front lines of a war.
—DR. DANIEL WILLIAM, a Manhattan physician
specializing in the treatment of AIDS, 1985

Everyone detected with AIDS should be tattooed on the upper forearm, to protect common-needle users, and on the buttocks, to prevent the victimization of other homosexuals.

—WILLIAM F. BUCKLEY, JR., 1986

AIDS is spreading and killing in every corner of the world. . . . It is an equal-opportunity merchant of death. . . . Ultimately, we must protect those who do not have the disease.

—Vice President and presidential candidate GEORGE BUSH, 1987

History will deal harshly with the Reagan administration for its failure to face up to the unprecedented threat of the AIDS pandemic. Not since Hoover has a president done less when he should have known better.

—Tennessee Senator and presidential candidate AL GORE, 1987

It simply became an overwhelming experience. You saw that quilt go down, and it was at dawn, and people were reading the names, and the names of all those people that have died. And all the talent gone, and the lives lost. And it simply became an overwhelming experience. It became a lot more than just my son.

—SUE CAVES, who sewed a panel in memory of her son, 1987

Lesbians are not an isolated community: there are lesbians who shoot drugs and share needles, there are lesbians who have been married, who have babies, who are in prisons, who have sex for money, who get raped. When examining the AIDS epidemic, it becomes obvious that stereotypes are useless: it's not who you are that puts you at risk, it's what you do.

—ZOE LEONARD, artist, filmmaker, activist, 1990

It is an excess of free speech . . . to resort to some of the tactics these people [ACT UP activists] use.

　　　　　　　　　　　—PRESIDENT GEORGE BUSH, 1991

I was very closeted about [having AIDS] at first. I didn't want the news to get out before the book did. I spent four years on Conduct Unbecoming; *it is my definitive statement on homophobia, and I didn't want all of the press to be about me having AIDS. I don't want to be a professional AIDS patient.*

　　　　　　　　　　　—RANDY SHILTS, 1993, author of *And the Band Played On*

I am the face of the HIV virus. You see me everyday, you pass me on the street, you work next to me, yet you don't know my secret. We are invisible. . . . Women are an invisible component of this disease for several reasons: fear of losing custody of children, fear of losing jobs or insurance, and fear of negative judgment.

　　　　　　　—An anonymous lesbian mother, 1993, quoted in *Until the Cure:
　　　　　　　Caring for Women with HIV*, edited by Ann Kurth

We would not be able to have the Year of the Queer, the decade of the 90s, if it were not for the last decade of the AIDS epidemic. . . . It has created such unstoppable, ferocious determination in all of us. It has telescoped what would have been decades of change.

　　　　　　　　　—TORIE OSBORN, former director of the National
　　　　　　　　　Gay and Lesbian Task Force, 1993

Gebbie was perfect for the position as it was defined: She wasn't good and she wasn't effective. But there was no way the office could be effective. It never had any real power.

　　　　　　　　　—ACT UP activist STEVE MICHAEL on Kristine
　　　　　　　　　Gebbie's resignation as AIDS czar, 1994

Too many of us have been in denial for far too long, whether about how we have been engaging in unsafe sex, or how we promote an often oppressive sexual culture that enables—and sometimes even encourages—others to do so.

—MICHAELANGELO SIGNORILE, 1994

Why are we spending so much on AIDS?

—REP. BOB LIVINGSTON (R-La.), 1995, to Donna Shalala, Health and Human Services Secretary

I just held my head in the hopes . . . I [didn't] know if I was cut or not. But I wanted to keep the blood in or just not let anybody touch it. Dealing with HIV was really difficult for me because I felt like, God, the U.S. Olympic Committee needs to know this. But I didn't anticipate hitting my head on the board. That's where I became paralyzed with fear.

—Olympic diver GREG LOUGANIS, 1995, on ABC's *20/20*

Women's access to health care is intrinsically linked to sexism, poverty, and racism. Remember that 75 percent of women with AIDS are women of color, many of whom are poor. So it's no surprise that research, treatment, and outreach efforts directed to this discounted group of women fall far short of meeting their needs.

—MARION D. BANZHAF, Executive Director, New Jersey Women and AIDS Network, 1995

HIV/AIDS STATISTICS

The following tables are reprinted from Centers for Disease Control and Prevention, *HIV/AIDS Surveillance Report,* 1994, Vol. 6, No. 2: pp. 11, 12, 20, 25, 35. Copies of the complete report are available free from the CDC National AIDS Clearinghouse, P.O. Box 6003, Rockville, MD 20849-6003; Phone: 800/458-5231.

MALE ADULT/ADOLESCENT AIDS CASES BY EXPOSURE CATEGORY AND RACE/ETHNICITY, REPORTED IN 1994, AND CUMULATIVE TOTALS, THROUGH DECEMBER 1994, UNITED STATES

EXPOSURE CATEGORY	White, Not Hispanic 1994 NO.	(%)	White, Not Hispanic CUMULATIVE TOTAL NO.	(%)	Black, Not Hispanic 1994 NO.	(%)	Black, Not Hispanic CUMULATIVE TOTAL NO.	(%)	Hispanic 1994 NO.	(%)	Hispanic CUMULATIVE TOTAL NO.	(%)
Men who have sex with men	21,536	(72)	153,150	(77)	7,959	(35)	44,597	(40)	4,945	(41)	28,232	(45)
Injecting drug use	3,224	(11)	16,632	(8)	8,290	(36)	40,580	(37)	4,385	(36)	23,911	(38)
Men who have sex with men and inject drugs	1,990	(7)	15,503	(8)	1,251	(5)	8,479	(8)	559	(5)	4,275	(7)
Hemophilia/coagulation disorder	353	(1)	2,848	(1)	68	(0)	338	(0)	48	(0)	285	(0)
Heterosexual contact:	584	(2)	2,374	(1)	1,651	(7)	5,876	(5)	689	(6)	2,320	(4)
Sex with injecting drug user	192		1,069		529		2,789		193		839	
Sex with person with hemophilia	1		14		2		4		—		6	
Sex with transfusion recipient with HIV infection	23		95		17		79		19		60	
Sex with HIV-infected person, risk not specified	368		1,196		1,103		3,004		477		1,415	
Receipt of blood transfusion, blood components, or tissue	220	(1)	2,711	(1)	137	(1)	790	(1)	59	(0)	443	(1)
Risk not reported or identified	2,003	(7)	5,604	(3)	3,482	(15)	10,298	(9)	1,331	(11)	3,468	(6)
Total	29,910	(100)	198,822	(100)	22,838	(100)	110,958	(100)	12,016	(100)	62,934	(100)

EXPOSURE CATEGORY	Asian/Pacific Islander				American Indian/Alaska Native				Cumulative totals[*]			
	1994		CUMULATIVE TOTAL		1994		CUMULATIVE TOTAL		1994		CUMULATIVE TOTAL	
	NO.	(%)	NO.	(%)	NO.	(%)	NO.	(%)	NO.	(%)	NO.	(%)
Men who have sex with men	377	(73)	2,085	(78)	94	(51)	544	(61)	34,974	(53)	228,954	(61)
Injecting drug use	22	(4)	120	(4)	32	(17)	110	(12)	15,968	(24)	81,491	(22)
Men who have sex with men and inject drugs	18	(3)	84	(3)	31	(17)	155	(17)	3,853	(6)	28,521	(8)
Hemophilia/coagulation disorder	5	(1)	41	(2)	6	(3)	24	(3)	483	(1)	3,545	(1)
Heterosexual contact:	19	(4)	49	(2)	2	(1)	12	(1)	2,946	(4)	10,641	(3)
Sex with injecting drug user	6		17		—		4		920		4,719	
Sex with person with hemophilia	—		—		—		—		3		24	
Sex with transfusion recipient with HIV infection	1		3		1		1		61		239	
Sex with HIV-infected person, risk not specified	12		29		1		7		1,962		5,659	
Receipt of blood transfusion, blood components, or tissue	11	(2)	84	(3)	2	(1)	7	(1)	432	(1)	4,047	(1)
Risk not reported or identified	66	(13)	204	(8)	17	(9)	36	(4)	6,935	(11)	19,690	(5)
Total	518	(100)	2,667	(100)	184	(100)	888	(100)	65,591	(100)	376,889	(100)

[*]Includes 620 men whose race/ethnicity is unknown.

FEMALE ADULT/ADOLESCENT AIDS CASES BY EXPOSURE CATEGORY AND RACE/ETHNICITY, REPORTED IN 1994, AND CUMULATIVE TOTALS, THROUGH DECEMBER 1994, UNITED STATES

EXPOSURE CATEGORY	White, Not Hispanic				Black, Not Hispanic				Hispanic			
	1994		CUMULATIVE TOTAL		1994		CUMULATIVE TOTAL		1994		CUMULATIVE TOTAL	
	NO.	(%)	NO.	(%)	NO.	(%)	NO.	(%)	NO.	(%)	NO.	(%)
Injecting drug use	1,259	(40)	6,141	(43)	3,360	(42)	16,069	(50)	1,099	(39)	5,519	(46)
Hemophilia/coagulation disorder	11	(0)	65	(0)	7	(0)	25	(0)	—	—	6	(0)
Heterosexual contact:	1,243	(39)	5,207	(37)	2,777	(35)	10,481	(33)	1,291	(46)	5,125	(43)
Sex with injecting drug user	503		2,408		1,013		5,498		498		3,045	
Sex with bisexual male	154		853		140		646		59		253	
Sex with person with hemophilia	36		189		11		32		7		16	
Sex with transfusion recipient with HIV infection	34		218		17		89		12		69	
Sex with HIV-infected person, risk not specified	516		1,539		1,596		4,216		715		1,742	
Receipt of blood transfusion, blood components, or tissue	129	(4)	1,551	(11)	133	(2)	776	(2)	48	(2)	413	(3)
Risk not reported or identified	506	(16)	1,202	(8)	1,739	(22)	4,470	(14)	376	(13)	846	(7)
Total	3,148	(100)	14,166	(100)	8,016	(100)	31,821	(100)	2,814	(100)	11,909	(100)

EXPOSURE CATEGORY	Asian/Pacific Islander				American Indian/Alaska Native				Cumulative totals[*]			
	1994		CUMULATIVE TOTAL		1994		CUMULATIVE TOTAL		1994		CUMULATIVE TOTAL	
	NO.	(%)	NO.	(%)	NO.	(%)	NO.	(%)	NO.	(%)	NO.	(%)
Injecting drug use	7	(14)	48	(17)	20	(48)	79	(50)	5,749	(41)	27,092	(48)
Hemophilia/coagulation disorder	—	—	1	(0)	—	—	—	—	18	(0)	97	(0)
Heterosexual contact:	22	(45)	129	(44)	18	(43)	56	(35)	5,353	(38)	21,021	(36)
Sex with injecting drug user	7		40		11		34		2,032		11,039	
Sex with bisexual male	7		38		3		6		363		1,798	
Sex with person with hemophilia	1		3		—		2		55		242	
Sex with transfusion recipient with HIV infection	1		12		—		—		64		389	
Sex with HIV-infected person, risk not specified	6		36		4		14		2,839		7,553	
Receipt of blood transfusion, blood components, or tissue	8	(16)	68	(23)	1	(2)	10	(6)	319	(2)	2,819	(5)
Risk not reported or identified	12	(24)	44	(15)	3	(7)	14	(9)	2,642	(19)	6,589	(11)
Total	49	(100)	290	(100)	42	(100)	159	(100)	14,081	(100)	58,428	(100)

[*]Includes 83 women whose race/ethnicity is unknown.

DEATHS IN PERSONS WITH AIDS, BY RACE/ETHNICITY, AGE AT DEATH, AND SEX, OCCURRING IN 1992 AND 1993; AND CUMULATIVE TOTALS REPORTED THROUGH DECEMBER 1994, UNITED STATES[1]

Race/Ethnicity and Age at Death[2]	Males 1992	Males 1993	Males Cumulative Total	Females 1992	Females 1993	Females Cumulative Total	Both Sexes[3] 1992	Both Sexes[3] 1993	Both Sexes[3] Cumulative Total
White, not Hispanic									
Under 15	54	47	408	27	43	295	81	90	703
15–24	181	181	2,084	39	44	313	220	225	2,397
25–34	5,429	5,432	40,377	377	435	2,709	5,806	5,867	43,086
35–44	7,844	8,007	53,979	382	537	2,404	8,226	8,544	56,383
45–54	3,460	3,630	23,330	167	196	918	3,627	3,826	24,248
55 or older	1,372	1,304	10,298	144	121	1,191	1,516	1,425	11,489
All ages	18,340	18,602	130,679	1,136	1,376	7,846	19,476	19,978	138,525
Black, not Hispanic									
Under 15	122	136	925	105	136	923	227	272	1,848
15–24	225	202	1,782	105	133	792	330	335	2,574
25–34	2,913	3,129	21,699	912	1,027	6,524	3,825	4,157	28,224
35–44	4,342	4,902	27,671	1,208	1,367	6,835	5,550	6,269	34,506
45–54	1,627	1,960	10,131	282	403	1,863	1,909	2,363	11,994
55 or older	730	785	4,330	157	184	942	887	969	5,272
All ages	9,960	11,114	66,637	2,769	3,250	17,911	12,729	14,365	84,549
Hispanic									
Under 15	57	61	430	37	54	381	94	115	811
15–24	102	100	1,005	42	54	324	144	154	1,329
25–34	1,907	1,896	13,576	395	392	2,592	2,302	2,288	16,168
35–44	2,333	2,502	15,321	376	490	2,316	2,709	2,992	17,637
45–54	923	935	5,659	121	164	719	1,044	1,099	6,378
55 or older	352	390	2,308	60	74	349	412	464	2,657
All ages	5,675	5,885	38,366	1,031	1,228	6,698	6,706	7,113	45,064
Asian/Pacific Islander									
Under 15	1	2	16	—	3	6	1	5	22
15–24	1	6	26	—	1	5	1	7	31
25–34	56	70	462	3	6	41	59	76	503
35–44	102	109	653	9	13	56	111	122	709
45–54	54	52	333	6	6	35	60	58	368
55 or older	12	16	124	4	4	28	16	20	152
All ages	226	255	1,614	22	33	172	248	288	1,786
American Indian/Alaska Native									
Under 15	—	2	10	—	1	4	—	3	14
15–24	1	3	20	—	—	2	1	3	22
25–34	36	42	206	4	4	27	40	46	233
35–44	19	42	167	4	4	22	23	46	189
45–54	5	14	59	—	1	6	5	15	65
55 or older	4	6	25	—	1	3	4	7	28
All ages	65	109	492	8	11	64	73	120	556
All racial/ethnic groups									
Under 15	234	248	1,790	172	237	1,615	406	485	3,405
15–24	510	493	4,921	186	232	1,437	696	725	6,358
25–34	10,358	10,580	76,407	1,694	1,864	11,904	12,052	12,445	88,312
35–44	14,667	15,581	97,941	1,985	2,417	11,657	16,652	17,998	109,598
45–54	6,080	6,604	39,569	577	770	3,548	6,657	7,374	43,117
55 or older	2,477	2,507	17,119	365	384	2,516	2,842	2,891	19,635
All ages	34,328	36,015	238,125	4,979	5,904	32,744	39,307	41,920	270,870

[1]Data tabulations for 1992 and 1993 are based on date of death occurrence. Data for deaths occurring in 1994 are incomplete and not tabulated separately, but are included in the cumulative totals. Tabulations for 1992 and 1993 may increase as additional deaths are reported to CDC.

[2]Data tabulated under "all ages" include 445 persons whose age at death is unknown. Data tabulated under "all racial/ethnic groups" include 390 persons whose race/ethnicity is unknown.

[3]Includes 1 person whose sex is unknown.

PERSONS REPORTED TO BE LIVING WITH HIV INFECTION (NOT AIDS) AND WITH AIDS, BY STATE AND AGE GROUP, REPORTED THROUGH DECEMBER 1994[1]

State of Residence (Date HIV Reporting Initiated)	Living with HIV (Not AIDS)[2]			Living with AIDS[3]			Cumulative Totals		
	Adults/ Adolescents	Children <13 Years Old	Total	Adults/ Adolescents	Children <13 Years Old	Total	Adults/ Adolescents	Children <13 Years Old	Total
Alabama (Jan. 1988)	3,544	31	3,575	1,318	16	1,334	4,862	47	4,909
Alaska	—	—	—	101	1	102	101	1	102
Arizona (Jan. 1987)	2,713	22	2,735	1,298	7	1,305	4,011	29	4,040
Arkansas (July 1989)	1,170	12	1,182	811	14	825	1,981	26	2,007
California	—	—	—	27,454	150	27,604	27,454	150	27,604
Colorado (Nov. 1985)	4,955	28	4,983	1,880	11	1,891	6,835	39	6,874
Connecticut (July 1992)[4]	—	85	85	2,677	75	2,752	2,677	160	2,837
Delaware	—	—	—	520	3	523	520	3	523
District of Columbia	—	—	—	2,926	55	2,981	2,929	55	2,981
Florida	—	—	—	17,890	467	18,357	17,890	467	18,357
Georgia	—	—	—	5,176	63	5,239	5,176	63	5,239
Hawaii	—	—	—	556	6	562	556	6	562
Idaho (June 1986)	264	2	266	116	—	116	380	2	382
Illinois	—	—	—	5,430	84	5,514	5,430	84	5,514
Indiana (July 1988)	2,382	17	2,399	1,456	14	1,470	3,838	31	3,869
Iowa	—	—	—	331	4	335	331	4	335
Kansas	—	—	—	485	2	487	485	2	487
Kentucky	—	—	—	519	8	527	519	8	527
Louisiana (Feb. 1993)	3,223	29	3,252	2,675	39	2,714	5,898	68	5,966
Maine	—	—	—	274	4	278	274	4	278
Maryland	—	—	—	4,400	119	4,519	4,400	119	4,519
Massachussets	—	—	—	3,651	64	3,715	3,651	64	3,715
Michigan (April 1992)	2,004	56	2,060	2,527	31	2,558	4,531	87	4,618
Minnesota (Oct. 1985)	1,944	20	1,964	974	10	984	2,918	30	2,948
Mississippi (Aug. 1988)	2,669	37	2,706	794	13	807	3,463	50	3,513
Missouri (Oct. 1987)	3,035	32	3,067	2,525	16	2,541	5,560	48	5,608
Montana	—	—	—	64	1	65	64	1	65
Nebraska	—	—	—	230	3	233	230	3	233
Nevada (Feb. 1992)	1,761	20	1,781	909	10	919	2,670	30	2,700
New Hampshire	—	—	—	248	3	251	248	3	251
New Jersey (Jan. 1992)	8,590	272	8,862	8,251	230	8,481	16,841	502	17,343
New Mexico	—	—	—	447	2	449	447	2	449
New York	—	—	—	25,417	642	26,059	25,417	642	26,059
North Carolina (Feb. 1990)	4,675	45	4,720	2,099	42	2,141	6,774	87	6,861
North Dakota (Jan. 1988)	50	—	50	23	—	23	73	—	73
Ohio (June 1990)	1,750	13	1,763	2,321	27	2,348	4,071	40	4,111
Oklahoma (June 1988)	1,493	9	1,502	893	5	898	2,386	14	2,400
Oregon	—	—	—	1,233	3	1,236	1,233	3	1,236
Pennsylvania	—	—	—	5,176	113	5,289	5,176	113	5,289
Rhode Island	—	—	—	509	6	515	509	6	515
South Carolina (Feb. 1986)	5,048	65	5,113	2,114	23	2,137	7,162	88	7,250
South Dakota (Jan. 1988)	123	4	127	32	2	34	155	6	161
Tennessee (Jan. 1992)	2,595	31	2,626	1,839	13	1,852	4,434	44	4,478
Texas (Feb. 1994)[4]	—	162	162	12,128	119	12,247	12,128	281	12,409
Utah (April 1989)	766	5	771	432	7	439	1,198	12	1,210
Vermont	—	—	—	98	1	99	98	1	99
Virginia (July 1989)	5,267	52	5,319	2,490	64	2,554	7,757	116	7,873
Washington	—	—	—	2,395	11	2,406	2,395	11	2,406
West Virginia (Jan. 1989)	341	2	343	202	2	204	543	4	547
Wisconsin (Nov. 1985)	1,727	19	1,746	959	12	971	2,686	31	2,717
Wyoming (June 1989)	60	—	60	46	—	46	106	—	106
Subtotal	**62,149**	**1,070**	**63,219**	**159,319**	**2,617**	**161,936**	**221,468**	**3,687**	**225,155**
Guam	—	—	—	4	—	4	4	—	4
Pacific Islands, U.S.	—	—	—	—	—	—	—	—	—
Puerto Rico	—	—	—	5,586	158	5,744	5,586	158	5,744
Virgin Islands, U.S.	—	—	—	129	5	134	129	5	134
Total	**62,149**	**1,070**	**63,219**	**165,038**	**2,780**	**167,818**	**227,187**	**3,850**	**231,037**

[1]Persons reported with vital status "alive" as of the last update.

[2]Includes only persons reported from states with confidential HIV reporting. Excludes 1,505 adults/adolescents and 18 children reported from states with confidential HIV infection reporting whose state of residence is unknown or are residents of other states.

[3]Excludes 244 adults/adolescents and 4 children whose state of residence is unknown.

[4]Connecticut and Texas have confidential HIV infection reporting for pediatric cases only.

GLOSSARY OF AIDS AND HIV-RELATED TERMS

Adjunct therapies: Interventions such as acupuncture and chiropractic used to supplement traditional medical treatments.

AIDS (aquired immunodeficiency syndrome): A viral suppression of the immune system that weakens the body's ability to withstand a variety of opportunistic infections, viruses, and malignancies.

Anonymous testing for HIV: Testing using anonymous identification numbers to insure that results are not publicly released but given only to the tested person. *See also* **Confidential testing for HIV**.

Antibodies: Cells manufactured by the immune system to target and protect against toxins and infectious agents.

Antibody test: A blood test that reveals the presence of antibodies to HIV, indicating that viral infection has occurred. The ELISA and Western blot tests are antibody tests.

Antigen: A virus, bacteria, or other foreign substance in the blood that stimulates the production of antibodies.

Antigen test: Blood test used to double-check positive results of the ELISA or Western blot antibody tests; checks for the presence of HIV itself, not antibodies to the virus.

Antiviral: A treatment that suppresses viral activity. AZT and ddI are antivirals.

ARC (AIDS-related complex): A variety of AIDS-related symptoms (such as swollen glands, fever, and diarrhea) that precede AIDS but are not severe enough to be included in the CDC definition of AIDS. This term is rarely used now and has been replaced by *HIV symptomatic*.

Asymptomatic: Being without the symptoms of HIV infection, even though one may test positive for HIV.

AZT (zidovudine): FDA-approved antiviral that slows down the replication of HIV within healthy cells and helps prevent the onset of opportunistic infections. AZT often has side effects, ranging from nausea to serious liver problems.

Bactrim: Drug used to treat PCP.

B cells: White blood cells that participate in the body's immune response to infection.

Bodily fluids: Any fluid produced by the human body, for example, blood, sweat, urine, breast milk, vaginal fluids, semen, precum, and saliva. Those bodily fluids known to transmit HIV are blood, semen, vaginal fluids, and breast milk.

Candidiasis: A chronic infection with the normally harmless yeast organism, *Candida albicans*. In the mouth, this yeast infection is called thrush.

CD4 cells (or lymphocytes): *See* **T4 (helper) cells**.

CD8 cells (or lymphocytes): *See* **T8 (suppressor) cells**.

CDC (U.S. Centers for Disease Control): Federal agency of the Public Health Service that tracks the incidence and trends of communicable diseases, conducts research, and licenses clinical laboratories.

Chronic: Persistent or of long duration.

Clinical trials: Drug trials using human subjects to prove drug safety and to determine dose levels.

CMV (cytomegalovirus): A virus related to herpes that can produce retinitis (inflammation of the retina that can lead to blindness), pneumonia, hepatitis, and colitis (inflammation of the colon).

Confidential testing for HIV: Often given by private doctors and public and private hospitals, testing whose results will be recorded in the tested person's medical charts and may be disclosed without his or her permission. *See also* **Anonymous testing for HIV**.

ddC (dideoxycytidine): FDA-approved antiviral used in the treatment of HIV/AIDS, particularly for patients who are intolerant of or ineligible for AZT, fail AZT, or are intolerant of or ineligible for ddI. ddC often has side effects, including peripheral neuropathy, pancreatitis, diarrhea, and dehydration.

ddI (dideoxyinosine): FDA-approved antiviral that slows down the replication of HIV within healthy cells and helps prevent the onset of opportunistic infections. ddI is used particularly for people who either do not respond well to AZT or who are in advanced stages of HIV infection with severe immunosuppression. ddI often has side effects, including peripheral neuropathy, pancreatitis, diarrhea, and dehydration.

Dementia: Loss of normal brain function, evidenced as loss of memory, learning ability, and motor control.

ELISA (enzyme-linked immunosorbent assay): A blood test that reveals the presence of antibodies to HIV, indicating that viral infection has occurred. Often called the HIV or AIDS test, it is the most common test for HIV.

Epidemic: A disease that spreads rapidly and affects a large number of people.

False positive: A positive test result, when the condition is in fact negative.

Food and Drug Administration (FDA): Federal government agency that tests and licenses drugs.

Full-blown AIDS: The state of a formerly asymptomatic HIV-positive person developing one or more diseases that are symptoms of immunosuppression.

Herpes: A family of viruses including herpes simplex (cold sores), herpes genitalia (affecting the genitals), CMV, chicken pox, and shingles.

High-risk behavior: Any activity that increases the risk of HIV transmission by allowing the exchange of body fluids. This may include, for example, unsafe sex and sharing IV needles.

HIV (human immunodeficiency virus): The virus thought to be the cause of AIDS.

HIV-negative: The state of having no antibodies to HIV present in the bloodstream. The person who tests negative is presumed to be uninfected with HIV. Also called seronegative.

HIV-positive: The state of having antibodies to HIV present in the bloodstream. The person who tests positive is presumed to be infected with HIV. Also called seropositive.

Host cell: Infected cell.

HPV (human papillomavirus): Virus associated with genital warts and cervical cancer, which is common for women with HIV/AIDS.

Immune system: The body's system of defense mechanisms, through which cells and proteins in the blood and other body fluids work together to attack infection and disease-producing agents.

Immunosuppression: Weakening of the immune system that occurs as a result of HIV infection.

Incubation period: Length of time between actual HIV infection and the appearance of the first signs and symptoms of that infection.

Indicator diseases: Opportunistic infections designated by the U.S. Centers for Disease Control as indicators of full-blown AIDS. PCP, KS, MAC, and CMV are among those indicator diseases.

Intravenous drugs: Drugs injected directly into the bloodstream through a hypodermic needle.

KS (Kaposi's sarcoma): A rare skin cancer that appears as purplish lesions.

Latency period: *See* **Incubation period**.

MAC (mycobacterium avium complex): Fungal infection normally seen in birds that attacks PWAs and is often misdiagnosed as the flu; the most common opportunistic infection in PWAs; also called MAI.

Macrophages: White blood cells that participate in the body's immune response to infection.

MAI (mycobacterium avium intracellulare): *See* **MAC**.

Nonoxynol-9: A spermicide found in some lubricants and condoms, which may help prevent HIV transmission.

Opportunistic infection (OI): An infection that takes advantage of immunosuppression to attack a person's immune system. The most commonly known opportunistic infections for PWAs are PCP, CMV, MAC, and toxoplasmosis. Some common opportunistic infections for female PWAs are PID, HPV, and chronic vaginitis.

Pandemic: A worldwide epidemic.

PCP (Pneumocystis carinii pneumonia): A common parasitic infection that attacks the lungs, leading to the most common cause of death for people with AIDS.

Pentamadine: A drug used to treat PCP.

PID (pelvic inflammatory disease): Infection that attacks a woman's fallopian tubes, ovaries, and/or uterus.

Precum: Clear fluid produced by a man's penis before ejaculation.

Prophylaxis: Preventive treatment.

Protease Inhibitors: A promising new class of antivirals in clinical trials that may prevent production of new virus in cells infected with HIV. Therapy opens up a different line of defense against HIV.

PWA: Person With AIDS.

Retrovirus: A virus that contains RNA rather than DNA as its genetic material. HIV is a retrovirus.

Safer sex: An array of sexual practices that may decrease the risk of HIV infection by preventing the transmission of bodily fluids during sex. The standard tools of gay male safer sex are condoms and latex gloves; some forms of safer sex are kissing, jerking off, phone sex, and rubbing.

Seroconversion: Development of antibodies to HIV.

Spermicide: A chemical that kills sperm.

STD (Sexually Transmitted Disease): Any disease that can be contracted through sexual behavior and practices. Besides HIV/AIDS, STDs include syphillis, gonorrhea, hepatitis B, herpes, chlamydia, and others.

T cell count: A reading of the number of T4 cells per millimeter of blood, used to determine how far a person's HIV infection has progressed.

T cells (or lymphocytes): White blood cells that direct the rest of the immune system and the targets of HIV; includes both T4 and T8 cells.

T4 (helper) cells (or lymphocytes): Antibody-triggered cells that attack invading organisms and infections; also called CD4 cells.

T8 (suppressor) cells (or lymphocytes): Cells that shut down the immune response when the infection or invading organisms have been destroyed; also called CD8 cells.

Thrush: *See* **Candidiasis**.

Toxoplasmosis: Infection affecting the brain.

Unsafe sex: High-risk sexual behavior, including sex without a condom or dental dam, that may lead to the exchange of bodily fluids and thus increase the odds of HIV transmission.

Vaginitis: Infection and inflammation of the vagina. When it is chronic, this can be a symptom of HIV infection in women.

Venereal disease: Another name for an STD.

Western blot test: A test believed to be even more specific than ELISA, which identifies specific antibodies to HIV. Used to double-check the results of ELISA.

White blood cells: All the cells of the immune system.

Window period: Period of time, usually six weeks to six months, between actual HIV infection and seroconversion, or the moment when the body has produced enough antibodies to the virus to be detected by a blood test. During the window period, HIV may be transmitted unknowingly.

Yeast infection: Vaginal infection that creates a white discharge.

SOURCES:

ACT UP/NY Women and AIDS Book Group. *Women, AIDS and Activism*. Boston: South End Press, 1990.

Ford, Michael Thomas. *100 Questions and Answers about AIDS: A Guide for Young People*. New York: New Discovery Books, 1992.

Hitchen, Neal. *Fifty Things You Can Do about AIDS*. Los Angeles: Lowell House, 1992.

Root-Bernstein, Robert. *Rethinking AIDS: The Tragic Cost of Premature Consensus*. New York: Free Press, 1993.

Siano, Nick. *No Time to Wait: A Complete Guide to Treating, Managing, and Living with HIV Infection*. New York: Bantam Books, 1993.

SOME TOOLS OF SAFER SEX FOR LESBIANS AND BISEXUALS

Condom: Latex shield placed over penis or sex toy during penetration. Lambskin condoms are not recommended for protection against HIV transmission.

Dental dam: A square sheet of thin latex (approximately 6" × 6") used to cover a woman's clitoris and vulva during oral sex or over the anus during rimming to prevent the transmission of bodily fluids. Its name comes from its original use by dentists to keep teeth dry during root canal, fillings, or other dental work. Saran Wrap is a scientifically proven alternative, and preferable to dental dams because it is thinner.

Finger cot: A small latex condom that fits over individual fingers and prevents the transmission of bodily fluids through cuts on the hands.

Lube: Lubricant for anal or vaginal sex for added moisture.

Rubber: A condom.

Safer sex: An array of sexual practices that can decrease the risk of HIV infection by preventing the transmission of bodily fluids during sex.

For definitions of specific sexual practices, see pages 77–93 of this book.

A Lesbian's and Bisexual's Guide to Safer Sex

Safer Activities

Body to body rubbing

Dry kissing

French kissing (as long as there are no open sores in the mouth)

Massage

Hugging

Masturbation

Fantasy and costumes

Voyeurism

Finger penetration of vagina or anus using latex gloves or finger cots

Hand penetration of vagina or anus using latex gloves

Individual vibrators or sex toys

Latex condoms with lubricant on dildos

Protected oral sex with a dental dam, plastic wrap, or cut-apart condom between the tongue and vulva

Spanking

S/M without drawing blood or exchange of bodily fluids

Any sex that doesn't exchange bodily fluids

Unsafe Activities

Unprotected oral sex (without a barrier), especially if either partner has a vaginal infection or her period

Unprotected rimming (mouth-anus contact)

Unprotected finger or hand penetration of vagina or anus (especially if you have cuts on your hands)

Any activity that could draw blood

Sharing unprotected or unwashed sex toys

Sharing needles for IV drug use or any other skin piercing activity

Note: For sex with a man, always use condoms for vaginal and anal penetration or for oral sex.

Source: *NYC Lesbian Health Fair Journal,* 1994

TWENTY-SEVEN AIDS INDICATOR DISEASES

Candidiasis, bronchi, trachea, lungs
  (thrush)
Candidiasis, esophageal (thrush)
Coccidiomycosis, disseminated or
  extrapulmonary
Cryptococcosis, extrapulmonary
  (crypto)
Cryptosporidiosis, chronic intestinal
Cytomegalovirus disease (CMV)
Cytomegalovirus retinitis (CMV/eyes)
HIV encephalopathy (dementia)
Herpes simplex, chronic ulcers (HSV)
Histoplasmosis (histo)
Invasive cervical cancer
Isoporiasis, chronic intestinal
Kaposi's sarcoma (KS)
Lymphoma, Burkitt's
Lymphoma, immunoblastic

Lymphoma, primary in brain
Mycobacterium avium complex
  (MAC/MAI)
M. tuberculosis, disseminated or
  extrapulmonary (TB)
M. tuberculosis, pulmonary (TB)
Mycobacterium of other species
Pneumocystis carinii pneumonia
  (PCP)
Progressive multifocal
  leukoencephalopathy (PML)
Recurrent pneumonias within a
  twelve-month period
Salmonella septicemia, recurrent
T4 cells under 200m or less than 14
  percent
Toxoplasmosis of brain (toxo)
Wasting syndrome

SOURCE: Centers for Disease Control

NATIONAL AIDS ORGANIZATIONS

So many of us have felt helpless in the face of the AIDS crisis: losing friends, family, and lovers, or dealing with our own illness. Our powerlessness to stop the pandemic and its shattering effects on our lives often leads to despondency. One way many of us have coped with the AIDS crisis is to get actively involved in groups and organizations that work on AIDS and HIV-related issues, either donating time or money or both. The following is a partial list of national AIDS organizations that need your support or that can direct you to services and programs in your area.

UNITED STATES

AIDS Coalition to Unleash Power (ACT UP)
496-A Hudson Street, #G4
New York, NY 10014
Phone: 212/564-2437
Sponsors direct actions at the national and local level to bring attention to the
  AIDS pandemic; also has chapters in Canada

AIDS National Interfaith Network
110 Maryland Avenue NE, Suite 504
Washington, DC 20002
Phone: 202/546-0807
Umbrella group of AIDS ministries
that mobilizes for education and
advocacy

AIDS Action Council
1875 Connecticut Avenue NW, #700
Washington, DC 20009
Phone: 202/986-1300
Lobbies Congress and watchdogs
national AIDS policy

AIDS Research Alliance
621-A North San Vicente Blvd.
West Hollywood, CA 90069
Phone: 310/358-2423
Conducts research on promising anti-
HIV therapies

American Foundation for AIDS
Research (AmFAR)
733 Third Avenue
New York, NY 10017
Phone: 212/682-7440
Research and lobbying group

AIDS Project/Lambda Legal Defense
and Education Fund
666 Broadway, 12th Floor
New York, NY 10012
Phone: 212/995-8585
Litigates test cases involving AIDS-
related discrimination

American Institute for Teen AIDS
Prevention
P.O. Box 136116
Fort Worth, TX 76136
Phone: 817/237-0230
AIDS education to teens, both in the
U.S. and internationally

Broadway Cares/Equity Fights AIDS
165 West 46th Street, Suite 1300
New York, NY 10036
Phone: 212/840-0770
Raises funds for PWAs in the
entertainment business

Community Research Initiative on
AIDS (CRIA)
275 Seventh Avenue, 20th Floor
New York, NY 10001
Phone: 212/924-3934
Conducts clinical trials on promising
therapies ignored by major drug
companies

Design Industries Foundation
Fighting AIDS (DIFFA)
150 West 26th Street, Suite 602
New York, NY 10001
Phone: 212/727-3100
Raises funds for organizations involved
in direct care, public policy, and
prevention programs

Gay Men's Health Crisis (GMHC)
129 West 20th Street
New York, NY 10011
Phone: 212/337-3519
Plays leadership role in AIDS
prevention and information
dissemination

Mobilization Against AIDS
584-B Castro Street
San Francisco, CA 94114
Phone: 415/863-4676
Lobbies for increased Congressional
funding for AIDS

National Leadership Coalition on
AIDS
1730 M Street NW, Suite 905
Washington, DC 20036
Phone: 202/429-0930
Conducts workplace initiatives to
educate employees about safer sex
and to protect the rights of
employees with AIDS

National Minority AIDS Council
(NMAC)
300 I Street NE, Suite 400
Washington, DC 20002
Phone: 202/544-1076
Develops new leaders in people of
color communities to address issues
of HIV and AIDS

People of Color Against AIDS
Network
1200 S. Jackson Street, #25
Seattle, WA 98144-2065
Phone: 206/322-7061
Education and advocacy group for
people of color communities

Project Inform
1965 Market Street, Suite 220
San Francisco, CA 94103
Phone: 415/558-8669
Operates treatment information hot
line, promotes immune-based
research, and influences research
regulations

Ryan White Foundation
101 West Washington Street, Suite
1135 East
Indianapolis, IN 46204
Phone: 800/444-RYAN
Focuses on support to teens and
hemophiliacs with AIDS and their
families

Test Positive Aware Network
1258 West Belmont Avenue
Chicago, IL 60657
Phone: 312/404-8726
Peer-led support services

Treatment Action Group
200 East 10th Street, #601
New York, NY 10003
Phone: 212/260-0300
Watchdogs AIDS research
establishment and influences
treatment policy and regulations

For a listing of local AIDS/HIV services, contact the U.S. Conference of Mayors, 1620 I Street NW, Washington, DC 20006; Phone: 202/293-7330. Many local AIDS groups and organizations are also listed by state in the *Gayellow Pages,* which can be ordered from Renaissance House, Box 292, Village Station, New York, NY 10014-0292.

CANADA

Canadian AIDS Society
170 Laurier Avenue West, #1101
Ottawa, Ontario K1P 5V5
Phone: 613/563-4998
Provides support services, education, and advocacy; also information about local
AIDS organizations

HIV/AIDS Information, Support, and Services Specifically for Women

Amigas Latinas en Accion Pro-Salud
47 Nichols Avenue
Watertown, MA 02172
Phone: 617/491-1268

Boston Women's AIDS Information
  Project
c/o Fenway Community Health Center
16 Haviland Street
Boston, MA 02115
Phone: 617/267-0900

Lesbian AIDS Project (LAP)
Gay Men's Health Crisis
129 West 20th Street, 2nd Floor
New York, NY 10011
Phone: 212/337-3532

Lyon-Martin Women's Health Services
1748 Market Street, Suite 201
San Francisco, CA 94102
Phone: 415/565-7683 or 415/565-7667

New Jersey Women and AIDS
  Network (NJWAN)
5 Elm Row, Suite 112
New Brunswick, NJ 08901
Phone: 908/846-4462

Sisterlove Women's AIDS Project
1132 W. Peachtree Street
Atlanta, GA 30309
Phone: 404/872-0600

Whitman-Walker Clinic, Women's
  Committee on AIDS
2335 18th Street NW
Washington, DC 20009
Phone: 202/797-3500

Women and AIDS Resource Network
  (WARN)
P.O. Box 020525
Brooklyn, NY 11202
Phone: 718/596-6007

Women and AIDS Risk Network
  Project L.A.
900 N. Alvarado, 2nd Floor
Los Angeles, CA 90026
Phone: 213/413-7779

Women in Crisis
Minority Women and AIDS Project
133 West 21st Street, 11th Floor
New York, NY 10011
Phone: 212/242-4880

Women's Action Committee/
Minority Task Force on AIDS
92 St. Nicholas Avenue
New York, NY 10030
Phone: 212/749-2816

Women's AIDS Network
P.O. Box 426182
San Francisco, CA 94142-6182
Phone: 415/864-4376

Women's AIDS Project
8235 Santa Monica Boulevard, Suite
  201
West Hollywood, CA 90046
Phone: 213/650-1508

Women's Council on AIDS
1441 Florida Avenue NW
Washington, DC 20009
Phone: 202/387-4898

WORLD (Women Organized Against
Life-Threatening Diseases)
P.O. Box 11535
Oakland, CA 94611
Phone: 510/658-6930

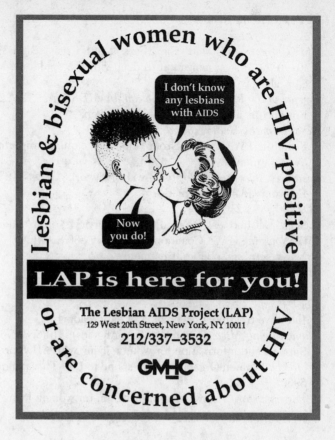

AIDS AND HIV-RELATED NEWLETTERS AND MAGAZINES

AIDS Treatment News: 800/873-2812
   One of the first newsletters; easy to read and informative
Art & Understanding: 800/841-8707
   Glossy magazine of literary and visual AIDS
Being Alive/Los Angeles: 213/667-3262
   Clear and factual
BETA (San Francisco AIDS Foundation): 415/863-2437
   Western and alternative therapies
Body Positive: 212/721-1346
   Treatment information plus personality profiles
Community Prescription Service InfoPack: 800/842-0502
   In-depth and easy-to-read articles
Critical Path AIDS Project: 215/545-2212
   For those who can't get information otherwise, like prisoners

Diseased Pariah News: 510/891-0455
An angry 'zine
GMHC Treatment Issues (Gay Men's Health Crisis): 212/337-3695
From the first organization to deal with the epidemic; lots of information on clinical trials
Journal of the Physicians Association for AIDS Care: 312/222-1326
For doctors and other health care workers
Notes from the Underground: 212/255-0520
From the PWA Health Group, a buyers' club; an important source on alternative treatments
Positively Aware (Test Positive Aware Network): 312/472-6397
Easy to read and informative
POZ: 800/883-2163
Slick, polished, easy to read; news, interviews, information
PWA Newsline (PWA Coalition/New York): 800/828-3280
News, activism, politics, treatment
SIDAahora (PWA Coalition/New York): 800/828-3280
PWA Newsline in Spanish
STEP Perspectives: 800/869-7837
Intensive treatment coverage, not easy reading
Women Being Alive (Being Alive/Los Angeles): 213/667-2735
Support and information for women living with AIDS or HIV
WORLD (Women Organized to Respond to Life-Threatening Diseases): 510/658-6930
Personal stories, news, and information for women living with AIDS or HIV

SOURCE: *POZ* magazine, Number 5, December 1994/January 1995

NATIONAL AIDS HOT LINES

AIDS Clinical Trials Information Services: 800/TRIALSA; TTY/TDD: 800/243-7012
AIDS Project Los Angeles: 800/922-2437
CDC (Centers for Disease Control) AIDS Hotline: 800/342-AIDS; in Spanish: 800/344-SIDA
National AIDS Hotline for Hearing Impaired: 800/243-7889
National Hospicelink: 800/331-1620
National Native American AIDS Hotline: 800/283-2437
National Sexually Transmitted Diseases Hotline: 800/227-8922
Project Inform National Hotline (AIDS treatment): 800/822-7422
Toll-free Directory Assistance (call for your state's own toll-free AIDS hot line): 800/555-1212

Reprinted with permission from *POZ* magazine, Number 5, December 1994/January 1995

The Centers for Disease Control operates an automated information line, through which you can get the latest statistics and facts about AIDS in the United

States and internationally, either by listening to a series of recordings or following the steps to get the information via fax. The telephone number is 404/639-3524 and operates continuously.

ONLINE: AIDS-SPECIFIC BULLETIN BOARDS

You can access information about AIDS treatment from the following computer bulletin boards, or join in an AIDS community discussion—right in your own home.

HIV/AIDS Information BBS (California): 714/248-2836
Fog City BBS (California): 415/863-9697
Black Bag Medical BBS (Delaware): 302/994-3772
AIDS Info BBS (Ohio): 614/279-7709
Midwest AIDS/HIV Information Exchange (Illinois): 312/772-5958
Critical Path AIDS Project (Pennsylvania): 215/463-7160
AIDSNet (New York): 607/777-2158

SOURCE: *POZ* magazine, Number 5, December 1994/January 1995

BUYERS' CLUBS

Buyers' clubs purchase experimental AIDS and HIV medications as well as FDA-approved drugs, vitamins, and supplements, and offer them for sale to the general public.

Atlanta Buyers' Club: 404/874-4845
PWA Coalition Boston: 617/266-6422
DBC Alternatives (Dallas): 214/528-4460
Colorado Health Action Project (Denver): 303/837-8214
Health Link (Ft. Lauderdale): 305/565-8284
DAAIR (New York City): 212/689-8140
PWA Health Group (New York City): 212/255-0520
PACT for Life Buyers' Club (Tucson): 602/770-1710
Healing Alternatives (San Francisco): 415/626-4053
AIDS Manasota (Sarasota, Fla.): 813/954-6011
Carl Vogel Center (Washington, D.C.): 202/289-4898

SOURCE: *POZ* magazine, Number 5, December 1994/January 1995

FIFTEEN MAJOR AIDS TREATMENT CENTERS IN THE UNITED STATES

- San Francisco General Hospital
- Johns Hopkins Hospital (Baltimore)
- Massachusetts General Hospital (Boston)
- University of California San Francisco Medical Center
- Memorial Sloan-Kettering Cancer Center (New York City)
- UCLA Medical Center (Los Angeles)
- New York University Medical Center (New York City)
- University of Miami Hospital and Clinics
- New York Hospital–Cornell Medical Center (New York City)
- Mayo Clinic (Rochester, Minnesota)
- Columbia-Presbyterian Medical Center (New York City)
- University of Washington Medical Center (Seattle)
- Deaconess Hospital (Boston)
- Mount Sinai Medical Center (New York City)
- Beth Israel Hospital (Boston)

FACTS ABOUT WOMEN AND AIDS

In North America, there are 171,000 reported cases of HIV among women, and 54,000 cases of women with full-blown AIDS.

Of the 6.5 million adults with AIDS worldwide, 3 million are women.

Women are the fastest-growing group of people with HIV/AIDS. Half of all new HIV infections are among women, with the disease being transmitted fastest in the United States among black and Latina women.

AIDS is the second leading cause of death for women ages fifteen to forty-four.

Since 1981, injection drug use has accounted for 57 percent of AIDS cases among women, and heterosexual transmission has accounted for 35 percent.

Women with AIDS are undercounted because the Centers for Disease Control definition of AIDS does not include most woman-specific infections and cancers (for example, chronic vaginal candidiasis, pelvic inflammatory disease, and cervical dysplasia). Invasive cervical cancer was added in January, 1993.

Seventy percent of babies born to women with HIV will *not* be infected.

SOURCE: *Ms.* magazine, March/April 1995; and New Jersey Women and AIDS Network

TEN THINGS YOU CAN DO ABOUT AIDS

Here is a list of ten things you can do to make a very personal difference in the fight against AIDS.

1. Donate blood to a local AIDS clinic or service organization. (There is no risk of HIV transmission in donating blood.)
2. Give a person with AIDS a ride to and from the doctor's office.
3. Volunteer an afternoon helping a person with AIDS with routine chores: go grocery shopping, walk the dog, make a bank deposit, clean, do the laundry, or make dinner.
4. Read to a friend with AIDS who has lost his or her eyesight to CMV retinitis.
5. Have a garage or apartment sale and donate the proceeds to a local AIDS organization.
6. If you're having a birthday party for yourself or your partner, ask guests to bring a check made out to the AIDS service organization of your choice in lieu of gifts.
7. AIDS caregivers often forget to take time for themselves or feel they aren't entitled to it. Offer to substitute as caregiver for an evening so the caregiver can go out with friends or have time to himself or herself.
8. Write a letter to your congressperson or senator about the need for a national health care plan that addresses the concerns of people with AIDS.

Senator _____   Representative _____
United States Senate   U.S. House of Representatives
Washington, DC 20510   Washington, DC 20515

9. Organize a canned food drive at work or at school and give the donations to a local AIDS service organization that provides meals to people with AIDS.
10. Contact the national television networks when they broadcast either noteworthy or inaccurate reports and programs about HIV and AIDS. Let the network presidents know you support or are displeased with their programming.

ABC   NBC
77 West 66th Street   30 Rockefeller Plaza
New York, NY 10023   New York, NY 10112

CBS   FOX
7800 Beverly Boulevard   P.O. Box 900
Los Angeles, CA 90036   Beverly Hills, CA 90213

Books and Pamphlets on AIDS Education, Treatment, and Prevention

AIDS Project Los Angeles. *AIDS: A Self-Care Manual*. (1987)

Baker, Ronald, Jeffrey Moulton, and John Tighe. *Early Care for HIV Disease*. (1994)

Bartlett, John G., and Ann K. Finkbeiner. *The Guide to Living with HIV Infection*. (1991)

Callaway, C. Wayne. *Surviving with AIDS: A Comprehensive Program of Nutritional Co-Therapy*. (1991)

Dalton, Harlon L., Scott Burris, and the Yale AIDS Law Project. *AIDS and the Law: A Guide for the Public*. (1987)

Dansky, Stephen. *Now Dare Everything: Tales of HIV Related Psychotherapy*. (1994)

Delaney, Martin, and Peter Goldblum. *Strategies for Survival: A Gay Men's Health Manual for the Age of AIDS*. (1987)

Eidson, Ted, ed. *The AIDS Caregiver's Handbook*. (1993)

Ford, Michael Thomas. *100 Questions and Answers about AIDS: A Guide for Young People*. (1992)

Gray, John, Phillip Lyons, and Gary Melton. *Ethical and Legal Issues in AIDS Research*. (1994)

Harding, Paul. *The Essential AIDS Fact Book*. Revised ed. (1994)

Hitchens, Neal. *Fifty Things You Can Do about AIDS*. (1992)

Kaiser, Jon D. *Immune Power: A Comprehensive Healing Program for HIV*. (1993)

Kittredge, Mary. *Teens with AIDS Speak Out*. (1991)

Kloser, Patricia, Craig Kloser, and Jane MacLean. *A Woman's HIV Sourcebook: A Guide to Better Health and Well-Being* (1994)

McCormack, Thomas P. *The AIDS Benefit Handbook*. (1990)

Madansky, Cynthia, and Julie Tolentino Wood. *Safer Sex Handbook for Lesbians*. Lesbian AIDS Project/Gay Men's Health Crisis, Inc. (1993)

Martelli, Leonard J., et al. *When Someone You Know Has AIDS*. Rev. edition. (1993)

Mikluscak, Cindy, and Emmett E. Miller. *Living in Hope: A Twelve-Step Approach for Persons at Risk or Infected with HIV* (1991)

Morales, Julio, and Marcia Bok. *Multicultural Services for AIDS Treatment and Prevention*. (1994)

O'Connor, Tom. *Living with AIDS: Reaching Out*. (1987)

O'Sullivan, Sue, and Pratibha Parmar. *Lesbians Talk Safer Sex*. (1992)

Patton, Cindy, and Janis Kelly. *Making It: A Woman's Guide to Sex in the Age of AIDS*. (1987)

Pinsky, Laura, and Paul Harding Douglas. *The Essential HIV Treatment Fact Book*. (1992)

Pohl, Mel, Densiton Kay, and Doug Toft. *The Caregiver's Journey: When Someone You Love Has AIDS*. (1990)

Richardson, Diane. *Women and AIDS*. (1988)

Shealy, C. Norman, and Caroline Myss. *AIDS: Passageway to Transformation*. (1994)

Siano, Nick. *No Time to Wait: A Complete Guide to Treating, Managing, and Living with HIV Infection*. (1993)

Tatchell, Peter. *Safer Sex: The Guide to Gay Sex Safely*. (1994)

Walker, Mitch. *Men Loving Men: A Gay Guide and Consciousness Book*. (1994)

AIDS IN LITERATURE: A READING LIST

NOVELS (N), SHORT STORY COLLECTIONS (S), YOUNG ADULT NOVELS (YA), ANTHOLOGIES (A), AND POETRY COLLECTIONS (P)

Avena, Thomas, ed. *Life Sentences*. (1994) (A)

Baker, James Robert. *Tim and Pete*. (1993) (N)

Barnett Allen. *The Body and Its Dangers*. (1990) (S)

Boucheron, Robert. *Epitaphs for the Plague Dead*. (1985) (P)

Bram, Christopher. *In Memory of Angel Clare*. (1988) (N)

Brown, Rebecca. *The Gifts of the Body*. (1994) (N)

Calhoun, Jackie. *Lifestyles*. (1990) (N)

Cameron, Lindsley. *The Prospect of Detachment*. (1990) (S)

Cameron, Peter. *The Weekend*. (1994) (N)

Chappell, Helen. *Acts of Love*. (1989) (N)

Claiborne, Sybil. *In the Garden of Dead Cars*. (1993) (N)

Coe, Christopher. *Such Times*. (1993) (N)

Cuadros, Gil. *City of God*. (1995) (N)

Daniels, Peter, and Steve Anthony, eds. *Jugular Defenses*. (1995) (P)

Davis, Christopher. *The Boys in the Bars*. (1989) (S)

———. *Valley of the Shadow*. (1988) (N)

de la Pena, Terri. *Latin Satins*. (1994) (N)

Dent, Tory. *What Silence Equals*. (1993) (P)

Donnelly, Nisa. *The Love Songs of Phoenix Bay*. (1995) (N)

Duplechan, Larry. *Tangled Up in Blue*. (1989) (N)

Feinberg, David B. *Eighty-Sixed*. (1989) (N)

———. *Spontaneous Combustion*. (1991) (N)

Ferro, Robert. *Second Son*. (1988) (N)

Hadas, Rachel. *Unending Dialogue: Voices from an AIDS Poetry Workshop*. (1991) (P)

Hansen, Joseph. *Early Graves*. (1987) (N)

Hite, Molly. *Breach of Immunity*. (1993) (N)

Hoffman, Alice. *At Risk*. (1988) (N)

Hunter, B. Michael, ed. *Sojourner: Black Gay Voices in the Age of AIDS*. (1993) (A)

Indiana, Gary. *Horse Crazy*. (1989) (N)

Johnson, Fenton. *Scissors, Paper, Rock*. (1993) (S)

Johnson, Toby. *Plague: A Novel about Healing*. (1987) (N)

Kerr, M. E. *Night Kites*. (1986) (YA)

Klass, Perri. *Other Women's Children*. (1990) (N)

Klein, Michael, ed. *Poets for Life: 76 Poets Respond to AIDS*. (1990) (A)

Leavitt, David. *A Place I've Never Been*. (1990) (S)

Lynch, Michael. *These Waves of Dying Friends*. (1989) (P)

McGehee, Peter. *Boys Like Us*. (1991) (N)

Mars-Jones, Adam. *Monopolies of Loss*. (S)

Martinac, Paula. *Home Movies*. (1993) (N)

Maso, Carole. *The Art Lover*. (1990) (N)

Maupin, Armistead. *Sure of You*. (1989) (N)

Mayes, Sharon. *Immune*. (1987) (N)

Micklowitz, Gloria D. *Good-bye, Tomorrow*. (1987) (YA)

Monette, Paul. *Afterlife*. (1989) (N)

———. *Halfway Home*. (1991) (N)

———. *Love Alone: Eighteen Elegies for Rog*. (1988) (P)

Mordden, Ethan. *Everyone Loves You: Further Adventures in Gay Manhattan*. (1988) (S)

Musto, Michael. *Manhattan on the Rocks*. (1989) (N)

Obejas, Achy. *We Came All the Way from Cuba So You Could Dress Like That?* (1994) (S)

Peck, Dale. *Martin and John*. (1993) (N)

Preston, John, ed. *Hot Living: Erotic Stories about Safer Sex*. (1985) (A)

Quinlan, Patricia. *Tiger Flowers*. (1994) (YA)

Rees, David. *Letters to Dorothy*. (1991) (S)

———. *The Wrong Apple*. (1988) (N)

Rule, Jane. *Memory Board*. (1987) (N)

Ryman, Geoff. *Was*. (1992) (N)

Saint, Assotto. *Saints*. (1989) (P)

Schreiber, Ron. *John*. (1988) (P)

Schulman, Sarah. *People in Trouble*. (1990) (N)

Uyemoto, Holly. *Rebel without a Clue*. (1989) (N)

Weir, John. *The Irreversible Decline of Eddie Socket*. (1989) (N)

White, Edmund, and Adam Mars-Jones. *The Darker Proof: Stories from a Crisis*. (1988) (S)

Wolverton, Terry, ed. *Blood Whispers: L.A. Writers on AIDS*. 2 vols. (Vol. 1, 1991; Vol. 2, 1994) (A)

BIOGRAPHIES, AUTOBIOGRAPHIES, MEMOIRS, AND PERSONAL NARRATIVES

Ascher, Barbara Lazear. *Landscape without Gravity: A Memoir of Grief*. (1992)

Callen, Michael. *Surviving AIDS*. (1990)

Chase, Clifford. *The Hurry-Up Song: A Memoir of Losing My Brother*. (1995)

Cox, Elizabeth. *Thanksgiving: An AIDS Journal*. (1990)

Fisher, Mary. *Sleep with the Angels*. (1992)

Fried, Stephen. *Thing of Beauty: The Tragedy of Supermodel Gia*. (1993)

Glaser, Elizabeth, and Laura Palmer. *In the Absence of Angels: A Hollywood Family's Courageous Story*. (1991)

Guibert, Herve. *To the Friend Who Did Not Save My Life*. (1991)

Hudson, Rock, and Sara Davison. *Rock Hudson: His Story*. (1986)

Jarman, Derek. *Modern Nature*. (1994)

Kramer, Larry. *Reports from the Holocaust*. (1989)

Mass, Lawrence D. *Confessions of a Jewish Wagnerite: Being Gay and Jewish in America*. (1994)

Monette, Paul. *Borrowed Time*. (1988)

———. *Last Watch of the Night: Essays Too Personal and Otherwise*. (1994)

Money, J. W. *To All the Girls I've Loved Before: An AIDS Diary*. (1987)

Petrow, Stephen. *Dancing in the Darkness*. (1990)

Preston, John. *Personal Dispatches*. (1989)

Reed, Paul. *The Savage Garden: A Journal*. (1994)

Rieder, Ines, and Patricia Ruppelt, eds. *AIDS: The Women*. (1988)

Rist, Darryl Yates. *Heartlands*. (1993)

Rudd, Andrea, and Darien Taylor, eds. *Positive Women: Voices of Women Living with AIDS*. (1992)

Solway, Diane. *A Dance Against Time: The Brief, Brilliant Life of a Joffrey Dancer*. (1994)

Valdiserri, Ronald. *Gardening in Clay: Reflections on AIDS*. (1994)

Whitmore, George. *Someone Was Here: Profiles in the AIDS Epidemic*. (1988)

Wiltshire, Susan Ford. *Seasons of Grief and Grace: A Sister's Story of AIDS*. (1994)

Wojnarowicz, David. *Close to the Knives: A Memoir of Disintegration*. (1991)

ESSAYS, THEORY, AND CRITICISM

ACT UP New York Women and AIDS Book Group. *Women, AIDS, and Activism*. (1990)

Altman, Dennis. *AIDS in the Mind of America: The Social, Political, and Psychological Impact of a New Epidemic*. (1986)

Baker, Rob. *The Art of AIDS*. (1994)

Bateson, Catherine, and Richard Goldsby. *Thinking AIDS*. (1988)

Boffin, Tessa, and Sunil Gupta, eds. *Ecstatic Antibodies: Resisting the AIDS Mythology*. (1990)

Browning, Frank. *The Culture of Desire: Paradox and Perversity in Gay Lives Today*. (1993)

Carter, Erica, and Simon Watney, eds. *Taking Liberties: AIDS and Cultural Politics*. (1989)

Corea, Gena. *The Invisible Epidemic*. (1992)

Crimp, Douglas. *AIDS: Cultural Analysis, Cultural Activism*. (1988)

Crimp, Douglas, and Adam Rolston. *AIDS DemoGraphics*. (1990)

Doyal, Lesley, Jennie Naidoo, and Tamsia Wilton, eds. *AIDS: Setting a Feminist Agenda*. (1995)

Fee, Elizabeth, and Daniel M. Fox, eds. *AIDS: The Burdens of History*. (1988)

Feinberg, David B. *Queer and Loathing: Rants and Raves of an Aging AIDS Queen*. (1994)

Fitzgerald, Frances. *Cities on a Hill*. (1986)

Kinsella, James. *Covering the Plague*. (1989)

McKenzie, Nancy F., ed. *The AIDS Reader: Social, Political, and Ethical Issues*. (1991)

Miller, James, ed. *Fluid Exchanges: Artists and Critics in the AIDS Crisis*. (1992)

Murphy, Timothy. *Ethics in an Epidemic: AIDS, Morality, and Culture*. (1994)

Murphy, Timothy F., and Suzanne Poirier, eds. *Writing AIDS: Gay Literature, Language, and Analysis*. (1993)

Nelson, Emmanuel S. *AIDS: The Literary Response*. (1992)

Pastore, Judith. *Confronting AIDS through Literature*. (1993)

Patton, Cindy. *Inventing AIDS*. (1990)

———. *Last Served? Gendering the HIV Pandemic*. (1994)

———. *Sex and Germs*. (1985)

Root-Bernstein, Robert. *Rethinking AIDS: The Tragic Cost of Premature Consensus*. (1993)

Schecter, Stephen. *The AIDS Notebooks*. (1990)

Schneider, Beth E., and Nancy E. Stoller. *Women Resisting AIDS: Feminist Strategies of Empowerment*. (1995)

Shilts, Randy. *And the Band Played On*. (1987)

Sontag, Susan. *AIDS and Its Metaphors*. (1989)

Watney, Simon. *Policing Desire: Pornography, AIDS, and the Media*. (1987)

———. *Practices of Freedom: Selected Writings on HIV/AIDS*. (1994)

AIDS on the Stage and Screen

The following are some of the depictions of AIDS on the stage and screen since the mid-1980s. For further reading, see *The Art of AIDS* by Rob Baker (1994).

PLAYS

Night Sweat, by Robert Chesley (1984)

The Normal Heart, by Larry Kramer (1985)

As Is, by William M. Hoffman (1985)

Jerker, by Robert Chesley (1986)

Beirut, by Alan Bowne (1987)

Safe Sex, by Harvey Fierstein (1987)

Dog Plays, by Robert Chesley (1989)

The Baltimore Waltz, by Paula Vogel (1992)

The Night Larry Kramer Kissed Me, by David Drake (1992)

Roy Cohn/Jack Smith, by Ron Vawter (1992)

Angels in America, by Tony Kushner (1993)

Jeffrey, by Paul Rudnick (1993)

The Destiny of Me, by Larry Kramer (1993)

Falsettos, by William Finn and James
   Lapine (1992)

FEATURE-LENGTH FILMS

Buddies (1985)
Parting Glances (1986)
Longtime Companions (1990)
Peter's Friends (1992)
Under Heat (1992)
The Living End (1993)

Philadelphia (1993)
Blue (1993)
Zero Patience (1993)
Savage Nights (1994)
Boys on the Side (1995)
The Cure (1995)

MADE-FOR-TV MOVIES

An Early Frost (1985)
Tidy Endings (1988)
Andre's Mother (1990)
Our Sons (1991)
Citizen Cohn (1992)

And the Band Played On (1993)
Roommates (1994)
A Place for Annie (1994)
My Brother's Keeper (1995)

INDEPENDENT DOCUMENTARIES

Chuck Solomon: Coming of Age (1986)
Dying for Love (1987)
Common Threads: Stories from the Quilt (1989)
Tongues Untied (1989)
Absolutely Positive (1991)
Non, Je Ne Regrette Rien (No Regrets) (1992)
One Foot on the Banana Peel, the Other Foot in the Grave (1992)
Sex Is . . . (1992)
Silverlake Life: The View from Here (1992)
The Heart of the Matter (1993)
Fighting in Southwest Louisiana (1994)
Living Proof: HIV and the Pursuit of Happiness (1994)

VIDEOS ON WOMEN AND AIDS

Dying for Love (1987)
Reframing AIDS (1988)
Doctors, Liars, and Women: AIDS Activists Say No to Cosmo (1988)
Her Giveaway: A Spiritual Journey with AIDS (1988)
The Second Epidemic (1989)
Absolutely Positive (1990)
Fighting for Our Lives: Women Confronting AIDS (1990)
DiAna's Hair Ego: AIDS Info Up Front (1990)
(In)Visible Women (1991)

Party Safe! with DiAna and Bambi (1992)
I'm You, You're Me (1993)
Fire in Our House (1995)

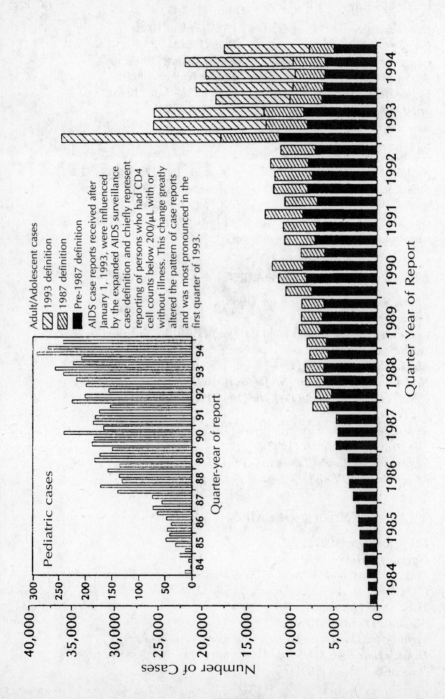

PART VIII

NATIONAL DIRECTORY OF LESBIAN
AND GAY COMMUNITY CENTERS

Compiled and edited by Richard D. Burns, Executive Director,
and Rhett Wickham, Executive Assistant,
Lesbian and Gay Community Services Center, Inc., New York, New York

THE LESBIAN AND Gay Community Services Center of New York is delighted to offer you a comprehensive guide to the gay and lesbian community centers serving our communities across the country. The national directory is now in its ninth edition and still growing.

Each year since 1987, lesbian and gay community centers from across the United States have gathered together in a session at the annual conference of the National Lesbian and Gay Health Foundation. In June 1994, representatives from more than thirty centers gathered for an all-day meeting at the New York Center and began the formation of a national association of lesbian and gay community centers.

Convened by the centers in Dallas, Los Angeles, Minneapolis, New York, and Colorado, the association will work to foster the growth of gay and lesbian community centers around the country and share ideas and program models. Meetings of the association in 1995 took place in June in Minneapolis at the National Lesbian and Gay Health Conference, and in November in Detroit at the annual National Gay and Lesbian Task Force Creating Change Conference.

ARIZONA

Valley of the Sun Gay and Lesbian Community Center

3136 N. 3rd Ave.
Phoenix, AZ 85013

Hours of operation: 10 A.M.–10 P.M. seven days a week
Phone: 602/265-7283; Fax: 602/234-0873

Major programs and services offered: Lesbian and Gay Community Switchboard;
Arizona AIDS Information Line; Valley One in Ten youth group; and VOIT, an antiviolence program

Publish a quarterly newsletter

Barb Jones and Tom Kinkel, Cochairs
Founded in 1993; annual budget for 1994: $100,000
One full-time staff member
Rent their building

Wingspan

422 North Fourth Avenue
Tucson, AZ 85705

Hours of operation: 1 P.M.–7 P.M. Mon.–Sat.
Phone: 602/624-1779; Fax: 602/620-6341

Major programs and services offered: youth group, meeting spaces, information
phone line, lending library, art gallery

Marcia Paris, President; Ernie Slaight, Volunteer Coordinator; David Eyde, Vice
President
Founded in 1988; annual budget in 1995: $21,000
No paid staff
Publish a newsletter called *The Center,* six times per year
Rent their building

CALIFORNIA

Deaf Gay and Lesbian Center

150 Eureka St., Suite 108
San Francisco, CA 94114

Hours of operation: Call for operating hours
Phone: 415/255-0700TTY; Fax: 415/255-9797
World Wide Web: http://www.hooked.net/users/dgrc/dglc.hrml

Major programs and services offered: counseling; advocacy and referrals; peer counseling; community education; workshops; and support groups

Publish DGLC Update newsletter

Founded in 1992; annual operation budget for 1995: $48,000
One full-time staff, one part-time staff
Rent their space

The Billy DeFrank Lesbian and Gay Community Center

175 Stockton Ave.
San Jose, CA 95126

Hours of operation: 6 P.M.–9 P.M., Mon.–Fri.; noon–6 P.M., Sat. and Sun.
Phone: 408/293-3040; Fax: 408/298-8986; Information and referral: 408/293-2429;
E-mail: BDFCPRES!AOL.COM
America Online address: BDFCPRES SERPER

Major programs and services offered: information and referral, peer counseling, youth services, social/recreational services, mental health program, addiction outreach program, volunteer resources, community drop-in, meeting space

Publish a monthly newsletter

Ralph M. Serpe, Program Director; Lisa Yamonaco, President; John Lindner, Executive Vice President
Founded in 1981; annual budget for 1994: $340,000
Two full-time staff, two part-time staff
Rent their building

The Edge

39160 State Street
Fremont, CA

Hours of operation: varied depending on staffing
Phone: 510/790-2887; Fax: 510/713-6679

Major programs and services offered: meeting space; drop-in space; community announcement bulletin boards; housing referral boards; gay men's support group; gay men of color support group; women's support group; men's social group; lesbian social group; and HIV education and prevention services

Mike Kemmerrer, Coordinator

Founded in 1995; operation budget for 1995 not provided
One full-time staff member
Rent their space

Gay and Lesbian Community Center

Mailing address:
P.O. Box 2206
Ventura, CA 93002

Building located at:
1995 East Main Street
Ventura, CA 93001

Hours of operation: 10 A.M.–4 P.M., 6–9 P.M. Mon–Fri.
Phone: 805/653-1979; no Fax

Major programs and services offered: 12-step meetings; rap groups; anti-violence project; counseling; youth program; arts program; library; resource and referrals; and meeting space

Publish a monthly newsletter, Out'About

Ron Cayou, Co-Chair; Edie Brown, Co-chair; Neil Demers-Gray, Founder/ Financial Officer

Founded in 1991; annual operating budget for fiscal 1995: $28,000
No paid staff
Rent their space

Gay and Lesbian Community Services Center of Long Beach

(previously Long Beach Lesbian-Gay Community Center)
2017 E. 4th St.
Long Beach, CA 90814

Hours of operation: 9 A.M.–10 P.M., Mon.–Fri.; 9 A.M.–6 P.M., Sat.
Phone: 310/434-4455; Fax: 310/987-5202

Major programs and services offered: support and rap groups; legal, psychological, and unemployment counseling; community activities program; information referral services; twelve-step programs

Publish a monthly newsletter

Jack M. Newby, Executive Director; Mary Martinez, Board Chair; Ernie Villa, Board Vice Chair

Founded in 1978; annual budget for 1995: $500,000
Nine full-time staff, three part-time staff
Housed in the building owned by ONE in Long Beach, a consortium of six organizations, including the center.

The Gay and Lesbian Community Services Center of Orange County

12832 Garden Grove Blvd., Suite A
Garden Grove, CA 92643

Hours of operation: 9 A.M.–10 P.M., Mon.–Fri.
Phone: 714/534-0862; Fax: 914/534-5491

Major programs and services offered: gay and lesbian support groups, special interest groups, youth services, referral, counseling, AIDS education, HIV support services

M. Dan Wooldridge, Executive Director; Kathy Yhip, Board Chair
Founded in 1972; annual budget for 1995: $800,000
Seven full-time staff, four part-time staff
Rent their building

Gay and Lesbian Resource Center

126 E. Haley St., Ste. A17
Santa Barbara, CA 93101
Phone: 805/963-3636; Fax: 805/963-9086

2255 So. Broadway, No. 4
Santa Maria, CA 19345
Phone: 805/349-9947; Fax: 805/349-8638

Derek Gordon, Executive Director; Kathy Hoxie, Santa Maria Office Manager;
Marian Bankins, Board President; Marsha Trott, Board Secretary
Founded 1976; annual budget for 1994: $1.25 million
Twenty full-time staff, five part-time staff

Gay and Lesbian Resource Center of Ventura County

363 Mobil Ave.
Camarillo, CA 93010
Hours of operation: 10 A.M.–10 P.M. seven days a week
Phone: 805/389-1530 or 646-5884

Major programs and services offered: counseling, support groups, speakers bureau,
classes and workshops, telephone information and referral, HIV/AIDS assistance
programs, various classes

Publish a newsletter four times per year

Ed Noel, Executive Director; Claire Connelly, President; Mary Long, Treasurer
Founded in 1983; annual budget in 1994: $12,000
One full-time staff
Rent their building

Lambda Community Center

P.O. Box 163654
Sacramento, CA 95816

Building Located at:
1931 L Street
Sacramento, CA 95814

Hours of operation: 10 A.M.–9 P.M., Mon.–Fri.; 12 P.M.–9 P.M., Sat. and Sun.
Phone: 916/442-0185; Fax: 916/447-5755

Major programs and services offered: AIDS education and prevention, youth program, health education for lesbians, Lambda Players Theatre Group, Lambda Letters letter writing campaigns

Publish a monthly newsletter

Joanna L. Cassese, Executive Director; Larry Hoover; Board President; Kath-
leen Finnerty, Board Vice President
Founded in 1978; annual operating budget for 1995: $250,000
Four full-time staff, two part-time staff
Own their building

Lavender Youth Recreation & Information Center (LYRIC)

127 Collingwood St.
San Francisco, CA 94114
Phone: 415/703-6150; Fax: 415/703-6153

Hours of operation: 10 A.M.–6 P.M.

Major programs and services offered: Youth Talkline, twenty-four-hour information and referral phone line, staffed by peer listeners in the evening; after school program, providing after school activities for youth under eighteen, five days a week; Pro Active Youth, providing job readiness training to youth under eighteen; young women's program, Young Tongues, a weekly rap group, ongoing workshops, and special events for women under twenty-four; Young Men's HIV Prevention & Education Program, a weekly rap group, ongoing workshops, and special events for men under twenty-four

Publishes a quarterly newsletter

Ken Bukowski, Interim Executive Director; Esperanza Macias and Vanessa Vishit-Vadakan, Board Cochairs
Founded in 1989; annual operating budget for 1995: $375,000
Six full-time staff; two part-time staff
Own their own building

The Lesbian and Gay Men's Community Center

P.O. Box 3357
San Diego, CA 92163

Building located at:
3916 Normal St.
San Diego, CA 92101

Phone: 619/692-2077; Fax: 619/260-3092
Hours of operation: 9 A.M.–9 P.M., Mon.–Sat.; 10 A.M.–7 P.M., Sun.

Major programs and services offered: mental health services for lesbian, gay, and HIV-related issues; lesbian health project; youth program; crisis line

Publish a quarterly newsletter

Karen Marshall, Executive Director; Ann Wilson, Board President
Founded in 1973; annual budget for 1995: $820,000
Seven full-time staff, twelve part-time staff
Own their own building

Los Angeles Gay and Lesbian Community Services Center

1625 N. Schrader Blvd.
Los Angeles, CA 90028

Hours of operation: 9 A.M.–10 P.M., Mon.–Sat.; 9 A.M.–6 P.M., Sun.
Phone: 213/993-7600; Fax: 213/993-7699
E-mail address: GAYLESBLA@aol.com

Major programs and services offered: employment training and placement, mental health services, addiction recovery services, youth services, homeless youth shelter, legal services, AIDS/HIV medical clinic, Audre Lorde Lesbian Health Clinic, anonymous HIV test site, HIV prevention education, cultural programming, computerized AIDS information network

Publish a quarterly newsletter

Lorri L. Jean, Executive Director; Gwen Baba and Loren Ostrow, Board Cochairs
Founded in 1971; annual budget for 1995: $13.8 million
200 full-time staff
Own their building

Pacific Center for Human Growth

2712 Telegraph Ave.
Berkeley, CA 94705

Hours of operation: 10 A.M.–10 P.M., Mon.–Fri.; 6 P.M.–10 P.M., Sat. and Sun.
Phone: 510/548-8283; Fax: 510/548-2938

Major programs and services offered: lesbian, gay, bi, trans speakers bureau; community space; peer support groups; HIV services; individual, couple, and family counseling; information and referral switchboard; Building Bridges, an antihomophobia training program for other organizations

Robert Fuentes, Board Chair
Founded in 1976; annual budget in 1995: $310,000
Ten part-time staff
Rent their building

Pride Center Sonoma County

205 Fifth Street
Santa Rosa, CA 95401

Hours of operation: not yet established as of this edition
Phone: 707/573-9463

Patrick Lancaster, Co-Chair
Mary Toth, Co-Chair
Founded in 1995; newly established
Rent their space

San Francisco Community Center Project

3543 18th St., Box 21
San Francisco, CA 94110

Phone: 415/255-4545

Currently a volunteer-run planning project; looking for a suitable site for the center
Planning began in 1994; annual operation budget for 1995: $40,000

Santa Cruz Lesbian, Gay, Bisexual, and Transgendered Community Center

Mailing address:
P.O. Box 8280
Santa Cruz, CA 95061

Building located at:
1328 Commerce Lane
Santa Cruz, CA 95060

Hours of operation: noon–10 P.M. daily, call ahead as schedule varies
Major programs and services offered: Pride Celebration, lending library, resource directory, information and referral, events sponsorship, meeting space, drop-in space

Publish *New and View of Santa Cruz,* a monthly newsletter

Mark Krikava and Merrie Schaller, Cochairs
Founded in 1980; annual operating budget for 1995: $20,000
No paid staff
Rent their space

Spectrum Center for Gay, Lesbian and Bisexual Concerns

100 Sir Frances Drake Blvd.
San Anselmo, CA 94960

Phone: 415/457-1115; Fax: 415/457-2838
Hours of operation: 9 A.M.–9 P.M., Mon.–Thurs., or by special arrangement

Major programs and services offered: Rainbow's End, teen program, young adult program, seniors' program, parenting program, support groups, special recreation program

Publish *Spectrum,* a newsletter, four times a year

Pat Tibbs, Executive Director; Tom Matteoli, President; Janice Azebu, Treasurer
Founded in 1982; annual operating budget for 1995: $321,000
Two full-time staff; six part-time staff
Rent their building

Stonewall Alliance Center

P.O. Box 8855
Chico, CA 95927

Building located at:
341 Broadway
Chico, CA 95928

Hours of operation: 3 P.M. to 6 P.M. Tues.–Fri.
Phone: 916/892-3336; no Fax

Major programs and services offered: crisis intervention phone line (916/893-3338); youth program; counseling; AIDS/HIV support and recreation services; library; community resources; and a memorial quilt project

Publish *Centerstone*, a monthly newsletter

Greg Williams, Executive Director; Dr. Robert Zadra, Co-Chair; Rae Morrison, Co-Chair
Founded in 1990; annual operation budget for 1995: $160,000
One full-time staff; three part-time staff
Rent their space

COLORADO

Gay, Lesbian & Bisexual Community Services Center of Colorado

P.O. Drawer 18E
Denver, CO 80218-0140

Cheryl Schwartz, Executive Director; Jill Olliver, MSW, Board President; John Bloechl, Board Vice President
Founded in 1976; annual budget for 1994: $194,000
Five full-time staff, one part-time staff

Lambda Community Center, Inc.

1437 East Mullberry, Suite #1
Fort Collins, Colorado 80524

Hours of operation: 12 P.M.–9 P.M.
Phone: 303/221-3247; Fax: 303/482-5815

Major programs and services offered: Youth group, antiviolence project, support groups, resource library, business referrals, educational workshops, recreational groups

Publish a bimonthly newsletter

Stacey Shelp, Executive Director; Ken Hoole, President; Gary Schluter, Secretary
Founded in 1994; annual budget for 1995: $12,000
One part-time staff
Rent their space

CONNECTICUT

Gay and Lesbian Community Center

(Previously Project 100)
1841 Broad St.
Hartford, CT 06114

Hours of operation: 2 P.M.–10 P.M., Mon.–Fri.; Sat. per event; 12 P.M.–5 P.M., Sun.
Phone: 203/724-5542; Fax: 203/724-3443

Major programs and services offered: AA recovery programs, health services, recreational programs, educational forums, theater company

Publish a monthly newsletter

Michael G. Louzier, Executive Director; Roy Moeckel, Board President; Thomas Bowie, Jr., Board Vice President
Founded in 1988; annual budget for 1995: $131,000
One full-time staff, one part-time staff
Rent their building

Tri-Angle Community Center, Inc.

Building located at:
25 Van Zant St., Suite 7-C
East Norwalk, CT 06855

Mailing address:
P.O. Box 4062
East Norwalk CT 06855

Hours of operation: 7 P.M.–10 P.M., Mon.–Thurs.; occasional weekend hours
Phone: 203/853-0600; Fax: 203/853-0600
America Online address: tccenter@aol.com

Major programs and services offered: discussion groups for gay, lesbian, bi, minority, and youth; resource room of books and periodicals; meeting space; community directory of businesses and services

Publish a monthly newsletter, *News and Views,* available on America Online at NewsViews@aol.com

Len Horey, President; David Carroll, Treasurer
Founded in 1989; annual budget for 1995: $50,000
No paid staff
Rent their building

FLORIDA

Lesbian, Gay, and Bisexual Community Center, Inc.

1335 Alton Rd.
Miami Beach, FL 33119

Hours of operation: 6 P.M.–9 P.M., seven days a week
Phone: 305/531-3666

Major programs and services offered: meeting space, information resource and referral, Miami Beach HIV/AIDS Project providing education and sponsoring support groups and services, anticrime project with Miami Beach Police Department, youth outreach, Community Organization Roundtable

Publish a bimonthly newsletter

Patricia Perreir-Pujol and Mitchell Haymes, Copresidents
Founded in 1992; annual budget for 1995: $42,000
Two part-time staff
Own their building

Compass, Inc.

2677 Forest Hill Boulevard, #106
West Palm Beach, FL 33406

Phone: 407/966-3050; Fax: 407/966-0039

Lisa McWhorter, M.S., Executive Director; Andy Amoroso, Board President; Sheldon Hartman, Board Treasurer; Kathryn Jakabein, Board Clerk
Founded in 1988; annual budget for 1994: $165,000
Four full-time staff

Gay and Lesbian Community Center of Greater Fort Lauderdale

Building located at:
1164 East Oakland Park Boulevard
Fort Lauderdale, FL

Mailing address:
P.O. Box 4567
Fort Lauderdale, FL 33338

Hours of operation: to be determined
Phone: 305/563-9500; Fax: 305/779-2680

Major programs and services offered: meeting space; telephone information and referral services, and various other programs in development

Publish a monthly newsletter

Delia Loe, Executive Director; Alan E. Schubert, President; Leon J. Van Dyke, Vice President
Founded in 1993; annual budget for 1995: $132,801

Gay and Lesbian Community Center of Tampa

1222 S. Dale Mabry, #350
Tampa, FL 33629

Phone: 813/273-8919

Major programs and services offered: phone tree; social, recreational and, fundraising events listed on the message of the above listed number, including locations, times, and dates

Dr. Craig Linden and Linda Hallgren, Board Cochairs; Trey Clark, Community Outreach Director
Founded in 1994; annual budget not established at time of writing
No paid staff
Raising funds for a space at time of publication

Gay and Lesbian Community Services of Central Florida, Inc.

Mailing address:
P.O. Box 533446
Orlando, FL 32853-3446

Building located at:
714 E. Colonial Drive
Orlando, FL 32803

Hours of operation: 11 A.M.–10 P.M., Mon.–Fri.; 12 P.M.–5 P.M., Sat.
Phone: 407/425-4527; Fax: 407/423-9904

Major programs and services offered: Social and support groups, professional counseling referral information, crisis intervention, *The Triangle* newspaper, media and library, advocacy, hate crime reporting, meeting space, and numerous social activities and events

Publish a monthly newspaper, *The Triangle*

Lyle C. Miller, Center Coordinator; Julie Whitley, Board President; Francis Ferguson, Board Treasurer
Founded in 1978; annual budget for 1995: $120,000
One full-time staff
Rent their building

Gay Switchboard of Gainesville

Box 12002
Gainesville, FL 32604

Phone: 904/332-0700

Doug Dankel, Coordinator
Founded in 1981; annual budget for 1994: $1,300
Ten part-time paid staff

GEORGIA

The Atlanta Gay Center

63 Twelfth Street
Atlanta, GA 30309

Phone: 404/876-5372

Joseph Lillich, Administrator; Donald W. Smith, Ph.D., Chairperson
Founded in1976; annual budget for 1994: $100,000
One full-time paid staff

Atlanta Lambda Center

Mailing address:
P.O. Box 15180
Atlanta, GA 30333

Building located at:
1518 Monroe Drive
Atlanta, GA 30324

No regular hours of operation
Phone: 404/662-9010; no Fax

Major programs and services currently under development

Publish an occasional newsletter, *Atlanta Lambda Center Newsletter*

David Herman, Board Co-Chair; Sandye Lark, Board Co-Chair
Founded in 1992, annual operating budget for 1995: $12,000
No paid staff
Rent their space

ILLINOIS

The Frank M. Rodde Fund

(operating as The Les-Bi-Gay Community Center of Chicago)
3023 N. Clark, #747
Chicago, IL 60657

Phone: 312/334-2174; Fax: 312/334-2174
E-mail address: MJH 123 @aol.com

Dale Muehler, Executive Director; Michael J. Harrington, President; Kenneth Allen, Vice President
Additional information not available at time of this printing

---

INDIANA

Up the Stairs Community Center
3425 Broadway
Fort Wayne, IN 46807

Hours of operation: 7 P.M.–10 P.M., Mon.–Thurs.; 7 P.M.–midnight, Fri. and Sat.; 7 P.M.–9 P.M., Sun.
Phone: 219/744-1199

Major programs and services offered: fund-raising dances for New Year's and gay/lesbian pride; gay/lesbian resource center and archives; open door chapel; gay/lesbian help line; Friday night drop-in; space rental to various groups including AA, HIV testing site, FAIR civil rights group, and Ladies After Dark (LAD)

Fred Hefter, spokesperson, treasurer, and board member
Founded in 1983; annual operating budget for 1995: $4,800
No paid staff
Own their building

IOWA

GLRC—Gay and Lesbian Resource Center

Box 7008
522 11th St.
Des Moines, IA 50309

Phone: 515/281-0634; Fax: 515/284-8909

Bill Crews, President; Todd Ruopp, Vice President
Founded in mid-1980's; annual budget for 1994: $30,000
No paid staff

KANSAS

The Center—Wichita

Mailing address:
P.O. Box 1357
Wichita, KS 67201

Building located at:
111 N. Spruce
Wichita, KS
Phone: 316/262-3991

Major programs and services offered: lesbian, gay, bi AA meetings; The Kansas Gay and Lesbian Archives; weekly coffee house; weekly lesbian coming out support group; Wichita Gay and Lesbian Alliance; HIV/AIDS clothes closet; community information center

Publish a monthly newsletter

Phil Griffin and Steve Aaron, Cochairs
Founded in 1993; annual operating budget for 1995: $20,000
No paid staff
Rent their space

LOUISIANA

Lesbian and Gay Community Center of New Orleans

816 N. Rampart St.
New Orleans, LA 70116

Hours of operation: noon–6 P.M., seven days a week
Phone: 504/529-2367; Fax: 504/527-5334

Major programs and services offered: information and referral service, weekly youth program, lending library, weekly movies, meeting space for groups, monthly art shows, seminars and forums, twenty-something group

Publishes a quarterly newsletter

Renee Parks and Clarke Broel, Cochairs
Founded in 1992; annual budget for 1995: $12,000
No paid staff
Rent their building

MAINE

Northern Lambda Nord, Inc.

Community Services Center
P.O. Box 990
Caribou, ME 04736

Phone: 207/498-2088

Founded in 1994
No other information available at time of printing

MARYLAND

Gay and Lesbian Community Center of Baltimore

241 W. Chase St.
Baltimore, MD 21201

Phone: 410/837-5445; Fax: 410/837-8512

Michael B. Linnemann, Center Coordinator: Karen Jordan, President
Founded in 1977; annual budget for 1995: $320,000
Five full-time staff, two part-time staff

MICHIGAN

Affirmations Lesbian and Gay Community Center

195 West Nine Mile Road
Ferndale, MI 48220

Hours of operation: 9 A.M.–11 P.M., Mon.–Fri.; noon–7 P.M., Sat.; noon–11 P.M., Sun.
Phone: 810/398-7105; Fax: 810/541-1943

Major programs and services offered: switchboard; peer support groups for men, women, couples, singles, and a mixed group; community outreach

Publishes a monthly newsletter

Jan Stevenson, Executive Director; Tom Wilezak, President; Shea Howell, Board Member
Founded in 1989; annual budget for 1995: $376,396
Five full-time staff, three part-time staff
Rent their building

MINNESOTA

Gay and Lesbian Community Action Council

310 E. 38th St., Room 204
Minneapolis, MN 55409

Phone: 612/822-0127 or 800/800-0350; Fax: 612/822-8786

Ann DeGroot, Executive Director; Tom Hoch, Board Chair
Founded in 1986; annual budget for 1994: $800,000
Ten full-time staff, two part-time staff

MISSOURI

Metropolitan St. Louis Lesbian, Gay, Bisexual and Transgendered Community Center

Mailing address:
Box 4589
St. Louis, MO 63108

Office located at:
438 N. Skinner Blvd.
St. Louis, MO 63130

Hours of operation: 10 A.M.–5 P.M., Mon., Wed., Fri.; 4 P.M.–10 P.M., Thurs.; Sat. and Sun. by arrangement
Phone: 314/997-9897; Fax: 314/862-8155

Major programs and services offered: Twenty-five-organization community voice mail system, education forums, candidates' forum for aldermanic president, lending library for books and videos

Publishes a monthy calendar of events

Mark Maloney, Office Manager; Robert Hollander and Sharon Cohen, Board Members
Founded in 1993; annual operating budget for 1995: $8,000
No paid staff

NEBRASKA

Panhandle Gay and Lesbian Support Services

P.O. Box 1046
Scottsbluff, NE 69363-1046

Phone: 308/635-8488

Diane Crystal, Director; Rae Ann Schmitz and Roni Reid, core group members
Founded in 1993; annual budget for 1994: $600
One part-time staff

NEW JERSEY

Gay and Lesbian Community Center of New Jersey, Inc.

Mailing address:
P.O. Box 1316
Asbury Park, NJ 07712

Building located at:
515 Cookman Ave.
Asbury Park, NJ 07712-1316

Phone: 908/775-4429 or 908/774-1809; Fax: 908/774-5513
Hours of operation: 12 P.M.–8 P.M., seven days a week

Major programs and services offered: meeting place of gay, lesbian, bi, and trans
groups; referral services; monthly socials; lecture series

Publishes a quarterly newsletter

Steve Russo, Board President; Kathy Taggart, Board Vice President
Founded in 1994; annual operating budget for 1995: $65,000
No paid staff
Rent their space

Pride Center of New Jersey

Building located at:
211 Livingston Ave.
New Brunswick, NJ 08901

Mailing address:
P.O. Box 1431
New Brunswick, NJ 08903

Hours of operation: 11 A.M.–1 P.M., and 7 P.M.–10 P.M., Mon. and Tues.; 7 P.M.–10
P.M., Wed. and Thurs.; call for other times
Phone: 908/846-2232

Major programs and services offered: Hot line, library, men's rap group, women's
group, P-FLAG, Log Cabin Club, teachers caucus, lesbian mothers, ACOA, SAGE,

Bisexual Network of NJ; OA; lesbian health services, monthly roller skating, winter and fall NJ gay lesbian street fairs

Ray Johnson and Gina Pastino, Cochairs
Founded in 1991; annual budget for 1995: $18,000
No paid staff
Rent their building

Rainbow Place of South Jersey

Building located at:
1103 North Broad Street
Woodbury, NJ 08096

Mailing address:
P.O. Box 682
Bellmawr, NJ 08099-0682

Hours of operation: call for specific hours
Phone: 609/848-2455; Fax: 215/951-0342
E-mail address: ALLEN219@AOL.COM America Online address: ALLEN219

Major programs and services offered: social and cultural events, referral information, peer support services

Publish a bimonthly newsletter

Laurin Stahl and Preston Brooks, Cochairs
Founded in 1993; annual budget for 1995: $15,000
No paid staff
Rent their building

NEW YORK

Capital District Gay and Lesbian Community Council

Building located at:
332 Hudson Ave.
Albany, NY 12210

Mailing address:
P.O. Box 131
Albany, NY 12201

Hours of operation: 7 P.M.–10 P.M., Mon.–Thurs.; 7 P.M.–11 P.M., Fri.–Sat.; 2 P.M.–10 P.M., Sun.
Phone: 518/462-6138

Major programs and services offered: support groups, programming throughout the Albany area, twenty-four-hour information line

Publish a monthly newsletter called *Community*

Bill Pape, President; Mark Daigneault, Vice President
Founded in 1970; annual budget for 1995: $100,000

No paid staff
Own their building

Gay Alliance of the Genesee Valley

179 Atlantic Avenue
Rochester, NY 14607

Phone: 716/244-8640; Fax: 716/244-8246

Tanya Smolinsky, Center Director; William Pritchard, Acting Board President
Founded in 1973; annual budget for 1994: $125,000
One full-time staff, two part-time staff

The Lesbian and Gay Community Services Center

208 West 13th Street
New York, NY 10011

Hours of operation: 9 A.M.–11 P.M., seven days a week
Phone: 212/620-7310; Fax: 212/924-2657
E-mail address: Igcsclnyc@aol.com

Major programs and services offered: meeting space for over 400 groups, Project Connect alcoholism and substance abuse recovery counseling, Center Bridge AIDS bereavement program, Youth Enrichment Services creative arts programming for young people ages twenty-one and under, Gender Identity Program, in-house and on-the-road community orientation, voter registration, Global Action Project for human rights, Center Kids lesbian/gay family project, Pat Parker/Vito Russo Library, National Museum of Lesbian and Gay History, dances twice a month, lesbian softball tournament, mediation services, information and referral, lesbian health fair, In Our Own Write creative writing classes and readers series, lesbian movie night, Center Stage theater parties, annual garden party kicks off NYC's Gay/Lesbian Pride Week

Publishes a newsletter, *Center Voice*, every other month and monthly calendar of events, *Center Happenings*

Richard D. Burns, Executive Director; Judith E. Turkel, Esq., Board President; Janet Weinberg and Michael Seltzer, Board Cochairs
Founded in 1983; annual budget for 1995: $3.3 million
Thirty-six full-time staff, nine part-time staff
Own their building

The LOFT

P.O. Box 1513
White Plains, NY 10602

Phone: 914/948-4922

Dr. Zelle W. Andrews and Lester Goldstein, Copresidents
Founded in 1990; annual budget for 1994: $50,000
No paid staff

Pride Community Center

P.O. Box 6608
Syracuse, NY 13217-6608

Phone: 315/446-4436

Projected opening date: Spring 1996, providing educational programs, support groups, and an information line

Publish a monthly newsletter, *Pride News*

John Brown, Founding Committee Chair
Founded in 1995; projected operating budget for fiscal 1996: $15,000
No paid staff
Currently seeking physical plant

NORTH CAROLINA

Gay and Lesbian Helpline of Wake Co.

P.O. Box 36207
Raleigh, NC 27606-6207

Phone: 919/821-0055

Noah Ranells, Codirector
No additional information as of this printing

OHIO

Dayton Lesbian and Gay Center

P.O. Box 1203
Dayton, OH 45401

Phone: 513/274-1776

Leon Bey, Chair; Debbie Ranard and Bob Daley, Board Members
Founded in 1976; annual budget for 1994: $25,000
No staff information provided

The Gay & Lesbian Community Center of Greater Cincinnati

Mailing address:
P.O. Box 141061
Cincinnati, OH 45250-1061

Building located at:
700 West Pete Rose Way
Cincinnati, OH 45203

Hours of Operation: 6-9 P.M. Mon.-Fri., 12-4 P.M. Sat. & Sun.
Phone: 513/651-0040; no Fax

Major programs and services offered: information and referral switchboard; library and archives meeting space; community calendar of events; community resource area for copying, faxing, and work on personal computer

Publish *Outlooks*, a quarterly newsletter

Jill Benavides, General Director
Founded in 1991; annual operating budget for fiscal 1995: $25,000
No paid staff
Rent their space

Lesbian/Gay Community Service Center

Mailing address:
P.O. Box 6177
Cleveland, OH 44101

Building located at:
1418 W. 29th St.
Cleveland, OH 44113

Phone: 216/522-0199; Fax: 216/522-0026
America Online address: CLEVLGCSC or RAINBROOK
E-mail address: CLEVLGCSC@AOL.COM

Hours of operation: 9 A.M.–5 P.M., Mon.–Fri.
Hot line open 3 P.M.–10 P.M., seven days a week
Computer hot line open twenty-four hours a day, seven days a week

Major programs and services offered: hot line, youth program (PRYSM), HIV positive program, meeting space, drop-in/information bulletin board, antidiscrimination work, speakers bureau

Publish a quarterly newsletter

Judith Rainbrook, Executive Director; Frank Lowery, Jr., Board President
Founded in 1975; annual budget for 1995: $230,000
Four full-time staff, one part-time staff
Rent their building

Stonewall Union Community Center

(previously Stonewall Community Center)
47 W. 5th Avenue
Columbus, OH 43201

Hours of operation: 9 P.M.–5 P.M., Mon.–Fri., evenings as scheduled
Phone: 614/299-7764; Fax/TTY: 614/299-4408

Major programs and services offered: antiviolence project, fight the right project, annual pride march (10,000 people in 1994); twice-weekly television program, booth at the Ohio State Fair

Publish a monthly newsletter

Gloria McCauley, Interim Executive Director; Susan Bader, President; Jeff Jones, Vice President
Founded in 1981; annual budget for 1995: $150,000
One full-time staff, three part-time staff
Rent their building

OKLAHOMA

The Oasis Gay, Lesbian and Bisexual Community Resource Center

2135 NW 39th St.
Oklahoma City, OK 73112

Phone: 405/525-2437

Christopher Bruce DeVault, Executive Director
Founded in 1982; annual budget for 1994: $50,000
One part-time staff

OREGON

Lesbian Community Project

800 NW 6th, Room 333
Portland, OR 97209

Hours of operation: 9 A.M.–4 P.M., Mon.–Thurs.; 9 A.M.–midnight, Fri.
Phone: 503/223-0071; Fax: 503/242-1967
Antiviolence hot line: 503/796-1703

Major programs and services offered: Antiviolence project and hot line; lesbian health project; the Oregon Lesbian Conference; voter registration; For Love and Justice: a Walk against Hate; lesbian film festival; over thirty-five group; safer sex workshops; coming out series; presentations to high school and college classes, business and social service organizations, churches, and other groups; some thirty other programs and services

Publish a monthly newsletter

Laverne Lewis, Executive Director; Susan Bryer, President
Founded in 1986; annual budget for 1995: $100,000
Two part-time staff
Rent their space

Lesbian Gay Bisexual Community Resource Center

P.O. Box 6596
Portland, OR 97208

Phone: 503/295-9732

Darci Chapman and Kim Grittner, Copresidents
Founded in 1993; annual budget for 1994: $1,000
No paid staff

PENNSYLVANIA

The Gay & Lesbian Community Services Center of Philadelphia

Mailing address:
537 N. 3rd Street
Philadelphia, PA 19123

Phone: 215/238-9792; Fax: 215/238-9263

A recently formed organization currently seeking information from other centers on programs, annual reports, start-up experience, and advice and structuring

Jonathan Cabiria, Board Member
Mission statement is, "To support the well-being of Philadelphia gay, lesbian, bisexual, and transgendered persons by providing essential human services to the community; by organizing and sponsoring community activities."

Penguin Place: Gay & Lesbian Community Center of Philadelphia, Inc.

Mailing address:
P.O. Box 12814
Philadelphia, PA 19018

Building located at:
201 S. Camac St.
Philadelphia, PA 19107

Hours of operation: 6 P.M.–10 P.M., Mon.–Fri.; 10 A.M.–6 P.M., Sat.; 3 P.M.–9 P.M., Sun.
Phone: 215/732-2220

Major programs and services offered: library and archives, counseling services, youth group, Out Music, team Philadelphia sports, art gallery

Publish a quarterly newsletter

Michael J. LoFurno and Pamila Florea, Board Cochairs
Founded in 1974; annual budget for 1994: $50,000
No paid staff
Rent their space

SOUTH CAROLINA

South Carolina Gay and Lesbian Community Center

Building located at:
1108 Woodrow St.
Columbia, SC 29205

Mailing address:
South Carolina Gay and Lesbian Community Center
P.O. Box 12648
Columbia, SC 29211

Hours of operation: 1 P.M.–6 P.M., Wed.; 7 P.M.–11 P.M., Fri.; 1 P.M.–8 P.M., Sat. and Sun.
Phone/Fax: 803/771-7713

Major programs and services offered: library, youth groups, lesbian coming out group, information and referral line, gay men's HIV and social group

Publish a bimonthly newsletter

Matt Tischler and Kristen Gregory, Cochairs
Founded in 1989; annual budget for 1995: $35,000
No paid staff
Own their building

TENNESSEE

Memphis Gay and Lesbian Community Center

P.O. Box 41074
Memphis, TN 38174

Phone: 901/728-4297

Michael Ricks, President; Vincent Astor, Vice President
Founded in 1989; annual budget for 1994: $12,000
No paid staff

TEXAS

Community Outreach Center

P.O. Box 64746
Lubbock, TX 79464-4746

Phone: 806/762-1019

Natalie Phillips, President; Bill Sommers, Vice President; Kara Carthel, Board Member
Founded in 1989; annual budget for 1994: $14,000
No paid staff

Cornerstone

Mailing address:
P.O. Box 3164
Austin, TX 78764

Building located at:
425 Woodward
Austin, TX 78704

Hours of operation not provided for this edition
Phone: 512/416-1616; Fax: 512/445-5518

Currently seeking physical plant to house numerous non-profit gay, lesbian, and bisexual service organizations; working in cooperation with Metropolitan Community Church of Austin

Publish a semi-annual newsletter, *The Cornerstone*

Gay and Lesbian Community Center

Building located at:
2701 Reagan Street
Dallas, TX 75219

Mailing address:
P.O. Box 190869
Dallas, TX 75219-0869

Hours of operation: 9 A.M.–9 P.M., Mon.–Fri.; 10 A.M.–6 P.M., Sat.; noon–6 P.M., Sun. and holidays
Phone: 214/528-9254; Fax: 214-522-4604
E-mail address: foundgay@onramp.net

Major programs and services offered: community hot line (214/528-0022); gay/lesbian help line, gay/lesbian speakers bureau, adult education, meeting spaces, Welcome Wagon, gay 101 workshops, community switchboard, community calendar, gay/lesbian archives, research library

Publish a monthly newsletter

John Thomas, Executive Director; Steve Hawkins, Board President; Jan Mock, Board Vice President
Founded in 1984; annual budget for 1995: $500,000
Four full-time staff, four part-time staff
Own their building (center is part of a larger multiorganizational program)

HAPPY Foundation

411 Bonham
San Antonio, TX 78205

Hours of operation: varies, best to call
Phone: 210/227-6451

Major programs and services offered: gay and lesbian archive collecting all kinds of history for research projects

Gene Elder, Executive Director
Founded in 1988; budget not provided

No paid staff
Own their building

Lambda Services

Mailing address:
P.O. Box 31321
El Paso, TX 79931-0321

Offices located at:
910 N. Mesa
El Paso, TX 79902

Hours of operation: 7 P.M.–11 P.M., Mon., Wed., Fri., Sat.; office open 8 A.M.–5 P.M., Mon.–Fri.
Phone: 915/562-4297; Fax: 915/532-6919
E-mail address: LAMBDAelp@aol.com
America Online address: LAMBDA ELP or LAMBDAtx

Major programs and services offered: HIV testing; twenty-four-hour switchboard, help line, and teen help line; antiviolence project; Youth OUTreach Services; Womyn's Services; public information speakers bureau

Publish a monthly newsletter

Rob Knight, President; Katherine Kelly, Vice President; Alejandro Herrera, Secretary
Founded in 1991; annual operating budget for 1995: $10,000
Five full-time staff, fifteen part-time staff
Rent their space

WISCONSIN

The United

14 W. Mifflin St., Suite 103
Madison, WI 53703

Phone: 608/255-8582

Jane Vaneerbosch, Director; Sande Janagold, Board Treasurer; Greg Hines, Interim Board President

Founded in 1978; annual budget for 1994: $51,000
One full-time staff, one part-time staff

AGENCIES WITH BUDGETS OF $10,000 OR UNDER

Wingspan
Tucson, Arizona

Gay Switchboard of Gainesville
Gainsville, Florida

Up the Stairs Community Center
Fort Wayne, Indiana

Metropolitan St. Louis Lesbian, Gay,
Bisexual and Transgendered
Community Center
St. Louis, Missouri

Panhandle Gay and Lesbian Support
Services
Scottsbluff, Nebraska

Lesbian Gay Bisexual Community
Resource Center
Portland, Oregon

Lambda Services
El Paso, Texas

AGENCIES WITH BUDGETS OF $20,000 AND UNDER

Gay and Lesbian Resource Center of
Ventura County
Camarillo, California

Santa Cruz Lesbian, Gay, Bisexual,
and Transgendered Community
Center
Santa Cruz, California

Lambda Community Center, Inc.
Fort Collins, Colorado

The Center—Wichita
Wichita, Kansas

Lesbian and Gay Community Center
of New Orleans
New Orleans, Louisiana

Pride Center of New Jersey
New Brunswick, New Jersey

Rainbow Place of South Jersey
Bellmawr, New Jersey

Memphis Gay and Lesbian
Community Center
Memphis, Tennessee

Community Outreach Center
Lubbock, Texas

AGENCIES WITH BUDGETS OF $50,000 AND UNDER

Deaf Gay and Lesbian Center
San Francisco, California

San Francisco Community Center
Project
San Francisco, California

Gay and Lesbian Community Center
Ventura, California

Tri-Angle Community Center, Inc.
East Norwalk, Connecticut

Lesbian, Gay, and Bisexual
Community Center, Inc.
Miami Beach, Florida

GLRC—Gay and Lesbian Resource
   Center
Des Moines, Iowa

Gay and Lesbian Community Center
   of New Jersey, Inc.
Asbury Park, New Jersey

The LOFT
White Plains, New York

Dayton Lesbian and Gay Center
Dayton, Ohio

The Gay and Lesbian Community
   Center of Greater Cincinatti
Cincinatti, Ohio

The Oasis Gay, Lesbian and Bisexual
   Community Resource Center
Oklahoma City, Oklahoma

Penguin Place
Philadelphia, Pennsylvania

South Carolina Gay and Lesbian
   Community Center
Columbia, South Carolina

The United
Madison, Wisconsin

Agencies with Budgets of $100,000 and Under

Valley of the Sun Gay and Lesbian
   Community Center
Phoenix, Arizona

The Atlanta Gay Center
Atlanta, Georgia

Capital District Gay and Lesbian
   Community Council
Albany, New York

Lesbian Community Project
Portland, Oregon

Agencies with Budgets of $250,000 and Under

Lambda Community Center
Sacramento, California

Stonewall Alliance Center
Chico, California

Gay, Lesbian and Bisexual Community
   Services Center of Colorado
Denver, Colorado

Gay and Lesbian Community Center
Hartford, Connecticut

Compass, Inc.
West Palm Beach, Florida

Gay and Lesbian Community Center
   of Greater Fort Lauderdale
Fort Lauderdale, Florida

Gay and Lesbian Community Services
   of Central Florida, Inc.
Orlando, Florida

Gay Alliance of the Genesee Valley
Rochester, New York

Lesbian/Gay Community Service
   Center
Cleveland, Ohio

Stonewall Union Community Center
Columbus, Ohio

AGENCIES WITH BUDGETS OF $500,000 AND UNDER

The Billy DeFrank Lesbian and Gay
   Community Center
San Jose, California

Gay and Lesbian Community Services
   Center of Long Beach
Long Beach, California

Pacific Center for Human Growth
Berkeley, California

Lavender Youth Recreation &
   Information Center
San Francisco, California

Spectrum Center for Gay, Lesbian and
   Bisexual Concerns
San Anselmo, California

Gay and Lesbian Community Center
   of Baltimore
Baltimore, Maryland

Affirmations Lesbian and Gay
   Community Center
Ferndale, Michigan

Gay and Lesbian Community Center
Dallas, Texas

AGENCIES WITH BUDGETS OF $1 MILLION AND UNDER

Gay Lesbian Community Services
   Center of Orange County
Garden Grove, California

The Lesbian and Gay Men's
   Community Center
San Diego, California

Gay and Lesbian Community Action
   Council
Minneapolis, Minnesota

AGENCIES WITH BUDGETS OVER $1 MILLION

Gay and Lesbian Resource Center
Santa Barbara, California

Los Angeles Gay and Lesbian
   Community Services Center
Los Angeles, California

The Lesbian and Gay Community
   Services Center
New York, New York

PART IX

NATIONAL DIRECTORY OF LESBIAN
AND GAY ORGANIZATIONS AND
RESOURCES

GENERAL/ACTIVIST

African American Lesbian and Gay
  Alliance
P.O. Box 50374
Atlanta, GA 30302

Network Linking Asian Lesbians in
  Asia and the Diaspora
P.O. Box 2594
Daly City, CA 94017-2594
Phone: 415/476-8180
Fax: 415/476-8887

Asian Pacific Lesbian and Bisexual
  Network
P.O. Box 460778
San Francisco, CA 94146-0778
Phone: 510/814-2422

Black Lesbian and Gay Leadership
  Forum
1219 South La Brea Avenue
Los Angeles, CA 90019
Phone: 213/964-7820

Gay, Lesbian, and Bisexual Speakers
  Bureau
Public Education Services, Inc.
P.O. Box 2232
Boston, MA 02117
Phone: 617/354-0133

Lesbian Avengers
c/o Lesbian and Gay Community
  Services Center
208 West 13th Street
New York, NY 10011
Phone: 212/967-7711 ext. 3204

National Coalition of Black Lesbians
  and Gays
P.O. Box 19248
Washington, DC 20036

National Gay and Lesbian Task Force
1734 14th Street NW
Washington, DC 20009
Phone: 202/332-6483

National Latino/a Lesbian and Gay
  Organization
P.O. Box 44483
Washington, DC 20026

National Lesbian Forum/Alliance
  Nationale des Lesbiennes
P.O. Box 482
Regina, SK, Canada S4P 3A2

Overlooked Opinions, Inc.
3712 North Broadway, #277
Chicago, IL 60613-9941
Phone: 312/929-9600

Queer Nation
c/o Lesbian and Gay Community
  Services Center
208 West 13th Street
New York, NY 10011
Phone: 212/260-6156

Trikone
P.O. Box 21354
San Jose, CA 95151
408/270-8776
Gay and lesbian South Asians

AIDS/HIV

AIDS Coalition to Unleash Power
  (ACT UP)
496-A Hudson Street, #G4
New York, NY 10014
Phone: 212/564-2437

AIDS National Interfaith Network
110 Maryland Avenue NE, Suite 504
Washington, DC 20002
Phone: 202/546-0807

AIDS Action Council
1875 Connecticut Avenue NW, #700
Washington, DC 20009
Phone: 202/986-1300

AIDS Research Alliance
621-A North San Vicente Blvd.
West Hollywood, CA 90069
Phone: 310/358-2423

American Foundation for AIDS
  Research (AmFAR)
733 Third Avenue
New York, NY 10017
Phone: 212/682-7440

AIDS Project/Lambda Legal Defense
  and Education Fund
666 Broadway, 12th Floor

New York, NY 10012
Phone: 212/995-8585

American Institute for Teen AIDS
  Prevention
P.O. Box 136116
Fort Worth, TX 76136
Phone: 817/237-0230

Broadway Cares/Equity Fights AIDS
165 West 46th Street, Suite 1300
New York, NY 10036
Phone: 212/840-0770

Canadian AIDS Society
170 Laurier Avenue West, #1101
Ottawa, Ontario K1P 5V5
Fax: 613/563-4998

Community Research Initiative on
  AIDS (CRIA)
275 Seventh Avenue, 20th Floor
New York, NY 10001
Phone: 212/924-3934

Design Industries Foundation
  Fighting AIDS (DIFFA)
150 West 26th Street, Suite 602
New York, NY 10001
Phone: 212/727-3100

Gay Men's Health Crisis (GMHC)
129 West 20th Street
New York, NY 10011
Phone: 212/807-6664
Hot line: 212/807-6655
See Lesbian AIDS Project, below

Mobilization Against AIDS
584-B Castro Street
San Francisco, CA 94114
Phone: 415/863-4676

National Leadership Coalition on
   AIDS
1730 M Street NW, Suite 905
Washington, DC 20036
Phone: 202/429-0930

National Minority AIDS Council
   (NMAC)
300 I Street NE, Suite 400
Washington, DC 20002
Phone: 202/544-1076

Project Inform
1965 Market Street, Suite 220
San Francisco, CA 94103
Phone: 415/558-8669

Ryan White Foundation
101 West Washington Street, Suite
   1135 East
Indianapolis, IN 46204
Phone: 800/444-RYAN

Test Positive Aware Network
1258 West Belmont Avenue
Chicago, IL 60657
Phone: 312/404-8726

Treatment Action Group
200 East 10th Street, #601
New York, NY 10003
Phone: 212/260-0300

AIDS/HIV—WOMEN

Amigas Latinas en Accion Pro-Salud
47 Nichols Avenue
Watertown, MA 02172
Phone: 617/491-1268

Boston Women's AIDS Information
   Project
c/o Fenway Community Health
   Center
16 Haviland Street
Boston, MA 02115
Phone: 617/267-0900

Lesbian AIDS Project (LAP)
c/o Gay Men's Health Crisis
129 West 20th Street, 2nd Floor
New York, NY 10011
Phone: 212/337-3532

Lyon-Martin Women's Health Services
1748 Market Street, Suite 201
San Francisco, CA 94102
Phone: 415/565-7683

Women's Action Committee/Minority
   Task Force on AIDS
505 Eighth Avenue, 16th Floor
New York, NY 10018
Phone: 212/563-8340

New Jersey Women and AIDS
   Network (NJWAN)
5 Elm Row, Suite 112
New Brunswick, NJ 08901
Phone: 908/846-4462

Sisterlove Women's AIDS Project
1132 W. Peachtree Street
Atlanta, GA 30309
Phone: 404/872-0600

Whitman-Walker Clinic
Women's Committee on AIDS
2335 18th Street NW
Washington, DC 20009
Phone: 202/797-3500

Women and AIDS Resource Network
   (WARN)
P.O. Box 020525
Brooklyn, NY 11202
Phone: 718/596-6007

Women and AIDS Risk Network
   Project L.A.
900 N. Alvarado, 2nd Floor
Los Angeles, CA 90026
Phone: 213/413-7779

Women in Crisis
Minority Women and AIDS Project
360 West 125th Street, Suite 11
New York, NY 10027
Phone: 212/316-5200

Women's AIDS Network
P.O. Box 426182
San Francisco, CA 94142-6182
Phone: 415/864-4376

Women's AIDS Project
8235 Santa Monica Boulevard, Suite 201
West Hollywood, CA 90046
Phone: 213/650-1508

Women's Council on AIDS
1441 Florida Avenue NW
Washington, DC 20009

WORLD (Women Organized Against
   Life-Threatening Diseases)
P.O. Box 11535
Oakland, CA 94611
Phone: 510/658-6930

For a listing of local AIDS/HIV services, contact the U.S. Conference of
Mayors, 1620 I Street NW, Washington, DC 20006; Phone: 202/293-7330.
Many local AIDS groups and organizations are also listed by state in the
Gayellow Pages (Renaissance House,
Box 292, Village Station, New York, NY
10014-0292).

AIDS HOT LINES

AIDS Clinical Trials Information
   Services
Phone: 800/TRIALSA; TTY/TDD:
   800/243-7012

CDC (Centers for Disease Control)
   AIDS Hotline
popularly known as the National AIDS
   Hotline
Phone: 800/342-AIDS; in Spanish,
   800/344-SIDA

National AIDS Hotline for Hearing
   Impaired
Phone: 800/243-7889

National Hospicelink
Phone: 800/331-1620

National Native American AIDS
   Hotline
Phone: 800/283-2437

National Sexually Transmitted
   Diseases Hotline
Phone: 800/227-8922

Project Inform National Hotline (AIDS treatment)
Phone: 800/822-7422

Toll-free directory assistance (call for your state's own toll-free AIDS hot line)
Phone: 800/555-1212

ARCHIVES/LIBRARIES

Archives Gaies du Quebec
4067 St.-Laurent, Suite 202
Montreal, QC H2W 1Y7C
Phone: 514/287-9987

Blanche Baker Memorial Library and
  Archives/ONE, Inc.
3340 Country Club Drive
Los Angeles, CA 90019
Phone: 213/735-5252

Canadian Gay Archives
P.O. Box 639, Station A
Toronto, Ontario M5W 1G2

Dallas Gay and Lesbian Historic
  Archives
2701 Reagan
Dallas, TX 75219
Phone: 214/528-4233

Douglas County Gay Archives
P.O. Box 942
Dillard, OR 97432-0942
Phone: 503/679-9913

Gay and Lesbian Archives of
  Washington, D.C.
P.O. Box 4218
Falls Church, VA 22044
Phone: 703/671-3930

Gay and Lesbian Historical Society of
  Northern California
P.O. Box 424280
San Francisco, CA 94142
Phone: 415/626-0980

Henry Gerber/Pearl M. Hart Library
  and Archives
Midwest Lesbian/Gay Resource
  Center
3352 N. Paulina Street
Chicago, IL 60657
Phone: 312/883-3003

Homosexual Information Center
115 Monroe Street
Bossier City, LA 71111

International Gay and Lesbian
  Archives
P.O. Box 38100
Los Angeles, CA 90038-0100

June Mazer Lesbian Collection
626 N. Robertson Blvd.
West Hollywood, CA 90069
Phone: 310/659-2478

Kentucky Collection of Lesbian Her-
  Story
P.O. Box 1701
Louisville, KY 40201

Lesbian and Gay Historical Society of
  San Diego
P.O. Box 40389
San Diego, CA 92164
Phone: 619/260-1522

Lesbian Herstory Archives
P.O. Box 1258
New York, NY 10116
Phone: 718/768-DYKE

National Museum and Archive of
Lesbian and Gay History
Lesbian and Gay Community Services
Center
208 West 13th Street
New York, NY 10011
Phone: 212/620-7310

New York Public Library
Division of Humanities, Social
Sciences, and Special Collections
Fifth Avenue and 42nd Street
New York, NY 10018
Phone: 212/930-0584

Pat Parker/Vito Russo Center Library
Lesbian and Gay Community Services
Center
208 West 13th Street
New York, NY 10011
Phone: 212/620-7310

Southeastern Lesbian Archives
Box 5502
Atlanta, GA 30307

Stonewall Library and Archives
330 SW 27th Street
Fort Lauderdale, FL 33315

ART AND DESIGN

International Lesbian Cartoonists'
Network
P.O. Box 6327
Daytona Beach, FL 32122

Lesbian Visual Artists
870 Market Street, #618
San Francisco, CA 94102

Organization of Lesbian and Gay
Architects and Designers (OLGAD)
P.O. Box 927, Old Chelsea Station
New York, NY 10113
Phone: 212/475-7652

ATHLETICS/SPORTS

Federation of Gay Games
584 Castro Street, Suite 343
San Francisco, CA 94114

International Gay Figure Skating
Union
P.O. Box 1101
New York, NY 10113
Phone: 212/691-1690 or 212/255-0559

International Gay Bowling Association
1730 Pendrell Street, #402
Vancouver, BC
Phone: 604/689-5146

International Gay Rodeo Association
900 East Colfax
Denver, CO 80218
Phone: 303/860-9105

Stonewall Climbers
P.O. Box 445
Boston, MA 02124
Rock and ice climbers worldwide

EDUCATION—TEACHERS/STUDENTS

American Federation of Teachers
National Gay and Lesbian Caucus
P.O. Box 19856
Cincinnati, OH 45219

Center for Lesbian and Gay Studies
  (CLAGS)
Graduate Center of the City
  University of New York
33 West 42nd Street, Room 404N
New York, NY 10036
Phone: 212/642-2924

Coalition for Lesbian and Gay Student
  Groups
Box 190712
Dallas, TX 75219
Phone: 214/621-6705
Fax: 214/528-8436

Gay Teachers Caucus of the National
  Education Association
32 Bridge Street
Hackensack, NJ 07606
Phone: 201/489-2458

Lesbian Teachers Network
P.O. Box 301
East Lansing, MI 48826

National Gay and Lesbian Task Force
  Campus Project
1734 14th Street NW
Washington, DC 20009
Phone: 202/332-6483

Network of Gay and Lesbian
  Alumni/ae
P.O. Box 53188
Washington, DC 20009

FILM/TELEVISION

Alliance for Gay and Lesbian Artists in
  the Entertainment Industry
P.O. Box 69A18
West Hollywood, CA 90069

DYKE-TV
P.O. Box 55, Prince Street Station
New York, NY 10012
Phone: 212/343-9335; 800/310-DYKE
Syndicated cable TV show

Frameline
346 Ninth Street
San Francisco, CA 94103
Phone: 415/703-8650

Gay and Lesbian Alliance Against
  Defamation (GLAAD)
150 West 26th Street
New York, NY 10001
Phone: 212/807-1700

In the Life
39 West 14th Street, Suite 402
New York, NY 10011
Phone: 212/255-6012
Monthly public TV program

Professionals in Film/Video
336 Canal Street, 8th Floor
New York, NY 10013-2022
Phone: 212/387-2022

FOUNDATIONS/FUNDING SOURCES

An Uncommon Legacy Foundation
150 West 26th Street, Suite 503
New York, NY 10001
Phone: 212/366-6507
Fax: 212/366-6509

Astraea National Lesbian Action
  Foundation
116 E. 16th Street, 7th Floor
New York, New York 10003
Phone: 212/529-8021

Colin Higgins Fund of Tides
  Foundation
1388 Sutter Street
San Francisco, CA 94109
Phone: 415/771-4308

Funding Exchange/OUT Fund
666 Broadway, Suite 500
New York, NY 10012
Phone: 212/529-5300

Ms. Foundation for Women
120 Wall Street, 33rd Floor
New York, NY 10005
Phone: 212/742-2300

National Network of Women's Funds
1821 University Avenue, #409N
St. Paul, MN 55104
Phone: 612/641-0742

North Star Fund
666 Broadway
New York, NY 10012
Phone: 212/460-5511

Out of the Closet Foundation
20084 Cherokee Station
New York, NY 10021
Phone: 212/472-3573

Paul Rapoport Foundation
220 East 60th Street
New York, NY 10022
Phone: 212/888-6578

Stonewall Community Foundation
825 Third Avenue, Suite 3315
New York, NY 10022

HEALTH AND MEDICINE

Association for Gay, Lesbian, and
  Bisexual Issues in Counseling
Box 216
Jenkintown, PA 19046

Association of Lesbian and Gay
  Psychiatrists
1439 Pineville Road
New Hope, PA 18938

Committee on Gay and Lesbian
  Concerns
American Psychological Association
1200 Seventeenth Street NW

Washington, DC 20036
Phone: 202/336-5500

Education in a Disabled Gay
  Environment (EDGE)
P.O. Box 305, Village Station
New York, NY 10014

Gay and Lesbian Medical Association
273 Church Street
San Francisco, CA 94114
Phone: 415/255-4547

International Advisory Counsel for Homosexual Men and Women in AA
P.O. Box 90
Washington, DC 20044-0090

Lesbian Community Cancer Project
Pat Parker Place
1902 W. Montrose Avenue
Chicago, IL 60613
Phone: 312/561-4662

Lesbian, Gay, and Bisexual People in Medicine
1890 Preston White Drive
Reston, VA 22091
Phone: 703/620-6600

Mary Helen Mautner Project for Lesbians with Cancer
1707 L Street NW
Washington, DC 20036
Phone: 202/332-5536

National Association of Lesbian and Gay Alcoholism Professionals
204 West 20th Street
New York, NY 10011

National Gay and Lesbian Domestic Violence Victims' Network

P.O. Box 140131
Denver, CO 80214

National Lesbian and Gay Health Association
1407 S Street NW
Washington, DC 20009
Phone: 202/939-7880
Fax: 202/797-3504

Pride Institute
14400 Martin Drive
Eden Prairie, NM 55344
Phone: 800/54-PRIDE

Project Connect
Lesbian and Gay Community Services Center
208 West 13th Street
New York, NY 10011
Phone: 212/620-7310

Society for the Psychological Study of Lesbian and Gay Issues
American Psychological Association
1200 Seventeenth Street NW
Washington, DC 20036
Phone: 202/336-5500

HOME AND FAMILY

Center Kids: The Family Project
Lesbian and Gay Community Services Center
208 West 13th Street
New York, NY 10011
Phone: 212/620-7310
Fax: 212/924-2657

Children of Lesbians and Gays Everywhere (COLAGE)
2300 Market St., #165
San Francisco, CA 94114
Phone: 415/206-1930

or
Box 187, Station F
Toronto, ON M4Y 2L5, Canada

Gay and Lesbian Parents Coalition International (GLPCI)
P.O. Box 50360
Washington, DC 20091
Phone: 202/583-8029

Gay Parents Coalition
P.O. Box 19891
Washington, DC 20036
Phone: 202/583-8029

Hetrick-Martin Institute for Lesbian
and Gay Youth
2 Astor Place
New York, NY 10003
Phone: 212/674-2400
Fax: 212/674-8650

Lavender Families (formerly Lesbian
Mothers National Defense Fund)
P.O. Box 21567
Seattle, WA 98111
Phone: 206/325-2643

National Coalition for Gay and
Lesbian Youth
P.O. Box 24589
San Jose, CA 95154-4589
Phone: 408/269-6125

National Federation of Parents and
Friends of Gays
8020 Eastern Avenue NW
Washington, DC 20012
Phone: 202/726-3223

National Register of Lesbian and Gay
Unions
125 Cedar Place Penthouse
New York, NY 10006

Parents and Friends of Lesbians and
Gays (P-FLAG)
1012 Fourteenth St. NW, #700
Washington, DC 20005
or
Box 27605
Washington, DC 20038
Phone: 202/638-4200
Fax: 202/638-0243

Partners
P.O. Box 8685
Seattle, WA 98109

Senior Action in a Gay Environment
(SAGE)
305 Seventh Avenue
New York, NY 10001
Phone: 212/741-2247

LEGAL ISSUES

American Civil Liberties Union
Lesbian and Gay Rights/AIDS
Project
132 West 43rd Street
New York, NY 10036
Phone: 212/944-9800

Gay and Lesbian Advocates and
Defenders (GLAD)
P.O. Box 218
Boston, MA 02112
Phone: 617/426-1350

Lambda Legal Defense and Education
Fund
666 Broadway, 12th Floor
New York, NY 10012
Phone: 212/995-8585

LeGaL: Lesbian and Gay Law
Association
799 Broadway #340
New York, NY 10003
Membership: 212/353-9118
Fax: 212/353-2970
Referral Service: 212/459-4873
E-mail: le-gal@interport.net

National Center for Lesbian Rights
(NCLR)
1663 Mission Street, 5th Floor
San Francisco, CA 94103
Phone: 415/392-6257

National Lesbian and Gay Law Association
Box 77130, National Capital Station
Washington, DC 20014
Phone: 202/389-0161

LITERATURE/PUBLISHING

Gay and Lesbian Task Force
American Library Association
50 East Huron Street
Chicago, IL 60611

Gay Writers Caucus
National Writers Union
13 Astor Place
New York, NY 10003
Phone: 212/580-2206

Lambda Literary Awards
c/o Lambda Book Report
1625 Connecticut Avenue NW
Washington, DC 20009
Phone: 202/462-7924

Gay and Lesbian Committee
PEN American Center
568 Broadway
New York, NY 10012
Phone: 212/334-1660

The Gaylactic Network
P.O. Box 127
Brookline, MA 02146-0001
Science fiction

The Publishing Triangle
P.O. Box 114, Prince Street Station
New York, NY 10012

MEDIA

DYKE-TV
P.O. Box 55, Prince Street Station
New York, NY 10012
Phone: 212/343-9335
Syndicated cable TV show

Gay and Lesbian Alliance Against
   Defamation (GLAAD)
150 West 26th Street
New York, NY 10001
Phone: 212/807-1700

Gay and Lesbian Press Association
P.O. Box 8185
Universal City, CA 91608-0185

GayNet
P.O. Box 25524
Albuquerque, NM 87125-0524
Phone: 505/243-2540
News wire service for gay publications

In the Life
39 West 14th Street, Suite 402
New York, NY 10011
Phone: 212/255-6012
Monthly public TV program

Lesbian and Gay Public Awareness
   Project
Box 65603
Los Angeles, CA 90065

National Gay and Lesbian Journalists
　　Association
874 Gravenstein Highway South,
　　Suite 4
Sebastopol, CA 95472
Phone: 707/823-2193
Fax: 707/823-4176

This Way Out
P.O. Box 38327
Los Angeles, CA 90038
Internationally distributed weekly
　　radio program

MISCELLANEOUS

Digital Queers
584 Castro Street, #150
San Francisco, CA 94114
Phone: 415/252-6282
Computers

Gay Officers Action League (GOAL)
P.O. Box 2038, Canal Street Station
New York, NY 10012
Phone: 212/996-8808

Lesbians and Gays in
　　Telecommunications (LEGIT)
P.O. Box 8143
Red Bank, NJ 07701

Lesbian and Gay Labor Network:
　　Coalition of Labor Union Activists
P.O. Box 1159, Peter Stuyvesant
　　Station

New York, NY 10009
Phone: 212/923-8690
Not a job-finding service

Liatris International
P.O. Box 1336
Davis, CA 95617-1336
Gay and lesbian horticulturists

National Organization of Gay and
　　Lesbian Scientists and Technical
　　Professionals
P.O. Box 91803
Pasadena, CA 91109
Phone: 818/791-7689

MILITARY

American Federation of Veterans
Veterans Hall
346 Broadway, Suite 811
New York, NY 10013
Phone: 212/349-3455

Gay and Lesbian Military Freedom
　　Project/National Gay and Lesbian
　　Task Force

1734 Fourteenth Street
Washington, DC 20009
Phone: 202/332-6483

Lambda Legal Defense and Education
　　Fund
666 Broadway, 12th Floor
New York, NY 10012
Phone: 212/995-8585

National Center for Lesbian Rights
1663 Mission Street, 5th Floor
San Francisco, CA 94103
Phone: 415/392-6257

PERFORMANCE

Gay and Lesbian Association of
  Choruses
P.O. Box 65084
Washington, DC 20035-5084
Phone: 202/467-5830

Lambda Performing Arts Guild of
  America
P.O. Box 140131
Denver, CO 80214

LEND, International (Lesbian
  Exchange of New Drama)
559 Third Street
Brooklyn, NY 11215
Phone: 212/874-7900 ext. 1103

Lesbian and Gay Bands of America
P.O. Box 57099
Washington, DC 20037-0099

OUTMUSIC: Gay/Lesbian Musicians,
  Composers, and Lyricists
P.O. Box 1575
New York, NY 10013
Phone: 212/330-9197

The Purple Circuit
Artists Confronting AIDS
684½ Echo Park Avenue
Los Angeles, CA 90026

Theatre Rhinoceros
2926 Sixteenth Street, 16th Floor
San Francisco, CA 94103
Phone: 415/552-4100
Produces lesbian and gay theater

POLITICS/GOVERNMENT

Egale
P.O. Box 2891, Station D
Ottawa, ON K1P 5W9
Phone: 613/230-4391

Gay and Lesbian Victory Fund
1012 Fourteenth Street NW, #707
Washington, DC 20005
Phone: 202/842-8679
Supports openly gay/lesbian political
  candidates

Human Rights Campaign Fund
1012 Fourteenth Street NW, #607
Washington, DC 20005

Phone: 202/628-4160
Lobbies Congress, undertakes political
  action, and grassroots organizing

International Gay and Lesbian Human
  Rights Commission
540 Castro Street
San Francisco, CA 94114
Phone: 415/255-8680

International Network of Lesbian and
  Gay Officials
3801 Twenty-sixth Street East
Minneapolis, MN 55406-1857

Log Cabin Federation
Phone: 212/886-1893
Gay Republicans

National Gay and Lesbian Task Force
1734 Fourteenth Street NW
Washington, DC 20009
Phone: 202/332-6483
Lobbying, political action, grassroots
  activism

RELIGION

A Common Bond
P.O. Box 405
Ellwood City, PA 16117
Phone: 412/285-7334
Ex–Jehovah's Witnesses

Affirmation/Gay & Lesbian Mormons
P.O. Box 46022
Los Angeles, CA 90046
Phone: 213/255-7251

Affirmation: United Methodists for
  Lesbian, Gay, & Bisexual Concerns
P.O. Box 1021
Evanston, IL 60204
Phone: 708/475-0499

American Baptists Concerned
872 Erie Street
Oakland, CA 94610-2268
Phone: 510/530-6562

American Gay & Lesbian Atheists
P.O. Box 66711
Houston, TX 77266
Phone: 713/862-3283

Axios: Eastern & Orthodox Christians
328 West 17th Street, #4-F
New York, NY 10011
Phone: 212/989-6211 or 718/805-1952,
  ask for Nick

Brethren/Mennonite Council for
  Lesbian & Gay Concerns
P.O. Box 65724
Washington, DC 20035-5724
Phone: 202/462-2595

Dignity USA
1500 Massachusetts Ave. NW, #11
Washington, DC 20005
Phone: 202/861-0017
Fax: 202/429-9898
Catholic

Emergence International: Christian
  Scientists Supporting Lesbians, Gay
  Men & Bisexuals
P.O. Box 6061-423
Sherman Oaks, CA 91413
Phone: 800/280-6653

The Evangelical Network
P.O. Box 16104
Phoenix, AZ 85011-1610

Evangelicals Concerned
c/o Dr. Ralph Blair
311 E. 72nd St., #1-G
New York, NY 10021
Phone: 212/517-3171

Friends for Lesbian & Gay Concerns
P.O. Box 222
Sumneytown, PA 18084
Phone: 215/234-8424
ask for Bruce

GLAD (Gay, Lesbian & Affirming
  Disciple) Alliance
P.O. Box 19223
Indianapolis, IN 46219-0223

Honesty: Southern Baptists Advocating
Equal Rights for Gays & Lesbians
P.O. Box 2543
Louisville, KY 40201
Phone: 502/637-7609

Integrity, Inc.
P.O. Box 19561
Washington, DC 20036-0561
Episcopal

Interweave (Unitarian Universalists for
Lesbian, Gay & Bisexual Concerns)
25 Beacon St.
Boston, MA 02108-2800
Phone: 617/742-2100

Lifeline Baptist
c/o Rev J. T. Williams
1635 Forest Hill Ct.
Crofton, MD 21114-1813

Lutherans Concerned/North America
P.O. Box 10461
Chicago, IL 60610-0461

Maitri Dorje: Gay & Lesbian
Buddhists
Phone: 212/619-4099, ask for Bill or
Peter

National Congress for Lesbian
Christians
P.O. Box 814
Capitola, CA 95010

National Council of Churches
Commission on Family Ministries &
Human Sexuality Office
Rev. Joe H. Leonard
243 Lenoir Ave.
Wayne, PA 19087-3908

National Ecumenical Coalition, Inc.
1953 Columbia Pike, #24
Arlington, VA 22204-4569

National Gay Pentecostal Alliance
P.O. Box 1391
Schenectady, NY 12301-1391
Phone: 518/372-6001

New Ways Ministry (Catholic)
4012 Twenty-ninth St.
Mount Rainier, MD 20712
Phone: 301/277-5674
Fax: 301/864-6948

Phoenix Evangelical Bible Institute
1035 E. Tyrney
Phoenix, AZ 85014
Phone: 602/265-2831

Presbyterians for Lesbian/Gay
Concerns
c/o James Anderson
P.O. Box 38
New Brunswick, NJ 08903-0038
Phone: 908/249-1016 or 908/932-7501

Radical Faeries
P.O. Box 1251
New York, NY 10013
Phone: 212/625-4505

Reformed Church in America Gay
Caucus
P.O. Box 8174
Philadelphia, PA 19101-8174

Seventh Day Adventist Kinship
International
P.O. Box 3840
Los Angeles, CA 90078-3840

Silent Harvest Ministries
P.O. Box 190511
Dallas, TX 75219-0511
Phone: 214/520-6655

Supportive Congregations
Network/Mennonite & Brethren
P.O. Box 479241
Chicago, IL 60647-9241

Unitarian Universalist Association
Office of Lesbian, Bisexual & Gay
Concerns
25 Beacon St.
Boston, MA 02108-2800
Phone: 617/742-2100

Unitarian Universalist Bisexual
    Network (UUBN)
P.O. Box 10818
Portland, ME 04104

United Church of Christ Coalition for
    Lesbian/Gay Concerns: Ohio
18 N. College St.
Athens OH 45701
Phone: 614/593-7301

United Community Church of
    America
Office of the General Superintendent
P.O. Box 7654
Jackson, MS 39284-7654
Phone: 601/924-3333

United Lesbian/Gay Christian
    Scientists
P.O. Box 2171
Beverly Hills, CA 90212-2171
Phone: 310/850-8258

Unity Fellowship Church
230 Classon Avenue (at Willoughby
    Ave.)
Brooklyn, NY 11205
Phone: 718/636-5646

Universal Fellowship of Metropolitan
    Community Churches
5300 Santa Monica Blvd., #304
Los Angeles, CA 90029
Phone: 213/464-5100

Witches/Pagans for Gay Rights
P.O. Box 4538
Sunnyside, NY 11104-4538

The Womyn's Spirituality Center
1405 Twenty-seventh Ave. NE
Seattle, WA 98155-7414
Phone: 206/547-3374

World Congress of Gay and Lesbian
    Jewish Organizations
P.O. Box 3345
New York, NY 10008-3345

TRAVEL

Gay Hospitality Exchange
    International
P.O. Box 612, Station C
Montreal, QC H2L 4K5

Gayroute: Tour Gay Canada
Box 314-G, Station deLorimier
Montreal, QC H2H 2N7

International Gay Travel Association
P.O. Box 4974
Key West, FL 33041
Phone: 800/448-8550

Olivia Cruises
4400 Market Street
Oakland, CA 94608
Phone: 510/655-0364 or 800/631-6277

INDEX

Page references to illustrations are cited in italics.